Concise
Dictionary
OF
Christianity
IN
America

Coordinating Editor
Daniel G. Reid

Consulting Editors
Robert D. Linder
Bruce L. Shelley
Harry S. Stout

Abridging Editor
Craig A. Noll

InterVarsity Press
Downers Grove, Illinois

© 1995 by InterVarsity Christian Fellowship of the United States of America

InterVarsity Press® is the book-publishing division of InterVarsity Christian Fellowship®, a student movement active on campus at hundreds of universities, colleges and schools of nursing in the United States of America, and a member movement of the International Fellowship of Evangelical Students. For information about local and regional activities, write Public Relations Dept., InterVarsity Christian Fellowship, 6400 Schroeder Rd., P.O. Box 7895, Madison, WI 53707-7895.

ISBN 0-8308-1446-9

Printed in the United States of America ∞

Library of Congress Cataloging-in-Publication Data

Concise dictionary of Christianity in America/editors, Daniel G.
  Reid . . . [et al.].
      p. cm.
   "A condensation of the Dictionary of Christianity in America,
which was published in 1990"—Pref.
   Includes bibliographical references.
   ISBN 0-8308-1446-9 (paper: alk. paper)
   1. Christianity—United States—Dictionaries.   2. United States—
Church history—Dictionaries.   I. Reid, Daniel G., 1949-
II. Dictionary of Christianity in America.
BR515.C665   1995
277.3'003—dc20

                                                                    95-40444
                                                                        CIP

| 21 | 20 | 19 | 18 | 17 | 16 | 15 | 14 | 13 | 12 | 11 | 10 | 9 | 8 | 7 | 6 | 5 | 4 | 3 | 2 | 1 |
| 13 | 12 | 11 | 10 | 09 | 08 | 07 | 06 | 05 | 04 | 03 | 02 | 01 | 00 | 99 | 98 | 97 | 96 | 95 |

CONTENTS

PREFACE

The *Concise Dictionary of Christianity in America* is a condensation of the *Dictionary of Christianity in America*, which was published in 1990. That volume quickly established itself as a standard reference book in the field of American religious studies and was widely acclaimed by reviewers and scholars.

The *Concise Dictionary of Christianity in America*, like its parent volume, covers the men and women, denominations and organizations, events and movements, ideas and practices that have contributed to shape the vibrant and complex history of Christianity in America. The *Concise Dictionary* is primarily concerned with history, though the time line of that history extends into the present. It seeks to be fair, accurate and objective in describing the lineage, beliefs and practices of the numerous and diverse expressions of Christianity in America. The geographical focus is primarily the United States, though a number of Canadian subjects are also included.

The *Concise Dictionary of Christianity in America* is intended to make available to a wider audience the basic information contained in the *Dictionary of Christianity in America*. The original 1,300 pages and approximately 1 million words have been reduced to about one-quarter of that length, presenting the most essential facts. Some of the larger, more wide-ranging articles in the original volume have not been included. The numerous bibliographies have also been dropped. These, along with the list of original contributors and an interpretative introductory essay, may be found in the larger volume. On the other hand, over fifty new articles have been added. These include some topics that reviewers brought to our attention and a number of biographical articles on significant individuals who have died since the late 1980s when the original volume was going to press.

The publishers once again express their gratitude to the work of the original consulting editors of the *Dictionary of Christianity in America* and to the many thoughtful reviewers and individuals who invested in the future of this project by contributing their ideas for enhancing future editions. Most of all, this volume owes its existence to the careful and diligent labor of Craig Noll, who skillfully condensed the *Dictionary of Christianity in America* to its concise essentials.

The Publishers

HOW TO USE
CROSS-REFERENCES

The *Concise Dictionary of Christianity in America* is designed to be an easily accessible reference book that provides basic information on the history and varied dimensions of Christianity in America. Articles are arranged alphabetically, and to assist readers in making the most of the material contained in the *Dictionary,* a system of cross-references has been used. Thus readers can more easily find subjects related to their interests.

Types of cross-references:

1. One-line, alphabetized entries direct the reader to the title of the article where the topic is treated:

Episcopal Church. *See* PROTESTANT EPISCOPAL CHURCH IN THE USA.

2. An asterisk after a word or phrase indicates that further relevant information will be found in an article approximating that title. Readers should note the following possibilities:

a. The *form* of the word asterisked will not always be precisely the same as that of the title of the article to which the asterisk refers. For example, "Methodism*" directs the reader to the article on **Methodist Churches** and "ordained*" to **Ordination**.

b. The asterisk sometimes applies to two or three words preceding the asterisk rather than to the word immediately preceding the asterisk. Thus "Social Gospel*" will refer the reader to **Social Gospel Movement** and not **Gospel**.

3. Cross-references such as (*see* Restoration Movement) have been used within the body of articles.

4. Cross-references have been appended to the end of many articles: *See also* HOLINESS MOVEMENT; PERFECTIONISM.

Abbott, Lyman (1835-1922). Congregational* minister and editor. Abbott's widest influence came through his editorial labors, as he edited the *Illustrated Christian Weekly* for six years and, beginning in 1876, the *Christian Union* (renamed *Outlook* in 1893) for forty-six years. Abbott's earlier evangelical* convictions gave way to a decidedly liberal* theology. Always interested in social reform, he championed Theodore Roosevelt's progressivism for nearly two decades.
See also BEECHER, HENRY WARD

Aberhart, William ("Bible Bill") (1878-1943). Radio pioneer and premier of Alberta. Aberhart first emerged into prominence as a Baptist* Bible teacher in Calgary, Alberta. Later he founded the Social Credit Party, which won provincial elections in 1935 and 1940. Aberhart died in office, having introduced education and farm reforms.

Abernathy, Ralph David (1926-1990). African-American civil rights leader and Baptist* pastor. Abernathy was pastor of First Baptist Church in Montgomery, Alabama, when he, along with Martin Luther King Jr.,* helped start the Montgomery bus boycott in 1955 and the Southern Christian Leadership Conference* in 1957. In 1961 Abernathy moved to Atlanta, the headquarters of the SCLC, and assumed the pastorate of West Hunter Street Baptist Church. After King's assassination in 1968, Abernathy was president of the SCLC until he resigned in 1977. His controversial book *And the Walls Came Tumbling Down* (1989) accused King of plagiarism and sexual indiscretion.

Abolition and the Churches. The growing emphasis on natural rights in the postrevolutionary era led many denominations* either to adopt pro-emancipation statements or to specifically condemn slavery. By the 1820s, however, accommodation to the Southern institution had again become the rule, and churches generally refused to take disciplinary measures against slaveholding members.

It was the movement for "immediate emancipation," developing primarily from the Second Great Awakening,* that began to challenge the equivocal stance of the traditionally evangelical* churches. Prominent leaders were Theodore D. Weld* as well as William L. Garrison* and his American Anti-Slavery Society. As this agitation for abolition continued within the denominations, schisms resulted among the Methodists (1844) and Baptists (1845) and others.

America thus abolished slavery not ultimately through moral or religious persuasion but through political and military means.
See also CIVIL WAR AND THE CHURCHES; EMANCIPATION PROCLAMATION.

Abortion. While Christianity in all its forms has never rested easy with abortion, European and American Christians historically have held a variety of opinions on the nature of the fetus and on whether its protection must be absolute. Even today they represent a wide range of convictions and viewpoints.

The Roman Catholic* Church has held to the view that the fetus receives its soul very early in its development. As ensouled, it was innocent humanity, to be protected against nearly every action that would destroy it.

Protestantism historically was even more forcefully opposed to abortion than was Catholicism. The Reformers had taught that the fetus inherited its sin* nature at conception and thus was fully human at that time. In American Protestantism, opposition to abortion was more likely to be grounded on the fact that it enabled people to evade the consequences of their sinful sexual behaviors.

A strong opposition to abortion under any circumstance except to save the mother's life is maintained by the various Orthodox churches.* At the other extreme, the United Church of Christ* urges that voluntary and medically safe abortions be available to all women. Others aligned with the strong antiabortion position include the Church of the Brethren,* the Reformed Church of America* and many smaller evangelical* bodies. Churches supporting individual choice in abortion decisions include the Evangelical Lutheran Church of America,* the Episcopal Church* and the Presbyterian Church (U.S.A.).

Biblical themes that tended to maintain an antiabortion stance include the value of each life as a divine creation, a stress on the woman's body as her responsibility for stewardship rather than as her possession, and an emphasis on the communal rather than individualistic nature of Christian believing. The dignity of the fetus and newborn also was implied by the tradition of infant baptism.*

In the years following the 1973 Supreme Court decision, evangelicals have entered into the abortion debate. Evangelical thinking has followed the work of Francis Schaeffer,* Harold O. J. Brown, James Dobson and others in repudiating abortion and in seeking legislation to make it unavailable.

See also BIRTH CONTROL; RIGHT TO LIFE.

Absolution. Declaration of forgiveness of sins. Absolution may be viewed as the human side of a sinner's finding forgiveness. It may be announced by a priest (in the Catholic* and Episcopal* Churches) or by public affirmation of God's forgiving sins through Christ (most Protestant* churches).

Abstinence. In its most technical sense, *abstinence* denotes a restricted form of fasting* that limits the type of food but not the quantity. A wider application of the term advocates refraining from other actions such as alcohol* consumption, marriage and participation in larger society.

Acadian Expulsion. The expelling of the French Catholic population of Nova Scotia from 1755 to 1763. The Acadians were the descendants of those settling in the French colony of Acadie (now Nova Scotia) in the early 1600s. Fearful of their Catholicism and suspected French sympathies, the Nova Scotia government sent some 10,000 into exile in the thirteen colonies, Eng-

land and France.

Adams, Hannah (1755-1831). Religious writer and historian. Adams's first book, in 1784, was a survey of the Calvinist-Arminian debate in America. Later books helped establish her reputation as a woman of learning and literary skill, and reflected her Unitarian* beliefs. She was the first self-supporting female author in America.

Adams, Theodore Floyd (1898-1980). Baptist* pastor, educator and leader in the Baptist World Alliance.* Adams's balanced ministry as pastor of the historic First Baptist Church of Richmond, Virginia (1936-1980), stressed missions,* pastoral care and social concern. He conducted a daily radio program for twenty-six years and became involved in television locally and nationally.

Addams, Jane (1860-1935). Settlement house* founder, social reformer, suffragist and peace activist. Addams is best known for her work with Ellen Gates Starr* in founding Hull House (1889) in Chicago. Hull House provided clubs, classes and activities to meet the needs of the primarily immigrant neighborhood. Politically, Addams was influenced more by pragmatism than by religious considerations. In 1931 she received the Nobel Peace Prize.

Adger, John Bailey (1810-1899). Presbyterian* minister and missionary. After missionary service to the Armenians in the Near East (1834-1847), Adger organized a church in Charleston (S.C.) and taught church history and church polity at Columbia Theological Seminary (1857-1874).

Adopting Act (1729). An action of the Synod* of Philadelphia whereby the Westminster Confession of Faith* and Catechisms* were adopted as the doctrinal position of the Presbyterian Church* in colonial America. This act represents a compromise between the dominant Scotch and Scotch-Irish party and those from England and New England, who did not want to see fallible, human documents imposed as tests of orthodoxy* and ordination.*

See also SCOTTISH PRESBYTERIANS IN AMERICA; SUBSCRIPTION CONTROVERSY.

Advent. A season of preparation for Christmas,*

more characteristic of Western liturgical* churches. The advent theme has focused on the coming of Christ at the consummation of history. While Advent has always been characterized by a heightened soberness, it has not been strictly penitential as has Lent. The four Sundays of Advent are popularly marked in homes by lighting, in order, four candles mounted on an evergreen "Advent wreath."

Africa Inland Mission. Interdenominational and international mission agency. The African Inland Mission (AIM) was founded in 1895 by Peter Cameron Scott,* with Charles Hurlbert serving as general director from 1896 to 1921. Hurlbert was assisted by the pioneering triumvirate of Lee Downing, Albert Barnett and John Stauffacher. Ministries of social concern began early and have continued as an integral part of the mission's primary commitment to evangelization, church planting and nurturing.

See also MISSIONS, EVANGELICAL FOREIGN.

African Methodist Episcopal Church. The largest African-American Methodist* denomination.* The African Methodist Episcopal Church (AMEC) was founded by Richard Allen* and his followers, who in 1787 refused to accept their second-class status in St. George's Methodist Episcopal Church in Philadelphia. Leaving the church in protest, Allen led in the formation of a congregation, later named Bethel. Bishop Francis Asbury* of the Methodist Episcopal Church dedicated Bethel Church in Philadelphia in 1793 and ordained Allen a deacon* in 1799.

A similar process happened in Baltimore, with Daniel Coker* there becoming the leader in 1801. In 1816 representatives from the Bethel churches met in Philadelphia to establish the AMEC.

After Reconstruction the AMEC expanded from 20,000 members in 1856 to over 200,000 members by 1876. The denomination currently has thirteen districts with thirteen bishops. As of 1991 there were a reported eight thousand congregations and an inclusive membership of 3.5 million.

African Methodist Episcopal Zion Church. Second-largest African-American Methodist* denomination.* In 1796 James Varick* and others led disaffected African-American members out of John's Street Methodist Episcopal Zion Church in New York. With the permission of Bishop Francis Asbury,* Varick and other African-Americans ultimately held their own meetings and in 1800 built their first church, called Zion.

Members of Zion Church later refused to join the African Methodist Episcopal Church.* In 1821, at their first annual conference, nineteen preachers representing six African-American Methodist churches organized the African Methodist Episcopal Zion Church (AMEZC), with Varick as the first bishop.

After the Civil War,* the AMEZ churches spread throughout the South. In 1991 the AMEZ Church reported some 1.2 million members in three thousand congregations.

African United Baptist Association. Canadian Black Baptist* convention. A meeting of black Baptist churches in Nova Scotia in 1854 led to the founding of the African United Baptist Association. Many of its members were refugees from slavery in the United States. By 1897 the denomination claimed twenty-two churches and 2,440 members. Presently the association has a membership of over 10,000.

Agassiz, Jean Louis Rodolphe (1807-1873). Naturalist, Harvard* professor. After distinguishing himself in Europe in natural history, zoology and geology, Agassiz immigrated to the U.S. in 1846. He soon emerged as the country's leading figure in natural sciences.

From 1855, however, Agassiz's involvement in the evolution controversy would diminish his stature and illustrate a transition in the intellectual climate of the nation. Agassiz resisted evolutionary theory on both religious and scientific grounds and increasingly found himself swimming against the tide of Darwinism.*

See also GRAY, ASA.

Aggiornamento. An Italian term broadly defined as modernization or adaptation. The term was popularized for Catholics* by Pope John XXIII,* who explained its meaning as "the renewal of traditions by interpreting them in harmony with the new conditions and needs of the time."

See also VATICAN COUNCIL II.

Agnosticism. The belief that humans cannot know the answers to the ultimate questions of the existence of God or the nature and destiny of the human soul. The term should not be confused with atheism,* which denies the reality of God.

This concept is rooted in the British skepticism of David Hume (1711-1776), who rejected the historical veracity of the New Testament miracles. It also owes much to Immanuel Kant (1724-1804), William Hamilton (1788-1856), Herbert Spencer (1820-1903) and William James (1842-1910). By the mid-twentieth century the term had come to be used loosely to describe all forms of skepticism.

Ahlstrom, Sydney Eckman (1919-1984). Historian of modern religion and American history. Teaching history at Yale from 1954 to 1983, Ahlstrom distinguished himself as one of the nation's foremost scholars in American religious and intellectual history. In 1957 he was lecturer for the Lutheran World Federation* throughout Europe. His encyclopedic study *A Religious History of the American People* (1972) received the National Book Award in Philosophy and Religion in 1973 and was honored in a *Time* magazine poll of book reviewers as the outstanding book on religion published in the 1970s.

Albright, Jacob (1759-1808). Itinerant* preacher, first bishop of the Evangelical Association. In 1791 Albright experienced a conversion, and in 1796, after being granted a Methodist exhorter's license, he began preaching throughout eastern Pennsylvania and Maryland.

Albright's abiding concern was the spiritual welfare of German-speaking people. When Methodist leaders failed to organize special meetings for Germans, Albright in 1800 organized his converts into three classes, after the Methodist fashion.

See also REVIVALISM, GERMAN-AMERICAN; UNITED METHODIST CHURCH.

Albright, William Foxwell (1891-1971). Biblical archaeologist. From 1929 to 1958 Albright was professor of Semitic languages at Johns Hopkins University. His career was characterized by extensive fieldwork, an ability to assimilate a wide range of historical and archaeological data, and a remarkable scholarly output and erudition. Albright's archaeological and historical studies led him to increasingly conservative conclusions regarding the historicity of the Bible, and he was influential in attracting many scholars in his field to similar conclusions.

Alcohol, Drinking of. While the Scriptures recognize alcohol as potentially evil, they do not normally prohibit its use. Christians have generally been in agreement that moderation is the clear Scriptural injunction on the use of alcohol.

New England Puritans* viewed alcoholic drinks as an enjoyable creation of God to be consumed along with other produce of the soil. Nineteenth-century American evangelicals,* influenced by revivalism* and perfectionism,* began to call not only for temperance* but for total abstinence.*

Nineteenth-century Catholics for the most part did not share the evangelical campaign against "demon rum," nor did many Protestants more closely identified with European confessional traditions.

See also PROHIBITION MOVEMENT; TEMPERANCE MOVEMENT.

Alemany, Joseph Sadoc (1814-1888). Dominican* missionary and archbishop of San Francisco. In 1850 Pope Pius IX* named Alemany bishop of Monterey, California, placing him in charge of church affairs not only in California but also in northwestern Mexico and parts of Utah, Nevada and Arizona. In 1853 he became archbishop.

Alexander, Archibald (1772-1851). First professor at Princeton Theological Seminary* and founder of the Princeton theology.* In 1812 Princeton Theological Seminary emerged as the first Presbyterian seminary in America, with Alexander as its first professor. By his academic diligence Alexander established Princeton's main themes and set a standard of excellence that his successors at Princeton vigorously maintained.

Undergirding his teaching, preaching* and writing was a fervent piety* and vital interest in religious experience* which had its roots in his revival* preaching and continued to be a characteristic feature of the Princeton theology.

Alexander, Charles M. (1867-1920). Singing evangelist with R. A. Torrey* and J. Wilbur Chapman.* In 1893 Alexander worked with Dwight L. Moody's* revival* meetings held during the Chicago World's Fair and then spent several years (1894-1901) with evangelist Milan B. Williams. The most notable phase of his ministry was his work with R. A. Torrey, with whom he traversed the globe (1902-1906).

From 1906 until the end of his life, Alexander

traveled internationally with evangelist J. Wilbur Chapman and supported the work of Pocket Testament League,* which was founded by his wife, Helen.

Alexander, Joseph Addison (1809-1860). Old School* Presbyterian* biblical scholar. The son of Archibald Alexander,* Joseph was instructor of ancient languages and literature at Princeton (1830-1833) and then taught Bible and church history at Princeton Theological Seminary* (1834-1860).

Alien Immersion. A term still used by many Baptists* in the South to refer to baptism* by immersion administered by non-Baptists. The term came to prominence through the Landmark movement, with the exclusivistic ecclesiastical theories of J. R. Graves,* J. M. Pendleton* and A. C. Dayton.

Alison, Francis (1705-1779). Presbyterian* educator and political theorist. As teacher and pastor, Alison became a major spokesperson for Old Side* Presbyterianism. In his teaching, Alison trained a whole generation of students in the inductive empiricism of Scottish Common Sense Realism,* demonstrating the relevance of Scottish academic philosophy to pressing American problems, particularly in political theory.

All Saints Day. A feast celebrated in the Western church on November 1 to commemorate Christian martyrs and all those who have led conspicuously holy lives. In the Eastern church it is observed on the first Sunday after Pentecost. It is also known as All Hallows, and so the popular celebration of Halloween began as a celebration of All Hallows Eve.

All Saints Day is in particular a recognition of those who have not been assigned a special day in the church year. On the day after the feast, All Souls Day, the Catholic Church* prays for all departed souls.

See also CHRISTIAN YEAR; PIETY, POPULAR CATHOLIC; SAINTS, CULT OF THE.

All Souls Day. See ALL SAINTS DAY.

Allen, Alexander V(iets) G(riswold) (1841-1908). Episcopal educator. Allen was a leading figure in the late nineteenth-century liberal* or broad church* movement within Anglicanism.*

Allen urged a revival of Greek theology with its emphasis upon divine immanence, and the connectedness between God, humanity and nature.

Allen, A(sa) A(lonzo) (1911-1970). Healing revivalist.* Converted in a "tongues speaking" Methodist* church in 1934, Allen for many years was a pastor and itinerant revivalist. Inspired by the success of Oral Roberts,* Allen began his own healing ministry and by 1951, claiming hundreds of healings in his meetings, had launched a tent ministry and radio network. His ministry was characterized by an appeal to the poor, an emphasis on eccentric healings and miracles, and an old-time Pentecostal message. An early forerunner of the faith movement,* Allen stressed financial as well as spiritual healing.

Allen, Cary (1767-1795). Presbyterian* revivalist* and home missionary. After experiencing a dramatic evangelical* conversion* in 1787, Allen helped precipitate a revival among fellow students at Hampden-Sydney College, which was one of the first outbreakings of the Second Great Awakening.* Allen was an extremely popular preacher.

Allen, Ethan (1738-1789). Revolutionary War* figure and controversial religious freethinker. Allen, who led the victory at Fort Ticonderoga in 1775, was an early representative of the antiauthoritarian, democratizing currents of thought that after the turn of the century effectively undercut New England's Congregational* establishment.

Allen, Richard (1760-1831). Black clergyman and founding bishop of the African Methodist Episcopal Church.* In 1786 Allen returned as a free man to his native Philadelphia. He joined the predominantly white St. George's Methodist Church but left the next year.

Convinced that African-Americans needed a distinct religious identity, Allen formally established the Bethel African Methodist Episcopal Church in 1794, with Bishop Francis Asbury* leading the dedication. For twenty-two years Allen sought its legal independence and throughout his life combined his experiential religion grounded in Methodism with widespread efforts to uplift African-Americans economically and socially.

See also BLACK RELIGION; FREE AFRICAN SOCIETY.

Alline, Henry (1748-1784). Leader of the Great Awakening in Nova Scotia. Alline became a forceful preacher of the "new birth."* His peculiar anti-Calvinistic mysticism* influenced the Free Will Baptist* movement in the U.S. Most of the Canadian "New Light"* churches he founded either collapsed or became Calvinistic Baptists.*

See also BAPTIST CHURCHES IN CANADA.

Allis, Oswald T(hompson) (1880-1973). Presbyterian* clergyman, Old Testament scholar and educator. From 1910 to 1935 Allis taught at Princeton Theological Seminary* and then at the newly founded Westminster Theological Seminary. He then devoted the rest of his life to writing and editing. In addition to compiling extended studies of English translations of the Bible, Allis focused on the Pentateuch and Old Testament prophecy.

Altar. In the Old Testament, a place of sacrifice, either of animal offerings or of incense; in Christian use, the table upon which the Eucharist* is celebrated and from which Holy Communion is distributed.

Altar Call. In the revivalistic* tradition the altar* call (or "invitation") is a period following the sermon* in which the hearers are challenged to respond publicly by coming to a designated place, usually in the front of the congregation. The altar call became popular during the first half of the nineteenth century, growing out of camp meetings* and in the "burned-over district"* of western New York.

See also MOURNER'S BENCH; REVIVALISM.

Altar Fellowship. The practice of Christians receiving Communion* at the same altar.* The issue of intercommunion was a major element in the heightening of denominational* sensitivity in the nineteenth century.

Altar Societies. The general name for a variety of groups formed in local Roman Catholic* parishes or congregations with the aim of assisting the clergy and serving God through care of the church appointments, especially the altar.* These societies are usually composed of women who take responsibility for the cleaning and decoration of the altar, the sanctuary area, the sacristy, church vestments, candles and flowers.

Altham, John (1589-1640). Jesuit* missionary in Maryland. In 1634, along with Father* Andrew White* and Brother* Thomas Gervase, Altham accompanied the first settlers who came to Maryland. Altham and the Jesuits began to evangelize* the Native Americans, a task for which Altham displayed unusual zeal.

Amana Church Society. Pietist* sect* previously known as the Community of True Inspiration. Formed in Germany in 1714, this sect believes that the age of true and direct divine inspiration has not ended. Immigrating to New York State in 1842 and then, between 1855 and 1864, to Iowa, the group established seven villages, known collectively as the Amana Colonies (Amana means "remain faithful"). Membership in the society reached its peak of 1,813 in 1880. In 1932 communal ties were dissolved and an independent church society was created.

American Baptist Association. A Landmark* Baptist* organization. The formation in 1905 of what later became the American Baptist Association was the culmination of the struggle of Landmarkism in the Southern Baptist Convention (SBC).* In that year, under the leadership of Ben M. Bogard, an effort was made to convert the SBC to Landmark views regarding mission methods. Although the attempt failed, Bogard's movement absorbed smaller Landmark bodies and was renamed the American Baptist Association in 1924.

American Baptist Board of International Ministries. Foreign mission* agency of the American Baptist Churches in the U.S.A.* This board traces back to the Baptist Board for Foreign Missions, formed in 1814 as a result of the Baptist convictions of missionaries Adoniram Judson* and Luther Rice.* In 1845 the board was renamed the American Baptist Missionary Union; in 1910, the American Baptist Foreign Mission Society; and in 1973, the American Baptist Board of International Ministries.

American Baptist Churches in the U.S.A. A major Baptist denomination,* formerly known as the American Baptist Convention (1950-1972) and the Northern Baptist Convention (1907-1950).

From the establishment of the first Baptist congregation in America at Providence, Rhode Island, around 1638, Baptists have cherished the local governance of their churches. Beginning in 1802, however, and modeled on English Baptist and American Congregationalist* bodies, Baptists in New England organized a series of benevolent societies to advance the denominational interests. From 1814, when the first national body was organized, the driving impulse of Baptists in the North was foreign missions. When financial exigency threatened around 1900, interagency agreements and planning meetings eventually led to the creation of a unified Northern Baptist Convention (NBC) in 1905.

After organization, the leaders of the NBC took some bold steps in ecumenism and centralization, some of which led to controversy and division. The main body of Northern Baptists in 1922 assumed a mediating position, affirming the New Testament as the "all-sufficient ground of faith and practice."

In 1950 Northern Baptists voted to rename themselves the American Baptist Convention (ABC) and to create an office of the general secretary. An open invitation was given to other Baptist bodies to unite with the ABC and achieve a national Baptist body.

In 1972 a second major revision of American Baptist denominational structures was adopted and a new, more connectional polity resulted in the American Baptist Churches in the U.S.A. In the 1990s the denomination claimed over 5,800 churches and over 1.5 million members in all fifty states. Theologically, American Baptists are broadly evangelical,* with churches and pastors representing conservative, neo-orthodox* and liberal* traditions.

See also THE BAPTIST CHURCHES IN THE U.S.A.

American Baptist Convention. See AMERICAN BAPTIST CHURCHES IN THE U.S.A.

American Baptist Foreign Mission Society. See AMERICAN BAPTIST BOARD OF INTERNATIONAL MINISTRIES.

American Baptist Missionary Union. See AMERICAN BAPTIST BOARD OF INTERNATIONAL MINISTRIES.

American Baptist Seminary of the West. American Baptist seminary. The seminary is a federation of Berkeley Baptist Divinity School (BBDS) and California Baptist Theological Seminary (CBTS). CBTS was founded in 1944 in Los Angeles and in 1951 moved to Covina, California.

BBDS was the result of a merger of California College, founded in 1871, and the Pacific Coast Theological Seminary, founded in 1884. This merged school moved to Berkeley, California, in 1904 and took the name Berkeley Baptist Divinity School in 1912. In 1968 BBDS and CBTS were incorporated as the American Baptist Seminary of the West, and today it is affiliated with the Graduate Theological Union in the San Francisco Bay area.

American Bible Society. A nondenominational organization dedicated to distributing the Bible throughout the world. In 1816, delegates from many of the regional Bible societies then active in the U.S. met in New York and formed the American Bible Society (ABS).

As time went on, the ABS began to see its mission in other lands more clearly. Working closely with missionaries of various denominations, the ABS has now printed Bibles in more than a thousand tongues. On the initiative of the ABS, the United Bible Society, which serves as an umbrella organization over the national societies, was formed in 1946.

American Bible Union. A nineteenth-century Baptist* Bible society. The American Bible Union grew out of a controversy over the translation of the Greek verb *baptizein,* which the King James Version translates "baptize" and Baptists wished to translate "immerse." The controversy split the American Bible Society* (ABS). The Baptists then formed the American and Foreign Bible Society in 1836, with the name becoming the American Bible Union in 1850. The rift between Baptists and the ABS was eventually healed, with Baptists in various conventions again loyally supporting the ABS.

American Board of Catholic Missions. A standing committee of the National Conference of Catholic Bishops* to distribute funds to the home missions. The board arose from a meeting of seventeen directors of Catholic home and foreign missionary societies at Notre Dame University,* Indiana, in 1919. Grants are distributed annually, especially in support of black and Hispanic parishes.

American Board of Commissioners for Foreign Missions. The first American foreign missions society. Many of the students who took part in the so-called haystack prayer meeting* were involved in moving to organize the American Board of Commissioners for Foreign Missions (ABCFM).

By 1870 the ABCFM had become basically Congregational in sponsorship. Nevertheless, both before and since that time about half the missionaries have come from other denominations. The board has always emphasized Bible translation, schools and hospitals, with evangelism gradually receding as a priority.

American Board of Missions to the Jews. An independent mission agency engaged in evangelism* to Jews. In 1894 the board was founded as the Williamsburg Mission by Leopold Cohn. In the 1920s, the mission expanded into several North American and European cities; in 1924 its name changed to American Board of Missions to the Jews. Leopold's son Joseph succeeded him as director upon his death in 1937.

See also JEWISH CHRISTIANS; JEWS, CHRISTIAN MISSIONS TO; JEWS FOR JESUS.

American Christian Commission. The first post-Civil War* Protestant* response to growing urban needs. By the end of the Civil War, Protestant leaders were becoming aware of the physical, moral and spiritual poverty in America's burgeoning cities. The American Christian Commission was formed in 1865 to meet this need.

American Colonization Society. An early nineteenth-century organization for the resettlement of freed African-American slaves in Africa. The American Colonization Society was founded in 1817 to raise funds to remunerate slave owners and establish a colony in Africa for the repatriation of American blacks.

The African-American colony of Liberia was founded in 1822, and as many as twelve thousand blacks immigrated to West Africa under the auspices of the American Colonization Society. But the organization failed in its ultimate purpose as many African-Americans and abolitionists rejected colonization.

American Council of Christian Churches. An agency representing separatist* fundamentalists.* The initial impetus for organizing the group (1941) was to witness to Protestant* orthodoxy* in the face of the modernism* represented by the Federal* Council of Churches—now known as the National Council of Churches*—and to provide a united organization of separatist churches. Carl McIntire,* a militant defender of orthodoxy, was the first president.

In the early 1990s the council reported a total membership of about 1.5 million, including denominations, independent churches, associations and individuals.

American Friends Service Committee. Independent Quaker* peace and service organization. Founded in 1917 to provide conscientious objectors with an opportunity to aid civilian victims during World War I,* today the committee carries on projects of service, development, justice and peace.

American Home Missionary Society. A cooperative and then Congregational* home mission agency. The competition and confusion resulting from independent actions of numerous locally based societies led in 1826 to the formation of the American Home Missionary Society (AHMS). As a coordinating body, it had some four hundred local auxiliaries within a few years. In 1893 it was renamed the Congregational Home Missionary Society (CHMS). By the turn of the century more than four-fifths of the 5,650 Congregational churches then in America had been planted by the AHMS/CHMS.

American Lutheran Church. A large Lutheran* denomination* that merged to form the Evangelical Lutheran Church in America (ELCA).* The American Lutheran Church (ALC) for the most part arose out of nineteenth-century Lutheran immigrants* to America who tended to stress a blend of confessionalism* and pietism.* In time these Lutherans formed various bodies, three of which merged to form the original ALC in 1930.

The ALC was joined in 1960 and in 1963 by Lutheran groups with Norwegian and Danish backgrounds. When the ALC merged to form the ELCA in 1987, it consisted of 2.3 million members.

American Missionary Association. A Congregational* mission* agency with a focus in the nineteenth century on ministry to African-Americans. Formed in 1846, the association sponsored some eighty missionaries in America and abroad. With the coming of the Civil War* the society focused on educating newly freed slaves. After the war, it resumed its earlier work among Native Americans, becoming the most significant of many such agencies.

American Missionary Fellowship. Nondenominational home mission* agency. The American Missionary Fellowship (AMF) traces back to the Sunday and Adult School Union (1817), which became the American Sunday School Union* in 1824. In response to changing patterns in American church life after World War II,* the union phased out its publication and literature ministry in 1968. In 1974 it changed its name to the AMF.

American Peace Society. The first nonsectarian national peace organization in the U.S. Formed in 1828 by William Ladd, the American Peace Society (APS) was one of the most idealistic antebellum expressions of evangelical* Protestant* millennialism* and perfectionism.* After the Civil War, the APS became an advocate of international arbitration.

American Protective Association. A nativistic* anti-Catholic society. Organized in 1887, the American Protective Association (APA) developed its strongest foothold in the Midwest. Chief among its concerns was a supposed Roman Catholic* plot to undermine American democratic institutions. Established upon a quixotic vision of salvaging the fleeting myth of a unified Protestant* social order, the APA did not long survive, dissolving in 1911.

American Revolution, Christianity and the. In 1776 religion and political sentiments merged in an unforgettable moment in history. The mingling of these two forces altered the nature of both the American Revolution and religion, examined here under three separate headings: religion shaping ideology, religion in wartime actions and the consequences of the war for religion.

Christianity and Other Ideological Causes of the Revolution. Ministers* from such diverse religious perspectives as libertarians, liberals* and evangelicals* all planted the seeds of rebellion. Lacking a coherent, all-encompassing worldview from which to work, the ministers tried to sort out a number of competing ideologies about the nature of society and government.

One major ideology came from Puritanism*—which stressed covenant theology*—for both the individual and the nation. In the past the special covenant people of God had been Israel, but now New England stood at the center of God's work in history. In return for obedience and acknowledgment of his sole sovereignty, God promised to defend and protect America. Drawing on the covenant concept, preachers in 1765 began to develop a rationale for armed revolt. They warned that further allegiance to England might result in God's displeasure and loss of America's special covenant relationship.

Many upper-class individuals and their pastors held a rival worldview: the commonwealth, or Whig, ideology. Whiggism warned that uncontrolled political power always degenerated into corruption, stressing that history was a struggle between power and liberty. Influenced by radical Whig writers, many Americans interpreted British actions as evidence of corrupt, unchecked power. Ministers applied the contractual notion to argue that King George III had broken his compact with the people and that the people therefore had a right to revolt.

After 1765 ministers increasingly strengthened their arguments for revolution by intertwining Whig ideology with Puritan covenant theology. They translated and elevated political arguments to the sacred plane of religious and moral language. A symbiosis of Puritanism and Whiggism was possible, since both ideologies held many similar beliefs: humans were basically sinful; governments must serve the common good; history was a struggle between good and evil; there were God-given "unalienable" rights.

Other, non-Christian ideologies stimulated armed revolt. These included (1) Adam Smith's economic liberalism, which enthroned self-interest and materialism as virtues; (2) the radical, popular ideology which, appealing to many lower-class townspeople, championed the leveling of society by advocating maximum power for the people; (3) the concepts of the European Enlightenment* theorists (1680-1789), who argued that rational thinking would bring liberal progress to civilization.

Ministerial Support for the War. Many ministers did not restrict their activities to preaching an ideology of revolution. They lent their names and spiritual support in local town committees and county conventions, and later at state conventions and national politics. Besides such political involvement, they also participated as chaplains

[17]

and sometimes as soldiers.

The most significant function of clergymen was in establishing a Christian milieu for the American revolutionary generation. Even if a majority of nonclerical members on local committees, or delegates to state conventions, or the "Founding Fathers" at the Continental Congress cannot be classified as godly men, all placed a high value on religion for the good of society.

The Religious Consequences of the War. Religion and politics entered the war locked arm in arm, but this partnership would prove to be short-lived. Unfortunately, the revolutionary fervor resulted in some negative religious trends. The blending of Whig and Puritan ideology during the Revolution produced an American civil religion* believing deeply that America was God's chosen people, a view that opens the door to insensitivity and arrogance.

The clergy's unreserved support for revolution meant forgoing criticism of revolutionary policies. Ministers ever since colonial days had played the role of Old Testament prophets, warning the people of sin or serving as critics of government policy. Yet, once evangelical pastors enthusiastically embraced the Revolution, it was difficult for them to maintain an objectivity about patriot policies.

Not all of the consequences, however, were negative. American independence could be obtained only with the support of the majority. Therefore, in a society so diverse—religiously, ethnically and ideologically—once the war began, most colonies attempted to build as broad a political and religious consensus as possible. This resulted in greater religious toleration and freedom after the war, including the removal of the churches from under state control.

American Society of Missiology. Ecumenical* society to promote mission studies in the U.S. Begun in 1973, the society promotes mission studies through its annual meetings, its journal *Missiology: An International Review* and its series of monographs.

See also MISSIOLOGY, PROTESTANT.

American Sunday School Union. Primary agency for the early development of the Sunday school.* Founded in 1824, the American Sunday School Union (ASSU) saw the Sunday school as a means to provide society with education in Christian and democratic* values. It was founded

on the "union principle," emphasizing a general evangelical* Protestant* Christianity. In 1970 the name was changed to the American Missionary Society.*

See also AMERICAN MISSIONARY FELLOWSHIP; SUNDAY-SCHOOL MOVEMENT.

American Tract Society. A nondenominational religious publisher. The American Tract Society (ATS) was the chief innovator of mass publication of religious material in early nineteenth-century America. Founded in 1825, the ATS quickly became a leader in the development of printing technology. By the late 1820s the ATS was annually printing and distributing more than five million tracts (plus books and magazines). By 1975—its sesquicentennial—the ATS was regularly publishing some thirty million tracts per year.

American Unitarian Association. Unitarian* denomination.* Established in 1825, the American Unitarian Association (AUA) rejected Calvinist* views of the divinity of Christ and the idea of predestination.* In 1961 the AUA merged with the Universalist Church of America to form the Unitarian Universalist Association.*

See also UNITARIAN CONTROVERSY.

Americanism. A nineteenth-century term for patriotism which entered the lexicon of Catholic theology in 1899 when Pope Leo XIII* used it in his apostolic letter *Testem Benevolentiae.** In the Catholic context, the term has several dimensions, including (1) the ideas censured in this letter, (2) a series of controversies between 1884 and 1899 dividing the U.S. Catholic community over the desired extent of accommodation to American culture and (3) ideas of American Catholic messianism held by the progressive or Americanist party.

Presuming a rigid Neo-Scholastic nature-grace distinction, *Testem Benevolentiae* condemned the notion that the church should adapt to the age in essentials and, more specifically, that the church should imitate contemporary states by introducing greater individual liberty. While noting the legitimacy of political Americanism, Leo rejected the term as applied to the censured opinions.

On Being American and Catholic: The Conflict, 1884-1899. Was the culture of the late nineteenth-century U.S. benign or hostile to the Catholic faith? Two views emerged. The Americanists, led by John Ireland,* archbishop of St. Paul, Minnesota, advocated mainstreaming immigrant Catholics into American society and adapting Catholicism, wherever doctrine allowed, to the genius of the American character. The Conservative party, led by Michael A. Corrigan,* archbishop of New York, thought Ireland and his friends minimized the hostility of the American environment to Catholicism and accused them of "a spirit of false liberalism."

These two approaches clashed for the first time over the "social question" raised by Catholic immigrant participation in the incipient American labor movement. Subsequent conflicts included a tangle of related issues, disagreement on which led to the bishops' appealing to the Vatican. The answer ultimately was *Testem*.

American Catholic Messianism. These ideas had come together nearly a decade before during the winter of 1886-1887, when the Americanist inner circle of Ireland with his allies Denis O'Connell and Bishop John J. Keane,* rector of Catholic University (Washington, D.C.), was formed at Rome. Having come to the Vatican for different purposes, the three became convinced of the need to grasp the present historical moment and committed themselves to a common body of ideas which would serve as a basis for church reform.

Their subsequent writings and speeches reveal a characteristic ideology of near-mythic proportions. The world had entered upon a new democratic* age. The U.S., with its institution of separation of church and state, embodied the spirit of the new age. As O'Connell would argue in an address in 1897, the church must adapt, always in nonessentials, to the new age. To American Catholicism fell the messianic mission of leading the Catholic Church into the new age.

With the adoption of this worldview, the Americanists had bought uncritically into the ambivalent Puritan* idea of American election.* A sense of the providential ripeness of the historical moment and a fascination with the prospect of contributing to history's movement account for the confident tone of apocalyptic* urgency which characterizes Americanist thought and distinguishes it from that of other Catholic thinkers who shared the concern to adapt Catholicism to the American situation.

See also IMMIGRATION AND ETHNICITY, CATHOLIC; LONGINQUA OCEANI.

Americans United for Separation of Church and State. An organization promoting a policy of strict separation of church and state.* This group began as a coalition of liberals* and conservatives, under the leadership of Joseph Dawson,* which opposed the Supreme Court's decision in *Everson v. Board of Education* (1947) to allow federal assistance in transporting children to parochial schools. It experienced rapid growth under Glen Archer, who served as executive director from 1948 to 1975. It now claims a membership of fifty thousand.

Ames, Edward Scribner (1870-1958). Philosopher, theologian and Disciples of Christ* minister. Ames's long and prominent career showed him to be among the most radical of the theological modernists* of the Chicago school.* Indebted to William James,* John Dewey (1859-1952) and Henri Bergson (1859-1941), his functionalism examined the search for human values in a universe characterized by process and social existence in which traditional dogma* had no positive meaning.

Ames, Jessie Daniel (1883-1972). Suffragist* and antilynching reformer. After her husband died in 1914, Ames became involved in Methodist women's groups, which led her into the women's suffrage movement. Ames was founding president in 1919 of the Texas League of Women Voters. She worked persistently for interracial harmony; in 1930 she founded the Association of Southern Women for the Prevention of Lynching.

Ames, William (1576-1633). British Puritan* theologian important to separating and nonseparating Congregationalists.* As professor of theology in Holland (1622-1632), Ames attracted students from all over Europe. His family settled in New England, bringing his library with them.

Ames's *Marrow of Theology* (1623) provided a good summary of Calvinistic theology, while his theological methodology *(Technometry)* affected generations of New England divinity* students.

Amillennialism. The view that the thousand years of Revelation 20:1-6 is not a literal millennial rule of Christ on earth but is a symbolic reference to the period between the ministry of Christ and his Second Coming. Amillennialism teaches that there will be a continuous development of good and evil in the world until the return of Christ, when the dead shall be raised and the last judgment conducted. Augustine is the most prominent amillennialist.

See also ESCHATOLOGY.

Amish, Old Order. One of several North American groups whose roots go back to the sixteenth-century Swiss Anabaptists.* In the 1690s the Swiss Brethren (today called Mennonites*) experienced a schism, with one faction, led by Jakob Ammann, rejecting the new spirit of Pietism* that was influencing many Swiss Mennonites. Some of these Amish families immigrated to North America. In 1878, in another schism, one group of Amish decided for the "Old Order"; the other accepted more progressive ideas.

Anabaptist Tradition and Vision. The term *Anabaptist,* from the Greek word meaning "to rebaptize," was given to the movement by its opponents in the sixteenth century. Anabaptists, who were neither Catholic* nor Protestant,* stressed pacifism, the separation of church and state,* and church membership* consisting of adult believers only. Mennonites,* Amish* and Hutterites* are the lineal and doctrinal descendants of that earlier movement.

The Anabaptists, who exhibited a significant doctrinal uniformity, did not announce a program for changing the social order, but their doctrine of a believers' church, their simple egalitarianism, as well as their missionary zeal so threatened both church and state in central Europe that persecution and martyrdom swiftly descended upon them.

Mennonites came to North America for many reasons, but the longing for freedom of religion* was primary. This included the freedom to exercise their pacifism, congregational autonomy, the right not to swear oaths and control over their own educational programs. In recent times, Mennonites have recovered their dynamic sixteenth-century missionary zeal. Instead of continued withdrawal from society, many Mennonites seek involvement and have become voices for social justice.

The Amish and Hutterite wings of the Anabaptist tradition reflect the values of their tradition in the most visibly distinctive ways. Their separation from the world is evident in their avoidance of agricultural mechanization, their legendary frugality and their ecologically efficient farming. In contrast to Old Order Amish, Hutterite farms are fully mechanized with modern equipment, but cars, radios and television are not permitted.

Anaphora. As a liturgical* term, *anaphora* refers to the Eucharistic prayer,* what medieval and Reformation writers spoke of as "the prayer of consecration." Twentieth-century liturgical studies have given a great deal of attention to this prayer. An earlier supposition that there could be but one Eucharistic prayer has given way to the writing of multiple forms in many traditions: Roman Catholic,* Episcopal,* Lutheran,* Methodist,* Presbyterian* and Reformed.*

See also EUCHARISTIC DEVOTIONS.

Anderson, Isaac (1780-1857). Presbyterian* minister and educator. Disappointed at the reluctance of Princeton* graduates to serve on the frontier, Anderson played a leading role at the Synod* of Tennessee in 1819 in the formation of the Southern and Western Theological Seminary. Anderson trained about 150 ministers in his lifetime and so contributed toward a broad base of New School* sentiment and support in Tennessee.

Anderson, Rufus (1796-1880). Missionary statesman and theorist. From 1826 until his retirement in 1866, Anderson was the foreign secretary of the American Board of Commissioners for Foreign Missions* (ABCFM).

Anderson became a strong advocate of decentralization that would encourage local initiative and make better use of overseas resources. He supported the ordination of national pastors and affirmed that all missionary institutions should be directed at strengthening the nascent church.

Anderson, William Madison, Jr. (1889-1935). Presbyterian* pastor and educator. Anderson's influence on Lewis Sperry Chafer* led to Dallas's becoming the home of what was later Dallas Seminary,* at which Anderson was vice president and professor of homiletics.* He also was a pioneer radio preacher in Dallas.

Andover Controversy. The debate over the doctrine of "future probation," involving the faculty of Andover Theological Seminary.* Conservative Congregationalists,* objecting when faculty members taught that heathen who die without knowledge of the gospel will have a chance to accept it or reject it in the future life, succeeded in removing faculty member E. C. Smyth in 1887. In 1892 his dismissal was voided by the Supreme Court of Massachusetts.

Andover Theological Seminary. Congregational* seminary. Andover Seminary was founded in 1808 in reaction to the takeover of Harvard by the Unitarians* in 1805. True to its mission, the seminary produced zealous ministers eager to resist growing Unitarian and Arminian* tendencies in Massachusetts and beyond. In later decades, the faculty adopted more liberal theological methods. In 1931 the trustees affiliated with a local Baptist seminary to form Andover-Newton Theological School—an institution that continues to train ministers today.

See also ANDOVER CONTROVERSY.

Andrew, James Osgood (1794-1871). Methodist* bishop. In 1832 the Methodist Episcopal Church made Andrew, from Georgia, one of its two bishops. At the General Conference of 1844, however, a majority of Northern delegates asked for Andrews's suspension. A Plan of Separation was adopted, and in 1845 Southern Methodists created the Methodist Episcopal Church, South, with Andrew as a bishop, in which capacity he served until 1866.

Angelus. A popular devotion* in honor of the Virgin Mary* which developed in the Middle Ages. From the twelfth century it became customary to say the *Ave Maria* at the sound of the evening curfew bell. Later, the prayers were said whenever the Angelus bell tolled.

Anglican Church of Canada. The Irish-born Loyalist Charles Inglis* became the first Anglican bishop in Canada, then British North America, in 1787. Inglis, who, like his successors in 1851, was appointed by the Crown, strongly believed in the establishment of the Church of England in Nova Scotia. The Clergy Reserves* Act of 1840, however, recognized religious pluralism* and rejected the principle of an Anglican establishment in Canada.

In 1860 Bishop Francis Fulford* was elected as the first Metropolitan* of the self-governing Ecclesiastical Province of Canada. There are now thirty dioceses grouped into four ecclesiastical provinces. In 1990 the Anglican Church of Canada (as it was called after 1955) claimed 1,767 churches and nearly 850,000 members, of whom almost half live in Ontario.

In this century, the Anglican Church of Canada has inaugurated many liberalizing policies involving significant changes in structure, theology* and outlook.

Anglican Churches in America. Historically Anglicanism* has put far greater emphasis on church unity than have other Reformation churches. Two communions, the Episcopal Church* of the U.S. and the Anglican Church of Canada,* compose almost 99 percent of the Anglican population of English-speaking North America. Since the organization of American Methodism* in 1784, there has been only one significant schism from these churches—the Reformed Episcopal Church* in 1873, organized by George D. Cummins* and others.

Organized between 1784 and 1789, the Episcopal Church comprises a house of bishops* and a house of deputies.* It is headed by a presiding bishop. Also in 1789 a revised American prayer book, combining elements from both the English and Scottish Episcopal liturgies, was given final shape. The Episcopal Book of Common Prayer* underwent further revision in 1893, 1928 and 1979.

The Anglican Church of Canada* was gradually organized over the course of the second half of the nineteenth century. Earlier it had been viewed as an extension of the Church of England and had received state support. Each province in the Canadian Church is governed by a synod* and headed by a metropolitan archbishop. In 1893 the churches in western Canada became autonomous from England, and the different provincial synods were united in one general synod. The head of this united church is known as the Primate of All Canada.

See also ANGLICAN COMMUNION; CHURCH GOVERNMENT: EPISCOPAL; PROTESTANT EPISCOPAL CHURCH IN THE U.S.A.; TRACTARIANISM.

Anglican Communion. A term for the worldwide churches that are the heirs of the Anglican Reformation and who stand in full communion with the archbishop of Canterbury. As of 1987 the Anglican Communion contained over sixty million members found in twenty-seven self-governing churches and distributed through approximately 164 countries.

See also ANGLICAN CHURCH OF CANADA; ANGLICAN CHURCHES IN AMERICA; CHICAGO-LAMBETH QUADRILATERAL; EPISCOPAL CHURCH; LAMBETH CONFERENCES.

Anglicanism. An ecclesiastical tradition arising from the British Reformation of the sixteenth century. The first phase of the Anglican Reformation (1531-1547) stemmed from England's King Henry VIII's failure to receive papal support for annulling his marriage to Catherine of Aragon. In response, both king and Parliament repudiated papal primacy and asserted the supremacy of the Crown over the church. His successor, Edward VI, attempted to place the English church more firmly into the Protestant camp, and then Mary sought unsuccessfully to bring the English church back to the Roman primacy.

With the accession of Elizabeth (1558)—and largely through her influence—Anglicanism began to take on its present form. Although firmly a Protestant church, it kept much of the organization of the pre-Reformation English church. It strove to be theologically flexible by allowing for various theological understandings, and it emphasized its Book of Common Prayer* as the center of worship. Opposition arose among more radical Protestants (later known as Puritans*), who wanted the English church more fully reformed. What resulted was the unique Anglican understanding of itself as a middle way between the excesses of both Geneva and Rome, theologically reflected by the balancing of Scripture,* tradition and reason. This was the religious heritage brought to the New World by the English explorers.

The revolutionary* era was a period of crisis for American Anglicans. As a result of the war, Anglicanism was legally disestablished in every colony and overall was greatly weakened.

In 1785 church representatives from a number of states met in convention, and the Protestant Episcopal* Church in America began organizing itself. In Canada, at approximately the same time, the English church began receiving increased support both from the Society for the Propagation of the Gospel* and from the legislature of Nova Scotia, as well as the British Crown.

In the early nineteenth century tensions arose in both America and Canada between those inspired by the English Revival and those characterized as high church.* This tension shaped much of Anglican religious life in the nineteenth century, reaching a peak during the 1840s and 1850s with the growing influence of the Oxford movement (see Tractarianism*).

Like many other mainline* denominations,* the U.S. Episcopal Church grew steadily through the mid-1960s, then declined markedly and stabilized in the 1980s. High church/evangelical party strife has declined in the twentieth century, though this has been at least in part replaced by a conservative/liberal* split on questions such as prayer book reform, social outreach and the ordination of women.*

See also ANGLICAN CHURCH OF CANADA; ANGLICAN CHURCHES IN AMERICA; ANGLICAN COMMUNION; ANGLO-CATHOLICISM; CHURCH GOVERNMENT: EPISCOPAL; EPISCOPAL CHURCH; REFORMED EPISCOPAL CHURCH; TRACTARIANISM.

Anglo-Catholicism. The common name for the most extreme wing of the high church* party within Anglicanism.* As a concept it arose out of the Oxford movement's emphasis upon the historic continuity of the Church of England with the pre-Reformation English church (*see* Tractarianism).

Anglo-Catholics, who are stronger in England than in America, have seen their task as reviving the spirit and forms of Catholicism within Anglicanism, particularly through emulating the theology and practice of the Middle Ages, Eastern Orthodoxy and post-Reformation Roman Catholicism.

Annual Conference. A geographic and organizational body within a Methodist* church, the annual conference is the heartbeat of Methodism. The Methodist *Discipline* requires an equal number of clergy and laity as conference members, who meet annually for three to five days to debate issues and do all necessary business.

Anointing. To apply oil or ointment as a sign of consecration* and invocation of the Holy Spirit. The term comes from the biblical practice of anointing persons or objects consecrated to holy service. Anointing, prayer and forgiveness of sins are associated with healing in James 5:14-15.

Protestant* commentators understand the efficacy of anointing the sick to arise from the "prayer of faith," while Roman Catholics* associate it with the Markan account of Jesus commissioning his disciples (Mk 6:7-11) and so speak of a sacrament* of anointing the sick.

See also BAPTISM; CHRISM; UNCTION.

Anointing of the Sick, Sacrament of the. *See* EXTREME UNCTION, SACRAMENT OF.

Anthony, Susan Brownell (1820-1906). Quaker social reformer. Anthony took on the moral zeal of her father, an early abolitionist,* and followed in the footsteps of outspoken women in her Quaker family tree. Her whole career reflected her devotion to reform. Following the Civil War* she devoted her life to endless lecture tours and state campaigns to win women the right to vote.

The suffrage crusade linked her with Elizabeth Cady Stanton* in one of the most productive intellectual partnerships in American history. In 1869 they organized the National Woman Suffrage Association (see Women's Suffrage Movement).

Anticlericalism. Opposition to perceived undue influence of clergy in church and society. Although a tradition of some individual scorn for ministers exists, anticlericalism has never taken root in the U.S. In the American Revolution* ministers were leading spokespersons, solidifying their place at the center of society. In the late 1980s, while polls showed ministers among the most admired people in America, a certain anticlericalism was perceptible in the secular media's treatment of news stories regarding popular religious figures.

Antimission Movement. A nineteenth-century Calvinistic Baptist* response to denominational* innovations and the growth of voluntary* societies. During the 1820s and 1830s, the development of state conventions as well as missionary, benevolence and educational societies evoked a hostile reaction among some Baptists living in the underdeveloped areas of the Ohio and Lower Mississippi River Valleys. Recent scholarship has tended to emphasize social and cultural factors that brought about the movement rather than the theological issues that were reportedly at stake.

See also BAPTIST CHURCHES IN THE U.S.A.; MISSIONARY BAPTISTS; PRIMITIVE BAPTISTS.

Antinomian Controversy. Meaning literally "against law," *antinomianism* describes a theological position in which the role of objective, external elements of Christianity (such as obedience to the moral law) are underemphasized and subjective, while internal elements of Christianity (such as the work of the Holy Spirit) are overemphasized.

In America this position is first associated with the teachings of Anne Hutchinson* of Boston, who believed that most of the Massachusetts Puritan* ministers were overly emphasizing external morality. The ensuing controversy nearly destroyed the colony.

Anti-Saloon League of America. A national Prohibition organization. Founded in 1895, the league had the professed goal of closing down the businesses which manufactured, distributed and sold alcoholic beverages; its ultimate goal was a "dry" society. The league reflected nineteenth-century evangelical antipathy toward the use of alcohol* and the demand that Christian standards govern the private behavior even of nonbelievers.

The league quickly gained ascendancy in the antiliquor crusade, using evangelical congregations as league units focusing on the single issue of Prohibition. Victory came in January 1919, with the ratification of the Eighteenth Amendment.

See also PROHIBITION MOVEMENT; TEMPERANCE MOVEMENT.

Anxious Bench. See MOURNER'S BENCH.

Apocalypticism. The expectation of imminent, cataclysmic events related to the Second Coming of Jesus Christ or the end of the age. Although similar to millenarianism,* it has broader applications and is not tied to any one millennial position. Particularly relevant for early American Christianity was the apocalyptic strand in seventeenth-century English Puritanism,* shaped by the Reformation view of the pope as antichrist and forged in the revolutionary traumas of the 1640s.

Since that time, many other persons and movements have also been viewed apocalyptically, including the British Empire, the French Revolution, a supposed conspiracy of Enlightenment* illuminati and the struggle against slavery.

In the twentieth century, the world wars have generated several antichrist candidates, dispensationalists* have viewed the Soviet Union apocalyptically, and some have portrayed the European Common Market, universal product codes and the New Age movement* as dangers of apocalyptic proportions.

See also ESCHATOLOGY.

Apologetics. Christian apologetics, broadly conceived, is argumentation on behalf of the Christian faith. Its substance is derived from revelation, while its packaging reflects the culture it addresses. Presumably, apologetics is directed toward those outside the Christian community, but in reality the audience is usually those within the Christian community.

Apologetics was imported to America ready-made from Great Britain. At the close of the eighteenth century, when English and French deism* penetrated most facets of American life, the British antideistic apologetic became the standard, particularly that of Joseph Butler (1692-1752) and William Paley (1743-1805). By the 1850s, new challenges were appearing on the horizon—first evolution* and then the new form of biblical interpretation,* higher criticism. After 1900, apologetics became more and more problematic. Liberals* and fundamentalists* could no longer talk with each other because the fundamentalists retained the older Lockean epistemology while the liberals followed first Hegel and then Kant or the pragmatists.

A revival followed World War II* with the apologetic theology of Paul Tillich* and the conservative apologetics of Gordon H. Clark,* Edward J. Carnell* and Bernard Ramm. By the late 1960s American intellectuals were increasingly fractured epistemologically, variously affirming logical positivism, language analysis, phenomenology, existentialism,* neo-Kantianism, process,* personalism, pragmatism and neo-Thomism.*

Apologist. See APOLOGETICS.

Apostasy. The abandonment of true Christian faith. In contrast to heresy,* apostasy refers to the total renunciation of Christianity through either word or deed. Apostasy may involve outright renunciation or the abandonment of a recognizably Christian lifestyle.

See also ASSURANCE OF SALVATION; ETERNAL SECURITY.

Apostolate. In general, *apostle* refers to both the mission and the representational authority* of one sent on a mission by a superior. *Apostle* refers to the authoritative mission conferred by Christ on his disciples. Later, *apostolic* referred to anything connected with the mission or apostolate of the Catholic Church. *Lay apostolate* or *apostolate of the laity* refers to the role or mission of the laity in contrast to but also in communion with the apostolate of the church hierarchy.

Apostolic Delegate. A papal diplomat. As official papal representative to the local (i.e., regional or national) church, this ecclesial diplomat promotes the unity of the Roman Catholic Church* by fostering Vatican-U.S. Catholic church relations.*

Apostolic Succession. In general, the whole church in any age may be viewed as the successor or follower of the apostolic church. In Catholic usage, *apostolic succession* is a technical term designating the college of bishops, in which the bishop of Rome, the pope, plays a special role. This college of bishops succeeds the college of apostles, especially the Twelve, in the administration and governance of the church.

Contemporary ecumenical* dialogue has often focused on the issue of apostolic succession and ministry, with a more biblical understanding of ministry emerging on both sides.

See also LAY MOVEMENT, CATHOLIC.

Apthorp, East (1733-1816). Episcopal* minister and founder of Christ Church, Cambridge, Massachusetts. The Congregational* establishment, concerned about the number of Anglican churches being formed in New England, made verbal attacks upon the spread of episcopacy.* Apthorp wrote a tract in defense, Thomas Mayhew* responded, and a pamphlet war erupted.

Archbishop. An episcopal office higher than that of bishop. The term usually designates those bishops whose jurisdiction extends over an ecclesiastical province, rather than over a single diocese.*

Archdiocese. A preeminent diocese* presided over by an archbishop. In a practice dating back to at least the fourth century, several neighboring dioceses are grouped into provinces. The most significant of these dioceses is then designated the metropolitan see, or archdiocese; the others are called suffragan dioceses. In the U.S. and Canada only the Roman Catholic Church* makes extensive use of the archdiocesan structure.

Argue, Andrew Harvey (1869-1959). Pentecostal* pioneer in Canada. Argue was a key figure in the emergence of the Pentecostal Assemblies of Canada in the late 1910s. He published several magazines promoting his views, notably the *Apostolic Messenger*.

See also PENTECOSTAL CHURCHES; PENTECOSTAL MOVEMENT.

Armenian Church. A non-Chalcedonian Orthodox* church. Christianity was proclaimed the official state religion in Armenia in 301, making it the first Christian nation. In 305 St. Gregory the Illuminator became the first *catholicos* (chief bishop) of Armenia. The Armenian Church belongs to the family of Eastern Orthodox churches commonly referred to as Oriental, or non-Chalcedonian, because of their opposition to the Council of Chalcedon (451) and their advocacy of the christological doctrine of St. Cyril of Alexandria.

Very few Armenians arrived on the shores of the U.S. until the first half of the nineteenth century. The first Armenian church was consecrated in Worcester, Massachusetts, in 1891. In 1933 an internal conflict within the community led to the establishment of a rival diocesan jurisdiction called the Armenian Apostolic Church of America, which in 1992 reported thirty-two congregations with an inclusive membership of 150,000. The schism remains unresolved to this day.

Beginning in the early 1970s, an ongoing wave of new immigrants from various Middle Eastern countries has brought the number of Armenians in the U.S. to an estimated population of over 750,000. In 1984 the Diocese of Canada was established. In 1991 the principal Armenian church body in the U.S., the Armenian Church of America, reported seventy-two churches and an inclusive membership of 414,000.

Arminianism. A theological reform movement within the Dutch Reformed Church in the early seventeenth century, Arminianism had considerable influence in Anglo-American theological developments, particularly as it came to be championed by Methodists.* The movement is traced to the work of Jacob Arminius (1560-1609), a convinced Calvinist* who eventually departed from the teachings of Calvin on several points of doctrine. In Arminius's view, God's decrees were based on his foreknowledge of the future faith of the elect and not foreordained so as to permit no room for a free human response to God's offer of saving grace. Moreover, this human response was not simply the exercise of free will, which would be to repeat the ancient Pelagian heresy. Arminius maintained that since the human will is enslaved to sin, it is necessary for God to assist people in responding to the invitation to salvation.* He does so by providing prevenient grace, thus enabling the will to respond freely to God. In his view, God also foreknows who will persevere in their Christian faith after conversion, although once again God's foreknowledge does not mean that he foreordains that they cannot fall from grace if they choose to do so.

The original tenets of Arminius enjoyed a restoration in the eighteenth century, emerging with evangelical* warmth in the Wesleyan* revival. Wesley overtly identified with the Arminian label during a dispute that erupted in 1770, when Methodists were labeled Arminians, although there is little indication that Arminius had heretofore been a major source in Wesley's theological reading. Wesley, accepting this label, named his new Methodist theological journal the *Arminian Magazine* when it began publication in 1778. There he advocated the case for "conditional salvation" in terms of "universal redemption" in Christ, in opposition to the Calvinist doctrines of predestination and the irresistibility of grace.

Methodism became the largest Protestant* denomination* within nineteenth-century America, and with it the Arminian ascendancy prevailed in the Second Great Awakening.* The Arminian outlook that informed this Methodist age of American Protestantism fit well with the emphasis upon voluntarism* and purposiveness that came to characterize American evangelical Protestantism.

Armitage, Thomas (1819-1896). Baptist* historian and pastor. Originally a Methodist Episcopal* pastor, Armitage is best known for his publication of *A History of the Baptists* (1887), in which he attempts to trace the continuation of Baptist teachings from the New Testament to the present.

See also AMERICAN BIBLE UNION; LANDMARK MOVEMENT.

Armstrong, Annie Walker (1850-1938). Leader of the Southern Baptist* Woman's Missionary Union. Armstrong led in the formation of the union in 1888 and also in the Lottie Moon* Christmas Offering. Perhaps more than any other person in the convention's history, Armstrong helped advance the cause of Southern Baptist home and foreign missions.

See also MISSIONARY MOVEMENT, WOMEN'S.

Armstrong, George Dod (1813-1899). Southern Presbyterian* pastor and scientist. As both a prominent pastor and as his denomination's* leading spokesman on the relationship between religion and science, Armstrong significantly influenced Southern Presbyterian opinion in the second half of the nineteenth century. His published works included a defense of slavery and persistent attacks on Darwinism.*

Armstrong, Laura Dell Malotte (1886-1945). Southern Baptist* missions* leader. Armstrong served on the executive committee of the Southern Baptist Convention from 1927 to 1945. She is best known for her leadership in the Woman's Missionary Union.

Armstrong, William Park (1874-1944). Presbyterian* New Testament scholar. Armstrong, a faculty member at Princeton Theological Seminary,* was on the board of the *Princeton Review* through all its years (1903-1929). He stayed at Princeton when J. Gresham Machen* and others left to form Westminster Theological Seminary.

Arndt, William Frederick (1880-1957). Lutheran New Testament scholar. Arndt, professor at Concordia Seminary, St. Louis (1921-1951), is best known for his work (1949-1955) with F. Wilbur Gingrich in producing an English translation and adaptation of Walter Bauer's magisterial Greek-German lexicon of the New Testament and early Christian writings.

Art, Liturgical. See LITURGICAL ART.

Articles of Religion (1784). Articles of doctrine prepared by John Wesley* for American Methodists.* When Methodists in America separated from the Anglican Church,* Wesley sent over, as standards of worship* and doctrine, a Sunday Service and the Articles of Religion, which the founding conference of the Methodist Episcopal Church* adopted in 1784. He sent twenty-four of the original Anglican articles, and the Americans added one more by inserting a statement affirming the new national government.

Asbury, Francis (1745-1816). First Methodist* general superintendent, or bishop, in America. In 1771, in response to a plea from John Wesley* for preachers to go to America to aid the fledgling Methodist work there, Asbury volunteered.

Aggressively evangelistic, Asbury was dis-tressed to find many Methodist preachers in America "settled" in one location. He was successful in prodding them into "circulation," which gave rise to the Methodist circuit rider.* Asbury himself traveled almost incessantly for forty-five years, covering an estimated 300,000 miles and preaching over 16,000 sermons.

By the end of the Revolutionary War, Asbury was the acknowledged leader of American Methodists. At the so-called Christmas Conference* (1784/1785), which formed the Methodist Episcopal Church, Asbury and Thomas Coke* were elected general superintendents.

Asbury used his office and influence to spur Methodism into a tremendous period of growth which continued well beyond his death in 1816.

Ash Wednesday. The first day of Lent* in Western churches, so designated from the custom in liturgical* churches of sprinkling ashes on the heads of the people as a sign of mortality, accompanied by the words "Remember that you are dust, and to dust you shall return" (Gen 3:19).

Asian-American Protestants. Protestantism has played a significant role among a variety of groups who are of Asian ancestry.

Chinese-Americans. The early period of Chinese immigration spans the years 1850 to 1882, when approximately 322,000 Chinese arrived in the U.S. With its newly discovered gold and with railroad and agricultural industries in need of cheap labor, California became the primary base of most Chinese immigrants. Nativist* sentiments culminated in the Chinese Exclusion Act of 1882, which effectively barred further Chinese immigration well into the twentieth century.

Protestant efforts among the Chinese became firmly rooted toward the end of the 1860s. By 1892 eleven denominations* were involved in home mission* efforts. Protestantism today claims the allegiance of only about 6 percent of the Chinese-American population, which, according to the 1980 census, is the largest Asian-American group, with approximately 820,000 persons.

Japanese-Americans. Japanese immigration to the U.S. began around 1860 and reached its peak at the turn of the century, when an estimated 130,000 Japanese filled the need for labor in the agricultural-, mining- and fishing-related industries of the West Coast and Hawaii.

The beginnings of Protestantism among the Japanese can be traced to San Francisco in 1877, when the Gospel Society was formed by several Japanese immigrants. Like the Chinese, the Japanese suffered from nativism and ethnic hysteria, culminating in the tragic incarceration of over 110,000 persons of Japanese ancestry during World War II.

Overall, the churches have not reached a large number of Japanese-Americans, with total membership representing about 3 percent of the current Japanese-American population of 720,000 (1980 census).

Korean-Americans. Between the years 1903 and 1905, a small group of Koreans left for the shores of Hawaii, and from there they traveled to the West Coast of the U.S. The overall Korean-American population did not grow much during the years 1910-1945 because it too suffered from the nativism and anti-Asian legislation that was imposed on other Asian-American groups. Not until the easing of immigration restrictions in 1965 did large numbers of Koreans begin to arrive in the U.S.

In contrast to the immigration patterns of the Chinese and Japanese, Korean-Americans have enthusiastically embraced Protestant Christianity, helped no doubt by some immigrants' being Christians before their arrival. As throughout the entire history of the Korean-American community, the Protestant church has been a central institution. It is estimated that there are one thousand Korean-American churches, accounting for approximately 65 percent of the Korean-American population (1990 census: 850,000).

Assemblies of God. Pentecostal* denomination.* Formed in 1914 in Hot Springs, Arkansas, the Assemblies of God (AG), with well over fifteen million adherents, is today the largest Pentecostal denomination in the world.

The people who formed the AG often shared backgrounds in one or another of the settings that had proved receptive to Pentecostal teaching— the Christian and Missionary Alliance;* John A. Dowie's* Zion City; Charles Parham's* Apostolic Faith movement in Texas; Elizabeth Baker's* Rochester Bible Training Institute; one or another local holiness* associations. Their sense of participation in a broader religious awakening was nurtured through such networks by a wide variety of Pentecostal periodicals, and frequent camp meetings* and conventions. Otherwise, they worked independently, with a strong stress on the restoration of New Testament Christianity, evangel-

ism,* healing* and the imminence of the Second Coming. They reveled in intense religious experiences;* for them Pentecostalism was a way of life, a way of perceiving reality.

Their initial reluctance to adopt a creed was challenged by the emergence of unorthodox trinitarian views within the constituency. In 1916 the fledgling denomination adopted a Statement of Fundamental Truths, which addressed the trinitarian question and defined a Pentecostal distinctive but omitted such doctrines as the virgin birth. In 1962, as the denomination asserted its evangelical* identity more formally, statements on the verbal inspiration of Scripture, the virgin birth and other doctrines affirmed in the National Association of Evangelicals'* statement of faith were added to the Statement of Fundamental Truths.

Those who formed the AG had already rejected the necessity of a crisis sanctification* experience. They anticipated that believers should experience one work of grace, not two (as their Holiness counterparts urged), and a crisis enduement with power, which they called the baptism with the Holy Spirit.* Their ideas on sanctification had been influenced by William Durham.*

From the outset the denomination supported a growing missions program. By the mid-1980s the Assemblies of God annually devoted some $135 million (nearly 75 percent of its total expenditures) to its various world ministries, in which some 1,500 missionaries served in 118 countries.

Assistant/Associate Pastor. An ordained* minister who works with the senior pastor of a larger congregation. The role of assistant pastor developed in response to the need for younger pastors to gain on-the-job training with the example, support and supervision of a more experienced senior minister.

Associate Reformed Presbyterian Church. *See* GENERAL SYNOD OF THE ASSOCIATE REFORMED PRESBYTERIAN CHURCH.

Associated Gospel Churches. A Canadian evangelical* denomination.* One of the few Christian bodies indigenous to Canada, the roots of the Associated Gospel Churches (AGC) lay in the intense evangelistic/revivalistic* and missionary movement of the late nineteenth century.

The key figure in the formation of the AGC was Peter W. Philpott,* who began the Gospel Tabernacle in Hamilton, Ontario. Satellite congregations were founded, which came together in 1921 to form the AGC. Growing steadily over the years, the group now has some ten thousand members in 115 congregations across Canada.

Association of Baptists for Evangelism in the Orient. *See* ASSOCIATION OF BAPTISTS FOR WORLD EVANGELISM.

Association of Baptists for World Evangelism. Independent Baptist* foreign mission* society. The fundamentalist-modernist controversy* in the Northern Baptist Convention led to the formation of the Association of Baptists for Evangelism in the Orient in 1927, which concentrated only on the Philippines. In 1939 it extended its operations into Peru and changed to its current name; today it oversees over seven hundred missionaries in twenty-nine countries.

Association of Evangelical Lutheran Churches. A Lutheran* denomination* now part of the Evangelical Lutheran Church in America.* It consisted of a group who left the Lutheran Church—Missouri Synod* after a conservative element took over in 1969.

Assumption of Mary. The Roman Catholic* doctrine that Mary, at the completion of her earthly life, was taken up to heaven, body and soul. It is attested to by New Testament apocrypha from the late fourth century onward and also found expression in feasts celebrating the death of Mary, perhaps as early as the fourth century.

Assurance of Salvation. The certainty or confidence which Christians have with respect to their own salvation.* There are two salient features that make up the doctrine of assurance: The first aspect is its objective basis, which Christians identify as being the death and resurrection of Christ. The second aspect, a subjective basis, entails the Christian's sense of acceptance before God.

While almost all Christian traditions affirm both the objective and the subjective bases of assurance, they vary in the emphasis and shape given to those affirmations. Roman Catholics,* for example, look to the sacramental* ministry of the church (especially penance* and the Eucharist*) as the means whereby assurance is communicated.

Reformed* Christians, following the Westmins-

ter Confession of Faith,* affirm "an infallible assurance of faith, founded upon the divine truth of the promises of salvation, the inward evidence of those graces upon which these promises are made, the testimony of the Spirit of adoption witnessing with our spirits that we are the children of God" (Article 18).

In a similar fashion, Christians differ over the constancy of the certainty they have about their salvation. For those, like Calvinists, who embrace doctrines of election and eternal security,* present assurance is directly connected to their future life with God. For others, including Roman Catholics and Wesleyan*-Arminians,* a present sense of assurance does not necessarily imply inclusion in a future state of blessedness, since salvation can be lost through faithlessness.

See also ETERNAL SECURITY.

Atheism. A transliteration of a Greek word which means "without God." The term has come to mean a disbelief in the existence of God.

Atheists have defended their position by appeals to the cruelty of nature (Charles Darwin), religion as a human invention to ease emotional pain (Karl Marx), God as a childish projection growing out of the wish for a father who would not die (Sigmund Freud), the impossibility of defining God in empirical terms (logical positivists) or the possibility of explaining everything that exists by scientific laws or human decisions (twentieth-century secular humanism*).

One of the most visible atheists in modern America has been Madalyn Murray O'Hair (b. 1919).

Athenagoras I (Aristoclis Spyrou) (1886-1972). Greek Orthodox* archbishop of North and South America and patriarch of Constantinople. Athenagoras was elected archbishop of the Greek Orthodox Church in the Western Hemisphere in 1931; in 1948 he was elected patriarch. He cultivated cooperation among the various Orthodox churches through a series of Pan-Orthodox Conferences, the first of which was held in Rhodes in 1961. He also developed a wide-ranging ecumenical ministry, meeting in Jerusalem in 1964 with Pope Paul VI.*

Atonement, Theories of. U.S. theologians have taught at least four views of the nature of the atonement.

The *substitutionary-penal* view was taught by

Jonathan Edwards* and other early American Calvinist* theologians. Christ's death primarily affects God; by his death, he paid the penalty for sin* to which humans were liable. This view emphasizes the holiness and righteousness of God and, consequently, the seriousness of humanity's sinful state.

The *governmental* view arose as strict Calvinism began to diminish. As taught by Joseph Bellamy* and others, the death of Christ primarily affects humanity and only secondarily affects God. Its primary purpose was to demonstrate the seriousness of sin by showing the extremity of God's action in putting his Son to death.

The *moral-influence* theory is primarily subjective in orientation. The leading American exponent was Horace Bushnell,* who emphasized that moral renovation of humanity requires more than mere good example and instruction. There must be some supernatural influence, which was accomplished by Christ's work.

The so-called *Socinian* or *example* theory of the atonement is perhaps the most subjective view. As taught by Unitarians,* human nature has not been radically corrupted by sin and thus needs not a moral and spiritual transformation or regeneration but a living example of virtue and righteousness. The death of Jesus Christ accomplishes this.

Conservative theologians have also debated the extent of the atonement. In general, Arminians* have held to an unlimited atonement, or general redemption (Christ died for the sins of the entire human race). Calvinists, in contrast, have espoused a limited atonement, or particular redemption (Christ died simply for the elect*). The Arminian view has been a potent theological rationale behind American Protestant revivalism,* with its broad invitation to the masses to "accept Christ."

An issue that has traditionally divided Protestants and Catholics* concerns the control and application of the benefits of Christ's atonement. Generally, conservative Protestants have held that the benefits of the atonement are available to all who believe. The traditional Roman Catholic position (expanded greatly by Vatican II*) has been that the church controls the "treasury of merit"* and that only those who are linked to its sacramental* system receive the benefits of Christ's death.

See also FUNDAMENTALS, THE; NEW ENGLAND THEOLOGY; NEW HAVEN THEOLOGY; PRINCETON THEOLOGY; REFORMED TRADITION.

Atwater, Lyman Hotchkiss (1813-1883). Princeton* College professor and apologist.* Along with Charles Hodge,* Atwater defended Old School* Calvinism against the mediating theologies of Nathaniel Taylor* and Horace Bushnell.* During the mid-nineteenth century he was probably the greatest champion of conservative Calvinist political, social and economic views.

Auburn Affirmation (1924). A document, entitled "An Affirmation," designed to safeguard the unity and liberty of the Presbyterian Church in the U.S.A.,* issued during the fundamentalist* controversy by a group of ministers meeting in Auburn, New York. It was intended as a liberal* protest against the Five Point Deliverance* of the 1910 General Assembly.*

See also FUNDAMENTALS, THE; PORTLAND DELIVERANCE.

Auburn Declaration (1837). A theological statement issued by New School* Presbyterians* in 1837 intended to confirm their Presbyterian orthodoxy.* The declaration defended the New School against accusations of heresy* made by the Old School* majority at the 1837 General Assembly* of the Presbyterian Church in the U.S.A.* The declaration affirmed a moderate but generally orthodox Calvinism, which its signers believed reflected Presbyterian doctrinal standards.

Augustinianism. A tradition of theological and philosophical thought based on the work of St. Augustine of Hippo (A.D. 354-430). Augustine's major writings include his *Confessions* (400) and *The City of God* (413-426). The Augustinian tradition in general has five emphases: (1) the primacy of the will over the intellect (I believe so that I may understand), (2) knowledge as illumination from God, (3) the soul as the human being, (4) the pervasive effects of the fall into sin* and (5) God's grace as manifested in divine election.*

In contemporary Catholic theology, Augustine's influence can still be seen wherever there is emphasis on action (the will) before abstract theology (the intellect), knowledge through self-knowledge or the centrality of the sacraments.

Among Protestants, Augustinianism can be seen in the various Calvinistic* or predestinarian theological traditions, as illustrated by the thought of Jonathan Edwards.*

Auricular Confession. See PENANCE, SACRAMENT OF.

Austin, Anne (d. 1665). Quaker* missionary. Austin arrived in Massachusetts Bay Colony in 1656 with Mary Fisher.* They were immediately imprisoned, and their books were burned. Austin ultimately became a housekeeper for a leading Quaker in England.

Authority. The power to author, command or sanction certain forms of life or ways of being, both corporate and personal, and to proscribe others. Within the traditions of Christian faith, all Protestants* and Roman Catholics,* and some Eastern Orthodox,* agree that the God of Jesus Christ is the ultimate source of both true authority and freedom. God's authority is the persuasive power of divine truth to create, sustain and perfect a historical community of royal, priestly and prophetic persons as the living image of divine freedom in the world.

The theological meaning of authority is an enduring issue in the West because of the breakdown of obedience to traditional sources and institutions of authority during the Reformation and the Enlightenment.* Authority was redefined in terms of individual consent to probable reason, and internal evidence was judged without invoking external theological authorities or doctrines. Autonomy radically redefined or replaced traditional modes of authority.

In the context of Protestant communities, North American religious history has witnessed a critical tension between institutional and charismatic forms of authority. The conflicts and conversations between these two forms of authority have encouraged a broader recognition among Protestants that their own churches and communities, like Catholics and Eastern Orthodox, also employ extrabiblical sources of authority in the interpretation and use of Scripture.

Autocephalous Orthodox Church. The status of a self-governing local Orthodox* church having the right to elect its own primate. In 1970 the Patriarchate of Moscow granted autocephaly to the jurisdiction in America known as the Metropolia. Since then, it has used the title The Orthodox Church in America. After the Greek Orthodox Archdiocese (Ecumenical Patriarchate),* it is the second-largest Orthodox jurisdiction in America, claiming about 350 parishes serving over 500,000 communicants.

As the first see of Orthodoxy, the Patriarchate of Constantinople has opposed the grant of autocephaly to the Metropolia, affirming that only the Patriarchate of Constantinople can grant autocephaly apart from the context of an ecumenical council.

Awakenings, College. Religious revivals* on university campuses. Perhaps the earliest religious awakening among students occurred at the University of Paris in the seventeenth century. Other student revivals touched Count Nicholas von Zinzendorf* in Halle (1710-1716) and John Wesley,* who in 1726 gathered the Holy Club at Oxford.

Meanwhile, in America revival had also touched university campuses. The "Haystack Prayer Meeting" (1806) at Williams College issued in the birth of the American foreign missionary movement.* The Second Great Awakening touched Yale College* (1802) and afterward spread to other colleges. Later in the nineteenth century, the focus of revival shifted to Oberlin College.*

After World War II* returning servicemen brought a renewed zeal for foreign missions to college campuses in Britain and America. This zeal has been fostered by the triennial Urbana Convention.*

Ayer, William Ward (1892-1985). Fundamentalist* Baptist* pastor, evangelist, radio voice and Bible conference* speaker. Converted* in 1916 at a Billy Sunday* revival meeting in Boston, Ayer later pastored churches in the U.S. and Canada. He is best remembered as minister of Calvary Baptist Church, New York City (1936-1949). Under Ayer's leadership the church grew from 400 to 1,600 members, and he had a weekly radio audience of some quarter million persons. Ayer traveled widely, making evangelistic trips to England and to Central and South America.

Azusa Street Mission. The site of early Pentecostalism's* legendary Azusa Street Revival,* which began in April 1906 under the leadership of William J. Seymour* and continued for approximately three years. Although not the point of origin of Pentecostalism, the mission provided the greatest impetus for its early growth and expansion.

During the revival, thousands of people from around the world made pilgrimages to Azusa

Street. Many, like Gaston B. Cashwell* and Charles H. Mason,* found their"'Pentecost" there and returned home as emissaries of the movement.

Azusa was noted for its fivefold doctrine of salvation,* sanctification,* tongues as evidence of Spirit baptism,* divine healing and the imminent Second Coming of Christ (*see* Eschatology).

B

Babcock, Rufus (1798-1875). Baptist minister in the North. In addition to his work as pastor, Babcock served as president of Waterville College of Maine (now Colby College) from 1833 to 1836 and as corresponding secretary of the American Bible Society* and the American Sunday School Union.* By advocating interdenominational cooperation, he helped Northern Baptists overcome their sectarian tendencies.

Bachman, John (1790-1874). Lutheran* minister, naturalist. Bachman won fame as a "Patriarch of Southern Lutheranism" and an American naturalist. While pastor of St. John's Lutheran Church, Charleston, South Carolina (1815-1868), he founded the South Carolina Horticultural Society (1833) and collaborated with John James Audubon on *Birds of America* (1827).

Backus, Isaac (1724-1806). Baptist* minister and champion of religious liberty.* Raised a Calvinist, Backus came slowly to Baptist beliefs but then plunged into evangelistic tours, pastoral responsibilities and the cause of religious freedom.

In 1773 his most important tract, *An Appeal to the Public for Religious Liberty Against the Oppression of the Present Day,* appeared—the best exposition of the eighteenth-century evangelical* concept of separation of church and state.* It is estimated that Backus traveled over sixty-seven thousand miles and preached close to ten thousand sermons in nearly sixty years of ministry.

Bacon, Leonard, Sr. (1802-1881). Congregational* minister and reformer. Bacon spent his entire ministerial career at New Haven's First Congregational Church (1824-1881). He also taught theology and church history at Yale Divinity School and edited the antislavery publication *The Independent* (1846-1881).

Bacon became a formidable polemicist, arguing particularly for a gradual emancipation of slaves. His volume *Slavery Discussed in Occasional Essays* (1846) influenced Abraham Lincoln.* Bacon was known as a diplomat who supported cooperation between churches as long as congregational autonomy was not at stake.

Bacon, Leonard Woolsey, Jr. (1830-1907). Congregational* minister and controversialist. From 1854 to 1892 Bacon pastored nine churches in regions as diverse as Geneva, Switzerland, and Savannah, Georgia. A forceful speaker and a combative writer, his niche was in polemics. His taste for historical investigation is evident in the capstone volume to the American Church History Series, *History of American Christianity* (1897).

Badin, Stephen Theodore (1768-1853). French Catholic* frontier missionary. In 1793 Badin became the first Catholic priest ordained* in the U.S. He played a key role in establishing Catholicism in Kentucky, Indiana and Tennessee. He donated property on which the University of Notre Dame was later built and is buried on the campus.

Bainton, Roland (1894-1984). Church historian. In 1927 Bainton was ordained* a minister of the Congregational Church,* though he also maintained an associate membership in the Society of Friends.* He taught church history at Yale from 1936 to 1962. Author of over thirty-two books, he is best known for *Here I Stand: A Life of Martin Luther* (1950). His scholarship combined with his clarity made him one of the most influential church historians in his time.

Baird, Robert (1798-1863). Presbyterian* minister, ecumenical* pioneer and leader of voluntary societies.* Baird's main concerns were temperance,* missions* and ecumenism.* His pioneering work as a leader and shaper of voluntary societies found him drawing support from several denominations* while frequently placing them under broad interdenominational governance. A prolific author, he charted the movements of voluntary societies, evangelicalism* and the American church scene in his classic *Religion in America* (1843).

Baker, Elizabeth V. (1849-1915). Faith healer* and educator. After an experience of healing in 1881, Baker devoted her life to Christian service. In 1895 she and her four sisters opened the Faith Mission in Rochester, New York, which later a variety of ministries. In 1907 they identified their work with the Pentecostal movement.

Balch, Hezekiah (1741-1810). Presbyterian* minister in East Tennessee. During a trip to New England in 1794, Balch met Samuel Hopkins,* whose "New Divinity" theology* Balch introduced on his return to Tennessee. This led to the growth of liberal currents that spurred defections of Tennessee Presbyterians into the New School* following the schism of 1837-1838.

See also DOAK, SAMUEL; NEW ENGLAND THEOLOGY.

Baldwin, Harmon Allen (1869-1936). Pentecost Band leader, Free Methodist* minister and theologian. A scholar of theology* and history, and a prolific author, Baldwin argued for a return to a Wesleyan* understanding of Christian perfection, for congruence with the patristic tradition and for Christian social responsibility.

Ballou, Hosea (1771-1852). Leader of New England Universalism.* Son of a Baptist minister, Ballou by 1791 had embraced Universalism. His *Treatise on Atonement* (1805), which reflects rationalist influences, presents a Unitarian* view of God that relegates Christ to the role of divine agent and makes God's love the central tenet, concluding that God through Christ's redeeming love will reconcile all to himself. Ballou started the *Universalist Magazine* in 1819, and in 1830 he founded the *Universalist Expositor*. For thirty-five years he was pastor of the Second Universalist Society in Boston. He saw Universalism grow to over 800,000 adherents.

Baltimore, Councils of. Meetings of the U.S. Roman Catholic* bishops in the nineteenth century to consider church concerns and to legislate uniform church discipline.* The first provincial council was held in 1829, with seven more over the next twenty years. Three times the hierarchy gathered for a plenary council: in 1852, 1866 and 1884. No further meetings of the entire hierarchy were held until the formation of the National Catholic War Conference* in 1917.

See also CONCILIAR TRADITION, AMERICAN.

Bangs, Nathan (1778-1862). Methodist* minister and editor. Bangs founded the Methodist Missionary Society, serving as its first secretary (1836-1841). He wrote a number of historical and doctrinal works, including a four-volume *History of the Methodist Episcopal Church* (1838-1840). His writings reflect his antipathy toward the Calvinist* doctrines of election* and predestination,* which he viewed as contrary to Scripture, reason and experience.

Bapst, John (1815-1887). Jesuit* missionary and educator. Bapst served in Maine on a missionary circuit of thirty-three towns (1848-1859), where he became noted for his converts to Catholicism* and his founding of several temperance* societies. In 1864 he served as the first president of Boston College.

Baptism. The initiation rite practiced by most Christian churches, in which water is applied to the participant. The rite is related to spiritual truths bound up with one's new status, including death and new life, cleansing from sin,* and the presence of the Spirit. Baptism has been controversial through much of Christian history, especially in America, where groups with divergent views have flourished and competed.

Some groups focus more on the underlying spiritual reality symbolized by baptism than on the rite itself. The Holiness* and Pentecostal* movements tend to separate Spirit baptism* from water baptism entirely, viewing the former as more significant than human rites such as water baptism. For the Evangelical Free Church of America,* baptism is optional, not required for local church membership. The Salvation Army* and the Society of Friends* do not practice water baptism at all, believing that the spiritual reality (Spirit baptism) has eliminated the need of its symbol.

In the first half of the seventeenth century the Puritans* of Massachusetts developed a distinctive form of church life known as the New England Way.* Full communicant status required not only the older requisites (acceptance of the doctrines of the church and baptism) but also verbal evidence of a religious experience* that had made the candidate aware of his or her elect status. The New England Way faced dissension, the first leading dissenter being Roger Williams,* who concluded that the principle of regenerate church membership required believers' baptism.

The face of American religion was radically changed by the Great Awakening* of the 1740s and the resultant rise of evangelical* fervor. The Awakening led to division in the churches and to the formation of separate congregations by many new converts. The renewed commitment to regenerate church membership that characterized the Separates,* or revivalists, reopened the question of baptism. Many adopted believers' baptism (seeing the rite as a profession of the participant's personal faith) and joined the Baptists.

The nineteenth century was characterized by debates between believers' baptists and pedobaptists (those who practice infant baptism) and by new developments, such as the Restoration movement* of Thomas Campbell* and his son Alexander,* which affected the older denominations. A second development, the Landmark movement,* nearly divided the Southern Baptist Convention.*

As the nineteenth century ended, the debates of the earlier era subsided. The rise of Protestant theological liberalism* led to a de-emphasis on traditional doctrine and a reduction of the role of the sacraments. In liberal theology baptism lost its stature as a regenerative rite or as a sign of the covenant. Instead it was viewed as a formality for church membership or, in the case of infant baptism, a dedicatory rite for parents. Likewise the nondenominationalism of liberalism called into question the importance of church divisions based on theology or polity.

Although many questions persist into the twentieth century, a new interest in ecumenism* has reshaped the outlook toward baptismal controversies, exemplified by the Faith and Order Commission, established in 1927. The commission produced *Baptism, Eucharist and Ministry* (1982), a document seeking to articulate a basic agreement among the churches on these topics. The understanding of baptism reflected in this document is inclusive: the act is both a divine gift and a human response. Churches are invited to see believers' baptism and infant baptism as "equivalent alternatives." At the same time, faith is necessary for the reception of the salvation set forth in baptism. In the case of infants, this personal response is to be offered later in the person's life. *Baptism, Eucharist and Ministry* holds forth the hope that the divisions produced or exacerbated by divergent understandings of baptism can be overcome.

See also ALIEN IMMERSION; BAPTISM IN THE SPIRIT; BAPTISMAL FONT; BAPTISTERY; SACRAMENTS AND ORDINANCES.

Baptism in the Spirit. The bestowal of the Holy Spirit on believers. One can distinguish five interpretations of the nature of Spirit baptism.

Classic Reformed Protestant.* The baptism of the Spirit occurred at the birth of the church as a singular historical event. Believers today receive the gift of the Spirit at conversion* unaccompanied by speaking in tongues* or any other signs.

Nineteenth-century Holiness movement. As a second work of grace, an enhanced sanctifying work of the Spirit lifts a believer to a new level of holiness. Those within the Keswick movement* often spoke of the lifelong work of sanctification* in a believer, aided by successive "fillings" of the Spirit.

Classic Pentecostal churches. For Keswick Pentecostals, Spirit baptism is part of the process of sanctification. For Holiness Pentecostals, Spirit baptism is a third event in Christian experience (in addition to regeneration and the "second blessing" of entire sanctification). Although Pentecostals have traditionally agreed that Spirit baptism is evidenced by speaking in tongues, this stance has been mitigated in the present day.

Protestant charismatics (or neo-Pentecostals). Charismatics as a whole are less inclined to identify speaking in tongues as the initial evidence of Spirit baptism, regarding it as one of several possible gifts accompanying Spirit baptism.

Roman Catholic charismatics.* Spirit baptism is the conscious experience of the Spirit, who has already been bestowed. Speaking in tongues is not regarded as an exclusive or necessary sign of Spirit baptism.

Baptismal Font. A vessel containing water used for baptism.* The shape and meaning of the baptismal font have changed considerably through the centuries, from a large basin in which an adult could be immersed to a small cup.

See also BAPTISTERY.

Baptist Bible Fellowship. Confederation of independent, fundamentalist Baptist churches. The Baptist Bible Fellowship was formed in 1950 as a result of a dispute over Texas Baptist fundamentalist J. Frank Norris's* autocratic leadership and control of Bible Baptist Seminary, Forth Worth. The protestors moved to Springfield, Missouri, where they founded another school, Baptist Bible College, the *Baptist Bible Tribune* and a fellowship of like-minded independent Baptist churches called the Baptist Bible Fellowship. The fellowship reflects fundamentalist doctrines and conservative political viewpoints. Though not a denomination, it functions as a source of identity and networking for its member churches and pastors.

Baptist Bible Union. An alliance of fundamentalist* Baptists (1923-1932). Support for the union came from three fundamentalist groups: the Northern Baptist Convention, led by William B. Riley;* those in the South, led by J. Frank Norris;* and those in Canada, led by Thomas T. Shields.* The two most significant fronts on which the union did battle with modernism* were missions* and education. In 1932 a new organization was begun, the General Association of Regular Baptist Churches.*

Baptist Board for Foreign Missions. *See* AMERICAN BAPTIST BOARD OF INTERNATIONAL MINISTRIES.

The Baptist Churches in the U.S.A. Members of a Christian denomination* that originated within seventeenth-century English Puritanism.* Baptists disagreed with most Puritans at two important points: (1) church membership* should be limited to those persons who could testify of the grace of God; (2) God had instituted the state as well as the church: the state was to bear the sword of justice, the church was to worship, preach* and grow by voluntary means alone, freed of the state's power.

Today in the U.S. there are over fifty distinct Baptist groups, with a total membership of some thirty million, the largest Protestant denominational family in North America. Four areas of dispute have helped divide Baptists: (1) Calvinists* (or Regular Baptists*) versus Arminians (or General Baptists*); (2) the use of "means" in church activity (missionary versus primitive,* or antimissionary,* bodies); (3) different cultural roots (North versus South); (4) issues of centralized denominational structures and liberalism.*

Colonial Period. Roger Williams* led in establishing the first Baptist church in America, at Providence, Rhode Island, in 1639. Due to Puritan opposition, however, the Baptist witness in New England remained weak throughout the seventeenth century.

Baptists found the Middle Colonies more favorable. In 1707 five churches in New Jersey, Delaware and Pennsylvania united to form the Philadelphia Baptist Association. By 1760 the association extended from Connecticut to Virginia. Most of this growth is traceable to the Great Awakening,* which drew to Baptist churches large numbers of awakened believers, called Separate Baptists,* from established Puritan Congregationalism.*

The Nineteenth Century. The missionary challenge provided the unifying cause that became the Baptists' major contribution to American life. In 1814 Luther Rice,* a missionary, rallied Baptists to form a General Convention of the Baptist Denomination (Triennial Convention*). Other independent societies were formed to meet a variety of needs.

The greatest challenge to Baptist unity was the slavery controversy. Failure to compromise led Southern churchmen in 1845 to organize the Southern Baptist Convention (*see* Civil War and the Churches).

The first African-American Baptist church was formed around 1773. But the great influx of African-Americans into Baptist churches awaited the Emancipation Proclamation.* Within fifteen years nearly one million African-American Baptists worshiped in their own churches.

The Twentieth Century. In 1905 Landmarkers* protested the "conventionism" of the Southern Baptist Convention. The result was the American Baptist Association.* In the 1950s, another group arose from Southern fundamentalism:* the Baptist Bible Fellowship.*

In Northern Baptist circles, theological differences centering in the fundamentalist-modernist* debate generated two conservative bodies: the General Association of Regular Baptist Churches* (1932) and the Conservative Baptists* (1940s). A third conservative body in the North, the Baptist General Conference,* was scattered across the North and the West.

See also BAPTISTS IN CANADA.

Baptist General Conference. A Baptist* denomination.* Originating in the evangelical revival* of the nineteenth century, the conference's specific roots were Swedish Pietism,* characterized by simple biblical faith, dedicated evangelism,* rejection of formalism and a demand for a regenerate clergy. The first Swedish Baptist congregation in America was founded in 1852 and in Canada in 1894.

The national body became known as the Swedish Baptist General Conference in 1879. In 1945 the conference dropped *Swedish* from its title.

Baptist Mid-Missions. An independent Baptist* foreign missionary agency. In 1920, William C. Haas organized the General Council of Cooperating Baptist Missions of North America and sent six missionaries to Africa. Expanding work there and opening new stations around the world, the council changed its name in 1953 to Baptist Mid-Missions. It emphasizes evangelism, church planting, theological education, medicine and Bible translation.

Baptist World Alliance. An international fellowship* of Baptist* organizations. The alliance, the first international Baptist organization of its type, was formed in 1905 in London but moved to Washington, D.C., in 1941. Two historic Baptist commitments have characterized the alliance: religious liberty and congregational autonomy. Another major purpose is coordinating relief efforts. At present the Baptist World Alliance consists of over 130 bodies in almost a hundred nations and dependencies, numbering over thirty million members.

Baptistery. The place of baptism.* The term has at least two meanings: (1) an area in a church building containing a font* for use in baptism and (2) a large tank, often below floor level, utilized by churches practicing immersion.

See also BAPTISM, BAPTISMAL FONT.

Baptistry. *See* BAPTISTERY.

Baptists in Canada. The roughly two thousand Baptist* congregations in Canada have a total membership of around 230,000, with some 700,000 total affiliated reported in 1981. Although they are only a small minority (2.9 percent) of the population, Baptists are the largest evangelical* denomination* in Canada.

Canadian Baptist Federation. The largest body (in 1992 a reported 1,150 churches, 131,349

members), representing the mainstream Baptist tradition, was organized in 1944 as the Baptist Federation of Canada (BFC) and renamed CBF in 1983. It coordinates programs in national, international and interdenominational spheres. Most programs are administered by each of the four constituent bodies: United Baptist Convention of the Atlantic Provinces, Baptist Convention of Ontario and Quebec, Baptist Union of Western Canada, and Union of French Baptist Churches.

Fellowship of Evangelical Baptist Churches in Canada. The second-largest group (in 1995 there were 503 churches with 66,612 members) formed in 1953 through the merger of two groups that appeared in central and western Canada (*see* T. T. Shields) after the fundamentalist-modernist controversy.

Ethnic Baptist Churches. The multiracial, multicultural Canadian society has been mirrored in ethnic Baptist churches for more than a century. Two conferences have formalized their independent status in Canada: Baptist General Conference of Canada* (originally Swedish) and North American Baptist Conference in Canada* (originally German).

Other Baptist Bodies. Other Baptist groups include the Canadian Convention of Southern Baptists (1985) and the Primitive* Baptist Conference of New Brunswick (1870s), which recently linked up with the Association of Free Will Baptists* in the U.S.

In the nineteenth century, Canadian Baptists made major contributions to the clarification of church-state relations (*see* Clergy Reserves) and to higher education. The various conventions and conferences now operate two colleges, eleven seminaries* and several Bible schools* and lay training centers.

See also BAPTIST CHURCHES IN THE U.S.A.

Barber, Virgil Horace (1782-1847). Roman Catholic* convert, missionary and educator. After being rector at two Episcopal churches, Barber and his family converted to Catholicism in 1816. In 1817 he entered the Jesuits* at Georgetown, and his wife entered the Visitandine convent there. In 1822 he was ordained* a priest and sent as a missionary to Claremont, New Hampshire. In 1830 he was recalled to the Georgetown area.

Barclay, Robert (1648-1690). Quaker* theologian and colonial governor. Barclay wrote *An Apology for the True Christian Divinity,* which became accepted as the authoritative statement of Quaker doctrines. Through William Penn* he became organizer and absentee governor of the Scottish committee that bought and settled East New Jersey as a colony.

Barnes, Albert (1798-1870). New School* Presbyterian* minister. In 1830, when the First Presbyterian Church, Philadelphia, called him as pastor, and again in 1835, Old School* conservatives brought charges against him, but each case was appealed to the General Assembly, which acquitted him both times. He supported revivalism and social reform, including the campaign against slavery, and wrote popular biblical commentaries, including the eleven-volume *Notes, Explanatory and Practical on the New Testament.* He provided leadership to New School Presbyterianism while he continued to serve his Philadelphia congregation until he retired (1868).

Barnhouse, Donald Grey (1895-1960). Presbyterian* fundamentalist* pastor, Bible expositor* and journalist. After World War I, Barnhouse served as missionary and pastor in Europe for six years. He became the pastor of Philadelphia's Tenth Presbyterian Church in 1927 and served there until his death. From that base he began a network radio program in 1928 and in 1931 a monthly magazine, *Revelation* (renamed *Eternity* in 1950). In doctrine and temperament he was a fundamentalist, but he never conformed to the party line.

Barth, Karl (1886-1968). Swiss Reformed* theologian. While serving as a pastor, Barth became convinced of the poverty of his liberal* theology* and began a reorientation that led him to a renewed theological quest in dialogue with Scripture and Protestant* orthodoxy.* Later he held a series of academic posts, ending up at Basel, Switzerland (1935-1962). Barth's best-known works are his commentary on Romans (1919; rev. ed. 1922) and his multivolume *Church Dogmatics* (1936-1969).

In America, liberal theologians criticized his emphasis on the "infinite qualitative distinction" between God and humanity for making God inaccessible and communication about God impossible. In contrast, conservative theologians feared he was producing a "new modernism,"* since he was building his theology on something other than rational foundations.

By the later 1930s, however, American theologians such as Reinhold Niebuhr* began to show Barth's influence in their own theologies. This led to the ascendancy of Barth's thought in the 1940s and 1950s. Barth's impact on American Protestantism has been strongest in the major Presbyterian* traditions but has also had an ongoing impact in American evangelicalism.*

See also NEO-ORTHODOXY.

Bartleman, Frank (1871-1936). Pentecostal* evangelist and author. By 1906 Bartleman was in contact with William J. Seymour* and soon became convinced of the Pentecostal message and launched into a career of itinerant ministry. A voice for unity among Pentecostals and a critic of sectarianism, he was also a pacifist and an advocate for the separation of church and state.* His book *How Pentecost Came to Los Angeles* (1925) is important for understanding the Azusa Street* Revival.

Barton, Bruce Fairfield (1886-1967). Journalist, advertising executive and popular religious author. In 1925 he published *The Man Nobody Knows,* a bestseller about Jesus. Ignoring the fundamentalist-modernist controversy,* Barton put the accent on a human Christ whose boundless energy, personal magnetism, physical strength and simple teachings revealed who God was and showed how people could live.

In 1918 Barton helped to start the advertising firm of BBDO. In 1937 he won a seat in Congress and then in 1940 returned to advertising.

Barton, Clarissa ("Clara") Harlowe (1821-1912). Founder of the American Red Cross. Her work as a nurse during the Civil War* led to her fame as she began direct aid to soldiers on the battle lines. Later, in Europe, during the Franco-Prussian War, she saw her first service under the Red Cross badge. In 1881 she formed the American Association of the Red Cross, and the agency first provided disaster relief in that year. She supervised aid for victims of natural disasters and the Spanish-American War* until her retirement in 1905.

Bashford, James Whitford (1849-1919). Methodist* pastor, educator, bishop in China. In 1889 Bashford became president of Ohio Wesleyan University. Later, as bishop in China, he helped establish Yenching University at Peking and the China Medical Board.

Bashir, Antony (1898-1966). Antiochian Orthodox* archbishop of New York. In 1936 the Lebanese-born Bashir was consecrated* bishop in New York, and his episcopacy saw the final separation of the Syrians from the Russian jurisdiction. He had a keen vision of what American Orthodoxy ought to be and pushed to achieve it. He created a youth-oriented Society of Orthodox Youth Organizations (SOYO) and instituted a Western Rite to accommodate converts.

Bauman, Louis Sylvester (1875-1950). Brethren pastor, evangelist, conference speaker. Bauman pastored churches around the country for nearly sixty years and served as secretary of the Brethren Foreign Missionary Sociey (1906-1945). His church in Long Beach, California, grew to be the largest in the denomination. His desire for a Brethren seminary saw fruit as Ashland College (Ohio).

Bäumler, Joseph Michael. *See* BIMELER, JOSEPH MICHAEL.

Bay Psalm Book. First American psalter. *The Whole Booke of Psalmes* was produced by the Massachusetts Bay clergy and published in 1640—the first book printed in English in North America. It incorporated the advances in scholarship included in the Bible of 1611, and most churches in Massachusetts Bay adopted it, hence the sobriquet Bay Psalm Book. In 1651 it was revised and enlarged.

Bayley, James Roosevelt (1814-1877). Catholic* archbishop of Baltimore. Bayley was ordained* in the Episcopal Church* in 1840, but after reading a biography of his aunt, Elizabeth Ann Seton,* he converted to Catholicism and was ordained a priest in 1844. Appointed to the faculty of St. John's College in Fordham, he subsequently served as vice president and president. In 1853 he was consecrated* bishop of the new Diocese* of Newark, New Jersey, where he established Seton Hall College and Immaculate Conception Seminary. In 1872 he was chosen as archbishop of Baltimore, the premier see of the U.S. Catholic Church.

Beatific Vision. A Roman Catholic* technical term for the vision of God experienced by the saved in heaven.* The vision comes not from human effort but as a gift of God, who grants the *lumen gloriae*—the light of glory. The notion of the beatific vision stems from the promise that the pure of heart will see God (Mt 5:8).

Beatification. A step toward the canonization* of a saint,* by which the pope permits religious honor to be paid to the deceased, or commands such veneration, but not with regard to the whole church. The process begins with an investigation of a would-be saint initiated by a local bishop. In 1988 two North Americans were beatified—Junipero Serra* and Katharine Drexel.*

Becker, Peter (1687-1758). First Brethren* minister in America. In 1719 Becker led a group of Brethren families from Germany to Germantown, Pennsylvania, where in 1723 he helped organize the first Brethren congregation in America. He was admired for his piety, ardent prayers and warm pastoral care.

Beecher, Edward (1803-1895). Congregational* minister, educator and abolitionist.* Son of Lyman Beecher,* he became pastor of Boston's Park Street Church in 1826, and then in 1830, president of Illinois College. His *Narrative of Riots at Alton* (1838) and his subsequent articles on the nature of "organic sin" helped galvanize the evangelical abolitionist cause.

Beecher later served in Boston as pastor and editor (1844-1853), in Galesburg, Illinois, as pastor (1855-1871), and in Brooklyn, where with his brother Henry Ward Beecher* he edited the *Christian Union* (1871-1873) and continued to preach and write.

Beecher, Henry Ward (1813-1887). Congregational* minister and religious editor. Son of Lyman Beecher,* Henry became one of the premier preachers of his time, ministering at Plymouth Church in Brooklyn Heights, New York (1847-1887). He became a proponent of "evangelical liberalism,"* also known as the new theology.

During the 1870s, he endured a public scandal for adultery, though he was finally acquitted. In the early 1880s, his lectures publicizing his adoption of evolution,* denial of eternal punishment and rejection of Calvinism* led to his resignation from the Congregational Association of New York.

Beecher, Lyman (1775-1863). Congregational* and Presbyterian* clergyman. Among his children were Edward Beecher,* Henry Ward

Beecher* and Harriet Beecher Stowe.* As a pastor in Connecticut, Beecher's reputation as a revivalist, social reformer and political observer grew. In 1826 he became pastor at the Hanover Street Church in Boston, where he campaigned against New England Unitarianism.*

In 1832 he began concurrent terms as president of Lane Seminary and pastor of the Second Presbyterian Church, both in Cincinnati, Ohio. Developing a keen sense of the power of voluntaryism* for social reform and revivalism led him to reshape his understanding of the doctrine of sin.* Influenced by Charles G. Finney* and Nathaniel W. Taylor,* Beecher adjusted the Calvinism* of the Puritans* and Jonathan Edwards,* a move that Beecher's ministerial colleagues resisted. In 1835 he was tried for heresy* but was cleared. He retired from his pastoral duties in 1843 and from the presidency of Lane Seminary in 1850.

Beecher, Willis Judson (1838-1912). Presbyterian* Old Testament scholar. After pastoring and teaching in New York and Illinois, Beecher served as professor of Hebrew at Auburn Theological Seminary in New York (1871-1908). With the influence in the U.S. of European higher-critical theories, Beecher felt called to prepare persuasive defenses of an orthodox* view of the Bible.

Beissel, Johann Konrad (1691-1768). Communitarian* leader. Leaving Germany for Pennsylvania in 1720, Beissel was later chosen as the leader of a Brethren group in what is now Lancaster County. In 1728 he broke with the Brethren and in 1732 founded the Ephrata Community.* Under his direction the community was noted for its choral singing, illumination of manuscripts (Fraktur), economic achievements and philanthropic* outreach. He was both revered and reviled for his highhanded leadership and brilliance, and historians still dispute his character.

Believers' Church. Those within the Free Church* tradition who regard the church as the gathering of regenerate, committed disciples. Membership* is based on a voluntary* confession of Jesus Christ as Lord, not on citizenship in a particular territory or on infant baptism.* Members accept the necessity of reproof by other members. Every believer participates in the full ministry of Christ and must share the gospel with

the world while remaining unstained by it.

Bell, Eudorus N. (1866-1923). Assemblies of God* founder. After seventeen years as a Southern Baptist* pastor, Bell accepted Pentecostal* teaching. He became editor of a paper, the *Apostolic Faith* (later called *Word and Witness*), and in 1913 he signed the call for the General Council, which created the Assemblies of God in 1914.

Bell, L(emuel) Nelson (1894-1973). Medical missionary and cofounder of *Christianity Today.* Bell was a Southern Presbyterian medical missionary in China from 1916 to 1941. In 1942 he founded the *Southern Presbyterian Journal* (renamed the *Presbyterian Journal* in 1959) in order to promote evangelical and Reformed* orthodoxy* within the Presbyterian Church in the U.S.* (PCUS). He served on the PCUS Board of World Missions (1948-1966). In 1956, along with his son-in-law Billy Graham,* Bell founded *Christianity Today.*

Bellamy, Joseph (1719-1790). Congregational* minister and a leader of the New Divinity movement.* In 1735 Bellamy went to Jonathan Edwards* for theological tutoring and emerged as one of the most fervent New Light* ministers. He began training young men for the ministry at Bethlehem, Connecticut, where he ministered from 1738 to 1790. In 1758 he published his most famous work, *The Wisdom of God in the Permission of Sin.* Scholars disagree on the impact of his theology.

See also NEW ENGLAND THEOLOGY.

Bellavin, Tikhon Basil (1865-1925). Russian Orthodox* archbishop in America and later patriarch of Moscow. Bellavin became bishop of the Aleutians and Alaska* in 1898, and in 1905 he was named archbishop. He was an early proponent of Orthodox unity in America and the use of English in liturgical services.

In 1917, following the abdication of Czar Nicholas II, Bellavin became metropolitan, and then patriarch, of Moscow. In 1918, in the face of the Bolshevik Revolution and the Russian Civil War, he excommunicated those whom he termed the "enemies of Christ, open or disguised."

Beman, Nathan S. S. (1785-1871). Presbyterian* minister and educator. Ordained* in 1810, Beman for many years was concurrently a pastor and a teacher. An eloquent preacher, he became the national leader of the New School* Presbyterian movement of 1837, displaying great evangelistic* and abolition* fervor. Later he became a signatory of the Auburn Declaration.*

Bender, Harold Stauffer (1897-1962). Mennonite* historian, educator and churchman. Bender served many years at Goshen College, beginning in 1924. He was general editor of *The Mennonite Encyclopedia* (1955-1959). He contributed significantly to recovering the history of sixteenth-century Anabaptism.*

Benedictines. A federation of independent monasteries under the Rule of St. Benedict (of Nursia, c. 480-c. 547). Some Benedictines from Europe came to North America as part of the tide of immigration* during the nineteenth century. Since then the Benedictine ministry has expanded across North America. By 1990 monks of the Benedictine Confederation in the U.S. numbered about 2,500, with Benedictine women numbering 4,000-5,000. The influence of individual Benedictines and their communities during the last century in the area of liturgical* reform, ecumenical* relations and spirituality* has reached beyond Catholic monastic circles and touched a widening number of American Christians.

Benevolent Fraternity of Unitarian Churches. Voluntary* association of Boston-area Unitarian* churches for support of local ministries to the urban* poor. Founded in 1834 at the urging of Ezra Stiles Gannett,* the fraternity underwrote a number of chapels* in working-class neighborhoods. It continues a wide range of local social ministries.

Benezet, Anthony (1713-1784). Quaker* educator and social reformer.* In Philadelphia, Benezet successfully urged the Friends to establish adequate schooling for girls (1755) and for African-American children (1770). By 1756 he had already begun to labor on behalf of slaves. Benezet's writings against slavery are probably what won John Wesley* to the antislavery* cause; the two corresponded for a decade. Benezet likewise sought better treatment of Native Americans, an unenviable task during the French and Indian War of the 1750s.

Bennett, Belle Harris (1852-1922). Southern Methodist* missions* leader and social reformer.* Bennett conceived the idea of and raised the funds for Scarritt Bible and Training School (1892) and was president of the Home Mission Society (1896) and, after 1898, of the Woman's Board of Home Missions (*see* Missionary Movement, Women's).

Bennett's major concern was the condition and needs of the cities. She established more than forty settlement houses* throughout the South for African-Americans. She was responsible for the development of the deaconess* movement in the South and worked for women's suffrage.*

Bennett, Mary Katharine Jones (1864-1950). Presbyterian home missions leader. Bennett served as president of the Woman's Board of Home Missions for the Presbyterian Church in the U.S.A.* (1909-1923). In 1916 she was the first woman to make a board report to the General Assembly,* and in 1923 she became vice president of the newly created National Board of Home Missions.

Berkenmeyer, Wilhelm Christoph (1686-1751). Lutheran* minister in New York. Ordained by the conservative Amsterdam Consistory for service in America, Berkenmeyer had a ministry encompassing New York and eastern New Jersey, which he divided into five parishes.* His failure to cut himself off from European ties hampered his ministry and led to a loss of authority, isolating him in his own parish.

Berkhof, Louis (1873-1957). Reformed* theologian. In 1906 Berkhof was appointed to Grand Rapids (later Calvin) Seminary, where he served the rest of his career as professor of biblical theology (1906-1914), New Testament (1914-1926) and, finally, systematic theology* (1926-1944). From 1931 to 1944 he served as president of the seminary.

For theology in particular, Berkhof insisted that Scripture is the only source and norm. On this bulwark he erected his systematics, hewing to a moderate line on the classic issues of Calvinist controversy and reproving modernist proposals. He rejected rationalistic* strictures on the Bible and orthodoxy, yet showed a rationalistic frame of mind himself. Faith alone could appropriate the saving truth of revelation, but reason's job of arraying these truths in systematic unity was vital.

Berlin Congress on World Evangelism. *See* WORLD CONGRESS ON EVANGELISM.

Berry, Martha McChesney (1866-1942). Southern educator. A devout Episcopalian,* Berry established nondenominational schools for boys (1902) and girls (1909) as well as Berry College (1926). Widely known in philanthropic circles as a consummate fundraiser, she was aided by Theodore Roosevelt, Andrew Carnegie and Henry Ford.

Bessette, Alfred ("Brother Andre") (1845-1937). Canadian Roman Catholic* saint.* Although only a lay brother,* Bessette became the most popular religious figure in French Canada, being credited with tens of thousands of miraculous healings. Pope John Paul II* beatified* Bessette in 1982.

Bethune, Joanna Graham (1770-1860). Founder of charitable societies. Devoting much of her life to educational and philanthropic causes, Bethune founded the Society for the Relief of Poor Widows with Small Children (1797), the Orphan Asylum Society (1806) and an Infant School Society (1827).

Bethune, Mary McLeod (1875-1955). African-American educator and advocate for African-American women. In 1904 Bethune opened the Daytona Normal and Industrial School for Girls, which later became Bethune-Cookman College, a fully accredited liberal arts college for African-Americans. She remained president of the college until 1942.

In 1927 she became president of the National Association for Colored Women (NACW), which advocated school desegregation, antilynching legislation, women's training programs and prison reform. She joined Franklin Roosevelt's "Black Cabinet" as director of the Division of Negro Affairs (1935-1943).

Bible, English Translations and Versions in North America. The Bible has been a significant feature of American culture since the first European settling of North America. The standard for English-speaking Americans became the King James, or Authorized, Version (AV) of 1611. Because the AV could be printed only by those authorized by the Crown, it was not until the Revolutionary War* that English Bible publishing

became an American concern. The story of Bible translation in America thus begins with the birth of the Republic.

In 1777 Robert Aitken printed the first American edition of the AV. Such was the appetite for Bibles in new and familiar forms that between 1777 and 1957 over 2,500 different English-language editions of the Bible were published in the U.S.

In 1870 British scholars of various denominations, with some American cooperation, began a major revision of the AV. The English Revised Version was completed in 1885; in 1901 the American committee produced the American Standard Version (ASV). The ASV became very popular in America, especially among students.

The arrival of the twentieth century marked the beginning of modern-speech versions. Translations by James Moffatt (1928, 1935) and Edgar J. Goodspeed* (1923, 1931) in particular were popular. Translations of the New Testament also appeared by Charles B. Williams (1937), Gerrit Verkuyl (1945, the Berkeley Version) and Kenneth Wuest (1956-1959).

Some forty denominations* in the U.S. and Canada cooperated in revising the ASV. The result was the Revised Standard Version (RSV) Bible (1952; rev. 1971). Sales of the RSV were phenomenal, with over fifty million copies sold in its first thirty years.

English-speaking Roman Catholics used the Douay-Rheims Bible as their "authorized version" up to 1937. With a change in the Vatican's policy in 1943 (*see* Divino Afflante Spiritu), members of the Catholic Biblical Association translated the Scriptures from the original languages, and in 1970 the New American Bible was published.

Other popular translations of the whole Bible in the twentieth century have been the New American Standard Bible (1971); the Living Bible (1971, a paraphrase by Kenneth N. Taylor); the Good News Bible (1976, translation spearheaded by Robert Bratcher); the New International Version (1978, work led by Edwin Palmer); and the New King James Bible (1982, a moderate revision of the AV).

Bible and Prophetic Conference Movement. As a series of conferences that helped to shape early fundamentalism,* the movement formed coalitions of conservative evangelicals,* trained new leaders and introduced dispensational* premillennialism* into the churches.

Borrowing an English practice, a group of Americans in 1868 began summer conferences for Bible study* and fellowship.* The most important of these was the Niagara Conference,* founded in 1875, which became a prototype for others. The Niagara Conference emphasized premillennialism, which many evangelicals did not accept at the time. Belief in premillennial doctrine in fact proved to be the undoing of the conference. As J. N. Darby's* dispensationalism became more popular, arguments over the any-moment, pretribulation rapture* of the church drove a wedge between the millenarians in charge, and the conference was canceled in 1901.

Evangelicals in different parts of the country, many of whom had Niagara connections, established annual Bible conferences at permanent sites. In 1878 Niagara Conference leaders organized the First American Bible and Prophetic Conference. These meetings gave premillennialism an unprecedented platform and increased the popularity of dispensationalism within millenarian circles.

By the early twentieth century, most of the promoters of the Niagara Conference had been replaced by new millenarian leaders, most of whom were important in the developing fundamentalist movement.

See also ESCHATOLOGY; SCOFIELD, C. I.; TORREY, R. A.

Bible Belt. Coined by H. L. Mencken to describe the fundamentalist* South, *Bible Belt* usually has a pejorative intent, referring to the literalistic reading of the biblical text on all matters. When used to describe rather than to evaluate, the phrase highlights the comprehensively Protestant* character of Southern society.

Bible Chairs. Programs of religious education* and nurture intended to supplement learning at state universities. In 1893 members of the Christian Church (Disciples of Christ)* concerned about their students in state universities established the first Disciples' Bible Chair—a program of religious studies adjacent to the University of Michigan in Ann Arbor. Similar chairs soon followed at other universities.

Bible Church Movement. The name generally applied to the hundreds of denominationally* unaffiliated churches that developed primarily in the U.S. during the twentieth century. Many of

these churches belong to organizations such as the Independent Fundamental Churches of America,* the American Council of Christian Churches* and the National Association of Evangelicals.*

The movement has its roots in the teaching of John Nelson Darby,* who rejected the concept of a state church and urged believers to deny the legitimacy of all denominations.* The movement received further support from D. L. Moody* and his successors.

Strict doctrine, including in most cases dispensationalism* as taught in the Scofield Reference Bible,* characterizes these churches. They typically shun any hint of a social gospel,* emphasize individual conversion,* interpret the Scriptures literally and advocate strict separation* from the world.

See also FUNDAMENTALISM.

Bible College. See BIBLE INSTITUTES AND COLLEGES.

Bible Commonwealth. The Puritan* application of scriptural teachings to political and ecclesiastical organization. In New England, the Puritans attempted to construct a society that emulated New Testament churches. The key element was that men judged to be converted* would control the society, granting access to both temporal and spiritual ordinances.

Bible Institutes and Colleges. The Bible college or institute (also popularly called Bible school) is primarily a North American evangelical* Protestant* development. Educationally, a Bible college is between a Bible institute and a Christian liberal arts college. Like a Bible institute, its students all major in religion and participate in Christian service. Like a liberal arts college, the Bible college enrolls all students in a series of general-education courses. The Bible college curriculum is generally four years and results in a B.A. degree, whereas the Bible institute program is shorter—frequently three years—and results in a diploma.

Origins of a Movement. The founders of the earliest American Bible schools were inspired by London pastors Charles Spurgeon and H. G. Guinness. But the movement blossomed in America in the late nineteenth and early twentieth centuries as a response to the revivalism* of D. L. Moody* and others, as a reaction to the growth of liberal* thought and as a reflection of the American move toward popular education. The first two Bible schools, Nyack in New York City and Moody* in Chicago, sought to provide quick, practical training for the increasing number of laypeople who wished to become full-time Christian workers. The first permanent Canadian school was Toronto Bible College (later Ontario Bible College).

Bible Colleges and the Evangelical Missions Movement. It is difficult to exaggerate the extent to which the early Bible schools emphasized foreign missions. This emphasis joined other forces to allow the U.S. by the early twentieth century to surpass England as the supplier of the majority of both personnel and funds for Protestant foreign missions.* By the mid-twentieth century the Bible colleges were probably producing the majority, and by the 1980s the large majority, of the Protestant missionary recruits in the U.S.

Development, Organization and Growth. The most significant recent development in the Bible college movement has been the evolution of Bible institutes to Bible colleges and even of Bible colleges to Christian liberal arts colleges. By 1960 about half of these schools identified themselves as Bible colleges rather than Bible institutes.

In the late 1940s an organization was formed to establish standards for Bible colleges, later named the Accrediting Association of Bible Colleges (AABC). In 1980, seventy-seven (out of some four hundred) North American institutions were fully accredited by the AABC. Canadian schools have participated in the AABC, but they have also organized the Association of Canadian Bible Colleges (1968). While 85 percent of the Canadian schools are affiliated with denominations, the most widely recognized are independent, including Ontario, Prairie (Alberta) and Briarcrest (Saskatchewan).

See also EDUCATION, PROTESTANT THEOLOGICAL; SEMINARY, CATHOLIC DIOCESAN.

Bible Presbyterian Church. A small Presbyterian* denomination* born out of the fundamentalist-modernist controversy.* Formed in 1937, the church at its first synod amended the Westminster* standards to teach premillennialism.* It called for separation from apostasy* as well as from those having fellowship with apostates.

Disagreements led to the withdrawal of Carl McIntire* and others in 1956. In 1961 the denomination changed its name to the Evangelical Presbyterian Church, and in 1965 it merged with another Presbyterian group to form the Reformed Presbyterian Church, Evangelical Synod.*

Bible Societies. Organizations founded for the purpose of distributing Bibles and portions of Scripture. The movement for Bible societies began with the Pietist* movement in Germany.

In 1808 the Philadelphia Bible Society was founded to supply Bibles in English, Welsh, German and French for all denominations* at no charge. Independent as well as interlocking Bible societies continued to form; by 1816 there were some 130 societies, all dependent on freewill offerings. The British and Foreign Bible Society (BFBS) contributed Bibles and finances to many of these.

In 1816 fifty-six delegates of various local societies met in New York and formed the American Bible Society* (ABS). Like the BFBS, its goal was to distribute the Scriptures "without note or comment." It was designed to help the existing regional societies, not to replace them. By 1817 forty-one established societies had joined the ABS as auxiliaries.

The charter of the ABS made clear that it was to serve not only Americans but also people living in other lands. Arrangements were made to lessen the potential for conflict and for overlap with the BFBS. The ABS decided to work with missionaries from various denominations in the country where these were active, with missionaries often carrying out the translation and the society printing the Bibles. As the ABS broadened its scope of mission, it relaxed its policy of printing Bibles without the Apocrypha or other helps. It also became a leader in printing translations based on modern linguistic theories.

The rapid growth of the ABS resulted in the establishment of similar societies in other countries. In 1946 the major Bible societies of Europe joined the ABS in forming the United Bible Society (UBS). As a result of the formation of the national Bible society in America (ABS), with its international connections (UBS), most of the regional Bible societies in the U.S. have disappeared.

See also BIBLE, ENGLISH TRANSLATIONS AND VERSIONS IN NORTH AMERICA.

Bible Study. Throughout American history, Bible study has been a dominant force in the spiritual and intellectual development of the populace. A central feature of colonial religious life was the exposition of Scripture through sermons,* supplemented by personal Bible reading. The Bible was also used to teach reading.

In the nineteenth century the popularity of William McGuffey's* *Eclectic Readers* reinforced the influence of the Bible on American education and society. Early in the twentieth century, the Protestant emphasis on Bible study was reflected in the Bible conference movement,* the establishment of Bible schools* and the publication of the Scofield Reference Bible.* Twentieth-century evangelicals* have used the Bible as their primary authority* for both faith and practice.

A significant move toward systematic Bible study occurred among Catholics in the late 1950s. Vatican II* reinforced this move by encouraging the reading and study of the Bible and its use in liturgy.*

Biblical Theology Movement.

An American movement generally believed to have begun in the 1940s and to have lasted until the early 1960s—roughly parallel to the flourishing of neo-orthodoxy* in America.

Though the movement was characterized by a diversity of methods, confessional orientations and results, James Barr has identified eight characteristics that were widely shared: (1) a contrast drawn between biblical and philosophical categories of thought; (2) a preference for the organic nature of biblical theology rather than the systematizing tendency of dogmatic theology; (3) an argument that the Bible was pervaded by Hebrew thought patterns in contrast to the Greek thought of later Christian theology; (4) a confidence in the unity of biblical theology and an optimism that a unifying theme could be found; (5) an emphasis on word studies as a legitimate approach to the meaning of biblical language; (6) a contrast drawn between the Bible over against its cultural and religious environment; (7) a stress on revelation in history; and (8) a conviction that theological concern should pervade biblical study, bearing fruit in preaching and the life of the church.

All of these features can be seen as a reaction against the sterility of the purely analytic biblical criticism that had prevailed for over half a century in America. The movement gave fresh impetus to scholars and publishers, who sought to bridge the gap between biblical exegesis and pulpit exposition. Biblical theology, if no longer a movement, remains today as a theological discipline that seeks to disclose the theological meaning of the Bible.

Biederwolf, William Edward (1867-1939).

Popular Presbyterian* evangelist. Beginning his evangelistic campaigns in 1906, Biederwolf combined soul-winning* with advocacy of civic reform, Prohibition,* Americanism and, in later years, premillennialism.*

Biederwolf became director (1923) and then president (1933) of the Winona Lake Bible School of Theology. From 1929 he also pastored the Royal Poinciana Chapel in Palm Beach, Florida, called by some the richest congregation in the world.

Bill of Rights.

See FIRST AMENDMENT TO THE CONSTITUTION.

Billings, William (1746-1800).

Composer and singing master. An untutored tanner by trade, Billings became the first important American composer and a major force in the development of New England musical practices. Alone among his American peers, he wrote or sought out original texts for his tunes, and he advocated the pleasure, as well as the spiritual benefits, to be derived from music.

Billington, Dallas Franklin (1903-1972).

Baptist* preacher. In 1934 Billington organized thirteen people into the Akron (Ohio) Baptist Temple. Under his ministry over the next thirty-eight years, the church grew to sixteen thousand members and physical assets of several million dollars. The church was among the first to have its own television studio.

Billy Graham Center.

An agency of Wheaton College* devoted to research, strategy and training for evangelism* and missions.* The center, which operates from a building dedicated in 1980, includes an archive, a library, a museum and a cluster of programs, including a missionary scholar in residence, professional workshops and conferences, and strategic institutes in the areas of Chinese studies, prison ministries and evangelism. An adjunct agency is the Institute for the Study of American Evangelicals.

Billy Graham Evangelistic Association.

The nonprofit religious corporation which conducts the ministries* of Billy Graham,* his associate evangelists and affiliated agencies. The Billy Graham Evangelistic Association (BGEA), founded in 1950, is the vehicle that has brought evangelist Billy Graham's gospel message to scores of millions around the globe and made him one of the best-known persons in the twentieth century. By the late 1980s, the BGEA had become a large and varied international religious agency, with offices serving every major continent.

Subsidiaries of the BGEA include the *Hour of Decision* radio program, World Wide Pictures, *Decision* magazine, two radio stations, World Emergency Fund and the Schools of Evangelism. Owing their existence to the BGEA are *Christianity Today,** the World Congress on Evangelism (Berlin, 1966), the International Congress on World Evangelism (Lausanne, 1974), the International Conferences for Itinerant Evangelists (Amsterdam, 1983 and 1986) and The Cove, a Christian retreat center (1988).

Bimeler (Bäumler), Joseph Michael (1778-1853). Communitarian leader. In 1817 Bimeler led a group of immigrants from Germany to Ohio. Calling themselves the Society of the Separatists of Zoar and adhering to a strict personal piety, they founded the community of Zoar, which survived until 1898.

Bingham, Hiram, Jr. (1831-1908). Missionary to the Gilbert Islands. Appointed a missionary in 1856, Bingham reduced the Gilbertese language to writing and provided the beginnings of a Christian literature in that language. He held a government appointment as protector for the colony of Gilbert Islanders.

Bingham, Hiram, Sr. (1789-1869). Pioneer missionary to Hawaii. In 1819 Bingham sailed with the first company of Protestant* missionaries to the Sandwich Islands. Bingham's force of personality and high moral principles won the general allegiance of the Hawaiians but brought him into conflict with foreigners who resented missionary interference with their own interests. Bingham was the first pastor of Kawaiahao Church and helped create a written Hawaiian language.

Bingham, Roland Victor (1872-1942). Evangelical* publisher and missionary. Following an early missionary venture to Africa, Bingham founded the Sudan Interior Mission* in 1898. In 1901 the first mission station was established in Patagi, West Africa, which, by the time of his death, had become the largest Protestant presence in Africa. Through his magazine *Evangelical Christian and Missionary Witness* and his summer conference, Bingham promoted British, American and domestic missions.

Bioethics. The intellectual discipline that attempts to resolve specific ethical problems brought about by innovations in biology. Until recently, religious and medical values were largely in fundamental agreement. Recent biological advances, however, especially in the areas of genetics, reproductive physiology and life-prolonging techniques, have given medicine new powers that go beyond its four traditional ends (preventive, diagnostic, curative and alleviatory). The gap between medical technology and traditional religious ethics* has prompted religious leaders and religious institutions to reevaluate their positions on medical ethics.

The most definitive and comprehensive ecclesiastical declaration on the matter of bioethics is that released by the Vatican in 1987, entitled "Instruction on Respect for Human Life in Its Origin and on the Dignity of Procreation."

See also ABORTION; BIRTH CONTROL; ETHICS, CATHOLIC PERSONAL; ETHICS, PROTESTANT PERSONAL.

Birth Control. In principle, any voluntary control of the reproductive effect of sexual intercourse; popularly used to refer to the various mechanical or chemical means used before, during or after coitus to prevent conception. In the latter sense it is often called contraception.

U.S. Catholic* and Protestant* views on birth control developed in the context of Christian thinking on marriage and its purposes, particularly in response to modern Western social conditions. Until about 1930, a broad consensus existed. Both Catholics and Protestants viewed voluntary prevention of conception by means other than abstinence as offensive to God's purposes for creation.

By the 1930s many U.S. Protestants were beginning to recognize contraception as a means to responsible Christian parenthood in a global perspective. Until the 1960s U.S. Catholic views on birth control were shaped largely by papal reaffirmations of the traditional consensus in terms of what was "natural," that is, in keeping with God's purposes for creation. When

*Humanae Vitae** appeared in 1968, a sizable majority of U.S. Catholics rejected its teaching on birth control.

In general Catholics and Protestants agree that, in the biblical view, procreation and mutual love are purposes of marriage. They also agree on the necessity of responsible parenthood. The official Catholic position excludes artificial contraception as a means to that end. U.S. Protestants in general would not oppose the use of contraception, including voluntary sterilization, in responsible family planning.

See also ABORTION; BIOETHICS; BODY, THEOLOGY OF THE; HUMANAE VITAE.

Bishop. The chief pastor or overseer in a church. In the Roman Catholic,* Eastern Orthodox* and Anglican* communions, the bishop stands in the ecclesiastical hierarchy above the priest and below the archbishop. Normally the bishop presides over a diocese* as its chief pastor, responsible for the full range of pastoral duties. Since the Reformation, most Protestant* churches have done away with the office.

Bishops' Pastoral Letters. There are two types: the individual pastoral, written by a bishop to his own diocese;* and the group pastoral, written by several bishops to all their dioceses. The latter are usually national pastoral letters and addressed to the faithful of an entire country and should be distinguished from statements issued by national episcopal* conferences.

Episcopal letters are the most common expression of the ordinary magisterium* of the bishops throughout the world. In the U.S. the national letters are usually the result of a general meeting of the hierarchy of the church. In recent years national bishops' pastoral statements on issues of justice and peace have had an influence in America far beyond the Catholic Church.

Bishops' Program of Social Reconstruction (1919). Social platform adopted by the American Catholic* hierarchy after World War I.* Written by Father John A. Ryan,* the program proposed practical ways of addressing crucial defects in the American system, including government agencies to find jobs and housing for returning veterans, vocational training programs, and minimum wage legislation. Labeled socialistic by its critics in the 1920s, much of the program was implemented during the New Deal years.

Bjerring, Nicholas (1831-c. 1883). Founder of first Orthodox* parish* in the eastern U.S. Originally a Roman Catholic* priest, Bjerring joined the Orthodox Church in 1870. His ministry, lectures and publications encouraged many American Protestants to examine Orthodoxy seriously.

Black Catholics. The earliest black Catholics in the U.S. were slaves. By the 1990s the number of black Catholics was approaching 2 million. Approximately 3 percent of all Catholics in the U.S. are black; approximately 4 percent of all blacks are Catholic.

Growth in the number of black Catholics is attributable to efforts of some inner-city priests to convert new black residents, the presence of parochial schools* in urban parishes and increased activism of the church in the 1950s and 1960s in social justice issues.

See also BLACK RELIGION.

Black Colleges. Of the 116 black colleges and universities in operation in the late 1980s, over fifty were founded by religious and voluntary associations.* Two organizations led the way in the move to educate African-Americans: the African Methodist Episcopal Church* founded over nine colleges between 1854 and 1890; the American Missionary Association, an evangelical* and abolitionist* organization formed in 1846, founded seven colleges.

The majority of these religious associations and black colleges viewed education as a way to Christianize newly freed slaves and prepare them for citizenship. To achieve these ends, many colleges and associations advocated a form of industrial education. By the twentieth century, most black colleges and universities had abandoned various forms of industrial education in favor of a liberal arts curriculum.

Black Religion. Black religion, in its Christian manifestation, has its origins in a synthesis of African traditional religions brought to the Americas by enslaved Africans and the evangelical* Christianity of North American Anglo-Saxons, shaped as it was by the revivalism* of the First and Second Great Awakenings.*

Black Denominations. The independent church movement among free African-Americans in the North, which began in the latter part of the eighteenth century, was primarily Methodist* (*see* Richard Allen; James Varick). The African Methodist Episcopal Church was formed in 1816, the African Methodist Episcopal Zion Church in 1821. Following the Civil War,* the memberships of the African Methodist churches grew dramatically as their missions extended to newly emancipated Southern African-Americans. In 1870, these two denominations were joined by a third: the Colored Methodist Episcopal Church, renamed Christian Methodist Episcopal* in 1954.

In the post-Civil War period, African-Americans organized separate Baptist* congregations, associations and conventions. In 1895 three such conventions merged to form the National Baptist Convention.* The Holiness movement* of the second half of the nineteenth century and the Pentecostal movement* in the first decade of the twentieth resulted in dozens of African-American Holiness-Pentecostal bodies, the largest of which is the Church of God* in Christ.

Character and Significance. Black religion has always held in tandem the emphases of spirituality* and social consciousness. Consequently, black religion has served two critical functions: survival under circumstances of the most extreme oppression, and struggle through liberation movements aimed at moderating the oppression.

The African-American churches figured largely in the civil rights movement;* organizationally, the church was most evident in the Southern Christian Leadership Conference* (SCLC). During the Black Power phase of the movement, SCLC and the more conservative National Black Evangelical Association* were joined by the National Conference of Black Churchmen,* which played a central role in the development of African-American liberation theology.*

Current Organization. In recent years, numerous neo-African religions have developed in urban settings. The most significant are Black Muslims, a product of the Nation of Islam, organized and led by Elijah Muhammad from the 1930s until his death in 1975.

The majority of African-Americans who claim a religious identity, however, are Christian. The overwhelming majority of church members—nearly twenty-five million—belong to one of the seven largest denominations: National Baptist Convention, U.S.A. (8.2 million), Church of God in Christ (5.5), National Baptist Convention of America (3.5), African Methodist Episcopal (3.5), African Methodist Episcopal Zion (1.1), Progressive National Baptist (2.5) and Christian Methodist Episcopal (0.7).

See also BLACK CATHOLICS; BLACK COLLEGES; BLACK THEOLOGY; MISSIONS, AFRICAN-AMERICANS AND.

Black Theology. Derived from both traditional African-American religion and the historical process of liberation, black theology focuses on God in Christ as deliverer of oppressed people, and blackness as the key to understanding that deliverance.

"It is my contention," wrote James H. Cone* in *A Black Theology of Liberation* (1970), "that Christianity is essentially a religion of liberation." In a society where people "are oppressed because they are black," he adds, "Christian theology must become black theology, a theology that is unreservedly identified with the goals of the oppressed community and seeking to interpret the divine character of their struggle for liberation."

A similar note was sounded by Albert B. Cleage Jr., author of *The Black Messiah* (1968). Like Cone, Cleage perceived an essential connection between the African-American experience of oppression and the liberating themes of Christianity. Both argued that this had been ignored or distorted by traditional white European and American theologians. To Cleage and Cone it appeared that any religion that did not meet the needs of a people was flawed in its theological understanding. As the two leading advocates of black theology in the late twentieth century, they have called for reorientation of Christian theology in both its theory and its applications. Blackness, defined more symbolically than physically, appears in their theology as the cornerstone of authentic Christian thinking. Jesus Christ, in this view, is "black" and embodies God's liberation of black (i.e., oppressed) people.

Black theology as a distinct movement within Christianity is relatively young. The civil rights movement* of the 1950s and 1960s not only quickened African-American political consciousness but also engendered widespread interest in African-American culture, identity and religious experience.* Dr. Martin Luther King Jr.,* a Baptist* minister and president of the Southern Christian Leadership Conference* (SCLC), constantly proclaimed a message of divine deliverance of African-American people. Throughout the organizational structure of SCLC and the broader civil rights movement, religious faith linked to a deliverance theology was the major energizing force.

Although he cannot be classified as an advocate of black theology as it is usually understood, King drew heavily on the tradition of liberation in African-American religion and contributed powerfully to the setting that produced black theology. This was recognized by Cone and Cleage, even as they disagreed with some of King's emphases, notably the principle of love as the energizing force of the nonviolent cement.

Diversity continued to characterize both African-American religion and the theology of African-American churches. There are wide differences among African-American ministers and teachers, as well as traditional laity, on such matters as the role of African culture, the relative weight of love and social pressure, and a host of other specifics. The theological approach that is defined formally as black theology thus exists within a shifting and complex matrix. What differentiates black theology from other forms is its persistent emphasis on the African-American experience as the pivotal reality of theology. "Blackness" is seen as both the quintessential human experience of suffering injustice and the focus of divine revelation. The action of God in history is directed toward its resolution.

Blackburn, Gideon (1772-1838). Presbyterian* minister, educator and missionary to Native Americans. In 1804 and 1805, Blackburn opened two schools for Cherokee youth in Tennessee. Later he became pastor of the Presbyterian church in Louisville, Kentucky, and in 1829 was made president of Danville (now Centre) College. His outspoken antislavery* and New School* views forced his resignation in 1830, and he moved to Carlinville, Illinois, where he became active in the formation of the Illinois Anti-Slavery Society.

Blackstone, William Eugene (1841-1935). Author and Christian Zionist.* Blackstone was a zealous dispensationalist* who authored *Jesus Is Coming* (1908). He is best remembered for his Zionist memorials sent to President Harrison (1891) and President Wilson* (1916).

See also JEWS, CHRISTIAN MISSIONS TO; MILLENNIALISM.

Blackwell, Antoinette Louisa Brown (1825-1921). First regularly ordained* woman in America. Ordained a Congregational* minister in New York in 1853, Blackwell eventually became a Unitarian,* pastoring All Souls' Unitarian Church in Elizabeth, New Jersey, from 1908 until her death. Throughout her life she was an ardent feminist*

and suffragist.*

Blackwood, Andrew Watterson (1882-1966). Presbyterian* minister and professor of homiletics.* Between 1925 and 1958 Blackwood taught at several institutions, including Princeton Theological Seminary. The author of twenty-two books, he was the most prominent homiletician among American Protestants in his era.

Blair, James (1656-1743). Anglican* commissary, and founder and president of the College of William and Mary.* After immigrating to Virginia in 1684, Blair became the first colonial commissary (or bishop's representative) in 1689. He was able to summon regular clergy conferences, secure the dismissal of two unfriendly colonial governors and found the College of William and Mary (1693). Near the end of his life, he was one of the few colonial commissaries to welcome evangelist* George Whitefield.*

Blair, John (fl. c. 1700). Early Anglican* missionary in North Carolina. In 1701 Blair visited the colony of North Carolina on a missionary tour. After baptizing* approximately one hundred persons, his funds ran out and he returned to England.

Blake, Eugene Carson (1906-1985). Presbyterian* minister, ecumenist* and civil rights* leader. Blake was the general secretary of the World Council of Churches* (1966-1972). As an ardent advocate of ecumenical relationships, he helped start the Consultation on Church Union.*

See also BLAKE-PIKE UNITY PROPOSAL; ECUMENICAL MOVEMENT.

Blake-Pike Unity Proposal. A suggestion for the union of major Protestant* churches in the U.S. At the request of Bishop James A. Pike,* Eugene Carson Blake* delivered a sermon in 1960 in which he invited interested denominations* to join Episcopalians and United Presbyterians in drafting a plan of union (*see* Consultation on Church Union).

Blanchard, Charles Albert (1848-1925). Congregational* minister and president of Wheaton College (Ill.).* Blanchard succeeded his father, Jonathan Blanchard,* as president of Wheaton (1882-1925). Under his presidency, the college made great advances as a center of conservative

Christian influence and as an academic institution. Blanchard became a leader in the fundamentalist* movement.

Blanchard, Jonathan (1811-1892). Presbyterian* minister, abolitionist* and president of Wheaton College.* Blanchard became an ardent abolitionist in 1834 and subsequently was unyielding in his attacks upon slavery. He was equally passionate in his attacks upon secret societies, especially the Masonic order.

In 1860 Congregationalists* called him to be the first president of Wheaton College. His son, Charles Albert Blanchard,* succeeded him as president in 1882.

Blanchet, François Norbert (1795-1883). Catholic* missionary to the Pacific Northwest and first archbishop of Oregon City. Blanchet arrived in the Oregon Territory in 1838 and in 1846 was elevated to the newly created archbishopric of Oregon City. He recruited missionaries and generally planted Catholicism in the Pacific Northwest. In 1862 he moved his see to Portland, where he built a cathedral,* college and hospital.

Bland, Salem Goldworth (1859-1950). Canadian Methodist* reformer. Bland, a professor and author, supported the labor movement, Sunday* observance, prohibition of alcohol,* the Cooperative Commonwealth Federation (a political party in Ontario), as well as doctrinal liberalization.

Bliss, Daniel (1823-1916). Missionary educator in the Near East. Going to Syria as a missionary in 1855, Bliss was instrumental in founding the Syrian Protestant* Collegiate Institute at Beirut, becoming its first president. In 1920 the college became the American University of Beirut.

Bliss, Philip Paul (1838-1876). Writer of hymns* and hymn tunes. Bliss joined Major D. W. Whittle* for several revival* meetings. He brought authentic personality to his music ministry, folksy humor to a newspaper column he published and spiritual dedication to every aspect of his short life. Representative of his hymn texts and tunes are "Almost Persuaded" and "Free from the Law."

Bliss, W(illiam) D(wight) P(orter) (1856-1926). Episcopal* priest, Christian socialist* and advocate for the Social Gospel.* In 1889 Bliss organized the Society of Christian Socialists, the first organization of its kind in America. From 1909 to 1914, Bliss and Josiah Strong* established the American Institute of Social Services.

As a liberal evangelical* and a supporter of the left wing of the Social Gospel movement, Bliss generally distinguished between the kingdom of God* and the secular vision of a socialist utopia. He believed that the solution to social ills lay not in an improved environment but in repentance, faith, baptism* and the sacraments.* Christocentric in theology,* his Christian socialism was rooted in the cross and resurrection of Jesus Christ. He was thoroughly committed to urban issues and attacked social evils of all sorts, particularly unjust labor practices.

Blue Laws. Civil legislation regulating Sunday* activities, including works, commerce, travel and public entertainment. All of the American colonies enacted and enforced such ordinances, which generally favored the Christian faith.

Blue Laws in the U.S. have constantly been a source of controversy and continuing legal action. Current Sunday laws are largely oriented toward public health, safety, recreation, welfare and cultural activities, but are gradually being eroded or are not enforced.

Boardman, George Dana (1801-1831). Pioneer Baptist missionary to Burma. After service in Calcutta (1825-1827), Boardman founded the mission station at Moulmein, Burma. In 1828 he founded a station at Tavoy, where he inaugurated extensive educational work.

Boardman, William Edwin (1810-1886). Presbyterian* minister and advocate of the higher Christian life.* In 1870, after service as a missionary of the American Sunday School Union* and then several years in business, Boardman became publicly associated with Holiness* teachings.

The Wesleyan and Oberlin* Perfectionist* teaching and expression that flow through his book *The Higher Christian Life* (1858) combined to produce a statement of the nature and reality of the holy life which was more widely received than the expositions in the more classic traditions. Boardman's ministry and writings were instrumental in opening the doors of non-Methodist churches to the teachings of the Holiness revival.

Body, Theology of the. Between September

1979 and November 1984, in 133 presentations, Pope John Paul II* developed what he calls a theology of the body, or teaching that deals with issues of marriage and gender. He delivered this publicly to large and enthusiastic throngs in St. Peter's Square.

Boehm, John Philip (1683-1749). German Reformed* pioneer in Pennsylvania. Arriving in Pennsylvania from Germany in 1720, Boehm became a leader in the German Reformed community, eventually founding twelve congregations.

When Moravian* leader Count Zinzendorf* arrived, Boehm through much effort succeeded in keeping his groups from joining the Moravians. In 1747 Boehm worked with Michael Schlatter* in establishing a German Reformed coetus (convention), which adopted the Heidelberg Catechism* and the Canons of Dordt as its confessional* standards.

Boehm, Martin (1725-1812). Cofounder of the United Brethren in Christ. Of Mennonite* upbringing, Boehm formed a long-lasting partnership with the German Reformed* pastor Philip W. Otterbein.* Under the leadership of Otterbein and Boehm, a revival* spread throughout the German communities of Pennsylvania, Maryland and Virginia. As the revival continued, many converts met in informal groups, which ultimately became a movement that in 1800 organized itself as the United Brethren in Christ, with Otterbein and Boehm as the first superintendents.

Bogardus, Everardus (1607-1647). Dutch Reformed* minister in New Netherland. In 1633 Bogardus arrived in New Amsterdam, where he became minister of the Dutch Reformed church. During his career in New Netherland, Bogardus ran afoul of two of the West India Company's directors-general, which led to his leaving America in 1647.

Bomberger, John Henry Augustus (1817-1890). German Reformed* minister. In 1870 Bomberger became president of Ursinus College at Collegeville, Pennsylvania. Some of his best-known writings were penned in opposition to the Mercersburg theology* of John W. Nevin* and Philip Schaff.* From 1868 to 1877 he edited the *Reformed Church Monthly,* which served as the primary organ for his anti-Mercersburg views. A main area of contention was the proposed revision of the liturgy* of the German Reformed Church.

Bompas, William Carpenter (1834-1906). Anglican* missionary and bishop in Canada. Arriving at Fort Simpson on Christmas Day 1865, Bompas until his death exercised a roving evangelistic* and pastoral ministry* to the Native American peoples of western Canada. A conservative evangelical,* he staunchly opposed ritualism and resisted any concession to Roman Catholic* missions.

Bonhoeffer, Dietrich (1906-1945). German Lutheran* pastor and theologian esteemed for his theological writings and life sealed by martyrdom. In Nazi Germany, Bonhoeffer was a leader in the resistance of the breakaway Confessing Church, which issued the famous Barmen Declaration (1934). Later he established a clandestine seminary for the Confessing Church. Two very influential books emerged from this period: *The Cost of Discipleship* and *Life Together.*

Bonhoeffer's influence in North America has risen in three successive waves. Post-World War II* Americans were especially receptive to his concept of "costly grace," with a corresponding church life that would nurture growth in grace. Next, radical thinkers—including the ephemeral "death of God"* theologians—picked up on Bonhoeffer's nascent thoughts about "religionless Christianity" in *Letters and Papers from Prison.* The third and most recent wave of Bonhoeffer's influence stems from detailed studies in the entire Bonhoeffer corpus, with special attention to church-state* relations.

Book of Common Prayer. The primary liturgical book of Anglican churches. The first Book of Common Prayer (BCP), primarily the work of Thomas Cranmer (1489-1556), archbishop of Canterbury, was issued in 1549. Subsequent revisions appeared in 1552, 1559, 1604 and 1662, with the last continuing in legal force as the BCP of the Church of England.

The Episcopal Church in the U.S. adopted its BCP in 1789 (revised in 1892 and 1928). The present American BCP was authorized in 1979.

See also LITURGICAL BOOKS.

Boone, William Jones (1811-1864). First American Episcopal* missionary bishop to China. In 1844 Boone was consecrated* missionary bishop to China, serving after 1845 in Shanghai. Boone was a significant participant in the committee that gathered in the late 1840s to make a new Chinese translation of the Bible.

Booth, Ballington (1857-1940). Salvation Army* leader and founder of the Volunteers of America.* Ballington, the second child of William and Catherine Booth,* was in command of army operations in the U.S. beginning in 1887. Becoming estranged from his father over the issue of the army's authoritarian international hierarchy, Ballington resigned from the army in 1896 and shortly thereafter established the Volunteers of America.

Booth, Catherine Mumford (1829-1890). Co-founder of the Salvation Army.* In 1855 Catherine married William Booth,* a licensed Methodist* preacher. Ten years later the Booths established an evangelistic mission in London, which in 1878 became the Salvation Army.

Catherine was a woman of strong moral conviction and an exacting sense of personal integrity, but at the same time she was known for her kindness and thoughtfulness toward others. She was a firm believer in women's rights to take roles equal to those of men.

Booth, Evangeline Cory (1865-1950). Salvation Army* leader. Evangeline was the seventh child of William* and Catherine Booth.* After directing army operations in Canada (1896-1904), Evangeline served as U.S. national commander from 1904 to 1934.

Flamboyant, melodramatic and strong willed, yet a capable administrator with the ability to attract and hold dedicated and efficient subordinates, Evangeline—the "Commander"—became famous beyond army circles.

Booth, Maud Charlesworth (1865-1948). Leader in the Salvation Army* and cofounder of Volunteers of America.* Maud married Ballington Booth,* the second son of William* and Catherine* Booth, and in 1887 they were sent to the U.S. as the national commanders. Both were indefatigable leaders, with Maud publicizing the work of the army through her writing and speaking.

Because of disagreement with William Booth over the autocratic governance of the army, the Ballington Booths resigned in 1896 and later that year founded the Volunteers of America.

Booth, William (1829-1912). English evangelist and founder of the Salvation Army.* In 1852 Booth became a licensed Methodist* minister; in 1861 he resigned to devote himself to the work of an independent evangelist.

Booth married Catherine* Mumford in 1855. Together they established the Christian Mission, opened in London's East End in 1865. Out of this mission grew the Salvation Army, with "General" William Booth at the apex. Catherine became the "Army Mother," and all of their eight children were eventually given high rank in the new organization. Within ten years, the Salvation Army was widely established throughout the British Isles and in the U.S., Canada, Australia and Europe.

William Booth was single-minded in his zeal for lost souls, subordinating everything to the work of evangelism. Influenced by Catherine, he streamlined the army's theology* to better serve its spiritual warfare. Everything else in the way of doctrine or practice was simply jettisoned—especially if, like sacramental* observances, these things were confusing or divisive.

The movement Booth founded remains an important force for spiritual and social redemption in many parts of the world.

Booth-Tucker, Frederick St. George de Lautour (1853-1929), and Emma Moss Booth-Tucker (1860-1903). National commanders of the Salvation Army in America.* In 1882 Frederick went to India to begin the work of the Salvation Army. Emma, the second daughter of William* and Catherine* Booth, was the principal of the first training home for women officers in 1880. The two were married in 1888.

In 1896 they were sent to the U.S. as national commanders of the Salvation Army, which was in disarray because of the resignations of Ballington* and Maud Booth.* They regained the confidence of the general public and greatly increased its social ministry.

Borden, William Whiting (1887-1913). China Inland Mission* missionary to Muslims. Born into a wealthy Chicago family, Borden early devoted himself and his wealth to serving others. In 1909 he entered Yale University* and later studied at Princeton Seminary.* While just beginning to serve the Muslims of northwest China, Borden met an untimely death from cerebrospinal meningitis; he was widely mourned.

Born Again. A phrase associated with revivalism* or any conversionist* form of Protestantism,* *born again* describes the experience of a person in shifting his or her life focus from any other center to Jesus Christ (from Jesus' words in Jn 3:7).

Bosworth, F(red) F(rancis) (1876-1958). Early Pentecostal* healing* evangelist. Bosworth established a successful independent healing ministry in the post-World War I* era, attracting large crowds in major cities throughout America.

During the post-World War II* healing revival, he joined the William Marrion Branham* team and functioned as a revered adviser to younger evangelists. Bosworth's teachings on faith healing made him an important precursor to the faith movement.*

Bouchard, Claude Florent (1751-?). French Catholic* priest in Boston. Bouchard deserted from the French fleet in 1788 and began an unauthorized ministry* as pastor of the School Street Church in Boston. He rapidly became controversial and eventually was suspended by the archbishop* of Paris. In 1790 Bouchard left Boston for Canada.

Boudinot, Elias (Galagina) (c. 1802-1839). Tribal leader and publisher among the Cherokee Indians. Converted* to Christianity at a mission school in Connecticut, Boudinot became widely influential as a Christian leader among his tribe. He translated a variety of religious and educational literature into the Cherokee language.

See also MISSIONS TO NATIVE AMERICANS, PROTESTANT.

Bounds, Edward McKendree (1835-1913). Methodist* minister and devotional writer. A chaplain during the Civil War, Bounds later served pastorates in Tennessee, Alabama and Missouri. Bounds taught a doctrine of entire sanctification* as a distinct second work of grace. His devotional* books, such as *Purpose in Prayer* (1920) and *The Necessity of Prayer* (1929), continue to appear in numerous new editions.

Bourget, Ignace (1799-1885). Catholic* bishop of Montreal. Living in Montreal, with its powerful Anglo-Saxon commercial community, Bourget was aware of the threat of Protestantism and of various forms of liberal thought. Consecrated* as bishop in 1840, Bourget made the Diocese* of Montreal the dynamic center of Canadian ultramontanism.* He did more than any other individual to make Francophone Quebec an unofficial theocracy,* a situation that would continue until the Quiet Revolution of the 1960s.

Bourne, Hugh (1772-1852). Cofounder of the Primitive Methodist Church.* Bourne, a Wesleyan Methodist in England, was excluded by the Wesleyans and, with William Clowes, founded the Primitive Methodist Church in 1811. In 1829 the conference, with Bourne as its leader, initiated a mission to America that later severed its connections with Britain.

Bowne, Borden Parker (1847-1910). Methodist* philosopher. In 1876 Bowne joined the faculty at Boston University, where he taught for thirty-five years. As the head of a prestigious philosophy department and an effective teacher, Bowne exerted a considerable influence on his contemporaries, including Edgar S. Brightman* an Albert C. Knudson.*

His philosophy increasingly centered on the role of personality and self-image in one's religious makeup and expressions. Bowne's career illustrates turn-of-the-century efforts to respond to social Darwinism and industrialization from a positive, modern Christian perspective.

Boyce, James Petigru (1827-1888). Southern Baptist* educator, theologian and seminary founder. In 1859 Boyce, who had an appreciation for Reformed* theology, helped to found the Southern Baptist Theological Seminary* in Greenville, South Carolina. Under his guidance the fledgling seminary survived the Civil War* years and a move to Louisville in 1877.

Bradbury, William Batchelder (1816-1868). Composer and compiler of Sunday-school tunes, music publisher and piano manufacturer. Bradbury studied with Lowell Mason* at Bowdoin Street Church, Boston, and held musical institutes with George F. Root,* Thomas Hastings and Mason. Bradbury tunes still familiar include "Bradbury" ("Savior, Like a Shepherd") and "Woodworth" ("Just as I Am").

Bradford, William (1590-1657). Governor of Plymouth Colony and historian. When the possibility of New World settlement arose, Bradford and other Separatist leaders embarked on the *Mayflower* in 1620. Within a year of the "Pilgrim"* settlement of Plymouth Colony, Bradford was elected governor and served in that capacity until his death.

Bradford also served as chief chronicler and historian of the first settlements. His manuscript *History of Plymouth Plantation* (written between 1630 and 1651) stands as the most profound testimony to the Congregational* vision and sense of destiny that prompted their New World settlement.

Bradley, Preston (1888-1983). Unitarian* minister and civic leader. In 1912 Bradley founded the People's Church, which he led until semi-retirement in 1968. His optimistic theism stressed human goodness and progress. He styled himself a heretic who disdained the traditions and creeds* of organized religion.

Bradstreet, Anne (c. 1612-1672). Puritan* poet. With her husband, Anne immigrated to Massachusetts Bay with the Winthrop party in 1630.

Bradstreet's poetry, written in the midst of demanding domestic duties, reveals a warm Puritan piety that accepted the joys and trials of life as from the hand of a sovereign and loving God. Her lyrics frequently expound the beauty and wonders of the natural world, through which she perceived the hand of God. She has the distinction of being America's first noteworthy poet.

Brainerd, David (1718-1747). Presbyterian* missionary in the Middle Colonies. Brainerd's most significant achievement as a missionary occurred near Trenton, New Jersey, between 1745 and 1746. There he led a revival* among small bands of Delaware Indians, baptized thirty-eight converts and formed a church.

Brainerd succumbed to tuberculosis in Northampton, Massachusetts. His friend and mentor Jonathan Edwards* fashioned Brainerd's diary into a heroic memoir and inspirational guidebook, which he published in 1749.

Branham, William Marrion (1909-1965). Healing* evangelist. The post-World War II* healing revival* in Pentecostalism* began in the ministry* of Branham, an independent so-called Holy Ghost Baptist* minister from Indiana. From 1946 to 1955 Branham conducted a healing ministry that only Oral Roberts* could match.

See also FAITH HEALING.

Brant, Joseph (Thayendanegea) (c. 1743-1807). Mohawk Indian statesman. Brant was converted while in a Connecticut school directed by Congregationalist* missionary Rev. Eleazar Wheelock.* During the American Revolution* he played an important role in keeping the Mohawks loyal to the Crown. Later he led a band of Mohawks to Canada.

Brattle, William (1662-1717). Harvard* academic and Congregational* minister. Although Brattle was in most respects a loyal son of the Massachusetts Congregational establishment, his catholic spirit and enthusiasm for Anglican* works of theology* smoothed the path for a number of students who subsequently entered the Church of England.

Bray, Thomas (1658-1730). Anglican* minister and promoter of missionary and philanthropic* causes. Bray was commissary to Maryland (1695-1704), although actually resident in Maryland only briefly in 1700. He succeeded in securing the establishment of the Church of England in Maryland in 1702.

Bray launched three organizations which still exist: the Society for Promoting Christian Knowledge* (1699), the Society for the Propagation of the Gospel in Foreign Parts* (1701) and, serving Native Americans and African-Americans, Dr. Bray's Associates (1724).

Brébeuf, Jean de (1593-1649). French Catholic* missionary and martyr. Brébeuf served among the Hurons near Georgian Bay, Lake Huron. In 1649 the Iroquois seized Brébeuf and other missionaries and tortured them ferociously. Brébeuf and seven companion martyrs were canonized* (1930) and named patron saints* of Canada (1940).

Breck, James Lloyd (1818-1876). Episcopal* missionary. Breck, influenced by the high church* principles of the Tractarian movement,* early determined to give his life to three goals: (1) missionary work in the West; (2) the establishment of a theological seminary in the West; and (3) the revival of a disciplined religious community life. He accomplished the first two, opening up schools for Indians in Nashotah, Wisconsin (1842, Nashotah House), in Faribault, Minnesota (1858, Seabury Divinity School), and in Bernica, California (St. Augustine's College). No priest did more for the Episcopal Church in the West than Breck.

Breck, Robert (1713-1784). Congregational* minister. Breck preached that the good heathen might be saved* and that some portions of the Scriptures are not inspired, which prompted an interrogation from Thomas Clap* and marked the beginning of the "Breck Affair." In the years following this affair, Breck had repeated clashes with Jonathan Edwards.*

Breckinridge, Robert Jefferson (1800-1871). Presbyterian* theologian. After serving as pastor and educator, Breckinridge founded Danville Seminary in Kentucky, where he was professor of theology* from 1853 to 1869. He became known as a controversial churchman, being an outspoken opponent of slavery, intemperance, Universalism,* sabbath* desecration and Roman Catholicism.* He helped define the Old School* party in the Presbyterian Church, which led to the denomination's division in 1837.

See also AUBURN DECLARATION.

Brenneman, John M. (1816-1895). Mennonite* Church minister and bishop. Despite his almost complete lack of formal education, Brenneman was an influential leader in his conference. Known as a skillful mediator, he assisted in the resolution of numerous church controversies.

Brent, Charles Henry (1862-1929). Episcopal bishop and ecumenical* pioneer. In 1901 Brent was elected by the Episcopal Church* in the U.S. as its first missionary bishop to the Philippines. Brent was an active participant in the famous Edinburgh Missionary Conference of 1910, expressing in his own person the shift of much missionary leadership to those who were not of an evangelical* position. Later, in 1927, he was elected president of the first World Conference on Faith and Order held in Lausanne, Switzerland.

Bresee, Phineas Franklin (1838-1916). Founder of the Church of the Nazarene.* In 1895 Bresee and J. P. Widney started the Church of the Nazarene. Opposing the tide of increasingly lux-

urious churches, they envisioned a denomination* with churches furnished to welcome the poor and in which holiness* would be preached.

Brethren in Christ Church. A small American denomination* with Anabaptist,* Pietistic* and Wesleyan* Holiness* roots. The Brethren in Christ emerged from the pietistic revival* movements in Lancaster County, Pennsylvania, during the latter years of the eighteenth century.

Beginning in the late 1940s the Brethren in Christ moved closer to the conservative, evangelical* mainstream of American religious life as they dropped requirements for plain dress and adopted a more ecumenical spirit by allowing open Communion. In 1992 there were a reported thirty-nine churches with 3,173 members in Canada and 184 churches with 16,697 members in the U.S.

See also OLD ORDER RIVER BRETHREN.

Brett, Pliny (fl. 1805-1840). Reformed Methodist* Church leader. Brett, with some laypeople, formed the Reformed Methodist Church in 1814. The new Methodist body kept much of the Methodist Episcopal Church structure but was congregational* in polity* and emphasized divine healing* and the attainability of entire sanctification.*

Breviary. The Roman breviary, or divine office,* containing the canonical hours,* composed of prayers,* psalms, scriptural readings and patristic lessons to be recited daily by the clergy and certain nonordained religious* in the Latin church. It has been superseded by the Liturgy of the Hours* (1971).

Brewer, Grover Cleveland (1884-1956). Church of Christ* preacher. A masterful orator, writer and preacher, Brewer has been considered one of the most influential second-generation leaders in the noninstrumental Church of Christ* during the first half of the twentieth century.

Brewster, William (c. 1564-1644). Elder* of Plymouth, Massachusetts. In 1620 Brewster sailed on the *Mayflower* and played a significant role in establishing Plymouth Colony, in governing the church and in providing spiritual guidance for the colonists. Since Plymouth had no settled minister until 1629, Brewster, as the only university-educated person in the colony, assumed virtually all pastoral duties except administering sacraments.* Brewster conducted services, prayed and preached* twice every sabbath to the satisfaction and edification of his brethren.

Briand, Jean-Olivier (1715-1794). First Roman Catholic* bishop of Quebec following the British conquest of New France. Briand assumed the leadership of the Canadian church at this critical point, and his actions ensured its survival. He managed to safeguard the rights of the church and prevent undue civil interference in its affairs, while at the same time remaining loyal to the British authorities.

Briant, Lemuel (1722-1754). Congregational* minister. In 1749 Briant preached a sermon opposing the view of the New Lights,* who stressed that the righteousness of the unregenerate was but "filthy rags." Briant instead held a "common sense," or Arminian,* view of human nature.

Bridgman, Elijah Coleman (1801-1861). First American missionary to China. In Canton (1830-1847) Bridgman edited the *Chinese Repository*, a monthly magazine which did much to enlighten foreigners in China and elsewhere about China. In Shanghai (after 1847) he devoted his time mainly to Scripture translation.

Bridgman, Eliza Jane Gillet (1805-1871). Episcopal* educator and missionary to China. Bridgman, wife of Congregationalist* Elijah Coleman Bridgman,* founded a day school for girls in Shanghai and, in Peking, Bridgman Academy, which eventually became the Women's College of Yenching University.

Briggs, Charles Augustus (1841-1913). Biblical scholar and Presbyterian* minister. Throughout the 1880s Briggs published works which championed the higher-critical method and questioned the orthodoxy* of Princeton theology.* The address he delivered upon his induction into the chair of biblical studies at Union Theological Seminary in New York* (1891) precipitated one of the most famous heresy trials* in American religious history.

In a polemical tone Briggs denied the verbal inspiration, inerrancy* and authenticity of Scripture. The 1891 General Assembly* responded by vetoing Briggs's professorial appointment. He remained at Union, however, and in 1898 entered the priesthood of the Episcopal Church.*

See also FUNDAMENTALIST-MODERNIST CONTROVERSY.

Brightman, Edgar Sheffield (1884-1953). Personalist philosopher and liberal* Methodist* theologian. Brightman, who taught philosophy at Boston University from 1919 until his death, was a prolific scholar and a major spokesperson for the philosophical movement known as Boston personalism. In this philosophical system persons are the sole or dominant metaphysical realities, as well as the only ultimate intrinsic values. While convinced of the truth of the Christian faith, Brightman learned much from other religions and particularly from Hinduism. There was for him no conflict between religion and philosophy. All he demanded was that every aspect of experience, including the religious, be included and tested before final judgments about truth were made.

Broad Church. A party within the Anglican Church* that has interpreted the Christian faith in its broadest and most inclusive sense. Today the term is seldom used; the theological descendants of the movement are known as modernists* or liberals.*
See also HIGH CHURCH; LOW CHURCH.

Broaddus, Andrew (1770-1848). Baptist* pastor and associational leader. Broaddus served as pastor of several rural churches in Virginia. An active leader and often moderator of the Dover Association, Broaddus resisted views of Alexander Campbell* and his followers in associational conferences. Regarded as a superb preacher and biblical expositor,* Broaddus declined invitations from influential city churches and remained a rural pastor.

Broadus, John Albert (1827-1895). Seminary professor and Southern Baptist* minister. Broadus long served as professor of New Testament interpretation and homiletics at the Southern Baptist Theological Seminary (1859-1895). Of his numerous books, pamphlets and tracts, his best known is his introduction to homiletics,* *On the Preparation and Delivery of Sermons* (1870), which became a textbook in many denominational seminaries and remains in print even today.

Brook Farm (1841-1847). Nineteenth-century transcendentalist* community in West Roxbury,

Massachusetts. George Ripley* and seventeen others formed the Brook Farm in 1841, attempting to give form to the philosophy of many members of the Boston Transcendentalist Club, which rejected Enlightenment* empirical philosophy and what the transcendentalists perceived to be its disintegrating effects on the social order. *See also* ROMANTICISM, CATHOLIC.

Brooke, John (d. 1707). Anglican* missionary in the Middle Colonies. Brooke served in New York and New Jersey under the Society for the Propagation of the Gospel.* In 1705 he signed a letter with thirteen other Anglican clergy in Burlington, New Jersey, asking the Church of England for a suffragan bishop.

Brookes, James Hall (1830-1897). Presbyterian* minister. Brookes, who is best known for his wide ministry as a conference speaker, was one of the founders of the Niagara Bible Conference,* which he presided over until his death. From 1875 until his death he was editor of *The Truth,* an influential premillennial* journal that assailed liberals and encouraged conservatives in their battle against Protestant apostasy. Brookes was a dispensational* premillennialist; C. I. Scofield* was a notable disciple.

Brooks, Phillips (1835-1893). Episcopal* preacher and bishop. Brooks, who early established his reputation as a premier preacher, was attractive, well read, and capable of impressive oratory and rapid delivery. He was the embodiment of his own belief that "preaching is the bringing of truth through personality."

In 1869 Brooks returned to his native Boston to become rector of Trinity Episcopal Church. A broad church* evangelical* of wide sympathies, his installation was opposed by conservatives and Anglo-Catholics alike. His Christmas carol "O Little Town of Bethlehem" remains popular to this day.

Brouwer, Arie (1935-1993). Reformed* minister and ecumenical* leader. Brouwer was ordained by the Reformed Church in America* (1959) and pastored churches in Michigan (1959-1963) and New Jersey (1963-1968) before moving into denominational administration and leadership, serving as the executive secretary of the denomination from 1977 to 1983. From 1985 until 1989 he was general secretary of the National

Council of Churches. From 1983 to 1984 he was deputy general secretary for the World Council of Churches* in Geneva, Switzerland. Brouwer was outspoken on issues of peace and justice both nationally and internationally and a strong opponent of apartheid in South Africa.

Brown, Arthur Judson (1856-1963). Presbyterian* clergyman, mission* executive. Brown traveled extensively for his denomination,* guided by his belief in the missionary character of the church, the necessity for Christian cooperation, and the call to Christian witness in both word and deed.

Brown was a leader and participant in numerous ecumenical* endeavors, including the 1910 Edinburgh conference. He contributed to the development of the World Council of Churches.*

Brown, Charles Reynolds (1862-1950). Congregational* minister and educator. From 1911 to 1928 Brown served as dean of the Yale University Divinity School.* His tenure was marked by increased student enrollment as well as a growth in faculty and funding. Brown exercised an enormous influence in mainline* Protestant* churches on behalf of theological liberalism* during the first half of the twentieth century through his distinguished career as a teacher, preacher and administrator, and through his thirty-nine published books.

Brown, Francis (1849-1916). Old Testament scholar and president of Union Theological Seminary (New York).* Brown became enmeshed in the controversies surrounding Charles A. Briggs* over higher criticism. He stood by Briggs and approved the severing of Union from the Presbyterian Church.* Brown remained a Presbyterian and was a leader among liberals.*

Brown, George (1818-1880). Canadian politician and founder of the *Toronto Globe.* Entering the Canadian Parliament in 1851, Brown spoke for the interests of many Protestants* in Canada West (now Ontario) in his opposition to perceived Roman Catholic* aggression and French-Canadian domination of the political union.

Brown, John (1800-1859). Militant messianic abolitionist.* By the 1850s Brown grew convinced that only violent action would end the wrong of slavery. On October 16, 1859, Brown and his raiders took control of the federal armory at Harpers Ferry, Virginia (now West Virginia). When the slaves of the area failed to rally to his cause, Brown was captured and later hanged for treason against the state. Brown became a martyr to the antislavery cause and a symbol of Northern conspiracy to the South.

Brown, Morris (1770-1849). African-American Methodist* minister. Brown, described as a preacher with an earnest and direct style and as a capable administrator, was the second bishop of the African Methodist Episcopal Church (AME) from 1820 until his death. During his tenure as bishop, the church moved into Canada and the Midwest and sponsored its first periodical, the *A.M.E. Church Magazine.*

Brown, Phoebe Hinsdale (1783-1862). Hymn* writer and essayist. Brown lived in New England and wrote for Congregationalists* there. Her essays were serialized in the *New Haven Religious Intelligencer* (1816-1837). Her stories traced the evils of drinking and gambling; many of her hymns paralleled those themes or are devotional* in tone.

Brown, R(obert) R(oger) (1885-1964). Christian and Missionary Alliance* pastor, district superintendent and radio preacher. In 1920 Brown was appointed superintendent of the Western District. He transferred the district office to Omaha, where he began the Omaha Gospel Tabernacle (1923).

To those outside his own group Brown was best known for his radio program *World Radio Chapel,* which he sustained from 1923 to 1964.

See also ELECTRONIC CHURCH.

Brown, William Adams (1865-1943). Presbyterian* educator and theologian. Brown spent his entire career at Union Theological Seminary* in New York, most significantly as professor of systematic theology* (1898-1930) and research professor in the field of applied Christianity (1930-1936). Throughout his career Brown was a strong advocate of theological liberalism.* He was a strong defender of both the Social Gospel* and the importance of religion in undergirding liberal democracy.

Brown University. An institution of higher education founded by colonial Baptists.* Founded in 1764 at Warren, Rhode Island, the school from its beginnings espoused principles of religious freedom.* In 1770 it moved to Providence, and in 1804, following a gift from Nicholas Brown, its name was changed to Brown University. Academically, Brown reached its nineteenth-century apex during the innovative presidency of Francis Wayland,* who introduced a largely elective curriculum.

Brownlow, William Gannoway (1805-1877). Controversial Methodist* preacher, journalist and governor of Tennessee. Because of his intense nativism* and anti-Catholicism, Brownlow became prominent in the Know-Nothing movement. At the end of the Civil War* his staunch Unionism led to his appointment as governor.

Brownson, Orestes Augustus (1803-1876). Preacher, author, editor and Catholic* lay apologist.* In his earlier years, Brownson successively followed or was influenced by Puritanism,* Presbyterianism,* Universalism,* radical humanism, Unitarianism* and transcendentalism.* In 1844, however, after seeing the Catholic Church as the only church capable of providing the spiritual power for social reform, he was baptized* a Roman Catholic.

Writing in his own *Brownson's Quarterly Review* (1844-1864; 1873-1875), Brownson defended Catholic doctrine against Protestant* thinking. Against the Know-Nothings and other nativist* groups, Brownson argued for the compatibility between Catholicism and American democracy. As a consequence of his doctrine of the supremacy of the spiritual (the Catholic Church) over the temporal (the state), he argued for the supremacy of the pope, not only in spiritual matters but even in temporal matters, insofar as the latter touched on spiritual concerns.

Brunner, H(einrich) Emil (1889-1966). Swiss Reformed* dialectical* theologian. Brunner, who occupied the chair of systematic* and practical theology at the University of Zurich (1924-1955), was the first to introduce neo-orthodoxy to the English-speaking world.

Although frequently associated with Barth,* Brunner developed his theology independently. A prominent motif in Brunner's theology, influenced by Kierkegaard* and Martin Buber (1878-1965), was his concept of revelational truth as "personal encounter." Special revelation is not the communication of facts but God's disclosure of himself.

Despite his negations of the historic orthodox* view of biblical revelation, Brunner did help restore to modern theology a sense of the transcendent reality of God and the personal commitment demanded by faith.

Brush Arbor. Overhanging tree branches sheltering the main area of a camp meeting* site. Lower limbs were broken off, creating a natural canopy with a cathedral-like effect.

Bryan, Andrew (1737-1812). Pioneer African-American Baptist* minister. In 1788 Bryan, while still a slave, was ordained—an early, if not the first, ordination of an African-American. His First Colored, later African, Baptist Church erected its first building in 1794, and the membership grew to 850 by 1802. After purchasing his freedom Bryan later organized two other Baptist churches in Savannah, Georgia.

Bryan, William Jennings (1860-1925). American editor, politician and antievolutionary leader. Bryan was a three-time candidate for president of the U.S. and secretary of state (1913-1915) under Woodrow Wilson.*

In 1896, although only thirty-six years old, Bryan won the Democratic presidential nomination (following his famous "Cross of Gold" speech) but lost to William McKinley.* Chosen two more times as the Democratic nominee, he lost to McKinley again in 1900 and to William Taft in 1908.

The end of Bryan's political career in 1915 opened the door for his reforming and religious leadership. He soon threw himself into the Prohibition* cause and played a significant role in securing the passage of the Eighteenth Amendment. In the spring of 1921, Bryan issued a series of attacks on evolution that instantly placed him in the forefront of fundamentalist* forces. Bryan's last great battle was the Scopes Trial.*

Bryant, William Cullen (1794-1878). Poet and editor. In 1811 Bryant composed the first draft of his best-known poem, "Thanatopsis," and by the 1820s was recognized as America's finest poet. Beginning in 1827, Bryant was editor and part owner of the *New York Evening Post*. Many of Bryant's poems deal with nature, in which he saw the presence of God. His popularity as a poet

and his use of religious themes contributed in a subtle way to the influence of Unitarianism* in nineteenth-century America.

Buchman, Frank Nathan Daniel (1878-1961). Founder and director of Moral Re-Armament.* A brilliant organizer, tireless promoter, charismatic leader and insightful counselor, Buchman founded a controversial religious movement in 1921 that for more than forty years had significant worldwide impact. Known successively as The First Century Christian Fellowship, the Oxford Group movement and Moral Re-Armament, Buchman's movement eventually spread to more than sixty countries. Its primary goal was to help individuals develop a deep spiritual commitment within the context of their own religious traditions.

Buck, Pearl S(ydenstricker) (1892-1973). Author. Buck spent her early years in China as the daughter of Presbyterian* missionaries. Following graduation from college she returned to China and there, in 1917, married missionary John Lossing Buck. From 1921 to 1931 she taught at Kiangan Mission in Nanking. Her first novel was *East Wind, West Wind* (1930), and her second, *The Good Earth* (1931), won her a Pulitzer Prize in 1932. Following controversy generated by an article she published that was critical of mission personnel, Buck resigned from the Presbyterian Board of Foreign Missions and returned to the United States in 1934. She obtained a divorce and in 1935 married her publisher, Richard J. Walsh. Buck wrote over 100 books, many of them having to do with China. She won the Nobel Prize for literature in 1938.

Buhlmaier, Marie (1859-1938). Baptist* home missionary. In 1893 Buhlmaier became a Southern Baptist Convention missionary to German immigrants in Baltimore.

Bultmann, Rudolf Karl (1884-1976). German biblical scholar and theologian. Professor of New Testament and early Christian history at the University of Marburg from 1921 to 1951, Bultmann is most widely known for his program for "demythologizing"* the New Testament.

Bultmann's own investigation of the New Testament was guided by form criticism, a method he was instrumental in developing. His research into the Synoptic Gospels yielded little reliable information about the historical Jesus and much that reflected the faith of the early Christians. But this paucity of reliable information about the historical Jesus did not trouble Bultmann. Heavily influenced by the existentialism* of his Marburg colleague Martin Heidegger (1899-1976), Bultmann interpreted the Christian message in terms of the Word of God that addresses moderns in their scientific and technological quest for security. To seek a historical Jesus was to abandon faith and engage in a quest for security and freedom apart from God.

Bultmann's influence among biblical scholars and theologians of the latter half of the twentieth century has been second to none. Yet his synthesis of literary-critical method, religious-historical approach and philosophical interpretation has gradually eroded. By the 1980s a new generation of scholars was more optimistic about clarifying its picture of the historical Jesus against the background of a newly enhanced understanding of first-century Judaism.

Burial Hill Declaration. A summary statement of belief issued in 1865 by Congregationalists* meeting in a national council, the first denomination-wide doctrinal statement since 1649. It was a short affirmation of evangelical* beliefs.

Burke, Edmund (1753-1820). First Catholic* vicar apostolic of Nova Scotia. Under Burke's leadership, Nova Scotia became a vicarate apostolic in 1817, which removed it from Quebec's jurisdiction. Burke was active in promoting the Roman Catholic interest in Nova Scotia and in defending his church and faith in exchanges with non-Catholics.

Burke, John Joseph (1875-1936). Catholic* publisher and founder of the National Catholic Welfare Conference.* Burke's major contribution was in founding and directing the Catholic War Council (later the National Catholic Welfare Conference), established originally to coordinate services to Catholics in World War I.* His broad record of public service, diplomacy and ecumenical* leadership earned him the admiration of many political and church leaders of his time.

Burned-Over District. An area located in New York State, bounded by the Catskill Mountains on the east and the Adirondack Mountains on the north and known for its concentration of relig-

ious experimentalism. Charles G. Finney* referred to the area as a "burnt district" and put his own mark on it by introducing a series of "new measures"* that provided a means for the excesses that characterized some movements during the 1820s and 1830s.

Burton, Ernest Dewitt (1856-1925). Baptist* biblical scholar and president of the University of Chicago. In 1892 Burton became head of the department of New Testament and early Christian literature at the university; in 1923 he became president.

Few writers surpassed Burton's usefulness in producing New Testament scholarship. He was among the first to develop biblical theology* as a historical discipline, arguing that the books of the Bible* represent a historical process.

Bush, George Herbert Walker (1924-). Forty-first U.S. president. Before becoming president, Bush served two terms in the House of Representatives, was ambassador to the United Nations under Nixon,* served as envoy to China under Ford* and was vice president in the Reagan* administration. Running as the Republican candidate in the 1988 presidential election, he won the election largely as the promising executor of the Reagan administration's legacy. Bush, a member of the Episcopal Church, preferred to keep his religious convictions a private affair and never seemed at home with religious language in his public pronouncements. During his administration Bush continued to express some of the moral themes of the Reagan administration, opposing abortion, pornography and special rights for homosexuals, and supporting prayer in public schools. In his 1992 bid for reelection, he clothed these and other concerns in the language of "family values." Nevertheless, the Religious Right, who helped Bush into office, felt neglected during his administration, enjoying little or no fulfillment of its social agenda. The strong conservative religious support (fifty-five percent of the evangelical vote) for Bush in his failed reelection campaign of 1992 was in large part due to the perceived threat of his opponent, Bill Clinton.*

Bushnell, Horace (1802-1876). Congregational* theologian and pastor. Bushnell was not a popular preacher, and his lack of success in effecting conversions abetted his search for a new system that would transcend the Old School*/

New School* debates then exercising New England Congregationalists. His *Christian Nurture* (1847) represented a covert attack on revivalism* as a source of church growth. In *God in Christ* (1849), he asserted that all religious language, including that of the creeds, must be understood as poetical and not literal. Such a view almost immediately involved him in charges of heresy.* His *Vicarious Sacrifice* (1866) advanced a "moral influence" theory of the atonement* that became influential among liberal Protestants.

Bushnell is thus often likened to Coleridge or Schleiermacher, battling the dry rationalism of Protestant scholasticism and restating religious truths in terms of human experience. More than any other single thinker, Bushnell laid the intellectual foundations for American Protestant modernism and the Social Gospel.*

Bushnell, Kathryn (1856-?). Physician and temperance* reformer. In 1885, after several years in China as a medical missionary, Bushnell became a full-time evangelist in the U.S. for the Social Purity department of the Women's Christian Temperance Union.* In 1891 she began worldwide lectures on behalf of temperance.

Buswell, J(ames) Oliver, Jr. (1895-1977). Presbyterian* fundamentalist* educator and organizational leader. Buswell was president of Wheaton College* (Ill.) (1926-1940) and taught at Covenant College and Seminary in St. Louis (1956-1970). A distinguished teacher of theology

and an ecclesiastical controversialist, Buswell's legacy included a vision for a vigorous evangelical* intellectual witness and a series of ecclesiastical separations. Both of these helped to shape the neo-evangelical* movement of the 1950s and 1960s.

Butler, Elizur (1794-1857). Medical missionary among the Cherokee Indians. Beginning in 1821, Butler worked among the Cherokee Indians in Georgia. In 1838 he accompanied the Indians when they were forced to remove to the Indian Territory, where he worked at the Park Hill and Fairfield missions.

See also MISSIONS TO NATIVE AMERICANS, PROTESTANT.

Buttrick, George Arthur (1892-1980). Congregational* preacher and theologian. After service as a British chaplain in World War I,* Buttrick came to the U.S. for health reasons.

After pastorates in Illinois and Vermont, Buttrick in 1927 was named to succeed Henry Sloane Coffin* as pastor of Madison Avenue Presbyterian Church, the largest church of its denomination in New York City. In his twenty-seven years at Madison Avenue, Buttrick distinguished himself in his preaching and writing. Known in some circles as "the preacher's preacher," he twice delivered the Lyman Beecher* Lectures on Preaching at Yale* and taught homiletics for two decades at Union Theological Seminary, New York.*

C

Cabrini, Francesca Xavier (1850-1917). Catholic* saint.* Born in Italy, Francesca founded the Missionary Sisters of the Sacred Heart in 1880. Witnessing the growth of this new institute, Pope Leo XIII* directed Francesca toward the Italians in America. Arriving there in 1889 and later becoming a U.S. citizen, Mother Cabrini provided evangelization through catechetical* instruction, prison work,* orphanages and schools throughout the country. She also established Columbus Hospitals in New York, Chicago and Seattle. In 1946 she was canonized,* the first American citizen to be declared a saint.

Cadbury, Henry Joel (1883-1974). New Testament scholar, Quaker* historian and humanitarian worker. Cadbury was Hollis Professor of Divinity at Harvard Divinity School (1934-1954). He became a leading New Testament scholar in America, specializing in Luke-Acts. In 1947 he received the Nobel Peace Prize.

Cadman, Samuel Parkes (1864-1936). Congregational* minister. Cadman was born in England and later immigrated to New York. From 1900 to his death, Cadman led Brooklyn's Central Church, making it one of the leading churches in the U.S. Cadman was an evangelical* liberal* who stressed the themes of divine Fatherhood, human brotherhood and the kingdom of God* with a christocentric focus. He was president of the Federal Council of Churches* (1924-1928) and, from 1928, their national radio preacher.

Cahensly, Peter Paul (1838-1923). German Catholic lay leader. An officer in the St. Raphaelsverein, an organization founded for the care of German Catholic immigrants, Cahensly sought to protect the faith of the immigrants to the U.S. by preserving their ethnic identity.

See also IMMIGRATION AND ETHNICITY, CATHOLIC.

Cain, Richard Harvey (1825-1887). Black Methodist* minister, editor and politician. Cain was an African Methodist Episcopal* (AME) pastor in Brooklyn during the Civil War.* At its close, he became a distinguished preacher-politician in South Carolina. He organized AME churches among the freed people, was an editor and served two terms in the U.S. Congress, where he spoke eloquently for civil rights and supported women's suffrage.*

Caldwell, David (1725-1824). Presbyterian* minister, educator and physician. A Scotch-Irish immigrant, Caldwell served in the North Carolina constitutional convention of 1776. After the war he devoted himself to his school, his church and his farm. He was offered, but declined, the presidency of the University of North Carolina.

California, Christianity in. California has had a significant influence in the shaping of American culture, including American Christianity. Roman Catholicism* was first brought to California during the era of Spanish control. Beginning in 1848, the gold rush attracted thousands of adventurers. Protestant* ministers soon arrived, and in 1852 the first Roman Catholic archbishop was appointed. Though the churches grew, the independent westerners were more attracted to unorthodox religious movements such as Spiritualism, Unitarianism* and Seventh-day Adventism.*

During the first quarter of the twentieth century, Southern California gained wide acclaim for its mild and healthful climate, attracting both solid citizens and unusual cultists. Coming to California in this era were such diverse religionists as radio-preacher Robert P. Shuler* and evangelist Billy Sunday,* joined by a wide variety of unorthodox movements such as Theosophy, New Thought and Christian Science.*

The 1906 Azusa Street Revival* in Los Angeles was a significant event in the birth of the Pentecostal movement.* Later the dynamic Aimee Semple McPherson* and her Foursquare Gospel Church* played a significant role in the development of Christianity in California. Since World War II,* California—and the Los Angeles area in particular—has produced a number of "super churches," such as Robert Schuller's Crystal Cathedral. The state also has spawned the Jesus movement,* the gay Metropolitan Community Church, the charismatic movement,* the Full Gospel Business Men's Fellowship* and, more recently, John Wimber's Vineyard Christian Fellowship.

Callahan, Patrick Henry (1866-1940). Catholic* layman. Callahan prospered as a leader in the paint and varnish business in Louisville from the 1890s until his death. A devout Catholic, he initiated a crusade during World War I* for religious toleration. His "Callahan Correspondence" was sent to leading political, religious and business figures to influence public opinion. The constancy of his political, economic, social and religious ideals makes Callahan the archetypal progressive.

Calvert, Cecilius (1606-1675). Catholic* colonizer of Maryland. Born in London, Cecilius established a colony in America as a refuge for his fellow Catholics. Cecilius appointed his brother Leonard* as governor and made sure that all settlers enjoyed religious liberty. He invited the Society of Jesus to care for the spiritual needs of Maryland's Catholics. In 1648 Cecilius appointed a Protestant as governor. His "Act Concerning Religion" (1649) helped allay Puritan suspicions.

See also CALVERT, GEORGE; COLONIAL CATHOLICISM; TOLERATION, ACT OF.

Calvert, Charles (1637-1715). Third Lord Baltimore, last Catholic* proprietor of Maryland. Charles served as governor of Maryland (1661-1684) and in 1675 became its proprietor. In 1689 a Protestant revolt to Maryland led to its becoming a royal colony and to the establishment of the Church of England* there in 1702.

Calvert, George (1580-1632). British Catholic* colonizer in America. Calvert, a member of the royal privy council and of Parliament, served James I and later Charles I. His interests increasingly turned to colonization as a means of providing fellow Catholics with refuge from England's

penal laws. He received rights to various lands in the New World, including land north of the Potomac. On his death, his son Cecilius* founded the new colony.

See also COLONIAL CATHOLICISM.

Calvert, Leonard (1610-1647). First colonial governor of Maryland. Appointed by his brother Cecilius,* Leonard, a Catholic, aimed to maintain a policy of toleration for all Christians. He supported Jesuit* missionaries' efforts to convert the Native Americans and constantly struggled to maintain peace between Catholics and Protestants.*

Calvinism. A doctrinal tradition originating with the Reformer John Calvin (1509-1564) and providing the foundational theology* of the Congregational,* Reformed* and Presbyterian* churches in America. Adhering to the fundamental Reformation principle of *sola Scriptura,* Calvinism claims to derive its doctrines entirely from Scripture—not reason or church tradition. It begins with the fundamental principle of the sovereign majesty of God and, consequently, emphasizes his exclusive initiative in salvation.* Otherwise known as Reformed theology, Calvinism as it came to America was defined by the Belgic Confession (1561), the Heidelberg Catechism (1563), the Thirty-Nine Articles* (1562, 1571), the Canons of the Synod of Dort (1619) and the Westminster Confession of Faith* (1647).

The Synod of Dort clearly defined in five summary points the salvific implications of Calvinism over against Arminianism:* (1) humanity is by nature totally depraved and unable to merit salvation; (2) some people are unconditionally elected by God's saving grace; (3) God's atonement* in Christ is limited in its efficacy to the salvation of the elect; (4) God's transforming grace, ministered by the Holy Spirit, is irresistible on the part of humans; (5) the saints must persevere in faith to the end, but none of the elect can finally be lost.

See also COVENANT THEOLOGY; ELECTION; PREDESTINATION; REFORMED TRADITION IN AMERICA.

Cambridge Platform (1649). Written codification of New England Congregational church government.* In 1646 the Massachusetts General Court convened the Cambridge Synod, which produced the Cambridge Platform (written largely by Richard Mather*). It described and gave biblical justification for the practices and government of New England churches. The platform soon came to be regarded as a higher law, binding on both ministers and congregations. Well into the nineteenth century it continued to serve as a fundamental statement of Congregational practice.

Cameron, Robert (c. 1845-c. 1922). Canadian Baptist* minister and prophetic writer. Cameron was a prominent figure in the Niagara Bible Conference* who rejected pretribulationism in favor of a posttribulation premillennialism.* He expounded his millenarian views in *Doctrine of the Ages* (1896) and *Scriptural Truth about the Lord's Return* (1922).

Camp Meeting. An outdoor revival* meeting, interdenominational in origin, during which the participants came prepared to encamp at the meeting site for several days. Beginning in Kentucky in 1800, the camp meeting proper developed under the auspices of Presbyterian revivalists,* shaping Protestant development in the trans-Allegheny West for several decades. In the later nineteenth century the camp meeting was significant in the Holiness* revival movement.

See also FRONTIER RELIGION; REVIVALISM, PROTESTANT.

Campaign for Human Development (1969). An organization launched by the National Conference of Catholic Bishops* (NCCB) to combat poverty and racism through fundraising and educational programs. The campaign represents the NCCB's response to the Catholic Church's growing awareness of its responsibility to the poor. It was also a response to indigenous American problems which exploded in the 1960s, especially the urban violence of 1967 and 1968.

Campanius, John (Johan) (1601-1663). Swedish Lutheran* minister and missionary. Although serving mainly in Sweden, Campanius ministered for five years to Swedish, Finnish and German settlers in the Delaware River area. He also translated Luther's Shorter Catechism into the Lenape language.

Campbell, Alexander (1788-1866). One of the founders of the Restoration movement* in America. Born in Ireland, Campbell immigrated to the U.S. in 1809 and spent several years itiner-

ating throughout Ohio, Indiana, Kentucky, Tennessee and West Virginia. Throughout his travels he emphasized a Christianity that recaptured the essence of New Testament faith and life, free from denominational and creedal restrictions and ecumenical* in its acceptance of all who confessed Jesus as Savior and had been baptized by immersion. Drawing largely from Baptists, Campbell formed groups of believers who called themselves Disciples of Christ* and were known to outsiders as Campbellites. In 1832 a group of 12,000 Disciples and 10,000 of Barton W. Stone's* group known as Christians came together for a meeting in Lexington, Kentucky. Within a few years the two groups were joined to form the Christian Church (Disciples of Christ).*

Campbell's theology,* with its emphasis on the simplicity of New Testament Christianity, free from the accretions of history and tradition, was readily wedded to the ethos of the American frontier.* The Bible provided the only authority* for restoring simple evangelical* Christianity, and this principle in turn protected individual freedom of opinion. Such emphases helped make his movement a vital force in American religion.

See also CAMPBELL, THOMAS.

Campbell, Thomas (1763-1854). Cofounder, with his son Alexander Campbell,* of the Restoration movement.* Immigrating to the U.S. from his native Ireland, Thomas founded an association to promote biblical Christianity and Christian union, its sole creed being "Where the Scriptures speak, we speak; where the Scriptures are silent, we are silent." He emphasized (1) the sinfulness of divisions within the body of Christ, (2) the sufficiency of the Bible as the only standard for doctrine, (3) love and forbearance as essential manifestations of Christian spirit.

See also CHURCHES OF CHRIST.

Campbell, Will D. *See* COMMITTEE OF SOUTHERN CHURCHMEN.

Campus Crusade for Christ International. An evangelistic* organization. Campus Crusade, founded in 1951 by William ("Bill") R. Bright,* is committed to spreading the gospel throughout the world, particularly among college students. Its *Have You Heard of the Four Spiritual Laws?* is a well-known booklet for converting people to Jesus Christ. Campus Crusade is ecumenical* in spirit, emphasizing commitment rather than doctrine.

Campus Ministries. Christian organizations and movements founded to nurture Christian faith in college students. Higher education began as a religious movement in America, as Harvard,* Yale,* Princeton* and a host of lesser colleges were founded with a vision of training Christian leaders. Over time, however, nearly all of these schools became secularized* and began to treat religion as little more than an academic discipline.

The advent of campus ministries can be understood largely as a response to this development. At first, small groups of Christians began to meet in secret to support one another, pray for revival* and plan strategies for evangelism.* By the late nineteenth century these small campus groups and organizations had spawned many larger organizations, such as the YMCA,* the YWCA,* the Student Volunteer Movement* and the World's Student Christian Federation.*

At the turn of the century, denominational leaders organized student foundations and commissioned pastors as campus ministers. Parachurch* groups like InterVarsity Christian Fellowship,* Campus Crusade for Christ* and the Navigators* were founded in the 1940s and 1950s as an alternative to mainline campus ministries. The Pax Romana and Newman* clubs and the World Union of Jewish Students provide similar ministries for Catholics and Jews on campuses.

See also AWAKENINGS, COLLEGE.

Cana Conferences. Spiritual and educational program for Roman Catholic* married couples. The conferences originated in the 1940s as a day of joint spiritual renewal* for Catholic married couples, during which they were instructed on the proper supernatural dignity and sacramentality of Christian marriage. In seeking to renew the Catholic family, the program aims to combat secularism and eventually effect a Christian reconstruction of American society.

Canadian Baptist Federation. A loose confederation of four autonomous Baptist Conventions/Unions. The federation (totaling some 1,100 churches, with over 130,000 members) includes the United Baptist Convention of the Atlantic Provinces, the Baptist Convention of Ontario and Quebec, the Baptist Union of Western Canada, and the Union of French Baptist Churches in Canada. Canadian Baptists support four theological colleges, one junior college and two lay training institutes.

The Federation emerged in 1944 as a national coordinating agency. Through its Canadian Baptist Relief and Development Fund, it cooperates with the Canadian Baptist Overseas Mission Board and numerous relief agencies overseas. In Canada today the Federation serves as the voice of Canadian Baptists before governments.

Canadian Council of Churches. An ecumenical organization founded in 1944 as a national expression of the worldwide ecumenical movement.* The Council was developed by the major Protestant* denominations* as a consultative body to help coordinate the growing number of cooperative ventures in the fields of social service, religious education,* evangelism* and overseas missions.* The Roman Catholic Church joined the Council as an associate member in 1985.

See also CHURCH UNION MOVEMENTS; ECUMENICAL MOVEMENT; ECUMENICITY; WORLD COUNCIL OF CHURCHES.

Candler, Warren Akin (1857-1941). Bishop, educator and leader of the Methodist Episcopal Church,* South. A strong supporter of Methodist missions, Candler's greatest contributions were in education. He was president, and later chancellor, of Emory College (University), whose school of theology was named in his honor.

Cane Ridge Revival. Largest and most famous camp meeting* of the Second Great Awakening.* In 1801 Barton W. Stone* organized a "sacramental meeting" at his Cane Ridge meeting house* (Presbyterian) in Bourbon County, Kentucky. Between ten and twenty-five thousand people gathered for a week of preaching and emotional expression. The resulting waves of revivalism* lasted for years, revitalizing western churches and bringing thousands of the unchurched into the fold of organized religion.

Cannon, James, Jr. (1864-1944). Methodist* bishop and temperance* advocate. Cannon was principal of Blackstone (Virginia) Female Institute for nearly twenty-five years. As bishop (1918-1938), he supervised overseas missionary activities and chaired the Commission on Temperance and Social Service. Cannon helped to organize the World League Against Alcoholism and was closely associated with the national Anti-Saloon League.* During the 1920s, he was the leading lobbyist for the "dry" cause in Washington, D.C.

A strong supporter of the Federal Council of Churches,* Cannon was one of the few American churchmen to participate in all the major ecumenical streams that joined to form the World Council of Churches* in 1948.

Canon. A religious standard or list. The word *canon* ("measuring rod") appears in the phrases *canon law* and *canonization* of *saints*. The most common American usage speaks of the Bible* as the canon because it is the authoritative, established collection of writings recognized as God's Word.

Canon Law. The various laws and prescriptions issued by ecclesiastical authority* for the governance of a given church. In the Roman Catholic* Church the code of canon law (applying only to the Latin rite*) was first promulgated in 1917. In 1983 Pope John Paul II* announced a revised code of 1,752 canons, which abrogates previous legislation and stands as the law for the Roman Catholic Church.

Canon of the Mass. Also called the Eucharistic* Prayer, it is the fixed formula in the Roman Catholic* liturgy* that the priest proclaims after offering the gifts of bread and wine. Its central focus is the formula of consecration: "This is my body; this is my blood." Other liturgically oriented churches use variations of the Canon.

See also MASS.

Canonization. The term used by Roman Catholics* to describe the formal process by which a deceased man or woman is defined and declared a saint* gloriously reigning in heaven, someone whose memory should be kept by the whole church and to whom prayers may be directed.

A regular process has been established for gathering data about a would-be saint. The Congregation for the Causes of Saints oversees the investigation, which requires the attestation of certain miracles before the subject is canonized, receiving the title *saint.*

See also BEATIFICATION; SAINTS, CULT OF THE.

Capers, William (1790-1855). Methodist* missionary and bishop. Capers earnestly tried to prevent the North-South schism which split his denomination in 1844. Eloquence and dedication brought Capers influence in his church and throughout the South. He was proudest of his missionary work among plantation slaves.

Capital Punishment. Execution carried out under authority of the law as the penalty for crime. Capital punishment in America has been characterized by three major trends: (1) limiting the types of crimes for which execution is permitted, (2) the unsuccessful effort to have capital punishment declared unconstitutional and (3) the development of standards for imposing the death penalty.

American Christians have taken one of three general positions on the issue. Some (including virtually every mainline* denomination*) have argued that when the Old and New Testament are considered together, a moral imperative against the use of the death penalty emerges. Others (including many contemporary evangelicals* and fundamentalists*) have held that Scripture offers at least a moral imperative, if not an outright mandate, for states to administer the death penalty. A third view is that the death penalty is neither mandated nor prohibited but is a permitted sanction as long as biblical conditions are met.

Cardinal. A member of the Sacred College of Cardinals, the chief Roman clergy. Now numbering more than one hundred, cardinals head up curial offices, Roman congregations and church commissions and (since 1179) vote to appoint a successor to a deceased pope.

Carlsson, Erland (1822-1893). Swedish-American Lutheran* pastor and home missionary. Carlsson immigrated to the U.S. in 1853 and became pastor of a Swedish Lutheran Church in Chicago. One of the founding fathers of the Evangelical Lutheran Church, or Augustana Synod, he was elected to the first board of directors of the Augustana College and Seminary, serving as its chairman for many years.

Carman, Albert (1833-1917). Canadian Methodist* leader. With the final union of Canadian Methodism, Carman became general superintendent (1884-1915). He brought to this position a deep concern for piety* and holiness.* He was convinced that the suspicions of supernaturalism evident in so much of biblical criticism were undercutting the roots of Christianity, eroding conversion* and Christian life and destroying the hope of church union* between the Methodists and Presbyterians.*

Carmelites. A family of Roman Catholic* religious orders.* The original Carmelite order began during the Crusades in Palestine on Mt. Carmel (c. 1154). Two celebrated members, St. Teresa of Ávila (1515-1582) and St. John of the Cross (1542-1591), initiated a reform that led to a parallel "Order of Discalced Brothers of the Virgin Mary of Mt. Carmel."

Carnegie Council on Ethics and International Affairs. An interfaith organization seeking to relate religion and ethics to international affairs. Founded in 1914, the organization was an early expression of interfaith cooperation between Protestants,* Catholics* and Jews. Now it sponsors lectures and seminars and publishes newsletters and books on peace.

Carnegie Hall Conference (November 15-21, 1905). Also known as the Interchurch Conference on Federation, it led to the establishment of Federal Council of Churches of Christ in America* (FCC) in 1908. Representatives of twenty-nine denominations attended, agreeing to overlook theological differences and emphasize cooperation.

Carnell, Edward John (1919-1967). Evangelical* theologian and educator. Earning doctoral degrees from Harvard and Boston University, Carnell served nineteen years at Fuller Theological Seminary.* He was the seminary's president from 1954 to 1959.

Carnell became one of the leaders in the intellectual awakening of conservative evangelicalism in America after World War II,* extending his influence through nine books, including *Introduction to Christian Apologetics* (1948) and *Christian Commitment* (1957).

Carrick, Samuel (1760-1809). Presbyterian* minister and college president on the Tennessee frontier.* In 1792 Carrick organized a congregation at Knoxville, the newly established capital of the Tennessee territory. The next year he opened a seminary in his home. In 1794 the school was chartered as Bount College, with Carrick as its president. After the Civil War* it became the University of Tennessee.

Carroll, B(enajah) H(arvey) (1843-1914). Southern Baptist* pastor, educator and controversialist. Carroll taught theology* at Baylor (1872-1905) and later was president of Southwestern Baptist Theological Seminary.* Carroll was an able spokesman for Southern Baptist doctrine and polity, promoting evangelism* and attacking heresy.*

Carroll, Charles (1737-1832). Roman Catholic* patriot and U.S. Senator. Educated in Jesuit* schools in Maryland and France, Carroll amassed a fortune in Maryland that made him one of the wealthiest men in the colonies. Elected to the Continental Congress in 1776, Carroll was the first to sign the Declaration of Independence. His leadership and risk-taking for the cause of independence encouraged American Catholics to give their overwhelming support to the Revolution.

Carroll, Daniel (1730-1796). Catholic* congressman. Daniel, older brother of Archbishop John Carroll,* amassed a fortune in Maryland as a tobacco planter and merchant. An early champion of colonial independence, Carroll attended the Constitutional Convention in Philadelphia in 1787-1788.

Carroll, John (1735-1815). First Roman Catholic* bishop in the U.S. Carroll's family was well-to-do, despite colonial penal laws against Roman Catholics. After study in Catholic institutions in Maryland and in Europe, John was ordained a Roman Catholic priest.

Carroll saw the Roman Catholic Church as a communion of basically self-governing national churches which chose their own bishops and educated their own clergy. He accepted the pope as head of the universal church and Rome as its center, but he understood church unity less in terms of governmental control from Rome than of shared belief and practice.

Carroll strongly supported separation of church and state* and religious toleration. He was deeply convinced that the "freedom and independence acquired by the united efforts and cemented by the mingled blood of Protestants and Catholics" should be shared equally by all. He founded the academy which became Georgetown University.

See also COLONIAL CATHOLICISM.

Carter, James Earl, Jr. (1924-). Businessman, farmer, statesman, Baptist* layman and thirty-ninth U.S. president. Jimmy Carter, owner of his family's farm in Plains, Georgia, capped an increasingly active career in state politics by winning election as governor in 1970. On completing his term in 1975, Carter began a run for the presidency. Despite the fears aroused by the fact that he was a self-acknowledged evangelical* Christian, a Southerner and a nonestablishment outsider, he won the presidency in 1976.

Carter's administration (1977-1981) received mixed reviews. He failed to seize the economic initiative in domestic affairs, and the country suffered increasing inflation, unemployment and federal deficits during his tenure in office. He succeeded in some matters, such as civil-service reform, environmental legislation and energy policies. In foreign affairs, Carter inaugurated full diplomatic relations with China, persuaded Israel and Egypt to sign the Camp David peace accord and, to some degree, established human rights as a basic tenet of American policy.

Carter displayed a combination of straightforwardness, an aura of moral rectitude that exemplified traditional values and a transparently authentic religious faith that struck the right note for the time. Carter was perhaps the most dedicated Christian ever to occupy the White House.

Much of the 1980 presidential campaign was played out under the cloud of the Iran Hostage Crisis, and Carter was criticized by his Republican opponent, Ronald Reagan,* for ineptitude and a lack of leadership. In addition, many evangelicals who had supported Carter in 1976 drifted away to the Reagan camp. Reagan was swept into office in a landslide victory. Carter's loss in the 1980 election was, in part, a reflection of public rejection of his prophetic civil religion* in favor of Reagan's politics of nostalgia for a bygone era of respected might and limitless plenty.

Cartwright, Peter (1785-1872). Methodist* frontier preacher. Referring to himself as "God's plowman," Cartwright preached an average of more than a sermon a day for the first twenty years of his ministry. With a keen wit, an uncompromising devotion to Christ and church, and a rugged physical constitution, his colorful exploits soon became well known throughout the American frontier.

After serving in the Illinois Legislature, Cartwright was defeated in a bid for Congress by Abraham Lincoln.* He strongly opposed slavery and championed the cause of Methodist colleges.

Carver, W(illiam) O(wen) (1868-1954). Southern Baptist* pastor, professor and missiolo-

gist.* Carver was missions instructor at the Southern Baptist Theological Seminary (1899-1943). An ecumenical* churchman and prolific writer, Carver sought to interpret the Baptist missionary imperative within the mission of the whole church.

Cary (Carey), Lott (c. 1780-1828). African-American Baptist* missionary. Born a slave in Virginia, Cary was converted* in 1807 and in 1813 bought his freedom and helped found the Richmond Baptist Missionary Society. He went to Africa under the society in 1821 and the next year was involved in the founding of the colony of Liberia. There he established churches and schools among the local inhabitants.

Case, Shirley Jackson (1872-1947). Baptist* New Testament scholar. Case taught at the University of Chicago Divinity School* (1908-1938). Refining the "socio-historical-environmental" method of the Chicago school,* he believed that he could find the historical Jesus and contended that the Jesus of history was in fact the Christ of faith.

Cashwell, Gaston Barnabas (1826-1916). Pentecostal* pioneer in the South. In 1906 Cashwell attended the Azusa Street* revival.* Returning to his home in North Carolina, he led a month-long revival and then engaged in a two-year preaching tour. The result was that many Holiness* ministers and two Holiness groups joined the Pentecostal ranks.

Catechetics, Catholic. The teaching and explanation of the Catholic* faith primarily to children, Native Americans* and African-American slaves. By the 1820s U.S. Catholics were following their Protestant* fellow-citizens in opening Sunday schools,* where priests and others taught the catechism lessons in a parish context. In the late nineteenth century catechetical activity became centered in the full-time Catholic schools. The twentieth-century movement known as the Confraternity of Christian Doctrine* (CCD) brought a renewed effort, especially in the 1930s, to reach out to children not in Catholic schools. Catholic catechisms have had a remarkably consistent content, with the Apostles' Creed functioning as the main framework. Young Catholics were led to interpret their situations as fallen and, short of God's intervention, hopeless and headed for eternal suffering. Christ's redemption, begged for in prayer, especially the Lord's Prayer, and received in the seven sacraments* of the Church, made possible the keeping of the commandments (meaning the Ten Commandments and those of the Church), which would lead to salvation after death.

The Second Vatican Council* had a profound impact on Catholic catechetics. The older format of memorizing questions and answers gave way to a more biblical and liturgical catechesis which goes beyond mere formulas about God. God now is portrayed as loving and revelation as interpersonal communion with God.

Catechisms, Protestant. A summary of Christian beliefs, usually set out in questions and answers to make doctrine more pedagogically accessible. Protestant catechisms often express the theological content of a doctrinal confession* or standard in simpler terms, for those without theological training. Often there is a larger catechism for adults and a shorter one for children.

The European catechisms brought to America by its settlers and immigrants were often the primary means of Christian education* until the Sunday-school movement.* An important use of private catechisms was in educating Southern slaves.

Catechist. One who systematically instructs students in Christian doctrine, usually by means of a catechism.* The term may refer specifically to (1) Roman Catholic lay teachers or (2) indigenous believers on the mission* field who instruct new believers.

Cathedral. A church, usually in a major city, containing the seat (Latin, *cathedra*) of a bishop, and therefore the central church of a diocese* or archdiocese.* Cathedrals are usually maintained by religious groups that adhere to the apostolic succession* of bishops.

Catholic Action. A term used to designate both a concept and an organization of laity, it has a variety of meanings, depending upon the decade and the region to which reference is made. Pope Pius XI* gave *Catholic Action* its classic definition in 1922 as "the participation of the laity in the apostolate* of the Church's hierarchy."

The type of Catholic Action which developed in the U.S. originally sought to Christianize economic and social institutions through a technique expressed in the formula "Observe, judge, act" applied in small groups. Many grassroots movements trained Catholics to influence the worlds of labor, race relations, marriage and family life, and local economics. In the 1970s and 1980s, however, the advent of lay ministry eclipsed Catholic Action in the U.S. by centering lay activity in the parish rather than the workplace.

Catholic Association for International Peace. *See* PEACE MOVEMENT, CATHOLIC.

Catholic Biblical Association of America. A Catholic society of biblical scholars. The fundamental goal of the Catholic Biblical Association (CBA), which first met in 1937, is to "devote itself to the scientific study of the Bible . . . in conformity with the spirit and instructions of the Catholic Church." The CBA has produced *The New American Bible* (Confraternity Version), publishes the *Catholic Biblical Quarterly* and helped launch *The Bible Today.* In the late 1980s CBA had over eight hundred active members, including priests, religious* and laity—as well as some Protestant and Jewish members.

Catholic Foreign Mission Society of America (Maryknoll Missioners). An American congregation of diocesan priests dedicated to foreign missions.* Founded in 1911, the Maryknoll Missioners are diocesan priests who do not take religious vows but an oath to serve in the missions and be faithful to the Society. Going first to China in 1918 and then to other countries in the Far East, by 1987 they were serving in twenty-seven countries.

Catholic Peace Fellowship. *See* PEACE MOVEMENT, CATHOLIC.

Catholic University of America. The only university belonging to the Catholic hierarchy of the U.S. Incorporated in the District of Columbia in 1887, the University initially offered only advanced degrees in ecclesiastical disciplines for clergy. It soon began offering graduate instruction in secular subjects, and in 1905 introduced lay undergraduate education. Presently the University, whose faculty and students are predominately lay, consists of ten schools along with an undergraduate college of arts and sciences.

Catholic Worker. Lay Catholic* movement.

Founded during the depth of the Great Depression* by Dorothy Day* and Peter Maurin,* the Catholic Worker encourages lay Catholic initiative in changing the social order and helping its victims. The movement views itself as a prophetic leaven for church and society, calling people to the essential teachings of Christ. Advocating nonviolent solutions to social problems and international conflicts, the Catholic Worker was the first Catholic pacifist* movement to emerge in the U.S.

Catholic Youth Organization. Catholic* archdiocesan youth organization founded in 1930 in Chicago by Auxiliary Bishop Bernard Sheil.* The organization developed a variety of services to help form Christian living habits in poverty's children.

Catholic Youth Organization has also referred to diocesan youth services that in 1937 began to affiliate with the National Council of Catholic Youth in the National Catholic Welfare Conference,* Washington, D.C.

Cauthen, Baker James (1909-1985). Southern Baptist* missionary, educator and missions executive. After service as pastor, missions professor and missionary to China, Cauthen became executive secretary of the Foreign Mission Board of the Southern Baptist Convention (1954-1979). He led Southern Baptists in building one of the largest missionary forces among Protestant denominations,* from 908 missionaries in 1954 to 3,008 in 1979, located in ninety-four countries.

Cavadas, Athenagoras (1885-1962). Greek Orthodox* bishop and educator. Cavadas was one of the most gifted and energetic of Greek clergymen in America. Serving as a roving evangelist in the U.S., he proved effective in healing the strife in the Greek-American community and stemming the tide of innovationism.

Cavanaugh, John Joseph (1899-1979). Catholic educator. In 1946, after being associated in various capacities with the University of Notre Dame for almost thirty years, Cavanaugh was named its fourteenth president. Cavanaugh presided over the transition of Notre Dame from an enclosed compound to an institution seeking integration into post-World War II American society. He developed the fundraising machinery that made possible the school's future expansion and development.

Caven, William (1830-1904). Canadian Presbyterian* leader. Migrating to Canada with his family from Scotland, Caven was a Presbyterian pastor, professor of theology and, from 1873, principal of Knox College, Toronto. He was staunchly conservative, yet without confessional rigidity; greatly interested in social questions of a moral kind; thoroughly committed to missions* and fearful of church and state too readily transgressing each other's boundaries.

Celebrant. The principal minister who presides at the Eucharist.* The celebrant may be a single priest, or, as in the early church and in recent (post-Vatican II*) practice, several may assist or share in the ceremony.

Celebritism, Christian. The practice of elevating certain well-known Christians to celebrity status, often in both Christian and secular communities. Celebritism is not new. In early church history desert fathers and hermits were famous for their piety.* The medieval papacy itself also attained a particular celebrity status. In some sense, the pope remains the world's most famous Christian person.

In the U.S. many flamboyant preachers and evangelists became famous (or infamous) in the larger society. Today Billy Graham* has become one of the most famous Protestant* preachers of the twentieth century. Television and the other modern media have contributed significantly to Christian celebritism.

Cell Group. A small group of individuals gathered into a particular unit of a larger organizational structure. It typically has a common purpose or task, with a common discipline or pattern of study and action. In Christian contexts cell groups are typically found within churches and parachurch organizations and may also be called small groups.

Chafer, Lewis Sperry (1871-1952). Presbyterian* minister, popular conference speaker and founder of Dallas Theological Seminary.* In 1901 Chafer began assisting in Dwight L. Moody's* famous summer conferences in Northfield,* Massachusetts. There he met C. I. Scofield* and later became an extension teacher for Scofield's Bible correspondence school.

Chafer gained prominence in the Bible conference movement* and eventually conceived the idea of founding a theological school that would combine the standard elements of seminary education with the distinctives of the Bible institute* and Bible conference movements. While pastoring Scofield's former church in Dallas, Chafer founded the Evangelical Theological College in 1924 (since 1936, Dallas Theological Seminary) and served as its president and professor of systematic theology* until his death. Within the evangelical*/fundamentalist* movement of the early twentieth century, Chafer emerged as a champion of the premillennial and dispensational* segment.

Chamberlain, Jacob (1835-1908). Dutch Reformed* missionary to India. After receiving degrees from seminary and medical school, Chamberlain went to India as a missionary under the Reformed Protestant Dutch Church (now the Reformed Church in America*). There he established two hospitals and also was instrumental in producing a Telugu translation of the Bible. In 1887 he founded what is reputed to be the first theological seminary on the mission field, in which he taught and later served as principal (1891-1902).

Channing, William Ellery (1780-1842). Unitarian* minister and theologian. Channing, long-time pastor of the Federal Street Church in Boston (1803-1842), defined the liberal movement in New England Congregationalism* that came to be known as Unitarianism. His defense of liberalism became the theological basis of the American Unitarian Association,* which was formed in 1825.

Channing argued that every individual possessed an innate spiritual potential and that the religious life consisted in the cultivation of that potential. Channing's theology of spiritual self-culture, which depicted human spiritual potential aspiring toward a benevolent God, became the hallmark of nineteenth-century Unitarianism. Much of Channing's later work was devoted also to social causes such as antislavery.

Chapel. A place of worship,* often small, for a special group or purpose. Some chapels are found adjoining the main sanctuary or along the aisles of churches or cathedrals.* Others may be contained within a larger institutional structure and may provide a central focus for a self-contained community.

Chaplain. A priest or minister who performs pastoral duties for special groups and in non-church, though sometimes church-related, institutions. The first chaplains were appointed to minister to bishops or royalty. In more recent times the work of the chaplain has been applied to the ministry of clergy who serve institutions separate from local churches.

The military chaplaincy in America began in 1776, with Roman Catholic chaplains added in 1824, Jewish in 1917. College chaplains began to gain prominence in the late nineteenth century. When criteria for selecting faculty, presidents and trustees changed, the religious life of many colleges and universities was entrusted into the hands of chaplains.

The work of the chaplaincy has proliferated in the twentieth century as institutions once controlled by churches and clergy have become increasingly secular. Many of these institutions now allow for official religious influence through the work of chaplains, including the U.S. Senate, many state governments, hospitals, prisons, industry and athletic teams.

Chaplain, Military. Chaplains have been part of Western armies since the fourth century and were transplanted to America with the earliest settlers. They served on a regular basis under the leadership of George Washington.* Chaplains serve both as staff officers and as religious leaders, responsible for religion, morale and morals. They conduct services of worship,* administer rites and sacraments* consistent with their own faith groups, and provide a full range of religious activities.

The military receives its chaplains through the recruiting efforts of forty-seven separate ecclesiastical endorsing agencies representing 120 denominations. These endorsing agencies certify a candidate's qualifications; in addition, clergy must meet the standard military requirements.

Chapman, John Wilbur (1859-1918). Presbyterian* pastor and evangelist. In 1903, after Chapman assisted Benjamin F. Mills* and Dwight L. Moody* in evangelistic endeavors, he devoted himself full time to such work. Teamed with musician Charles Alexander,* Chapman conducted meetings across the U.S. and around the world, with outstanding success in Boston (1909) and Chicago (1910).

Chapman introduced the method of the simultaneous campaign into urban evangelism (one central meeting, with other meetings in various parts of a target city). Chapman was also the first director of the Winona Lake (Indiana) Bible Conference.

Chappell, Clovis Gillham (1882-1972). Methodist* minister. Born in Tennessee, Chappell began his ministry in Texas and served pastorates throughout the South. Chappell was an outstanding preacher, widely known for his biographical sermons.

Chapter. Term used of various clerical bodies. The term arose from the meeting of monks* to hear a chapter of their rule or of Scripture read. It then began to designate the meeting itself, and finally the monks themselves.

Charismatic Movement. The classic Pentecostal movement* usually traces its origin to New Year's Day, 1901, when Agnes Ozman* first spoke in tongues in Charles F. Parham's* Bible school in Topeka, Kansas. Many ridiculed the movement that ensued as the religion of the economically deprived, the socially disinherited, the psychologically abnormal and the theologically aberrant. However, by the 1960s many sociological, psychological and theological theories had given way under the increasing evidence that Pentecostals were becoming middle class and educated. At the same time, their characteristic teachings were gaining acceptance among Christians within mainline* Protestant* denominations,* as well as the Catholic Church.* As the national media publicized this new movement, American Christians began to grapple with a phenomenon that would come to be known as the charismatic, or neo-Pentecostal, movement.

Undoubtedly the most prominent figure in founding the charismatic movement was the Southern California dairyman Demos Shakarian.* As founding president of the Full Gospel Business Men's Fellowship International* (1953), his efforts were the catalyst for the Pentecostal experience penetrating the mainline Protestant and Catholic churches.

Mainline Protestant and Nonaligned Charismatics. The early 1960s witnessed the movement's spread into every major stream of traditional Protestantism. An Assemblies of God* minister, Ralph Wilkerson, founded the Melodyland Christian Center, a large charismatic congregation that hosted numerous conferences and supported various educational ventures. A parachurch organization known as Women's Aglow gained widespread influence. Larry Christenson became a prominent Lutheran* charismatic, and his denomination became fertile ground for charismatics. The other major denominations also felt the effects of the movement.

Among nonaligned charismatics, the trend is toward denominationalism rather than the celebrated ecumenicity of the charismatic movement as a whole. In its embryonic stage this denominationalism led to the controversial Discipleship/Shepherding movement* of the 1970s. A number of groups are taking on increasingly denominational characteristics, such as Chuck Smith's Calvary Chapels, Bob Weiner's Maranatha Christian Churches, Larry Lea's Churches on the Rock and John Wimber's Vineyard Christian Fellowships. Among the leading charismatic parachurch organizations are Youth With A Mission* and Bethany Fellowship.

Typically middle class and higher in social standing, non-Catholic charismatics are frequently well educated, yet seldom theologically literate. They are avid proponents of inner healing and consider spontaneous, revelational prophecy* a commonplace. Their doctrinal centerpiece remains baptism in the Spirit.

The Catholic Charismatic Movement. An indirect result of the extensive changes arising from Vatican II,* the Catholic charismatic movement is perhaps the most remarkable segment of the large charismatic movement. Catholic historians and theologians are careful to point out that the movement is not new to Catholic history. However, in more recent times, the Cursillo movement* was foundational for the specific events that took place in 1967 at Pittsburgh's Catholic Duquesne University. The movement spread to the University of Notre Dame* and then Michigan State University in 1968, followed by rapid diversification.

The movement has enjoyed official encouragement, beginning with the 1969 report by the Committee on Doctrine submitted to the Catholic Bishops of the U.S.A., the response of Pope Paul VI* in 1973, and the more recent encouragement of Pope John Paul II.* Catholic theologians seem generally to be of the opinion that, regardless of temporal discontinuity, Spirit baptism is related to Christian initiation, whether that be defined as water baptism,* confirmation* or some other experience. They uniformly deny any graduated experience of the Spirit's work and resist the idea that tongues-speech is the initial evidence of Spirit baptism.

Chase, Philander (1775-1852). Episcopal* bishop and missionary. While attending Dartmouth College,* Chase discovered the Book of Common Prayer* and became an avid Episcopalian. Following his ordination,* he became a most energetic missionary, serving in New York State and then New Orleans and Hartford. Effectively combining the hearty self-reliance of the frontiersman with the evangelistic fervor of the missionary, Chase was bishop of Ohio (1818-1831) and of Illinois (1835-1852).

Chauncy, Charles (1589-1672). Puritan* pastor-scholar and second president of Harvard College.* A stringent Calvinist,* Chauncy nevertheless differed from his Puritan colleagues in his support of the practice of immersing, rather than sprinkling, infants presented for baptism.* By most accounts he was unusual in his ability to balance erudition with plain, accessible preaching.*

Chauncy, Charles (1705-1787). Boston* minister and Arminian* theologian. Great-grandson of Harvard's second president (and having the same name), Chauncy served the First Church in Boston from 1727 until his death.

As the Great Awakening* developed, Chauncy initially approved of the spiritual renewal. Becoming concerned, however, about emotional excesses, between 1742 and 1745 he led the Old Lights* in resisting the revival. Chauncy became the leader of the liberal, or Arminian, movement which became increasingly apparent within New England Congregationalism after midcentury. Reasoning from his belief in God's benevolence, Chauncy eventually became convinced of the doctrine of universal* salvation.

A man of strong beliefs, Chauncy was often involved in controversy. Much of the final quarter-century of his life he spent resisting an Anglican* episcopate in the American colonies and supporting the American Revolution.*

Chautauqua Movement. Educational movement. From August 4 to 18, 1874, John H. Vincent,* general agent of the Methodist Episcopal Sunday School Union, along with Lewis Miller,

held at Lake Chautauqua, New York, an institute to give instruction in Sunday-school* organization and instruction. Interest and support for the program grew, and in 1876 the session was extended to three weeks. The course offerings quickly expanded to include a variety of subjects, from literature to music and physical education, with the grounds and facilities of Chautauqua expanding to accommodate as many as 25,000 people at once. The Chautauqua meetings developed into an extensive lay educational movement that transcended denominational affiliation. Numerous local "Chautauquas" sprang up around the country, and after the turn of the century a traveling Chautauqua carried its benefits from town to town.

Cheney, Charles Edward (1836-1916). Second bishop of the Reformed Episcopal Church.* As priest in the Episcopal Church,* Cheney became embroiled in the contest between evangelicals* and the Tractarian movement* and ultimately was deposed from the ministry.* He joined the Reformed Episcopal Church upon its founding (1873) and later organized the Synod* of Chicago and was its presiding bishop (1876-1877, 1887-1889).

Cheverus, Jean Lefevre de (1768-1836). First Roman Catholic* bishop of Boston. French-born Cheverus ministered to Passamaquoddy Indians in Maine and Catholics in the Boston area. In 1808 he was appointed head of the newly created Diocese* of Boston, which encompassed all of New England. He was successful in fostering good relations with the dominant Protestant* majority.

Chicago Declaration of Social Concern. An evangelical declaration of commitment to social involvement. Drafted in 1973, primarily by William Pannell, Jim Wallis and Stephen Mott (reworking a manuscript prepared by Paul Henry), this landmark document heralded the arrival of a new period of evangelical* social involvement.

Chicago School of Theology. A theological movement centered at the Divinity School of the University of Chicago. In the early years of the School, from its founding (1892) to the mid-1920s, three central motifs characterized the Chicago school: a sociological orientation, use of the historical-critical method and an appropriation of pragmatism as developed by William James* and, especially, John Dewey.

Faculty members Shailer Mathews* and Shirley Jackson Case* saw Christianity as a social movement whose origins and development were to be studied by the method of secular historical criticism. Edward Scribner Ames* viewed religion as one of humanity's many ways of adapting to its environment. In the 1920s Henry Nelson Wieman* introduced the empirical metaphysics of Alfred North Whitehead to the Divinity School. Dean Bernard M. Loomer organized the entire curriculum around process thought and in so doing firmly identified the Chicago school with process theology.*

The addition of Paul Tillich* to the Divinity School faculty (1955) signaled the end of the dominance of pragmatism and process thought at Chicago. In the 1960s, several new appointments to the faculty completed the transition to a more pluralistic methodology and thus marked the end of the Chicago school.

See also HARPER, WILLIAM RAINEY.

Chicago-Lambeth Quadrilateral. Authoritative document of four articles held by the Episcopal Church* and the worldwide Anglican Communion* as a minimal basis for any discussions that may lead to church unity. Adopted by the American Episcopalian bishops in 1886 and by the Lambeth Conference* of 1888, the Quadrilateral considers (1) the Holy Scriptures, (2) the Apostles' and Nicene Creeds, (3) the sacraments* of baptism* and the Lord's Supper,* and (4) the "historic episcopate."

Child Evangelism Fellowship. An international evangelistic* organization working with children. Founded in 1937, the Fellowship has the goal that "every child . . . have a chance to accept Christ." It focused originally on children's Bible classes and over the years has added prayer programs, "Radio Kids Bible Club," a magazine, summer programs, an Overseas Summer Missions program for college students, a radio program, a children's television program, telephone outreach, video training and a summer camping program.

Children, Christian Ministries to. The nature of Christian ministries* to children has paralleled historical shifts in attitudes toward children. Whereas Christianity was an integral part of child-

hood in seventeenth-century Puritan* New England, the impact of industrialization, urbanization and immigration* in subsequent centuries has served to institutionalize responsibility for religious training.

Early nineteenth-century revivals* and reform movements* prompted the formation of numerous Christian organizations directed toward children. Late nineteenth-century Christian ministries to children were typified by the example of the Student Volunteers for Foreign Missions.* Twentieth-century ministries have burgeoned and continue to respond to changes in society, with most being age-specific and highly organized in order to fit the fast-paced age of advanced industrialized society in the U.S.

See also CATHOLIC YOUTH ORGANIZATION; CHILD EVANGELISM FELLOWSHIP; CHRISTIAN ENDEAVOR SOCIETY; CHRISTIAN SERVICE BRIGADE; EPWORTH LEAGUE; SUNDAY-SCHOOL MOVEMENT; YOUNG LIFE; YOUTH FOR CHRIST.

Children of God. *See* FAMILY OF GOD.

China Inland Mission. *See* OVERSEAS MISSIONARY FELLOWSHIP.

Choir. Any group musical performance, such as a male chorus, a brass ensemble or bells; usually a mixed choral group singing in four parts. Before the twentieth century, choral literature was typically sacred, arising in a church context.

Chornock, Orestes (1883-1977). Metropolitan* of the American Carpatho-Russian Orthodox Greek Catholic Diocese of the U.S.A., bishop of Agathonikia. Czech-born Chornock became a priest of the Greek Catholic Church in 1906 and later served in several parishes* in the U.S. In a dispute with the Vatican* over married priests, which were permitted to Carpatho-Russians by the Union of Uzhorod (1646), Chornock was ultimately suspended from the priesthood. He then was instrumental in forming a new Greek Catholic diocese, which eventually was accepted into the Orthodox Communion. Chornock was consecrated* bishop (1938) and later (1965) elevated to the rank of metropolitan.

Choruses. A broad term that now includes the "worship music" of charismatic* improvisation and group singing at popular Christian entertainers' concerts, as well as songs used in children's worship and instruction.

Chrism. The early Christian name for a mixture of olive oil, balsam and (in Eastern Christianity) perfumes used sacramentally* and liturgically.* Eastern Orthodox* anoint newly baptized infants; Roman Catholics* anoint older children as part of confirmation rites.

Christian. Believers in Christ were first called Christians *(christianos)* in Antioch of Syria (Acts 11:26). The Greek term perhaps signifies a slave or soldier belonging to the divine Christ. Such persons are bought with a price (1 Cor 6:19-20) and are "born again" or "born from above" (Jn 3:7) through faith in Christ (Jn 3:16; Eph 2:8-9).

Over the centuries, the meaning of *Christian* has fluctuated. For the Reformers and those in the modern evangelical tradition, for example, the emphasis has been on conversion—on the turning of one's life that involves personal repentance and belief. Throughout the Middle Ages and for today's mainline denominations, in contrast, the emphasis has more been on being a member of the church, having typically undergone the steps of baptism and confirmation.

Christian Action. *See* FELLOWSHIP OF SOCIALIST CHRISTIANS.

Christian and Missionary Alliance. Evangelical* denomination* with strong emphases on overseas missions* and personal holiness.* The century-long history of the C&MA is essentially the story of a parachurch* organization evolving into a denomination. The Alliance was begun by A. B. Simpson,* who in the 1880s began to gather like-minded people in New York City with a burning interest in evangelism,* world missions and a deeper Christian life. In 1992 there were a reported 1,923 churches with 289,391 members in the U.S. and 348 churches with 80,681 members in Canada. In 1991 the denomination had 1,185 missionaries from the U.S. and Canada.

The doctrinal statement of the C&MA includes such themes as the inerrancy* of Scripture, sanctification* as both a crisis and a progressive experience, physical healing* and the imminent and premillennial* return of Christ (*see* Eschatology).

Christian Booksellers Association. A retail management organization. Christian Booksellers Association was organized in 1950 to service the specific needs of Christian bookstore owners and managers. Sponsoring management training, con-ventions, a monthly journal and other services, the Association is the vehicle for uniting over three thousand Christian bookstores in the U.S.

Christian Camping. Christian camping has been defined as an experience in guided Christian living in the out-of-doors. Its uniqueness as an agency of Christian education is in the combination of a round-the-clock living experience in a group setting of peers with qualified leadership in the out-of-doors, especially the world of nature.

The antecedents of Christian camping may be found in the frontier camp meeting,* the educational assemblies (such as Chautauqua*), Bible conference* grounds, the appeal of outdoor adventure associated with the Civil War* and the exploration of the West, and the ardor of evangelical* men and women who creatively evangelized* and discipled youth.

In the early part of this century camping was largely agency-related and Christian in orientation. As camping became a broader educational and social institution after World War II, evangelical church-related camps developed.

Christian Century, The. An ecumenical* Protestant* journal of news and opinion. Beginning in 1884 as the *Christian Oracle* (published by the Disciples of Christ*), the *Christian Century* received its current name in 1900 and dropped its denominational affiliation in 1916. It now describes itself as "An Ecumenical Weekly."

Throughout its history the *Christian Century* has reflected and communicated the social and theological agenda of mainline* American Protestantism, which has included the Social Gospel,* the ecumenical movement,* pacifism,* Prohibition,* liberal* theology* and civil rights.*

Christian Church (Disciples of Christ). A denomination* arising out of the Restoration movement.* The Christian Church (Disciples of Christ) was formed in 1831 from the merger of Barton W. Stone's* "Christians" and Alexander Campbell's* "Disciples." By the end of the nineteenth century the movement represented the fastest growing religious body in America.

Over most of its history the Christian Church (Disciples of Christ) has maintained the practices common to most Restoration churches: the local autonomy of individual congregations, the plurality of elders,* Communion* every Sunday* and baptism* by immersion for the remission of sins as a condition for church membership.* Today, however, most congregations practice open membership and accept nonimmersed believers into fellowship as full members.

See also CHRISTIAN CHURCHES/CHURCHES OF CHRIST (INDEPENDENT); CHURCHES OF CHRIST (NONINSTRUMENTAL); RESTORATION MOVEMENT.

Christian Church (Disciples of Christ) in Canada. A denomination* in the Restoration* tradition. The Disciples in Canada trace their origins to two separate streams of missionary enterprise. One was a movement involving Scottish immigrants in the Maritimes; the other was contact with followers of the Christian movement in the U.S. The two movements coalesced in 1832, and Disciples churches appeared in Ontario (c. 1820) and in western Canada (1881).

Disciples congregations observe the Lord's Supper* weekly and believers' baptism by immersion. Although historically the congregational polity of Disciples militated against centralization, they eventually accepted "cooperations" or associations of churches. They were formal participants in the ill-fated General Commission on Church Union (1973) with the United and Anglican churches.

Christian Churches/Churches of Christ (Independent). An association of churches arising out of the Restoration movement.* The Christian Church/Churches of Christ (Independent) arose from the 1831 merger between Barton W. Stone's* "Christians" and Alexander Campbell's* "Disciples," which formed the Christian Church/ Disciples of Christ. In 1927 a group of "Independents," who objected to the liberalism* of the International Convention of the Disciples, formed the North American Christian Convention.*

Doctrinally, the Independents have also been distinguished by their belief in the necessity of baptism* by immersion for the remission of sins as a condition for church membership* (in obedience to what they believe to be the injunction of Acts 2:38).

See also CHRISTIAN CHURCH (DISCIPLES OF CHRIST); CHURCHES OF CHRIST (NONINSTRUMENTAL).

Christian Coalition. Conservative Christian political action organization. Founded in 1988 by Pat Robertson after his unsuccessful run for the Republican presidential nomination, the Christian Coalition is self-described as "a pro-family citizen action organization to impact public policy on a local, state, and national level" and committed "to teach Christians effective citizenship and to promote Christian values in government." Led by executive director Ralph Reed, the Coalition's membership is mainly white evangelicals and Roman Catholics who wish to maintain traditional middle-class American family values and provide a unified voice in public affairs. The political power of the Coalition was demonstrated in the November 1994 elections when it distributed thirty-three million voter guides prior to the elections and was judged a significant factor in the Republicans' major upset of the Democrats. In May 1995 the Coalition made public its Contract with the American Family, which articulated its specific goals in addition to those of the Republican Contract with America. In 1995 the Christian Coalition claimed more than 1.6 million members in 1,600 county chapters throughout all fifty states. The Coalition publishes a monthly newsletter called *Religious Rights Watch* and a national newspaper entitled *Christian America.*

Christian Connection. An association of Restorationist* groups of the nineteenth century. The three major components were the movements associated with James O'Kelly* in Virginia-North Carolina, Abner Jones* in New England and Barton W. Stone* in Kentucky. In 1931 the Connection merged with the Congregational Church.*

Christian Education. The intentional and organized efforts to teach the Christian faith, its methods of reflection and action and lifestyle. In the mid-nineteenth century, churches began to use the phrase *Christian education* to refer to their practice of religious instruction.

Denominations* influenced by the Sunday-school movement,* including the Methodists,* Baptists* and Congregationalists,* used the Sunday school as a primary means for teaching the content of the Bible as well as their specific denominational distinctives. Other religious bodies, such as the Catholic Church* and a variety of Lutherans,* had the additional concern of preserving their ethnic* identities and built their educational programs around parochial schools.*

Today many educators are concerned about the function of Christian education within the plurality of educational influences present in

American culture.

See also CATECHETICS, CATHOLIC; CATECHISM; CATECHIST; SCHOOLS, PROTESTANT DAY; CHRISTIAN NURTURE; PAROCHIAL SCHOOLS, ROMAN CATHOLIC; SUNDAY-SCHOOL MOVEMENT.

Christian Endeavor Society. An evangelical* and interdenominational youth ministry.* Founded in 1881 by Congregationalist* minister Francis E. Clark,* Christian Endeavor quickly became a big success and was evangelicalism's first interdenominational youth ministry. Its purpose was to incorporate young people into the total life of the local church and prepare them for future leadership. In the late 1980s societies existed in seventy-eight nations.

Christian Family Movement. A Catholic Action* organization for married couples. A typical CFM group consists of five or six couples from the same parish or neighborhood who meet regularly in one another's homes. The group follows a program of prayer, discussion and action based on the "observe, judge and act" technique of Catholic Action. The couples in the group work to educate themselves to better their own family situation.

Christian Front. A nativistic* American fascist organization. The Christian Front was organized by popular "radio priest" Father Charles E. Coughlin.* Capitalizing on the economic distress of the Depression* years, Coughlin called for an American version of fascism as a bulwark against godless communism and Jewish interventionism. Before its demise in late 1940, the Christian Front and its journal *Social Justice* commonly baited Jews, communists and labor unions.

Christian Holiness Association. Association of Holiness churches,* originally known as the National Campmeeting Association for the Promotion of Christian Holiness. Formed in the aftermath of an 1867 camp meeting* in New Jersey, the Association began as an evangelistic* organization with the special task of restoring what it regarded as John Wesley's* teaching on Christian perfection. Camp meeting revivalism was the Association's principal method. In 1971 the group changed its name to the Christian Holiness Association.

See also HOLINESS CHURCHES AND ASSOCIATIONS; HOLINESS MOVEMENT.

Christian Literature Crusade. A nondenominational foreign missionary* and literature-distribution agency. Founded in England in 1941, Christian Literature Crusade (CLC) has focused primarily on the distribution of evangelical* Christian literature. It also cooperates with other missions in evangelism* and church planting. Today CLC operates in forty-five countries on all continents, supported by over six hundred workers representing forty different nationalities.

Christian Methodist Episcopal Church. An African-American Methodist* denomination.* Formally organized in 1870, the Colored Methodist Episcopal Church (CME)—its official name until 1954—was the fourth African-American denomination to separate from biracial connections in nineteenth-century American Methodism. The product of both the Southern Methodist program to evangelize* the slaves and the African-American initiative to embrace the Christian faith, the CME Church evolved at local and annual conference levels, beginning in 1867.

In this century the CME Church has moved into the mainstream of African-American social and political involvement, with public condemnations of lynching, cooperation with the civil rights* programs and participation in the Social Gospel* orientation of the Federal (later National*) Council of Churches.*

Christian Nationals Evangelism Commission. An organization for supporting Chinese evangelists. Adopting its present name after the communists seized power in China, the organization has retained its vision of using Western funds to assist strategic ministries that would otherwise be hampered for lack of finances.

Christian Nurture. The instilling of Christian beliefs, devotion,* character and lifestyle through intentional and sustained participation in the caring community of the church, through the agency of the Holy Spirit. Originally proposed by Horace Bushnell* in the mid-nineteenth century, "Christian nurture" as a paradigm for Protestant* Christian education* was most influential from the end of World War II* to the mid-1960s.

Christian Reformed Church in North America. A small Reformed* denomination,* principally of Dutch descent, centered in the American Midwest. The Christian Reformed Church (CRC) grew out of the later (1840s-1920s) wave of Dutch immigration* to the U.S. The CRC, having been consistently defined by traits from its Netherlandic past, stresses (1) heartfelt conversion* and piety,* (2) confessionalism* and orthodoxy,* and (3) Christian cultural engagement, especially as enunciated by Abraham Kuyper.*

Christian Schools. *See* SCHOOLS, PROTESTANT DAY.

Christian Science. An indigenous American religion noted for its theory and practice of religious healing.* Christian Science was born in 1866 when Mary Baker Eddy's* spontaneous recovery from a severe injury led her to conclude that reality is completely spiritual and that evil—as well as sickness and death—is only an illusion. She thus denied the Christian doctrines of creation, fall and redemption.

Eddy published *Science and Health* (1875) and *Key to the Scriptures* (1883). In 1892 she established a central church organization, the Mother Church, in Boston which was to organize evangelistic lectures and monitor educational standards. She also founded the *Christian Science Monitor* (1908). These missionary activities enhanced the growth of Christian Science, spreading it to Europe and Asia by the early twentieth century. Local churches now number about three thousand worldwide, with the vast majority of Christian Scientists, including practitioners (currently about 2,884), still in the U.S. Christian Science church services do not permit preaching, but are carried out by first and second readers who read selections from Scripture and from *Science and Health.*

Christian Service Brigade. An international discipleship program for boys. Arising from a weekly boys' club program of games and Bible study* started in 1937 by Joseph Coughlin, Christian Service Brigade (CSB) experience rapid growth in the 1950s and 1960s. Today over two thousand churches across North America conduct some form of the Brigade program. The purpose of CSB has remained "to train men to cultivate friendships with boys and prepare them for future leadership in their families, churches, and communities."

Christian Social Union (1891-1911). An Episcopal* organization concerned with social questions. Modeled on an English organization of the same name, the Christian Social Union (CSU) was organized by Robert A. Holland, an Episcopal minister. To fulfill its goals the CSU encouraged sermons and lectures on, and investigations of, social conditions in major U.S. cities and published a large number of pamphlets.

Christian Socialist Fellowship. A voluntary society promoting Christian socialism.* In 1906 the Christian Socialist Fellowship grew out of the *Christian Socialist*, a journal arguing that socialism was a necessary economic expression of the Christian life. The Fellowship affiliated with the Socialist Party and helped produce the nearly one million votes for Eugene V. Debs in the 1912 presidential race against Roosevelt, Taft and Wilson.

Christian Year. *See* CHURCH YEAR.

Christianity Today. The leading evangelical* periodical. Launched in 1956 largely at the initiative of Billy Graham* and his father-in-law, L. Nelson Bell,* *Christianity Today (CT)* was aimed at ministers and thoughtful laypeople and attempted to foster a broader sense of church and social responsibility for independent evangelicals.

As a biweekly (now eighteen times yearly) journal of evangelical opinion and religious news, *CT* has succeeded in overtaking the prestigious liberal weekly *Christian Century** in paid subscribers and in becoming the most widely quoted religious journal in the secular press.

Christmas. The festival observed on December 25 celebrating the nativity of Jesus Christ. The date for the celebration, which does not in any way accurately mark the birth date of Jesus, comes either from a Christian appropriation of a Roman holiday or from a calculation nine months after March 25, a date already assigned to Christ's crucifixion and to his conception. At least since the mid-nineteenth century the celebration has gained in popularity so that today it extends well beyond Christianity itself.

Christmas Conference. The organizing meeting of American Methodism.* Convened in Baltimore on December 24, 1784, the Conference recognized Thomas Coke* and Francis Asbury* as the first independent ecclesiastical leaders of Methodism in America. It also made a commitment to John Wesley's* ideal of spreading scriptural holiness.*

Christology. A technical theological term for the doctrine of Christ, usually consisting of carefully formulated statements describing his person and nature. The Puritans* shared with Roman Catholics* the creedal definitions of Christ and his nature formulated by the early church. But while Catholic Christology in the New World was to remain relatively unchanged in its formal expressions, the Protestant* understanding of Christ was subject to various influences.

Unitarianism. Beginning in New England as early as 1710, some Congregationalists* began to reject the deity of Christ and thus also the Trinity. By 1750 this view had become quite widespread among the Congregational pastors in the Boston area. The most influential later proponent was William Ellery Channing.*

Christology and Liberal Protestantism. In the late nineteenth and early twentieth centuries, Protestant liberals* continued to use the term *divinity** in speaking of Christ, but for them the word took on new meaning and nuance. To some the divinity of Christ was a matter of degree—something he held in common with other humans but possessed to a greater degree than they. American liberal theology was in some ways a blend of two streams of German liberalism—one from Friedrich Schleiermacher, which stressed feeling as piety, and one influenced by Albrecht Ritschl, which emphasized ethical activity.

Orthodoxy and Neo-Orthodoxy. Because the reference to Christ's divinity had been so generalized, conservatives increasingly sought to affirm unequivocally the deity of Christ. The litmus test for orthodox Christology became the doctrine of the virgin birth, whose most notable defense was J. Gresham Machen's* *Virgin Birth of Christ* (1930). In emphasizing the deity of Christ, the historical Jesus was somewhat neglected by the neo-orthodox* movement. In their case, and even more so in the followers of Rudolf Bultmann,* there was a conviction that the search for the historical Jesus would inevitably fail.

Late Twentieth-Century Christologies. The late twentieth century has seen several attempts to recast Christology into terms responsive to the needs of the age. One development has been the secularization of theology, the most extreme branch of which flowered briefly in the mid-1960s as the Death of God theology,* with Thomas

as J. J. Altizer its most prominent exponent.

Existential* theology has also produced a significant redefinition of Christology in the twentieth century. Paul Tillich* developed his theology around the concept of God as the Ground of Being, the force or cause of being for all that is.

Process theology* has also given rise to a distinctive Christology. In process thought, God is active in every event of history, and in this sense every event is an incarnation and none exclusively so. Consequently, many process theologians find it difficult to speak of the uniqueness of Jesus and tend to speak of the degree to which Jesus fulfilled or actualized God's purpose.

Since the early 1970s various forms of liberation theology* have arisen, the one most indigenous to America being black theology.* Another distinctly twentieth-century type of Christology is found among feminist* theologians, who tend to minimize belief in Jesus' deity, which they identify with patriarchalism.

American Roman Catholic theology prior to the Second Vatican Council* held the same orthodox view of Jesus Christ that was found throughout Roman Catholicism worldwide. Vatican II opened the possibility of a greater variety of positions on doctrinal matters, and more recently Christology has come in for more concentrated attention.

Church. Historically, the Christian church is a community founded on the teachings of Jesus Christ and striving to bear witness to Christ's gospel in its worship* and faith, work and memory. Theologically, the church is a spiritual communion of the whole people of God, a living organism of persons closely related to Christ and to one another.

Roman Catholics* unite around apostolic authority* based on Scripture and church tradition mediated through the bishops and ultimately the pope. The Orthodox* and Anglican* traditions also stress the role of the episcopacy* in defining the truly apostolic church.

The churches of the Reformation reasserted Scripture as the true measure of apostolicity. The Reformed Tradition* generally favors a presbyterian* form of church order represented in pastors, teachers, deacons* and elders.* Congregationalists* and Baptists* emphasize the authority of Christ as expressed through the congregation.

See also CHURCH GOVERNMENT; CULT; DENOMINATIONALISM; SECT; VOLUNTARYISM.

Church and State, Separation of. In the American experience, separation of church and state is the exclusion of civil authority from religious affairs and the institutional independence of organized religion from government sanction or support. The American tradition in church and state, the nonestablishment of religion and the free exercise of religion, represented on behalf of the Founding Fathers a bold experiment unparalleled in human history. Not until the twentieth century were the American guarantees of the First Amendment* constitutionally and unequivocally enunciated anywhere else in the world. The uniqueness of this American tradition in church and state is of profound importance in understanding both the political and the religious history of the nation.

With independence, there was a move on the part of religious dissenters throughout the states to bring an end to religious establishment in the various states and the privileges that it assumed. By the time of the nation's founding, religious freedom was eloquently championed by religious and political leaders alike. For both theological and political reasons, it was argued, religion should be free of the state, and government should be denied the right of jurisdiction over religion.

The only reference to religion in the original Constitution, Clause 3 of Article VI, is written in the form of an unequivocal prohibition on giving any consideration to religion in determining one's qualifications for public office: "No religious test shall ever be required as a qualification to any office or public trust under the United States." Article VI not only removed the basis for any preferential treatment of one religion over another for holding public office, but also denied the right of any preferential status of religion over nonreligion in matters of one's political participation in the life of the Republic.

From dissenters, especially Baptists,* Presbyterians,* Methodists,* Unitarians,* deists* and Quakers,* came the demand in the form of a Bill of Rights to guarantee the separation of church and state and to provide some explicit assurance of the free exercise of religion. Consequently, an establishment of religion, at least on a national level, was expressly prohibited by Congress on September 25, 1789, with the adoption of the First Amendment, which begins with the words "Congress shall make no law respecting an establishment of religion or prohibiting the free exercise

thereof." Only with the ratification of the Fourteenth Amendment in 1868 were the religion clauses of the First Amendment specifically applied to the states.

Church Government: Congregational. Congregationalism is a Protestant* tradition of ecclesiology and church government maintaining that local congregations can minister* and govern themselves through congregational vote, covenant and participation. Brought to America by the Puritans,* the congregational tradition has the ideal of recognizing Jesus Christ as head of the local church, not any earthly ecclesiastical authority external to that body. The ordained ministry is revered but has no power of government.

Congregational government is used not only by churches directly in the congregational tradition but also by Baptists,* independents, churches in the Restoration* tradition and many other denominations standing in the Free Church* tradition.

See also CONGREGATIONALISM; NEW ENGLAND WAY.

Church Government: Episcopal. A form of church government distinguished from presbyterian* and congregational* forms insofar as local churches are subject to the more or less monarchical authority* of a bishop (from the Greek *episkopos,* meaning "overseer"). Roman Catholics,* Orthodox* and Episcopalians* maintain the doctrine of apostolic succession,* signifying that the episcopacy derives in direct line from the beginnings of Christianity and is indispensable to the church.

Roman Catholic bishops of an ecclesiastical province or archdiocese* meet regularly to compile a list of priests considered suitable for the episcopacy. The list is then sent to Rome, where the Congregation for Bishops studies the materials and makes its own recommendation to the pope, who actually makes the choice. The diocesan bishop appoints all the pastors and diocesan officials as well as assigns every priest belonging to the diocese.

The archbishop and the bishops in the Greek Orthodox Church are appointed by the synod in Constantinople (Istanbul), presided over by the ecumenical patriarch.* The Orthodox Church in America provides that the Diocesan Assembly nominate a candidate for the office of diocesan bishop to be submitted for approval to the Holy Synod, which is the supreme canonical authority in the Church.

[79]

An Episcopal bishop is elected by a convention of all the clergy and lay representatives of the parishes of the diocese which the bishop is to head. The presiding bishop of the Church is elected at a General Convention by the House of Bishops.* Although Methodists do not regard the episcopacy and apostolic succession as essential to the Church or as an order different from that of elder, they do consider it to be scripturally warranted, and American Methodists accord bishops a key role.

Church Government: Presbyterian. A form of church government consisting of a graduated series of councils from the congregational to the national level. In the U.S., Presbyterianism is organized under a presbyterium, or a graduated series of councils: the local church session* of laity, men and women, moderated by the pastor; presbyteries,* made up of several congregations and composed equally of clerical and lay representatives from sessions; synods,* larger regional bodies with similar representatives; and a General Assembly,* a national body made up of clergy and lay commissioners from the presbyteries.

Congregations elect their own ministers under presbytery advice and consent, as well as other officers called elders* and deacons* who are ordained* by the congregation.

Church Growth Movement. A missiological* movement founded by Donald A. McGavran* and characterized by a pragmatic approach to planting and nurturing the growth of churches, based on a systematic analysis of growing churches. The church growth movement arose in response to the crisis in missions,* especially after World War II.* McGavran's seminal work *The Bridges of God* (1955) introduced the concept of "people movements" as the key to mission strategy. Emphasizing the Great Commission (Mt 28:18-20) as the foundation for mission, McGavran has warned of the tendency of the church to neglect the discipling of those who have never heard the gospel.

Response to the movement has been most positive among evangelicals.* In addition to Fuller's School of World Mission, which has trained hundreds of students from all parts of the world, most evangelical seminaries in North America have been influenced by the movement's concepts.

Church Membership. Two different traditions of church membership have characterized Christianity in America. An inclusive tradition carried over from European Christendom the concept of the church's being coextensive with the territory—that is, that everyone located geographically within a parish* is eligible for baptism.* In contrast, an exclusive tradition confined church membership to those who could give a credible profession of personal faith.

During the Great Awakening,* Jonathan Edwards* insisted that one must be genuinely converted* to have access to the sacraments* and the privileges of church membership. By the early twentieth century, however, membership requirements in mainline* denominations were less demanding.

Church Missionary Society. An evangelical* voluntary missionary* organization within the Church of England. The Church Missionary Society (CMS) was founded in 1799 as part of the first phase of the modern Protestant missionary movement. During the nineteenth century it was the largest English missionary society and was looked to as the leader in missionary thought and practice. In North America the work of the CMS was restricted almost entirely to ministry among Canada's native peoples, beginning in 1822.

Church of England. *See* ANGLICAN CHURCH.

Church of God in Christ, Mennonite. A small conservative Mennonite* denomination.* The group was founded by John Holdeman,* who in 1859 left the main body of Mennonites when they failed to ordain* him. As a symbol of nonconformity the men of the church wear a neatly trimmed beard and no ties; the women wear full dresses, plain in character and without ornamentation. All jewelry is shunned. Higher education is not permitted.

Church of the Brethren. Founded in Germany in 1708 by Alexander Mack* and seven others as an Anabaptist*/Pietist* sect.* By 1719 persecution had forced a group to immigrate to the U.S. By 1948 the Brethren had become an ecumenically* oriented Free Church* known for its service outreach and peace emphasis.

Brethren resist creedal statements but accept basic Protestant* doctrines. In patterning church life after the early Christians, they practice believer's baptism* by threefold immersion, the love feast and foot washing.* Brethren polity combines congregational* and presbyterian* elements, with an authoritative annual conference.

See also FREE CHURCH TRADITION IN AMERICA.

Church of the Nazarene. A denomination originating from the union of several religious bodies with roots in the Holiness movement.* Consonant with its origins, the Church of the Nazarene* emphasizes the doctrine of entire sanctification* as a second definite work of grace subsequent to conversion* and advocates a disciplined lifestyle for its members reflecting "holiness of heart and life." Doctrinally the Church of the Nazarene has been shaped most by that branch of the Christian tradition associated with John Wesley* and his Methodist movement.

The Church of the Nazarene began in the U.S. as a result of the proliferation of independent Holiness associations, missions and churches during the second half of the nineteenth century and early part of the twentieth century. Eventually a "union movement" favoring a national Holiness church arose among some of these bodies, encouraged notably by Phineas F. Bresee,* who in 1895 organized the first group to use the name Church of the Nazarene. After 1908 the church continued to grow through numerous accessions of Holiness groups in North America and the British Isles, as well as through an aggressive evangelistic* and missionary* program.

Church of the New Jerusalem. A religious body founded on the spiritual teachings of Emanuel Swedenborg. Claiming to have communicated with the spirit world, Swedenborg (1688-1772) attempted to extract the Bible's spiritual or allegorical meaning. He apparently denied the orthodox doctrines of the Trinity, original sin,* the vicarious atonement* and the bodily resurrection.

Following Swedenborg's teachings, Robert Hindmarsh launched the New Jerusalem Church in London in the 1780s. It spread to other countries and today exists in the General Conference (England), the General Convention of the New Jerusalem (U.S.), and the General Church of the New Jerusalem, which in 1890 broke from the parent group in the U.S.

Church of the United Brethren in Christ, The. An evangelical* denomination* with roots in German-American revivalism.* The church began in 1800 as a result of the preaching of Martin Boehm* and William Otterbein* among German settlers. Methodist* in doctrine, church government* and practice, it maintains a lifestyle that forbids alcoholic beverages,* membership in secret societies and engaging in aggressive (but not defensive) war.

Church Peace Union. See CARNEGIE COUNCIL ON ETHICS AND INTERNATIONAL AFFAIRS.

Church Union Movements. Beginning in the early 1800s, specific concerns brought individuals and denominations* together in voluntary societies* such as the American Board of Commissioners for Foreign Missions* (1810) and the American Bible Society* (1816). Also active in the nineteenth century were American ecumenists like Samuel Schmucker* (Lutheran*), Alexander Campbell* (Disciples of Christ*), William Reed Huntingdon* (Episcopalian*) and Elias B. Sanford* (Congregationalist*).

In twentieth-century America, ecumenical cooperation across denominational lines increased as groups came together in the Federal Council of Churches* (1908), the World Council of Churches* (1948) and the National Association of Evangelicals* (1943). Organic unions among American denominations, which also became more frequent in the twentieth century, included the American Lutheran Church* (1930), the United Church of Christ* (1957), the Presbyterian Church (U.S.A.)* (1983) and the Evangelical Lutheran Church in America* (1988).

In Canada, denominational mergers occurred earlier in the nation's history as this country's great expanses and sparse population, particularly in the West, necessitated a coordinated effort in the mission field. Thus Presbyterians united (1875), as did Methodists (1884) and Anglicans (1893). The biggest step of union on the continent occurred in 1925, when Canadian Presbyterian, Methodist and Congregational bodies merged to become the United Church of Canada.*

Church World Service. Ecumenical relief agency. Founded in 1946, the Church World Service (CWS) became an independent division in the National Council of the Churches of Christ in the USA* (NCCC) in 1985. Supported by over thirty Protestant and Orthodox churches in its worldwide mission to "carry on works of Christian mercy, relief, technical assistance, rehabilitation, and interchurch aid," CWS is noted for its prompt aid to victims of disasters and wars and has assisted thousands of refugees to resettle in North America.

Church Year. The annual liturgical cycle of Christian feasts and seasons. Historically the Christian church has celebrated principal events of salvation in Christ with an annual cycle of feasts and seasons. In the West the cycle of seasons consists of Advent* (the four Sundays leading up to Christmas* Day), Christmas (the twelve days from Christmas to Epiphany* on January 6), Epiphany, Lent* (beginning with Ash Wednesday* and ending with Holy Week), Easter* (Easter Sunday through Pentecost) and the season after Pentecost. The principal feast is Sunday,* as a celebration of the Resurrection, and other feasts throughout the year commemorate aspects of the life, death and glorification of Jesus, the events of Mary,* and the lives of various martyrs and saints* of the church.

Churches of Christ (Noninstrumental). A brotherhood of churches spawned by the nineteenth-century Restoration movement.* First recognized as distinct in 1906 and the most conservative of the three groups arising out of the movement, the Churches of Christ retain early Restorationist motifs. This entails congregational independence, believer's baptism* by immersion, weekly observation of the Lord's Supper,* teaching elders* and traveling nonsalaried evangelists. Proponents are strongly anticreedal, arguing that creeds* have generated schisms in the body of Christ. The controversies leading to the 1906 separation were over state and national mission societies and over musical instruments in worship;* the Churches of Christ were opposed to both practices.

Churches of God. Over two hundred religious groups have adopted this name, with most being Holiness* or Holiness/Pentecostal.* Their ordinances* are typically baptism (by immersion), Communion* and foot washing.* Five major Christian denominations* go by this name.

Church of God (Anderson, Ind.). This group was founded by Daniel Sydney Warner,* who in 1877 experienced sanctification* and then, in 1881, announced his freedom from all sects.* He issued a call to reject sectarianism, and soon persons from various denominations were joining him. Arminian* in orientation, the church teaches

faith healing* and the Second Coming of Christ without a millennium.* Emphasizing the guidance of the Holy Spirit, the movement from the start has ordained women.

Since 1906 the *Gospel Trumpet* (since 1962, *Vital Christianity*) has been published in Anderson, Indiana, the church's national headquarters. In 1992 the church had a reported 214,743 members in the U.S. in 2,330 congregations.

Church of God (Cleveland, Tenn.). The oldest Pentecostal body in the U.S., this church traces back to a group formed in 1886 by eight people with the goal of restoring primitive Christianity, promoting Holiness doctrine and uniting all denominations. Church members first spoke in tongues* in 1896.

In 1920 the group had an auditorium built in Cleveland, Tennessee, which became the general headquarters. Originally decrying creeds, the church formulated a declaration of faith in 1948 affirming belief in the verbal inspiration of the Bible, the premillennial* Second Coming of Christ and divine healing. The church has maintained its Holiness doctrine of sanctification and believes that this experience is followed by the baptism of the Spirit,* evidenced by speaking in tongues. In 1992 there were a reported 672,000 members in the U.S. worshiping in 5,776 churches.

Church of God of Prophecy. When Ambrose J. Tomlinson,* the first general moderator of the Church of God (Cleveland, Tenn.), was removed from his office in 1923, he founded a rival church known as Tomlinson Church of God. At his death in 1943 the church chose for its leader Milton R. Tomlinson, one of Tomlinson's two sons. The name eventually became Church of God of Prophecy, which maintained its headquarters in Cleveland, Tennessee. Membership in 1992 was reported at 72,465 with 2,072 churches.

Church of God in Christ. The Church of God in Christ is the largest African-American Pentecostal group in the world. Its founder was Charles H. Mason,* who in 1907 spoke in tongues at the Azusa Street* revival.* Mason then called together other African-American preachers who believed in speaking in tongues, and in 1907 the group organized itself as a general assembly of the Church of God in Christ. As general overseer and chief apostle, Mason maintained full control over the church until his death in 1961. Since 1968, a general board of twelve bishops has overseen the work of the church.

The church is trinitarian and premillennialist,* believes in divine healing and holds that tongues is a gift for all Christians. Church members engage in an active worship style that includes dancing and shaking. In 1991 there were a reported 5.5 million members in 15,300 churches.

Church of God (Seventh Day). Adventists who refused to endorse Ellen White's* visions and writings departed from her church in 1858 and organized the General Conference of the Church of God in 1884. "Seventh Day," added to the name in 1923, reflects their distinctive observance of the sabbath. In 1990 there were a reported 153 churches.

Circuit Rider. An early American Methodist preacher who was appointed to a circuit, sometimes as large as a state. Their labors were strenuous, with half of them dying before completing five years of service. They spoke first to awaken and then to convert* and sanctify* through faith in Jesus Christ by the power of the Holy Spirit.

Civil Religion. A scholar's term which embodies and describes a religio-political phenomenon considered by anthropologists, sociologists and historians to be as old as organized human communities. Civil religion is a way of thinking which makes sacred a political arrangement or governmental system and provides a religious image of a political society for many, if not most, of its members. Also called civic, public, political or societal religion or public piety, civil religion is the general faith of a state or nation that focuses on widely held beliefs about the history and destiny of that state or nation. It is a religious way of thinking about politics which provides a society with ultimate meaning (thus making it a genuine religion) which, in turn, allows a people to look at their political community in a special sense and thus achieve purposeful social integration. In short, it is the social glue which binds a given society together by means of well-established ceremonies—rituals, symbols, values—and allegiances which function in the life of the community in such a way as to provide it with an overarching sense of spiritual unity. Therefore, it is not a particular or specific religion or expression thereof but is of such a nature that those who hold specific beliefs can read into it whatever meaning they choose. Civil religion has no formal organization and no central authority, yet it can be highly institutionalized in the collective life of a society.

Jean-Jacques Rousseau actually coined the term in his *Social Contract* (1762) when he identified civil religion as something which could deal with religious pluralism* and at the same time cement people's allegiances to civil society, thereby achieving and ensuring social peace. In the Western world in modern times, civil religion has developed along Rousseauean lines, especially in terms of his insistence that it be kept general with simple, positive beliefs. The more recent popular use of the term and the ensuing debate over its conceptual utility was inaugurated in 1967 by the publication of sociologist Robert N. Bellah's seminal essay "Civil Religion in America."

Evidence of the civil faith in the U.S. includes the biblical imagery and references to Almighty God and Providence that have pervaded the speeches and public documents of the nation's leaders from earliest times, the trappings of religious celebration at presidential inaugurations, the religio-political symbolism of much of the architecture of the nation's capital, patriotic songs in church hymnals,* the display of the nation's flag in church sanctuaries, the celebration of national holidays in which themes of "God and country" are skillfully blended, the inclusion of *under God* in the Pledge of Allegiance and, above all, the national motto "In God We Trust."*

Historical American civil religion continues to challenge Christians to sort out the sometimes conflicting, sometimes complementary, dimensions of public religion and personal faith and to make necessary distinctions between the national mission and the Great Commission. Most important, a knowledge of the existence and nature of civil religion will force followers of Jesus Christ to make conscious choices concerning the proper relationship of the Christian faith, especially in its catholicity, to the political culture of the day.

See also CHURCH AND STATE, SEPARATION OF.

Civil Rights Movement and the Churches. The civil rights movement (1954-1966), the struggle for equal civil rights for African-American people in America, was one of several events that culminated in the convulsive decade of the 1960s. Although most churches entered the civil rights struggle late and with reservations, their beliefs were basic to the moral premises of the movement.

During the decade following the 1954 Supreme Court* decision that overturned the "separate but equal" approach of the earlier *Plessy v.*

Ferguson decision (1896), American churches remained essentially passive toward civil rights. Thus the original impetus for civil rights activism came from outside the institutional church. It was the Montgomery bus boycott (1955) and the rapid development of other centers of nonviolent activism in the South that spurred the increased involvement by African-American pastors in the movement. The Southern Christian Leadership Conference* (SCLC), created in 1957 and led by Dr. Martin Luther King Jr.,* provided the movement with both leadership and a framework for collective action. Based largely in local churches, the SCLC drew upon the traditional linkage of religion and liberation indigenous to African-American experience.

As African-American churches became the single most decisive factor in the nonviolent civil rights movement, white congregations and clergy wrestled with the tension between their support of law and order and the direct action taken by movement leaders. Equally problematic was the apparent contradiction between the churches' message of love and their de facto segregation. As time passed, however, church courts, assemblies and ministerial associations increasingly reflected the progress of civil rights in America.

See also BLACK RELIGION; BLACK THEOLOGY.

Civil War and the Churches. The middle years of the nineteenth century marked a traumatic convulsion for America's churches quite as much as for the nation at large. For decades a conflict over slavery had been simmering as an inner civil war within the churches. When armed hostilities began in 1861, most churches, North and South, offered massive support to their side in the conflict. Their behavior before and during the war led to a long-lasting legacy of suspicion and bitterness between the sections.

Pro- and Antislavery Forces. In the revolutionary* and early national periods, when exalted ideas of liberty and human equality occupied many Americans' minds, several church bodies issued strong proclamations against slavery. Actual emancipations by church members, however, were few. Slaveholders resisted efforts to tamper with "the peculiar institution," and soon even the formal proclamations softened or ceased altogether.

Abolitionist* activity increased sharply after 1830. In the South, its main effect was to harden support for slavery.

Divided Churches. The first church rupture came in 1837, when the Presbyterian Church in the U.S.A.* divided as a result of a dispute in which sharply differing attitudes toward slavery figured significantly, if not decisively. In 1857 the final break occurred, completing the North-South division of the Presbyterian Church.

Methodists* had regularly expressed disapproval of slavery since 1784, although leaving to local option how to formulate its own rules. A sizable defection of abolitionist Methodists occurred in 1843, when Orange Scott* organized the Wesleyan Methodist Church.* The following year matters came to a head in the General Conference, when the Southerners withdrew and organized the Methodist Episcopal Church,* South, as a proslavery denomination.

Baptists* had no single national judicatory; their strict congregational* polity allowed only single-purpose societies for missionary* and related endeavors. Leaders of these societies ruled repeatedly that consideration of slavery was not among the objects for which their organizations existed. In 1845, however, disagreement over slavery led to the forming of the Southern Baptist Convention.*

A Divided Nation. The Southern members of the three denominations that divided over irreconcilable views of slavery represented 94 percent of the churches of the South. Because these schisms represented such an ominous division of the nation, observers from all quarters noted the possibly fateful consequences to political union.

The positions of smaller denominations such as Congregationalists* and the Society of Friends* reinforced the growing sectional estrangement. Episcopalians,* Lutherans* and Roman Catholics* maintained official silence on slavery until political rupture and war forced them into temporary sectional divisions supporting their respective governments. The Disciples of Christ* had members on both sides of the conflict.

Southern preachers denounced with increasing stridency the "rationalism and infidelity" that underlay the "meddling spirit" of Northern churches. They supported the Confederacy by encouraging men to join the army, preaching that God favored their cause and doing all in their power to maintain Southern morale.

Yankee Protestants were equally fervent for the Northern crusade. They preached with apocalyptic thunder that the Union was God's cause. They ministered through the U.S. Christian Commission* to the soldiers, whom they regarded as God's instruments in trampling out the grapes of divine wrath against the sinful South.

The Enduring Legacy. Denominations that had not been torn apart by the slavery controversy reunited easily after the war. The denominations that had divided before the war, however, found that they had invested themselves so heavily in the sectional conflict that postwar reconciliation became next to impossible. Northern and Southern Methodists remained apart until 1939. Presbyterians began coming back together only in the 1970s, and the reunion of white Baptists remains as remote as ever. The predominantly African-American denominations, having long ago achieved organizational maturity and moderate financial strength, seem destined to continue separate existence into the foreseeable future.

Perhaps the most significant religious legacy of the Civil War is the impetus it gave to civil religion.* Sometimes called the "spiritual center" of the nation's history, the war exposed the flaws in America's earlier claim to be "God's New Israel," a special people with a divinely ordered destiny. In the late twentieth century, as the nation continues its struggle to achieve the ideals of unity, freedom and equality, the nineteenth-century "time of testing" furnishes many clues to the meaning of "one nation under God."

Clap, Thomas (1703-1767). Congregational* minister and president of Yale College.* Clap originally opposed the emotional excess of the Great Awakening* and the methods of George Whitefield* and Jonathan Edwards.* Later, as the pro-revivalist wing moderated in the 1750s and Old Lights* tended toward Arminianism,* Clap joined the evangelicals.

Clark, Francis Edward (1851-1921). Congregational* minister and founder of the Christian Endeavor Society.* Clark founded the first society in Maine in 1881, and within six years the movement had grown to over a half million "Christian Endeavorers" in seven thousand local societies. This became American evangelicalism's* first national and interdenominational youth ministry.

Clark, Gordon Haddon (1902-1986). Calvinist* philosopher. From 1936 to 1943, Clark taught at Wheaton College* (Ill.), where he had a decisive influence on a number of future evangelical* intellectual leaders, including Edward J. Carnell*

and Carl F. H. Henry.* Henry regarded Clark as "one of the profoundest evangelical Protestant philosophers of our time."

Released from Wheaton because of his challenge to its Arminianism,* Clark joined the faculty of Butler University in Indianapolis, Indiana, where he came to chair the department of philosophy for twenty-eight years. From that secular campus he continued to exert a notable influence on the evangelical intellectual world, and the Reformed sector in particular, through over thirty publications.

Clark, William Smith (1826-1886). Educator and administrator. After teaching for many years in Massachusetts, Clark went to Japan in 1876 to help establish an agricultural college, which in time became Hokkaido University. An earnest Christian and a former colonel in the Union army, Clark insisted on rigorous standards and the teaching of the Bible as a textbook in ethics.

Clarke, James Freeman (1810-1888). Unitarian* transcendentalist* minister. Belonging to the transcendentalist, or "New School,"* movement, Clarke was an active church reformer. He theorized about a democratic,* reformist "Church of the Future," which was to be an eclectic combination of what he considered the best elements in Catholicism,* Protestantism,* Unitarianism, transcendentalism and humanitarian reformism. As minister, Harvard educator and church reformer, Clarke had a strong impact on nineteenth-century Christian liberalism.*

Clarke, John (1609-1676). Baptist* minister, cofounder of Rhode Island Colony and advocate of religious freedom.* Emigrating to Massachusetts Bay in 1637, Clarke championed the cause of Anne Hutchinson* in the antinomian controversy.* Searching for refuge from persecution, Clarke went to what later became Rhode Island, where he helped found Newport (1639). In Newport Clarke became the miniser of the local congregation, which by 1644 became identified as a Baptist church.

In 1652 Clarke traveled with Roger Williams* to London to secure a new charter for Rhode Island Colony. Clarke finally received the charter in 1663, which gave the colonists permission to attempt "a lively experiment" in which they could enjoy complete religious liberty.*

Clarke, Sarah Dunn (1835-1918). Cofounder of the Pacific Garden Mission.* Burdened for Chicago's poor, Sarah Clarke (whose husband eventually shared this burden) founded what was the second rescue mission in the U.S. and became deeply involved in every facet of its operation. One of her converts was Billy Sunday.*

Clarke, William Newton (1841-1912). Baptist* minister and theologian. After pastoring several Baptist churches, Clarke became professor of theology* at Colgate Theological Seminary (1890-1908), where he became a leader in the New Theology.* Clarke wrote America's first systematic theology* from a liberal* perspective—*An Outline of Christian Theology* (1898). Following Friedrich Schleiermacher (1768-1834), he believed that the starting point for theology was "religious sentiment," not the irreducible facts of Scripture.

Classis. An organizational unit within a Reformed* church's governmental structure. A number of churches in a limited geographic area are grouped into a classis; the classes in turn are responsible to the synod* (*see* Presbytery*).

Clayton, Thomas (?-1699). Pennsylvania Anglican.* In 1698 Clayton was sent to Christ Church in Philadelphia as the first rector in Pennsylvania. Within two years he had increased the membership of the church from about fifty persons to seven hundred. He was successful in converting many Quakers* to the Church of England.

Clergy. Persons ordained* by a denomination* or local church to serve as priests or ministers. Roman Catholic,* Eastern Orthodox* and Episcopal* churches in particular emphasize the distinction between clergy and laity.

Clergy Reserves. Lands in Upper and Lower Canada allotted by the Constitutional Act of 1791 "for the support and maintenance of a Protestant* clergy." Proceeds went to the Church of England* until the mid-nineteenth century. After various conflicts, the reserves were secularized entirely in 1854.

Cleric. A member of the clergy; one ordained* by a church to serve as minister or priest.

Clericalism. The rule or influence of clergy in church and society. Authority* varies with church polity,* ranging from government by bishops or elders* (presbyters) to congregationalism,* with authority vested in the people. In most traditions lay boards of trustees at least share authority.

Clinton, William (Bill) J. (1946-). Forty-second U.S. president. Clinton was Democratic governor of Arkansas (1978-1980; 1982-1992) when in 1992 he won the U.S. presidential race against Republican incumbent George Bush* and the independent candidate H. Ross Perot. Clinton, a Southern Baptist* and active member of Immanuel Baptist Church, Little Rock, Arkansas, could claim a "born again" experience and comfortably invoke religious imagery in his public speeches. Nevertheless, his prochoice views on abortion, his liberal views of sex education and his open attitude toward homosexual rights raised vigorous and heated opposition from the Religious Right. In the November elections fifty-five percent of white evangelicals voted for George Bush, who, though his religious commitment was somewhat ambiguous, supported the policies of his predecessor Ronald Reagan* in advocating "traditional family values." Clinton's election was viewed as a defeat by the Religious Right, and their fears were fulfilled in the first days of the Clinton administration. Within hours of taking office Clinton lifted the ban on homosexuals in the military and rescinded all of the abortion-related executive orders enacted by his presidential predecessors, Reagan and Bush. While Clinton maintained dialogue with some prominent evangelical leaders and expressed opposition to government interference in religious concerns, many conservative evangelicals* and fundamentalists* continued to view him with suspicion and deep-seated antipathy. The sweeping triumph of the Republican Party in the 1994 elections and the consequent Republican majority in Congress was understood by some commentators as a conservative rejection of Clinton's presidency and a strong reflection of the ascendant political power of the Christian Coalition.*

Clough, John Everett (1836-1910). Baptist* missionary to India. In 1866 Clough founded a church as he ministered among the outcaste Madigas. His relief work during the terrible famine of 1876-1878 was widely respected and led to thousands of baptisms and widespread influence.

Cobbs, Nicholas Hamner (1796-1861). Episcopal* bishop. Ordained to the priesthood in 1825, Cobbs was a zealous missionary in his native Virginia and later Episcopal chaplain* to the University of Virginia. In 1844 he was consecrated* first Episcopal bishop of Alabama. Although the evangelicalism* of Virginia influenced him throughout his life, he subsequently combined high* and low* church emphases in a way that many thought paradigmatic of Anglicanism.

Cody, John Patrick (1907-1982). Catholic* archbishop of Chicago (1965-1982). As archbishop of New Orleans, Cody earned a reputation for racial liberalism by working for the desegregation of that city's parochial schools.* In 1965 he was transferred to Chicago, where he angered liberal Catholics by closing many inner-city schools for financial reasons. Perhaps his most permanent legacy was the decision not to build Catholic schools in new suburban parishes. He was named a cardinal in 1967.

Coe, George Albert (1862-1951). Professor of religious education. Coe held professorships at Northwestern University (Evanston, Ill.), Union Theological Seminary (New York)* and Teachers College, Columbia University.*

Coe was the leading theorist in liberal* religious education during the first half of the twentieth century. He appealed to Horace Bushnell's* theory of Christian nurture,* arguing that people could be educated into Christian faith with no need for religious conversion.* He also drew heavily on John Dewey's pragmatism and the social Darwinism of his time.

Coe, Jack (1918-1957). Pentecostal* healing* revivalist.* Ordained* by the Assemblies of God* in 1944, Coe's dynamic revivalist style led to a tent ministry and to a prominent role in the nationwide healing revival of 1947-1952. Expelled from the Assemblies of God in 1953, Coe opened his Dallas Revival Center in 1954. His *Herald of Healing* reached a circulation of 250,000 in 1956.

Coffin, Henry Sloane (1877-1954). Presbyterian* minister and educator. As pastor of the prestigious Madison Avenue Presbyterian Church in New York City (1905-1926), Coffin became known as one of America's great preachers. He later served as president and professor of homiletics* at Union Theological Seminary* (1926-

1945). Calling himself an "evangelical liberal," Coffin attempted to find a mediating position between extreme conservative and liberal factions in the Presbyterian Church of his day.

Coffin, Levi (1789-1877). Quaker* merchant and president of the Underground Railroad. Levi and his cousin Vestal Coffin initiated the Underground Railroad in 1819. Levi Coffin's house in Old Newport (now Fountain City), Indiana, where Coffin resided from 1826 to 1847, was dubbed the "Grand Central Station of the Underground Railroad" by frustrated slave hunters. By the time of the Emancipation Proclamation,* he had aided three thousand slaves on their way to freedom.

Coffman, John S. (1848-1899). Pioneer Mennonite* Church evangelist. Coffman was a writer for Mennonite publications and educational organizer, but his greatest contribution was as an evangelist, as his gentle style and tact helped break down opposition to such work within the conference.

Coffman, S(amuel) F(rederick) (1872-1954). Canadian Old Mennonite* bishop and educator. Coffman, the (first) principal of Ontario Mennonite Bible School in Kitchener (1907-1948), was one of Ontario's most influential Mennonites. He opposed liberalism* but without the negative tone of American fundamentalism.*

Coke, Thomas (1747-1814). Methodist* bishop. In 1776 Coke offered his services to John Wesley,* who used him extensively in drafting deeds and documents, anticipating the organization of the Methodists in both England and America. In 1784 Coke was ordained* by Wesley as the first bishop for the American Methodist Episcopal Church. In the U.S., Coke joined with Francis Asbury* to establish the Methodist Episcopal Church at the Christmas Conference* of 1784.

In eight subsequent trips to America (1787-1803), Coke found the American Methodists moving away from the direct rule of Wesley and even challenging Asbury's authority.* Back in England, Coke's influence remained considerable until his death.

Coker, Daniel (born Isaac Wright) (1780-1846). African Methodist Episcopal* minister. Born a slave, Coker later gained his freedom and was ordained* a Methodist* deacon* by Bishop Francis Asbury.* He was one of the founders of the African Methodist Episcopal Church (1816) and later conducted missionary work in Africa.

Cole, Nathan (1711-1783). Lay leader of the separatist* movement in New England. Cole was converted under George Whitefield* and later joined Ebenezer Frothingham's* separatist congregation. He produced a number of controversial works, including a defense of his rejection in 1778 of pedobaptism.

Coleman, Alice Blanchard Merriam (1858-1936). Home missions leader. Coleman was president of the Woman's American (later Chicago's Woman's) Baptist Home Mission Society (1890-1909 and 1920-1928) and the Council of Women for Home Missions (1908-1916).

Colgate, William (1783-1857). Manufacturer, philanthropist* and Baptist* layman. By the 1840s Colgate had become an acknowledged leader in the soap and toiletry industry. He helped found several Bible societies,* including the American Bible Society* and the American and Foreign Bible Society.

Collect. A short, structured public prayer* which follows a distinctively formalized pattern including (1) an address to God, (2) an appeal to an attribute of God, (3) the petition, (4) a statement of the divine purpose of the prayer and (5) a conclusion.

College of New Jersey. *See* PRINCETON UNIVERSITY.

College of Rhode Island. *See* BROWN UNIVERSITY.

Collegiality. The principle that the church is a communion (college) of local churches which make up the church universal. As a mode of decision-making, collegiality emphasizes collaboration at all levels of the church.

Colonial Catholicism. Catholicism came to North America with the three major colonial powers: England, France and Spain. In the French and Spanish domains, the union of church and state* and the privileged position enjoyed by Roman Catholicism* assisted that church's growth and development (*see* Missions to North America,

French; Missions to North America, Spanish). Catholics in the English colonies, however, were generally subject to severe civil penalties.

In Maryland in 1649, the Catholic-controlled assembly passed a Toleration Act,* guaranteeing religious toleration for all Christians. This law was repealed in 1654 when the Puritans* seized control of the colony. In 1702 the Church of England was established, and the assembly instituted a harsh penal code.

German and Irish Catholics were among the earliest settlers in Philadelphia, where Catholics were tolerated, though they could not hold public office. New York briefly enjoyed religious toleration during the proprietorship of the Duke of York (James II), who had converted to Catholicism in 1672. Leisler's rebellion in 1689, however, ended toleration.

At the time of the Revolution, most colonial Catholics allied themselves with the revolutionary cause. They were led by Charles Carroll* of Carrollton, who attended the First Continental Congress in Philadelphia, signed the Declaration of Independence and was the first Catholic to hold political office in Maryland since the seventeenth century.

Colporteur. Itinerant hawkers of religious tracts and books in nineteenth-century America. The chief promoter of the colportage system was the American Tract Society,* which had more than five hundred colporteurs at work by 1851, mainly in the frontier regions of the West and South.

Columbia University. Educational institution with colonial Anglican* roots. Opening in Trinity Church in Lower Manhattan in 1754 as Kings College, and largely under Anglican control, the school was dispersed in 1776 as a result of the Revolutionary War.* It reopened in 1784 as Columbia College. In 1857 the college moved to more spacious quarters in midtown Manhattan. Continued growth resulted in its final move to a 28.5-acre campus in Upper Manhattan. Enrollment presently averages around seventeen thousand students.

Columbian Catholic Congress. National conference of Catholic* laity. In November 1889, a congress of Roman Catholic laymen met in Baltimore. The second Catholic Congress of the U.S., held in 1893 in Chicago, was organized to coincide with the Columbus Exposition and World's Fair.

Columbus, Christopher (1451-1506). Sailor, chartmaker, navigator and discoverer of the New World. Obsessed with the idea of finding a west-ward sea route to Asia, Columbus made four voyages between 1492 and 1504, always con-vinced he was headed for the Asian Indies but always landing in Caribbean America, land here-tofore unknown to Europe.

Columbus himself was a strong-willed, am-bitious, industrious, bold and above all pious person whose religious devotion* and practice usually surpassed that of all his companions. In American history the Anglo-Puritan* "Errand in the Wilderness" is a well-known motif. "The conversion to our Holy Faith" of millions of pagans in Asia was equally the errand of Colum-bus, however much gold the Spanish monarchs may have expected and been promised.

Columbus is a hero not only to sailors and navigators but especially to American Catholics, who have used him as an inspiration and patron in their own efforts to establish themselves social-ly and religiously.

Commission of the Churches on Interna-tional Affairs. Ecumenical* agency seeking Christian solutions to international problems. Or-ganized in 1946 at a conference in Cambridge, England, and then placed under the World Coun-cil of Churches* in 1948, the commission has di-rected studies of long-term problems and coun-seled governments to forgo violence, seek mediation and use the services of the United Na-tions. The CCIA is given substantial credit for the religious-freedom clause in the Universal Decla-ration of Human Rights (1948).

Committee of Southern Churchmen. A small nondenominational Christian service network based in Nashville and led by Will D. Campbell. This committee, which emerged in 1963-1964 from the dormant Fellowship of Southern Church-men,* continued the racial justice emphasis of the previous fellowship, participating in the major Southern nonviolent campaigns of the 1960s. Evan-gelism,* prophetic social criticism, reconciliation and promotion of a christocentric human commu-nity are basic to the committee's perspective.

Common Sense Philosophy. *See* SCOTTISH REALISM.

Communion of Saints. The universal fellow-ship* of Christians and the solidarity they have with one another. The term stems from the Apos-tles' Creed, "I believe . . . in the communion of saints." The concept is suggested by New Testa-ment texts indicating that Christians have inti-mate fellowship with God and with one another through their union in Christ and by the power of the Holy Spirit. In this broad sense, *saints* de-scribes all Christians.

See also ALL SAINTS DAY; SAINTS, CULT OF THE.

Communion Table. The table on which the elements of bread and wine rest during the Eu-charist* and from which Holy Communion is dis-tributed, often ornamented with a text taken from the narrative of the Last Supper.

Community of True Inspiration. *See* AMANA CHURCH SOCIETY.

Concelebration. The reciting of the central prayer* of the Christian Eucharist* by a number of presiders simultaneously at the same altar.* Concelebration was discouraged as the church progressively moved toward requiring all priests to say Mass daily; since Vatican II,* however, it has been stressed more.

Conciliar Tradition, American. Ancient Chris-tian tradition traced the origin of holding coun-cils or synods* to decide doctrinal or disciplinary questions to the meeting of apostles and elders at Jerusalem (Acts 15:1-29; Gal 2:1-10). General, or ecumenical, councils began with Nicaea (A.D. 325) and in Roman Catholic* usage have con-tinued to Vatican Council II* (1962-1965).

Beginnings in Baltimore. The structured Ro-man Catholic Church of the U.S. is descended from the church community begun in 1634 in Maryland. For 150 years, until John Carroll's* ap-pointment as superior of the missions in 1784, Jesuit* priests managed church affairs in Maryland and Pennsylvania with only nominal supervision by a bishop in London. In America hostility to the office of bishop had kept both Anglicans and Catholics from establishing the position.

The Diocese of Baltimore was created in 1789. Bishop John Carroll held two meetings during his twenty-six-year tenure as leader of the American church: a synod of priests in 1791 and, after his diocese was divided, an informal session in 1810 with three of the new suffragan* bishops. Later, seven provincial councils of Baltimore* were held (1829-1949), each led by the current archbishop of Baltimore. Their chief result was to fix the pattern of a church firmly dominated by bishops.

Three nationwide plenary councils (1852, 1866, 1884) were also held at Baltimore, with the archbishop of Baltimore in each instance named by the pope as apostolic delegate* and president. Their legislation, binding on all U.S. dioceses, reinforced general Roman Catholic doctrinal and disciplinary norms.

Provincial councils have been infrequent, and there has been no plenary council since 1884. The archbishops of the U.S. met annually after 1890 until World War I,* and a more formal organization developed from the National Catholic War Council, organized to coordinate church cooperation in providing social services in the 1917-1918 war effort.

Modern Conciliar Tradition. In 1966, after the Second Vatican Council encouraged establishment of permanent bishops' conferences, the National Council was succeeded by the National Conference of Catholic Bishops* (NCCB), with the U.S. Catholic Conference* (USCC) as its operational arm. American bishops attended the First* (1869-1870) and Second* (1962-1965) Vatican Councils, where their approach was primarily pastoral and pragmatic.

See also BALTIMORE, COUNCILS OF; NATIONAL CATHOLIC WELFARE CONFERENCE; VATICAN COUNCIL I; VATICAN COUNCIL II.

Confession of 1967. Most recent theological standard of the Presbyterian Church (USA).* In 1958 the church appointed a committee to draw up a brief contemporary confession* of faith. A draft was presented in 1965 and a revised form accepted by the 1967 General Assembly.

The confession's overriding theme is Christian reconciliation, needed in four areas: the discrimination dividing the family of humanity, conflict between nations, "enslaving poverty" in an affluent world, and male-female relations. The confession regards the Bible as "the witness without parallel," yet in the "words of men" and so approachable only "with literary and historical understanding."

Confessionalism. The practice of defining a religious body's faith and identity by reaffirming historical creeds* and confessions of faith. In ad-

dition to the ancient ecumenical creeds, the Lutheran* and Reformed* bodies of Europe ascribed to their own confessions. Presbyterians and, to a lesser degree, Congregationalists have held to the Westminster Confession of Faith.*

The most popular forms of American Protestantism have been conversionist rather than confessional, oriented toward a direct personal experience of God rather than subscription to a creed.

Confessor. A person, usually a priest, to whom one confesses sin. In the early church, the title "confessor" was given to those who, despite great suffering, did not deny their Savior. Later, it referred to outstanding Christians whose lives were models for others.

Confirmation. A postbaptismal sacrament* or rite of prayer* and laying on of hands* and sometimes anointing.* Confirmation has been associated variously with (1) the reception, strengthening, sealing, gifts or anointing of the Spirit; (2) the fulfillment and appropriation of baptism* and preparation for the first reception of Holy Communion;* (3) the increasing of sanctifying grace to equip the baptized believer to live the Christian life faithfully; (4) the personal confession of faith required for active church membership* and/or (5) the ordination* of the laity for service in the world.

Confraternity of Christian Doctrine. A Catholic association concerned with the religious education of Catholics, particularly youth who do not attend a Catholic elementary or high school. Originating in 1905 and developing nationally throughout the U.S. in the 1930s, the Confraternity of Christian Doctrine (CCD) evolved as the primary means of providing formal religious education* through the local parish* for millions of American Catholics, from preschool children to adults.

Congregation for Divine Worship. Catholic* administrative body. Formerly known as the Congregation of Sacred Rites, the congregation (1) supervises the liturgy* of the Catholic Church, including all ceremonies, rites and celebrations, and (2) recommends candidates to the pope for beatification or canonization.

Congregation for the Doctrine of the Faith. A Catholic agency, formerly known as the Holy

Office and located in the Vatican, whose task is to assist the pope and the whole church in preserving the integrity of doctrines concerning faith and morals and in alerting the church to errors. The need for such a churchwide office was felt at the time of the Protestant Reformation as Pope Paul III established what is considered the earliest permanent structure in 1542. In 1965 Pope Paul VI renamed the organization and reformed its procedures.

Congregation of Holy Cross. Roman Catholic* religious order. Founded in France in 1837 by priest Basil Moreau and today established in more than a dozen countries, the congregation has long been active as educators. In 1841, seven members were sent to work in the Diocese of Vincennes, Indiana. Their first permanent foundation was at Notre Dame, Indiana, in 1842, where they opened a school that in 1844 was chartered as the University of Notre Dame du Lac (see Notre Dame, University of).

Congregation of Sacred Rites. See CONGREGATION FOR DIVINE WORSHIP.

Congregation of the Missionary Society of St. Paul the Apostle. An officially recognized association of Roman Catholic* priests and seminarians. Popularly called "Paulists," the congregation was founded in 1858 in the state of New York by Isaac Thomas Hecker.*

Recent reassessment of Hecker's hopes and aims has led the Paulists to affirm three main emphases: (1) reconciliation of Catholics alienated from the church, (2) evangelism* and (3) ecumenism.* Members work in parish* settings as well as in universities, the media, information centers and ecumenical ventures.

Congregational Home Missionary Society. See AMERICAN HOME MISSIONARY SOCIETY.

Congregationalism. A Protestant* tradition of ecclesiology and church government,* Congregationalism maintains that local congregations, consisting of men and women who acknowledge the lordship of Jesus Christ and seek his will, can minister* and govern themselves through congregational vote, covenant and participation. Although there are specific Congregational denominations,* this type of church government also occurs in many other churches and denominations in America, particularly among Baptist* and independent churches. Here we focus, however, on historic Congregationalism in America and its present manifestation in the United Church of Christ.*

Historic Congregationalism came to America with the Separatist* Pilgrims* of Plymouth and the Puritans* of the Massachusetts Bay Colony. From 1646 to 1648 the religious leaders of New England met several times in a synod* at Cambridge, Massachusetts, and there decided to accept the Westminster Confession of Faith* as their doctrinal* statement. They also drafted and adopted the "Platforme of Church Discipline"—better known as the Cambridge Platform*—defining their polity.* It is the earliest document setting forth American Congregational faith and church government and served as the constitution of the "Congregational Way" well into the nineteenth century. Only in 1865 was this platform superseded, by the so-called Boston Platform.

The Great Awakening* had a great impact on New England Congregationalism. On the one hand there was the revival* of a heartfelt religion that was profoundly evangelical* in character, led by Jonathan Edwards,* Congregationalist minister and theologian of the movement. On the other hand, a significant number of Congregational clergy opposed the revivals, and a rift developed that was to divide Congregationalism into liberal and evangelical wings.

In the nineteenth century, Congregationalism was again influenced by theological liberalism, the leading voice being that of Congregational minister Horace Bushnell.* Liberalism has continued to hold a prominent place in twentieth-century Congregationalism, although evangelicals and evangelical theology have maintained a presence, with Harold John Ockenga* (1905-1985) and Donald G. Bloesch (1928-) representing this tradition. In 1871 American Congregational churches, which have typically formed fellowships beyond the local church, formed the National Council of Congregational Churches. In the late nineteenth century, Congregationalists began to consider whether their fellowship might not extend beyond their National Council. Consultations began with other denominations, two of which were ultimately successful. Talks with a Restorationist* group, the Christian Connection,* led to a merger of the two bodies in 1931, when they formed the General Council of Congregational and Christian Churches. This council in turn merged with the Evangelical and Reformed Church in 1961, forming the United Church of Christ.

Congress of National Black Churches. Black ecumenical* organization. Formed in 1978 by black churchmen and scholars, the Congress of National Black Churches (CNBC) provides a continuing forum for leaders of black denominations* with national constituencies.

CNBC is concerned with neither doctrinal conformity nor structural merger but with cooperative social and economic action to empower the black community. The dominant emphasis is on economic institution-building, including collective insurance, purchasing, banking and community development programs.

Connecticut Missionary Society. Early nineteenth-century organization that funded missions to the American West. Founded in 1798 by the General Association of the Congregational* Church, the society reflected growing concern about the moral fate of the western territories.

The first missionaries were sent on tours lasting one or two months, preaching* the gospel and distributing thousands of religious books and tracts.* Later the society funded settled ministers.* In 1826 the society became an auxiliary of the American Home Missionary Society.*

Connelly, Cornelia Augusta Peacock (1809-1879). Roman Catholic* convert,* founder of the Society of the Holy Child Jesus. After marriage in 1831 to Pierce Connelly and his subsequent decision to become a priest, Cornelia professed a solemn vow of chastity in 1845. In 1846 she succeeded in establishing a religious order* which provided teacher training and first-rate education for all classes.

Conner, Walter Thomas (1877-1952). Baptist* theologian and educator. Teaching from 1910 to 1949 at Southwestern Baptist Theological Seminary, Conner was a frequent contributor to theological journals, a popular teacher and a dedicated scholar. He published fifteen books. Through his teaching and writing he shaped the theology of thousands of Southern Baptists, becoming one of the most influential and respected Southern Baptist theologians of the twentieth century.

Conscience. A human faculty or capacity used in judging how to live morally. At the time Puritans settled New England there were two important views of how conscience functioned. William Perkins* argued that conscience had to be informed through instruction and left free to decide right and wrong for itself. His student, William Ames,* took a different view, arguing that moral issues had one and only one answer. Most Puritan settlers in America ultimately followed Perkins's view of freedom (liberty) of conscience—Roger Williams* being a prominent example.

Consecration. The act by which a person, a place or an object is set apart for holy use by ritual words and gestures. Consecration is used for (1) the Eucharistic bread and wine, (2) the induction into office of church workers and (3) the dedication of church buildings and furnishings.

Conservative Baptist Association of America. An association of Baptist* churches, chiefly in the northern and western areas of the U.S. Organized in 1947, the association is closely allied with the Conservative Baptist Foreign Mission Society (CBFMS), the Conservative Baptist Home Mission Society and several seminaries. In 1992 the total membership of 1,084 churches in the association was approximately 200,000.

The association emerged from the fundamentalist-modernist controversy* within the Northern (now American*) Baptist denomination. After unsuccessful efforts over several years to establish doctrinal standards for the missionary* agencies of the Northern Baptist Convention, in 1943 several hundred conservative churches formed the CBFMS and, beginning in 1947, hundreds of Northern Baptist churches left their national convention to join the conservatives. In the late 1950s internal conflict and intense debate over separation* led eventually to an exodus of a militant minority, consisting of about two hundred churches.

Conservative Congregational Christian Conference. An evangelical* association of Congregational* churches. This group of churches and ministers was organized in 1948 in order to provide a fellowship for evangelical Congregationalists who did not wish to become a part of the emerging United Church of Christ.* In 1992 there were a reported 188 churches with a total membership of 30,387.

Consistent Calvinism. *See* HOPKINS, SAMUEL; NEW ENGLAND THEOLOGY.

Constantinides, Michael (1892-1958). Greek Orthodox* bishop. After ministry in Asia Minor following World War I, Constantinides served in London and then Greece. In 1949 he was sent to New York to succeed the newly enthroned Ecumenical Patriarch Athenagoras* as archbishop. His nine-year tenure was marked by taking measures to stabilize the archdiocese's finances and to promote the Hellenic spirit in parish* schools and youth organizations.

Constructive Theology. A theological movement which emerged in the mid-1970s. The movement was formed in an attempt to promote collaborative work among systematic theologians.* Members share the perspective that theology, for all of its reliance on tradition, is a constructive project. At the heart of this contention is the view that the Scriptures of the Old and New Testaments, along with their doctrinal interpretations, no longer occupy an indispensable place of authority* for Christian faith and practice. Theology must thus be reshaped to meet the needs of the modern world.

Consubstantiation. The doctrine which teaches that the substance of the bread and of the body are coexisting in the consecrated host at the Lord's Supper.* Although this doctrine, which is an alternative to transubstantiation,* is often erroneously described as the Lutheran* position on the real presence of Christ in the sacrament* of the altar,* it is specifically rejected by the Lutheran confessions and all of the early Lutheran theologians.
See also LUTHERAN TRADITION IN AMERICA.

Consultation on Church Union. A movement toward church union among mainline* U.S. churches. The Consultation on Church Union (COCU) grew out of a proposal for a united church in a sermon preached by Eugene Carson Blake* in 1960. Several COCU commissions and plenaries produced *Principles of Church Union* (1966), which revealed a consensus on the issues of Scripture and tradition; the threefold ministry* of bishops, presbyters* and deacons;* and the faith of the church and the sacraments.* COCU represents predominantly African-American churches and predominantly white churches

seeking to overcome racism, sexism and nationalism and to express a truly inclusive church in which ethnic and cultural diversity is celebrated yet brought into communion.
See also BLAKE-PIKE UNITY PROPOSAL; CHURCH UNION MOVEMENTS; ECUMENISM.

Contraception. *See* BIRTH CONTROL.

Conversion. In its most basic sense, conversion means a turning from one way of life to another. For Christians it is a turning from sin* to a new life in Christ, an experience of the saving power of God. Early colonial Puritans* frequently viewed conversion as an extended process of spiritual struggle as the individual waited on God's irresistible grace. Nineteenth-century evangelicals put greater emphasis on individual free will and immediate regeneration.*
See also NEW BIRTH.

Conversion Narratives. Speeches given before the congregation for admission to full membership.* One of the distinguishing marks of colonial New England church polity* was the practice of testing applicants for full membership. The most important ingredient in this exaination process was the conversion* narrative, a short speech describing the narrator's experience of grace.

Conwell, Russell Herman (1843-1925). Inspirational lecturer and writer, Baptist* pastor. In 1882 Conwell became pastor of the Baptist Temple in Philadelphia, which by 1893 had become the largest Protestant church in America. Conwell also was the founder of Temple University.

Conwell wrote over thirty inspirational books but is best remembered for "Acres of Diamonds," a sermonic lecture he delivered over six thousand times nationwide. The central theme is that it is one's Christian responsibility to become wealthy in order to help the cause of Christ.

Cook, David C. (1850-1927). Sunday-school* curriculum author and publisher. Wishing to meet the need for inexpensive curriculum materials for mission schools, Cook founded a publishing company in Illinois in 1875. A pioneer in his field, Cook became a national and international leader in the Sunday-school movement. The publishing firm bearing his name continues as a leader in the field of Christian educational curriculum publishing.

Cook, Joseph (Flavius Josephus) (1838-1901). Congregational* lecturer. In the 1870s Cook was catapulted into international prominence as a popular spokesman for the concerns of American Protestantism.* Riding the crest of nineteenth-century America's regard, Cook developed a successful career as a lecturer. Cook primarily used his lectures as a forum to attempt the reconciliation of orthodox* Christianity with other pressing issues of modernity—especially Darwinism.*

Cooke, Terence James (1921-1983). Archbishop of New York. A gifted fundraiser and administrator, Cooke in 1957 was appointed personal secretary to Cardinal Spellman.* After Spellman's death in 1967, Cooke was appointed archbishop in 1968. Although known as an enlightened conservative in matters of doctrine, most notably supporting Pope Paul's* encyclical* on artificial birth control, he was considered a liberal in his stand on racial, economic and social issues.

Cooper, Samuel (1725-1783). Calvinist Boston preacher. Pastor of Brattle Street Church (1743-1783), Cooper was an able and eloquent preacher. Cooper actively supported the American Revolution* and was a friend of John Adams and Benjamin Franklin.

Copley, Thomas (Philip Fisher) (c. 1595-1652). Jesuit* missionary in Maryland. Born in Spain of English parents, Copley sailed to Maryland as a missionary in 1637. There he fought bitterly with Governor Leonard Calvert* over restrictions on Jesuits. Later deported, Copley returned to minister in Maryland, sometimes under the pseudonym Philip Fisher.

Corcoran, James Andrew (1820-1889). Catholic theologian* and educator. Corcoran, the first native of South Carolina to become a priest, taught at the Charleston Seminary and was rector of the cathedral.* Corcoran's reputation as a theologian was earned in his role as secretary for the Eighth Baltimore Council* of 1855 and his similar work for the Ninth Council.

In 1868 Corcoran was sent to the Vatican as the sole representative of the U.S. archbishops on the preparatory commission for Vatican I.* Corcoran

also was founding editor of the *American Catholic Quarterly Review* (1876-1889).

Corpus Christi, Feast of. A festival in the Roman Catholic* church year* celebrating the presence of Christ in the Eucharist.* Corpus Christi ("the body of Christ"), now known as the Solemnity of the Body and Blood of Christ, is celebrated on Thursday of the first week of Pentecost.* From the fourteenth century the public procession with the Blessed Sacrament assumed an increasingly important role.

Corrigan, Michael Augustine (1839-1902). Archbishop of New York. In 1873 Corrigan was consecrated* bishop of Newark (N.J.), where he focused attention on the plight of Italian immigrants and promoted the founding of parochial schools,* orphanages and hospitals. In 1886 he was installed as archbishop of New York.

A vigorous conservative, Corrigan opposed the Knights of Labor,* Catholic membership in secret societies and the so-called heresy* of Americanism.* But history has remembered him as a masterful administrator and builder who greatly increased the number of churches, priests, schools and charitable institutions in his diocese.

Costas, Orlando (1942-1987). Hispanic missiologist.* Born in Puerto Rico, Costas grew up in the U.S. and was converted to evangelical* faith at age seventeen during a Billy Graham* crusade in New York. After college and seminary education in the U.S. and in Puerto Rico, Costas obtained his doctorate in missiology from the Free University of Amsterdam and launched a short but productive career as a minister, educator, evangelist and missiologist. His influence and leadership was felt in the Hispanic church in the U.S. as well as in Latin America. At the time of his death he was dean at Andover Newton Theological Seminary. Among his writings are *Christ Outside the Gate* (1982) and *Liberating News: A Theology of Contextual Evangelization* (1989).

Cotton, John (1584-1652). Seventeenth-century Puritan* minister and spokesman for New England Congregationalism.* After earning a reputation in England as a great and learned preacher, Cotton departed for the New World, where he became teacher of the First Church of Boston and the most eminent minister in Massachusetts. Cotton's evangelical* preaching sparked a large number of conversions* within the first two years of his arrival.

Cotton may justly be considered the father of early New England Congregationalism. Though ministers agreed upon most of the larger principles of church government,* many practical questions concerning baptism,* election of officers and other church procedures remained unresolved during the first years of settlement. Church authorities frequently looked to Cotton to turn to the Scriptures for answers to such problems.

Coughlin, Charles Edward (1891-1979). Radical Roman Catholic* priest and radio preacher. Born in Ontario, after his ordination in 1916 he spent most of his life in Michigan. In 1926 Coughlin began an effective radio ministry in an effort to explain Roman Catholicism after the Ku Klux Klan burned a cross in the churchyard of his church. By 1930 he had turned from strictly religious topics and had begun to preach anticommunism and anti-Semitism on the radio; in time he became pro-Nazi. He was eventually forced off the air by church authorities.

See also CHRISTIAN FRONT.

Council on Religion and International Affairs. *See* CARNEGIE COUNCIL ON ETHICS AND INTERNATIONAL AFFAIRS.

Counsels of Perfection. Poverty, chastity and obedience. Christian tradition teaches that this is a threefold remedy for a threefold obstacle (namely, "the lust of the flesh and the lust of the eyes and the pride of life," 1 Jn 2:16) to the perfection of love. These fundamental weaknesses in human nature, if left unattended, can keep the soul separated from God. Individuals, particularly members of Catholic religious orders,* may bind themselves by vows to a life of poverty, chastity and obedience.

Covenant Theology. A doctrine or system of theology* explaining the relationship between God and humankind in terms of a compact, or covenant (also called federal theology). Theologians* who have taught the covenant doctrine have based it on biblical themes, especially God's covenant with Israel as recorded in the Old Testament.

Although the concept of covenant is ancient, the rigorous development of an overall, systematic covenant theology grew out of the Protestant* Reformation. Reformed covenant theology has taught that God offers grace and salvation* to humankind. To those who by faith accept God's offer of salvation—on his terms—he assuredly grants salvation.

The covenant approach to theology strongly affected English Puritanism,* and through Puritanism's influence in the New World came to have a significant influence in America. The appeal of the covenant among Puritans of England and America was varied, but most noteworthy was its rational and easily understood organizational structure. Moreover, the doctrine offered absolute assurance of God's eternal graciousness.

Covenant Theology and the Church. Although rooted in theological speculation, the covenant ideal had many applications in America. From the individual covenant of grace, American Congregationalists* deduced the corporate church covenant, whereby the believers would band together to carry out their covenant responsibilities.

When religious zeal waned, as it did within a few decades, the problem of maintaining pure, saintly churches became a dilemma. Many respectable citizens, baptized* as infants into the church, could not as mature persons point to a particular experience of true conversion.* Thus, they were not allowed to take up active membership in the church. To solve this dilemma, the New England Congregationalists created the policy of the Half-Way Covenant* (1662).

Covenant Theology and Public Life. Just as God had covenanted with humankind in salvation and in gathering churches, so groups within society were to covenant with one another as they carried out their ordinary affairs. In fact, the seventeenth century was an age of compacts, contracts and secular covenants, through which the public business was transacted. Theological covenants and sociopolitical covenants thus sprang out of the same milieu in America.

Although the reign of covenant theology began to fade in the late eighteenth century, the covenant ideal, with its teaching about mutual obligation and communal responsibility, continued to influence American life, although in ever more secularized forms. The pervasive ideal that America has a moral mission in the world, beyond the mundane, owes much to covenant theology.

See also MANIFEST DESTINY; NEW ENGLAND THEOLOGY; NEW ENGLAND WAY.

Cowley Fathers. *See* SOCIETY OF ST. JOHN THE EVANGELIST.

Cowman, Lettie Burd (1870-1960), and Charles Elmer Cowman (1864-1924). Missionaries to Japan and founders of OMS International.* The two labored together in Japan and Korea until Charles suffered a heart attack in September 1918. For nearly sixty years Lettie played a crucial role in OMS International. She is best known for her devotional book *Streams in the Desert* (1925), compiled during her husband's illness. It is the all-time bestseller among devotional books, with more than three million copies in print in English and more than a dozen foreign languages.

Craig, John (1710-1774). Pioneer Presbyterian* minister in western Virginia. Craig, an Old Side* Presbyterian, had a parish that originally extended over more than six hundred square miles; today thirteen Presbyterian churches owe their origin to his missionary* activity.

Cramp, John Mockett (1796-1881). Canadian Baptist* leader and educator. A historian, prolific writer and tireless preacher, Cramp became a Maritime Baptist leader and also gave direction to the temperance* and education causes. In helping to integrate the British and American traditions, Cramp shaped a generation of Maritime Baptist scholars.

Crapsey, Algernon Sidney (1847-1927). Episcopal* priest. In 1879, Crapsey became the rector of St. Andrew's Church, Rochester, New York, where he worked with Walter Rauschenbusch.* After publication of his *Religion and Politics* in 1905, Crapsey's orthodoxy was challenged in a heresy* trial and he was deposed from the ministry.

Crawford, Alexander (c. 1785-1828). Pioneer Baptist* preacher on Prince Edward Island. In 1812 Crawford performed the first adult believer's baptism on Prince Edward Island, where he later founded Baptist churches and served as an itinerant* preacher. Both the Baptists and the Disciples of Christ* look to him as their founding father on the island.

Crawford, Florence (1872-1936). Founder of the Pentecostal* Apostolic Faith movement. After experiencing tongues speaking and healing at the Azusa Street revival* of 1906, Crawford began an itinerant ministry of Pentecostal evangelism* which led ultimately to a permanent ministry in Portland, Oregon. Her movement emphasized strictness and separation, which helped keep it on the fringe of evangelical* and Pentecostal* circles.

Crawford, Percy B. (1902-1960). Evangelical* youth minister, educator and broadcaster. Crawford was a significant figure in pre- and post-World War II* fundamentalism* and evangelicalism. He launched Saturday night rallies (1930), one of the first national Christian radio broadcasts (1931) and the first fundamentalist coast-to-coast television program (1950). He also established King's College (N.Y.).

Creation Science. As used by its defenders, the view that God created the world some ten thousand years ago, doing so in six twenty-four-hour days, and that a worldwide flood best explains all geological data. Early advocates of creation science gained visibility in the early 1920s through their antievolution articles in the *Princeton Theological Review* and in 1925 in the well-publicized Scopes Trial.* In 1926 George McCready Price typified the evolutionary principle of uniformity as "essentially pagan or atheistic" and declared the literal creation of all the primal types as recorded in Genesis 1 to be the only fact that modern science needed to deal with.

In recent decades civil engineer Henry Morris has spearheaded the modern creationist revival, publishing *The Genesis Flood* (1961) with theologian John Whitcomb and becoming president of the newly founded Institute for Creation Research (1972).

See also DARWINIAN EVOLUTION AND THE AMERICAN CHURCHES.

Creationism. *See* CREATION SCIENCE.

Creed. A confession of adherence to selected essentials in the Christian faith. Creeds have been used to confess the faith of a Christian individual or group (most commonly in corporate worship), to teach the young or prospective church members, to provide a basis for founding or uniting churches, to warn against error, and for many other purposes. The earliest Christian creed may be embedded in the New Testament (e.g., Rom 10:9). Most widely known are the Apostles' Creed and the Nicene Creed.

Cridge, Edward (1817-1913). Bishop of the Reformed Episcopal Church.* In 1865 Cridge was made dean of Victoria (British Columbia) and rector of Christ Church Cathedral. His years as dean were marred by his growing unhappiness with the influence of Tractarianism* in the Anglican Church in Canada.* A dispute with the bishop led to half the cathedral* congregation's seceding and joining the evangelical* Reformed Episcopal Church.

Crittenton, Charles Nelson (1833-1909). Businessman, evangelist and philanthropist.* Crittenton experienced a dramatic conversion* in 1882, which soon rechanneled his efforts from business into evangelism in urban slums. His first such effort convinced him that he should work to provide practical assistance to the destitute persons to whom he was witnessing, which he did effectively in New York City and around the country.

Cronyn, Benjamin (1802-1871). First Anglican* bishop of Huron (Canada West, now Ontario). Cronyn's evangelicalism* involved him in controversies with high churchmen* like John Strachan* and George Whitaker, provost of Trinity College, Toronto. This led in 1863 to Cronyn's establishing a theological* college in his own diocese, Huron College.

Crosby, Thomas (1840-1914). Canadian Methodist* missionary to British Columbia. In 1869, two years before his ordination,* he took charge of the Methodist missions to the Native Americans in southern British Columbia. Crosby's ministry, which emphasized material and cultural improvement, was the first to include medical work.

Crosby (Van Alstyne), Fanny Jane (1820-1915). Gospel song* writer, musician, preacher and evangelist. Blind from the age of six weeks, Crosby (who married Alexander Van Alstyne in 1858) established the style of poetry which still characterizes gospel songs and made her familiar to an entire generation. Her texts were set to music by the most popular American tunesmiths of the century, including Ira D. Sankey.* Among her thousands of familiar hymns and gospel songs are "Blessed Assurance" and "To God Be the Glory."

Croswell, Andrew (1708-1785). Itinerant* Congregational* preacher and radical supporter of the Great Awakening.* A much-published controversialist, Croswell used unorthodox methods in preaching. His outspoken criticism of Old Lights* (as well as moderates like Jonathan Edwards*) earned him a reputation for extremism.

Crowell, Henry Parsons (1855-1944). Manufacturer and Christian philanthropist.* Influenced by Dwight L. Moody* during Moody's visit to Cleveland in 1873, Crowell later ensured the financial survival of Moody Bible Institute,* serving as chairman of the board (1902-1944) and influencing its theological development.

Crucifix. A cross bearing the figure of Christ. During the Middle Ages, the crucifix came to have very extensive devotional* use. Fearing idolatry, many sixteenth-century Reformers eliminated crucifixes. More recently, though, some U.S. Protestants* are regarding the crucifix as a valid way of recalling the Passion.

Crummell, Alexander (1819-1898). Episcopal* minister and missionary to West Africa. Born a free African-American in New York, Crummell became an Episcopal priest in 1844. He dedicated his life to the liberation of African-American people in the U.S. and in Africa and was one of the earliest leaders of the Pan-African movement. Crummell believed that unity among African-American people was a necessary ingredient for the unity of all humankind.

Crumpler, A(bner) B(lackman) (1863-1952). Holiness* evangelist. A pioneer leader of the Holiness movement in North Carolina, Crumpler left his church, the Methodist Episcopal, South, to found the Holiness Church at Goldsboro in 1899. Inspiring demonstrative worship* and deep loyalty, Crumpler was repeatedly elected convention president. In 1907, despite his disapproval, almost the entire ministerium was swept into the Pentecostal* camp under G. B. Cashwell.* Crumpler then withdrew and joined the Methodist Church.*

Crusade Evangelism. *See* MASS EVANGELISM.

Culbertson, William (1905-1971). Bishop of the Reformed Episcopal Church* and president of Moody Bible Institute.* Culbertson's reputation as a preacher* and his long-standing interest in Christian education* led to his serving as president of Moody (1948-1970), where he managed to preserve the idea of the Bible institute* as a viable evangelical* educational entity. Culbertson repudiated liberal* theology and called for strict separation* from liberal church bodies.

Cullis, Charles (1833-1892). Physician and faith healer.* A devout Episcopalian* inspired by Wesleyan/Holiness* spirituality,* Cullis established a home to care for "consumptives." Cullis became famous for his efforts in "Faith Cures Through Prayer" and was influential in the larger Keswick,* Wesleyan/Holiness and Pentecostal* movements around the world.

Cult. Although widely used by scholars, journalists and the public, the term *cult* lacks precise definition. Social and behavioral scientists define cults as religious groups lying outside the American religious mainstream, incorporating beliefs and practices in tension with the dominant culture. Evangelical* Christians tend to define cults as religious groups which deviate significantly from orthodox* Christianity.

See also SECT.

Cumberland Presbyterian Church. Presbyterian* denomination* with churches predominantly in the South and West. An outgrowth of the frontier revivals* of 1800 in Kentucky, this denomination originated in 1810 in Tennessee following controversy with the Presbyterian Church in the U.S.A.* over the Westminster Confession.* Reunion with the Presbyterian Church in the U.S.A. was approved in 1906, although a continuing Cumberland Presbyterian Church was perpetuated by a sizable minority which feared that doctrinal harmony between the two churches had not been achieved.

Cumberland Presbyterian Church in America. Presbyterian* denomination* of predominantly African-American membership. Initially known as the Colored Cumberland Presbyterian Church, the denomination emerged from the Cumberland Presbyterian Church* during Reconstruction. In 1869 African-American ministers, desiring autonomy, petitioned the Cumberland Presbyterian General Assembly to allow the formation of "presbyteries of colored ministers." By 1895 the church claimed about fifteen thousand members in twenty-two presbyteries. The denomination has gone through three name

changes: Colored Cumberland Presbyterian Church in the U.S.A. and Liberia, Africa (1949), Second Cumberland Presbyterian Church (1960) and the present title of Cumberland Presbyterian Church in America (1992). It now consists of 148 congregations in four synods and sixteen presbyteries.

Cummins, George David (1822-1876). Founding bishop of the Reformed Episcopal Church.* An Episcopalian, Cummins became assistant bishop of Kentucky in 1866. As bishop, Cummins's principal inspiration was the catholic evangelicalism* of William A. Muhlenberg,* which brought him into opposition to high church* ideas concerning the exclusive validity of Episcopal ordinations. A dispute in 1873 led to his "Call to Organize" a new Episcopal church.

Curate. Orignally, any clergyman or ordained* person. In English practice, the term *curate* has been reserved for the assistant to a rector. Most Protestant* groups do not use the term.

Curse of Ham. An argument used to justify slavery, based on Noah's curse of Canaan, the son of Ham. In America the use of the story can be traced to the beginning of the eighteenth century. After 1830 the story became one of the most popular defenses of slavery, being used by clergy of many different denominations.* Writers in the antebellum South especially used the philological argument that Japheth's name could mean "whiteness" and Ham's name "dark," "hot" and "black."

Cursillo. A twentieth-century Catholic* movement emphasizing spiritual growth within small groups. Individuals become involved in the movement by participating in an intense, same-sex weekend experience which includes lectures delivered by trained leaders and punctuated by opportunities for individual and group response. The weekends result in the formation of small groups of *cursillistas* who meet weekly to build upon the spiritual renewal and sense of community achieved through the initial Cursillo.

Cushing, Richard James (1895-1970). Cardinal* of Boston. Possessed of a gruff voice, Archbishop Cushing was habitually informal and breezy and always identified with his working-class Irish origins. He was regarded as an outstanding administrator and raised millions of dollars for numerous charities. His special interests were missions and retarded children, but his gifts—often unpublicized—went to a wide variety of causes.

A long-time friend of the Kennedy family, Cushing politically appeared to be a bundle of contradictions. His apparent inconsistencies stemmed from the fact that he seldom held a systematically thought-out position but usually reacted to events and to people on the basis of intuition and feeling, considering himself a man of the heart rather than of the head.

Cutler, Timothy (1684-1765). Anglican* rector in Boston. Originally a Congregational* pastor in Connecticut, Cutler defected to Anglicanism* in 1722, a move that paved the way for Anglican growth in Puritanism's* back yard.

In Boston Cutler established himself as a formidable opponent of Congregationalism and as the city's leading spokesperson for Anglican prerogatives. With his theology* giving him little sympathy for the religious enthusiasm of the Great Awakening,* he long combated what he called the "madness" of revivalism.*

Cuyler, Theodore Ledyard (1822-1909). Presbyterian* minister and prolific author. From 1860 to 1890 Cuyler was pastor of the Lafayette Avenue Presbyterian Church in Brooklyn. His sermons were forceful and evangelical* in tone, and he became one of New York City's most popular preachers.

D

Dabbs, James McBride (1896-1970). Southern Presbyterian* civil rights* advocate. A fervent Christian, Dabbs wrote tirelessly about the South, bringing faith to bear on issues import to the region. Theologically, Dabbs reiterated classic themes of Reformed tradition.*

Dabney, Robert Lewis (1820-1898). Southern Presbyterian* theologian and educator. Dabney was professor of church history and polity* (1859-1883) at Union Seminary (then located at Hampden-Sydney College). A respected churchman, Dabney was elected moderator of the Southern Presbyterian General Assembly* in 1870.

A loyal Southerner to the end, Dabney never wavered from his belief that the cause of the South was right and would eventually be vindicated. Embittered by Reconstruction policies, he vigorously opposed reunion with the Northern Presbyterians.

A man of wide learning and a teacher of great intensity and clarity, Dabney was recognized as the leading Southern Presbyterian theologian after the Civil War.* His theology was the moderate but consistent Calvinism* of the Westminster Confession* and catechisms and was comparable to other nineteenth-century Old School* Presbyterian theologians such as Charles Hodge* of Princeton.* Because of his willingness to wrestle with difficult theological issues and make his own critical observations, some have regarded Dabney's systematic theology as more profound than that of Charles Hodge.

Dagg, John Leadley (1794-1884). Baptist* minister, educator and theologian. After serving as pastor in Virginia and Philadelphia, Dagg gave himself to teaching, educational administration and writing. From 1844 to 1854 he was president of Mercer University in Penfield, Georgia.

Dagg's aim overall was to assist in the prep-

aration of ministers. His theology may be described as essentially biblical and moderately Calvinistic,* and it earned him the reputation as the pioneer Baptist theologian in America.

Daggett, Naphtali (1727-1780). Congregational* minister, professor of divinity* at Yale College.* In 1756 Yale president Thomas Clap,* wanting to move Yale in a New Light* direction, named Daggett the college's first professor and pastor to students. Though a dull teacher and preacher, Daggett established the college on a firm institutional footing.

Dake, Vivian Adelbert (1854-1892). Free Methodist* pastor and founder of the Pentecost Bands. In 1882 in the Midwest Dake organized the first Pentecost Band, a team of youth devoted to short-term evangelistic and missionary endeavors. The bands were active in evangelism* and social reform in the U.S. and abroad.

Dallas Theological Seminary. A professional graduate-level institution, training men and women for ministry.* Opening in 1924, this institution was the fulfillment of the aspirations of popular Bible teacher Lewis Sperry Chafer,* who in effect institutionalized the theological distinctives of the Bible conference movement.*

By the late 1930s the seminary began to emerge into a place of increasing prominence in the evangelical* community. Because of shifting theological currents and alignments in the 1930s and 1940s, the school has become a major training center for the nondenominational, or separatist,* evangelical movement in America. Presidents appointed after Chafer's passing have been John F. Walvoord (1952), Donald K. Campbell (1986) and Charles Swindoll (1994).

Damien, Father (Joseph de Veuster) (1840-1889). Missionary-priest to the lepers of Molokai,

Hawaii. Joseph served in Hawaii as priest and then as a worker among lepers, caring spiritually and physically for Catholics and non-Catholics. In 1884 he himself was declared a leper.

Dana, James Dwight (1813-1895). Geologist and mineralogist. As a young scientist, Dana—in his day America's foremost geologist—underwent a conversion* to evangelical* faith.

By 1883 he had, with qualifications, accepted Darwin's principle of natural selection. Humans, he argued, were derived from a lower species, albeit by a special work of divine creativity. Dana thus was an influential force in advocating a theistic Darwinism among evangelicals of the late nineteenth century.

See also DARWINIAN EVOLUTION AND THE AMERICAN CHURCHES.

Danforth, Samuel (1626-1674). Puritan* minister. Danforth was a fellow of Harvard and accomplished preacher. His election sermon of May 11, 1670, "A Brief Recognition of New England's Errand into the Wilderness," has provided historians of New England Puritanism with a useful metaphor by which to describe the Puritan mission in America.

Darby, John Nelson (1800-1882). British promoter of ecclesiastical separatism* and dispensational* premillennialism.* After a short ministry in the Church of England,* a disenchanted Darby left the church and joined a gathering of people meeting privately in Dublin for worship,* Bible instruction, and the breaking of bread. In 1831 he joined others of like sympathies in Plymouth, England, where they spawned a remarkably influential movement known as the Plymouth Brethren.*

Darby called for ecclesiastical separation from a corrupt, organized Christianity. He also taught a unique view of prophetic events that would come to be known as dispensationalism.

Darby traveled extensively, spreading his ideas throughout the expanding Brethren movement. He deeply influenced the Bible conference movement* in America after 1870 and the rise of the separatist fundamentalist* movement in America early in the twentieth century.

Dartmouth College. An American college with roots in the Great Awakening.* Originally sponsored in Connecticut by pro-revival Congrega-

tionalists,* and developing from Moor's Indian Charity School begun by Eleazar Wheelock* in 1754, the institution relocated to Hanover, New Hampshire, where the new state charter named it Dartmouth College.

The important U.S. Supreme Court case of *Dartmouth College v. Woodward* (1818) clarified the distinction between private and public institutions, carefully protecting the former from state control.

Darwinian Evolution and the American Churches. In defense of evolution, Darwin presented a wealth of evidence to support a possible mechanism—the concept of natural selection. Darwin's controversial theory stirred passionate debate, but not along clearly drawn lines between scientists and theologians. During the decades before 1920 the evangelical movement showed a surprising diversity of response to Darwin's theory of evolution. In the 1920s, however, the lines quickly hardened in a shift from moderation to militancy.

Conservative anti-Darwinians (e.g., zoologist Louis Agassiz* and theologian Charles Hodge*) relied on the observed design in nature as a crucial argument for the existence of God. Conservative Darwinians (e.g., botanist Asa Gray* and theologian Benjamin Warfield*) staked out a "middle ground" with confidence in both biblical theology* and evolutionary theory. Liberal Darwinians interpreted evolution in the light of an Enlightenment* progressivism that went far beyond the competence of science and the content of biblical teaching.

See also CREATION SCIENCE.

Davenport, James (1716-1757). Presbyterian* minister and revivalist.* Great-grandson of the founding divine of New Haven, John Davenport,* James graduated from Yale College* in 1732, an acknowledged prodigy who was prey to emotional instability. Deeply affected by the preaching of George Whitefield* in 1740 and the outbreak of the Great Awakening,* he abandoned his congregation to become an itinerant* revivalist. As a revivalist, his tendencies toward outlandish behavior and his refusal to cooperate with settled ministers raised serious opposition in his path. Though unrepresentative of the Great Awakening, his activities were seized upon by critics as examples of the logical conclusion of revivalist principles.

Davenport, John (1597-1670). Congregational* minister. In 1637 Davenport assisted in organizing a company of 250 settlers bound for New England. Arriving in Boston in the midst of the antinomian* crisis, he participated in the examination of Anne Hutchinson.*

In April 1638, Davenport and the settlers moved to Quinnipiac on Long Island Sound and organized the colony of New Haven. Elected pastor of the New Haven church, his ministry soon became noted for its strict Congregational practices. He was an early advocate of premillennial* eschatology.*

See also DAVENPORT, JAMES.

Davies, Samuel (1723-1761). Presbyterian* minister and educator. An organizer of dissenting congregations in Virginia, Davies gained the reputation of fomenting a Southern Great Awakening* during colonial times.

A model preacher and intellectual leader, Davies has been remembered for his skill as an orator, his academic leadership at the College of New Jersey (later named Princeton University*) and as a champion of religious freedom* who helped break the grip of established* religion in the colonies.

Davis, John Merle (1875-1960). Missionary and social researcher. Davis served the YMCA* in Japan and later, working with the International Missionary Council, called attention to the importance of social and economic environments. Studies of Latin America, the Caribbean and Africa broadened his impact.

Dawson, John William (1820-1899). Canadian geologist and principal of McGill University. Dawson was principal of McGill from 1855 to 1893, rescuing it from the brink of ruin and establishing it as a world-class institution. Dawson was Canada's best-known scientist of the nineteenth century. He was also its most outspoken critic of Darwinism,* being a proponent of the "day-age theory" of creation.

Dawson, J(oseph) M(artin) (1879-1973). Southern Baptist* minister, denominational* executive and advocate of civil liberty. Dawson was best known as an outspoken representative of the Baptist position on religious freedom, peace, social justice and civil liberty. He was particularly concerned that Baptists know and understand their heritage as defenders of religious liberty.

Day, Dorothy May (1897-1980). Journalist, social activist and cofounder of the Catholic Worker* movement. Leaving her earlier socialism and radicalism, Day converted to Catholicism* in 1927. With Peter Maurin,* a like-minded street philosopher, she started the Catholic Worker. Under Day's leadership, the Catholic Worker practiced a radical social activism, even in the face of an FBI investigation of the group for possible subversiveness.

Much of Day's influence came from her writing. Her best-known work, *The Long Loneliness* (1952), a classic of conversion literature, has been reprinted in several foreign-language editions.

Day Schools. *See* SCHOOLS, PROTESTANT CHRISTIAN DAY.

Deacon. The early church appointed official "deacons" (from Greek *diakonos,* "servant") to look after the basic needs of the community. During the fourth and fifth centuries, deacons became influential administrators of large, wealthy churches; in the Middle Ages the diaconate declined in importance.

Since the Reformation, only Catholics,* Anglicans,* Swedish Lutherans* and the Orthodox* have deacons who are ordained by a bishop through the laying on of hands.* In the Reformed tradition,* deacons are ordained by the pastor and the elders* of the local congregation.

Deaconess Movement. A Protestant* movement of single women who gave themselves to Christian service, ministering particularly to the sick, the dying and the disadvantaged. The precedent for this ministry is found in the early church, where women such as Phoebe (see Rom 16:1-2) carried out a ministry of service *(diakonia)*.

The deaconess movement in America received its impetus in the mid-1800s from the European Lutheran* deaconess movement, and in 1883 the movement began in the Methodist Episcopal Church. Deaconesses frequently ministered in urban settings among the poor immigrants* who were then flooding U.S. cities. In their efforts to apply the message of the gospel creatively to physical and spiritual needs of the cities, the deaconess movement reflected many of the same concerns of the Social Gospel movement.* While the movement prospered from the 1880s until the early years of the twentieth century, by the 1920s it had declined.

Death of God Movement. During the 1960s, several American theologians used the phrase *Death of God* to describe what they felt to be an important event in modern Western culture, which they saw as secularized and having lost any sense of the sacred. Five authors are frequently identified as the primary figures in the Death of God movement, each one meaning something quite different by the phrase: Gabriel Vahanian (1927-), Paul M. van Buren (1924-), William Hamilton (1924-), Thomas J. J. Altizer (1927-) and Richard L. Rubenstein (1924-).

The Death of God movement was a sensational event while it lasted, attracting the attention of the popular press and making the cover story of *Time* magazine. But it was not of enduring significance except as a reminder of the poverty of twentieth-century theologies that had lost their roots in Christian theism.*

Declension. A theory describing changes leading to the breakdown of Puritanism* in seventeenth-century New England. By the end of the seventeenth century, many pastors indeed saw increased moral laxity and lowered standards for participation in the church (*see* Half-Way Covenant) as evidence of a spiritual decline.

Dederer, Anna (1902-1976). Missionary to Micronesia. Serving first under the German Liebenzell Mission and, beginning in 1948, under the American Board of Commissioners for Foreign Missions,* Dederer focused on work with youth and women.

Dedham Decision (1820). A court decision effectively ending the established* Congregationalism*—or "Church of the Standing Order"—of Massachusetts. In a suit involving the First Church of Dedham, a Unitarian*-dominated Massachusetts Court ruled in 1820 that title to all Standing Order property was vested in parishes, not in communicant membership. As a result of this decision, over one hundred parishes became Unitarian.

See also ESTABLISHED CHURCHES IN NEW ENGLAND.

DeHaan, M(artin) R(alph) (1891-1965). Author and radio preacher. Trained as a medical

doctor, DeHaan established one of the most successful national radio and Bible literature ministries, the Radio Bible Class. He also was a powerful and persuasive Bible conference* speaker and engaging pulpiteer.

Deism. An Enlightenment* religion particularly influential during the late eighteenth century. Deism became popular among some upper-class Americans at the time of the American Revolution. It is essentially a rationalistic religion, which assumes that each person naturally possesses the ability to know the universe's Deity through reason and that the creator of the universe was a rational architect who revealed himself in nature and through reason.

In the post-Revolutionary War era, the most forceful deist was Thomas Jefferson,* who wed Enlightenment religion with the ideals of American democracy. By 1810 deism had lost its momentum in its bid for becoming a popular religious option.

DeKoven, James (1831-1879). Episcopal* educator and ritualist leader. Ordained priest in 1855, DeKoven long served as warden of Racine (Wis.) College. An advanced high churchman* and brilliant orator, he was the acknowledged leader of the ritualist movement in the Episcopal Church after the Civil War.* A man of vast learning and holiness of character, he is today commemorated in the calendar of the Episcopal Church.

Demythologization. A method of interpreting the New Testament. Advocated by Rudolf Bultmann* in his essay "New Testament and Mythology" (1941), demythologization represents an effort to communicate the gospel of Jesus Christ to modern men and women by speaking of God and the world apart from reference to "myths" such as angels and a heavenly redeemer.

Denomination. An association or fellowship of congregations within a religion that have the same beliefs or creed,* engage in similar practices and cooperate with each other to develop and maintain shared enterprises. Similar religious groups like the many Baptist* bodies in the U.S. constitute a "denominational family."

Religious bodies that accommodate themselves to the power structures and values of society came to be labeled by the term *denomination.* In contrast, sects are in tension with society, uphold differences from it, oppose it or separate themselves from it. The types overlap and merge into each other, for most denominations began as sects. Cults also overlap; they are either newly created religious innovations, imports from other cultural settings or groups formed by syncretistic merger and adaptation of elements from more than one religious tradition. The words *sect* and *cult* have negative connotations, so the more neutral label of *new religious movement* is now often used. All are included in American denominationalism.

Scholars like H. Richard Niebuhr,* who value the organizational unity of Christians, interpret the proliferation of Christian denominations as an indication of moral failure, hypocrisy and scandal. The ecumenical movement* has tried to vanquish the struggles for power that divide and weaken Christianity, to achieve cooperation among denominations so that they will be more influential in society and even to build structural unity. Others have tried to regain the unity that presumably existed in the New Testament church by drawing people out of denominations into the "true church." Their efforts to unite all Christians and defeat denominationalism by applying such labels as *Brethren,* *Church of God,* *Disciples of Christ,* *Restoration movement* or *Bible Church* have instead been equivalent to founding additional new denominations.

Alongside the ecumenical movement are other tendencies toward Christian unity.* Cooperative evangelistic,* educational, social-action and service ministries are bringing evangelicals* together with fundamentalists,* charismatics* and other Christians. This "spiritual ecumenism" often is mediated through parachurch* organizations supported by individual Christians outside of denominational channels.

American Christianity shows greater vitality than that of most other nations. Religious diversity and competition have contributed to broader opportunities to satisfy people's spiritual needs and stronger efforts to recruit them for church membership and Christian ministries. Denominationalism does not necessarily violate the spiritual unity of the body of Christ. It is consistent with the competitive free enterprise system, the voluntary* principle of individual freedom and other liberties deeply engrained in American society.

See also MAINLINE DENOMINATIONS; PLURALISM, RELIGIOUS; VOLUNTARYISM.

Deposit of Faith. Roman Catholics* understand the deposit of faith to be the entirety of those truths communicated explicitly or implicitly to the apostles by Jesus Christ, in both his earthly life and his risen glory. The church guards this deposit as a sacred trust and may not add to or subtract from it.

The concept of the deposit of faith, however, is closely related in any given age to the opinions held concerning the development of doctrine and the role and status of religious authority.* The notion of the deposit as a closed and self-contained reality impervious to historical adaptation has been challenged since the nineteenth century by several Roman Catholic thinkers. Many of these have maintained that the church guards this deposit most effectively when it demonstrates its salvific relevance to every age and mentality.

See also DEVELOPMENT OF DOCTRINE.

Development of Doctrine. The problem of how Christian doctrine develops over time has primarily been the concern of Catholic theologians. Along with the doctrine of papal infallibility* has been the obvious fact that articles of faith have emerged in the dogmatic tradition which were not explicit in the primitive deposit of faith.* Throughout much of church history, however, Christian doctrine was believed to be a precise formulation of what the church had always explicitly and consciously believed.

In the late nineteenth century the issue became particularly acute as a developmentalist worldview (spread by Hegel, Darwin, Marx and others) took hold in Western thought and challenged traditional understandings of Christian doctrine.

Christian theologians responded in various ways. Some, labeled by Karl Rahner* as dogmatic positivists, continued to hold an exclusively propositional concept of faith and understood development as a process in which revealed truth logically unfolds.

In contrast, transformists, influenced by German Pietists, argued that unchangeable doctrine is not the essence of Christianity. Revelation and faith are experiential, with revelation always at work in human experience, gradually creating, purifying and clarifying a consciousness of communion with God in the individual and in humanity. The continuity between contemporary faith and apostolic faith is not in doctrine but in inspiration.

A third option, the theological theory of development, argues that God gives to his church not only a doctrine of salvation* expressed in human words but also a light by which it enters into living communion with its Savior. This inner light does not reveal anything independent from God's publicly and prophetically revealed truth, but God continues to unveil truth through a historically conditioned process guided by the light of the Spirit.

Dialectical Theology. A European theological movement during the 1920s, centering on Karl Barth* and Emil Brunner,* known also as crisis theology. For Barth, God is revealed as reconciler in Christ, in whom "two worlds meet and go apart, two planes intersect, the one known and the other unknown." As Christ faces humanity, it must turn either toward or away from the Word of God. Only God-given faith can hold together both poles of the dialectic in the divine/human dialogue.

Dickinson, Emily Elizabeth (1830-1886). American poet. A shy recluse from Amherst, Massachusetts, Dickinson spent most of her life in her home and garden, yet the lines that she penned and stored there have made her one of America's foremost poets. Dickinson published only seven poems during her lifetime, but after her death, over 1,500 of her poems were found, which reveal her true poetic genius. Her intense interest in death, immortality and nature led to a rather pronounced treatment of religious themes.

Dickinson, Jonathan (1688-1747). Presbyterian* minister and theologian. A strong Calvinist,* Dickinson was nonetheless opposed to the rigid confessionalism* of Scotch*-Irish Presbyterians who wished to impose the Westminster Confession* and Catechism as a test of orthodoxy.* He led the antisubscriptionists (see Subscription Controversy), arguing for the strict examination of the ministerial candidate's religious experience.*

Leading colonial Presbyterians through several controversies, Dickinson defended Calvinism against Arminianism* and deism,* presbyterianism against episcopacy,* and Nonconformity against Anglicanism.* He was arguably the most distinguished Presbyterian minister in the colonial period, with an international reputation as a theologian

second only to that of Jonathan Edwards.*

Diehl, Nona May (1894-1981). United Lutheran* missionary leader. As secretary of the Women's Missionary Society of the United Lutheran Church, Diehl brought new prominence to the role of women in the missionary cause.

Dietz, Peter Ernest (1878-1947). Labor priest. Although he began and ended his priestly career in parish ministry,* between 1909 and 1922 Dietz was involved in attempts to develop the social ministry of the American Catholic Church.* Thus, he devoted his energies to educating American Catholics in the social teachings of the church and to establishing ties with the American labor movement. He formed the Militia of Christ for Social Service (1910) and, to train Catholic social workers, the American Academy of Christian Democracy (1915).

Diocesan Pastoral Council. An advisory group of clergy and laity to aid the bishop in fulfilling his ministerial responsibilities. Such a group functions in the Roman Catholic Church,* the Greek Orthodox* Archdiocese* of North and South America, and the Protestant Episcopal Church.*

Diocese. A geographic area over which a bishop has jurisdiction. For the Episcopal,* Roman Catholic* and Orthodox* churches, the diocese, not the congregation, is the primary ecclesiastical unit.

Disciple, Discipleship. In Christian usage a disciple is a follower of Jesus Christ. *Discipleship* identifies the lifestyle or process whereby individuals or groups live out their understanding of what it means to be a disciple. Dietrich Bonhoeffer's* classic *Cost of Discipleship* (1937) has helped to shape the current usage of these terms.

Discipleship Movement. *See* SHEPHERDING MOVEMENT.

Discipline, Church. The church's efforts to rebuke, correct and reform its membership through the use of censures that range from admonition through suspension from the Lord's Supper* (and from office) to excommunication* or expulsion from the fellowship of the church. The goal of church discipline has ordinarily been threefold:

the restoration of the sinner, the deterrence of other church members from such offenses and the honor of Christ as head of the church.

The Puritans* brought to America a concern for discipline aimed at producing a purer visible church that would approach conformity with the invisible church. In contrast, churches in twentieth-century urban American society have tended to neglect church discipline except for the most obvious cases—usually of sexual sin.*

Dispensationalism. A hermeneutical approach to the Bible that became a movement within American evangelicalism* after the 1870s. At the heart of dispensationalism is the dividing of all time into separate dispensations, which are seen as different stages in God's progressive revelation. Though many Christians have used historical periodization, John Nelson Darby* (1800-1882) was the first to use it to create a full-blown system of interpretation. Especially controversial was his doctrine of the pretribulation rapture of the church, which split his own Plymouth Brethren.

Darby's dispensationalism came to America in the 1870s. Dispensational views spread into conservative evangelicalism through the Bible and prophetic conference* movement, the Bible institutes* and, most important, the Scofield Reference Bible* (1909, revised 1967). By the 1920s it had eclipsed other kinds of premillennialism* and became closely identified with the fundamentalist* movement. In the U.S. today dispensationalism is the most common view of eschatology* taught in fundamentalist schools and churches.

See also APOCALYPTICISM.

District. A subunit of the Methodist* annual conference.* Districts are organized to carry out the programs of the conference and the general church, to promote good will in the local area and to provide for initial screening of candidates for ordination.* Their chief spiritual overseer is the district superintendent.

Divine, Major J. ("Father Divine") (c. 1880-1965). African-American cult* leader. In 1919 Divine began a ministry to the poor on Long Island. This became a movement of perhaps two million followers, known for its social services, its strict moral code, claims of healings, emphasis on racial equality and fierce loyalty to Father Divine, who proclaimed himself God.

Divine Office. *See* LITURGY OF THE HOURS.

Divinity. A term frequently used prior to the twentieth century to refer to the study of theology, or the "science of divine things." It could also refer to God himself and to the quality of being divine. In the early nineteenth century, Protestant* seminaries were frequently called divinity schools.

Divino Afflante Spiritu. Encyclical* promoting biblical studies.* Issued by Pope Pius XII* in 1943, it commemorated the fiftieth anniversary of Pope Leo XIII's* encyclical *Providentissimus Deus* (1893). Pius wished to encourage a renewed study of Scripture in the midst of the chaos of World War II,* as well as point to the progress in modern biblical scholarship which might advance Catholic* understanding of God's purposes as revealed in Scripture. The result was a renaissance of Catholic biblical scholarship in which Catholic scholars began to share the same critical concerns and tools of other Western biblical scholars.

Divorce. *See* MARRIAGE AND DIVORCE.

Dixon, A(mzi) C(larence) (1854-1925). Baptist* pastor and evangelist. As well as serving several pastorates in the South, Dixon became a popular Bible conference* speaker in America and England. His most prestigious pulpit was Spurgeon's Tabernacle in London, where he pastored from 1911 until 1919. Dixon then spent several years in an itinerant evangelistic and Bible teaching ministry across the U.S.

Dixon was a staunch fundamentalist* and premillennialist,* an opponent of Darwinism* and biblical criticism.* He served as the first executive secretary and editor of *The Fundamentals.**

Doak, Samuel (1749-1830). First Presbyterian* minister to settle in Tennessee. A man of sober and even grave disposition, Doak was nevertheless irenic, and the early success of Presbyterianism in east Tennessee is largely attributable to his skill and indefatigable labors. In the New Divinity* controversies, he was a vigorous leader of the orthodox* party.

Doane, George Washington (1799-1859). Episcopal* bishop of New Jersey. While bishop, Doane served as rector of St. Mary's, in Burlington, New Jersey, and was a leading promoter of the missionary movement and a founder of Episcopal schools. He founded St. Mary's Hall for girls in 1837 and Burlington College for men in 1846. Doane was a high churchman* and supported the Tractarian movement.*

Doane, William Howard (1832-1915). Layman and hymn* composer. Doane was a wealthy Cincinnati business executive and manufacturer. A civic leader and philanthropist, he was also an active Christian layperson. Doane had a gift of song, which he used as a song leader and soloist for YMCA* evangelist Thane Miller. Doane composed many favorite gospel hymns, such as "To God Be the Glory," "Tell Me the Old, Old Story," "Rescue the Perishing," "Near the Cross," "More Like Jesus" and "Take the Name of Jesus with You." His daughter Marguerite T. Doane (1868-1954) was a prominent supporter and benefactor of Northern Baptist* overseas missions and the principal founder of Houses of Fellowship, a missionary furlough residence center in Ventnor, New Jersey.

Dock, Christopher (c. 1690-1771). Colonial Mennonite* schoolmaster. Dock is best known for his *Schulordnung* ("School-Management"), written in 1750, the earliest known essay in North America on the theme of pedagogy. Other articles reveal the customs of the colonial Pennsylvania Germans.

Dogma, Dogmatic Theology. The truths and systematic presentation of those truths which all Christian believers are obligated to accept, particularly within a Roman Catholic* context. Dogma refers to the points of doctrine which are essential to Christianity. Apart from believing in them, one cannot be Christian; thus their denial constitutes heresy.* In Roman Catholic theology, what constitutes dogma is defined by the teaching office of the church primarily through ecumenical councils* and the pope.

See also CONGREGATION FOR THE DOCTRINE OF THE FAITH; MAGISTERIUM; SYSTEMATIC THEOLOGY.

Dominicans. Catholic* mendicant religious order.* In 1805 four Dominican friars set out from Maryland to establish in frontier Kentucky a new American province of their worldwide Order of Preachers. Near Bardstown, they established their church, college and preaching center. As the pop-

ulation grew and the numbers of Dominicans increased, they founded parishes and colleges in the heartland of the nation from the Canadian border at Mackinac to Louisiana, and eastward to Washington, D.C., and New York. The order has continued to expand in numbers and ministries throughout the nation and to peoples of Asia, Africa and South America.

Foundations of Dominican Sisters began in the U.S. soon after that of the friars. In 1822 nine young women, experiencing the spiritual needs of their people in Kentucky, formed there the first American community of Dominican Sisters. There are now forty congregations of Dominican Sisters serving in the U.S., each having many branch communities.

Dominion Theology. *See* RECONSTRUCTIONISM, CHRISTIAN.

Dongan, Thomas (1634-1715). Catholic* governor of colonial New York. Appointed governor of New York in 1682, Dongan convened an assembly which adopted a "Charter of Liberties" which included religious toleration* for Christians. Dongan worked to establish the boundaries of New York against the threat from the French and their Iroquois allies.

Dooyeweerd, Herman (1894-1977). Dutch Calvinist* philosopher. Dooyeweerd developed the core ideas of Dutch neo-Calvinism into a wide-ranging and tightly argued system known as the philosophy of the cosmonomic idea. His influence in North America rose with the post-1945 Dutch immigration to Canada and the subsequent building there of academic and other institutions bearing his inspiration.

Dorchester, Daniel, Jr. (1827-1907). Methodist* minister in New England. Dorchester served as a minister in the Providence Conference of the Methodist Episcopal Church until 1855, when he was elected state senator from Mystic, Connecticut. In 1882 he was elected to the Massachusetts legislature and in 1899 was appointed commissioner of Indian education by President Harrison.

Doremus, Sarah (1802-1877). Founder and first president of the Woman's Union Missionary Society of America. Responding to the need for single women to minister* to women overseas, Doremus organized what was to become the first of more than forty female missionary agencies founded between 1860 and 1900.

Dorsey, Thomas A. (1899-1993). Father of gospel music. Dorsey's father was a Baptist* revivalist* preacher. In 1918 Dorsey moved to Chicago, where he worked and attended the Chicago Musical College. After some time as a successful blues musician and composer, Dorsey began to draw on black church music, combining it with elements of blues and jazz and creating a new form of church music he called "gospel music." In the late 1920s Dorsey, with Sallie Martin, formed the first "gospel choir" at Ebenezer Baptist Church in Chicago, and in 1932 he founded the National Convention of Gospel Choirs and Choruses, associated with the National Baptist Convention, U.S.A., Inc.* Famous Dorsey gospel music includes "Precious Lord, Take My Hand" and "I Will Put My Trust in the Lord." He was ordained* in 1964 and in 1979 became the first African-American elected to the Nashville Song Writers Association International Hall of Fame.

Dougherty, Dennis J. (1865-1951). Catholic* cardinal. In 1903 Dougherty became the first American bishop to the Philippines. Later he was installed as bishop of Buffalo, New York, and then in 1918 was the first native son to become archbishop of Philadelphia. Three years later he was the fifth American named a cardinal. Calling himself "God's bricklayer," he vastly extended the facilities of his archdiocese, where, among other institutions, he created a unique system of free high-school education for all Catholic teens.

Douglas, Thomas Clement "Tommy" (1904-1986). Baptist* minister and political figure. Douglas was for two full terms a member of Parliament before resigning to become the leader of the Co-operative Commonwealth Federation (CCF) party in Saskatchewan in 1944. His party won the election, becoming the first socialist government to be elected in North America. Douglas was the leader of this CCF government for seventeen years before becoming the leader of the federal New Democratic Party.

Douglass, Frederick Augustus Washington Bailey (1817?-1895). Former slave, orator, journalist and abolitionist.* After escaping to freedom in 1838, Douglass became an outspoken advocate for the abolition* of slavery and for temperance*

and women's rights. Douglass lectured widely in America and abroad, edited four newspapers, and wrote three autobiographies in support of such causes.

Doukhobors (Dukhobors). A mystical, communal Christian sect* with Russian origins. This word, derived from one meaning "spirit wrestlers," was adopted by a mystical, pacifist, communal sect of Christians appearing around 1740 in the Dnieper River region of the Ukraine. Dissenting from the Orthodox Church,* they taught that the "inner light" or voice of God, what they also identified as the "Christ Spirit," inhabited all things and persons. Hence, they denied the authority* of the church and took an anarchist position toward government.

Fleeing sporadic persecution in Russia, eight thousand Doukhobors immigrated to Canada in 1898. Known as the Christian Community of Universal Brotherhood, most settled ultimately in British Columbia. In 1987 there were an estimated thirty-four thousand Doukhobor descendants, half of whom continue to speak Russian and remain religiously active.

Dow, Lorenzo (1777-1834). Itinerant* evangelist. Working only briefly under Methodist appointment, Dow traveled ceaselessly throughout the U.S., Canada and Great Britain. His peculiarities, prescience, directness and powerful preaching regularly attracted large crowds.

Dowie, John Alexander (1847-1907). Healing* evangelist and founder of religious colony. In Australia and then in Chicago, Dowie made divine healing a focus of his ministry. In 1896 he founded the Christian Catholic Church in Chicago and in 1900 began "Zion City," a utopian colony under his theocratic leadership. Dowie's ministry ended ignominiously with the colony's financial failure and a paralyzing stroke in 1905.

Doxology. Any ascription of praise offered to God in Christian worship.* More specifically, for American Protestants* "the Doxology" refers to the response "Praise God from Whom All Blessings Flow." Written by Thomas Ken around 1700, it is often sung to the tune "Old Hundredth" as the public offering is presented to God.

Dreher, Godfrey (1789-1875). Lutheran* minister, evangelist. A patriarch of South Carolina Lutheranism and an ardent evangelist, Dreher was a prime mover of the South Carolina Synod (1824). Dreher's confessionalism* caused him to oppose revivalism,* the General Synod* and synodical connectionalism. Following the "Dreher controversy" (1834-1837)—a conflict involving the synod and Dreher's neighboring pastors—Dreher became an independent Lutheran minister.

Drexel, Katharine (1858-1955). Heiress, founder of the Sisters of the Blessed Sacrament for Indians and Colored People. In 1887 Drexel asked Pope Leo XIII* for missionaries to Native Americans,* but he challenged her to become one herself. As a result, she determined to found a new order for that purpose. In 1891 she professed vows as a Sister of the Blessed Sacrament for Indians and Colored People. As long-time superior general of the order, Drexel established numerous missions and schools for African-Americans and Native Americans. The cause for her canonization* was introduced in 1964, and she was beatified* in 1988.

DuBose, William Porcher (1836-1918). Episcopal* theologian. DuBose served at the University of the South (Sewanee, Tenn.), where he was chaplain (from 1871) and dean of the School of Theology (1894-1908).

DuBose's theological position developed out of early evangelical* convictions into a liberal Catholicism,* stressing the incarnation and evolution.* While Christ was the particular incarnation of God, all of humanity shares in a generic incarnation. Largely uninfluential in his own day, DuBose's intellectual creativity has since been recognized, and he has been called the American Episcopal Church's greatest theologian.

DuBourg, Louis William Valentine (1766-1833). Catholic* educator and bishop. Forced by the Revolution to flee from France, DuBourg made his way to the U.S. In Baltimore he began ministering to the African-American refugees from Santo Domingo. In 1796 Bishop John Carroll* appointed DuBourg president of Georgetown College. In 1812 Bishop Carroll sent DuBourg to New Orleans as the administrator of the Diocese* of Louisiana and the Floridas, where he struggled with the problems of the War of 1812.

Duchesne, Rose Philippine (1769-1852). Pioneer, missionary, founder of the Society of the Sacred Heart. In 1818 Duchesne and four other nuns left their native France for St. Louis. Mother Duchesne then spent over thirty years in the Sacred Heart schools in the St. Louis area. She insisted on high standards of education but also on rigid adherence to French custom and discipline. Her ardent nature endeared her to intimates.

Although Philippine Duchesne considered her own work a failure, in 1918 the Historical Society of Missouri named her the greatest benefactor among the state's pioneer women, and in 1940 she was beatified* by Pius XII.*

Duffy, Francis Patrick (1871-1932). Catholic* military chaplain.* Duffy, the best-known American chaplain in World War I,* wrote *Father Duffy's Story* (1919). In the presidential campaign of 1928, he helped prepare Governor Alfred E. Smith's* reply to charges that American Catholics were not loyal citizens.

Dukhobors. *See* DOUKHOBORS.

Dulles, John Foster (1888-1959). U.S. secretary of state and Presbyterian* layman. In 1917 Dulles accepted an assignment by President Woodrow Wilson* to Central America, the beginning of a career in public service that climaxed in his role as secretary of state (1952-1959) in the Eisenhower* administration.

Throughout these years, Dulles remained active in the life of his church. He worked in ecumenical* church circles as well. Beginning in 1921, he became closely associated with the Federal Council of Churches of Christ in America,* chairing their Commission on a Just and Durable Peace. The commission's influential support for the development of a United Nations organization marks an important point in American Protestantism.*

Duncan, William (1832-1918). Anglican* lay missionary in British Columbia and Alaska. In 1856 Duncan was sent by the Church Missionary Society* (CMS) to evangelize* and teach the Tsimshean Indians at Fort Simpson, British Columbia. There he built a model Victorian town and light industry for the Tsimshean that became the showpiece of all CMS missions.

Dunkers. *See* EPHRATA SOCIETY.

Dunster, Henry (1609-1659). First president

of Harvard College.* Dunster immigrated to Boston in 1640, where New England magistrates and ministers immediately elected him president of Harvard College, which had languished since opening its doors in Cambridge in 1638. Dunster established the academic curriculum, completed buildings, raised funds, secured the college charter (1650), attracted students and taught full time. A controversy over his rejection of infant baptism led to his dismissal.

Du Plessis, David (1905-1987). Leader of charismatic movement.* Known as "Mr. Pentecost," du Plessis in 1947 was the organizing secretary of what later became the World Pentecostal Conference.* In 1949 he came to the U.S. and affiliated with the Assemblies of God.* Throughout the 1960s and 1970s, du Plessis served as a catalyst for the spread of the charismatic movement, speaking at hundreds of gatherings. Unique among Pentecostals,* du Plessis was a zealous ecumenist,* once being called a "WCC gadfly" by *Christianity Today.**

Durham, William (1873-1912). Pentecostal* leader. Criticizing Holiness teaching on instantaneous sanctification* and promulgating a baptistic view of progressive sanctification, Durham was largely responsible for forging a non-Wesleyan view of sanctification as an option for Pentecostals. Today his views on the subject are best represented by the Assemblies of God.*

Dutch Reformed. *See* REFORMED CHURCH IN AMERICA.

Dutton, Anne (1692-1765). English evangelical* author. Editor and author of devotional literature, Dutton carried on an extensive correspondence with revivalist* George Whitefield,* who encouraged her writing and admired her devotion to the evangelical cause.

Dwight, Louis (1793-1854). Prison reformer.* Dwight was instrumental in replacing a system of solitary confinement and solitary labor with one of cell blocks and group labor, reforms that made U.S. prisons a model for the rest of the world.

Dwight, Timothy (1752-1817). Congregational* clergyman, theologian, poet and educator. Grandson of Jonathan Edwards,* Dwight was president of Yale College* from 1795 to 1817. Soon after he became president, Yale College experienced a series of small revivals* that were a product of the larger religious movement known as the Second Great Awakening.

Dwight erected his theology on the conviction that unbounded reason inevitably produced theological distortions. In the face of the New Divinity's* stress on divine omnipotence in evangelism,* Dwight elevated the utility of human activity in the conversion* process.

A traditionalist in theology and politics, Dwight supported Federalist attempts to protect the Connecticut Congregationalist churches from disestablishment* at the hands of Jeffersonian Baptists.* His Federalist views found their greatest expression in his literary works, which look backward to the Puritan* images of the city on a hill and the errand into the wilderness, and forward to a vision of American harmony, in which a moderate Calvinist ethos would prevail.

Dyer, Mary (c. 1605-1660). Quaker* martyr in Boston. With her husband, Mary Dyer came from England to Boston, where she became a friend of Anne Hutchinson.* Later the Dyers were excommunicated and in 1651 went back to England.

In England Mary became a Quaker. Convinced that she must testify to her new faith, in 1656 she returned to the New World to New York and traveled overland to carry God's warning to an intolerant Massachusetts. Mary was imprisoned in Boston and ultimately was hanged in Boston Common.

E

Easter. An annual celebration of the resurrection of Jesus Christ. The early church likely celebrated the event of Christ's resurrection annually as a parallel to the Jewish Passover celebration.

The celebration of Easter developed as part of a liturgical* complex including the events of Holy Week* and the preparatory period of Lent.* Churches with a strong liturgical tradition reflect in their worship the drama of Christ's movement toward the cross and the climax in the victory of the resurrection. In Western liturgical churches *Easter* also designates the eight-week season from Easter Day through Pentecost.*

For Anglo-Saxons, the celebration of Easter originally seems to have supplanted a pagan celebration of spring. With the growth of religious pluralism* and secularism* in American culture, vestiges of the original pagan celebration—such as the fertility symbols of eggs and rabbits—have tended to erode the formerly dominant Christian interpretation of the day.

Eastern Baptist Theological Seminary. American Baptist* seminary. The seminary was organized in 1925 in Philadelphia by fundamentalists* in the Northern Baptist Convention. A collegiate department, begun in 1932, was chartered in 1952 as a separate college, Eastern College, on its own campus in St. Davids, Pennsylvania. Affiliated with the American Baptist Churches in the U.S.A., the school is broadly ecumenical in spirit and practice, and is supported and attended by Baptists and non-Baptists. In 1993-1994 there were about 380 degree students.

Eastern Rite Catholics. Churches from the Eastern Orthodox* tradition that have returned to the Catholic Church,* yet retain their own liturgies,* canon law* and customs.

Sometimes referred to with the more pejorative term *Uniates,* several of these Eastern rite bodies have been led by historical developments to seek communion with the Roman Catholic Church. The Second Vatican Council's* "Decree on the Catholic Eastern Churches" significantly affirmed the place within the church of these Eastern churches.

Easton, Burton Scott (1877-1950). Episcopal* priest and New Testament scholar. After earning a Ph.D. in mathematics at the University of Pennsylvania (1901), Easton was ordained* a priest in the Episcopal Church (1905). Easton is primarily remembered for his work on Jesus and the Gospels, seen in his magnum opus, *The Gospel According to St. Luke* (1926).

Eaton, Nathaniel (c. 1609-1674). First master of Harvard College.* Appointed in 1638 at the infant Harvard College, Eaton aroused criticism for his treatment of students and was removed from his position, fined and excommunicated by the church. He eventually returned to England, where he became a vicar* and a rector.

Eaton, T(homas) T(readwell) (1845-1907). Southern Baptist* pastor and editor. Eaton succeeded J. R. Graves* as leader in the Landmark movement.* His influence as editor of the *Western Recorder* forced W. H. Whitsitt* to resign as president of Southern Baptist Seminary* in Louisville.

Ecumenical Movement. The name given in modern times to the concerted drive toward the attainment or restoration of unity among Christians and their communities throughout the world.

Americans on the World Scene. As early as 1747, Jonathan Edwards* struck the authentic missionary and eschatological note of ecumenism* in his *Humble Attempt to Promote Explicit Agreement and Visible Union of God's People.* In 1867 an American branch of the Evangelical Alliance* was formed, and the Alliance's annual Week of Prayer, together with the Octave of Prayer for Unity from the Roman Catholic* Graymoor Community under Paul Wattson (1863-1940), has helped to establish the Week of Universal Prayer for Christian Unity, now sponsored by both the World Council of Churches* (WCC) and the Roman Catholic Church.

Other American ecumenical leaders include John R. Mott,* Charles Henry Brent,* John Courtney Murray* and Lutheran* theologian George A. Lindbeck. North America has hosted two assemblies of the WCC: the second, in Evanston,* Illinois (1954), and the sixth, in Vancouver* (1983). American churches and theologians also played an important part in the preparation of the WCC Faith and Order Lima document *Baptism, Eucharist and Ministry* (1982).

The American Scene Then and Now. In 1838 the Lutheran Samuel Schmucker* proposed a confederated American Protestant* Church, and later in the century Swiss Reformed* historian and theologian Philip Schaff* argued for a federal view of Christian unity.

In 1908 the Federal Council of the Churches of Christ in America* was founded. Its theme of cooperative agency for the sake of a Social Gospel* has remained predominant in the successor organization, the National Council of Churches* (1950).

Since 1962 the most comprehensive project has been the Consultation on Church Union.* Methodist,* Presbyterian,* Episcopalian* and UCC* theologians have largely agreed on an "emerging theological consensus" (1976, revised 1980). Other discussions involve the Episcopal Church with the Evangelical Lutherans and the Southern Baptists* with Roman Catholics and Greek Orthodox.*

E Pluribus Unum? While competition has tended to recede in favor of cooperation, the generally increasing friendliness of the larger U.S. churches toward one another has still not produced union. Several impeding factors exist: (1) continuing divisions at the level of doctrine and church government,* (2) understandable doubts about the wisdom of a super church conceived on the lines of a big-business merger and administered by a national bureaucracy, (3) difficulty in agreeing how to adapt the gospel to contemporary cultural circumstances and (4) differences in ecclesiological vision as to what really constitutes the unity of Christians and of the church.

Ecumenism. The efforts of Christians and their communities to live in such unity that they may with one heart and one voice glorify the God and Father of our Lord Jesus Christ (Rom 15:5-6), and by their witness bring the world to believe in the divine mission of the Son (Jn 17:21). In recent American usage, *ecumenical* is sometimes opposed to *evangelical.* The falsity of this opposition is revealed when it is noted that (1) the modern ecumenical movement was evangelistic* and missionary* in its very origins; (2) *evangelical* is properly no more a party word than *catholic* or *orthodox;* (3) modern ecumenism is no liberal* Protestant* preserve but has from the start engaged the classic churches of the Reformation, then the Orthodox* and finally the Roman Catholic Church.*

Eddy, G(eorge) Sherwood (1871-1963). YMCA* secretary for Asia. Inspired by Dwight L. Moody* and John R. Mott,* Eddy sailed to India in 1896, beginning a long career with the YMCA. Eddy, who once described his life as moving from personal to shared to social religion, was ecumenical* in spirit. Through his over thirty books and his speaking, Eddy was a self-appointed ambassador for both personal and social salvation.

Eddy, Mary Baker (Glover, Patterson) (1821-1910). Founder of Christian Science.* A dramatic recovery from severe pain in 1866 led Eddy into a career of healing and teaching that culminated in the establishment of the Christian Science movement. In 1875 Eddy published the first of many editions of *Science and Health.* Eddy taught a radical idealism. Only God, his manifestations and synonyms that express the completeness of his nature exist; all else, especially body, matter, death, error and evil, is merely an illusion. Healing is the experience of physical and spiritual wholeness that follows from a recognition of these truths.

Edman, V(ictor) Raymond (1900-1967). Missionary, college professor and president. After missionary service in Ecuador, Edman became pastor of the Christian and Missionary Alliance* Tabernacle in Worcester, Massachusetts (1929-1935), and earned a Ph.D. in Latin American history at Clark University (1933). He served many years at Wheaton College,* where he was appointed professor (1936), president (1940) and chancellor (1965).

Education, Protestant Theological. American graduate theological education, in its modern form, emerged in the early nineteenth century. Before then ministerial trainees who acquired a formal education usually studied in one of the eastern undergraduate colleges or with a practicing minister in one of the western theological academies or "log colleges."*

Andover (in Massachusetts) opened in 1808 as the first major theological seminary. It came into existence as an expression of protest by the evangelicals* of New England against the growing influence of Unitarianism,* especially at Harvard. Other seminaries appeared soon thereafter, and by 1860 there were a total of sixty seminaries. This rapid increase occurred because of a growing sense of the inadequacy of the informal apprentice system, the desire for regionally trained clergymen in the expanding frontier* and the fact that the Second Great Awakening* (1800-1835) had greatly stimulated both the supply of and demand for ministerial candidates.

Pioneering seminaries Andover and Princeton* introduced a curricular structure which provided the model for later nineteenth-century schools and, to a large extent, for present-day curriculum. The three-year course of study included major work in biblical literature, Christian theology, practical theology and church history.

The most significant period of change in seminary history occurred during the generation following 1890. The faculty became increasingly professional, the curriculum became broader and the seminaries increasingly began to cast doubt on the supernatural elements of the Christian faith. Such liberal thought was especially prominent at Harvard,* Yale,* Union* (New York) and Chicago.*

Since 1960 the overall enrollment has nearly doubled, primarily because of large growth in the conservative seminaries. Another major change is the increase in the number of curricular options.

The Canadian experience in theological education, while in many ways parallel to that of its southern neighbor, differs markedly from the U.S. in its relationship to the general pattern of graduate seminary education. Whereas in the U.S. the typical seminary has been a self-standing institution, in Canada most theological colleges and seminaries have been federally related or affiliated with a university and more completely supported by public funds than has been the case in the U.S.

See also Bible Institutes and Schools; Seminary, Catholic Diocesan.

Edwards, Jonathan (1703-1758). Colonial Congregational* preacher and theologian. Edwards's overall contribution places him in the ranks of the greatest American theologians and most famous colonial figures.

In 1734-1735 a sermon by Edwards on justification* caused a widespread awakening among his congregation in Northampton, Massachusetts. In 1737 Edwards published a description of the conversions in *A Faithful Narrative*, which turned out to be a pattern for revivals* that swept through the colonies in the next few years. The fame of Edwards's preaching* and writing on revivals placed him in the forefront of American Christianity just prior to the Great Awakening.* He became the leading spokesman against established Old Light* clergy who found the revivals disruptive and too emotional.

In 1741 Edwards delivered his most famous sermon, "Sinners in the Hands of an Angry God"—perhaps the most famous sermon in American religious history.

In his later years, Edwards accepted a call to a Native American mission in Stockbridge, Massachusetts (1750), and to the presidency of the College of New Jersey* (later Princeton College; 1758).

See also Great Awakening; New England Theology.

Edwards, Jonathan, Jr. (1745-1801). Congregational* theologian and president of Union College. The ninth child and namesake of colonial New England's most brilliant theologian, Jonathan Edwards Jr.'s clerical career followed the model that his father and his father's New Divinity* ministers provided for him. He published theological treatises and essays dealing with the doctrinal and ecclesiastical problems that preoccupied the Congregational* ministers of his day. He was active in reform efforts, including antislavery.

Edwards, Morgan (1722-1795). Baptist* preacher, evangelist, historian and educator. Edwards became pastor of the Baptist church in Philadelphia in 1761 and was active in the Philadelphia Baptist Association* as clerk, moderator, evangelist and historian.

Edwards's concerns for an educated American Baptist clergy were fulfilled, with the aid of James Manning* and Hezekiah Smith,* in the founding of Rhode Island College (Brown University*). He was an early supporter of the separation of church and state.*

Edwards, Sarah Pierpont (1710-1758). Wife of Jonathan Edwards,* early worker in women's ministries. Raised in a cultured and pious* household, Edwards had a deep spiritual experience as a youth that well prepared her for her future ministry.

Like many wives of Puritan divines, she viewed her marriage and ministry as a true partnership. A picture of Puritan piety, Edwards was known for her beauty, wit and hospitality. She was active in women's ministries at a time when it was considered improper.

See also EDWARDS, JONATHAN; EDWARDS, JONATHAN, JR.; MINISTER'S WIFE.

Edwardseanism. *See* NEW ENGLAND THEOLOGY.

Eells, Cushing (1810-1893). Congregational* missionary to the Oregon Territory. In 1838 the American Board of Commissioners for Foreign Missions* assigned Eells and his bride to a new mission to the Native Americans in Oregon. After years of little success, Eells in 1869 began an itinerant* ministry of travel throughout Oregon, establishing churches and promoting educational activities.

Eisenhower, Dwight David (1890-1969). Soldier, statesman, thirty-fourth U.S. president and inspirational leader of American civil religion.* Young Dwight (or "Ike," as he became known locally) grew to manhood in Abilene, Kansas, in an intensely devout, religious home. The Eisenhower home all during Ike's youth emphasized traditional evangelical* Mennonite* values.

In World War II* Eisenhower was supreme commander of the Allied Expeditionary Forces in Europe, where he brilliantly led the most powerful military organization ever assembled.

Recruited as the Republican candidate for president in 1952, the enormously popular war hero with the charismatic smile won a landslide victory in that year and again in 1956. As president (1953-1961), Eisenhower brought the Korean War (1950-1953) to a speedy conclusion, developed a doctrine of containment in dealing with world communism and began the process of integration of the nation's public schools.

In 1953 Eisenhower made a public profession of faith and was baptized,* being received into

membership at the National Presbyterian Church in Washington, D.C. As chief executive, Eisenhower frequently spoke about religious values, signed an act making "In God We Trust"* the national motto in 1956, established the practice of opening cabinet meetings with silent prayer and in general promoted civil religion. Perhaps Eisenhower's most enduring legacy was his rejuvenation of the nation's public faith, which has continued strongly into the last decade of the twentieth century.

Elaw, Zilpha (c. 1790-c. 1850). Methodist* Episcopal exhorter and preacher. Born to free and pious African-American parents, Elaw in 1817 felt herself sanctified* and called to exhort from house to house. In 1823 she began an itinerating* ministry, which included a very successful tour of the slave states.

Election. As a biblical term, *election* refers to God's choosing a particular people to receive his salvation* from sin,* guilt and condemnation (see Ephesians 1 and Romans 9). The Westminster Confession of Faith* of 1647 clearly expressed this doctrine for American Presbyterians,* Congregationalists* and a large number of Baptists.*

Such a view of election gradually gave way to a more Arminian* emphasis, which focused on the subjective experience of salvation. In the nineteenth century the New School* theologians accommodated orthodox* Calvinism* to meet the needs of the revivals* of the Second Awakening,* as has happened also in the twentieth century, with revivalism's emphasis on the freedom of the will.

Electronic Church. Since 1980 the term *electronic church* has referred increasingly to prominent television programs produced by independent Protestant evangelists* from Pentecostal,* charismatic,* fundamentalist* and evangelical* traditions. Although the term is new, the motivations and attitudes animating the electronic church are rooted deep in the American cultural and religious experience. American Protestants have always shaped the gospel to the latest media, from the spoken proclamations of early American itinerant* evangelists to the printed pronouncements of nineteenth-century religious periodicals. The electronic church is the most recent attempt by conservative Protestants in the U.S. to fashion the gospel for the latest media technologies—broadcasting, satellites and cable television.

Electronic evangelism began in the 1920s with the rapid development of radio broadcasting. Churches* and evangelical educational institutions were among the first radio station owners and operators. During the 1930s and 1940s, Charles E. Fuller* and Walter A. Maier* successfully built radio audiences in the millions.

In the 1950s various evangelists began experimenting with paid television broadcasts, including Tulsa evangelist Oral Roberts* and Roman Catholic* Bishop Fulton J. Sheen,* who probably had the largest audience of any regular religious program during the decade.

The electronic church emerged slowly in the 1970s and 1980s as a hodgepodge of different program styles and evangelistic strategies, from the old-style revivalism* of Jimmy Swaggart* to the charismatic talk-show formats of the 700 Club and the PTL Club. Some television evangelists, including Jerry Falwell* and James Robison, addressed current political issues and established specific political agendas on their programs.

In 1987 religious broadcasting was shaken by the public revelation that Jim Bakker of the PTL Club had committed adultery and received an annual salary of over $1 million. Donations to nearly all of the major television ministries quickly declined, and many religious broadcasters called for higher standards of accountability among television preachers.

Meanwhile, the number of religious broadcast stations grew rapidly in the 1980s. Religious radio expanded at the rate of one new station every week, while television added a new station every month, with over 200 nationally in 1987. The Roman Catholics and the Southern Baptists* started their own satellite broadcasting systems, as did numerous independent evangelical organizations.

Eliot, John (1604-1690). Puritan* minister, missionary, linguist and Bible translator. Living in Massachusetts from 1631, Eliot there prepared an Algonquian catechism* and grammar, as well as a translation of the Bible in Algonquian, the first edition of the Bible printed in North America.

In 1649 Eliot motivated the establishment of the Society for the Propagation of the Gospel in New England.* By 1674 Eliot had gathered converts into fourteen self-governing communities of "praying Indians,"* with a total population of about 3,600.

Elliot, James (1927-1956). Missionary martyr. Elliot, along with Nathanael Saint, T. Edward McCully, Peter Fleming and Roger Youderian, all missionaries with Wycliffe Bible Translators, Inc.,* were attempting in the early 1950s to establish relations with the Auca tribe in the jungles of Ecuador. In 1956 all five men were murdered by some Aucas. This event, widely publicized and regarded by North American evangelicals as an outstanding example of missionary martyrdom for the cause of Christ, inspired many to give themselves to the evangelical* missionary cause. In 1958 Saint's sister, Rachel, and Elliot's widow, Elisabeth Howard Elliot, returned to live among the Aucas and win many converts. Elisabeth Elliot's account of her husband's life and martyrdom, *Through Gates of Splendor* (1957), quickly became a classic among evangelicals and served to memorialize the name "Jim" Elliot.

Elliott, Stephen, Jr. (1806-1866). Episcopal* bishop. Elliott was chaplain* at South Carolina College and then, in 1841, was consecrated* the first Episcopal bishop of Georgia. After the Civil War, Elliott took a leading role in reuniting the separated Northern and Southern dioceses* of the Episcopal Church.

Ellis, John Tracy (1905-1992). Roman Catholic* historian and educator. Ellis began his teaching career after obtaining his Ph.D. from the Catholic University of America* in 1930 and later studied at Sulpician Seminary, Washington, D.C. (1934-1938). He served at a number of Catholic institutions throughout his career as a church historian, most notably at Catholic University of America and the University of San Francisco. A leading figure among historians of American Catholicism, Ellis was managing editor of the *Catholic Historical Review* (1941-1964). His many books include *The Life of James Cardinal Gibbons*, 2 vols. (1952), and *American Catholicism* (rev. ed., 1969).

Ellyson, Edgar P. (1869-1954). Minister, theologian and a founder of the Church of the Nazarene.* Ellyson, president of several colleges and a leader in the Church of the Nazarene's educational endeavors, laid out the plans for the Nazarene Board of Education, was chief editor for the denomination's Sunday-school* publications and chaired the committee that revised the Nazarene manual of discipline* in 1924.

Ely, Richard Theodore (1854-1943). Economist. Ely introduced in America the German "historical" school of economics, emphasizing the social, cultural and political factors that shaped economic systems, rather than classic theories, which stressed universal laws. Ely, who emphasized the ethical function of economics, was an Episcopal* layperson and a central figure in the growth of the Social Gospel movement.*

Emancipation Proclamation. On September 22, 1862, President Abraham Lincoln* proclaimed that on January 1, 1863, "all persons held as slaves within any state or designated part of a state . . . shall be then, thenceforward, and forever free." The practical effect of the proclamation was to transform the Civil War* from a struggle to preserve the Union into a crusade for human freedom. It exposed the South as fighting to maintain an institution that the rest of Western civilization had renounced.

Northern church leaders had long been pleading for such a measure, and Lincoln had received many petitions from Quakers,* evangelicals,* Unitarian-Transcendentalists* and others, urging him to proclaim emancipation. Among the Northern denominations, only Episcopalians* and Roman Catholics* failed to issue a public endorsement of emancipation.

The Emancipation Proclamation was given permanent force by the Thirteenth Amendment, ratified in December 1865.

Embury, Philip (1728-1773). Methodist* minister. Baptized a Lutheran,* Embury immigrated to New York from Ireland in 1760. In 1766 he began preaching to a group of five gathered in his own home, a congregation that ultimately grew to fill the Wesley Chapel erected on John Street. Embury was the first Methodist preacher in North America, though he was not an official minister.

Emerson, Ralph Waldo (1803-1882). Transcendentalist* essayist and poet. Young Emerson, after three years as a Unitarian* minister, rejected what he called the "corpse-cold" rationalism of Unitarianism in favor of the New England variation of European romanticism* called transcendentalism.*

Unable to tolerate Calvinism's* emphasis on

original sin,* Emerson found in romanticism a language with which to celebrate the Spirit without what he called the "Hebraic mythology" of Christianity.

Although they angered many, Emerson's essays and lectures inspired generations of churched and unchurched Americans, including Walt Whitman, Henry Ward Beecher* and John D. Rockefeller.

Emerson, William (1769-1811). Unitarian* minister. In 1799 Emerson accepted a call to the First Church of Boston, a position he held until his death. He also served as chaplain* of the state senate and overseer of Harvard College.* His eight children included the noted essayist Ralph Waldo Emerson.*

Emmons, Nathanael (1745-1840). Congregational* minister and theologian. Emmons quickly acquired a reputation for being the most radical of the New Divinity Men. In the interests of preaching consistent Calvinism,* he followed Joseph Bellamy* and Samuel Hopkins* in advocating a governmental theory of the atonement, and he followed Jonathan Edwards* in teaching both the moral inability of sinners to repent and the natural blameworthiness of those who do not. In a further reflection of Edwards, he also dismissed the need to speak of an underlying "nature" or "substance" and described human self-consciousness in phenomenological terms as a continuous creation of God.

Empirical Theology. Early twentieth-century theologians who sought a new departure for theology consistent with modern methods of thinking, especially as found in the empirical sciences, were termed *empirical theologians.* Theology was the search for pragmatic religious truth that finds its validity in its practical workableness. The movement developed strongly at the University of Chicago Divinity School under the influence of Shailer Mathews,* who emphasized a sociohistorical approach to Christianity.

Endecott, John (c. 1589-1665). Political and military leader of Massachusetts Bay Colony. In 1628 Endecott was appointed the first governor of Massachusetts Bay. Endecott's leadership was characterized by his rigid principles and discipline. He led the force that broke up Thomas Norton's settlement at Mt. Wollaston.

Engel, Jacob (1753-1833). One of the founders of the Brethren in Christ Church.* Engel was strongly influenced by the pietistic* revival* movement, a contemporary feature of Lancaster County (Penn.) life. Because of tension with his Mennonite* background, Engel and others organized their own group, known first as River Brethren but legally, since the Civil War,* as Brethren in Christ.

England, John (1786-1842). Catholic* bishop of Charleston (S.C.). Born in Cork, Ireland, England received his early education in one of the Protestant* schools there. His education and his Irish experiences made him sympathetic to the republican and Enlightenment* values of his day. In 1820 Rome appointed England to be the first bishop of Charleston. From 1820 to 1842, England not only served the small Catholic community in his diocese* but also became the leading Catholic apologist in the U.S. Through the episcopal* government of his diocese and public lectures throughout the nation and the press,* England tried to help Catholics identify themselves as Catholics and Americans. The central focus of his ministry was to establish not only the compatibility of but also the similarity between American republicanism and Catholicism.

Enlightenment Catholicism. Enlightenment Catholicism* refers to the Christian rationalism and republicanism that arose during early antebellum American Catholicism.

In the realm of thought, the American Catholic Enlightenment emphasized harmony and order in the universe, the role and capacity of reason in understanding both the created and revealed orders and the rights of individual conscience in society and in Christianity. Enlightened Catholics also asserted that the American values of religious freedom,* separation of church and state,* voluntaryism* and republican political theory were historically and theoretically compatible with the Catholic tradition.

The primary issue in American Catholic thought was not the question of establishing the grounds for the possibility or necessity of revelation and Christianity but of vindicating the reasonableness of Catholicism. Catholics were preoccupied with constructing responses to the nativist* and Protestant* charge that Catholicism represented mental slavery.

As an intellectual movement, the Catholic Enlightenment gradually came to an end in the 1840s when the romantic* impulse replaced it as a mode of thought for explicating the Catholic tradition to the American people.
See also ENLIGHTENMENT PROTESTANTISM.

Enlightenment Protestantism. The Enlightenment was an intellectual movement that stressed reason as the way to truth, a world based on perfectly ordered natural laws, and a self-confident and optimistic belief in human ability to make progress. Truth, it was believed, had been obscured by revelation and dogma,* but at last people could be enlightened through reason, science and education. The intellectual and religious implications of the Enlightenment were profound, constituting a massive shift in Western thought.

The Enlightenment began in England, spread to Europe (especially France) and flourished in America (c. 1750-1800) as the new nation was forming. It followed the Great Awakening* (1740-1760) and preceded the era of romanticism* (1800-1850). It was not a mass movement but was advocated by an influential elite group of writers. American Enlightenment thought relied heavily on European writers, including Isaac Newton, John Locke, David Hume and Voltaire.

Restructuring a Reasonable Religion. Enlightenment thinkers believed that the basic ideas of religion could be derived from reason alone. First, God is chiefly a great designer who created the world and devised natural laws for its perpetual motion. Second, people everywhere experience the sense of obligation or ethical demands toward neighbors. Proper treatment of others is what pleases God, not a particular manner of worship* or a collection of doctrinal statements. Third, because of the sense of right and wrong, it is reasonable to conclude that there will be an afterlife in which right and wrong will be rewarded and punished. Thus there is an attempt to reduce religion to its simplest and most permanent features.

So pivotal were its theological ideas that many interpreters suggest that the Enlightenment closed the medieval era and began modernity. These concepts shaped American deism* and Unitarianism* and raised important questions for all Christian traditions.

Organizing and Disseminating Reasonable Religion. Ethan Allen,* Elihu Palmer* and Thomas Paine* clearly articulated the ideas of American deism. Deism was not a denomination, but rather a system of religious thought, adopted by Benjamin Franklin,* John Adams, Thomas Jefferson* and others. Paine's work in particular alarmed many readers, prompting countless replies, and organized deism lost momentum after 1810. Two denominations* grew out of rational religion: American Unitarianism* (1825) and Universalism* (1790).

See also ENLIGHTENMENT CATHOLICISM.

Ephrata Society. Colonial Pietist* community founded by Johann Conrad Beissel.* The mystically inclined Beissel immigrated to Pennsylvania in 1720 from the Palatinate (Germany) in search of spiritual peace.

In 1732 Beissel and a small group removed to remote Lancaster County, where the semimonastic Ephrata community was formed. It believed in threefold immersion baptism* and nonresistance and observed a love feast with foot washing.* Ephrata was an important force in colonial Pennsylvania cultural life.

Epiphany. A festival on January 6 celebrating, in Western liturgical* churches, the visit of the wise men to the newborn Jesus in Bethlehem. Epiphany also designates the season in the church year* extending from January 6 to Ash Wednesday.* In early Eastern church tradition this festival celebrated both the nativity and the baptism of Jesus, a custom retained by the Armenian Church* today.

Episcopacy. The office of bishop, a body of bishops in a church or geographic region, or episcopal church government* generally (comprising the orders of bishop, priest and deacon*). From A.D. 200 until the Reformation, a threefold ministry centering on the episcopal office was normative.

Episcopal Church. *See* PROTESTANT EPISCOPAL CHURCH IN THE U.S.A.

Epp, Theodore Herman (1907-1985). Religious broadcaster. After earlier work as pastor and church planter, in 1939 Epp moved to Lincoln, Nebraska, to begin his radio ministry, *Back to the Bible Broadcast,* which grew to include more than six hundred stations. He also published seventy books and two periodicals.

Epworth League (1889-1930). Methodist* youth organization. The product of a fusion of five Methodist young people's groups, the Epworth League was named for the place of John Wesley's* birth. Its objectives included the promotion of "an earnest, intelligent, practical, and loyal spiritual life in the young people of our church." The Epworth Leagues stressed the importance of church loyalty, Christian education, commitment to Methodist missions, and spiritual and social development.

Erb, Paul (1894-1984). Mennonite Church* educator and journalist. Erb achieved his greatest influence as editor of the *Gospel Herald,* the organ of the Mennonite Church, from 1944 to 1962. His book *The Alpha and the Omega* (1955) highlighted his role as diplomat and mediator.

Erdman, Charles Rosenbury (1866-1960). Presbyterian* clergyman and educator. Son of premillennialist* leader William J. Erdman,* Charles Erdman in 1906 assumed the chair of practical theology at Princeton Seminary,* which he held until his retirement in 1936.

In 1925, at the height of the fundamentalist-modernist controversy* in the Presbyterian Church, Erdman won election as moderator of the General Assembly* and at a crucial moment broke the momentum of fundamentalist exclusivists.

Erdman, William Jacob (1834-1923). Presbyterian* pastor and Niagara Conference* speaker. Erdman, a premillennialist,* often appeared as a Bible expositor at the Niagara Conference and served as its secretary. His son, Charles R. Erdman,* figured in the fundamentalist-modernist debate* within the Presbyterian Church.

Esbjorn, Lars Paul (1808-1870). Swedish Lutheran* pastor, missionary and educator. In Illinois and at Princeton,* Esbjorn organized Swedish Lutheran congregations. In 1859 he led a movement of Swedes and Norwegians out of the Illinois Lutheran synods,* which became the Scandinavian Evangelical Lutheran Augustana Synod of North America (later known simply as the Augustana Synod).

Eschatology. Traditionally, eschatology is the doctrinal study of last things and may refer either to the fate of individuals (death, resurrection, judgment and afterlife) or to events surrounding the end of the world. In America, when tied to expectations of a coming millennium, such concerns have produced powerful movements with significant religious and social effects.

Broadly speaking, Christian millennialism is the belief, deeply rooted in Revelation 20, that there will be a long period of unprecedented peace and righteousness closely associated with the Second Coming of Christ. Historically, Christians have divided themselves into three groups, depending on whether they expect a literal millennium on the earth and where they place Christ's return in relation to it. Premillennialists* take Revelation 20 quite literally and expect the Second Coming of Christ to occur before the millennium (*see* John Nelson Darby; Dispensationalism; Jehovah's Witnesses; William Miller; Mormonism). Postmillennialists* believe that the kingdom of God is already in the world and is now being extended through the preaching* of the gospel and the work of the Holy Spirit (*see* Lyman Beecher, Jonathan Edwards, Charles Finney, Reconstructionism, Restoration Movement). Amillennialists* do not expect a literal millennium of any kind on the earth. Because amillennialists view the millennium as having no material expression this side of the new creation, their views tend to need no institutional expression. But pre- and postmillennialists have frequently translated their beliefs into powerful and popular movements which have affected American society.

The social ramifications of these millennial views are significant and often predictable. Although there are important exceptions, it is safe to conclude that historically the Christian social conscience and commitment to social righteousness have tended to atrophy during times of premillennialist ascendancy. People who believe that nothing can be done to alter the present age's rendezvous with the antichrist and total apostasy generally do not waste their energy trying to change things in the meantime. By World War I,* most premillennialists had decided to leave social involvement to postmillennialists and theological liberals* and concentrate on evangelism.* Not until the 1970s have premillennialists been willing to reevaluate their social responsibility.

See also APOCALYPTICISM; FUNDAMENTALISM.

Established Churches in New England. "Established churches" are those enjoying privileged status. In New England, the early settlers founded "gathered" churches in which the locus of authority was the body of communicant members. Within the boundaries of a town, however, this church functioned as in an English parish. No religious competition was allowed. The town government assessed all taxpayers for support of the minister and maintenance of the meetinghouse, and everyone was expected to attend services.

Tensions arose within this system as some lost interest in church membership and others formed separatist* churches of their own. By the end of the eighteenth century, competitors to the established Congregational* churches dotted the New England landscape: Baptists,* Shakers,* Anglicans,* Quakers* and even Universalists.* Not until 1818, when a coalition of Baptists, Methodists,* Anglicans and Jeffersonians controlled the ballot box, did Connecticut completely disestablish its churches. New Hampshire followed a year later. The last legally privileged churches in New England, those of the Commonwealth of Massachusetts, were not disestablished until 1833.

See also ANGLICANISM; TOLERATION, ACT OF.

Eternal Security. The belief that a person who has been truly justified* by faith in Christ has eternal salvation* and cannot lose it. Sometimes termed *absolute final perseverance*, this doctrine is an integral part of a Calvinistic* doctrine of salvation which affirms predestination,* unconditional election* and irresistible grace.

American Puritans,* like Jonathan Edwards,* embraced final perseverance because of the immutability of God's decree of election. On the frontier, Wesleyan* Arminians,* like circuit-riding Bishop* Francis Asbury,* stressed instead the cooperation of divine grace with human wills. Classic Calvinistic affirmations of eternal security continued in Princeton theologians* such as Charles Hodge* and Benjamin B. Warfield.*

See also ASSURANCE OF SALVATION.

Ethics, Catholic Personal. Ethics in Catholic thought is distinguished from mores, morals, metaethics and moral theology.* Mores are actual behavior patterns approved by a social group. Morals are principles specifying right and wrong behavior. Ethics is the philosophical science of moral principles. Metaethics examines the criteria of meaning in ethical statements. Moral theology is based on faith in divine revelation and is the study of ethics from the viewpoint of God's law.

In practice, the Catholic tradition has usually joined philosophy and theology, reason and faith, while clearly distinguishing them in theory.

Traditionally, ethics has been divided into three parts: (1) social ethics* (how we should treat each other); (2) personal or individual ethics* (what sort of individuals we should be); and (3) metaphysical ethics (what the *summum bonum* is, the greatest good or ultimate end). Modern ethical philosophies, except for the existentialists, typically concentrate on (1), less on (2) and hardly ever on (3), which raises ultimate metaphysical and theological questions.

Natural Law. Natural law is perhaps the most important and distinctively Catholic ethical teaching, though a few secular thinkers (such as Mortimer Adler) and a good number of Protestant thinkers (such as C. S. Lewis) also embrace the idea, which was held by nearly all premodern thinkers. Three kinds of law are distinguished: (1) eternal law (God's nature and will); (2) natural law (human reason's participation in eternal law, aware of the laws of human nature as designed by God); and (3) human-posited or manmade law. The distinction between (2) and (3) corresponds to that between mores and morals, between the legal and the moral. Ethical positivism denies categories (1) and (2).

Application of Moral Law. The three moral determinants or factors that cause any freely chosen human act to be morally good or evil are (1) the moral nature of the act itself as specified by the moral law, (2) the intention or motive of the actor and (3) the circumstances, or situation. Natural law specifies (1) but must be applied to ever-changing and multifarious circumstances (3) by a prudent and well-intentioned individual (2). Though the principles of natural law are unchanging and universal, the applications of them are not.

Revelation, Tradition and Reason. Catholic ethics is more traditional and less individualistic than Protestant ethics because of the Catholic emphasis on the authority of the church as a single worldwide community stretching back in time to Christ. Contributing to this tradition are both divine revelation and human reason. Revelation includes (1) the Word of God in person—Christ, (2) the Word of God in writing—the Scriptures and (3) the teaching of the body of Christ—the church. Reason includes (1) objective reason, the intelligible nature of things; (2) the individual's native power of intelligence and (3) the written

works of great thinkers and saints, especially Aquinas and Augustine, the latter being the chief common source for both Catholic and Protestant philosophers.

Ethics, Protestant Personal. Christian personal ethics is concerned with how one conducts one's life in the family, in the workplace and in the community, and it touches on issues of honesty, sexuality, the use of force and influence, and the management of resources.

There are significant differences in method between Protestant personal ethics and Roman Catholic* and Orthodox* approaches. Catholic ethics recognizes two sources of moral knowledge, revelation and reason, as it discerns the natural law. This gives it greater access to the results of philosophical reflection and to the Christian ethical tradition. By contrast, the Scriptures are the primary focus in Protestant thinking (*see* Sola Scriptura). Protestants not only emphasize Scripture but insist on individual freedom of interpretation and reject the tradition of detailed interpretation of quasi-legal ethical principles known as casuistry.

The Protestant emphasis on Scripture as the authoritative source of ethical thinking was tested in this century when the fundamentalist-modernist controversy* erupted over the inspiration and ultimately the normative force of Scripture. As a result of this schism, fundamentalist and evangelical* Christianity began to emphasize personal ethics to the virtual exclusion of social ethics.* Liberal* Protestant Christianity, in contrast, led by Walter Rauschenbusch,* Reinhold Niebuhr* and others, focused on the social mission of the church.

See also ETHICS, CATHOLIC PERSONAL.

Ethnicity. *See* IMMIGRATION AND ETHNICITY.

Eucharist, Holy Communion or Lord's Supper. A liturgical* act utilizing bread and wine (or grape juice) and celebrating the death of Christ. Instituted by Jesus at the Last Supper, this liturgical act is celebrated by nearly all Christians, though with wide disagreement about its practice and meaning.

Roman Catholics* usually use the term *Mass* and believe that the elements of bread and wine are in their underlying reality changed into the body and blood of Christ (*see* Transubstantiation).

Eastern Orthodox* Churches refer to Holy Communion as *the Divine Liturgy* and teach that after the prayer of consecration* the bread and wine have become the body and blood of Christ, but the way this happens is a mystery.

The Episcopal* Churches usually use the term *thanksgiving* for the Eucharist and affirm (without explanation) that Jesus Christ is present in the meal.

Lutherans* usually refer to the meal as *Holy Communion* and teach the real presence—Christ's body and blood are present "with, in and under" the bread and wine (*see* Consubstantiation).

Presbyterian,* Congregational* and Reformed* Churches follow Calvin in rejecting the doctrine of the presence of Christ's body. Churches in the Methodist,* Baptist* and Restorationist* traditions regard the Lord's Supper as a memorial recalling Jesus' death and sacrifice.

See also SACRAMENTS AND ORDINANCES.

Eucharistic Congress. *See* INTERNATIONAL EUCHARISTIC CONGRESS (XXVIII).

Eucharistic Devotions. Acts of homage and adoration rendered by Roman Catholics* to the true presence of Jesus Christ under the Eucharistic* elements of bread and wine. Many such devotions* have appeared, most of them developing either in the medieval period or in the period of the Catholic Reformation as a countersign to the Eucharistic theology of the Protestant* Reformation.

Euthanasia. The deliberate killing of a human being, by acts of either omission or commission, where the alleged intent is the benefit of the one being killed. Often referred to as mercy killing, it is usually directed at the physically or mentally handicapped, the chronically ill or the elderly.

The Judeo-Christian* tradition always condemned euthanasia, with agitation for its legalization beginning in the U.S. only in the 1930s. In the 1960s a number of state legislatures introduced bills to legalize it. Euthanasia has joined abortion on the agenda of activists supporting the sanctity of human life.

Evald, Emmy Carlsson (1857-1946). Lutheran missionary leader. Evald is best known for helping to organize the Woman's Home and Foreign Missionary Society of the Augustana Lutheran Church (later Lutheran Church Women of the Lutheran Church in America) in 1892, and serving as its first president.

Evangelical Alliance. One of the earliest attempts to bring about Protestant* cooperation. The alliance was formed in London in 1846 at a large convention at which more than fifty evangelical* groups from Europe and America were represented. The individuals gathered in London agreed to a very broad creedal basis, but no long-range program was established for the future. Sharp disputes between the English and American delegates about the morality of slavery ruined the Evangelical Alliance as a worldwide organization. The outcome was a consensus that each nation represented should form its own Evangelical Alliance.

The Evangelical Alliance in the U.S. was formed in 1867. By 1900, however, its influence was waning in America, and it became clear that its goals could not be accommodated to the contemporary individualism* of laissez-faire economic and social philosophies. In 1908 it was followed by the Federal Council of Churches in Christ in America.*

Evangelical Alliance Mission, The. An evangelical* foreign mission* society, originally known as the Scandinavian Alliance Mission. Founded by Fredrik Franson* in 1890, the mission changed its name in 1949 to The Evangelical Alliance Mission (TEAM).

TEAM is primarily committed to ministries of evangelism,* church planting and church development but has initiated and maintained supporting ministries in medicine, linguistics, literature, education, Christian camping and radio.

Evangelical Church. *See* GERMAN-AMERICAN REVIVALISM; UNITED METHODIST CHURCH.

Evangelical Covenant Church of America. A free church* denomination.* Founded in Chicago in 1885 as the Swedish Evangelical Mission Covenant of America, the Evangelical Covenant Church of America traces its roots back to the pietistic* revivals* in eighteenth- and nineteenth-century Sweden.

Doctrinally, the group holds the final authority* of Scripture, along with affirmations of the historic creeds of the church, particularly the Apostles' Creed. The church has been described as evangelical,* but not exclusive; biblical, but not doctrinaire; traditional, but not rigid; and congregational,* but not independent.

Evangelical Fellowship of Canada. A national fellowship of Canadian evangelicals.* Begun in Toronto in 1964, the Evangelical Fellowship of Canada (EFC) includes pastors* serving in both mainline* and uniformly evangelical denominations.* In the early 1990s it included twenty-eight denominations, 115 organizations, 1,025 local churches and over ten thousand individual members.

Evangelical Foreign Missions Association. A fellowship of about ninety evangelical* missionary* organizations which either send missionaries or directly support the North American missionary endeavor. Founded in 1945 and led by Clyde W. Taylor* and, since 1974, by Wade T. Coggins, the association has been a voice for mission concerns, providing a channel for cooperation and many services, including conferences, seminars, workshops, publications, government liaison and visa procurement. With the Interdenominational Foreign Mission Association* it publishes *Evangelical Missions Quarterly* and *Pulse.*

Evangelical Free Church of America. An evangelical* denomination* with roots in the Scandinavian free church* movement. Born out of revival among the scattered immigrants who had left the Lutheran* state church in Scandinavia to come to America, the denomination dates officially to a conference of free churches held in Iowa in 1884. In 1950 the Evangelical Free Church of America (Swedish) and the Evangelical Free Church Association (Norwegian-Danish) merged into the present body.

Evangelical Friends Alliance. An organization of evangelical* Friends* churches. Formed in 1965, the alliance united Friends who had been influenced by evangelicalism. The Evangelical Friends now consists of four regional yearly meetings or districts.

Evangelical Liberalism (1880-1930). A Protestant* movement, also termed *New Theology* or *Progressive Orthodoxy,* arising in the decades after the Civil War.* Its members attempted a synthesis between the old faith and the new scientific thought, hoping to preserve the main lines of Christian orthodoxy* in an expression more suitable for modern times.

Evangelical liberalism represented a transformation of Calvinistic* orthodoxy, even though it retained the traditional theological language. Its most popular representatives were Henry Ward Beecher,* Phillips Brooks,* Lyman Abbott* and Harry Emerson Fosdick.*

See also LIBERALISM/MODERNISM, PROTESTANT.

Evangelical Lutheran Church in America. The largest Lutheran* denomination* in America. Formed in 1988, the church represents the merger of three Lutheran bodies: the Lutheran Church in America,* the American Lutheran Church* and the Association of Evangelical Lutheran Churches.*

Evangelical Lutheran Church in Canada. The largest Lutheran* body in Canada. The Evangelical Lutheran Church in Canada (ELCC) is the product of a number of mergers, most of which took place in the U.S. Because Canadian Lutheranism has had close links with the U.S., both official and unofficial, these unions were experienced north of the border as well. They involved mergers of the Canadian districts of the American Lutheran Church,* the Evangelical Lutheran Church, the Danish United Evangelical Lutheran Church and the Lutheran Church in America.*

Evangelical Mennonite Brethren Conference. *See* FELLOWSHIP OF EVANGELICAL BIBLE CHURCHES.

Evangelical Presbyterian Church. Presbyterian* denomination.* The Evangelical Presbyterian Church was organized in 1981 by churches that had withdrawn from the United Presbyterian Church and the Presbyterian Church in the United States* in protest over their theological pluralism. While some churches that withdrew from these denominations joined the Presbyterian Church in America (founded in 1973), those with women elders and deacons,* and those with a charismatic* presence found themselves incompatible with any of the existing conservative Presbyterian denominations. A centrist and moderate alternative denomination was thus founded that maintained doctrinal faithfulness to the Westminster Confession* while allowing differences in matters of eschatology,* gifts of the Holy Spirit and the ordination of women. From the original 14,000 members, forty-three ministers and fifteen founding churches in 1981, by 1993 the denomination had grown to 52,360 members, 375 ministers and 175 churches.

Evangelical Protestant Church of North America. *See* UNITED CHURCH OF CHRIST.

Evangelical Theological Society. An organization of North American theologians and Bible scholars. Organized in 1949, the Evangelical Theological Society (ETS) officially holds to a belief in the inerrancy of the Bible in the original autographs. Despite occasional tensions within the group, the ETS has remained for some four decades a society of healthy theological discussion and exploration in the context of a firm commitment to the truthfulness of Holy Scripture.

Evangelical United Brethren Church. *See* UNITED METHODIST CHURCH.

Evangelical United Front. A network of benevolent societies formed by Protestants* to define America in Christian terms. Beginning in 1816, Protestant leaders in the Northeast founded over one hundred interdenominational, voluntary societies* to foster religion, morality and education, the pillars of a Christian republic. By the 1840s the effort was in decline.

Evangelicalism. A movement in North American Christianity that emphasizes the classic Protestant* doctrines of salvation,* the church and the authority* of the Scriptures; in the American context it is characterized by stress on a personal experience of the grace of God, usually termed the *new birth** or *conversion.** Estimates of evangelical strength in the U.S. and Canada run as high as fifty million, making it one of the major expressions of Christianity in North America. Three significant periods of modern Christianity have shaped evangelicalism: the Protestant Reformation, the evangelical revivals* of the eighteenth century and fundamentalism.*

The Protestant Reformation, 1517-1560. Although not questioning the orthodox* tradition of early Christianity, the Reformation was in a special way a restatement of the gospel. Challenging the medieval doctrines of salvation and the church, the Reformers argued that faith in Christ alone brought salvation (vs. faith plus good

works), authority lay in Scripture (vs. in the church; *see* Sola Scriptura); the church is a community of faith (vs. a hierarchical and priestly institution); and the essence of Christian living is serving God in one's calling, whether sacred or secular (vs. monasticism).

The Evangelical Revivals, 1720-1860. During the seventeenth century the vigorous defense of the gospel in the Protestant Reformation was replaced by an unyielding spirit of Protestant orthodoxy, as Protestantism became legal, acceptable and generally lifeless. Justification by faith was a doctrine to debate more than a life to experience. A series of renewal movements changed this traditional Protestantism and gave fresh meaning to the term *evangelical.* This term came to mean "born again"* Christianity, the experience of the Holy Spirit in a life-changing way.

The first of these revivals was a movement in Germany termed *Pietism,** which stressed heartfelt faith through Bible study,* prayer* and mutual care within the church. One group arising from these revivals was the Moravians,* which in turn influenced John Wesley.* Preaching in the open fields through England, Wesley became the prime human mover in England's greatest spiritual awakening.

The American colonial counterpart of the Methodist* revival in the British Isles was the Great Awakening.* The revival appeared first in the 1720s as a series of regional awakenings. But under the incendiary preaching* ministry of Wesley's friend George Whitefield,* the regional revivals merged into a Great Awakening that continued until the American Revolution.

The evangelical call for an instantaneous conversion to Christ continued through the nineteenth century in camp meetings* and revivals and classrooms all across America. Under this influence, evangelical Christianity emerged as the dominant faith in America before the Civil War.*

The Fundamentalist Movement, 1920-1960. During the critical years between the Civil War and World War I,* evangelicalism was dethroned as the reigning religious perspective of American society. This loss is explained mainly by the fears and reactions of conservative evangelicals in the face of three rapid changes that swept over America after the Civil War: (1) the immigration of millions of Catholics,* Jews and others who did not share the Puritan* and revivalistic traditions of American evangelicals; (2) the growing influence of Darwin's *Origin of Species;* (3) the rise of higher criticism, an approach to the Bible that undercut the idea of special revelation and a supernatural gospel.

In the first three decades of the twentieth century, modernists* tried to retain the traditional Protestant hold on America by modifying the traditional doctrines of the Christian faith in order to reconcile them with science, evolution and religious pluralism.* Fundamentalists resisted changes in American society and defended a supernatural Christianity by emphasizing an infallible Bible and Jesus Christ as the divine Savior. This threw them into conflict with American society and made them appear outdated and irrelevant.

A dramatic turnaround occurred after World War II.* Harold John Ockenga,* Carl F. H. Henry,* Bernard Ramm and other heirs of fundamentalism questioned the movement's tendency to justify denominational separatism,* social and cultural irresponsibility, and anti-intellectualism. Playing important roles in the resurgence of evangelicalism were the National Association of Evangelicals,* *Christianity Today,* Fuller Theological Seminary,* evangelist* Billy Graham* and the charismatic movement.*

See also NEW EVANGELICALISM.

Evangelism and Evangelists. In the New Testament, evangelism is the spread of the gospel, or good news, by means of proclamation or announcement. An evangelist is the person who carries out evangelism, proclaiming the good news of Jesus Christ. In the New Testament, the word refers generally to one who is called and empowered by God to proclaim the good news of Jesus. In North America *evangelist* has most often been used of mass evangelists in the revivalist tradition.

The forms and methods of evangelism have evolved along with the nation, with evangelists George Whitefield,* William and Gilbert Tennent,* Charles G. Finney,* Dwight L. Moody,* R. A. Torrey,* Billy Sunday* and Billy Graham* each playing an important role. Their respective effectiveness reflects their ability to speak the simple but profound truth of the gospel in the language of everyday experience.

Since World War II there has been an increasing emphasis on evangelism that is more personal, relational* and dialogic, as opposed to the approach of preaching. Personal evangelism, small-group evangelism and other such methods have become more common and have been extensively used by parachurch* groups.

See also REVIVALISM.

Evangelism-in-Depth. A strategy for comprehensive evangelization* of a particular nation or region. Formulated by the American missionary R. Kenneth Strachan,* it was first implemented in Nicaragua in 1960. The plan was subsequently put into operation in many other countries of Latin America, Africa and North America. In Africa it was known as New Life for All.

Evans, Evan (1671-1721). Anglican* clergyman and missionary to Welsh immigrants. In 1700 Evans was sent by the bishop of London to serve as rector of Christ Church, Philadelphia. There he had an immensely successful ministry* for the next eighteen years. His warm piety* won many Quakers* to the Anglican Church.

Evans, James (1801-1846). Methodist* missionary, linguist and inventor. Ordained* as a Methodist minister in 1833, Evans was appointed general superintendent of the Northwest Indian Methodist Missions in 1840. He developed a written language for Cree and published hymns,* prayers* and the Scriptures in Cree.

Evans, William (1870-1950). Evangelical* Bible teacher and theologian. A pastor and Christian educator, Evans was considered one of the outstanding Bible teachers of his time. Beginning in 1918, Evans was a director of World Bible Conferences, spending most of his time traveling and lecturing.

Evanston Assembly. Second assembly of the World Council of Churches* (WCC), in 1952 at Evanston, Illinois. Meeting under the christological* theme "Christ—the Hope of the World," 1,500 participants, including 500 delegates from 163 Protestant* and Orthodox* churches (as compared with 150 at the Amsterdam Assembly in 1948), tried to declare Christian faith and hope to a postwar, secular world. The assembly revealed a WCC willing to address the tough spiritual questions of the 1950s and to seek in its membership to stretch across the political, cultural and confessional divisions in the world.

Evening Service. Church services held in the evening. The historic roots of the evening service go back to Jewish practice (Ex 29:39; Ps 141:2) and early Christian continuance of temple worship (Acts 2:46; 3:1). The spiritual awakenings of the eighteenth and nineteenth centuries gave rise to the revivalistic* tradition that undergirds the evangelistic nature of many evening services in the twentieth century.

Evensong. *See* VESPERS.

Evolution. *See* DARWINIAN EVOLUTION AND THE AMERICAN CHURCHES.

Ewart, Frank (1876-1947). Oneness Pentecostal* minister. In 1913 Ewart participated in the Pentecostal camp meeting* in Los Angeles that sparked an intense interest in the definitive biblical formula for water baptism.* His understanding that true baptism was in the name of Jesus alone led to a rejection of trinitarian theology. He contributed specifically to the church now known as the United Pentecostal Church.*

Ewer, Ferdinand Cartwright (1826-1883). Anglo-Catholic* preacher and theologian. After an earlier period of skepticism, Ewer was ordained rector of Grace Church in San Francisco and then Christ Church, New York, where he achieved wide fame as a gifted preacher. Ewer emerged as the foremost apologist* for Anglo-Catholicism, although his ritual practices aroused much hostility and led to his resignation in 1871.

Ewing, Finis (1773-1841). Principal founder of the Cumberland Presbyterian Church.* In 1810, while in the throes of a lengthy dispute between revival* and antirevival Presbyterians, Ewing and two others started the Cumberland Presbyterian Church. The primary cause of the schism was the revivalists' moderating the Calvinism* of the Westminster Confession* in order to give greater place to the human will in conversion. This modified Calvinism became the new evangelical* orthodoxy* of the Second Great Awakening.*

Excell, Edwin Othello (1851-1921). Gospel singer, songwriter and publisher. Excell became best known for his work with evangelist Sam P. Jones,* with whom he traveled for more than twenty years. He wrote more than two thousand gospel songs.

Excommunication. Censure barring a Christian from the privileges and rights of church membership.* Excommunication is practiced, at least in theory, by nearly all Christian churches, although its definition and application vary widely.

Competition among church bodies in America, social mobility, the threat of litigation, the value placed upon tolerance and the popularity of therapeutic psychology make the consistent practice of excommunication particularly difficult in the modern American church.

See also DISCIPLINE, CHURCH.

Exegesis. The practice of discovering the meaning of a text in its original cultural, historical, literary and theological contexts. Exegesis is to be distinguished from hermeneutics, which is the theory of interpretation. An exegete is one who engages in exegesis.

The most prominent exegetical tradition in America's religious history was shaped by the Reformation principle of literal and grammatical (rather than allegorical) interpretation.

The historical-critical method interpreted the biblical text as it would any other ancient text. Modern critical exegesis attempts to uncover not only the originally intended meaning of a text (or oral tradition preserved within a text) but subsequent meanings and layers of interpretation introduced by later editors and compilers.

Existentialism, Christian. Christian existentialism stresses the role of human experience in discovering truth. Søren Kierkegaard,* the Danish philosopher whose writings inspired the movement, maintained that truth cannot be found by means of detached intellectual reasoning. It must be personally appropriated and demands the involvement and commitment of the whole self. Within the context of Christian faith, Kierkegaard argued, one becomes a Christian only by a "leap of faith," by which one accepts God's claim on his or her life and embraces the Christian gospel, with all its ethical demands for obedience to God. This frees the person to an open future in which the responsible self discovers Christian truth in encounter and action.

Many of Kierkegaard's philosophical and theological insights were adopted by Karl Barth* and others who promoted dialectical theology during the 1920s. Existential themes continued to emerge in the thought of Continental philosophers and theologians such as Karl Jaspers, Gabriel Marcel, Nicolai Berdyaev, Dietrich Bonhoeffer,* Rudolf Bultmann* and Paul Tillich.*

These and contemporary American theologians have shaped Christian existentialism, yet the existentialist impulse has also been especially strong in the arena of Christian ethics.*

Expositor. One who defines and explains the meaning of a biblical text, whether in a classroom, from a pulpit, over electronic media, or in published popular or scholarly commentary. In expository preaching,* a popular preaching method in America since the days of the Puritans,* a text rather than a topic determines the preacher's theme and conclusion.

Extreme Unction, Sacrament of. One of the traditional seven sacraments* of the Roman Catholic Church,* it is more commonly called today the Sacrament of the Anointing of the Sick. Documents from Vatican II* insist that this sacrament is not to be reserved for those who are on the point of death but for those who are ill, so that the church might recommend to the Lord, who suffered and died for his people, that he might bring relief and salvation to the sufferer.

F

Faith Healing. A practice of many Christians, though frequently associated with the Pentecostal* and charismatic* movements in particular, based on the belief that Jesus' promise of healing recorded in Mark 16:18 is for every generation of believers.

The postapostolic church continued the tradition of first-century believers by teaching and practicing a healing ministry to the sick. By the ninth century, however, evidence indicates that prayers for the sick had fallen from regular practice. The sixteenth-century Protestant Reformation* brought with it a revival of prayers for the sick. The Catholic Church* has maintained the Sacrament of the Anointing of the Sick* since the eleventh and twelfth centuries. It has recognized also other means of miraculous healings, including healing power associated with places (e.g., Lourdes, France) or prayers to a saint.*

The present-day faith-healing movements look to the late nineteenth century for their immediate antecedents, as led by Charles Cullis, Carrie Judd Montgomery,* Maria B. Woodworth-Etter,* A. B. Simpson,* A. J. Gordon,* R. A. Torrey,* John Alexander Dowie,* R. Kelso Carter and others.

At the turn of the century, individuals within the Holiness movement,* as well as isolated evangelicals,* were reporting divine healings. The Pentecostal movement in particular was making faith healing an important part of its teachings and practices. Charles F. Parham,* William J. Seymour,* Florence Crawford* and others believed it was God's will that anyone who was sick should be healed. Prior to World War II,* popular evangelists such as Aimee Semple McPherson* and others held salvation-healing meetings and attracted crowds numbering in the thousands.

Even more dramatic were the faith healers after World War II, especially William M. Branham* and Oral Roberts.* They were followed by Kathryn Kuhlman,* A. A. Allen,* Jack Coe* and others. By the 1960s the charismatic movement had begun to surface in mainline* denominations* and in the Catholic Church, bringing faith healing a newfound respectability.

From 1982 to 1986 Fuller Theological Seminary* offered a well-attended course entitled "Signs, Wonders and Church Growth." A parallel and equally controversial development has been the growth of John Wimber's Vineyard Fellowship, a nationwide network of congregations emphasizing the miraculous gifts of the Spirit.

See also FAITH MOVEMENT.

Faith Missions Movement. Arising from the founding of the China Inland Mission by Hudson Taylor in 1865, the movement in North America has grown to include at least fifteen thousand missionaries representing more than seventy-five different agencies. The typical financial policy of faith missions expresses the faith that God will provide funds and generally does not guarantee salaries for missionaries.

See also MISSIONS, EVANGELICAL FOREIGN.

Faith Movement (Word Movement). A movement arising within charismatic* Christianity during the early 1970s stressing the power of faith in obtaining the divine blessings of physical health and financial prosperity. The acknowledged patriarch of the movement is Kenneth Hagin (1917-).

The first of the movement's three main emphases is that physical health is always the will of God, as assured by Jesus' atonement, with lack of faith being the main obstacle to receiving healing. Second, God wants his people to prosper in every area of life, including financially. Third, drawing primarily from the writings of E. W. Kenyon,* the faith movement teaches that God's promises are obtained through positive confession—a positive statement of confident faith.

Praised by some for encouraging victorious living and unquestioning trust in God's promises, the movement has also been labeled a "charismatic humanism," a spiritualized "American dream" which inflicts guilt and confusion on sick and physically handicapped followers, and accused of favoring speculation and "revelation knowledge" over sound biblical interpretation.

Falckner, Justus (1672-1723). Lutheran* pioneer pastor and hymn writer. In 1703 Falckner accepted a call to serve the Lutheran Church in New York. For two decades he served a parish extending from Perth Amboy, New Jersey, to Albany, New York.

Falckner composed a number of German hymns. He is remembered for his tireless and varied contributions to the establishment of German Lutheranism in Pennsylvania.

Family, Christian. The family as an entity and the role of its individual members changed dramatically from the seventeenth century to the twentieth.

Seventeenth-century New England Christian families were influenced by the Puritans'* strong commitment to the family and by the necessity of working together to survive in a somewhat hostile environment. Late eighteenth-century European Enlightenment* thought emphasized the concept that human nature is basically good. The industrial revolution, while raising the general standard of living, also drew the workers out of the home and into an environment in which they worked with and for strangers.

The twentieth-century family structure has faced the challenges of materialism, world wars,* the Great Depression,* and more women working outside the home. Since the late 1940s Catholics* and others have participated in the Christian Family movement.* Since the 1970s evangelical* parachurch agencies have given increasing attention to the family, the most notable effort being James Dobson's Focus on the Family.

Family Life Division of the United States Catholic Conference. Prompted by Pope Pius XI's* 1930 encyclical* on marriage and family life, a Family Life Section was established in 1931 in the Social Action Department of what later became the U.S. Catholic Conference.* Its purpose was to aid Catholic family life activities.

Family of Love. A cultic* group arising from the Jesus movement* of the 1960s. Founded in 1968 by David Berg in southern California, the move-

ment has been known as Teens for Christ, Revolution for Jesus, Children of God and, since 1983, the Family of Love.

Originally an ultrafundamentalist sect,* the group devolved into a sex cult, as its leader, affectionately known as Moses David or "Mo" to his followers, promoted a form of religious prostitution known by members as Flirty Fishing.

Fanning, Tolbert (1810-1874). Church of Christ* preacher and editor. In 1844 Fanning founded Franklin College in Nashville and conducted it until the Civil War.* In 1855 he began editing the *Gospel Advocate,* which he continued with David Lipscomb* after the war.

Far Eastern Gospel Crusade. *See* SEND INTERNATIONAL.

Farley, John Murphy (1842-1918). Cardinal and fourth archbishop of New York. Farley received a series of papal honors, ultimately crowned by the title of cardinal priest in 1911. A learned man himself, he took particular interest in education, and under his leadership parochial schools* in the archdiocese doubled in number. He supported the Catholic University of America.* Farley's career was characterized by a pastoral care dominated by his cautious and peace-loving nature.

Fast Day. A day devoted to fasting as a sign of penitence and dependence on God. The fast day was an English Puritan* response to the Anglican* holy days. Plymouth Colony observed the first such day in 1636. The other Puritan colonies followed suit and imposed fines on those who recreated or labored on government-appointed fast days.

During the revolutionary era, other colonies proclaimed fast days, and special days for "publik humiliation, fasting and prayer" were set aside by the Continental and Confederation Congresses. Later, fasts were proclaimed by Presidents Adams (1798, 1799), Madison (War of 1812), Lincoln* (Civil War*) and Wilson* (1918).

Father. A form of address usually used by Catholic* laity to address a priest. Early Christians frequently called their spiritual leaders *father.* The modern custom apparently began in Ireland and, as a result of Irish immigrations, spread to the U.S., where it became firmly established during the second half of the nineteenth century.

Feast of Circumcision. A feast celebrated on January 1, the eighth day after Christmas,* since the sixth century, in Gaul and Spain; since the eleventh century, in Rome; and then throughout the Eastern and Western churches. The developed liturgy* includes four motifs: (1) the New Year, (2) the octave of Christmas, (3) the circumcision of Jesus and (4) Mary* as the Virgin-Mother of God.

Feasts of the Church. For almost all Christian groups, the principal feast day of all Christian churches is the Lord's Day—Sunday.* Within the cycle of the year, however, most denominations* have designated special feasts connected with the life of Christ (such as Easter* or Christmas*) or Sundays which are given over to a special emphasis (such as Mission* Sunday or Reformation Sunday). The Roman Catholic Church* also celebrates feast days of the Blessed Virgin,* the apostles and the other saints.*

Federal Council of Churches. Ecumenical* association of denominations* studying and acting upon matters of social importance. Founded in 1908, the Federal Council of Churches (FCC) initially comprised thirty-three denominations, numbering eighteen million American Protestants.*

Only the preamble to the constitution contained any hint of doctrinal conformity; it proclaimed simply that the FCC was "to manifest the essential oneness of the Christian churches of America in Jesus Christ as their divine Lord and Savior."

Several Eastern Orthodox* churches joined the FCC in 1938. As a leader in ecumenical relations, the FCC was able to lend its expertise and moral support to establishing of the World Council of Churches* in 1948. In 1950 the FCC merged with thirteen other interdenominational agencies to become the National Council of Churches.*

See also ECUMENISM.

Fee, John Gregg (1816-1901). Abolitionist* minister and founder of Berea College. Fee established antislavery churches in Kentucky and in 1855 founded an abolitionist school (now Berea College). He consistently joined conversion* with a Christian commitment to socially relevant causes.

Feehan, Patrick Augustine (1829-1902). First Catholic* archbishop of Chicago (1880-1902). Feehan devoted most of his time and energy in Chicago to "brick and mortar" activities, establishing a total of 140 new parishes. He also founded St. Mary's Training School, an orphanage and industrial school in Des Plaines, Illinois.

Feeney, Leonard (1898-1978). Jesuit* poet and controversialist. In 1943 Feeney began giving weekly lectures at Cambridge, Massachusetts, and quickly gained a large following. By 1946, however, he began teaching a rigorist interpretation of the ancient church doctrine that "outside the church there is no salvation."

In 1949 the Vatican's Holy Office officially condemned Feeney's interpretation of church doctrine, and in 1953 he was excommunicated.* This "Boston Heresy Case" made Feeney the most publicized heretic in American Catholic history.

Fellowship of Evangelical Bible Churches. Formerly Evangelical Mennonite Brethren Conference, the Fellowship of Evangelical Bible Churches (FEBC) was organized in 1889 by Mennonites* who emigrated from Russia to the U.S. in the 1870s. In recent years the conference has identified more closely with its pietist*/evangelical* heritage, dropping the word *Mennonite* from its name in 1987. Membership is roughly 4,500 in thirty-six congregations in North and South America.

Fellowship of Grace Brethren Churches. A conservative Brethren denomination.* Although related to other evangelicals* and fundamentalists,* the Grace Brethren differ from them in their emphasis on a peculiar observance of the Lord's Supper* which includes the love feast* and the service of foot washing.* The Brethren also practice adult baptism* by triple forward immersion. In 1986 the group had a membership of 41,249 in over three hundred congregations, most heavily concentrated in California, Ohio and Pennsylvania.

Fellowship of Reconciliation. Nondenominational Christian pacifist* and social-reform organization. The American branch of the Fellowship of Reconciliation (FOR) was organized in 1915 at a meeting of a group of Quakers,* Social Gospel* ministers* and leaders of the YMCA.* By the end of World War I,* FOR had become a meeting place for left-wing reformers attracted to pacifism and Christian pacifists. In 1942 Chicago FOR members organized the Congress of Racial Equality, which pioneered the use of nonviolence in the postwar crusade for black civil rights.*

Fellowship of Socialist Christians. Organized in 1932 in the crisis of the Great Depression,* the Fellowship of Socialist Christians was to develop critical socialist theory and action. The fellowship's guiding spirit was Reinhold Niebuhr,* for whom it served as a chief outlet for action from 1934 to the end of the decade. It sought to develop Christian social theory in order to critique capitalist individualism* while rejecting the secularism and reductionism of Marxism. Its journal was *Radical Religion* (1935), later named *Christianity and Society* (1940-1956).

Fellowship of Southern Churchmen. A nondenominational Christian social reform organization. Founded in 1934, the fellowship combined prophetic radicalism, neo-orthodoxy* and a strong sense of Christian vocation in supporting labor unions, tenant farmers and minorities. In 1964 it was reorganized as the Committee of Southern Churchmen.*

Feminism, Christian. A movement for women's equality rooted in Scripture and Christian faith. In America, Christian feminism mobilized in the climate of nineteenth-century revivalism* where the Spirit's call, not necessarily ordination* or education, qualified one to preach.

Religious freedom* and disestablishment in America contributed to new denominations* which were able to utilize women however they chose. Free-Will Baptists* had female preachers as early as 1797. In 1853 Congregationalists* became the first U.S. denomination to fully ordain a woman.

Temperance,* abolition* and women's suffrage* helped spur Christian feminism. Also, the rise of female foreign missionaries after the Civil War* meant that women now studied Bible and theology* in training schools (see Missionary Movement, Women's).

Diversity marks twentieth-century feminism. Early Pentecostals* (e.g., Aimee Semple McPherson*) and charismatics (e.g., Kathryn Kuhlman*) continued the tradition within Methodist-Holiness* churches of advocating women's public ministry. All of the Protestant* mainline* denominations now ordain women to the ministry.

Feminist theology has become a recognized theological movement among both Protestant* and Roman Catholic* theologians.

See also INCLUSIVE LANGUAGE MOVEMENT; ORDINATION OF WOMEN.

Fenwick, Benedict Joseph (1782-1846). Second Catholic* bishop of Boston. After serving as president of Georgetown College, Fenwick was head of the Boston diocese* from 1825 until his death. There he contended against anti-Catholicism and started new parishes. In 1843 he founded the College of the Holy Cross, the first Catholic college in New England.

Fenwick, Edward Dominic (1768-1832). Dominican* missionary bishop and founder of the first province of Dominicans in the U.S. In 1821 Fenwick was named the first bishop of Cincinnati, with responsibility for the spiritual welfare of Catholics in the vast area north to Canada and west across Lake Michigan to the Upper Mississippi River. Upon his death, Bishop Fenwick was mourned as the "apostle of Ohio."

Ferrill, London (Loudin) (?-1854). African-American Baptist* minister. Freed upon the death of his owner, Ferrill moved to Lexington, Kentucky, where the white First Baptist Church sponsored his ordination* and the membership of his First African Church in the Elkhorn Association in 1822. Respected by whites and especially by younger African-Americans, Ferrill became a man of wealth and fame.

Fideism. An epistemological perspective emphasizing the priority of faith over reason in religious knowledge. Fideists maintain that religious truth is apprehended by faith rather than evidential reasoning or rational arguments. Used pejoratively, *fideism* refers to a reliance on faith at the expense of reason.

Fielde, Adele (1839-1916). Baptist* missionary to China. After missionary service in Siam, Fielde went to China in 1872. There she began training Chinese women to become "Bible women"—lay Bible teachers and assistants to missionaries. She also organized a school, wrote textbooks, taught classes and conducted field training.

Fifield, James William, Jr. (1899-1977). Congregational* minister. A controversial libertarian conservative, Fifield founded Spiritual Mobilization in 1935 to rally the clergy to resist collectivism, including the New Deal. Its monthly *Faith and Freedom* (1949-1960) spread his anticommunist* views.

Fillmore, Myrtle Page (1845-1931), and Charles Sherlock Fillmore (1854-1948). Cofounders of the Unity School of Christianity.* Myrtle and Charles, married in 1881, each experienced a healing (she from tuberculosis, he from a withered leg), which was instrumental in the birth and development of what came to be known as the Unity School. Myrtle was the inspirational force in the early days of the movement, carrying on a ministry of prayer for those in need of healing. Though the Fillmores incorporated many aspects of orthodox* Christianity, their basic emphasis was on the necessity of obeying the divine laws by right thinking and right living, being unified with the Christ mind in prayer and thereby receiving the benefits of health and prosperity.

Finley, James Bradley (1781-1856). Itinerant* Methodist* minister. Finley succeeded in every circuit he served, spending most of his fifty ministerial years in Ohio. In the General Conference of 1844, Finley moved that a slaveholding bishop "desist from the exercise of this office so long as the impediment remains." That motion passed and became the catalyst for the sectional split of the Methodist Episcopal Church.

Finley, Samuel (1715-1766). New Side* Presbyterian* evangelist and fifth president of the College of New Jersey (later Princeton).* As a scholar, teacher and one of the most successful and respected of the New Side Presbyterians, Finley was a logical choice for the presidency of the College of New Jersey. He served from 1761 to 1766.

Finney, Charles Grandison (1792-1875). Leading revivalist* of the nineteenth century. Finney, known as the Father of Modern Revivalism, experienced a dramatic religious conversion* in 1821. After his ordination* in 1824, Finney began work as a missionary to the settlers of upstate New York. Under his preaching,* a series of revivals broke out in a number of little villages throughout Jefferson and St. Lawrence counties,

and by 1825 his work had spread to the towns of Western, Troy, Utica, Rome and Auburn. These revivals, in which Finney exercised "new measures"* such as the anxious seat,* protracted meetings and allowing women to pray in public, brought Finney national fame. During the years 1827-1832, Finney's revivals swept urban centers such as New York City, Philadelphia, Boston and Rochester.

Forced in 1832 to curtail his travels because of medical problems, Finney became pastor of churches in New York and Ohio and, from 1851 until 1866, president of what is now Oberlin College.*

Theologically, Finney can best be described as a New School* Calvinist.* His preaching and teaching—always pointed and dramatic—stressed the moral government of God, the ability of people to repent and make themselves new hearts, the perfectibility of human nature and society, and the need for Christians to apply their faith to daily living.

Fire-Baptized Holiness Movement. An early radical Holiness* movement characterized by "third blessing" theology.* In 1895 Benjamin Hardin Irwin* founded the Fire-Baptized Holiness Church. Irwin became an ardent advocate of a crisis experience of sanctification* subsequent to new birth* and also advocated a "third blessing," a "baptism with the Holy Ghost and fire." This distinction between an experience of sanctification and a subsequent baptism of the Spirit* prepared the way for the modern Pentecostal* revival.

Irwin traveled widely, first throughout the Midwest, later the South, propagating his views. His meetings were marked by considerable emotional display. Some who received the baptism reported seeing balls of fire and feeling a burning sensation within. Irwin's evangelistic activity led to the formation of state Fire-Baptized Holiness associations, beginning with Iowa in 1895.

In 1911 and in 1915 the movement was absorbed by merger with Pentecostal churches which, in 1975, became the International Pentecostal Holiness Church. In 1990 there were a reported 131,674 members.

First Amendment to the Constitution. The First Amendment, part of the so-called Bill of Rights, protects the most treasured rights of U.S. citizens—freedom of religion, speech, press, and the right to peaceably assemble and petition. Invariably the courts and scholars insist that a proper judicial interpretation, especially the clause on religious freedom, the Christian's most treasured legacy, must be based on the history of the First Amendment and the intent of the Framers.

See also CHURCH AND STATE, SEPARATION OF.

Fisher, George Park (1827-1909). Congregational* clergyman and Yale* church historian. Rooted in the later New England theology* as a student of Nathaniel William Taylor* and Edwards Amasa Park,* Fisher, a liberal,* epitomized the effort of church historians to be impartial in judgment and to apply to the history of Christianity the same methodology as would be applied to any social institution.

Fisher, Henry L. (1874-1947). Bishop of the United Holy Church of America.* Fisher was without a doubt the single most influential person in the United Holy Church of America during its early development. Following rather undistinguished predecessors, Fisher was elected to the office of president in 1916 and served with distinction until his death in 1947. Highly esteemed for his powerful preaching and endearing fatherly ways, Fisher traveled widely, preaching holiness,* establishing convocations and promoting missions.*

Fisher, Mary (1623?-1698). Quaker* traveling preacher. Arriving from England via Barbados, Fisher and Ann Austin* became the first Quakers to set foot in Boston. Later, after preaching in the West Indies and in the Middle East, Fisher sailed to South Carolina, where she became a pillar of the tiny Charleston Quaker Meeting.

Fisk, Pliny (1792-1825). Pioneer missionary to the Near East. In 1819 Fisk embarked on the first American mission to the Near East. First based at Smyrna, Fisk reached Jerusalem in 1823. His extensive journal and correspondence helped lay the foundation for a very large mission.

Fisk, Wilbur (1792-1839). Methodist* minister and educator. Fisk, the first president of Wesleyan University in Connecticut (1830-1839), spoke and wrote on behalf of missions* and temperance* and against Calvinism* and Universalism.* He was the first American Methodist theologian* to achieve recognition outside of his denomination.*

Fiske, Fidelia (1816-1864). Missionary to Persia. In 1843 Fiske went to the Nestorian Mission in Persia. For fifteen years she headed the school for girls at Oroomiah, which became a center for religious revival among women of the Nestorian community.

Five Point Deliverance. A doctrinal* statement adopted in 1910 by the Presbyterian Church (U.S.A.)* for licensing ministerial candidates. The deliverance, a victory for conservatives, was an integral part of a fifty-year struggle over revision of the creedal foundation (the Westminster* Standards) and control of the denomination.*

Flaget, Benedict Joseph (1763-1850). First bishop of Bardstown (Louisville), Kentucky. Flaget's diocese* covered most of the U.S. beyond the Alleghenies. Within a few years of his appointment, he had convoked a diocesan synod, established St. Thomas Seminary and authorized the foundation of two communities of religious women. Flaget's diocese was divided eleven times as Catholicism developed in the West. In forty years of tireless missionary activity, Flaget became widely respected for his administrative skill and personal holiness.*

Fleming, Paul William (1911-1950). Founder of New Tribes Mission. In 1942 Fleming recruited Cecil Dye, who led a small band of workers to Bolivia, representing the first efforts of the New Tribes Mission. In 1943 Fleming formed the New Tribes Institute for the training of missionary personnel.

Fletcher, Joseph F. (1905-1991). Ethicist. Fletcher was professor of social ethics at the Episcopal Theological School, Cambridge, Massachusetts. His early interest in biomedical ethics led to his first book, *Morals and Medicine* (1954). But his *Situation Ethics: The New Morality* (1966) was his most famous and controversial work, the title of which quickly worked its way into popular terminology and, for conservatives, symbolized much of what had gone wrong in modern society. The final years of his teaching career were spent as a visiting lecturer in medical ethics at the University of Virginia.

Florovsky, Georges Vasilievich (1893-1979). Russian Orthodox* theologian. As a middle-aged student in Paris, Florovsky quickly became a leader of the "Parisian School" of émigré Russian theologians. In 1948 he immigrated to America, teaching at St. Vladimir's Orthodox Theological Seminary in New York, Harvard* Divinity School and Princeton University,* all the while remaining active in the ecumenical movement.

Flower, Joseph James Roswell (1888-1970). Assemblies of God* founder and leader. In 1907 Flower identified with a newly formed Pentecostal* group that had been part of the local Christian and Missionary Alliance* branch. In 1908 he began to edit a monthly paper, *The Pentecost,* as well as to travel in evangelistic* ministry. In 1914 Flower participated in the convention in Hot Springs, Arkansas, which organized the General Council of the Assemblies of God. From 1914 until his retirement in 1959, he served that organization in various offices. He also was influential in organizing the National Association of Evangelicals.*

Font. *See* BAPTISMAL FONT.

Foot Washing. A religious rite, regarded as either an ordinance or sacrament,* practiced by a number of American church groups. It is based on Jesus' words in John 13:14, its presence in the early church (1 Tim 5:10), and its practice, especially on Maundy Thursday, by various groups throughout church history.

Foote, Julia A. J. (1823-1900). African Methodist Episcopal Zion* exhorter and preacher. Foote held meetings in upstate New York, Ohio, Michigan and Canada. Eventually recognized by her church, she became her denomination's* first female deacon* in 1894 and was ordained* its second woman elder* in 1900.

Ford, Gerald Rudolph (1913-). Thirty-eighth U.S. president and devout Episcopalian* churchman. Elected to Congress in 1948 as a Republican from the Grand Rapids area for the first of thirteen times, Ford was House minority leader from 1965 to 1973.

In 1973 Ford became vice president of the U.S., and in 1974 president, the first person to occupy the White House without being elected either president or vice president. A conservative on domestic issues and an internationalist in foreign affairs, Ford was widely known as a thoughtful man of prayer* whose public addresses often reflected both his personal faith and his civil religion.*

Ford became the Republican nominee for president in 1976, only to lose to fellow evangelical* Jimmy Carter* in a close race.

Ford, Reuben (1742-1823). Baptist* pastor and apologist for religious liberty.* Ford spent much of his career clarifying church-state relations through his contacts with Patrick Henry,* Thomas Jefferson* and James Madison. In 1776 he helped eliminate compulsory tax support for the clergy.

Foreign Missions Conference of North America. An interdenominational group of cooperative mission bodies. Arising out of a meeting in 1893 of interested ecumenists and representatives of twenty-one mission boards and other organizations, the Foreign Missions Conference of North America (FMC) held meetings annually beginning in 1895. In 1950 the FMC voted to become a constituting member of the National Council of the Churches of Christ in the U.S.A.* as its Division of Foreign Missions.

Fosdick, Harry Emerson (1878-1969). Liberal* Baptist* preacher. After serving in a pastorate in New Jersey and then as a chaplain during World War I,* Fosdick became pulpit minister at First Presbyterian Church, New York City (1918-1925). There he gained national attention in 1922 when he preached his most famous sermon, "Shall the Fundamentalists Win?" It was intended as a plea for greater tolerance and understanding between fundamentalists* and liberals. Fosdick essentially asked fundamentalists to tolerate other opinions on three central issues: the virgin birth, the inerrancy* of the Bible and the literal Second Coming of Christ.

Resigning from his church in 1924, Fosdick next became pastor of Park Avenue Baptist Church (1925-1930). By 1930 the congregation had erected a new building named Riverside Church, where Fosdick served until his retirement in 1946. At Fosdick's insistence, the ministry of Riverside Church was nonsectarian. The program was one of Christian personalism, a people-centered ministry emphasizing personal spiritual growth and social consciousness.

Foster, Frank Hugh (1851-1935). Theologian and historian. Foster began his career as a defender of Calvinism.* By the time he concluded his most important and best-known work, *A Genetic History of the New England Theology* (1907), he had become a radical naturalist. Foster's analysis of the history of ideas in American theology marked an advance over contemporary sentimentalism and denominational allegiances.

Foster, George Burman (1858-1918). Baptist* theologian and educator. One of the seminal thinkers of the late nineteenth century, Foster for most of his career taught systematic theology* or philosophy of religion* at the University of Chicago* (1895-1910). Given the rising reputation of the Chicago school* of theological studies, Foster had a broad influence on philosophical approaches to religion and on the next generation of theologians.

Four Spiritual Laws. Formulated by William ("Bill") R. Bright,* the Four Spiritual Laws were designed to be a tool for evangelism* among college students. These laws, supported by Bible verses and diagrams, provide a step-by-step approach for converting* an individual to Christianity.

Foursquare Church. *See* INTERNATIONAL CHURCH OF THE FOURSQUARE GOSPEL.

Fox, George (1624-1691). Founder of the Religious Society of Friends* (Quakers). Fox reached maturity during great political, social and religious upheaval in England. In a time of great personal despair, he had an experience of Christ's spiritual presence, which he subsequently communicated in his travels throughout England and abroad.

Fox's influence in America was primarily indirect, although his one visit to America, traveling up and down the Atlantic seaboard in 1672-1673, strengthened American Quakerism.

See also PENN, WILLIAM.

Foxe's Book of Martyrs. A Protestant* martyrology influential among colonial Puritans.* Written in 1563 by John Foxe (1517-1587), the book recounts the lives of Protestant reformers and martyrs through the reign of Queen Mary (1553-1558).

The martyrdom of Protestants is dramatized as a spiritual warfare of the elect, who are sustained by a confident expectation of the final triumph of the forces of Christ over those of the antichrist

and the inauguration of a new age. For Puritans, this providential conception of history led to the English believing themselves an "elect nation" with a special role to play in God's redemptive plan.

Franciscans. A common designation for various religious communities professing to live according to the ideals of Francis of Assisi (d. 1226). Franciscans, who had always cultivated popular preaching and missionary* activities, took an active role in evangelizing the Americas under the patronage of the Catholic* colonial powers.

In the republic, Franciscans were reintroduced in 1844, when Austrian friars volunteered to minister to German Catholics in Cincinnati. Other missions soon followed. Because of the needs of the church, North American Franciscans became heavily involved in parochial* and educational ministries, in addition to their traditional preaching activity.

See also MISSIONS TO NORTH AMERICA, FRENCH; MISSIONS TO NORTH AMERICA, SPANISH.

Franson, Fredrik (1852-1908). Evangelist and missionary statesman. Deeply influenced by D. L. Moody,* Franson became the preeminent evangelist and revivalist* to the late nineteenth-century Scandinavian communities of the north central and western U.S. Franson is credited with founding some nineteen or twenty missionary societies in Europe and the U.S.

Free African Society. Early African-American voluntary association. Organized in 1787 by former slaves Richard Allen* and Absalom Jones, the society initially was a mutual-benefit association. It increasingly assumed religious functions, in 1791-1792 becoming "the Elders and Deacons of the African Church."

See AFRICAN METHODIST EPISCOPAL CHURCH.

Free Church Tradition in America. The term *free church* emerged in nineteenth-century England among non-Anglican denominations as a more positive self-description than *Nonconformist, Dissenter* or even *Protestant.* Emphasizing the principled separation from the established church, the term denoted a voluntary covenanting of believers in self-supporting and self-regulating gathered churches. The term has been widely used in North America since the 1950s. American denominations derived from Continental free churches can be categorized into three church families: (1) radical reformers, (2) Brethren and (3) pietists.*

Radical Reformers. Alongside mainstream Lutheran* and Reformed* churches emerged reformers dedicated to a more radical revision of church life. Called Anabaptists (rebaptizers) because they rejected infant baptism and practiced baptism of covenanting believers, by 1525 they had appeared in various parts of Europe. Anabaptists often understood themselves as uncompromising disciples of the Protestant reformers, determined to complete the reform of doctrine by reformation of life.

Anabaptists were bloodily suppressed by Catholics* and Protestants alike. The earliest free development of this tradition took place in the Netherlands, where the movement took the name "Mennonite,"* after Menno Simons, who became a leader of the movement after 1536. In the late seventeenth and early eighteenth centuries, many Mennonites, leaving Switzerland and the Palatinate, migrated to America, with Pennsylvania as their favored destination.

Two other Anabaptist-derived movements garner wide attention for their determinedly nonconformist ways: the Amish* and the Hutterian Brethren.*

Brethren. Initiated as a merging of Pietist and Anabaptist strands in 1708 in central Germany, Brethren emigrated to America after 1719. Known colloquially as "Dunkers," the movement has experienced various schisms, leading to the Ephrata Community,* the Old German Baptist Brethren ("Old Orders"), the Brethren Church (Ashland, Ohio), the Church of the Brethren, the Dunkard Brethren and the Fellowship of Grace Brethren Churches* (Winona Lake, Indiana).

Pietists. Pietism was a renewal movement beginning among late seventeenth-century German Lutheran and Reformed Churches seeking to inculcate true piety in individual believers. Although the Moravian Church* originated in the fifteenth century, it experienced pietistic revitalization in 1727 under Count Zinzendorf.*

Two remaining Continental free churches stem from Scandinavia. The Evangelical Covenant Church* developed from pietist Bible study* conventicles in nineteenth-century Sweden. A similar group, the Evangelical Free Church of America,* was formed in 1950 when two independent Scandinavian bodies of pietist derivation united.

See also AMANA CHURCH SOCIETY; ANABAPTIST TRADITION AND VISION; MENNONITE CHURCHES; PIETISM.

Free Methodist Church of North America. Founded in 1860 by two reform movements expelled from the Methodist Episcopal Church, the group added the word *Free* to its name to show that it stood for free pews,* freedom for the slaves and freedom in worship.* The church today remains close to its theological roots.

Free Will. *See* PREDESTINATION.

Free Will Baptists. Formed in opposition to Calvinist* predestination* among Regular Baptists,* Free Will Baptists arose in this country from two streams—one in North Carolina (1720s) and another in New England (1780). In 1935 representatives from these groups formed the National Association of Free Will Baptists (NAFWB). The Free Wills are distinguished from other Baptists by their intense conservatism, centralized organizational structure and the practice of foot washing.*

See also THE BAPTIST CHURCHES IN U.S.A.; PALMER, PAUL; RANDALL, BENJAMIN.

Freed, Arvy Glenn (1868-1931). Church of Christ* educator, preacher and debater. With his former student Nicholas B. Hardeman,* Freed established the National Teachers' Normal and Business College (in Henderson, Tenn.), which eventually became Freed-Hardeman College. Although highly regarded as a preacher, Freed's real influence was in education.

Freeman, Hobart (1920-1984). Cult* leader. After being dismissed from the Fellowship of Grace Brethren Churches* in 1963 for promulgating extreme antidenominational views, Freeman later was associated with the charismatic* "Glory Barn" near North Webster, Indiana. In 1978 he left to establish the "Faith Assembly" near Warsaw, Indiana, which grew rapidly. Freeman's most controversial tenet involved faith healing,* rejecting all use of traditional medicine.

Frei, Hans Wilhelm (1922-1988). Theologian. Frei was born in Breslau, Germany, but immigrated to the U.S. in 1938, where he received his postsecondary education. He taught in the religious studies department of Yale University* from 1957 until his death in 1988. Frei's books include *The Identity of Jesus Christ* (1975) and *Types of*

Christian Theology (1992), but his best known work is *The Eclipse of Biblical Narrative* (1974). In this and other work he made an important contribution to narrative theology and the emerging postliberal "Yale School" of theology.

Frelinghuysen, Theodorus Jacobus (1691-c. 1747). Dutch Reformed* minister in New Jersey. A fervent pietist,* Frelinghuysen settled in the Raritan Valley of New Jersey, where he enjoyed considerable success among the Dutch. He flouted ecclesiastical conventions and excoriated the Dutch Reformed hierarchy back in Amsterdam for failing to send pietist ministers to the New World.

Frelinghuysen's evangelical* fervor and his itinerancy* contributed to the onset of the Great Awakening* in the Middle Colonies. Gilbert Tennent,* Jonathan Edwards* and George Whitefield* spoke highly of Frelinghuysen's ministry.

Friar. A member of one of the mendicant orders of Roman Catholicism.* The four chief orders, recognized in the thirteenth century, are Franciscans,* Dominicans,* Carmelites and Augustinians.*

Friends, The Religious Society of (Quakers). The Society of Friends was one of many religious groups which arose from the ferment of the English Puritan* revolution. The movement dates its origin from a vision that George Fox* had in 1652. The nickname *Quaker* was early used to describe the Friends because they were known to tremble when they fell under the power of God. "Friends" or "Society of Friends" is the preferred title.

The burden of Fox's preaching was to turn every person to the Light of Christ within. For Fox, this Light was the transcendent God perceptibly breaking into human consciousness. Quakers came to esteem Scripture for self-examination and as a test of morals and doctrine but always placed it under the authority of the living Christ.

Fox refused to participate in war or to take an oath because he understood these to be prohibited by the Sermon on the Mount. In America, Quakers have suffered for their pacifist* stance during every war since the colonial period, often being accused as traitors.

Quakers, believing that the gift of ministry is not distributed according to gender, have fostered female leadership since the movement's earliest days.

Almost immediately after the movement was born, Quakers began immigrating to America. Although suffering early persecution, by 1657 a number of Quakers had found a more tolerant home in Rhode Island. When William Penn,* the most prominent Quaker in American history, received a charter for his colony of Pennsylvania in 1681, it immediately became a haven for persecuted Quakers and other religious groups.

The bright flower of eighteenth-century American Quakerism was John Woolman.* Woolman, sensitive in conscience, early recognized the evils of slavery (*see* Abolition and the Churches) and eventually persuaded the Society of Friends of his view.

The flush of revolutionary ardor and the exaltation of free thought over against Scripture and religious authority captured the imagination of Elias Hicks* and resulted in the Hicksite schism of 1827-1828. The Hicksites equated the Light with reason, disparaged the deity of Christ,* his substitutionary atonement,* biblical authority, mission* activity, most evangelical* philanthropies* and cooperation with other denominations.*

Other divisions led to the Gurneyites* and the Wilburites. British Quaker Joseph John Gurney* and his followers were orthodox regarding the authority of Scripture, the deity of Christ and the significance of his death and resurrection for the forgiveness of sins. Gurney himself defended the traditional Quaker style of silent worship, without benefit of prepared sermon,* hymns* or paid clergy, but his followers on the American frontier gradually adopted these innovations.

New England Quaker John Wilbur* was also orthodox in his belief in the deity of Christ and the significance of his death on the cross. He feared, however, that Gurney was placing too much stress on biblical authority and losing the traditional Quaker reliance on the immediate presence of Christ.

Though presently numbering only 112,000 members in some 1,000 congregations in the U.S., there is as much theological diversity among American Quakers as there is among Protestants* generally. Members of the Evangelical Friends Alliance* are theologically conservative evangelicals and use music and prepared sermons in their worship services. Friends General Conference is the liberal wing; worship in these meetings is generally silent and without reliance upon paid leadership or prepared messages. Friends United

Meeting roughly corresponds theologically to mainline Protestantism.

Frontier Fellowship. *See* FELLOWSHIP OF SOCIALIST CHRISTIANS.

Frontier Religion. A term loosely applied to popular Protestantism* of the Second Great Awakening* as it developed in the trans-Allegheny West during the first decades of the nineteenth century.

Some broad generalizations may be made. First, popular religion was decidedly evangelical,* emotionally intense, often individualistic and anti-intellectual. These characteristics are best illustrated by camp meeting* revivalism,* particularly the great Cane Ridge revival* of 1801, and the experiences of dedicated backwoods preachers, such as Methodist* Peter Cartwright.*

Second, those denominations which used western revivalism and best adapted to frontier conditions reaped the most benefits in terms of expansion and growth. The Baptists* and Methodists were most successful.

A third characteristic of frontier religion was its plurality and the opportunity it provided for experimentation.

Although the census department officially closed the frontier in 1890, the religious diversity and individualism nurtured on the frontier have continued to shape American church life.

Frost, Henry Weston (1858-1945). Mission society* director. Frost established the American branch of the China Inland Mission (Overseas Missionary Fellowship*) and at first served as secretary of the Mission (1889-1893) and later was home director at Philadelphia (1893-1919).

Frost, James Marion (1848-1916). Southern Baptist* pastor and Sunday School* Board executive. The proposal for a Sunday School Board was adopted in 1891, and Frost served as its leader for over two decades. Under his leadership it gained denominational confidence, developed into publishing curriculum materials and books, and launched programs designed to strengthen Sunday schools and the denomination. Today it is the largest denominational publishing agency in the world.

Frothingham, Ebenezer (1719-1798). Congregational* Separatist.* Frothingham was the leading apologist of the pro-revival Separatists (or "Strict Congregationalists") of the Great Awakening.* His *Articles of Faith and Practice* (1750) was the first comprehensive treatment of Separate beliefs, particularly the new birth* and regenerate church membership.*

Frothingham, Octavius Brooks (1822-1895). Unitarian* minister. Frothingham's ministry from 1847 to 1879 in New England and New York City marked a transition in Unitarianism. Frothingham guided the "de-Christianization" of a large segment of that movement through the founding of the Free Religion Association.

Frothingham's religious beliefs became increasingly unorthodox throughout the 1860s when he began to describe himself as a "theistic* humanist." He criticized the revivals* of Henry Ward Beecher* and Dwight L. Moody* and accused Christianity of becoming institutionalized.

Fry, Franklin Clark (1900-1968). Lutheran* leader and ecumenist.* Fry's successive service to Lutherans at large tasks revealed his gifts. As president of the United Lutheran Church in America (1944-1962) and of the consolidated Lutheran Church in America* (1962-1968), Fry linked confessional* loyalty and ecumenical endeavor, emphasizing the oneness of Christ's church. To many, he was "Mr. Protestant."

Fulford, Francis (1803-1868). Anglican* bishop of Montreal. Widely respected for his gifts as a conciliator, Fulford worked to establish links between the Church of England and the Protestant Episcopal Church* in the U.S.

Full Gospel Business Men's Fellowship International. A lay organization within the charismatic* movement. The fellowship is a nondenominational association of charismatic businessmen who emphasize fellowship* and world evangelism,* being united in their belief in the full gospel (salvation,* divine healing,* Spirit baptism* accompanied by the sign of speaking in tongues* and the imminent personal return of Jesus). The founder and president is Demos Shakarian.* In 1993 there were a reported 60,000 members in the U.S.

Fuller, Charles E. (1887-1969). Radio evangelist and cofounder of Fuller Theological Seminary.* In 1937 Fuller took his radio program airing in Southern California to a national audience. Renamed *The Old-Fashioned Gospel Hour,* the program by 1939 reached an estimated ten million listeners on Sunday evenings. In 1947 Fuller joined Harold John Ockenga,* pastor of Park Street Church in Boston, in founding Fuller Theological Seminary in Pasadena, California.

Fuller, Richard (1804-1876). Prominent Baptist* pastor and leader in the formation of the Southern Baptist Convention.* Fuller, who published a scriptural defense of slavery in 1845, served as convention president for two years, preaching the first annual sermon in 1846.

Fuller, Samuel (?-1632). Deacon and physician of Plymouth, Massachusetts. As Plymouth's surgeon, Fuller was sent in 1630 to offer medical help to the settlers of Massachusetts Bay. In the process he explained Plymouth's separatist* church polity,* which led to establishing religious ties between the two colonies.

Fuller Theological Seminary. A leading seminary in the evangelical* renaissance following World War II.* Fuller was founded in Pasadena, California, in 1947, primarily through the efforts of Charles E. Fuller* and Harold John Ockenga.* At a time when the lines between fundamentalism* and evangelicalism were indistinct, the seminary increasingly was identified with the "new evangelicalism"* (Ockenga's term).

Since 1963, under the leadership of David Hubbard, Fuller has become the undisputed leader in progressive evangelicalism. Thanks to Hubbard's ability to develop a new constituency from mainline* evangelicals and Pentecostals,* by the 1980s Fuller had become the largest nondenominational seminary in the U.S.

Fundamental Theology. The systematic reflection on the possibility and legitimacy of Christian theology prior to revealed doctrinal content (not to be confused with fundamentalist* theology). Fundamental theology has been a particular concern of modern Roman Catholic* theologians such as Karl Rahner.*

Fundamental theology is apologetic* in nature and can be understood as a part of natural theology.* It attempts to demonstrate certain truths without reference to what is revealed to the church* in Scripture. Its basic premises come from the world at large and from within the human person.

Fundamentalism. A movement organized in the early twentieth century to defend orthodox* Protestant* Christianity against the challenges of theological liberalism,* higher criticism of the Bible, evolution* and other modernisms* judged to be harmful to traditional faith.

Changing Interpretations of Fundamentalism. Beginning in the 1930s, most scholars viewed fundamentalism in terms of cultural lag or social displacement. By the late 1960s, however, historians had begun looking at fundamentalism as a bona fide religious, theological and even intellectual movement in its own right. The most sophisticated thesis to date has been offered in George M. Marsden's *Fundamentalism and American Culture* (1980), which defines fundamentalism as "militantly anti-modernist Protestant evangelicalism."*

Such shifts in historiography suggest that fundamentalism should be seen as a rather distinctive modern reaction to religious, social and intellectual changes of the late 1800s and early 1900s, a reaction that eventually took on a life of its own and changed significantly over time. In fact, one can detect five distinct but overlapping phases in the history of American fundamentalism.

Forming Conservative Coalitions, 1875-1900. After the Civil War* various intellectual, social and religious changes undermined the foundations of the evangelical empire. Many Protestants adjusted to these challenges by adopting a New Theology;* others developed a Social Gospel.* Most conservative evangelicals, however, found such adjustments unacceptable.

During this period conservatives engaged in many cooperative efforts. They built their own Bible institutes* and gathered in their summer Bible conferences.* Such associations cut across denominational* lines and provided the personal and organizational framework for a later fundamentalism that was more self-conscious.

Finding a Fundamentalist Agenda, 1900-1920. During this period conservatives were articulating a core of nonnegotiable beliefs and developing a stronger sense of mutual identity. They produced *The Fundamentals* * (1910-1915) in an effort to identify and overcome what was wrong with modern religion and society.

In 1910 the General Assembly of the Northern

Presbyterian Church affirmed five essential doctrines (see Five Point Deliverance) that it (and many others) believed had come under attack: the inerrancy of the Bible, the virgin birth of Christ, his substitutionary atonement,* his bodily resurrection and his miracles.

Battling Modernism in the Public Arena, 1920-1935. During the 1920s and early 1930s fundamentalists engaged in a series of public disputes in order to purge liberals from the evangelical denominations and took action to eliminate the teaching of evolution in the public schools.

The fiercest battles were waged in the Northern Baptist* and Presbyterian* denominations. In both cases liberals turned back efforts by conservatives to adopt more restrictive statements of faith.

Establishing New Institutions, 1930-1950. Having failed in their two crusades, many fundamentalists decided to start institutions of their own. Conservative groupings of Baptists and Presbyterians were formed, as well as literally thousands of independent Baptist and Bible Churches.*

Equally important was the vibrant subculture that separatistic fundamentalists created for themselves, as they built their own schools,* publishing houses and mission agencies. They continued or founded their own Bible conferences and Bible institutes and even engaged in their own brand of ecumenism.* Militants founded the American Council of Christian Churches* (1941), while moderates founded the slightly less separatistic National Association of Evangelicals* (1942).

Rebuilding and Regrouping, 1945-1980s. After World War II,* fundamentalists continued to change. In the late 1940s Harold J. Ockenga* called for a "new evangelicalism"* devoid of fundamentalism's shortcomings. Carl F. H. Henry* criticized fundamentalism for its anti-intellectualism, divisiveness, lack of social conscience and uncritical alliance with political conservatism. Other evangelicals founded *Christianity Today** as the journal for the new movement and looked to the leadership of a young evangelist named Billy Graham.*

By the 1980s fundamentalism was more divided than ever. Militants still argued over the limits of separatism and fretted over how many of their own had moved toward neo-evangelicalism. More moderate evangelicals became equally concerned about the growing diversity in their ranks over biblical inerrancy, Christian feminism,* char-

ismatic* gifts and political involvement.

See also FUNDAMENTALIST-MODERNIST CONTROVERSY.

Fundamentalist Baptist Fellowship. A movement of conservatives in the Northern Baptist* Convention. In 1921 a group that came to be called the Fundamentalist Fellowship sought unsuccessfully to rid Northern Baptist Convention schools of liberal* teachers.

The Fundamentalist Fellowship stayed within the denomination until the 1940s. In 1943 the fundamentalists organized the Conservative Baptist Foreign Mission Society and laid the foundation for the Conservative Baptist* movement.

Fundamentalist-Modernist Controversy. The fundamentalist*-modernist* controversy was an extended conflict in the Protestant* churches and American society at large between religious liberals, who sought to preserve Christianity by accommodating the traditional faith to modern culture, and militant theological conservatives, determined to save evangelical* Christianity and American civilization from the advances of modernism and Darwinism.*

In 1865 most Americans thought of their country as a Christian nation and, demonstrating an impressive unity of beliefs and values, looked on evangelical Protestantism as the national religion. In the years between the Civil War* and World War I,* this consensus dissolved. Differing responses to the profound intellectual and social changes of the late nineteenth and early twentieth centuries produced sharp divisions in American Protestantism which, in the wake of World War I, erupted in the fundamentalist-modernist controversy.

Evangelical Protestants responded to these changes in different ways. Many, accepting the advances in science, history and biblical studies, set out to save Christianity by adjusting the traditional faith to modern intellectual trends. These were the liberals, or so-called modernists.

Around the turn of the century, conservative Protestants began to forge alliances to defend supernatural Bible-based Christianity against the advances of liberalism. The clearest manifestation of this nascent coalition was the publication of *The Fundamentals** (1910-1915).

In the heat of the cultural crisis that gripped America after World War I, fundamentalism emerged as a distinct movement, and the long-developing differences between liberals and conservatives exploded in the fundamentalist-modernist controversy. Modernists, more aggressive and influential than ever, and fundamentalists, sure that liberal theology and Darwinism were undermining Christianity and American civilization, squared off for battle.

They fought on two fronts: the churches and the culture at large. In the major denominations and their mission* fields, conservatives sought to halt liberalism by requiring subscription to traditional doctrines of supernaturalist Christianity. Liberals insisted that they were evangelical Christians and appealed to the American sense of liberty and tolerance. By 1926 the liberal appeal to tolerance had essentially succeeded.

In the culture generally, a variety of interdenominational groups and individuals sought to save American civilization from the effects of Darwinism. This effort led to the Scopes trial* of 1925, which did irreparable damage to the fundamentalist cause.

Fundamentalism and modernism underwent significant changes after 1930. Conservatives regrouped and emerged later in the century as evangelicals and fundamentalists. Liberals abandoned their sanguine view of humanity and history. Henceforth, divisions between conservative and liberal Christians would far overshadow differences based on formal denominational ties.

See also EVANGELICALISM; HERESY TRIALS; LIBERALISM/ MODERNISM, PROTESTANT.

Fundamentals, The. A twelve-volume paperback series, published between 1910 and 1915, containing essays testifying to the truth of traditional Protestant* orthodoxy.* *The Fundamentals,* usually regarded as a signal of the beginning of the organized fundamentalist* movement, was one of the sources for the movement's name. Lyman Stewart,* with his brother Milton, financed the project, sending out some three million sets gratis to English-speaking Protestant religious workers all over the world.

The central themes of the volumes were that conservative evangelical* Protestantism could be defended on two major counts. First, its affirmations of miraculous divine interventions were fully compatible with modern science and rationality. Second, the testimony of personal experience was also important in confirming Christian belief.

See also FUNDAMENTALIST-MODERNIST CONTROVERSY.

Funerals. A ceremony customarily performed to mark the death of a person and to dispose of the body in a respectful manner. Historical records and archaeological evidence suggest that all societies have developed funeral rituals, sometimes elaborate and mostly religious. Contemporary American funeral rites and customs vary greatly from one part of the country to another, yet there are common elements, particularly among Christian communities.

Christian burial practices evolved out of the customs of Judaism but emphasized reverence for the body as "the temple of the Holy Spirit" and the positive message of the resurrection.

Funk, John Fretz (1835-1930). Mennonite* leader. Funk was an innovator, introducing methods such as Sunday schools* and evangelism* to the Mennonites. During the period from roughly 1870 to 1900, Funk was the outstanding leader of the Mennonite Church. He was instrumental in helping the church move from a German-speaking immigrant church to a predominantly English-speaking church that was increasingly at home in America.

Furman, Richard (1755-1825). Early eighteenth-century Baptist* leader in the South. Considered the most important Baptist leader of the antebellum South, Furman was a pioneer denominational statesman. Besides serving as president of several Baptist conventions, he was most responsible for developing the organizational concepts that prevailed in the creation of the Southern Baptist Convention* (1845). In 1822 Furman, an aristocratic slave owner, wrote the classic Southern biblical defense of slavery.

G

Gaebelein, Arno Clemens (1861-1945). Fundamentalist* Bible teacher and editor. Adopting dispensational premillennialism* in the late 1880s, Gaebelein soon became one of its most articulate advocates.

Gaebelein was a forerunner of the militant fundamentalism that emerged after World War I.* In 1899, believing the Methodist Church* to be apostate, he left that church and promoted ecclesiastical separatism* long before it became fashionable among other conservative evangelicals.*

Gailor, Thomas Frank (1856-1935). Episcopal* bishop. Over the years Gailor became synonymous with The University of the South (Sewanee, Tennessee) and the Diocese* of Tennessee. Besides serving as professor and chancellor of the university, Gailor was bishop of Tennessee and president of the National Council of the Episcopal Church.

Gallicanism. An ancient doctrine concerning the proper relationship between the papacy and the French church, stressing the limitation of papal power. Its defeat was sealed at the First Vatican Council* by the declaration of papal infallibility.*

See also PAPACY AND U.S. CATHOLICS; ULTRAMONTANISM.

Gallitzin, Demetrius Augustine (1770-1840). Pioneer Catholic* missionary in Maryland and Pennsylvania. Gallitzin was ordained* in Baltimore in 1795, the first priest to receive all his training and orders in the U.S. After missionary work in Maryland, he established a Catholic community in Loretto, Pennsylvania.

Gambrell, James Bruton (1841-1921). Southern Baptist* pastor, editor and denominational* leader. Gambrell served four terms as president of the Southern Baptist Convention (1917-1921). Known for his practical wisdom and keen wit, he stressed isolation from ecumenical* involvement.

Gannett, Ezra Stiles (1801-1871). Unitarian* minister and denominational* statesman. Gannett was president of the American Unitarian Association* (1847-1851) and the Benevolent Fraternity of (Unitarian) Churches* (1857-1862). A conservative whose preaching stressed the primacy of faith in Christ, Gannett opposed the transcendentalists'* efforts to reduce Unitarianism to a species of ethical humanism.

Gano, John (1727-1804). Baptist* pastor, itinerant* evangelist in the South, Revolutionary War* chaplain.* In 1754 Gano began a series of trips into the South as an evangelist of the Philadelphia Association,* distinguishing himself as a warm-hearted preacher and peacemaker among the struggling churches. He was instrumental in establishing and reorganizing churches conforming to the Regular* Baptist (Calvinist) order.

Garden, Alexander (1685-1756). Anglican* leader in colonial South Carolina. Creating an effective working arrangement between clergy and political leaders, Garden moved the provincial Anglican Church toward more independence from England, opposed pluralism and significantly strengthened Anglicanism.

Garfield, James (1831-1881). Twentieth president of the U.S. and first chief executive openly to confess that he had been "born again."* According to his own account, Garfield's conversion* occurred in 1850.

After serving as a Republican congressman from Ohio from 1862 to 1880, Garfield won election to the Senate but, before he could take his seat, a deadlocked Republican national convention nominated him as a compromise candidate for the office of president. Winning comfortably, Garfield took office in March 1881, only to be shot four months later by a deranged lawyer. He died in September.

As a politician, Garfield was both devout and scholarly and often reflected on the relationship between religious commitment and political participation. Although his presidency was too brief to yield extensive change, his efforts eventually resulted in broad civil-service reform.

Garnet, Henry Highland (1815-1882). Presbyterian* preacher and abolitionist* orator. Born in slavery on a Maryland farm, at age nine Garnet fled to New York City, where he was educated. Ordained in 1842, he served Presbyterian churches in various places and also involved himself with the politically active wing of the antislavery movement.

Garrettson, Freeborn (1752-1827). Itinerant* Methodist* minister. Converted in his early twenties under the preaching* of Francis Asbury,* Garrettson freed his slaves and started an itinerant ministry in 1775. He traveled widely, preaching a message of Christian perfection,* pacifism* and aggressive abolitionism.* The first to push Methodism beyond the Alleghenies, apart from Asbury, Garrettson was the most important figure in early American Methodism.

Garrigus, Alice Belle (1858-1949). Pentecostal* evangelist. After service as a teacher and itinerant* preacher, Garrigus went to Newfoundland as a missionary in 1910. She is credited with founding the Pentecostal movement in Newfoundland.

Garrison, James Harvey (1842-1931). Disciples of Christ* editor. Garrison was a moderate in a time of great change within the Christian Churches* and Disciples of Christ. A theological conservative, he nevertheless was open to scholarly opinion regarding higher criticism and supported the involvement of the Disciples in the Federal Council of Churches.* As one of the preeminent elder-statesmen among the Christian Churches, he helped lead them into national recognition.

Garrison, William Lloyd (1805-1879). Reformer and journalist. The indifference of many clergymen to the slavery issue brought Garrison into open conflict with orthodox* churches. He himself eventually became openly unorthodox.

He espoused peaceful means to his antislavery goals but personally was uncompromising and inflammatory.

Garvey, Marcus (Mosiah) (1887-1940). African-American nationalist and founder of the Universal Negro Improvement Association. Garvey, influenced by Booker T. Washington's Tuskegee Institute, designed his association to promote education, self-help and racial solidarity among African-American people. By 1922, rising criticism of Garvey's black nationalism and allegations of mail fraud led to a prison sentence and then deportation.

Garvey, a forerunner of black theology,* held that African-Americans needed to conceive of God as black rather than white and so undo the oppression of European theology over blacks.

Gay, Ebenezer (1696-1787). Early Arminian* and "patriarch" of Unitarianism.* Despite his theological unorthodoxy and Tory sympathies, Gay was a pastor in Hingham, Massachusetts, for fully seventy years. An Arminian and an Arian, Gay opposed the Great Awakening* of the 1740s.

As one no longer able to accept either the seemingly arbitrary, inscrutable deity of the Calvinists* or their assumptions of a humanity utterly depraved and corrupt, Gay represents the front lines of change in the transition between seventeenth-century Puritanism* and nineteenth-century liberalism.*

Geddie, John (1815-1872). Canadian missionary to the South Seas. Geddie and his family sailed for the South Seas in 1840, settling finally on Aneitium Island in the New Hebrides. There, despite harassment, he won the confidence of the people by ministering through word, print and medicine. In 1854 the whole population became Christian.

General Assembly. Central governing body of the Presbyterian* churches. The General Assembly, which includes delegates from each of the presbyteries, serves as a unifying force in the church. Any innovations it suggests require the consent of a majority of the presbyteries.

General Association of Regular Baptist Churches. An association of fundamentalist* Baptist* churches. The General Association of Regular Baptist Churches (GARBC) was founded at the final meeting of the Baptist Bible Union* in May 1932. The GARBC early came under the guiding influence of Robert T. Ketcham (1889-1978), who served as national representative from 1948 to 1960.

Theologically, the issues of separation* (from worldliness and apostasy) and a premillennial* eschatology* have been distinctive of the GARBC. In 1992 the association reported 1,532 fellow-shiping churches with a total membership of 160,123.

General Baptists. Those Baptists named for their adherence to the Arminian* doctrine of general atonement,* which claims that Christ died for all persons. The earliest American churches appeared in Providence (1652), Newport (1665) and Swansea (c. 1680). Also known as Six-Principle Baptists, they opposed singing in worship and required hands to be laid upon new converts.

After a period of decline, a new movement led by Benoni Stinson culminated in the formation of the General Association of General Baptists (1870).

General Conference Mennonite Church. The second-largest organized body of Mennonites* in North America. The General Conference Mennonite Church (GCMC) was organized in 1860 as an agency for Mennonite denominational unity, mission* work, Christian education* and publication. Its progressive agenda attracted Mennonite congregations who were becoming Americanized and wanted to move beyond Mennonite traditionalism, legalism and separation from the world. The conference holds to traditional Anabaptist*-Mennonite teachings, including nonresistance. It does not have an official creed* and follows a congregational* polity.

General Conference of German Baptist Churches. *See* NORTH AMERICAN BAPTIST CONFERENCE.

General Conference of Mennonite Brethren Churches of North America. A Mennonite* denomination* growing out of Mennonite immigrants* from Russia and Crimea. Among the thousands of Mennonite immigrants to North America between 1874 and 1884 were some two hundred families affiliated with the Mennonite Brethren Church. Today this group has grown to five district conferences in sixteen states and six provincial conferences in Canada. Total membership in 1985 was 41,700.

General Confession. A corporate or personal act of repentance. In the Anglican Book of Common Prayer* the term refers to the set form of public confession. In the Roman Catholic Church* the term is also applied to a private confession.

General Council of Cooperating Baptist Missions of North America. *See* BAPTIST MID-MISSIONS.

General Missionary Convention and the Baptist Board for Foreign Missions. *See* AMERICAN BAPTIST BOARD OF INTERNATIONAL MINISTRIES.

General Synod. An early Lutheran* denomination.* Organized in 1820 from several regional synods, the General Synod benefited from the strong leadership of Samuel Schmucker.* After suffering several schisms in the 1860s, the groups reunited in 1918 with the formation of the United Lutheran Church in America.

General Synod of the Associate Reformed Presbyterian Church. A small Presbyterian* denomination.* Deriving mainly from Scottish* seceder heritage, the Associate Reformed Presbyterian Church (ARPC) members immigrated to the American colonies in the 1700s. The seceders formed the ARPC in 1782 through union with Reformed, or covenanting, Presbyterians. By 1858, however, synodic defections left only the Synod of the Carolinas to continue the heritage of the ARPC. In 1935 it added *General Synod* to its name.

General War-Time Commission of the Churches. An interdenominational agency organized in response to World War I.* In May 1917, with the encouragement of the federal government, the Federal Council of the Churches of Christ in America* organized the commission to coordinate the wartime activities of the Protestant* denominations* and such interdenominational agencies as the YMCA.*

Gerhart, Emanuel Vogel (1817-1904). German Reformed* theologian. A theology professor at the Reformed Church Seminary in Lancaster

(1868-1904), Gerhart—along with Philip Schaff* and John W. Nevin*—helped shape the direction and theology of the German Reformed Church during the second half of the nineteenth century.

German Baptist Brethren. *See* EPHRATA SOCIETY.

Gibbons, James (1834-1921). Catholic* vicar apostolic of North Carolina, bishop of Richmond and archbishop of Baltimore. In 1876 Gibbons published his best-known work, *Faith of Our Fathers*, a popular presentation of Catholicism based on his pastoral experience in the South. Translated into six European languages, it became one of the most widely used expositions of Catholicism in the nineteenth century.

Named a cardinal in 1886, Gibbons found himself in the midst of the controversies which split the hierarchy and the Catholic community during the last two decades of the nineteenth century. His authentic devotion to American ideals led him to sympathize with the Americanist* party.

Gibbons, who became a kind of civic symbol of the compatibility of Catholicism and American institutions, presided over the founding of the National Catholic War Council (1917) and the National Catholic Welfare Conference* (1919). He is perhaps the best-known Catholic bishop in U.S. history.

Gideons International. A voluntary organization devoted to the worldwide distribution of Scripture. Growing out of a meeting in Wisconsin in 1898 between John Nicholson and Samuel Hill, the Gideons began distributing the Bible in 1908, placing Scripture in hotel rooms, hospitals, prisons and schools, and engaging in personal evangelism. The Gideons today have more than twenty thousand members active in at least seventy-five countries.

Gillespie, Eliza (Mother Angela) (1824-1887). Educator and superior of the Sisters of the Holy Cross. In 1857 she became the first sister to be elected superior of the Sisters of the Holy Cross, who were centered at Notre Dame,* an office she held until 1860. Under her leadership her order expanded its educational and medical ministry in America, opening forty-five foundations, including three hospitals.

Gillis, James Martin (1876-1957). Catholic* preacher, editor and author. Gillis joined the

Paulists* in 1898 and was ordained* in 1901. After serving as a parish* mission preacher (1910-1922), Gillis was editor of the *Catholic World* (1922-1948). He also wrote a widely syndicated column and for eleven years appeared on *The Catholic Hour* radio program.

Gladden, Solomon Washington (1836-1918). Congregational* minister. Profoundly influenced by Horace Bushnell's* writings and friendship, Gladden advocated a liberal* Christianity from early in his ministry. Gladden was a popular writer and speaker and lectured widely, becoming one of the most influential clergymen of his day. Above all, he stressed the importance of character and urged people not to segregate religion from their work week but to act morally and justly in all aspects of their lives.

Remembered as the father of the Social Gospel,* Gladden's efforts were a significant force in awakening Protestants* to the needs of society and the claims of the kingdom of God.*

Glebe Lands. Farm lands (glebes), together with homes, barns and slaves, set aside for the support of clergymen and their families, a provision wherever the colonial Anglican Church* was formally established.

Glossolalia. *See* TONGUES, SPEAKING IN.

Glover, Goodwife Ann (d. 1688). Colonial Catholic* executed for witchcraft.* An Irish Catholic woman living in Boston, Glover was a casualty of the witchcraft hysteria that swept Massachusetts Bay Colony in the late seventeenth century.

Glover, Robert Hall (1871-1947). Missionary educator and statesman. In 1913 Glover was named foreign secretary for the China Inland Mission* (CIM); from 1930 to 1943 he was its home director. His enduring contribution to the missionary enterprise was his survey text *The Progress of World-Wide Missions* (1924), based on mission lectures he gave at Moody.*

God. *See* THEISM.

God's Will. An expression derived from Scripture referring to the work of God both in creation at large and in the lives of individual men and women. It is composed of two aspects: God's immutable plan (his sovereign or determined will), which cannot be frustrated (Acts 2:23; Eph 1:11) and his desired wish (his moral will), involving the cooperation of individual people (Eph 5:17; 1 Thess 4:3).

The expression *God's will* is used by evangelical* Christians in different ways. For some, it refers primarily to God's guidance and specific plan for the lives of individuals. In Pentecostal* and charismatic* circles it is customary for people to speak of a variety of means of divine direction (visions, prophecies, etc.). For others, the expression refers to the need to understand general biblical principles, to make good and wise decisions and to live obediently and draw upon the Spirit's wisdom in each situation.

Goetschius, John Henry (1717-1774). Dutch Reformed* minister in Middle Colonies. Originally denied ordination* because of his Pietist* leanings and schismatic tendencies, Goetschius in 1740 managed to secure an appointment among the Dutch churches on Long Island. His tenure, however, was marked by bitter contention.

Goforth, Jonathan (1859-1936). Canadian Presbyterian* missionary. In 1888 Goforth and his bride, a cultured artist, left for China, where for years their ministry would be centered in Honan.

Goforth was a deeply spiritual person and a man of iron determination and indefatigable activity. Theologically a Calvinist,* he learned premillennialism* at the famous Niagara Bible Conference.* A strenuous opponent of theological liberalism* wherever he encountered it, he refused to enter the United Church* in 1925.

Good Friday. The Friday before Easter* and an important Holy Week observance. Since the early days of Christianity, Good Friday has been a time of somber reflection, penance and meditation. In Roman Catholic* tradition the Mass* is not celebrated on that day.

Goodell, William (1792-1867). Pioneer missionary in Turkey. In 1831 Goodell began a mission in Constantinople and became a leader among the men of the Near East Mission of the American Board of Commissioners for Foreign Missions.* He translated the Bible from Hebrew and Greek into Armeno-Turkish.

Goodpasture, B(enjamin) C(ordell) (1895-1977). Church of Christ* editor and evangelist. As a preacher, Goodpasture served churches in Alabama, Tennessee and Georgia. From 1939 until his death he edited the *Gospel Advocate.* His moderate stance on most matters of controversy was considered a strong force for stability within the denomination.*

Goodrich, Chauncey (1836-1925) Missionary to China. Goodrich was the first preacher at Tungchow (1866) and settled there in 1873 as dean of Gordon Memorial Theological Seminary. He was deeply involved from the beginning with the creation of a Union version of the Bible in *baihua* (common-speech Mandarin).

Goodspeed, Edgar Johnson (1871-1962). Baptist* New Testament scholar and Bible translator. In 1900 Goodspeed began teaching New Testament at the University of Chicago,* where he spent his entire career. An industrious scholar, he rose rapidly through the academic ranks and succeeded Ernest D. Burton as chairman of the New Testament department (1923-1937). Under his leadership the department became a center for New Testament manuscript and textual studies.

As a Bible translator Goodspeed first published *The New Testament: An American Translation* (1923), a work that received praise and established him not only as a translator but also as a popular communicator of scholarship. He was one of the most prolific and versatile American New Testament scholars of the twentieth century.

Gordon, A(doniram) J(udson) (1836-1895). Baptist* minister and missions* leader. From 1869 until his death, Gordon was pastor of the Clarendon Street Church in Boston, which he transformed into one of the leading missions-minded* churches in America and a leading fundraiser for Baptist foreign missions. He is best remembered for founding, in 1889, the Boston Missionary Training School, the forerunner of Gordon College and Gordon-Conwell Theological Seminary.

Gordon was a prolific writer on Christ's Second Coming. Well known for his emphasis on the Holy Spirit and his advocacy of faith healing,* Gordon was also a leading evangelical* supporter of women's suffrage* and of women's work in the Prohibition movement.*

Gordon was one of the most influential evangelicals of the late nineteenth century. His popularity permitted him to bridge the ranks of separatist* fundamentalists* and denominational* loyalists.

Gordon, Charles William (1860-1937). Canadian novelist and Social Gospel* activist. Gordon, an ordained* Presbyterian* minister and Social Gospel activist, was involved with such issues as immigration,* temperance,* moral reform and industrial relations. Under the pseudonym Ralph Connor, he was the most popular Canadian writer of his generation.

Gordon, George Angier (1853-1929). Congregational* preacher and theologian. Becoming pastor in 1884 of Boston's prestigious Old South Church, Gordon reigned for over two decades as one of the most outspoken leaders of the "New Theology."* His *Christ of Today* (1895) popularized a "progressive orthodoxy" that combined an emphasis on divine immanence within human culture, an "experiential Christianity" defined as a progressive encounter between persons in history rather than a creed* or set of doctrines.

Gordon, S(amuel) D(ickey) (1859-1936). Devotional writer. After years of service with the YMCA,* Gordon initiated a ministry* of preaching* and lecturing on religious issues. He is probably best known for his "Quiet Talks" devotional books.

Gorton, Samuel (c. 1592-1677). New England religious radical. From 1637 until his departure for England in 1644, Gorton was involved in a series of controversies in Massachusetts and Rhode Island. His difficulties stemmed in part from his promulgation of the radical ideology of John Saltmarsh, prominent English radical of the time.

Gospel Hymns and Songs. The musical term *gospel* refers to a range of styles which grew from the popular-based music used in American camp meeting* revivals* of the early nineteenth century and the Sunday-school movement* tunes of the late nineteenth century. The tradition has parallels in popular church music throughout the history of the church, such as the New Testament "spiritual songs" (Eph 5:19; Col 3:16), the hymns* of early church evangelists, the *Laude* of St. Francis and the Dissenter's hymns of Isaac Watts. Gospel hymns are personal expressions of

faith. Characteristically, they are strophic with a refrain, rhythmic, popular and easily learned. If the past is any measure of the future, churches will continue to need and use music that is accessible, straightforward and popularly based. Gospel hymns of the future will undoubtedly take many forms as they respond to popular culture.

Gospel Missionary Union. Evangelical* foreign missionary* society. Organized in 1892 as the World's Gospel Union, the group early sent missionaries to Sierra Leone and Morocco, and later to other countries in Africa and Central and South America.

In 1992 the Gospel Missionary Union had 240 full-time missionaries from the U.S. and Canada working in nineteen countries, primarily in evangelism,* church planting and leadership development.

Gospel of Wealth. *See* WEALTH, GOSPEL OF.

Gould, Thomas (?-1675). Early colonial Baptist* pastor from Boston. Gould (Goold) first came to notice through his association with Henry Dunster,* ousted president of Harvard* (1654), over the issue of infant baptism.* Separating from his church, Gould ministered to Baptists in East Boston.

Grabau, Johannes Andreas Augustus (1804-1879). Lutheran* pastor, teacher, writer and synodic leader. In Buffalo, New York, Grabau founded the Martin Luther Seminary (1840), where he served as president and major professor. Grabau, an exponent of Old Lutheranism, gathered the Synod of the Lutheran Church Emigrated from Prussia (Buffalo Synod) in 1845.

Grace, Charles Manuel ("Sweet Daddy") (1881-1960). Founder and bishop of United House of Prayer for All Peoples. Grace's first success occurred when he opened a branch of his church in Charlotte, North Carolina, in 1926. The church prospered, growing to include 375 branches from coast to coast and about 25,000 members by the time of his death.

The flamboyant Grace had his greatest appeal among urban African-American women. The core of his ministry was his alleged gift of healing.

Grace Brethren. *See* FELLOWSHIP OF GRACE BRETHREN CHURCHES.

Grady, Henry Woodfin (1850-1889). Editor and layman in Methodist Episcopal Church,* South. Grady took the vanguard in championing worthy social issues. Through his efforts, impetus was given to the renewal of spirit in the churches and culture of the post-bellum South.

Graham, Isabella Marshall (1742-1814). Pioneer of organized charity and Sunday schools.* In 1789 she came to America and opened a school for girls in New York City. She helped found one of America's first organized charities—the Society for the Relief of Poor Widows with Small Children.

Graham, William (Billy) Franklin (1918-). International evangelist. In 1949 Graham's evangelistic efforts in Los Angeles first brought him to national attention. In 1950 he founded the Billy Graham Evangelistic Association* and also began his weekly radio program *The Hour of Decision*. A successful ministry in England in 1954 ushered Graham onto the international stage. In 1956 he was a major force in establishing the publication *Christianity Today.** Graham's stature within American society led him to become an unofficial spiritual adviser and confidant to many U.S. presidents, beginning with Dwight D. Eisenhower.*

Characterized by sterling integrity and a genuine humility, Graham has weathered criticism by not responding to it and has remained one of the most respected public figures of his generation and the most influential evangelical of the twentieth century. He has preached the gospel to more people than any evangelist in the history of the church, reaching nearly one hundred million individuals in person and untold numbers by radio and television throughout the world.

See also BILLY GRAHAM CENTER; REVIVALISM, PROTESTANT.

Grail, The. An international Catholic* laywomen's movement. The Grail has its origins in the Women of Nazareth, a spiritual movement (or apostolate*) established by a Dutch Jesuit* in 1921. In May 1940 the Grail's first American headquarters opened in Libertyville, Illinois.

Since 1944 The Grail has offered courses at Grailville, the group's new headquarters near Loveland, Ohio. These have touched the lives of countless Catholic women who stayed for a few weeks, a summer or a year.

Grant, Frederick Clifton (1891-1974). Episcopal* priest and biblical scholar. In addition to being editor of the *Anglican Theological Review,* Grant is primarily remembered for his critical studies in the Gospels, as well as his investigation of the Jewish and Hellenistic backgrounds of the New Testament.

Grant, George Monro (1835-1905). Canadian Presbyterian* educator. In 1877 Grant became principal of Queen's University in Kingston, Ontario, and had a powerful impact on fellow Presbyterian clergy through an annual theological conference* held at Queen's. Grant pioneered the Social Gospel* in Canada and strongly opposed secularism.*

Graves, James Robinson (1820-1893). Southern Baptist* preacher, editor and publisher who led in the formation of the Landmark movement.* Moving to Nashville in 1845, Graves soon became the editor of the *Tennessee Baptist,* which, by the eve of the Civil War,* had the largest circulation of any denominational paper in the South. Graves also formed a publishing company which became one of the most influential and prolific religious presses* in the South during the second half of the nineteenth century.

During the decade before the Civil War, Graves became the dominant figure of a developing movement in Baptist life known as Landmarkism.

Gray, Asa (1810-1888). Harvard* botanist. The preeminent American botanist of the nineteenth century, Gray in his career combined an outstanding scientific reputation with an evangelical* Christian faith. He employed both in his efforts to urge the compatibility of theism with Charles Darwin's* biological theory of evolution.

Gray, James Martin (1851-1935). Reformed Episcopal* clergyman and first dean and president of Moody Bible Institute.* Gray first became associated with Dwight L. Moody* in 1893, when he began preaching at Moody's Northfield, Massachusetts, summer conferences. In 1904 he became the first dean of the Moody Bible Institute in Chicago, a position which he held until his death. Gray was responsible for the sharpening of the institute's conservatism after Moody's death, especially during the fundamentalist-modernist controversies* of the 1920s.

[147]

Great Awakening. Although the term *Great Awakening* was not used by eighteenth-century Americans, it soon came into use by historians to describe a unique wave of intercolonial religious revivals* that peaked throughout many of the colonies in the years 1740-1742. Historians described these revivals as a "Great Awakening" because they saw in those revivals novel qualities that would transform pulpit and pew in early America and that would mark the beginning of popular evangelicalism* in the American churches.

Religious revivals per se were not new to the eighteenth century. The religious revivals that peaked in 1740 in conjunction with the preaching tour of England's famed revivalist George Whitefield* were unique, however. First, they differed in expanse, encompassing several colonies, not just individual towns. The second difference was in leadership, with the outsider Whitefield eclipsing local pastors in captivating the crowds, who seemingly materialized out of nowhere to hear him speak in the most stirring terms about the "new birth."*

By 1743 America's clergy were evenly split over whether the revivals were a work of God or a work of the devil. Opponents of the revivals, led by Boston's Charles Chauncy,* detected symptoms of mental illness throughout the ranks of their "enthusiastic" opponents. Supporters of the revivals, led by Northampton's Jonathan Edwards,* insisted that they did not lead necessarily to separations and discord, nor were impassioned calls for an immediate conversion experience necessarily a form of madness or hysteria. Such disputes ended the long record of accommodation that had existed before the revivals, and the results were cataclysmic.

More than any other movement, the Great Awakening tipped the balance of religious authority in America firmly and decisively in the laity's direction. Suddenly it was the people—guided by their self-made leaders—who had to take responsibility for their religious lives to retain God's special favor for America. The Great Awakening thus represented a crucial index of democratization that would lead to the creation of "evangelical" religious movements, whose authority emerged from beneath, among ordinary people, rather than in Old World fashion from the top down.

Yet if the Great Awakening promoted discord and democratization in social and political terms,

it also represented a profound spiritual movement that produced America's greatest "theologian of the heart"—Jonathan Edwards. Alongside the social legacy of the midcentury revivals has been a spiritual legacy from Edwards that has endured in American religion and made the Great Awakening "great."

See also NEW LIGHTS; OLD LIGHTS; REVIVALISM; SECOND GREAT AWAKENING.

Great Depression, The Churches and the. The Great Depression of the 1930s marks a distinctive period in American church history. The economic upheaval and its contrast to the relative prosperity of the 1920s adversely affected the life of most churches. Whereas most large denominations* struggled to maintain their membership size and financial stability, churches of the more traditionally disinherited (such as black congregations), plus the aggressively fundamentalist* Holiness* and Pentecostal* churches, grew notably.

Distinctions among Protestants* widened, moreover, as they responded to the liberal New Deal social programs identified with President Franklin D. Roosevelt. A distinctively new Protestant thrust, however, critiqued both reactionary conservatism and idealistic liberalism. Largely an intellectual movement within academic circles, but with widespread influence, the "crisis theology" and "social realism" of neo-orthodoxy* sought to recover Reformation Protestant identity within the modern world.

During the 1930s, American Roman Catholics* manifested a fresh expression of social thought* organization and action within the civil order that marked the continuing Americanization of the church. After 1932 the New Deal program received large (though critical) Catholic support.

World War II brought an end to the Great Depression and fueled revolutionary social forces on a global scale. The American churches emerged from the experience with a chastened and more mature determination to engage the modern social-intellectual-technocratic world with effective Christian faith and order, life and thought.

Greater Europe Mission. Evangelical,* nondenominational mission* agency. The Greater Europe Mission (GEM) was founded by Noel Lyons and Robert P. Evans, a World War II* navy chaplain* who became burdened with the spiritual needs of the European continent. Evans's vision was to train Europeans to evangelize* and disciple* their own peoples.

In Paris in 1949, Evans founded the European Bible Institute. Other schools have since been established in ten other European countries. Evangelism and church planting have become increasingly emphasized. By the mid 1990s over forty churches were reported to have been started by GEM personnel and over half of GEM's 400 missionaries were involved in evangelistic initiatives to start new churches.

Greek Orthodox Archdiocese of North and South America. The largest Orthodox* jurisdiction in the U.S. The first Orthodox arrived in Florida in 1768, but not until the years following the Civil War* did Orthodox Christianity began to grow in the U.S. As a result of the massive influx of immigrants from Greece and Asia Minor between 1880 and 1920, some 150 parishes were established throughout the U.S.

In 1921 the Greek Orthodox Archdiocese was formally incorporated in New York, and in 1922 the Archdiocese of North and South America was canonically established, with Archbishop Alexander (Demoglou) (1876-1942) elected as its first archbishop.

The second archbishop (1930-1948) was Athenagoras (Spyrou), who united the parishes and established a college and theological school. Next was Michael (Konstantinides or Constantinides*), during whose archbishopric (1949-1958) important demographic changes began to take place. The majority of the members were now persons born and raised in the U.S. and not all were of Greek ethnic background.

Archbishop Iakovos* (Coucouzis) has headed the archdiocese since 1959. It now consists of about five hundred parishes and claims two million communicants throughout the U.S., Canada, and Central and South America. The entire archdiocese is a province of the Patriarchate of Constantinople.

Green, William Henry (1825-1900). Presbyterian* theologian. Teaching Old Testament at Princeton* from 1851, Green was firmly committed to the divine inspiration and inerrancy* of Scripture. He steadfastly resisted the mounting influence of biblical criticism* and led the opposition to the documentary hypothesis of the origin of the Pentateuch.

Grellet, Stephen (1773-1855). Quaker* minister, missionary and evangelical* social reformer. Arriving in New York from France in 1795, Grellet was greatly influenced by his reading of William Penn's *No Cross, No Crown* and converted to Quakerism. He became one of America's greatest Quaker leaders.

In 1796 he became a missionary, pleading the cause of the poor, sick and imprisoned before most of the crown heads of Europe.

Grenfell, Wilfred Thomason (1865-1940). Missionary to Labrador. Influenced to become a medical missionary by a Dwight L. Moody* campaign, Grenfell devoted himself to alleviating the misery of the poor in Labrador. The fruit of his more than forty years of labor included many hospitals, schools and cooperative stores.

Griffin, Edward Dorr (1770-1837). Congregational* minister and president of Williams College. From 1811 to 1814 Griffin served as pastor of Park Street Church in Boston and built its reputation as a bulwark of trinitarian theology. In his final years he effectively served as president of Williams College (1821-1836), where he enlarged the curriculum and injected evangelical* fervor.

Grimké, Sarah Moore (1792-1873), and Angelina Grimké Weld (1805-1879). Quaker* abolitionists* and women's rights activists. Born into a wealthy slaveholding family, the sisters' abolitionist convictions took root after they left the Episcopal Church to become Quakers. In 1836 they moved to New York and began a career mobilizing women for the abolitionist cause.

The Grimké sisters became popular public speakers, touring New England as agents of the American Anti-Slavery Society in 1837. Angelina married the prominent abolitionist Theodore Weld* in 1838.

Griswold, Alexander Viets (1766-1843). Episcopal* bishop of the Eastern Diocese.* After serving several Episcopal churches in Connecticut, Griswold in 1810 was elected bishop of a diocese encompassing New Hampshire, Vermont, Massachusetts and Rhode Island. In 1836 he became the fifth presiding bishop of the Episcopal Church, serving until his death.

Griswold is credited with re-creating the Episcopal Church in New England, outside of Connecticut, following the Revolutionary War.* As a moderate evangelical,* he stressed the teachings of the gospel rather than the distinctive doctrines of the Episcopal Church.

Grundtvig, N(ikolai) F(rederik) S(everin) (1783-1872). Danish Lutheran* theologian, hymn writer and minister. Grundtvig was said to influence other Christians to "joy of life, openness and freedom." Though he never visited the U.S., he was influential in American religion through Lutheran "happy Danes" (Danish Evangelical Lutheran Church in America).

Gulick, Orramel H. (1830-1923). Congregational* missionary to Japan. Born in Hawaii to pioneer missionary parents, Gulick served there for some time and then in 1869 was assigned to Japan. In 1875 he started Japan's first Christian periodical, which initiated a vigorous tradition of Christian journalism.

Gunsaulus, Frank Wakeley (1856-1921). Congregational* minister, author and educator. Moving to Chicago after several eastern pastorates, Gunsaulus gained national renown at Plymouth Congregational Church (1887-1899) and the nondenominational Central Church (1899-1919). He was a great orator, as well as a lover of the arts.

Gurney, Joseph John (1788-1847). Quaker* leader, banker and philanthropist.* Although Gurney adopted many elements from evangelical* revivalism,* he did so without sacrificing such traditional Quaker doctrines as pacifism,* plain dress and worship* in silence.

Gurney, an Englishman and the leading evangelical Quaker theologian of the first half of the nineteenth century, left his impression upon a segment of the Quaker tradition now best represented in the Evangelical Friends Alliance* and the Friends United Meeting.

See also FRIENDS.

Gurneyites. A branch of the Religious Society of Friends* (Quakers). Gurneyite Quakers stem from Joseph John Gurney,* who paid an influential visit to America from 1837 to 1840. Modern descendants of the Gurneyites are included in the Evangelical Friends Alliance* and Friends United Meeting.

Guyart, Marie de l'Incarnation (1599-1672). Pioneer Ursuline* missionary and mystic. In 1639 Guyart departed for Canada, where she built a European-style monastery and recruited French nuns for the first institute for women's education in Canada. Her correspondence provides important sources for the early history of Canada. In 1980 she was beatified* by John Paul II.*

H

Haas, Francis Joseph (1889-1953). Catholic labor priest and bishop of Grand Rapids. A staunch supporter of organized labor and of government assistance to the poor, Haas was appointed to numerous government positions during the New Deal years. As special commissioner of conciliation for the Department of Labor, he mediated some of the nation's most nettlesome strikes during that turbulent period. Liberal in political and economic matters, Haas was conservative theologically. He was comfortable with traditional church teachings and structures and was unhesitatingly loyal to the Holy See.

Hague, Dyson (1857-1935). Canadian Anglican* minister. As rector, professor and writer, Hague was one of the most influential evangelicals* within the Church of England and a leader of Canadian fundamentalism.*

Haldeman, I(saac) M(assey) (1845-1933). Baptist* pastor. For nearly fifty years, Haldeman was pastor of the First Baptist Church of New York City. He was deeply committed to the fundamentalist* crusade against "worldliness" and was active in the fundamentalist-modernist controversy.* A dispensationalist* with radical views of cultural pessimism, Haldeman had no time for reform movements.

Hale, Edward Everett (1822-1909). Unitarian* minister, author and reformer. Hale was exceedingly active in ecclesiastical, political, social and literary affairs. He was a moderate Unitarian who helped found the National Conference of Unitarian Churches in 1865.

Hale, a prolific author of fiction and historical works, was best known for his patriotic story *The Man Without a Country* (1863). Hale's career epitomizes the way nineteenth-century liberal Protestants* adapted secular means to apply religious principles to social issues.

Hale, Sarah Josepha Buell (1788-1879). Magazine editor. After the death of her husband in 1822, Hale began a literary career. From 1837 to 1877 she was the editor of *Godey's Lady's Book* and became the popular arbiter of feminine taste. She encouraged careers for women in education, foreign missions* and medicine.

Half-Way Covenant. Modified colonial Congregational* church membership* requirements. By 1636 New England Congregationalists agreed that only "elect,"* or regenerate, individuals merited church membership. Only these church members, in turn, were allowed to present their children for baptism.* Within a few years, however, the elders faced an unforeseen question: Did the children of baptized but unregenerate parents retain a right to baptism?

In 1656 seventeen clergymen in Boston debated the issues, arriving at what opponents later derisively labeled the Half-Way Covenant. Under its provisions, unregenerate children of regenerate parents could baptize their offspring, providing the children led an upright life and agreed to own the church covenant before the assembled congregation. As adults, "half-way" members did not enjoy the privileges of voting or participation in the Lord's Supper.*

See also COVENANT THEOLOGY; DISCIPLINE, CHURCH; NEW ENGLAND WAY.

Hall, John (1829-1898). Presbyterian* preacher. In 1867 Hall received a call to the Fifth Avenue Presbyterian Church in New York City. It grew to become the largest congregation in the city, and Hall remained there until his death.

Hall, a gifted preacher and a conservative, was especially noted for his pastoral labors, including an extensive program of regular visitation to each family in his large congregation.

Hallelujah. An expression of praise to God used

formally and informally in numerous Christian traditions. The word, which appears throughout the Psalms, means "Praise God!"

Hallinan, Paul John (1911-1968). Archbishop of Atlanta. In 1962 Hallinan became the first archbishop of Atlanta when it became an archdiocese in 1962. He was active in efforts to end racial segregation in the South.

Ham, Mordecai Fowler (1877-1961). Fundamentalist* Baptist* evangelist and pastor. Concern for evangelism led Ham into a life of itinerant* ministry through the Southern U.S. At the close of his ministry, he claimed one million converts, including Billy Graham,* who had made a decision at the Charlotte, North Carolina, meetings in 1934.

Hamlin, Cyrus (1811-1900). Missionary educator in Turkey. Sent to Constantinople in 1839 by the American Board of Commissioners for Foreign Missions,* Hamlin opened Bebek Seminary. In 1859 he became the founding president of Robert College (today University of the Bosporus).

Hammet [Hammett], William (d. 1803). Founder of the Primitive Methodist Church.* Ordained* by John Wesley* in 1786 to work in Newfoundland, Hammet later went to Charleston, South Carolina. He engendered a short-lived schism, which he named the Primitive Methodist Church (not to be confused with the later denomination of that name).

Hammond, Lily Hardy (1859-1925). Southern Methodist* advocate of interracial justice. Hammond addressed issues of racial discrimination, mob violence, labor peonage and poverty, arguing that such problems must be viewed in light of Christian precepts.

Hardeman, N(icholas) B(rodie) (1874-1965). Church of Christ* evangelist, educator and debater. Hardeman is considered one of the builders of the Church of Christ in the South. He is best known for his Nashville "Tabernacle Meetings," held between 1922 and 1942. From 1925 until his death, he was president of Freed-Hardeman College.

Harkness, Georgia (1891-1979). Methodist* theologian and ecumenist. Harkness's long teaching career included positions at Elmira College for Women (1923-1937), Mt. Holyoke College (1937-1939), Garrett Biblical Institute (1939-1950) and Pacific School of Religion (1960-1974). She attended the Madras Conference (1938) and the Amsterdam and Evanston* meetings of the World Council of Churches* (1948 and 1954).

Harkness was a twentieth-century pioneer, both as a woman theologian and in her service to the Methodist Church. She was a prolific writer, publishing thirty-six volumes in her lifetime.

Harper, Frances Ellen Watkins (1825-1911). African-American writer and reformer. Employed by the Maine Anti-Slavery Society, Harper delivered lectures throughout the Northern U.S. and Canada from 1854 to 1860. She became the nation's most popular African-American poet of the late nineteenth century.

Faced with discrimination within the suffrage* and temperance movements,* Harper helped African-American women organize an independent, autonomous movement in 1896—the National Association of Colored Women.

Harper, William Rainey (1856-1906). Baptist* Old Testament scholar and founding president of the University of Chicago.* Harper was chosen by John D. Rockefeller to be the founding president of the University of Chicago (1892), and in a short time he created a major comprehensive research university. Because of his own interests, biblical studies flourished at the new institution.

As a scholar Harper's greatest contribution lay in his promotion of the study of Hebrew. Theologically, he was a liberal* and adamant in insisting on a modern critical approach to Scripture.

Harris, George (1844-1922). Congregational* minister and theologian. Harris was professor of Christian theology* at Andover Theological Seminary* (1883-1899) and later became president of Amherst College (1899-1912). At Andover, Harris was a part of the "new theology," or "progressive orthodoxy" (see Evangelical Liberalism).

Harris, Merriman Colbert (1846-1921). Methodist* missionary to Japan and Korea. Harris enjoyed an illustrious career that included work with East Asians in Hakodate, Tokyo, Seoul and San Francisco. Between 1904 and 1916 Harris served as bishop, first in Japan and then in Korea. He wrote three books about Japan and its Christianity.

Harris, Samuel (1814-1899). Congregational* theologian. From 1855 to 1867 Harris was professor of systematic theology* at Bangor Seminary, Maine, and was then called to be president of Bowdoin College. From 1871 to 1895 he was Dwight Professor of Systematic Theology at Yale* Divinity School.

Hartshorne, Charles. See PROCESS THEOLOGY.

Harvard University. First institution of higher education founded in North America. Founded by the Puritans* in 1636 to train their future ministers, Harvard has led the nation's schools in curricular planning. Under President Charles Eliot (1869-1909), it introduced an elective curriculum; under President Abbott Lawrence Lowell (1909-1933), it adopted general education and major requirements.

Harvard was the early leader in the process of secularization* in American higher education, moving early in the nineteenth century from Calvinism* to Unitarianism* en route to secularism. Today Harvard continues its premier reputation in higher education, holding a multibillion-dollar endowment and maintaining the largest university library in the world.

See also EDUCATION, PROTESTANT THEOLOGICAL.

Hasselquist, Tufve Nilsson (1816-1891). Pioneer Swedish-American Lutheran* pastor, church president, educator and journalist. Immigrating to the U.S. in 1852, Hasselquist was one of the organizers of the Scandinavian Evangelical Lutheran Augustana Synod (Church) in 1860. He also was president and theological professor of the denomination's infant Augustana College and Theological Seminary.

Hatcher, William Eldridge (1834-1912). Baptist* minister and editor. In 1875 Hatcher assumed the pastorate of Grace Street Church in Richmond, Virginia, where he remained for twenty-six years. From 1882 to 1885 he edited the *Religious Herald.* A gifted preacher and master pulpiteer, Hatcher was known in the South for his leadership in Baptist circles.

Haury, Samuel S. (1847-1929). First mission-ary sent by the North American Mennonites.* From 1880 to 1887 Haury and his wife worked within the Arapaho tribe in Indian Territory (now Oklahoma) under the mission board of the General Conference Mennonite Church. Later he practiced medicine in Kansas and California.

Haven, Gilbert (1821-1880). Methodist Episcopal* bishop and abolitionist.* Throughout his life, Haven served as professor, pastor, chaplain* and editor. His published writings provided him a forum for articulating his progressive views on abolition and racial equality; he also supported prohibition* and women's suffrage.* He was forthright in championing his social views, even in hostile settings, and sought to base them on Scripture and the Wesleyan tradition.*

Haviland, Laura Smith (1808-1898). Quaker* abolitionist* and Underground Railroad conductor. Haviland helped organize the first antislavery association in Michigan. During the Civil War* she worked at army hospitals and prisons and assisted freed slaves in the South. After the war she undertook relief efforts in the South and Kansas.

Hawaweeny, Raphael (1860-1915). First Orthodox* bishop ordained* in America. A native of Damascus, Syria, Hawaweeny came to New York in 1895 to serve the growing numbers of Arab Orthodox there. At the time of his death, some thirty Orthodox parishes were serving about 25,000 Arab immigrants.

Hawthorne, Nathaniel (1804-1864). New England fiction writer. Hawthorne captures in his fiction the themes and atmosphere of Puritan* New England while simultaneously pointing the American mind toward the ambiguities and complexities of the later nineteenth and twentieth centuries. Themes Hawthorne explores in his *Scarlet Letter* and *House of the Seven Gables* include the horror of secret sin, the sacredness of the human heart, the consequences of a sinful past (especially the Puritan past) on the present, the inevitability of the loss of innocence, and the impact of pride and selfishness on the human personality.

Hayes, Patrick Joseph (1867-1938). Cardinal archbishop of New York. In 1914 Hayes was made an auxiliary bishop of New York in 1914. The

[153]

following year he became pastor of St. Stephen's Church in New York City. In 1919 Hayes was named archbishop of New York and in 1924 was made a member of the College of Cardinals.

Within his own diocese* Hayes devoted most of his energies to the works of charity and social welfare. His successful reforms in this area earned for him the epithet "The Cardinal of Charity."

Haygood, Atticus Greene (1839-1896). Methodist Episcopal,* South, bishop, editor and educator. Haygood pastored until 1870, when he became editor of Sunday-school publications for the denomination.* He later served as president of Emory College (1875-1884), where he introduced practical courses such as bookkeeping and telegraphy into the curriculum. He also contributed significantly to the establishment of Paine College in Augusta, Georgia.

Haygood, Laura Askew (1845-1900). Methodist* educator and missionary to China. In 1884 the Woman's Board of Foreign Missions appointed Haygood to the task of organizing missions for women in Shanghai. She organized extant day schools, launched new programs and in 1896 became the director of all Women's Board work in China.

Hays, Lawrence Brooks (1898-1981). Lawyer, congressman and Southern Baptist Convention* president. An active advocate of civil rights for all citizens, Hays opposed the views of Arkansas Governor Orval Faubus during the school desegregation crisis in Little Rock (1958). Later he was special assistant to Presidents Kennedy* and Johnson. Hays was president of the Southern Baptist Convention for two terms (1957-1959).

Haystack Prayer Meeting (1806). Founding event of the American foreign missionary movement.* Occurring at Williams College (Mass.), this student prayer meeting under a haystack led to widespread mission involvement.

Haywood, G(arfield) T(homas) (d. 1931). Oneness Pentecostal* minister. By 1908, Haywood was pastoring an African-American Assemblies of God* congregation in Indianapolis that would grow to over 450 members. In 1915 Haywood and his congregation accepted a new "oneness" doctrine of a baptism* in "Jesus only." Under his persuasive leadership a number of other African-American Pentecostal ministers and congregations joined the Oneness movement.

Healy, James Augustine (1830-1900). Catholic* bishop of Portland, Maine. Consecrated* in 1875 the second bishop of Portland, Healy established several parishes, schools and welfare institutions. A gifted administrator and eloquent preacher, Healy was the first priest and bishop in the U.S. with African ancestry, yet he never identified personally with the African-American community.

Heaven and Hell. The final states of everlasting bliss for the righteous (those saved) and of everlasting torment for the wicked (those lost, or damned). The traditional Christian doctrines of heaven and hell, while formally accepted by most North American believers, are increasingly slighted or reinterpreted, or both, except among fundamentalists* and other conservatives.

The Puritan* concept of heaven was theocentric and otherworldly, with worship the preeminent activity. During the eighteenth century a more material concept of heaven began to gain currency, with human love and progress characterizing life in the new order. This anthropocentric view became more prominent in the nineteenth century.

Contemporary Christian scholars often stress as a substitute for the old hope of heaven (and fear of hell) the biblical promise of "a new heaven and a new earth" (Rev 21:1). Universalism* has gained ground among more liberal Christians who, in an ever-shrinking world, have entered into dialogue with other world religions, but it is usually rejected by evangelicals.*

Heck, Barbara Ruckle (1734-1804). Mother of American Methodism.* In 1760 Barbara Ruckle married Paul Heck and with him and her cousin Philip Embury* immigrated to New York from Ireland. There, in 1766, she stirred up Embury, who had previously been converted under John Wesley,* to conduct services in his own home—the first Methodist meeting in New York. Two years later Heck herself whitewashed the walls of the first Methodist chapel in America.

Hecker, Isaac Thomas (1819-1888). Catholic* priest,* missionary,* journalist and founder of the Missionary Society of St. Paul the Apostle (Paulist Fathers).* Hecker converted to Catholicism in

1844. During the early 1850s, he and three other American-born converts made plans for a mission band dedicated to work with non-Catholic Americans. Founding the Paulist Fathers in 1858, Hecker went on to become an internationally known figure for his fresh presentation of Catholicism as a religion best suited for the demands of modern democratic society.

The 1860s were the high point of his active ministry, during which he founded the *Catholic World* magazine and the Catholic Publication Society, which later became the Paulist Press. As a missionary, he toured the country, giving parish missions to Catholics and lecturing to non-Catholics, often on the lyceum circuit.

Heidelberg Catechism. A German Reformed* catechism* published in 1563. The catechism begins with humanity's misery and guilt before the unreachable perfection of God's law, then focuses on redemption through Christ's suffering and resurrection for all who repent and accept him, and concludes with a section on the human joy and gratitude arising from the reception of divine grace.

This catechism was the first Protestant* confession to be brought to America by Europeans (1609). It has been the most widely accepted doctrinal standard among Reformed denominations in America up to the present day.

Hell. *See* HEAVEN AND HELL.

Helm, Lucinda Barbour (1839-1897). Methodist* missions leader and reformer. An early Sunday-school* worker and teacher of black and white children, Helm shifted her energies to the newly formed Woman's Foreign Missionary Society in 1876. Helm is best known for her work in conceiving and organizing the Woman's Department of the Board of Church Extension, serving as its general secretary from 1886 to 1890.

Hemmenway, Moses (1735-1811). Old Calvinist* minister. A staunch Whig, Hemmenway spent more than fifty years as pastor of the First Church in Wells, Maine. He was a friend and correspondent of his Harvard* classmate President John Adams.

Hemmenway is remembered today for his writings that were attacked by New Divinity* Calvinists. In spite of the controversies, Hemmenway was a strong voice for infant baptism,* and against

Arian, Socinian and Universalist* tendencies in New England.

Henkel, Paul (1754-1825). Lutheran* evangelist. In 1776 Henkel heard evangelist George Whitefield,* experienced the new birth,* and resolved to be a preacher. A prolific promoter of Lutheranism, Henkel formed three synods*— North Carolina (1803), Ohio (1818) and Tennessee (1820).

Committed to a fervent confessionalism* and an ardent evangelicalism,* by the time of his death, Henkel was recognized as one of the major founders of Lutheranism in America.

Hennepin, Louis (c. 1626-1705). Priest, missionary, explorer and historiographer of New France. Upon arrival in Canada in 1675 (*see* Missions to North America, French), Hennepin went through the St. Lawrence countryside preaching the gospel. Beginning in 1678 he accompanied La Salle on explorations of the West, helping to map and explore much of the Upper Mississippi. Hennepin soon returned to Europe and published his unusually successful *Description de la Louisiane* (1683).

Henry, Patrick (1736-1799). Revolutionary statesman and governor of Virginia. Henry is best known as an orator, an opponent of the ratification of the Constitution and a five-term governor of Virginia. His father belonged to the local Anglican church,* but his mother embraced Presbyterianism* following her conversion* during the Great Awakening.* Despite his mother's earnest pleas and his hearing the sermons of Samuel Davies,* Henry continued steadfast in the Anglican faith.

Hepburn, James Curtis (1815-1911). Pioneer Protestant* missionary to Japan. After service as a medical missionary in Singapore and China (1841-1845), Hepburn went to Japan in 1859. There he carried on medical work and also made significant contributions because of his knowledge of Japanese. He compiled the first Japanese-English dictionary and had a key role in translating the Bible into Japanese.

Heresy Trials (1878-1906). A series of ecclesiastical and civil trials within Protestant* denominations* aimed at checking the inroads of theological liberalism.* The Congregationalists* and

Baptists,* with their loose form of denomination-al government, offered few barriers to the spread of liberalism. While the Methodists* had better structures for addressing liberalism, their tests of fellowship tended to stress morality rather than doctrine.

The most publicized heresy trials were in Presbyterian ranks in the North, especially the cases brought in the 1890s against Charles A. Briggs* at Union Theological Seminary* in New York and against Henry Preserved Smith* at Lane Theological Seminary in Cincinnati. Both men were eventually suspended, with Briggs ultimate-ly becoming an Episcopalian,* and Smith, a Con-gregationalist.

Herman, St. (c. 1756-1836). First Orthodox* saint canonized* in America. Little is known of the life of the Monk Herman before he entered the monastic life near present-day Leningrad. He eventually volunteered for missionary service in Kodiak Island, Alaska, where he proved himself the mission's most steadfast and important member.

More than anything else, Herman lived a life of simplicity and holiness which attracted others. Thirty years after his death, followers began to collect stories about him and about reputed mir-acles, which led ultimately to his glorification in 1970.

Herron, George Davis (1862-1925). Radical social prophet. In the 1890s Herron attained a national following through his lectures and writ-ings as the central figure in the controversial "Kingdom Movement," which gained a wide hearing in the churches and won many to social Christian views. This support fell away as Herron adopted more radical, socialist views. During World War I* Herron was an interpreter to Europe of Wilson's* war and peace aims.

Hewit, Augustine Francis (1820-1897). Co-founder of the Paulists.* In 1858 Hewit, along with Isaac Hecker* and three others, established the Paulists. For almost forty years, Hewit contrib-uted richly to the life of the young community and to Catholic* letters. He wrote the first rule, educated the candidates and served as theologian at the Second Plenary Council of Baltimore.* He established the Columbus Press (1891), now Paulist Press, began missions* to non-Catholics (1893), sent the Paulists to San Francisco (1894),

and founded the Catholic Missionary Union (1896).

Hickok, Laurens Perseus (1789-1888). Con-gregational* theologian and philosopher of relig-ion. Hickok was one of several late nineteenth-century Congregationalists who drew on German thought, particularly Kant, in order to form a phi-losophical foundation for Calvinism.* While some acclaimed him as having achieved the height of speculative thought, his critics charged him with being an idealist and even a pantheist.

Hicks, Elias (1748-1830). Farmer and leader of the Hicksite* schism among the Religious Society of Friends (Quakers).* From 1774, when he un-derwent a religious crisis, until his death in 1830, Hicks devoted himself to serving Quaker commu-nities as far afield as Virginia, Indiana and Canada, covering over forty thousand miles in his itinerant ministry.

A liberal in his stress on reason, Hicks repre-sented the great commoner, who earned his liv-ing by the sweat of his brow and sought to throw off the yoke of wealthy Quaker bankers and in-dustrialists.

Hicksites. A branch of the Religious Society of Friends (Quakers).* Hicksites derive their desig-nation from the Long Island farmer and Quaker minister Elias Hicks,* who led a schism among American Quakers which began in Philadelphia in 1827-1828. Modern Hicksites compose the Friends General Conference with a membership of 25,000.

Higginson, Francis (1588-1630). Teacher of Salem, Massachusetts. Higginson arrived in New England in June 1629. In July the settlers of Salem appointed by ballot Higginson as their teacher and Samuel Skelton* as pastor. The church cov-enant* composed by the pair established Salem as the first nonseparating congregational* Puri-tan* church in New England. The covenant al-lowed into Communion only those who were doctrinally sound and who had an experience of grace.

High Church. A term referring to individuals and congregations within the Anglican Church* who interpret the episcopate,* priesthood and Book of Common Prayer* in a Catholic* sense, stressing the continuity of the Anglican Church with Catholic Christianity.

See also BROAD CHURCH; LOW CHURCH; TRAC-
TARIANISM.

Higher Christian Life. A late nineteenth-century Protestant* movement emphasizing experiential holiness* as a distinct work of grace clearly distinguishable from justification.* The Higher
Christian Life movement, with its cornerstone of
experiential holiness, originated among North
American Protestants and was eventually to move
worldwide by means of the British Keswick
movement.

The figures most prominently associated with
the phrase *Higher Christian Life* are William E.
Boardman,* who published *The Higher Christian
Life* (1859), and the husband-wife team of Robert
Pearsall Smith,* who wrote *Holiness Through
Faith* (1870), and Hannah Whitall Smith,* who
published the immensely popular *The Christian's
Secret of a Happy Life* (1875). Their basic theology was that while justification dealt with the
guilt of sin,* sanctification* dealt with its power
and led to a happy, or higher, Christian life.

See also HOLINESS MOVEMENT; PERFECTIONISM; VIC-
TORIOUS CHRISTIAN LIFE.

Hillenbrand, Reynold Henry (1904-1979).
Seminary rector, liturgical pioneer and social activist. In his native Chicago, Hillenbrand served as
a professor at Quigley Seminary and then, from
1936 to 1944, as rector of St. Mary of the Lake
Seminary. There his interest deepened in the
cause of liturgical renewal, which he saw as intimately connected with the cause of social reconstruction. He also was extensively involved with
labor unions and the sponsorship of labor
schools for the growing number of unskilled la-
borers being organized by the C.I.O. in Chicago.

His lifelong interest was the Specialized Catholic Action (*see* Catholic Action) work of Canon
Joseph Cardijn of Belgium—a successful cell
technique of Christian action drawing small
groups of students and workers together to effect
change in the social order.

Hillis, Newell Dwight (1858-1929). Congregational* clergyman and pulpiteer. After three pastorates in Illinois, Hillis moved to the Plymouth
Church of Brooklyn, New York (1899-1924),
where he became an immensely popular
preacher in both the U.S. and Great Britain.

Hillis's influence moved well beyond the pulpit, as he developed an interest in urban planning
and preached on the subject. His illustrated lecture "A Better America" was used by the U.S. government during and following World War II.

Hills, Aaron Merritt (1848-1935). Church of
the Nazarene* theologian. Hills became greatly
interested in Christian holiness* through the influence of Charles G. Finney* and during his later
pastorates increasingly identified with the Holiness movement.*

Hills founded three Wesleyan*-Holiness colleges. He wrote nearly thirty books, including the
first Nazarene systematic theology (1931).

Himes, Joshua V. (1805-1895). Early Adventist* preacher and leader of the Millerite movement. In 1839 Himes accepted the views of William Miller* regarding the immediacy of Christ's
Second Coming. Through Himes's promotional
skills, Miller became a nationally known figure.

Hispanic Churches in America. The Hispanic
churches in America consist primarily of Catholics* and Protestants,* although there is a growing
number of Hispanic adherents to other religious
sects. Traditionally, active Catholics and Protestants have each made up about 10 percent of the
Hispanic population, with the remaining 80 percent considered to be nominal Catholics. Recently the proportion of Protestant Hispanics has risen
to over 20 percent, with Pentecostal* groups
showing the largest gains.

For Protestants the major thrust among Hispanics began in the early 1800s, when mainline* denominations sent missionaries to evangelize the
existing Hispanic populations then concentrated
in the American Southwest and in Puerto Rico
and Cuba. After an initial openness to Hispanic
congregations, an integrated form of polity all but
absorbed the Hispanic churches. In the late twentieth century a new stage of self-determination
and liberation is now beginning to stir among
Hispanics.

Hispanic Catholics faced a similar situation.
When the present Southwest was annexed to the
U.S. in the mid-nineteenth century, the Catholic
Church within the region was in a state of near
collapse. In Latin America a long tradition of
Spanish colonialism and a long-standing conflict
between the church and state left a divided and
weakened church. A new openness began taking
place within the Catholic Church during the

1960s. By the mid-seventies, a Secretariat of Hispanic Affairs had been appointed, and the first Hispanic archbishop had been named. The *Comunidades Eclesiales de Base* (base communities) are offering the laity a new opportunity for involvement in the church.

Hitchcock, Edward (1793-1864). Congregational* layman and geologist. Hitchcock was long associated with Amherst College in Massachusetts, as professor (1825-1864) and president (1845-1854), where he distinguished himself as an eminent geologist.

Hitchcock's geological work was a conscious attempt to reveal (usually through analogical means) the evidences of God in nature. Not disposed to endorse any evolutionary scheme, Hitchcock's work argued for the complementarity of Christian faith and science, even if the latter required accepting an old earth.

Hobart, John Henry (1775-1830). Episcopal* bishop and controversialist. During his career Hobart was a vigorous champion of the high church* (*see* Tractarianism) vision of Episcopalianism, in numerous tracts and books emphasizing the value of the liturgy* and forms of the Episcopal Church.

Through his labors Hobart did much to extend the Episcopal Church. His thought and labor made him one of the most important figures in the revitalization of the Episcopal Church in America after the Revolutionary War.*

Hocking, William Ernest (1873-1966). Philosopher of religion* and critic of Protestant* foreign missions.* Hocking, who taught from 1914 until 1943 at Harvard,* was in the idealist tradition in modern philosophy, in a form he identified as "objective idealism."

Hocking's major contribution to missions involved his service as chairman of the Commission of Appraisal of the Laymen's Foreign Missions Inquiry* which visited American Protestant missions in Asia in 1931. In its report the commission criticized much of the Protestant missionary effort, arguing that missions ought to emphasize social effort apart from evangelism,* aim for cooperation rather than conversion* and foster greater unity with members of other religions.

Hodge, A(rchibald) A(lexander) (1823-1886). Princeton* theologian. Born the eldest son of Princeton theologian Charles Hodge,* A. A. Hodge came to defend Calvinist* theology and its worldview in the tradition begun by his namesake, Archibald Alexander.* From 1878 until his death he taught at Princeton Theological Seminary.* His writings reflect the warm evangelicalism* which nourished Princeton's stout theology, conservative Presbyterianism's* resistance to all attempts to revise the Westminster Confession of Faith* and a breadth of vision extending to America's political and social milieu.

In *Outlines of Theology* (1878) Hodge responded to liberals* who used a naturalistic worldview to interpret Scripture. To critics who claimed contradictions existed in the biblical text and between the Bible and what scientists have found in nature, Hodge made explicit Princeton's doctrine of plenary and verbal inspiration. He believed church and state should be separate, but as an ardent postmillennialist* he also thought religion must be closely integrated into American political, economic and social institutions.

See also PRINCETON THEOLOGY.

Hodge, Charles (1797-1878). Princeton* theologian. A committed disciple of Archibald Alexander,* Hodge faithfully transmitted his teacher's tradition of defending Reformed* orthodoxy* by combining a firm grasp of Calvinist* theology,* undergirded by a fervent evangelical* piety,* with a rigorous adaptation of Scottish Common Sense philosophy.*

In an era when theological ideas powerfully influenced American culture, Hodge became the central figure in one of the most prestigious graduate schools of the country. Under his leadership the *Biblical Repertory,* later renamed the *Princeton Review,* became a respected theological journal renowned for its staunch support of Old School* Calvinism. He defended an authoritative Bible* and a Reformed perspective of its teaching when theological and cultural tides were shifting toward Arminian,* revivalist and Unitarian* views.

As the most prominent American Presbyterian theologian of the nineteenth century, Hodge trained more than two thousand students in the Princeton theology from 1822 to 1878.

Hodge, Margaret E. (1869-1943). Presbyterian* foreign missions* leader. In 1920, Hodge became president of the Woman's Board of Foreign Missions. With Katherine Bennett she coauthored "Causes of Unrest Among Women in the Church"

(1927) and argued for wider equality for women in all aspects of church life.

Hogan, William (1788-1848). Schismatic Catholic* priest. Hogan immigrated to the U.S. in 1819 and obtained a pastoral assignment in Albany from the bishop of New York. In 1820 Hogan moved to St. Mary's Church in Philadelphia, though without the approval of his bishop in New York. Subsequent criticism of the bishop of Philadelphia led to his excommunication.

Subsequently Hogan became a lawyer, worked as a newspaper editor in Boston and in 1843 served as American consul in Cuba.

Hogan Schism. A division within the Catholic diocese of Philadelphia (1820-1831). When William Hogan,* a popular pastor at St. Mary's Church, lost his permission to act as a priest, the trustees of the church claimed the right to select their own priests. Hogan was excommunicated, but not until 1831 did a new bishop prevail against the trustees.

See also TRUSTEEISM.

Hoge, Moses Drury (1819-1899). Southern Presbyterian* preacher. From 1845 until his death, Hoge was the pastor of the Second Presbyterian Church of Richmond, Virginia. He was an extremely able speaker, and his church became one of the largest and most influential Presbyterian churches in all the South. An orthodox* Calvinist,* he worked hard for reconciliation with the Northern church after the Civil War.*

Holdeman, John (1832-1900). Founder of the Church of God in Christ, Mennonite.* Extensive reading in early Mennonite sources convinced Holdeman that the Mennonite Church of his day had fallen into "decay," having departed from the teachings of the Mennonite fathers and from the enforcement of church discipline.* In 1859 he organized the church referred to popularly as the Holdeman Mennonites. It fused conservative Mennonite practices with what Holdeman had apparently learned from the revivalism* of John Winebrenner.*

Holiness. In Christian theology* the term *holiness* first of all describes God's unblemished moral character and majesty. Objects, institutions and people may be holy inasmuch as they are consecrated to God, separated from that which is un-clean and renewed for holy use. Three general approaches to holiness can be identified within the Christian traditions that have flourished in America.

Sacramental *holiness,* emphasized in the Roman Catholic Church* and by certain high church* Anglicans,* is premised on the holiness of the church, inasmuch as it has been granted by God the deposit of faith, the ministry of the gospel and the sacraments.

Positional *holiness,* espoused by those in the Reformed tradition,* emphasizes the status of holiness before God for those that have been justified* by faith.

The quest for *personal holiness* characterizes churches of the Holiness* or Wesleyan* tradition. John Wesley's theology provided the foundation for the emergence of a distinctive holiness theology in nineteenth-century America.

See also HOLINESS MOVEMENT; PERFECTIONISM; SANCTIFICATION.

Holiness Churches and Associations. The quest for unity is a recurring theme in the history of the Holiness movement.* John Wesley,* the movement's forefather, fostered holy living through pietist* cell groups. Likewise, collective spirituality* (or social holiness) was emphasized in American Methodism* from the 1830s on by Phoebe Palmer* of New York City, in whose weekly Tuesday Meetings a large segment of the American Holiness movement was born. After the Civil War,* associations emerged as enlarged means for pursuing "unity in holiness," while in the 1880s the rise of Holiness sects* added new dimensions to the impulse. Twentieth-century Holiness denominationalism* developed from sectarianism, assuming a dominant role in the movement's search for unity in holiness.

Early Associations. The first, most influential and longest continuing association was organized in 1867 at Vineland, New Jersey, as the National Camp Meeting Association for the Promotion of Holiness,* known popularly as the National Holiness Association (NHA) until 1971, when officially it became the Christian Holiness Association (CHA). The NHA was the archetype that inspired a large network of regional, state, county and local Holiness associations that operated as independent entities.

Sectarian Heyday. The Holiness movement began losing cohesion in the 1880s. Its sectarian heyday (1880-1910) was followed by a period of merger and consolidation and then, after midcentury, by new sect formation in reaction to cultural accommodations.

Other Traditions. The Holiness movement also affected existing Methodist and non-Methodist groups. The Wesleyan Methodist Church (1843) and the Free Methodist Church* (1860) were participants in the holiness revival by the 1880s, as were the Salvation Army* and the Brethren in Christ.* Holiness thought also spread in nineteenth-century Quaker* circles.

Consolidation and Contemporary Associations. Two other factors shaped the mosaic: "unitive holiness," which was increasingly important to leaders pondering the limited ability of regional bodies to carry out a mission to the world, and the rise of Pentecostalism.*

Following the shift from "Holiness movement" to "Holiness churches," the CHA changed from a Methodist body into an ecumenical one. The CHA presently lists nineteen denominations as affiliated or cooperating members, representing over 1.5 million constituents in the U.S. and Canada. The Inter-Denominational (now Inter-Church) Holiness Convention was formed as a fellowship of conservatives in 1952.

Holiness Movement. The Holiness movement grew from seeds planted in the 1830s, although it did not take definite institutional form until after the Civil War.* It emphasized the complete sanctification* of Christian believers, often conceiving of it as something like a second conversion* experience, instantaneous and dramatic. The movement drew support from persons of many different ecclesiastical traditions and denominations,* although Methodists* were always prominent among its leaders. At first more or less tolerated, if not actually embraced warmly by the existing churches, many Holiness advocates eventually came into open conflict with denominational leaders. This led by the 1880s and 1890s to the founding of numerous independent Holiness churches, many of which have continued to the present.

Pre-Civil War Beginnings. The immediate antecedents of the Holiness movement lie in pre-Civil War American revivalism* and the growing influence of Methodism over American Protestantism* in the early decades of the nineteenth century. The revivalism associated with the Second Great Awakening* helped to create a religious climate in which the power and active presence of God in the world and in Christian believers' lives were expected—and perceived—on every hand. Revivals of religion encouraged Christians to believe in great spiritual possibilities, including the full perfection of individuals and society. As a result several varieties of perfectionist* teaching had sprung up by the 1830s and 1840s, most notably at Oberlin College,* led by Charles G. Finney* and Asa Mahan.*

One of the most effective of the Methodist promoters of Holiness was laywoman Phoebe Worrall Palmer.* Most significant was her leadership of the Tuesday Meeting for the Promotion of Holiness, a "social religious gathering" in New York City which for more than sixty years helped shape the views of many ministers and laypeople* both inside and outside of Methodism.

The Post-Civil War Holiness Crusade. The Civil War brought the first phase of the Holiness movement to an end. The division and distraction the war occasioned, as well as the exhausting moral debate over slavery leading up to it, combined to sap the movement's momentum and at the same time to undermine the fortunes of organized religion generally. Desiring to revive the sagging fortunes of the quest for holiness, a group of ministers met two years after the war's end to organize a camp meeting* for promoting holiness.

This first "general camp meeting" for the promotion of holiness was held in 1867 in the Methodist village of Vineland, New Jersey, out of which came the National Campmeeting Association for the Promotion of Holiness.* This new development significantly changed the course of the Holiness movement, giving it an organizational center it had not previously had.

About this time the influence of the Holiness movement was spreading to the British Isles, due largely to the work of the American husband-and-wife team of Robert Pearsall Smith* and Hannah Whitall Smith,* who visited Britain from 1873 to 1875. They were central figures in the Oxford Union Meeting for the Promotion of Scriptural Holiness held in 1874 and a similar gathering held at Brighton in 1875.

These were not unlike the American Holiness camp meetings, and they gave a central focus to higher life activity in Britain. This was made permanent with the founding of the Keswick* Convention in 1876, a higher-life institution which continues to the present. Keswick teaching was eventually imported to the U.S. in the 1880s and 1890s via the celebrated Northfield Conferences* organized by Dwight L. Moody.*

Separation. By the 1880s and 1890s large numbers of Holiness advocates had become alienated from their churches. Opposition of ecclesiastical officials to the highly independent and rapidly multiplying Holiness associations and bands led to tension and conflict. Beginning in 1881 with Daniel Sidney Warner's* Church of God* (now Church of God, Anderson, Indiana), the Holiness movement began to produce numerous independent churches. Several other churches already in existence also came to identify themselves as Holiness churches and to associate themselves with the new groups, including the Salvation Army,* the Wesleyan Methodist Church, the Free Methodist Church,* the Brethren in Christ Church* and the Evangelical Friends.*

Holiness and Pentecostalism. By promoting entire sanctification, the Holiness movement helped to make possible the rise of Pentecostalism* in the early twentieth century. But a significant factor during the second half of the nineteenth century was the growing popularity in Holiness circles of using the term *baptism of* (or *with*) *the Holy Spirit* to describe the "deeper work of grace," or "second blessing," of entire sanctification. This term was embraced by Wesleyan, Oberlin and Keswick segments of the movement alike, and the biblical account of the gift of the Spirit to the early church on the Day of Pentecost became an important resource for preaching and teaching Holiness. In time, some within the Holiness movement began to identify speaking in tongues* as the outward sign of receiving the baptism with the Spirit. This new teaching led to a fracture in the movement and the emergence of still more new churches in the years following the 1906 Azusa Street Revival* in Los Angeles.

Holmes, Obadiah (c. 1607-1682). Colonial Baptist* minister. In 1650, while living in Plymouth Colony, Holmes became a Baptist. Persecution led to his settling in Newport, Rhode Island. Holmes's greatest legacy was his *Last Will and Testimony* (1675), which remains the best example of Baptist theology,* preaching* style, piety* and family life to come out of the seventeenth century.

Holocaust and the American Churches. The Holocaust refers to the colossal tragedy of the attempted annihilation of European Jewry at the hands of the Nazis. During the twelve years of the Third Reich (1933-1945), under the despotic leadership of Adolf Hitler, six million Jews were killed. Countless others also suffered persecution, imprisonment, dehumanization and death—including Protestant* pastors and laity, Catholic* priests, Jehovah's Witnesses,* gypsies, Slavs, political opponents, homosexuals and the intelligentsia—but by far the most harassed, persecuted, humiliated and murdered people were the Jews in Germany and the occupied territories.

During this crisis the responses of the churches proved to be totally inadequate and ineffective. Although there were published reports in American church journals, a few denominational* and ecumenical* public statements, attempts now and then to influence political leaders, and assistance to fleeing refugees, it would be difficult to dispute the following conclusion of a renowned Holocaust scholar: "At the heart of Christianity is the commitment to help the helpless. Yet, for the most part, America's Christian Churches looked away while European Jews perished" (D. Wyman).

Holy Name Society. A Roman Catholic* spiritual group encouraging reverence for the name of Jesus. Established in Spain in the fifteenth century, the society was officially approved by Pope Pius IV a century later. By 1963, at about the height of the society's activities, membership numbered five million worldwide, including some women.

Since Vatican II,* the Holy Name Society in America has been joined, and often supplanted, by many other groups which further the mission and spirituality* of parishes.

Holy Office. *See* CONGREGATION FOR THE DOCTRINE OF THE FAITH.

Holy Orders. Catholic* term for the sacrament* of the priesthood. More generally, the term refers to the rank of bishop, priest or deacon* in the Roman Catholic, Orthodox* and Anglican* churches.

Holy Rollers. A derisive term from the early twentieth century, describing groups who give extreme emotional expression to their faith.

Home Missions Council. Interdenominational network of home mission agencies. Organized in

1908 under the chairmanship of Charles L. Thompson,* the Home Missions Council promoted fellowship, conferences and cooperation among Christian organizations doing missionary work in the U.S., Canada and their dependencies. The council grew until the early 1930s, when it served as agent for forty-two Protestant home mission boards and societies, representing twenty-seven denominations.

Homecomings, Church. A Southern tradition of reunion of present and former members of a local congregation, usually celebrated annually on a designated Sunday.* These gatherings have great sentimental value because of the interrelatedness of church, community and family in rural areas.

Homiletics. The study of the content, manner and method of preaching.* Preaching has been central to the Christian faith from the church's inception. Homiletics has followed accordingly, as preachers have reflected on the act of preaching and tried to teach the art of preaching to others.

Homiletics has traditionally maintained a creative tension between the authority* of the Bible and the ethos of culture. Homiletics is the discipline which enables the preacher to understand the text, discern the spirit of the times and bring the two together.

See also EXPOSITOR.

Homosexuality and the Churches. Until the latter half of the twentieth century, the American churches gave little public attention to the phenomenon of sexual attraction and sexual behavior between members of the same sex. The traditional view of most ecclesiastical bodies condemned homosexuality, finding justification for the condemnation in natural law* and in several biblical texts (e.g., Gen 19:4-11; Lev 18:22; 20:13; Rom 1:27; 1 Cor 6:9; 1 Tim 1:10).

The first sign of a reevaluation of the issue appeared in 1955 with the publication in England of *Homosexuality and the Western Christian Tradition* by Rev. Derrick Sherwin Bailey, an Anglican* priest. Bailey challenged the church's traditional view with current findings from the behavioral sciences and a reinterpretation of relevant biblical passages.

In 1969 the Universal Fellowship of Metropolitan Community Churches (UFMCC) was founded by the Rev. Troy D. Perry. The UFMCC, affirming homosexuality as a gift of God and welcoming both homosexual and heterosexual Christians into its fellowship, has grown to include over 100,000 members in more than 150 congregations throughout the world.

Meanwhile, inside the traditional churches, lesbian and gay advocacy groups began forming to lobby for full acceptance of homosexual Christians within the church. In some denominations their presence stimulated the formation of opposing caucuses. As a result of discussions among these various groups, most American and Canadian denominations have gone on record as supporting civil rights for the homosexual community; opposing homosexual practice, though recognizing that sexual orientation is rarely chosen; calling for ministry* to lesbians and gays; and denying ordination* to self-affirming, practicing homosexuals.

Homrighausen, Elmer George (1900-1982). Reformed* pastor and educator. In 1938 Homrighausen became professor of Christian education at Princeton Seminary.* He was dean of the seminary from 1955 to 1965 and retired in 1970. He also served as director of the National Council of Churches'* Department of Evangelism. An early, enthusiastic supporter of Karl Barth's* theology, Homrighausen helped introduce Barth's early thought to American theologians.

Hooker, Thomas (1586-1647). Puritan* minister, theologian and political theorist. In 1634 Hooker became pastor of the church in Newtown (present-day Cambridge) and then in 1636 led his congregation in an exodus to the banks of the Connecticut River, founding the town of Hartford. Hooker's political perspective sharply distinguished between the national (religious) covenant* and all civil covenants. He refused to make church membership* a prerequisite for the franchise, as was the pattern in Massachusetts.

Hoover, James Matthew (1872-1935). Methodist* missionary to Southeast Asia. In 1899 Hoover went to Malaya as a missionary of the Methodist Episcopal Church (1899). He established more than forty churches and schools, accomplishing a high degree of self-support through improved farming and marketing.

Hoover, Willis Collins (1856-1936). Methodist* missionary and founder of the indigenous Chilean Pentecostal* movement. In 1902 Hoover became pastor of a Methodist church in Valparaiso, Chile. By 1910 he and as many as six hundred Chileans had left the Methodist Church and formed the parent organization of the contemporary movement.

Hopkins, Emma Curtis (1853-1925). Leader of New Thought. After initial participation in the Christian Science* movement, Hopkins broke with Mary Baker Eddy* and in 1886 established what became the Christian Science Theological Seminary. Hopkins taught a brand of Christian Science that freely borrowed from a variety of the world's mystical and religious traditions.

Hopkins, John Henry (1792-1868). Episcopal* bishop. Bishop of the Diocese* of Vermont (from 1832), Hopkins was a prolific controversialist. His basic argument was that religious doctrine be grounded on Scripture, as interpreted through the witness of the primitive church. In the 1840s he thus opposed the Tractarian movement* and, during the 1850s and 1860s, the abolitionist movement.*

Hopkins, Mark (1802-1887). Moral philosopher and president of Williams College. Hopkins, an ordained* Congregational* minister, served as president of Williams from 1836 to 1872. Convinced that the religious and philosophical truths that stood the test of time provided sufficient answers to all facets of human life, Hopkins stood in opposition to many of the intellectual currents of his day, including transcendentalism* and nascent Darwinism.*

Hopkins, Samuel (1721-1803). Congregational* clergyman and theologian. Profoundly influenced by the thought of Jonathan Edwards,* Hopkins became one of Edwards's closest friends and most influential disciples. With his colleague Joseph Bellamy,* another of Edwards's protégés, Hopkins helped to shape a highly nuanced version of Edwards's theology. By the final decades of the eighteenth century, Hopkins and Bellamy had won a group of some sixty like-minded ministers to their way of thinking. This first indigenous school of American Calvinism* has borne a plethora of names, with *New Divinity** being the most common.

Hopkins taught that sin* is manifested in self-ishness or inordinate self-love, even for those trying to use the means of grace. He argued further that the center of regeneration lay in the convert's new access to "disinterested benevolence." Seeing the heart of Christian virtue as selflessness—disinterested charity for all of God's creation—Hopkins erected a powerful Calvinistic apologia for social reform.

Hopkinsianism. *See* Hopkins, Samuel.

Horner, Ralph Cecil (1853-1921). Father of the Canadian Holiness movement.* Horner led evangelistic* campaigns marked by conversions,* sanctifications* and speaking in tongues.* Deposed as a Methodist* minister in 1895, he organized the Holiness Movement Church and became its first bishop.

Horton, Douglas (1891-1968). Congregational* leader and advocate for Christian unity.* Horton was an active proponent of the merger of the Congregational Christian Churches with the Evangelical and Reformed* Church, leading in 1957 to the creation of the United Church of Christ.* He served on the General Committee of the World Council of Churches,* and from 1957 to 1963 he chaired its Faith and Order Commission.

Horton, T(homas) C(orwin) (1848-1932). Minister and cofounder of the Bible Institute of Los Angeles (now known as Biola University). In 1906, while serving at Los Angeles's Immanuel Presbyterian Church, Horton founded the Fishermen's Club. Established to train laymen in Bible and evangelism,* the club eventually became an international organization.

In 1908, with the financial backing of oilman and Christian layman Lyman Stuart,* Horton founded and served as the superintendent of the Bible Institute of Los Angeles, whose aim was to prepare young people for Christian service.

Horton, Walter Marshall (1895-1966). Neo-orthodox* theologian. Ordained* a Baptist* minister in 1919, Horton began his teaching career at Union Theological Seminary,* New York (1922-1925), but soon moved to Oberlin College* Graduate School of Theology, where he spent the rest of his career as Fairchild Professor.

Horton, rightly regarded as a founder of the field of pastoral psychology, analyzed religious experience in terms of its behaviorial dimensions, integrating moral values and human development with traditional theological doctrines such as theism,* sin,* salvation* and human destiny.

Hospice. Holistic care for the terminally ill and their families. A hospice represents a skilled community dedicated to (1) enabling those whose life expectancy is measured in months or weeks to experience the fullest possible quality of life before their death, (2) making the patient-family the primary focus of concern and (3) supporting the family in its bereavement. To provide a holistic program of physical, emotional, psychological and spiritual care, as well as symptom control, hospices often employ physician-directed interdisciplinary teams, including nurses, social workers and the clergy.

Hostetter, C(hristian) N(eff), Jr. (1899-1980). Brethren in Christ* bishop* and educator. Hostetter, president of Messiah College (1934-1960), was active in his denomination* as an evangelist, board member and moderator of the General Conference. He also served on the Mennonite Central Committee* (1948-1967).

Hotovitzky, Alexander (c. 1870-c. 1935). Russian Orthodox* priest. Hotovitzky arrived in America fresh out of seminary, one of Bishop Nicholas Ziorov's finest recruits—honest, idealistic and deeply religious. He married* in the U.S. and quickly became the trusted adviser of all the East Coast Orthodox clergy.

Houghton, William Henry (1887-1947). Fundamentalist* Baptist* minister and president of Moody Bible Institute.* After evangelistic work and several successful pastorates, Houghton became president of Moody in 1934. At Moody he built up the faculty and student body (from 848 in 1934 to 1,428 in 1945) and edited and expanded the circulation of *Moody Monthly* (from 35,000 in 1934 to 75,000 in 1945). Houghton, with Irwin A. Moon, initiated the idea of a periodic meeting of Christians involved in science, which eventually became the American Scientific Affiliation.

House Churches. Gatherings of believers held in the home of a Christian individual or family. House churches have existed from the time Christianity began; the apostle Paul frequently mentioned "the church in the house of _____"

(Rom 16:5; Col 4:15; etc.). Contemporary house churches, which are not limited to any particular theological tradition, in some cases are temporary arrangements in the course of establishing a new congregation with a new church building; in other cases they represent a quest for intimacy and community that members have not found in a large church.

House of Bishops. A legislative body that, along with the House of Deputies,* constitutes the General Convention of the Episcopal Church* in the U.S. It includes all Episcopal bishops.

House of Deputies. A legislative body that, along with the House of Bishops,* constitutes the General Convention of the Episcopal Church* in the U.S. It includes four ordained* and four lay persons from each diocese.*

Howe, Julia Ward (1819-1910). Unitarian* author and social reformer. Howe published several volumes of poetry, essays and drama, but her chief fame came from a single poem, "The Battle Hymn of the Republic," which she composed in 1861 after visiting a Union army camp.

After the war Howe was active in various reform causes. In the end she preached a gospel of culture to a society she believed had grown neglectful of basic American values.

Howell, R(obert) B(oyte) C(rawford) (1801-1868). Southern Baptist* pastor and denominational* leader. A proponent of theological education* among Baptists, Howell was instrumental in the founding of various Baptist institutions, including the Southern Baptist Theological Seminary* (1859). He is best known for his opposition to the movement called Old Landmarkism.*

Howell, Vernon. See KORESH, DAVID.

Hughes, John Joseph (1797-1864). Roman Catholic* prelate and controversialist. Named New York's first archbishop (1850), Hughes was an aggressive prelate and created a centralized diocesan* authority that also maintained its Roman identity. He founded St. John's College, later Fordham University (1841), and laid the cornerstone for St. Patrick's Cathedral (1858).

Hughes enjoyed national prominence. His rhetorical skill gained him an invitation to speak before Congress (1847) and even a request to represent the Union before Pius IX* and Napoleon III (1861).

Huguenots. The popular name for the Calvinist* French Protestants,* officially the Reformed* Church of France. In the sixteenth and seventeenth centuries, the word was often used to describe the French Protestants as both a religious movement and a political faction.

Under the intellectual and spiritual leadership of their exiled countryman John Calvin, French Protestants grew rapidly in numbers from about 1540 to 1560. Efforts to suppress the French Reformed Church led to a series of inconclusive Wars of Religion in France between 1562 and 1598. A resolution of the civil conflict came when the Huguenot leader Henry of Navarre succeeded to the throne as Henry IV (1589-1610), declared himself a Catholic* and in 1598 issued the Edict of Nantes, granting the Protestants religious toleration and full civil liberties.

During the reigns of Louis XIII (1610-1643) and Louis XIV (1643-1715), these rights were undone. First the Huguenots' military and political prerogatives were removed, and then the revocation of the Edict of Nantes (1685) abolished completely their religious rights. With Protestantism made illegal in almost all of France, over 400,000 of the more than two million Huguenots immigrated to Prussia, the Netherlands, Switzerland, the British Isles and North America.

Between 1562 and 1750, about twenty thousand Huguenots immigrated to America. Most of them settled in and around Charleston, South Carolina, but large numbers also landed in Pennsylvania, Virginia, New York, Rhode Island and Massachusetts. Though small in numbers, the Huguenots wielded a considerable influence in colonial life because most of them were merchants, bankers, skilled craftsmen or members of the legal and medical professions.

The story of the Huguenots in America constitutes one of the great mysteries of ethnic refugee assimilation in American history. By 1750, as a group, they had largely disappeared into the larger Anglo-Saxon culture and assimilated almost flawlessly into Protestant America, contrary to the normal pattern that sustained immigrant identity (*see* Immigration and Ethnicity, Protestant).

Humanae Vitae. An encyclical letter of Pope Paul VI* (July 1968) on the topic of birth control.* The context for the encyclical is the twentieth-century debate over the nature and purpose of Christian marriage.*

In 1966 a papal commission, while strongly rejecting arbitrary contraception, advocated leaving decisions about how to achieve responsible parenthood in the context of fruitful married life to the consciences of Christian parents. Published two years later, *Humanae Vitae* rejected this report's conclusions. In it the pope defended the principle that married love cannot be isolated from the responsibility of parenthood, that every act of marital intercourse must remain open to the possibility of procreation.

Because of the widespread controversy and public dissent attending its publication, some have interpreted *Humanae Vitae* as a kind of turning point in U.S. Catholic* history, dividing so-called liberals and conservatives. Its impact on the Catholic Church in the U.S. is still a matter of debate.

See also ETHICS, CATHOLIC PERSONAL.

Humanism. *See* SECULAR HUMANISM.

Hunt, Robert (c. 1568-1608). First Anglican* priest in America. Hunt was chaplain* of the Virginia Company's 1607 expedition to Jamestown. He led the morning and evening prayer, preached two sermons each Sunday and presided at Holy Communion every three months.

Huntington, Frederic Dan (1819-1904). Unitarian* minister, convert* to theism* and first Protestant Episcopal* bishop of central New York. In 1855 Huntington became the first incumbent of the Plummer Professorship of Christian Morals, making him preacher to Harvard College.* A spiritual struggle ensued, and in 1860, having accepted a trinitarian theism and the deity and redemptive work of Christ, he resigned his professorship at Harvard—one of the most famous conversions in Harvard College history.

Huntington, William Reed (1838-1909). Episcopal* priest, ecumenical* leader and liturgical* reformer. In 1862 Huntington became rector of All Saints' Church in Worcester, Massachusetts (1862-1883), and later of Grace Church, New York City (1883-1909). For many years he was the most influential member of the House of Deputies of the Episcopal Church's General Convention. His seminal work *The Church Idea* (1870) was the major source of the Chicago-Lambeth Quadrilateral.*

Huron Mission. During the middle decades of the seventeenth century, the outstanding French missions* were those of the Jesuits* among the Hurons in modern Ontario, a group held in bitter enmity by the Iroquois.

In 1634 Champlain induced a group of Hurons on a trading visit to Quebec to take back some Jesuits, led by Jean de Brebeuf,* to reside with them. Before long a number of converts* were gathered. In 1640 a college and seminary for Huron children was established at Quebec.

Attacks by the Iroquois were devastating, however, leading in 1649 to Brebeuf's martyrdom and the end of the Huron mission.

Hutchinson, Anne Marbury (1591-1643). Puritan* Massachusetts religious dissenter. Shortly after immigrating to Massachusetts in 1634, Hutchinson began teaching that God granted salvation* to whomever he pleased and that human actions could in no way influence his decision or help establish proof of election.* The established ministers, she believed, placed too much emphasis upon deeds. So began the celebrated antinomian* crisis in Massachusetts Bay. Excommunicated in 1638, Hutchinson left for Rhode Island and later moved to Long Island Sound, where she was killed in an Indian uprising.

Hutterites (Hutterian Brethren). A communal form of sixteenth-century Anabaptism* that has survived and flourishes in North America. Hutterite origins may be traced to Moravia, where persecuted Anabaptists found refuge in the mid-1520s. Jacob Hutter (martyred in 1536) reorgan-ized the struggling group into the movement that still bears his name. Distinctive features of Hutterian life include believer's baptism,* nonresistance, separation of church and state,* distinctive dress and communitarian living.

Hymns, Hymnals. In 1640 the first book printed in North America for the English-speaking colonies was *The Bay Psalm Book.* Benjamin Franklin reprinted Isaac Watts's hymns (1729), and John* and Charles Wesley printed *Hymns and Sacred Poems* (1739). In 1784 John Wesley himself prepared a hymnal for America as a safeguard on the excitable American scene. Asahel Nettleton's* *Village Hymns for Social Worship* (1824) was to supplement Watts, as was Joshua Leavitt's *Christian Lyre* (1831). Lowell Mason* and Thomas Hastings published their *Spiritual Songs for Social Worship* (1832). Beginning in 1875 Ira D. Sankey* collaborated successively with Philip P. Bliss,* James McGranahan and George C. Stebbins* to publish *Gospel Hymns.* Throughout the nineteenth century, denominations* produced hymnals, as many of them did around the 1940s. In the 1980s another set of denominational books was produced, including the *Lutheran Book of Worship,* the Episcopal* *Hymnal 1982,* the Roman Catholic* *Worship III,* and *Rejoice in the Lord* for the Reformed Church in America.*

Editors of all these publications had to struggle with language, including dealing with King James English, battle symbolism, discriminatory language (*see* Inclusive Language Movement) and language about God.

I

Icon. A painting on a flat surface depicting a person or event venerated as holy in the Eastern Orthodox Church.* Icons are used in the corporate worship of the Eastern Orthodox Church and are prominently displayed in church buildings. Believers display devotion by genuflecting, kissing, incensing and lighting candles before icons, which are considered channels of grace and miracles. However, a distinction is made between the honor given to the saints and the worship that belongs to God alone.

Illinois Band (Yale Band). A group of Yale* students who in 1829 formally pledged to establish a seminary and plant churches* in Illinois. All eventually became Congregational* ministers. The band was responsible for the rapid spread of Congregationalism in Illinois and strongly influenced the abolitionist* and temperance movements* there.

Immaculate Conception. A teaching of the Roman Catholic Church* that the Blessed Virgin Mary,* by a singular grace and privilege of God, through the merits of her son Jesus Christ, was preserved from the stain or effects of original sin* from the first moment of her conception by her parents. Although many Catholic scholars and theologians had serious problems with this view, eventually a consensus arose, which enabled Pope Pius IX* to declare this official Catholic teaching in 1854.

See also ASSUMPTION OF MARY; MARIAN DEVOTIONS; MARIOLOGY.

Immigration and Ethnicity, Catholic. No nation can match the U.S. in the size and diversity of its immigrant population. Such diversity first became apparent in the nineteenth century, when a major migration of people took place in Europe. Between 1820 and 1920 over fifty-two million people left Europe, with some thirty-four million coming to the U.S.

Two Waves of Immigration, 1820-1920. In the first wave, 1820-1860, most immigrants came from Germany and the British Isles, especially Ireland. In the second wave, from the 1880s until the outbreak of World War I,* the immigrants came from other parts of Europe. In response to the influx of so many immigrants, various denominations* began to establish foreign-language churches, and missionary* efforts among immigrant communities became commonplace.

Changing Demographics. Immigration changed the Catholic Church* in a number of ways. First of all, it altered the ethnic mix of the people. In the early nineteenth century most Catholics were of Irish or Anglo-American descent, with some German and a large number of French clergy. By the end of the century Catholics came from as many as twenty-eight different countries, the largest groups being the Irish, German, Italian and Polish. As a result of immigration the number of Catholics increased substantially, so that by 1850 the Catholic Church had become the largest single denomination in the country, a distinction it has retained ever since.

Ethnic Churches. One of the first major acts of a settled immigrant community was to organize a religious society of some type. Once established, the society then became the catalyst for the building of a church. The language was the cement that held the community together, and anything that threatened the survival of the mother tongue was judged to be destructive of the community.

Ethnic Schools. A key institution in the immigrant neighborhood was the school. Since the public school was permeated with the ethos of American Protestantism,* immigrant Catholics launched a crusade on behalf of the Catholic parochial school.* Many viewed the parish school as a key agent in the effort to maintain the culture of the old country.

Ethnic Societies and Organizations. In some communities the church and the school were just the beginning of an extensive institutional complex. It was not unheard of to have a large Polish or German congregation supporting a hospital and orphanage, as well as numerous societies that appealed to the needs of various age groups. Such communities were a church within a church, where the immigrant pastor often presided with papal-like authority.*

Immigration and Ethnicity, Protestant. As a nation of immigrants, the U.S. contains in microcosm the religious and cultural diversity of the world's peoples.

Ethnicity and Identity. Because ethnicity and religion are so intertwined, scholars recognize that in some societies distinctive faiths may provide the source for ethnic identity, just as distinctive peoples may in other societies develop unique religious beliefs and practices. For state-church adherents like the German Lutherans,* Dutch Reformed* and English Episcopalians,* a shared nationality, language and homeland may overshadow religious beliefs and practices as the source of ethnicity. For religious dissenters, however, like the Huguenots* and the Quakers,* religious beliefs are their very reason for existence and survival.

Self-Preservation and Accommodation. Initially, the desire for self-preservation was overriding, especially for non-English-speaking groups who faced nativist* attacks. Preserving the mother tongue and Old Country customs and practices in church, school and family was deemed to be essential. These immigrant groups fostered Christian day schools,* promoted economic exchange within the group and waged bloc voting in public elections. Ethnicity and religion had merged into one force for survival.

But eventually, usually by the second generation, the forces of Americanization pressed immigrant churches to choose between accommodation or extinction. Pragmatic methods of revivalism,* a theology of individualism,* congregational* forms of church governance and, above all, the adoption of the English language in worship* for the sake of the young people became appealing if not mandatory reforms. Many third-generation immigrants, however, again sought to revive the waning ethnic heritage.

Sanctuary and Community. Christian beliefs and churches also had a direct bearing on the success of immigration. Religious convictions undergirded immigrants in their crises as "strangers in a foreign land." Churches served as agencies of the transplanting process, as immigrants' home away from home.

The role of the church differed, depending on whether immigrants settled in colonies or scattered and dispersed themselves. Immigrants who wished to take the fast track to Americanization refused to settle in the colonies, or they departed as soon as possible. These assimilators usually joined indigenous Protestant churches, often Presbyterian* congregations if they were of Reformed background or American Lutheran congregations if they hailed from Lutheran lands. The transcultural Christian heritage that was stressed in these churches helped immigrants to leave their former identity and to adopt the new one.

See also ASIAN-AMERICAN PROTESTANTS; HISPANIC CHURCHES IN AMERICA; IMMIGRATION AND ETHNICITY, CATHOLIC; REVIVALISM, GERMAN-AMERICAN; SCOTTISH PRESBYTERIANS IN AMERICA.

Imprimatur. Translated as "it may be printed," this Latin phrase signifies a Roman Catholic* bishop's permission for publication of a book by a Catholic author. According to Canon Law* (1983), this consent is required for translations of Scripture, liturgical books* and catechisms,* and theological textbooks.

In God We Trust. National motto of the U.S. In 1865 legislation was first passed which authorized the placement of "In God we trust" on certain U.S. coins. Legislation in 1955 required the phrase on all U.S. coins and, for the first time, paper money. In 1956 Congress made the phrase the national motto.

The inspiration for the phrase seems to have come from the last stanza of the "Star Spangled Banner," which contains the words "And this be our motto—'In God is our trust.' "

See also CIVIL RELIGION.

Inclusive Language Movement. A movement to make the language of worship,* Scripture and Christian education materials more inclusive in terms of gender, race and ability. The idea first emerged among public-school educators concerned that the exclusive use of male terms gave students the message that women were excluded from various professions and roles, and that the use of illustrations containing no people of color encouraged racial discrimination. In the church the movement promotes more inclusive language about both people and God.

Independence Day (July 4). The day commemorating the signing of the Declaration of Independence (1776). Public speakers often invoke themes of American civil religion,* and ministers—particularly conservative Protestants*—frequently eulogize the faith of the nation's Founding Fathers.

Independent Fundamental Churches of America. An organization of independent fundamentalist* churches and agencies. In 1930 thirty-nine men met with William McCarrell, pastor of the Cicero Bible Church, Cicero, Illinois, and began the IFCA.

The bylaws state that IFCA's purpose is to unify those who have "separated from denominations which include unbelievers and liberal teachers" and to encourage one another in world evangelism.* In 1992 the IFCA reported 71,672 members in 708 churches and a ministerial membership of 1,369.

Index of Forbidden Books. An alphabetical catalog specifying books Roman Catholics* could not publish, read, defend, retain or sell. Evolving from magisterial concerns to protect the faith and morals of the church, the index emerged during Catholic reaction to the Reformation.

Individualism. The concept of individualism gained currency in America with the publication of Alexis de Tocqueville's* *Democracy in America* (1835). He defined it as the tendency of Americans to draw apart into smaller circles defined by family and friendship, and he feared that eventually it would destroy the virtues of American public life. Religious writers have used the term in discussing four topics: the church, doctrinal authority,* the economic order and psychological well-being.

In the early nineteenth century a number of theologians argued that American Protestants,* formed by revivalistic* piety,* had lost the traditional sense of the church as a corporate organism.

Other theologians debated the principle of "private judgment" in the interpretation of Scripture and the formation of doctrine, arguing that the refusal to acknowledge a controlling authority

beyond the individual mind when interpreting Scripture promoted sectarian* disunity.

The primary debate over individualism resulted from the need to redefine the relationship between Christianity and the social order after the maturing of industrial capitalism in the late nineteenth century. A number of theologians warned that economic individualism threatened to produce social disorder and flouted the Christian ethical precept of care for the neighbor.

Sociologists of religion and culture have recently observed that individualism remains a powerful ideology in America and that it has now assumed new forms. They distinguish the older economic individualism from an expressive individualism that exalts the goal of self-fulfillment and that has proved to be increasingly attractive in American culture and Christianity.

Indulgence. Release from temporal punishment for sins* already forgiven. This Catholic* doctrine teaches that purification from sin's corruption comes through the sacrament of reconciliation* (penance). By indulgence, the church accepts good works of charity or devotion in lieu of such discipline.

See also MERIT; PURGATORY.

Inerrancy Controversy. One of the most vexing controversies within conservative Protestantism* since World War II has focused on the doctrine of biblical inerrancy. In the 1950s fundamentalists,* most evangelicals* and most Roman Catholics* upheld the inerrancy of the Bible, meaning that the Bible, when correctly interpreted, is "truthful," regardless of the topic it broaches, whether in the area of doctrine and ethics,* or history and the natural world.

In the late 1950s a small number of evangelical scholars had become uncomfortable with the doctrine, believing that the Bible does in fact contain material errors. In 1967 Fuller Theological Seminary* removed the doctrine of biblical inerrancy from its Statement of Faith. Since the 1970s, conservatives interested in promoting the doctrine of biblical inerrancy have gained control in the Lutheran Church—Missouri Synod* and in the Southern Baptist Convention.* The debate currently shows few signs of slackening.

Ingersoll, Robert Green (1833-1899). Agnostic controversialist. Ingersoll's greatest notoriety resulted from his frequent and highly popular lectures in which he promoted "freethinking." Though he recognized the ethical authenticity of Jesus Christ, Ingersoll advocated a thoroughgoing scientific skepticism. Known by religious contemporaries as "the great agnostic," Ingersoll posed the period's most visible and potent arguments for freethinking and against orthodoxy* and Christianity in general.

Inglis, Charles (1734-1816). Anglican* bishop of Nova Scotia. Loyalist sympathies that Inglis expressed in 1776 led to some American patriots' burning his New York church a year later. Leaving for England in 1784, he returned to North America in 1787 as the first bishop appointed to a colony by the Church of England.

Institutional Church Movement. A turn-of-the-century effort by Protestant* Social Gospel* leaders to regain ground the church had lost in the city, and particularly among the laboring poor. Pioneered by William A. Muhlenberg* and Thomas K. Beecher, the first significant expression of this idea was William S. Rainsford's St. George's Episcopal Church in New York, beginning in 1882. Rainsford sought to devise daily church programs that would meet practical needs of the people.

Interchurch World Movement. A short-lived ecumenical movement.* At a meeting in 1918, some 135 church and agency leaders decided to pursue a post-World War I* vision of a united church uniting a divided world. An overambitious budget and other flaws led to the movement's demise two years later.

Interdenominational Foreign Mission Association of North America. A fellowship and accrediting agency for nondenominational faith missions.* The association began in 1917 through the efforts of several mission societies committed to world evangelization.* Today over one hundred mission groups from the U.S. and Canada are affiliated with the association. These agencies represent over eight thousand missionaries from North America and another three thousand from other nations.

International Bible Reading Association. An organization established to encourage personal Bible reading and study. Founded in England in 1882 by the National Sunday School Union, the association spread rapidly beyond England's shores. It continues to publish daily Bible notes, along with reading aids for children, young people and adults.

International Bible Society. A society distributing Scripture worldwide. The International Bible Society (IBS) is an outgrowth of the New York Bible Society,* which was established in 1809. In 1967, under the leadership of its executive secretary, Y. R. Kindberg, the New York Bible Society undertook the financial sponsorship of the New International Version of the Bible, which was eventually published in 1978.

Today the IBS is involved in projects in ninety-nine different languages in thirteen countries. It currently supplies Bibles for prisons, hospitals and hotels, and maintains a full-time staff of evangelists in New York City.

International Church of the Foursquare Gospel. Pentecostal* denomination.* The church grew out of Pentecostal evangelist Aimee Semple McPherson's* Angelus Temple in Los Angeles. McPherson founded the church in 1927. The "Foursquare Gospel" was derived from the four-faced figures of Ezekiel 1, which McPherson reported seeing in a vision in 1921. The faces were interpreted as the fourfold gospel of salvation,* baptism in the Holy Spirit,* divine healing and the Second Coming of Christ.

Church growth in the 1920s was spectacular but then leveled off until about 1970. In 1992 there were reported to be over 200,000 members in 1,558 churches in the U.S.

International Congress on World Evangelization (Lausanne, Switzerland, 1974). A ten-day conference attended by 3,700 representatives from 150 nations to consider world evangelization* by the year A.D. 2000. With its theme "Let the Earth Hear His Voice," the meeting has been called the most global and representative such undertaking to date.

The congress, which provided ample room for debate, produced a statement on the primacy of evangelism drafted by the British churchman John R. W. Stott. It also decided to organize continuing discussions at the regional and national levels.

International Council of Biblical Inerrancy. *See* INERRANCY CONTROVERSY.

International Council of Christian Churches. A separatist* fundamentalist* association of churches. After World War II* there were many conservative Protestants* who were concerned about what they regarded as a growing apostasy in American mainline* churches. One was Carl McIntire,* who in 1948 organized the International Council of Christian Churches (ICCC) to offset the influence of ecumenism.* In America much of the message of the ICCC is spread by the affiliate organization, the American Council of Christian Churches.*

International Council of Religious Education. An interdenominational religious education* organization. The International Council of Religious Education (ICRE) was formed in 1922 as a merger of the International Sunday School Association* and the Sunday School Council of Evangelical Denominations. It was the leading voice in religious education in North America until 1950, when it merged with other denominational* agencies to form the National Council of Churches.*

International Eucharistic Congress (XXVIII). A biannual Catholic* devotional event celebrated in Chicago in 1926. Started in France in 1881, the congresses honor Christ in the Blessed Sacrament. George Cardinal Mundelein* of Chicago convened the twenty-eighth congress in his city to highlight the rapid growth of Catholicism in the U.S.

International Federation of Gospel Missions. *See* INTERNATIONAL UNION OF GOSPEL MISSIONS.

International Missionary Council. An ecumenical* missionary organization. A direct outgrowth of the Edinburgh World Missionary Conference (1910), the council was organized in 1921 under the leadership of John R. Mott.* It was constituted by several missionary councils and national organizations from North America and Europe, but also represented groups in China, Japan, India, Burma and Ceylon.

The council's first conference was in Jerusalem (1928). In 1961 it merged with the World Council of Churches.*

See also MISSIONS, PROTESTANT MAINLINE FOREIGN.

International Sunday School Association. A nondenominational Sunday-school* agency. Al-

though the association was formally named in 1905, it had existed since 1860 as the National Sunday School Convention system, the organization responsible for popularizing the Sunday school.

See also SUNDAY-SCHOOL MOVEMENT.

International Union of Gospel Missions. An association of urban rescue missions. The union was begun in 1913 as a continuation of the National Federation of Gospel Missions, which encompassed mission works active for over two decades. In the early 1990s the union included approximately 250 member missions.

See also RESCUE MISSION MOVEMENT.

InterVarsity Christian Fellowship. An evangelical* interdenominational organization working with Christian student groups in North American universities and colleges. The movement began in Great Britain in 1873. In 1928 InterVarsity work began in Canada, and in 1939 the first chapter opened in the U.S.

By 1994 InterVarsity Christian Fellowship was ministering to nearly 27,200 students on 580 campuses in forty-eight states. Its triennial Urbana Convention* and InterVarsity Press, its book-publishing division, are widely known outside the student and university world.

Ireland, John (1838-1918). Archbishop of St. Paul. When St. Paul became an archdiocese in 1888, Ireland became archbishop. His life centered on Catholic reform, as he worked to bring Catholics to the West, supported Catholic education, defended labor organizations and worked with the Roosevelt wing of the Republican Party. In 1876 Ireland founded the Catholic Colonization Society, with the belief that Catholics would thrive in the new western agrarian environment as opposed to their miserable lives in eastern ghettos.

His greatest educational accomplishment was to assist in the founding of the Catholic University of America,* traveling to Rome to argue the case for the American Catholic school system.

Ireland's greatest struggle for American Catholics was in the Americanist* movement, which eventually caused him much trouble with Rome. He desired to stop foreign influence on American Catholics, to teach English exclusively in American schools and to turn immigrant* Catholics into American nationalists.

Ironside, Henry ("Harry") Allen (1876-1951). Fundamentalist* Bible expositor. Ironside's fame as a Bible teacher, evangelist and author grew steadily, but his only pastorate, at the Moody Memorial Church in Chicago (1930-1948), brought him to the center of the fundamentalist network and the peak of his influence. His lively style and clear-cut interpretations frequently made Ironside the final authority* on the sacred text in fundamentalist pulpits and Bible-study* circles.

Irwin, B(enjamin) H(ardin) (b. 1854). Holiness* evangelist. In 1891 Irwin, a Baptist,* came into contact with Wesleyan* teaching, claimed entire sanctification* and became, he said, a "John Wesley Methodist." He adopted the theory of John Fletcher, Wesley's coworker, that the full baptism of the Holy Spirit* might require effusions of the Spirit beyond entire sanctification, a belief confirmed to him in 1895 when in a vision he saw "a cross of pure transparent fire." Proclamation of the baptism of fire, the so-called third-work heresy, cost Irwin his support within establishment Methodism.* In South Carolina in 1898 he organized the Fire-Baptized Holiness Association of America.

Shortly thereafter Irwin was reportedly seen drunk in public and also divorced his wife. His career after 1907 is uncertain.

Itinerancy. The practice of preaching* on an irregular basis to randomly visited pulpits or parishes.* Beginning at about the time of the Great Awakening,* itinerant preachers started moving about calling for revivals* and preaching in an extemporaneous style that established a special rapport with their audiences. The most famous eighteenth-century itinerant preacher in America was the Englishman George Whitefield.*

Ives, Levi Silliman (1797-1867). Episcopal* bishop and Roman Catholic* apologist. After ordination* to the Episcopal priesthood in 1823, Ives served in a number of churches in Pennsylvania and New York until his election in 1831 as second bishop of the Diocese* of North Carolina. Ives strongly supported the Oxford movement's* attempt to reclaim the Catholic heritage of his church. While in Rome in 1852, Ives resigned his episcopate and entered the Roman Catholic Church.

J

Jackson, Samuel Macauley (1851-1912). Presbyterian* educator and author. In 1876 Jackson was ordained* and served for four years as pastor of a Presbyterian Church in New Jersey. Finding himself temperamentally unsuited to the pastoral ministry, he became involved in charitable work and historical scholarship. He edited several major reference works and later taught church history at New York University (1895-1912).

Jackson, Sheldon (1834-1909). Presbyterian* missionary to frontier West and Alaska. From 1859 until 1869 Jackson labored in western Wisconsin and southern Minnesota, beginning his long career of pioneering Presbyterian work on the western frontier. During this period he helped organize twenty-three churches and secured twenty new ministers from seminaries* in the East.

In 1877 Jackson began superintending work in Alaska. Jackson, known as the "Bishop of All Beyond" (or "Apostle to Alaska"), was tireless in his efforts to establish the American frontier as a Christian society. His pioneering efforts ultimately led to the founding of over 150 churches.

Jackson, Thomas Jonathan ("Stonewall") (1824-1863). Confederate general and Presbyterian* layman. Sometime after the Mexican War, Jackson began a serious study of religion, finally affiliating with the Presbyterian Church in 1851. Southern preachers often referred to him as a prophet-warrior. He consistently observed the sabbath* and was in the habit of rising for prayer several times during the night on the eve of battle.

During the Civil War* Jackson distinguished himself as an outstanding Confederate officer, earning the nickname "Stonewall" because of his stout resistance at the First Battle of Bull Run.

Jacobs, Benjamin Franklin (1834-1902). Sunday-school movement* leader. Jacobs organized the national Sunday-school convention system and the uniform lesson curriculum system; in 1889 he helped form the World's Sunday School Convention System.

Jacobs, Henry Eyster (1844-1932). Lutheran* theologian and historian. Jacobs served the Lutheran Theological Seminary in Philadelphia as professor of systematic theology* (1883-1932), dean (1894-1920) and president (1920-1928). Through his translations from the German, Jacobs was a key figure in the confessional* and liturgical* renewal and reunion of Lutherans.

James, William (1842-1910). Philosopher and psychologist of religion. James's career as professor at Harvard* (1872-1907) led him through a varied intellectual pursuit in the areas of physiology, psychology and philosophy. He is best known as an advocate of pragmatism and as a founder of the field of the psychology of religion. His work in both areas gave support to liberal trends in American Protestantism,* particularly liberalism's* emphasis on the role of feeling in religion and its hesitancy to regard religious claims as absolutes.

James's Gifford Lectures (1901-1902) appeared as *The Varieties of Religious Experience* (1902), one of the first systematic attempts to analyze religious experience since the time of Jonathan Edwards.*

Janes, Leroy Lansing (1837-1909). Independent evangelist to Japan. In Japan Janes led a group of students—later known as the Kumamoto Band—to conversion.* Some of its members became leaders in the Congregational Church* and its educational institutions; others played distinguished roles in secular society.

Jansen, Cornelius (1822-1894). A leader of the Mennonite* immigration from Russia to the

U.S. in the 1870s. In Russia Jansen became an ardent advocate of immigration to North America, for which he was expelled in 1873. The family eventually reached the U.S., where Jansen and his son Peter worked tirelessly for immigrants, raising money, securing homes in the Midwest and petitioning the U.S. government.

Jarratt, Devereux (1733-1801). Anglican* revivalist* of the Great Awakening.* Ordained* in 1762 in England as an Anglican priest, Jarratt returned to Virginia the next year and served his parish until his death.

Jarratt played a leading role in the Southern Awakening. From 1764 to 1772 he led a revival among Southern Anglicans, itinerating* extensively throughout Virginia and North Carolina and organizing religious societies. In 1773 Jarratt joined forces with the Methodists,* a cooperation that climaxed in the revival of 1775-1776, the so-called Methodist phase of the Southern Awakening.

Jefferson, Charles Edward (1860-1937). Congregational* minister. In 1898 Jefferson became pastor at Broadway Tabernacle in New York City, where he remained until his retirement in 1930. Jefferson became known as a lucid thinker who expressed the gospel in a clear, passionate yet conversational pulpit style. Theologically a liberal evangelical,* Jefferson could stress orthodox* doctrines such as the deity of Christ, yet he was comfortable with the modern critical approach to the Bible.

Jefferson, Thomas (1743-1826). Principal author of the Declaration of Independence, Enlightenment* philosopher, diplomat, statesman and third U.S. president. Jefferson served the province and commonwealth of Virginia and the young American republic for almost forty years as a public official. He wrote the main draft of the Declaration of Independence (1776) and the Virginia Statute of Religious Freedom (adopted 1786). His election as president in 1800 and again in 1804 furthered the development of political democracy and checked in the U.S. the tide of political reaction then sweeping the Western world. A distinguished architect and naturalist, a remarkable linguist, a noted bibliophile and the principal founder of the University of Virginia, he was the chief patron of learning and the arts in this country in his generation.

In many ways, Jefferson was a living paradox. Widely hailed as a "man of the people," he was a person of wealth and a natural aristocrat. Highly tolerant of the views of others, he was highly intolerant of those he believed unfaithful to republicanism. An individual who kept his personal opinions concerning religion to himself, Jefferson was often charged with being "an infidel and atheist" and was well known for his insistence on a thoroughgoing separation of church and state.* In reality, he was one of the most thoughtfully religious men ever to occupy the White House. As president, Jefferson clearly articulated in his two inaugural addresses and many public speeches that he believed in God, valued piety* for its civic utility, and accepted the basic framework of American civil religion.*

Jehovah's Witnesses. A religious body originating with Charles Taze Russell,* also known as The Watchtower Bible and Tract Society of New York, Inc. Russell started with an independent Bible study in 1870 and then in 1876 began publishing *Zion's Watchtower,* which eventually became today's *Watchtower* (over 18 million copies published bimonthly in 106 languages).

At Russell's death, most of his followers joined J. F. Rutherford and, in 1931, adopted the name Jehovah's Witnesses. By the late 1980s the Witnesses reported almost three million members worldwide, with over 800,000 in North America. After Rutherford, the movement was led by Nathan H. Knorr* and then Frederick W. Franz (1893-).

Although the group lacks a well-defined systematic theology,* in many respects it resembles traditional Roman Catholicism* rather than Protestantism* because of its understanding of doctrinal and ecclesiastical authority.* The Witnesses deny orthodox* teachings about the person and work of Christ, holding instead to a pseudo-Arianism emphasizing Jesus as the "Second Adam" who was essentially a perfect man.

Three other doctrines are key for the Witnesses. First is their eschatology,* which, due to their habit of setting dates, has repeatedly proved false. Second, their belief in the sacredness of life and refusal to imbibe blood in any form has led to a rejection of both military service and blood transfusions. Third, their door-to-door preaching work—done to earn salvation—has brought them into many neighborhoods throughout North America.

Jeremiad. A sermon* of woe and promise. Originating with the Puritans,* the jeremiad was preached as an occasional sermon on public occasions and on days set aside by the civil authorities for fasting, prayer or thanksgiving. Focusing attention on contemporary moral failure and natural disasters, the jeremiad attempted to create an anxiety that would lead the audience to reform and renewal of the covenant.

Jessup, Henry Harris (1823-1910). Presbyterian* missionary to the Near East. Arriving in Beirut in 1856, Jessup was pastor for thirty years of the Syrian church there and head of its school. Jessup's ministry led him to associations with the journal *El-Nesbrah,* a hospital for the emotionally disturbed and the Syrian Protestant College, now known as the American University of Beirut.

Jesus Christ. *See* CHRISTOLOGY.

Jesus Movement. Christian countercultural youth movement of the late 1960s and early 1970s. Parallel to the counterculture movement generally of this same period, a new counterculture spirituality* emerged on the American religious landscape variously called the Jesus movement, the Jesus revolution or the Jesus people movement.

The Jesus people phenomenon must be viewed in the context of the changing American culture of the decade of the sixties. It was a period of transition, protest, uncertainty and social upheaval. In such a setting the Jesus people movement developed as an unorganized, diverse movement consisting of many widely scattered subgroups. Despite its diverse natures the Jesus people shared common interests and certain basic concerns. Above all, the Jesus movement was characterized by its intense evangelistic zeal and emphasis on experience.

As the faddish elements and excessive emotionalism of the movement waned and as the teenage participants matured into early adulthood, the Jesus movement tended to dissolve in two directions. One segment, consisting of groups like the Children of God* and The Way, became increasingly authoritarian and assumed cultic* characteristics. Another segment of the Jesus people drifted toward more conventional evangelicalism.* This segment is represented by churches like Calvary Chapel (Orange County, California) and the Christian World Liberation Front.

Jeter, J(eremiah) B(ell) (1802-1880). Southern Baptist* pastor, editor and denominational* leader. Although he was self-taught as a minister,* Jeter was a very effective pastor of several large churches, including the First Baptist Church, Richmond, Virginia, where he served for more than thirteen years. He also was the first president of the Foreign Mission Board of the Southern Baptist Convention (1845-1849).

Jewett, Paul King (1919-1991). Evangelical* theologian. Jewett spent most of his teaching career (1955-1990) at Fuller Theological Seminary,* where he was professor of systematic theology. Though raised and ordained a Baptist,* and always a strong proponent of believer's baptism, by 1970 he had joined the Presbyterian Church, U.S.A.* Jewett's *Man as Male and Female* (1975) was a controversial evangelical attempt to argue for the full equality and complementarity of the sexes. His *God, Creation and Revelation: A Neo-Evangelical Theology* (1991) was the first in a projected multivolume systematic theology.

Jewish Christians (or Messianic Jews). Jews converted* to Christianity. These individuals typically insist that their conversions do not invalidate their Jewishness and that they have actually become more aware of their traditional heritage after their acceptance of Christ as the Jewish Messiah.

Sometimes a distinction is made between Messianic Jews and Jewish Christians. The former tend more to maintain Jewish symbols and liturgy* and may follow the Mosaic law as a cultural practice, not as a means of salvation,* and belong to "messianic congregations." The latter, who are less interested in preserving Jewish culture, typically associate themselves with traditional churches.

Jewish-Christian Dialogue. The general climate of Christian-Jewish relations in America until the middle of the twentieth century was stormy. In the last few decades, however, more positive changes have taken place between synagogue and church than in the entire period since these bodies irreversibly split following the biblical period.

Mainline* liberal* Protestants* were the first major group with which the Jewish community in America entered serious dialogue. This came about largely through the pioneering efforts of such leading interfaith voices as Martin Buber, Abraham Heschel and Marc Tanenbaum.

Among Catholics,* the work of Pope John XXIII* in calling together Vatican II* (1963-1965) has done more to eradicate Catholic-Jewish misperceptions than any other single force.

Evangelical*-Jewish dialogue did not begin to take serious shape until the mid-1970s. Israel's unstable position in the Middle East has led Jews to value the solid support of Israel often given by evangelicals.

Jews, Christian Missions to. Christian missions to Jews began in the U.S. in 1820, with the organization of the American Society for Meliorating the Condition of the Jews, which claimed fifty converts in the 1850s. Since the turn of the century, dispensationalists* have shown the greatest interest in evangelizing Jews.

With the growth of liberal* theology* and ecumenism* following World War I,* American Christians lost a good deal of interest in evangelizing Jews. In the Jesus movement* of the 1970s, however, many young Jews became Christians and formed the nucleus of both a rejuvenated missionary effort and an ambitious attempt to found "messianic congregations" of converted Jews.

See also JEWISH CHRISTIANS; JEWS FOR JESUS.

Jews for Jesus. A term referring to both a contemporary movement of young Jews to Christianity and a specific mission agency. The former began in the late 1960s with the so-called Jesus movement.* By the 1970s enough Jews had accepted Christianity that leaders from both communities noticed the phenomenon. Jews for Jesus as an organization grew out of this revival in 1973, when Moishe Rosen, a career missionary with the American Board of Missions to the Jews,* established it as an independent evangelistic agency.

Jogues, Isaac (1607-1646). Jesuit* missionary and martyr. Shortly after his ordination* in 1636, Jogues began his decade of missionary work among the Huron* Indians in Canada. On a canoe trip in 1642 Jogues and several others were ambushed by a party of Iroquois, carried off as prisoners into Mohawk territory and put to the most appalling tortures, all of which Jogues bore with extraordinary fortitude.

Rescued by the Dutch in 1643, Jogues later willingly returned to Quebec, where he was killed by the Iroquois. His self-sacrifice stimulated and inspired the cause of French Canadian missions.

See also MISSIONS TO NORTH AMERICA, FRENCH.

John XXIII (1881-1963). Pope. Born Angelo Giuseppi Roncelli, he served the Vatican* in a variety of posts until becoming pope in 1958. Considered a caretaker, he surprised everyone by convening all the bishops of the church in the Second Vatican Council* (1962), which was to initiate the "aggiornamento"* of the church. Dying before the second session of the council began, he nonetheless opened a new period in the church, in America as elsewhere.

John Birch Society. Far-right political society. Founded in 1959 by Robert Welch, the society was named after Capt. John M. Birch, a Baptist* missionary and Army Air Force officer killed by the Chinese communists in 1945. For much of the 1960s the John Birch Society played a major role in defining the far-right agenda: boycott of UNICEF, restoration of prayer* in the public schools,* opposition to civil-rights* legislation and elimination of the welfare state. At its peak, the Society is estimated to have had a membership of about 100,000.

John Paul II (1920-). Pope. Born in Poland, Karol Wojtyla broke the cycle of Italian popes when he became Pope John Paul II in 1978. He has combined relentless concern for the poor and laboring people with opposition to liberation theology* and Marxism, and has joined devotion to church renewal with a rigorous defense of the church tradition. On his papal journeys to the U.S. and Canada, he has enhanced the prestige of the Catholic Church* through his evident charisma and integrity.

Johnson, Carrie Parks (1866-1929). Methodist* advocate of human rights for women and minorities in the South. Johnson worked long for lay representation for women in the conferences and councils of her church. In 1922 she led a concerted opposition to mob violence and lynching.

Johnson, Charles Oscar (1886-1965). Baptist* minister. Johnson's final pastorate was at Third Baptist Church, St. Louis, Missouri (1931-1958), which under his leadership grew by over ten thousand members. He was president of the

Northern Baptist Convention and of the Baptist World Alliance* (1947-1952).

Johnson, Samuel (1696-1772). Anglican* minister, philosopher and president of King's College.* Johnson served with the Society for the Propagation of the Gospel* as a missionary rector in Stratford, Connecticut (1723-1754, 1764-1772), and as president of King's College (1754-1763). As the unofficial leader of New England's Anglicans, he led them in numerous public controversies, including his criticisms of strict Calvinism* and the Great Awakening.*

Johnson, William Bullein (1782-1862). Southern Baptist* minister and leader. Throughout Johnson's several pastorates, he maintained an active interest in education, serving as headmaster of a number of schools and chancellor of the Johnson Female University (1853-1858). His interest in Baptist missions* led him to suggest the first meeting of the General Baptist Missionary Convention. Johnson was the major architect of the Southern Baptist Convention and was its most important spokesman as well as its first president.

Joliet (or Jolliet, Jollyet), Louis (c. 1645-1700). French-Canadian explorer and entrepreneur. Recognized, with Jacques Marquette,* as the codiscoverer of the Mississippi River, Joliet, a Quebec-born Jesuit,* achieved distinction in several fields. After training for the priesthood, he became the first Canadian to study music in France. A classics scholar and teacher at the Jesuit college in Quebec, Joliet left the priesthood in 1667 in favor of fur-trading and exploration.

Jones, Abner (1772-1841). Pioneer leader of the Christian Connection.* By 1804, working together with Elias Smith, another former Baptist* preacher, Jones developed a whole movement of Christian churches following the Bible only and known as the Christian Connection.
See also RESTORATION MOVEMENT.

Jones, Bob, and Family. Robert R. "Bob" Jones Sr. (1883-1968), Robert R. "Bob" Jones Jr. (1911-), Robert R. "Bob" Jones III (1939-). Fundamentalist* educators. As an evangelist fighting against modernism* and what he judged to be sinful social practices, Bob Jones Sr. became convinced of the need for conservative religious educational institutions. He founded Bob Jones College in

Florida in 1926 and eventually, in 1947, moved the campus to Greenville, South Carolina.

Fearing regulation and scrutiny by government and secular educators, Bob Jones University has remained outside the regular U.S. educational system and is unaccredited. Bob Jones Jr. was its president from 1947 to 1971; Bob Jones III since 1971.

Fear of compromise caused the Jones family to break relations with many evangelical organizations, including the Billy Graham Evangelistic Association,* a disagreement that marked a major split between evangelicals and fundamentalists.

Jones, Charles Colcock, Sr. (1804-1863). Presbyterian* minister. Jones is best known as the devoted "Apostle to the Blacks." Although he impugned slavery while studying in the North (1825-1830), upon returning to his family's plantations, Jones joined Southern clergymen in biblically defending the "peculiar institution." He developed a system for evangelizing* slaves and convinced masters throughout the South to adopt it.
See also MISSIONS TO THE SLAVES.

Jones, Clarence Wesley (1900-1986). Pioneer missionary broadcaster. During the 1920s, Jones founded the AWANA youth program, which today is used across the country. In 1930 Jones moved to Quito, Ecuador, where in 1931 he helped establish radio station HCJB. After retiring in 1961, Jones traveled extensively promoting Christian radio.

Jones, E(li) Stanley (1884-1973). Methodist* missionary to India. An innovator in his approach to missions, Jones founded Christian ashrams (retreat centers for study and meditation) to share Christ with higher-caste Hindus. He also utilized roundtable conferences, gathering groups of fifty persons for informative presentations of Christ, followed by discussion. Such approaches of witness to non-Christian Indians he described in his bestselling *The Christ of the Indian Road* (1925). Written in haste during one of his trips to America, the book sold over 600,000 copies and brought him international recognition.

Jones, Jim (1931-1978). Founder and leader of Peoples Temple. In the early 1950s Jones began in Indiana what eventually would become known as Peoples Temple. In 1964 he was ordained as a minister ιιι the Christian Church (Disciples of Christ),* and in 1965, in response to a vision of nuclear holocaust, he moved his congregation to Ukiah, California. Jones received public recognition for his work among the poor, but by the early 1970s his church was increasingly engaged in spiritualism and healing, and Jones was exercising greater control over his church members. In 1977 Jones and many members moved to an agricultural colony called Jonestown in Guyana, South America, which he had founded in 1973. With Jonestown's population exceeding 900 and amidst increasing signs of Jones's suspicious and paranoid behavior, U.S. Congressman Leo Ryan visited the colony in November 1978. Ryan and his party were murdered and the Jonestown residents, along with Jones, committed mass suicide. The tragedy was widely publicized, with "Jonestown" becoming a byword for extremist cults.

Jones, John William (1836-1909). Baptist* minister, Confederate soldier and author. Appointed as missionary to China in 1860, Jones instead served in the Civil War.* In *Christ in the Camp* (1877) he recorded the history of the famous revival services which swept through Lee's army during the winter of 1862-1863.

Jones, Rufus Matthew (1863-1948). Quaker* mystic,* philosopher, educator and humanitarian. Jones spent the major portion of his career at Haverford College, where he was professor of philosophy for over forty years (1893-1934). He served the Friends by editing the *American Friend* (1894-1912) and was active in the formation of the Five Years Meeting of Friends (now Friends United Meeting). In 1917 Jones helped found the American Friends Service Committee* and served as its chairman for many years.

Jones, Samuel ("Sam") Porter (1847-1906). Methodist* minister and evangelist. Converted* to Christianity in 1872, Jones became a pastor and then a powerful revivalist.* In his effort to reach the common people, he used blunt, homespun language which some considered irreverent. Nevertheless, his effectiveness as an evangelist earned him the title "The Moody of the South."

Jordan, Clarence (1912-1969). Founder of Koinonia Farm. In 1942, in company with Martin England, Jordan founded Koinonia Farm on four hundred acres near Americus, Georgia. The farm was established as a racially integrated witness of Christian community, brotherhood and peace.

Jordan's response to the segregated South was his four-volume Cotton Patch Version of the New Testament (1968-1973).

Jowett, John Henry (1864-1923). English Congregational* minister. Following two pastorates in England, Jowett came to New York's Fifth Avenue Presbyterian (1911-1918). In his day Jowett was reputed to be one of the greatest evangelical* preachers, with his sermons noted for their expository style.

Judeo-Christian Tradition. A religious and political slogan which has played a critical role in defining the spiritual ideology of the U.S. since World War II. During the war, *the Judeo-Christian tradition* served in America as a mobilizing slogan for the Allied cause. Once the war was over, it played a similar role in the rhetorical arsenal of anticommunism.

Since it burst upon the scene, *the Judeo-Christian tradition* has functioned more as a rallying cry than as an identifiable piece of religious common ground. Useful in polemic, the phrase is most meaningful for what it discloses about the spiritual politics of the U.S. in the latter part of the twentieth century.

See also CIVIL RELIGION.

Judson, Adoniram (1788-1850). Pioneer missionary to Burma. In Rangoon, Judson succeeded in gathering a small group of converts.* In 1824 he was imprisoned when war broke out between England and Burma and for twenty-one months suffered intolerable confinement and deprivation. Ann Judson* died in 1826, not long after Judson's release. Judson remarried in 1834 (*see* Sarah Boardman Judson) and in 1846 (*see* Emily Chubbuck Judson). Not returning to the U.S. until thirty-three years after the beginning of his missionary career and having sustained such hardship and loss in pursuit of his calling, Judson became an inspiring example of missionary sacrifice and dedication for several generations of young people.

Judson, Ann Hasseltine (1789-1826). Baptist* missionary to Burma. Shortly after Ann married Adoniram Judson* in 1812, the two departed as missionaries to India. Ann Judson was the first woman to leave America as a missionary, a move regarded by her family and friends as wild and romantic.

In Burma Ann quickly learned the language and soon began teaching Burmese women and doing translation work. Her most important contribution to missions was her written account of their years in Burma (1823), for a generation of Americans had little knowledge of overseas missions.

See also JUDSON, EMILY CHUBBUCK; JUDSON, SARAH HALL BOARDMAN.

Judson, Emily Chubbuck (1817-1854). Popular author and missionary. Adoniram Judson* selected Emily to write the biography of his second wife, Sarah.* This association led to marriage, and they sailed for Burma in 1846. There Emily wrote Sarah's biography and nursed others while fighting her own illness.

Judson, Sarah Hall Boardman (1803-1845). Missionary to Burma. Sarah married George Dana Boardman* in 1825 and that year sailed to the Far East. In Burma Sarah established a girl's school and worked on the Talaing translation of the New Testament. Upon George's death in 1831, Sarah remained in Burma. In 1834 she married Adoniram Judson* and continued with her translation work, finally completing the New Testament.

Jurisdictional Conference. An organizational body within the United Methodist Church.* The 1939 merger that created the Methodist Church established six jurisdictions—five geographic, and the sixth an organizational unit for African-American Methodists. The principal function of each conference is the election of bishops.

Justification. Derived from the Pauline epistles, especially Galatians and Romans, and generally understood to be a term that arose within a judicial context as a statement of a person's just status before a court, *justification* has been closely associated with the doctrines of divine grace and human faith in describing what God does for and to believers in Jesus Christ.

Justification became a rallying center of the Protestant Reformation, and hence a crucial issue in dispute between Protestants* and Roman Catholics,* beginning in the sixteenth century. The magisterial Reformers held that sinners are declared or reckoned to be righteous as God's free gift by the imputation of the righteousness of Christ and through faith. Hence to be justified is to have a new standing before God, not a new nature. This teaching found its way to the English colonies in North America, especially through the Puritans.*

The fathers of the Council of Trent (1547), in contrast, held that sinners are made righteous by the infusion of God's justice through Christ's merits so that believers are justified to the extent that they are, in Protestant terms, sanctified. Moreover, individuals cannot be certain that they are justified, and they can cease to be justified. Such conciliar teaching was brought by Roman Catholics to North America.

Jonathan Edwards* related justification to covenantal theology* in that Christ, as the elect's federal representative, made available through his death his imputed righteousness. Methodists* have held to an Arminian* view that the gift of justification is extended to all and not limited to a select number of elect.*

K

Kauffman, Daniel (1865-1944). Mennonite* leader and theologian. Kauffman was the leading spirit within the Mennonite Church from around 1898 to 1930. He made his mark as a theologian with his *Manual of Bible Doctrines* (1898), and as a church leader in the creation of the Mennonite General Conference (of the [old] Mennonite Church). He also edited the *Gospel Herald,* the church paper.

Keach, Elias (1667-1701). Baptist* minister in the Middle Colonies. Keach traveled throughout the Middle Colonies, preaching to groups of English, Irish and Welsh settlers. When numbers were sufficient a church was gathered in each location. Contact between the churches of the area was maintained, evolving into the Philadelphia Association of Baptists,* formally established in 1707.

Keane, John Joseph (1839-1918). Roman Catholic* prelate and founder of the Catholic University of America.* A variety of interests occupied Keane throughout his life: temperance,* Protestant-Catholic relations, the black apostolate, and the education and formation of youth. From 1887 until the Vatican's censure of Americanism* in 1899, Keane worked closely with John Ireland* and Denis O'Connell* at the center of the Americanist movement.

Keane is best remembered as the founding rector* (1889-1896) of the new Catholic University of America, for which he recruited a distinguished international faculty. An energetic pastor, a popular speaker and a prolific writer, Keane was one of the most visible Catholic figures of his day.

Keeble, Marshall (1878-1968). African-American evangelist. Around 1900 Keeble began preaching* part-time, and twenty years later he became a full-time evangelist. As many as 350 congregations, mostly African-American churches in the South, trace their origins to his evangelistic efforts, and approximately thirty thousand people were baptized* by him.

Kehuckee Baptist Association. Baptist* anti-missionary* group in North Carolina. In 1769 Baptist churches along Kehuckee Creek in North Carolina formed their own association, which in 1826 voted to "discard all Missionary Societies." *Kehuckeeism* became a synonym for antimissions among Baptists.

Keith, George (1638-1716). Quaker* teacher and controversialist. In 1689 Keith became a schoolmaster in Quaker Philadelphia. In 1691 Keith was accused by local Quakers of preaching salvation* through the historical death of Christ independently of Christ within. He in turn wrote tracts* on the dispute, organized a faction of followers as "Christian Quakers" and was disowned by the Philadelphia Yearly Meeting.

Keith's concern for the Bible and the historic Christ took him into the Church of England,* where he was ordained* a priest in 1702.

Kellogg, John Harvey (1852-1943). Physician and health reformer. In 1876 Kellogg became superintendent of a Seventh-day Adventist* institution later named the Battle Creek (Mich.) Sanitarium. Advocating "biologic living," he invented corn flakes and various meat substitutes.

Kellogg, Samuel Henry (1839-1899). Presbyterian* missionary and pastor. Ordained* a missionary to India in 1864, Kellogg served mostly at the Theological School at Allahabad. In 1875 he completed a monumental grammar of the Hindi language. After his wife died, he returned to the U.S. and was a pastor and professor of theology. In 1892 he returned to India to assist in revising the Hindi Old Testament.

Kelpius, Johannes (1673-c. 1708). Communitarian mystic.* Arriving in Philadelphia in 1694 from Europe as head of a group of forty scholars and mystics awaiting Christ's return, Kelpius and many of the others pursued an ascetic lifestyle. They taught the children around them, helped the sick and became known as the Society of the Woman in the Wilderness (Rev 12:6). The group disbanded with Kelpius's death.

Kennedy, John Fitzgerald (1917-1963). First Roman Catholic* president of the U.S. The first Catholic to run for the presidency since Alfred E. Smith* in 1928, Kennedy initially encountered strong opposition because of his religion, some of it from secularists, some from Protestants* and Jews. On numerous occasions Kennedy explained that his religion was a purely personal affair and that he would not allow religious considerations to dictate his conduct as president.

Kennedy's response to the religious issue in 1960 became a model for a number of later politicians, both Catholic and Protestant. It left unanswered, however, the question to what degree a public official should follow the dictates of a religiously formed conscience, and it left the way open for a purely secular approach to public policy.

Kennedy was buried with full Catholic rites following his assassination in 1963.

Kenrick, Francis Patrick (1796-1863). Roman Catholic* prelate and scholar. As bishop in Philadelphia, Kenrick found his leadership tested by trustees of St. Mary's Church, who refused to recognize episcopal* parish* appointments until Kenrick's 1831 interdict, which ended trusteeism* in Philadelphia.

When nativist* riots in 1844 left churches razed and several Catholics dead, Kenrick fled the city, closed churches and condemned retaliation.

Kenrick's final challenge was the Civil War.* His scholastic approach, placing national stability above slavery's abolition* and states' rights, antagonized both sides.

Kenrick, Peter Richard (1806-1896). First Roman Catholic* archbishop of St. Louis. Kenrick became bishop of St. Louis in 1841, and archbishop in 1847. After the Civil War,* when Missouri adopted a constitution requiring clergymen to take an oath of loyalty to the state, Kenrick won an appeal at the U.S. Supreme Court.*

Kenyon, E(ssek) W(illiam) (1867-1948). Pastor, radio preacher and author. In 1923 Kenyon moved from New England to the West Coast, where he became a pioneer in radio ministry. Not widely known during his lifetime, Kenyon's teachings on faith, healing,* positive confession and similar topics have directly influenced the Pentecostal* faith movement.*

Kerr, Hugh Thomson (1909-1992). Presbyterian* theologian. After graduate study at the University of Edinburgh (Ph.D., 1936), Kerr taught at Louisville Presbyterian Theological Seminary (1936-1940) before moving to Princeton Theological Seminary* (1940-1974), where he became professor of systematic theology.* Kerr authored and edited a number of books, including *A Compend of Calvin's Institutes* (1938, rev. 1989) and *A Compend of Luther's Theology* (1963), and was long-time editor (1944-1992), with a few interludes, of Princeton's influential journal *Theology Today.*

Kerygmatic Theology. A mid-twentieth-century emphasis, associated with Rudolf Bultmann,* grounding theology* in the New Testament proclamation of Jesus as the Christ rather than in the historical figure of Jesus of Nazareth. Kerygmatic theology takes as its starting point the proclamation of the early Christian community recorded in the Gospels that Jesus is the Christ, and that in his life, death and resurrection God's redemptive purposes for humankind are accomplished. For Bultmann this kerygma had to be demythologized* in order to arrive at its essence.

More recently, however, New Testament scholars have tried to understand Jesus within the Jewish environment of his day, and theologians have pursued more direct lines between the Jesus of history and the Christ of faith.

Kester, Howard Anderson ("Buck") (1904-1977). Congregational* minister and social activist. Kester served with the pacifistic Fellowship of Reconciliation* and the Fellowship of Southern Churchmen,* doing grassroots work on racial and economic issues.

Keswick Movement. An evangelical* movement stressing personal holiness,* commonly disseminated through summer conferences and Bible schools* in North America. The Keswick teaching had its genesis in the writing and speaking ministries of three Americans: William E. Boardman* and the husband-wife team, Hannah Whitall* and Robert Pearsall Smith.* In London, during Dwight L. Moody's* 1873 campaign, the Smiths joined Boardman for a series of breakfasts designed to promote Holiness. By this means 2,400 ministers heard their message. A series of conferences followed, including one at Keswick in 1875, which became the center of Holiness teaching in England and gave its name to the movement. Annual conferences at Keswick followed.

Largely through Moody's Northfield Conferences in Massachusetts, the Keswick teaching spread throughout the U.S. and Canada, and captured many evangelical Bible schools and missionary agencies. Since 1923 Keswick conferences have been held at Keswick Grove, New Jersey.

Ketcham, Robert Thomas (1889-1978). Fundamentalist* Baptist* minister. A member of the Baptist Bible Union,* Ketcham withdrew from the Northern Baptist Convention in 1928 and became president of the newly formed Ohio Association of Independent Baptist Churches. He led in the development of the General Association of Regular Baptist Churches.*

Key, Francis Scott (1780-1843). Author of "The Star Spangled Banner," Episcopal* layman and Sunday-school* statesman. During the War of 1812, after witnessing the British bombardment of Fort McHenry, Key penned the words to "The Star Spangled Banner." Published that year, it became the U.S. national anthem in 1931.

Less known is Key's work in the Sunday-school movement. One of the founders of the American Sunday School Union* in 1824, he presided over the 1830 Sunday-school meeting in Washington, D.C., that launched a fifty-year outreach program known as the Mississippi Valley Campaign.

Key 73. A 1973 evangelistic effort by American evangelicals.* The program, sparked by a 1967 *Christianity Today*** editorial, was sponsored by over 130 denominations* and religious organizations. Although results were mixed, Key 73 represented an important attempt at grassroots cooperation among American evangelicals.

Kierkegaard, Søren Aabye (1813-1855). Danish philosopher. Given to deep melancholy and introspection, Kierkegaard lived much of his short life withdrawn from society. Having undergone a deep religious experience in 1848, Kierkegaard began to reflect on the radical difference between authentic Christianity and that of the Danish state church. His later writings are characterized by the themes of personal authenticity, the profound distinction between God and humanity, and the need for a personal, subjective engagement with truth.

Kierkegaard's influence was not felt in America until the century after his death. Christian existentialism* is the appropriation of Kierkegaard's insights for Christian theology* and ethics,* stressing human experience, freedom and the commitment of faith.

King, Jonas (1792-1869). Pioneer missionary to the Near East and Greece. From 1822 to 1827 King observed and did missionary work in Palestine, Lebanon and Syria. In 1831 he settled in Athens for thirty-eight years of pioneer missionary work. His special contribution was the translation of the Bible into Armeno-Turkish.

King, Joseph Hillary (1869-1946). Holiness* and Pentecostal* leader. After several years as a Methodist* pastor in north Georgia, in 1898 King became vice president of come-outist Benjamin Irwin's* fledgling Holiness group, the Fire-Baptized Holiness Church.* In 1900 he succeeded Irwin as president. In 1908 King embraced Pentecostalism and brought the Fire-Baptized Holiness Church with him into the Pentecostal movement.

King, Martin Luther, Jr. (1929-1968). African-American Baptist* minister and civil rights* leader. In 1955 King gained national acclaim as the leader of the Montgomery bus boycott. During this first major campaign of the modern civil rights movement King developed his philosophy and tactic of nonviolent protest to bring about social change. Following the boycott, King became associate pastor of his father's church, Ebenezer Baptist, in Atlanta. In 1957 King became president of the newly organized Southern Christian Leadership Conference.*

King is perhaps best known for his 1963 "I Have a Dream" speech, which reflected the goal of integration, the ideology of reform and the strategy of moral persuasion that characterized the first phase of the civil rights movement.

He was assassinated on April 4, 1968, in Memphis, Tennessee. His birthday, observed on the third Monday in January, became a national holiday in 1986.

King Philip's War (1675-1676). The most bloody and destructive Native American war of the seventeenth century. King Philip, who became leader of the Wampanoag tribe in 1662, deeply resented the power of the English and the expansion of their settlements. Following the execution of three Native Americans for the murder of one of missionary John Eliot's* "praying Indians," Philip and his warriors began looting houses in the town of Swansea in June of 1675. The violence spread, leaving little of New England untouched. Philip was finally captured and killed in August 1676.

By the war's end, more than a dozen towns were almost completely destroyed, and several thousand people had died. For Native Americans, the war meant utter destruction.

Kingdom of God. The biblical term *kingdom of God* has taken on various meanings in American religious history. For the nonseparating Puritans* of the Massachusetts Bay Colony, *kingdom of God* represented not only an internal lordship over the individual conscience but an external sovereignty of God over corporate society, whether in the church or in the civil sphere. By the era of the Great Awakening* the individual, internal sense of the term was receiving greater emphasis.

During the nineteenth century, revivalists* of the Second Awakening* and those who followed extended the sense of the reign of Christ through love to active social reform. The social application of the gospel stressed by liberalism* was further enunciated by the Social Gospel movement.*

Among evangelicals* at the turn of the century, postmillennialists* tended to identify advancement of the kingdom with social and cultural progress, whereas premillennialists* tended to be pessimistic about secular culture and to view the kingdom as coming visibly only with the return of Christ.

For some, the kingdom of God came to be so closely identified with the American nation that it served as a basis for civil religion* in the U.S. Such American values as democracy, liberty, equality and capitalism were associated with Christian virtues and were exported together as the kingdom in some foreign missions work.

Kings College. *See* COLUMBIA UNIVERSITY.

Kingsbury, Cyrus (1786-1870). Missionary educator among the Cherokee and Choctaw Indians. Beginning in 1817, Kingsbury established Indian missions in Tennessee and Mississippi. In 1836 he went to Indian Territory, where the Choctaws were settling after being pushed west once again. There he worked among Native Americans for the remainder of his life.

Kino, Eusebio Francisco (1645-1711). Jesuit* missionary to the American Southwest. Arriving in Mexico in 1681, the following year he joined the Atondo expedition to Baja California and stayed to help establish Jesuit missions in the area. In 1687 he went to Pimeria Alta, astraddle today's Mexico-U.S. border, where he thereafter labored, becoming renowned as the "Apostle of Sonora and Arizona." He baptized approximately 4,500 Pima Indians and helped launch a cattle industry for the region.

See also MISSIONS TO NORTH AMERICA, SPANISH.

Kirk, Edward Norris (1802-1874). Congregational* evangelist and pastor. As a successful New York pastor, Kirk went to Great Britain, where his protracted meetings enhanced his reputation as a polished and powerful preacher and opened the door for evangelistic campaigns in several major eastern cities upon his return to America. His success in Boston led to the formation of Mt. Vernon Congregational Church, where he pastored from 1842 to 1871. There Kirk combined his evangelism* with antislavery,* temperance* and other reform* activities.

Kirkconnell, Watson (1895-1977). Linguist, poet, Milton scholar and university president. In 1948 he became president of Acadia University, a Baptist* institution in Wolfville, Nova Scotia. One of the most prominent Baptist laymen in the country, he was one of the key founders of the Baptist Federation of Canada* in 1944.

Kirkland, John Thornton (1770-1840). Unitarian* minister and Harvard* president. In 1793 Kirkland became pastor of Boston's New South Church. When the Harvard presidency became vacant in 1810, Kirkland, the ideal gentleman scholar, was chosen for the post without opposition. His tenure marked the emergence of Harvard as a true university, with new law and divinity* schools.

Knights of Labor. The first national labor union

and focus of a controversy among Catholics* in the late nineteenth century. Founded in 1869, the Knights aroused suspicions in certain Catholic quarters. The Vatican, however, refused to condemn the Knights. In the larger Americanism* controversy, this decision was regarded as a victory for those within the American Catholic Church who wished to accommodate their church to American culture.

See also RERUM NOVARUM.

Knorr, Nathan H. (1905-1977) Leader of Jehovah's Witnesses.* In 1923 Knorr began working in the Watchtower Society's publishing office and, in 1942, succeeded Joseph F. Rutherford* as president of the Jehovah's Witnesses.

Knox, John (c. 1817-1892). Disciples of Christ* pioneer on Prince Edward Island. Deeply influenced by the ideas of men like Barton W. Stone* and Alexander Campbell,* Knox for about forty years pioneered the Disciples' work in Canada's Maritime Provinces. A powerful preacher, Knox did much to establish his denomination* in the area.

Knubel, Frederick Hermann (1870-1945). Lutheran* Church president. A New York City pastorate (1896-1918) revealed Knubel's gifts of leadership, and his guidance of a wartime Lutheran welfare commission made him known nationally. From 1918 to 1944 he was president of the United Lutheran Church in America.

Knudson, Albert Cornelius (1873-1953). Methodist* Old Testament scholar and theologian. Knudson spent most of his career at Boston University, as professor of Hebrew and Old Testament exegesis* (1906-1921), professor of systematic theology* (1921-1943) and dean of the School of Theology (1926-1938). In his teaching and writing he became an important advocate of personalism in pre-World War II Protestant* liberalism.*

Kohlmann, Anthony (1771-1836). Jesuit* priest and vicar general of the Diocese* of New York. In 1808 Kohlmann was assigned to New York City, where he became the vicar general of the newly established Diocese of New York.

In 1813 Kohlmann was involved in a celebrated case concerning the secrecy of the confessional, which brought him wide recognition. Ultimately the state of New York upheld Kohlmann, recognizing the confidentiality of the confessional.

Going to Washington, D.C., in 1815, Kohlmann served as president of Georgetown and superior of the American Jesuits.

Konstantinides, Michael. *See* CONSTANTINIDES, MICHAEL.

Koresh, David (1960-1993). Branch Davidian leader. Through a series of internal power struggles, by 1988 Vernon Howell had gained succession to the "Throne of David" of the Branch Davidian community of Mount Carmel, near Waco, Texas, and in 1990 changed his name to David Koresh. The sect dated back to a break from Seventh-day Adventism* in the mid-1930s. Koresh held to an apocalyptic theology centered in the book of Revelation and incorporating other portions of Christian Scripture. These texts were interpeted in light of the Davidian community, Koresh's role as its leader and their place in the perceived apocalyptic scheme of Revelation. Koresh considered himself to be the "Lamb" of Revelation 5, a "sinful messiah" called *Koresh* (Hebrew for Cyrus in Isaiah 45:1), who was prophesied to appear at the end time, open the seven seals of Revelation, defeat Babylon and initiate his marriage feast.

On February 28, 1993, the Bureau of Alcohol, Tobacco and Firearms (ATF), suspicious of the community's possession of a large number of armaments, arrived in force and assaulted the compound with tear gas and explosivelike "distraction devices." The ATF assault was repelled by automatic gunfire, and casualties, including several deaths, were sustained on both sides. A standoff ensued that lasted until April 19, 1993, and was the focus of sustained national media attention. Federal authorities became increasingly frustrated by their inability to bring the conflict to a negotiated conclusion and were apparently unable to comprehend the intricacies of Koresh's beliefs. Heedless of warnings from experts in religion, the FBI played into the fulfillment of Koresh's apocalyptic interpretation of the events based on Revelation 6:9-11. On April 19 the FBI initiated a concerted riot-gas assault on the Mount Carmel compound. The result, its immediate cause unknown, was a fire that, whipped by winds into a conflagration, consumed the compound and killed some seventy-five Davidians, including Koresh. The federal government's role in the incident was investigated and the remaining Davidians tried and sentenced. The incident was decried by some as a tragedy that could have been avoided.

Krauth, Charles Philip (1797-1867). Lutheran* church leader and theologian. Krauth served as the first president of what later became Gettysburg College (1834-1850). Krauth, like his son, Charles Porterfield Krauth,* was a staunch defender of strict Lutheran confessionalism* within the General Synod.

Krauth, Charles Porterfield (1823-1883). Lutheran* clergyman, theologian and educator. Son of Charles Philip Krauth,* Krauth became a serious student and a bibliophile. While serving pastorates in Pittsburgh (1855-1859) and Philadelphia (1859-1861), he began an intensive study of German theological literature virtually unknown among native American Lutherans. Of particular interest to him were the Lutheran dogmaticians and the confessional* standards of the sixteenth and seventeenth centuries.

This development in Krauth's thought coincided with the Great Immigration* of the 1840s and 1850s, which brought close to one million Germans to America, among them many conservative Lutherans. In the crisis that developed out of the increasing tension between native and European Lutheranism, Krauth became a spokesman for the conservative or European theological position.

Kugler, Anna Sarah (1856-1930). Lutheran* medical missionary to India. Going to India in 1883 under the auspices of the General Synod (Lutheran) and its Women's Missionary Society, Kugler founded a women's dispensary (1893) and hospital (1898). Her medical skill and regard for Indians won their respect.

Kuhlman, Kathryn (1907-1976). Healing* evangelist. At the age of sixteen Kuhlman began an itinerant* preaching* ministry* throughout the Midwest. In 1948 two spontaneous healings occurred during the course of her preaching which caused her to turn her attention to healing ministry. In 1950 she moved to Pittsburgh, where her meetings earned favorable treatment from both the media and church leaders. In the 1960s her ministry expanded to include national and international appearances. Her book *I Believe in Miracles* (1968) sold millions of copies.

Kuhn, Isobel Miller (1901-1957). Missionary to China. From 1929 to 1950, with the exception of the World War II* years, Isobel and her husband worked among the Lisu tribe in China. Kuhn's writings about her mission's work among tribal people became very popular among evangelicals.*

Kurtz, Benjamin (1795-1865). Lutheran* pastor, editor and advocate of social reforms. As editor (1833-1861) of the *Lutheran Observer,* Kurtz entered stridently into the many issues of the day, advocating religious revival* methods and the causes of temperance,* antislavery* and Christian unity among evangelicals.*

Kuyper, Abraham (1837-1920). Dutch Calvinist* theologian and statesman. As founder and leader of the Dutch Neo-Calvinist movement (1875-1925), Kuyper worked to mobilize the conservative Reformed sector of the Dutch population against the theological and cultural modernism* ascendant at the time.

His influence in North America has descended chiefly along Dutch immigrant lines, especially those connected with the Christian Reformed Church.* His legacy includes the drive to engage every domain of society and culture from a distinctly Christian point of view.

Kyle, Melvin Grove (1858-1933). Presbyterian* fundamentalist* educator and biblical archaeologist. Kyle served long at Xenia Theological Seminary, as professor (1908-1922) and then president (1922-1930). He brought the seminary into national prominence by his archaeological research and writing. He also was active in establishing the League of Evangelical Students, a forerunner of InterVarsity Christian Fellowship.*

Kynett, Alpha Jefferson (1829-1899). Methodist* minister and temperance* advocate. During his career as a minister Kynett worked at the highest levels of his denomination* to increase lay participation, particularly by women.

Like so many reform-minded evangelical* Protestants* of his generation, Kynett sought to destroy the liquor traffic. He was the primary figure behind the calling of a national convention in Washington, D.C., in 1895, which organized the Anti-Saloon League.*

L

LaBerge, Agnes N. Ozman (1870-1937). Pentecostal* evangelist. On the evening of January 1, 1901, Charles Parham* laid hands on Ozman and prayed that she would receive the baptism with the Holy Spirit;* in response, Ozman spoke in tongues.* Her experience convinced others that they had rightly believed that such speech should uniformly attest Spirit baptism* and became the basis for the emergence of a distinct Pentecostal movement.*

Lacombe, Albert (1827-1916). Catholic* missionary. Lacombe, who was one of the first Roman Catholic missionaries to the Northwest, worked primarily with Blackfoot Indians.

Ladd, George Eldon (1911-1982). Evangelical* New Testament scholar. Ladd taught at Fuller Theological Seminary* from 1950 to 1980. His years there were characterized by hard work, well-reasoned but passionately held views and a driving, Socratic classroom style. In his *New Testament and Criticism* (1967), he moved evangelical biblical interpretation beyond the horizons of defensive fundamentalism,* accepting the positive gains of modern critical method while challenging the negative results of critical scholars on their own ground.

LaFarge, John (1880-1963). Jesuit* editor and pioneer for interracial justice. LaFarge served as college teacher, prison and hospital chaplain,* and, for fifteen years, missionary in rural Maryland. From 1926 until his death, he served in various editorial capacities at the Jesuit weekly *America* and was editor in chief from 1944 to 1948. In 1926 LaFarge also founded the *Interracial Review.* He was the chief Catholic spokesperson for the civil rights movement.*

Laity. A term normally referring to people in the church who are not ordained* clergy. Since the colonial period lay leadership has characterized the American church. In many cases, particularly on the western frontier, congregations were formed and maintained by clergy-recruited lay leaders.

See also LAY MOVEMENT, MODERN CATHOLIC; LAYPEOPLE, PROTESTANT.

Lalemant, Jérôme (Achiendassé) (1593-1673). Jesuit* missionary and superior in New France. As superior in New France (1645-1650 and 1659-1673), Lalemant initiated a great resurgence in missions and was highly respected for his skills, devotion to the poor, personal piety* and discretion.

See also HURON MISSION; MISSIONS TO NORTH AMERICA, FRENCH.

Lalemant (L'Allemant), Gabriel (1610-1649). Jesuit* missionary martyr in Canada. Lalemant began his brief but famous missionary career in 1646 along the St. Lawrence River. In 1649 he went to assist Father Jean de Brebeuf* at the St. Louis mission to the Hurons.* That year the two were captured, tortured and killed by the Iroquois.

See also MISSIONS TO NORTH AMERICA, FRENCH.

Lalor, Teresa (1769-1846). Roman Catholic* founder of Order of Visitation. In 1816, Lalor became superior of a group of thirty-five fully accredited Visitation nuns. She held the post until 1819, after which she established other houses in Mobile, St. Louis, Baltimore and Brooklyn.

Lambeth Conference. Assembly of Anglican* bishops representing the Anglican Communion.* The first conference was in 1867, at Lambeth Palace, the official residence of the archbishop of Canterbury. Except during World War I,* the conferences have been held in every decade since. While conference recommendations are not binding on individual national churches, the deliberations of the body do strongly affect the decisions that national churches make for themselves.

See also CHICAGO-LAMBETH QUADRILATERAL.

Lamy, John Baptist (Jean Baptiste) (1814-1888). First Catholic* archbishop of Santa Fe, New Mexico. Lamy's territory included eastern Colorado and most of Arizona as well as New Mexico. Lamy unified and expanded the Catholic Church in New Mexico, preaching* and traveling as well as overseeing his diocese.* By 1865 there were 100,000 Catholics under his jurisdiction, and many churches and schools (including a seminary) had begun to prosper.

Landis, Benson Young (1897-1966). Congregational,* social activist and researcher. Landis conducted surveys and research in industrial, social and moral issues and was particularly interested in rural and agricultural problems.

Landmark Movement. A nineteenth-century Baptist* movement in the South asserting the sole validity and unbroken succession of Baptist churches since the New Testament era. This exclusivistic ecclesiology arose among Baptist churches in the South during the mid-nineteenth century and was linked with the concept that the church is always a local and visible institution. In the latter half of the nineteenth century, Landmarkism made deep inroads in the Southern Baptist Convention,* affecting concepts of missions,* ordination,* ordinances* and even eschatology.* The dominant figure behind the movement was James R. Graves.*

Lankford, Sarah Worral. See PALMER, SARAH WORRAL LANKFORD.

Lard, Moses E. (1818-1880). Disciples of Christ* minister and editor. Lard took a moderate position among Disciples, halfheartedly approving mission societies but opposing creeds,* open Communion, instrumental music and a settled ministry. He was a pacifist* and argued against everlasting punishment, for which he was charged with Universalism.*

Larkin, Clarence (1850-1924). Baptist* pastor and author. At the age of thirty-two Larkin joined the Baptist Church and was ordained* two years later. Larkin subsequently became a premillennialist* and published books on prophetic themes. Utilizing his background as an engineer, Larkin included his numerous memorable charts, many illustrating prophetic themes.

Larsen, Peter Laurentius (1833-1915). Lutheran* minister and college president. At the founding of Luther College, Larsen became president (1861-1902) but also served as professor, pastor, editor and synodic officer. He advocated both orthodox* Lutheran doctrine and careful attentiveness to the American setting.

Lartigue, Jean-Jacques (1777-1840). First Roman Catholic* bishop of Montreal. Lartigue was appointed bishop of Montreal in 1836 at a time when the political situation in Lower Canada was reaching critical proportions. He enjoined obedience and submission to the rule of law, and when rebellion occurred in 1837-1838 he stood firmly against it.

La Salle, René Robert Cavalier Sieur de (1643-1687). French explorer of North America. In 1666 La Salle went to New France, where he became interested in exploring the interior. In 1679 he led an expedition into Lake Michigan and central Illinois. In 1682 he went through the Illinois territory and down the Mississippi to the gulf, the first white man to do so. Here he claimed the entire Mississippi River Valley for the King of France, naming it Louisiana in his honor.

Lathrop, John (d. 1653). Puritan* minister and English Congregational* leader. Lathrop, copastor of a London church of Congregational independents, went to America in 1634 with thirty followers.

Latin America Mission. A service agency to extend and assist the evangelical* church in the Spanish-speaking republics. Founded in 1921 by Harry and Susan Strachan, missionaries to Argentina, Latin America Mission (LAM) attempted to replace the slow-moving approaches to evangelism* then in use. The Strachans undertook aggressive, concentrated efforts in fourteen of the twenty Hispanic-American republics in the next decades.

Administrative oversight of LAM was assumed by R. Kenneth Strachan at the death of his father in 1945. Out of concern for the awakening masses, Strachan developed Evangelism-in-Depth* in the 1960s.

Latin Rite. The term *rite* here refers primarily to the whole way of being a particular Christian church. In summary, this includes the church's liturgical* rites, legal code and spiritual heritage. In this sense, the Latin Rite is distinguished from the Eastern Rites,* all of which have their own distinct way of being a Christian church. The Latin Rite has its center of unity in the church at Rome, overseen by the bishop of Rome, the pope. Hence it is also called the Roman Rite.

Latitudinarianism. A term used to describe the beliefs of a prominent group of Anglican* divines in the late seventeenth and early eighteenth centuries. Reacting against the dogmatic Calvinism* of the Puritans* and the liturgical* practices of the high church,* they sought a common ground between Anglicans, Presbyterians* and Nonconformists. They were theologically ambiguous but possessed a strong ethical emphasis.

Latourette, Kenneth Scott (1884-1968). Distinguished scholar of Asian and missions history. Involvement with the Student Volunteer Movement* led Latourette to a brief term of missionary service in China (1910-1912). He later was professor of missions and Oriental history at Yale Divinity School,* where he taught for thirty-two years. He wrote *History of the Expansion of Christianity* (7 vols., 1937-1945) and *Christianity in a Revolutionary Age: A History of Christianity in the Nineteenth and Twentieth Centuries* (5 vols., 1958-1962). Placing the church in the context of unfolding historical developments, Latourette perceived God's work in the world through human institutions.

Laubach, Frank Charles (1884-1970). Congregational* missionary. In 1929 as a missionary to the Philippines, Laubach began a literacy work among the underprivileged people on Mindanao. He developed the approach "Each One Teach One," which came to be known as the Laubach Method. The program eventually spread to more than one hundred countries.

Lausanne Committee for World Evangelization. International evangelical* council committed to world evangelization. The Lausanne Committee for World Evangelization was formed as a continuing body that would carry forward the vision and spirit of the International Congress on World Evangelization* held in Lausanne, Switzerland, in 1974. This was an international evangelical conference dedicated to the purpose of world evangelization by A.D. 2000. The seventy-five member Lausanne Committee is international in its membership and maintains the evangelical commitments expressed in the Lausanne Covenant. The Committee has sponsored numerous congresses, conferences and publications aimed at furthering its goals.

Lausanne Congress on World Evangelism. *See* INTERNATIONAL CONGRESS ON WORLD EVANGELIZATION.

Lausanne Covenant. World evangelization document. The Lausanne Covenant was drafted at the International Congress on World Evangelization* and represents a milestone statement of the theological basis of international evangelicalism's* commitment to world evangelization. Framed under the leadership of John R. W. Stott, the Covenant is 3,000 words in length and is organized under fifteen articles that articulate evangelical beliefs and their implications, particularly for evangelism.* It forms the doctrinal basis for the ongoing work of the Lausanne Committee for World Evangelization, and it has been widely adopted as a statement of basic evangelical belief and commitment.

Laval de Montmorency, François Xavier (1623-1708). First bishop of Quebec. In 1659 as a member of the Quebec Council, Laval opposed the governor and others who sought to control the church. Laval's development of a strong church structure independent of the French crown and of a Canadian clergy enabled the Catholic Church* to hold its own after British conquest. It also contributed to the ultramontane* movement in Quebec during the nineteenth century.

Laws, Curtis Lee (1868-1946). Baptist* clergyman and editor. In 1913 Laws became editor of the Baptist weekly the *Watchman-Examiner.* In an editorial in 1920, he coined the name *fundamentalist* for those "who still cling to the great fundamentals and who mean to do battle royal for the faith." Laws was a prominent leader of the conservative reaction to modernism* in the

Northern Baptist Convention from 1920 through the 1940s.

Lay Movement, Modern Catholic. The modern American Catholic* lay movement has experienced three periods of prominence: the lay renaissance (c. 1889-1894), the 1930s and the 1960s. During the first period Catholic leaders in a broad array of Catholic social and educational movements launched the lay congress movement. At several congresses, nonordained Catholics took a critical look at their church and proposed future changes.

The 1930s witnessed an upsurge in lay social activism prompted both by the socioeconomic problems of the Depression* and by a growing awareness of European Catholic movements.

Such lay movements produced a whole new generation of educated, self-conscious laypeople who, in the wake of the Second Vatican Council,* found new opportunities for spiritual growth and leadership, such as in Cursillo,* the charismatic* renewal and on the parish councils.*

See also LAYPEOPLE, PROTESTANT.

Lay Reader. A licensed, unordained worship* leader in the Episcopal Church.* In most liturgical churches in the U.S., laypeople are allowed to read certain Scripture lessons in public worship without formal license. Since 1972 the Roman Catholic Church* has regulated readers as an unordained ministry.

Laying on of Hands. A religious rite in which the imposition of hands suggests consecration, blessing and invocation of the Holy Spirit. The New Testament evidences three main usages of the rite: healing,* ordination* or setting apart for service and communication of the Holy Spirit, often in conjunction with Christian baptism.*

Laymen's Foreign Missions Inquiry (1930-1932). An inquiry into missions* conducted by prominent Protestant* laypersons. Financed by John D. Rockefeller Jr., the inquiry was confined to missions connected with churches in Burma, China, India and Japan. After field visits, a commission of appraisal headed by William E. Hocking* of Harvard* University drafted the final report. Most controversial was the report's proposal that Christian missions reinforce the nobler aspects of other religions rather than seek to convert their adherents.

Laymen's Missionary Movement. An interdenominational program to raise funds for Christian missions.* First proposed by John B. Sleman, a participant in the Student Volunteer Movement,* the movement helped increase total missionary giving for denominations from $9.0 million in 1906 to $45.3 million in 1924.

Laypeople, Protestant. Throughout the history of American religion, Protestant* laypeople have played an exceptionally active role. In so doing, they have realized the vitality of the Protestant doctrine of the priesthood of all believers* and the national doctrine of democratic* equality. During the colonial period (1607-1789), laypeople had considerable control over religious life in the Protestant colonies. The Great Awakening* (1720-1760) spelled a profound victory for the role of the laity, especially among the Baptists* and Methodists.* During the Revolutionary War era (1775-1800), the churches were disestablished and religious liberty* was guaranteed. This made all the churches voluntary associations (denominations*) and promoted lay activity and control.

The nineteenth century experienced several revivals, which greatly increased church membership.* Especially significant were voluntary associations, especially the Sunday-school movement,* which cut across denominational lines and were basically lay movements.* Another significant development of the nineteenth century was the activity of laywomen, who taught in the Sunday schools and who were the backbone of the missionary societies (see Missionary Movement, Women's) and of the temperance movement.*

Lay activity reached something of a climax in the early twentieth century with the organization of the interdenominational Laymen's Missionary Movement* in 1906 and the Men and Religion Forward Movement* in 1911. The resurgence of lay activity after World War II* has been called a lay renaissance.

See also LAY MOVEMENT, MODERN CATHOLIC.

Leachman, Emma (1868-1952). Southern Baptist* social ministries pioneer. In 1921 "Miss Emma" was appointed as the first general field worker of the Home Mission Board of the Southern Baptist Convention. In this capacity she traveled widely throughout the South enlisting support for city missions* projects and promoting the cause of Christian social ministries.

League for Social Reconstruction. Canadian social reform organization arising out of the Great Depression.* The league was established in Toronto and Montreal in 1931-1932 by a group of academics, businessmen and ministers, many of whom had close ties to the Social Gospel movement* in Canadian Protestantism.* League members emphasized "the common good rather than private profit." The group disbanded in 1942.

Leavell Family. Landrum Pinson (1874-1929); Frank Hartwell (1884-1949); Roland Quinche (1891-1963). These three brothers served Southern Baptist Churches* and agencies.

Landrum became (1907) the first secretary of the Baptist Young People's Union and (after 1918) directed the Sunday School Board. Frank was the executive leader of the Inter-Board Commission and later directed the Department of Student Work. Roland became the first superintendent of evangelism* for the Home Mission Board (1937-1942) and later president of the New Orleans Baptist Theological Seminary (1946-1958).

Lectionary. A regular cycle of assigned Scripture readings to be used in worship* on specific occasions. Contemporary lectionaries commonly include four readings for each Sunday service: Old Testament, Psalms, New Testament (Epistle, Acts or Revelation) and Gospel. A lectionary provides for the systematic coverage of a large portion of the Bible over a cycle which may vary from one to four years or even more. Readings are normally chosen according to the church year, with the Gospel text as central.

Lectureships. Annual gatherings of members of the Churches of Christ.* The lectureships feature sermons and classes for inspiration, motivation and information. Also there are meetings and various exhibits. The most influential and largest (15,000) lectureship meets annually at Abilene Christian University.

Lee, Ann (Mother Ann) (1736-1784). Shaker* leader. In 1774 Lee and a few other English Shakers went to a community at Niskeyuna (Watervliet), New York. "Mother Ann" was revered by the community for her prophetic powers, healings, ecstatic singing and praying.*

A belief later arose among Shakers that she was the Second Coming of Christ in female form. This belief was held most strongly during the Shaker spiritual revival, known as Mother Ann's Work, that occurred over fifty years after her death (c. 1837-1847).

Lee, Daniel (1807-1896). Methodist* missionary to Oregon. Lee served in Oregon from 1834 to 1843. After returning to New England, Lee published, with J. H. Frost, *Ten Years in Oregon* (1844), which served to awaken the interest of the church in the Oregon mission.

Lee, Jarena (1783-c. 1850). African Methodist Episcopal* exhorter and preacher. Converted under the ministry* of Richard Allen,* Lee began preaching as an itinerant* in 1819. She continued this work tirelessly, despite obstacles, for more than thirty years. She was active in the movement for women's full access to the pulpit.

Lee, Jason (1803-1845). Methodist* missionary to the Pacific Northwest. Lee traveled to the Oregon Territory in 1834, accompanying a party of fur traders. He is credited that year with preaching* the first Protestant* sermon* delivered west of the Rocky Mountains. Lee was instrumental in founding the Oregon Institute (1842), which became the basis for the first collegiate institution in the Far West, Willamette University.

Lee, Jesse (1758-1816). Methodist* preacher. Lee received his first appointment as a circuit rider* in North Carolina and Virginia in 1783. Francis Asbury,* whom Lee met in 1785, soon recognized his gifts and graces and took him as a traveling companion for three years. Lee then ministered in New England for over a decade. Returning later to Virginia, he was elected chaplain* of the U.S. House of Representatives (1809) and of the Senate (1814). Lee is regarded as the father of Methodism in New England.

Lee, Robert E(dward) (1807-1870). Confederate general, commander of the Southern armies. Lee, who loved the Union and opposed slavery and secession, nevertheless could not betray his native Virginia and accepted command of the Army of Northern Virginia in June 1862. Though always outnumbered, Lee's armies won several strategic victories before the crucial defeat at Gettysburg in July 1863.

A devout Episcopalian,* Lee was esteemed throughout the South as a Christian knight and was often compared to Christ.

Lee, Robert Greene (1886-1978). Southern Baptist* minister. Lee served seventeen short pastorates before going in 1927 to Bellevue Baptist in Memphis, Tennessee. When he retired from there in 1960, he had received 24,071 new members, 7,649 by baptism.* His ministry was marked throughout by an evangelistic* emphasis.

Legalism. The act of putting law above gospel by establishing requirements for salvation* beyond repentance and faith in Jesus Christ. Legalism reduces the broad, inclusive and general precepts of the Bible to narrow and rigid codes. Ultimately, it creates a system that obligates God to bless those who have proven themselves worthy. It thus tends to underestimate both the sinfulness* of humanity and the holiness* of God.

While legalism has been abhorred in the history of the church, so has license. American Christians have often found it difficult, however, to balance the two. Roman Catholics* sometimes err on the side of ritual legalism. American fundamentalists* gravitate toward moral and doctrinal legalism. Pentecostals* are sometimes guilty of experiential legalism. Many mainline* Protestants* lean toward political legalism. All such propensities tend to undermine the once-for-all work of Christ and alienate other Christians who approach the Christian faith from a different, though equally legitimate, perspective.

Leiper, Henry Smith (1891-1975). Missionary and ecumenist.* After ministries in Siberia, China and France, Leiper became involved with ecumenical agencies. He was foreign secretary of the Federal Council of Churches* (1930-1948) and associate general secretary of the World Council of Churches* (1948-1952).

Le Jeune, Paul (1591-1664). Jesuit* missionary and superior in New France. In 1632 Le Jeune became superior of the Jesuit Missions in Quebec. There he completely rebuilt the Quebec mission after its demise under English rule. He initiated Native-American language study for missionaries and established schools, seminaries and hospitals for Native Americans.

Leland, John (1754-1841). Baptist* preacher and religious libertarian. As a Baptist pastor and evangelist in Virginia, Leland for years faced hostility from legal and church authorities.

Through his preaching, writing and personal friendship with Thomas Jefferson* and James Madison,* Leland exercised notable influence in the struggle to disestablish the Anglican* Church and establish religious liberty.* He led the Baptists in support of Jefferson's bill establishing religious liberty in Virginia. Leland, like Isaac Backus,* proposed a Bill of Rights to the Constitution.

In 1792 Leland moved back to Massachusetts, where he spent his next fifty years in itinerant* ministry that took him throughout New England, as well as on several return trips to Virginia.

Lenski, R(ichard) C(harles) H(enry) (1864-1936). Lutheran* minister and biblical scholar. Lenski is most famous for his eleven-volume series Interpretation of the New Testament, which is still in print.

Lent. A six-week period of spiritual preparation prior to Easter.* The season is characterized by penitence, which is reflected in the Lenten liturgy of the Catholic Church.* Lent has continued to be observed in the Anglican* tradition and was particularly encouraged by the Tractarians.* It is observed by Lutherans* and by other Protestant* denominations affected by the liturgical movement.*

See also MARDI GRAS.

Leo XIII (1810-1903). Pope. Leo, elected pope in 1878, deeply influenced the growth of the Catholic Church* in the U.S. During his pontificate, the Catholic population grew tremendously, owing largely to European immigration.* By 1884 there were 12 million Catholics in the U.S. in a total population of 76 million.

Leo's pronouncements on capital, labor as well as other social issues were set forth in his well-known encyclical *Rerum Novarum,* in which he supported the working classes and labor unions.

In 1895 Leo sent his first encyclical* to the American Church, *Longinqua Oceani,* in which he praised the prosperity of the church and the freedom it enjoyed. Shortly thereafter, in the late 1890s, the crisis of Americanism* developed. Doctrines it allegedly upheld were condemned in Leo's letter *Testem Benevolentiae* (1899).

LeTourneau, Robert Gilmour (1881-1969). Protestant* layman, educator and industrialist. In 1946 LeTourneau founded and generously endowed a school to train students in mechanical and industrial arts, LeTourneau College in Longview, Texas.

Leverett, John (1662-1724). Massachusetts lawyer, political leader and president of Harvard College.* In 1699 Leverett was a cofounder of Boston's Brattle Street Church. Elected Harvard's first nonclerical president in 1707, he led the college in an entirely new direction, introducing Anglican* divinity,* broader readings in secular literature and a freer style of campus life.

Lewis, C(live) S(taples) (1898-1963). British scholar, writer and Christian apologist.* At Oxford, Lewis was a fellow in English language and literature at Magdalen College (1925-1954); at Cambridge, he was professor of medieval and renaissance English (1954-1963).

Lewis's enormous reputation stems largely from his extensive and diverse list of publications. His fame was further enhanced by his popular BBC radio broadcasts on Christianity during World War II,* as well as his numerous public lectures and sermons.

Though Lewis never visited North America, he has had an immense impact on North American Christians. Over three dozen of his titles are available, with over forty million copies in print, making him the bestselling Christian author of all time and perhaps the most frequently quoted in sermons, lectures, books and articles. The list of people who claim to have become Christians or have been aided in their spiritual growth because of his books is seemingly endless.

Lewis, Edwin (1881-1959). Methodist* theologian. Lewis was a professor of theology at Drew Theological Seminary from 1916 to 1951. In the 1920s his theology reflected the evangelical* liberalism* which prevailed in mainline* Protestantism.* In the late 1920s, however, he underwent a radical reorientation in his thinking "from philosophy to revelation"; from this emerged Lewis's most influential work, *A Christian Manifesto* (1934), in which he passionately urged American Protestantism to return to its historic, biblical beliefs.

Lewis, Tayler (1802-1877). Biblical scholar.

One of Lewis's chief interests was the relationship between science and religion, particularly regarding creation. He wrote *The Six Days of Creation* (1855), arguing that biblical interpretation need not be harmonized with scientific theories that were notably defective and subject to change.

Liberal Catholic Church. A religious movement based on Theosophy and founded in Great Britain. Founded by James Ingall Wedgwood in London in 1916, the church also recognizes Charles W. Leadbeater as its cofounder. Its historical and theological roots can be traced to the Old Catholic Church, from which it emerged; the Anglican Church,* with which its early leaders were formerly affiliated; but most significantly the Theosophical Society, whose mystical* tradition it adapted to Catholic ritual.

The church was established in the U.S. in 1919. In 1987 there were 127 clergy active in the United States and thirty-four churches with 2,800 members.

Liberalism/Modernism, Protestant (c. 1870s-1930s). A movement in the late nineteenth and early twentieth centuries seeking to preserve the Christian faith by adjusting traditional Christianity to developments in modern culture.

Liberals found precedent in the theology of Unitarianism,* transcendentalism* and Horace Bushnell,* who was perhaps the most important precursor of the religious liberals who followed later in the nineteenth century. In his books, Bushnell developed many of the themes that came to dominate modernism: the immanence of God, the importance of Christian experience, the necessity of doctrinal revision and the poetic nature of religious language.

In the decades after the Civil War,* profound intellectual and social changes rocked the U.S. The spread of Darwinism* and evolutionary thought, massive immigration,* rapid industrialization, skyrocketing urban growth and the gradual secularization of society resulted in pervasive tensions in American society. The new intellectual and social trends nourished the liberal impulse in America which, by the 1880s, had given rise to an identifiable movement known as the New Theology or Progressive Orthodoxy. By 1920 liberals dominated perhaps half of the country's Protestant seminaries and publishing houses and a third of the Protestant pulpits.

For modernists, ethics replaced doctrine as the

theological centerpiece. The value and truth of religion was demonstrated by the moral impact it had on individuals or society. Concern for this world overshadowed interest in the life hereafter. This stress on morals was nowhere clearer than in the liberal view of Jesus which often attributed his divinity to his ethical and religious excellence. The mission* of the church was to help bring in the kingdom of God through religious education and social reform.

Having reached its zenith by the 1920s, liberalism found itself assaulted by fundamentalists* on the right and scientific humanists on the left. Both argued that modernism was not Christianity and demanded that liberals make a clean and honest choice between the orthodox* faith and humanism. By the 1930s neo-orthodoxy* also was challenging American modernism. Unable to withstand these attacks, liberals executed a strategic retreat.

The most persistent legacy of modernism to American Protestantism was its insistence that Christian theology acknowledge and exploit the inevitable involvement of religion and culture.

See also FUNDAMENTALISM; FUNDAMENTALIST-MODERNIST CONTROVERSY; HERESY TRIALS; MODERNISM, CATHOLIC.

Liberation Theology. Liberation theology was introduced to North Americans in 1973 with the English translation of Gustavo Gutiérrez's *Theology of Liberation*. As a movement for both the reform of theology* and a Christian commitment to radical social change, liberation theology has had a profound influence on theology in North America and elsewhere.

Historical Roots. In the early 1960s some Latin American theologians saw the need for a theological response to widespread conditions of poverty and injustice. Their concerns made a strong impact on the Roman Catholic Church* at the Second General Conference of the Latin American Episcopate (CELAM), held in Medellín, Colombia, in 1968. The bishops recognized and encouraged the development of "base communities," small groups of Christians gathered together for Bible study,* prayer* and reflection on the gospel in their context. These groups have become the major vehicle for the spread of liberation themes beyond academic circles. By 1980 there were as many as 100,000 base communities meeting in Latin America.

Since becoming a North American and world-wide movement in theology, liberation theology has appealed primarily to people committed to addressing situations of economic, racial and sexual exploitation.

Liberation Method. Liberation theology employs a method whose principal source is not reason, tradition, the Bible,* the voice of the Spirit or social analysis but a Christian praxis which enlists all of the above. Liberation theologians argue that praxis—the unity of theory and practice in a concrete historical situation—is the starting point for theology. Theology is seen as the second step. First we must have a fundamental commitment to the poor and/or oppressed that is expressed in the way we live.

Orthodoxy* gives way to orthopraxis. Liberation theology reflects a revolution in the way theology has traditionally been conceived. The measure of theological adequacy is not orthodoxy but conformity to the actual process of liberation that God is bringing about in the world. In practice this means that theology is measured by orthopraxis—by whether or not it leads to concrete action designed to liberate people from their oppression.

Liberty, Christian. Christian freedom from the necessity of good works and religious practices, particularly regarding their necessity for salvation.* The Protestant* Reformers affirmed Christian liberty as a corollary to justification* by faith alone. Martin Luther wrote, "A Christian is perfectly free, lord of all, subject to none. A Christian is a perfectly dutiful servant of all, subject to all."

In American revivalism* the Puritan* vision of a godly commonwealth was expanded to encompass the nation and was infused with the Wesleyan* conception of sanctification,* linking stewardship of the human body with a mandate to reform society through the prohibition* of alcohol,* tobacco and unholy practices. Baptists* and various Holiness* churches typically incorporated into their standards for church membership* prohibitions against alcohol, profaning the Lord's Day and various indications of worldliness.

License. Licensing to preach* is an early stage of ordination* in many Protestant* churches, particularly in the free church* tradition, practiced in many churches since the nineteenth century.

Liele, George (c. 1750-1820). African-American Baptist* preacher. In 1775 Liele was ordained* to work as a missionary among slaves on Georgia plantations. Considered the first formally ordained African-American minister in America, Liele was freed by his master to carry out his ministry. In 1784 he obtained permission to preach in Jamaica, becoming the first African-American foreign missionary.

Lifting of Hands. A gesture of worship* generally, though not exclusively, associated with charismatic* and Pentecostal* Christianity. The gesture is one of joy and exuberance but also of gratitude, devotion or surrender to God, the object of worship.

Limbo. In Roman Catholic* theology,* the region or state proximate to heaven in which reside departed souls who do not enjoy the beatific vision but do not suffer any other privation. Limbo (an idea traceable back only to the high Middle Ages) comprises Old Testament believers and unbaptized infants. Since 1900 some theologians have denied the existence of limbo altogether.

Lincoln, Abraham (1809-1865). Lawyer, statesman, political theologian and sixteenth U.S. president. After serving in the U.S. House of Representatives (1847-1849), Lincoln lost the 1858 Senate race to incumbent Stephen A. Douglas. Lincoln's many speeches and debates during that period made him a national figure, however, and in 1860 he won the Republican nomination for president on the third ballot. Judged by its consequences, the election of 1860 was the most momentous in American history.

He entered office at a critical juncture in U.S. history, the Civil War* (1861-1865), and died from an assassin's bullet at the war's end before the greater implications of the conflict could be resolved. Even though relatively unknown and inexperienced when elected president, he soon proved to be a consummate politician. Above all, he was firm in his convictions and dedicated to the preservation of the Union.

More has been written about Lincoln, including his religion, than about any other president. Although not particularly religious as a young man, Lincoln became increasingly thoughtful about spiritual matters during his last years. Although he appears to have rejected his parents' Baptist* faith, he never discarded the teachings of the Bible as he understood them.

It was not Lincoln's personal faith but rather his public religion which grew from it that profoundly affected the course of American history. Lincoln, as heir of the Puritans,* was convinced that the U.S. was more than an ordinary nation, that it was a proving ground for the idea of democratic government. He was the person most responsible for fusing the dominant evangelical-biblical religion of his day with democratic ideals and for creating a civil-religion* version of the old Puritan quest to build a "city upon a hill."

Lincoln's assassination on April 15, 1865, made him a redeemer-savior-martyr figure and created a new focus of American civil piety. He thus joined George Washington* as the second great hero of the public faith.

Lind, Jenny (Goldschmidt) (1820-1887). Swedish soprano and philanthropist* who toured America from 1850 to 1852. By 1840, Lind had become Sweden's premier opera and concert coloratura.

In 1850 she accepted P. T. Barnum's offer of a 150-concert tour throughout the eastern U.S., hoping to raise funds for charitable enterprises. Each concert included her singing "I Know That My Redeemer Liveth." Believing her art was God's instrument by which she could reach out to others, Lind used the proceeds of her performances primarily to benefit needy individuals and institutions.

Lindsay, Gordon (1906-1973), and Freda Schimpf Lindsay (1916-). Charismatic* mission* strategists and leaders of the healing* movement. Gordon published the influential magazine *Voice of Healing* from 1948 to 1967.

In 1970 Gordon opened Christ for the Nations Institute (CFNI) as a center of theological and spiritual formation for the charismatic and Pentecostal* movements. Upon his death, Freda was elected president of CFNI, which has grown under her leadership.

Lipscomb, David (1831-1917). Church of Christ* preacher and editor. In 1866 Lipscomb reactivated the *Gospel Advocate,* which was sympathetic to the South and reflected the more conservative viewpoint of the Southern Churches of Christ. It became—and still is—the leading paper among the Southern churches of the Restoration movement.* In 1891 Lipscomb founded Nashville Bible School, which later was renamed David Lipscomb College.

Litany. A form of liturgical* prayer in which a leader voices petitions and the people affirm these with a short, repeated refrain. Its primary purpose is to enable the people to participate actively together in expressing corporate prayers. Litanies, used in Christian churches by the fourth century, have their most comprehensive role in Eastern Orthodoxy.* Protestant litanies have been in continuous use since the time of Luther.

Liturgical Art. Art which serves the worship* or devotional* life of the Christian community. It forms a separate category within religious art in general.

Because of the fear of idolatry, Puritan* colonists in New England eschewed visual representations of religious subjects in their meetinghouses and churches. An emphasis on dignified simplicity continued through the eighteenth century, not only among Puritans, but also among Lutherans,* Quakers,* Methodists* and Presbyterians.*

Beginning in the nineteenth century, several forces conspired to change the direction of liturgical art in the U.S. Massive waves of Roman Catholic,* Lutheran and Orthodox* immigration introduced into the American liturgical art scene fresh infusions of the European artistic vocabulary. By the end of the nineteenth century, the Gothic Revival had given a medieval look to the liturgical art of nearly every mainstream denomination* in the U.S.

The twentieth century, however, saw the coalition between the liturgical movement* and proponents of well-designed art in a contemporary style for liturgical use. In recent years a renewed theological emphasis on the function of symbols and images in religious life has led many denominations back to a serious consideration of liturgical art.

Liturgical Books. Service books used in the public worship* of several American liturgical traditions. For Roman Catholics,* use of approved books is mandatory in most forms of public worship; for Lutherans* and Episcopalians,* the forms of public worship are in prescribed books which are normally used; and for United Methodists* and Presbyterians,* liturgical books provide forms for public worship, but use, while common for the sacraments,* is not enforced on congregations.

Most Roman Catholic liturgical books were revised after the Council of Trent (1545-1563). After the Second Vatican Council* massive changes occurred in all the Roman liturgical books.

Similar drastic revisions have occurred in many Protestant* churches. Among Lutherans, largely concentrated now in the Evangelical Lutheran Church in America,* the service book is the Lutheran Book of Worship. The service books of the Episcopal Church have been the Book of Common Prayer* (BCP) and various hymnals. Methodist services were part of the Methodist *Discipline* until 1968. Hymnals have been used ever since John Wesley* published the first American hymnal in 1737. The various Presbyterian bodies have operated under the general supervisions of a series of the Directory for Public Worship as well as series of hymnals.

Liturgical Commissions. Organizations within many American denominations,* regional bodies or local churches that work for the promotion of good liturgical practice. Many of the national liturgical commissions produce publications and conduct workshops and seminars to stimulate developments in thought and practice. Several ecumenical* groups also exist, including the Commission on Worship of the Consultation on Church Union.*

Liturgical Movement. A movement to reform the Roman liturgy* and thereby renew the attitude of the faithful toward worship* and its relationship to the Christian life. The modern liturgical movement had its origin in the French Benedictine* monk Prosper Guéranger (1805-1875), who sought to purify Catholic* religiosity of its popular or culturally derived liturgical and devotional elements by following the Romantic* impulse and Catholic ultramontanism* in a return to the Middle Ages and the Roman liturgy.* In the early twentieth century Pope Pius X* pointed the way toward liturgical renewal in urging more frequent reception of the Eucharist* and the restoration of Gregorian chant for the universal church.

Dom Virgil Michel,* a Benedictine monk of St. John's Abbey, Collegeville, Minnesota, became the center of the movement in North America. In 1926 he began the Liturgical Press and the journal *Orate Fratres,* which continues to be published as *Worship* magazine, to disseminate liturgical reform.

The Second Vatican Council,* in its Constitution on the Sacred Liturgy, incorporated in its recommendations many of the earlier proposals of the liturgical movement. It encouraged full participation on the part of the laity and thus introduced the vernacular language and a simple and clear liturgy designed to educate the faithful. The increased use of Scripture in the liturgy was emphasized, the Divine Office and liturgical calendar were ordered revised and restored, and the common celebration of vespers* on Sundays* was encouraged. Gregorian chant, referred to as having "pride of place," was to be returned to popular use, although contemporary sacred music was not excluded.

Ultimately, the liturgical movement was not limited to the Catholic Church but spilled over into a liturgical renewal in mainline* Protestant* churches.

Liturgical Year. See CHURCH YEAR.

Liturgy. Broadly, any regular form of public worship.* In America, there are a wide variety of liturgical traditions, each with distinctive characteristics. They include several traditions of the Eastern (Orthodox* or Oriental) churches and seven Western traditions: Roman Catholic,* Lutheran,* Reformed,* Anglican,* free church* (including Mennonites* and Quakers*), Methodist* and Pentecostal.* The term *liturgical tradition* denotes a definite body of inherited patterns of worship practices and understanding of such practices. Most Christian worship in America has been historically shaped within a single tradition, although such traditions frequently interact. Within each tradition there are ethnic and cultural styles (e.g., frontier Reformed practice or the worship of black Methodists).

As worship traditions mature, they seem more willing to recognize the values of other worship traditions and to borrow from them. Thus, spontaneous prayer appears in Episcopal services and set forms attract some free church people. Greater variety seems to be evolving within each tradition, yet without abandoning its distinctive characteristics.

Liturgy of the Hours. Also known as the Divine Office, the term refers to the public celebration of prayer, distinct from the Eucharistic liturgy (Mass*) in the Roman Catholic Church.* Since Vatican II* the office has been revised and is now celebrated in the vernacular. Since 1970 its name has been changed to Liturgy of the Hours and is considered the official public prayer and praise of the church, keyed to times of the day, days of the week and seasons of the year.

While the Divine Office is most commonly celebrated in monastic* and religious houses, cathedrals where there are resident canons and by the ordained* clergy who are bound to its private recitation, it has become once again a prayer of the Catholic Church for the church by laity.*

Livermore, Mary Ashton Rice (1820-1905). Temperance* and women's suffrage* leader. Livermore became convinced that women needed the vote to fight poverty, drunkenness and sexual exploitation, so she convened Illinois's first suffrage convention in 1868 and served as its president. In Massachusetts she was president of the state Women's Christian Temperance Union* (1875-1885) and Woman Suffrage Association (1893-1903).

Livingston, John H. (1746-1825). Dutch Reformed* minister and president of Queen's (Rutgers) College.* An ardent patriot during the Revolution, Livingston became an ecclesiastical peacemaker, assisting an ethnic church in finding its new identity and status in the emerging republic. From 1810 to 1825 he served as president of Queen's College in New Brunswick, New Jersey.

Loehe, Johannes Konrad Wilhelm (1808-1872). German Lutheran* pastor, writer and pioneer in mission* work. Loehe recruited and trained hundreds of "Christian emergency pastors" to work among the American settlers and to evangelize* the Native Americans—though he himself never left Germany.

Loetscher, Lefferts A. (1904-1981). Presbyterian* historian. Loetscher taught church history at Princeton Theological Seminary* from 1941 until 1974. His published work in church history, particularly Presbyterianism, is well known and includes *A Brief History of the Presbyterians* (3rd ed., 1978), *The Broadening Church* (1954) and *Facing the Enlightenment and Pietism: Archibald Alexander and the Founding of Princeton Theological Seminary* (1983).

Log College. Colonial school for training Presbyterian* ministers in the revivalist* tradition.

The "college" was a small school founded and run by William Tennent* in Neshaminy, Pennsylvania, during the 1730s and 1740s, the purpose of which was to train men for the Presbyterian ministry. In spite of severe criticism of Tennent's work, the college continued to turn out New Side*-type Presbyterian ministers until the early 1740s, when it ceased to function. The college was exceptionally influential in the crucial formative years of the Presbyterian Church.

Lonergan, Bernard J. F. (1904-1984). Canadian Catholic* theologian. Lonergan's main contribution was to bring Thomistic thought into dialogue with modern science and propose a new method for doing theology.

Followers of Lonergan have acclaimed him as a new methodological master, doing for his age what Aristotle and Francis Bacon had done for theirs. Lonergan provides for experience, understanding, judgment and decision. He distinguishes such realms as common sense, theory, art and prayer.

Long, Ralph H. (1882-1948). Lutheran* minister and director of the National Lutheran Council.* Long's vigorous leadership rescued the council during the financially precarious Depression* years. In the emergencies of World War II,* the council blossomed, proving highly effective under his wise direction.

Longinqua Oceani. A papal encyclical* by Pope Leo XIII* to the bishops of the U.S. in January 1895. It mixes warm praise for "the young and vigorous American nation" and its burgeoning Catholic Church,* with pointed warnings about trying to promote separation of church and state* and heavy emphasis on the role of the recently (1893) appointed apostolic delegate.*

The pope's comments disturbed the Americanists,* contradicting their hope that American-style separation of church and state could strengthen the church's embattled position in Europe. The encyclical marked the beginning of the decline of Americanism.

Loras, Jean Mathias Pierre (1792-1858). First Catholic* bishop of Dubuque, Iowa. At Loras's appointment in 1837, the virtually empty Diocese* of Dubuque encompassed most of present-day Iowa and Minnesota. During his tenure Loras attracted many new Catholic settlers and added dozens of priests and churches.

Lord, Daniel Aloyisius (1888-1955). Roman Catholic* writer, composer and playwright. In 1928 Lord organized the first national Leadership School for lay Catholics and in 1931 the national Summer School of Catholic Action, which had held 190 sessions by 1963. In 1943 he became director of the Jesuits' Institute of Social Order.

Lord's Day Act. Canadian federal act regulating Sunday activities. Introduced by the government of Prime Minister Wilfrid Laurier and passed by the Canadian Parliament in 1906, the act sought to limit work, commerce, pleasure traveling, games and public performances on the Lord's Day. Support for this law came from the Lord's Day Alliance, organized labor and Catholic* bishops. The act was repealed in 1985.

Love Feast. A worship* practice based on a shared common meal. European Pietism* revived the ancient practice of the love feast, and it became part of the worship of Mennonites,* Brethren,* Moravians* and early Methodists.* Today, the love feast is particularly associated with the Church of the Brethren and the Moravians.

Lovejoy, Elijah Parish (1802-1837). Presbyterian* minister and abolitionist* martyr. In St. Louis, Lovejoy became the editor of a Presbyterian newspaper. As he moved toward the radical position of immediate abolition, he became increasingly unwelcome and, in 1836, moved his paper to Alton, Illinois. There he again met with hostility, with mobs destroying his press on three occasions and ultimately shooting him down. Lovejoy in his death played a notable role in galvanizing antislavery sentiment.

Low Church. A term referring to individuals and congregations within the Anglican Church* who interpret the episcopate,* priesthood and Book of Common Prayer* from a distinctly Protestant* point of view.
See also HIGH CHURCH.

Lowrie, Walter (1868-1959). Episcopal* minister and Kierkegaard* scholar. Lowrie was deeply influenced by his reading of German dialectical theologians and began reading the Danish philosopher Søren Kierkegaard in German translation. At the age of sixty-five Lowrie taught himself

Danish and embarked on a study and translation of Kierkegaard's works, which contributed greatly to later interest in Kierkegaard.

Loy, Matthias (1828-1915). Lutheran* minister, theologian and educator. Loy was called in 1865 to be professor of theology* at the Lutheran seminary in Columbus, where he served until his retirement in 1905. During and after his tenure Loy was the leading theologian and churchman of the Evangelical Lutheran Joint Synod of Ohio and Adjacent States. He edited the *Lutheran Standard* (1864-1891) and the *Columbus Theological Magazine* (1881-1888).

Loyalist, United Empire. *See* AMERICAN REVOLUTION; ANGLICANISM.

Lutheran Church in America, The. The largest Lutheran* denomination* prior to its merger to form the Evangelical Lutheran Church in America (ELCA). The lineage of the Lutheran Church in America* (LCA) reached back to Henry Melchior Muhlenberg* and Samuel Simon Schmucker.* When the LCA merged to form the ELCA in 1987, it brought with it 2.9 million members. Like all Lutherans in America, the members of the LCA would be classed as theologically conservative, but they were the most moderate and, to the ultraorthodox, represented the Lutheran Left.

Lutheran Churches in America. The vast majority of Lutherans in America are members of three bodies: the 1988 merger called the Evangelical Lutheran Church in America (5.5 million members at the time of merger), the Lutheran Church—Missouri Synod* (2.6 million members) and the Wisconsin Evangelical Lutheran Synod* (400,000 members).

Lutheran Diversity. Lutherans in America have been noted for their existence in a great number of small and totally independent bodies. There are still a number of very small independent, unlinked churches, the largest of which has only eleven thousand members.

This great diversity of Lutheran churches resulted from two factors: immigration* and doctrinal differences. Lutherans arrived from northern and central Europe over more than a three-century period. These European churches had virtually no contact with each other until the twentieth century, having developed separately since their formation. Doctrinal differences further separated

these groups. Many of the immigrant groups represented "free" (nonestablished), schismatic or sectarian movements that resulted from revivalist* or pietist* movements in Europe. Still others were expressions of extremely conservative "confessionalism,"* which meant that they adhered to sixteenth-century Lutheran creeds* or confessions and resisted modern rationalism or forced movements of union with Reformed* churches in parts of Germany.

The Evangelical Lutheran Church in America. The largest, most dispersed and most complex of the Lutheran churches in America is the Evangelical Lutheran Church in America (ELCA), the result of a merger between the Lutheran Church in America* (LCA), the American Lutheran Church* (ALC) and the Association of Evangelical Lutheran Churches* (AELC). The LCA itself, the most moderate component, resulted from a merger in 1962. The ALC, with its background of both confessionalism and pietism, often found the ancestors of the LCA to be too "worldly." The AELC consisted of congregations that had left the Missouri Synod after an ultraconservative element took over leadership of the latter body in 1969.

Lutheran Church—Missouri Synod. During all this merging activity, the Missouri Synod (LC—MS) and the Wisconsin Evangelical Lutheran Synod (WELS) went their separate ways. The LC—MS has come to be known distinctively not only for their standing apart but because they established a very extensive network of elementary and secondary parochial schools,* one of the most elaborate outside Catholicism.*

Wisconsin Evangelical Lutheran Synod. When formed in 1850, the ancestor of the current WELS was a moderate group, but since 1917, when it absorbed several other Upper Midwest synodic groups, it has prided itself in being the most conservative sizable Lutheran group. It has ecumenical* relations with no one. The history of the Lutheran churches in America, then, has been a history of immigrations, doctrinal controversies and mergers down to the three main groups. This history has seen the churches leaving behind many ethnic customs, non-English languages and European memories. They have become thoroughly at home in America but in their "evangelical Catholicism" tend to see themselves situated somewhat independent of both mainstream and Reformed evangelical* Protestantism. They differ from the former in their confessionalism and from the latter in their consistent practice of infant baptism* and their belief in "the Real Presence" of Christ in the Lord's Supper.*

See also LUTHERAN TRADITION IN AMERICA.

Lutheran Church—Missouri Synod, The. A large Lutheran* denomination* of German background. In 1847 a group of German-American pastors* and their congregations organized the German Evangelical Lutheran Synod of Missouri, Ohio, and Other States. The word *German* was dropped from the name in World War I,* and in 1947 the present name was adopted.

Under the leadership of its first two presidents, Carl F. W. Walther* (1847-1850; 1864-1878) and F. C. D. Wyneken (1850-1864), the synod developed a strong defense of its biblical theology, anchored in the sixteenth-century Lutheran confessions of the Book of Concord, and its congregational* polity.* The leaders of the synod early recognized that the immigrant church would have to acculturate, a process hastened by persecution of German-Americans during World War I.

During the 1960s and early 1970s, tensions arose over the proper interpretation of the synod's traditional confessional stance. The controversy culminated in 1974, when the majority of students and faculty at Concordia Seminary, St. Louis, walked out and formed the Christ Seminary-Seminex and the Association of Evangelical Lutheran Churches. The group represented 4 percent of the synod's membership.

The synod currently continues its commitment to a strict interpretation of the Lutheran confessions, a strong educational program at every level and a firm commitment to evangelism and missions. In 1992 the membership numbered 2.6 million, making it the second-largest Lutheran denomination in the U.S.

See also LUTHERAN CHURCHES IN AMERICA; LUTHERAN TRADITION IN AMERICA.

Lutheran Council in Canada. A cooperative organization of Lutheran* denominations* in Canada. Formed in 1967, the council included such activities as missions, chaplaincies, social service, public relations, theological studies and work among university students and faculty. It serves the participating church bodies in their dealings with the federal government and in their ecumenical* interests of nationwide scope. As the movement for Lutheran union has advanced, the LCC has diminished.

See also LUTHERAN CHURCHES IN AMERICA.

Lutheran Tradition in America. The churches and culture derived from northern Europe and transplanted to the U.S. make up a religious tradition that has had considerable influence on the nation. In the Scandinavian nations or in the parts of Germany from whence the vast majority of the American Lutheran ancestry derives, Lutheranism was the dominant, established,* state-supported religion. In America, while it has attracted millions of participants, Lutheranism has been a minority in a culture more shaped by Reformed* Protestantism,* Roman Catholicism* and the religious ethos of the Enlightenment.* The act of surviving and prospering in such an environment has led to considerable adjustment and adaptation.

Three Theological Motifs. Doctrinally, the Lutheran tradition in America has perpetuated the historic outlook of its European ancestry, including the three great motifs of the sixteenth-century Reformation: *sola gratia* (a person is saved solely by the divine initiative), *sola fide* (the bond between God and the redeemed is formed entirely by faith) and *sola scriptura** (the Bible is the only source and norm for Christian teaching).

Another strand of Lutheranism stresses that this authority and the divine inspiration of the Bible center in the concept of the "inerrancy"* of the Bible. The Lutheran Church—Missouri Synod* and the Wisconsin Evangelical Lutheran Synod* stand apart from other Lutheran groups in large measure because of their insistence on inerrancy.

Confessionalism. Lutheran churches and members respond to the ecumenical creeds of the early Christian centuries and the formal writings of the Lutheran churches in the sixteenth century, which together make up the Book of Concord of 1580. Not all American Lutherans treat all the writings of this book equally. Some are most concerned only with Martin Luther's Small Catechism and Large Catechism and the decisive Augsburg Confession* of 1530.

Lutheran Tradition/American Experience. Lutheran polity in America has been quite varied. Lutherans like to speak of "the priesthood of all believers" and to assure that the laity has considerable voice in Lutheran affairs and especially in congregational and synodic life.

Lutherans have not made a cultural impact commensurate with their size in America, in part because of their relatively late arrival on the American scene after the mid-nineteenth century; because most of them came speaking German or

Scandinavian languages and not English; and because they inherited traditions of political passivity from Europe. Few of them have risen to positions of political leadership until recent years. In recent decades Lutherans have made considerable effort to downplay their reliance on ethnic heritages and to be inclusive.

See also IMMIGRATION AND ETHNICITY, PROTESTANT; LUTHERAN CHURCHES IN AMERICA.

Lutheran World Federation. A free association of ninety-nine Lutheran churches* from fifty countries. The federation succeeded the Lutheran World Convention that met in 1923, 1929 and 1935 as a result of contacts made by American and European Lutheran leaders in post-World War I* relief efforts. It meets in assembly every six years.

Lutheran-Catholic Dialogue. Lutheran-Catholic dialogue in the U.S. began in July 1965. Seven rounds of theological discussion had been completed by 1987, and the eighth was in progress. Common statements resulting from each completed round have been published, together with some of the preliminary essays.

Though the dialogue has been widely hailed by the press as an ecumenical* breakthrough and celebrated by theologians for their depth of theological investigation, assessments differ on the degree of consensus achieved. The published documents on justification by faith have been strongly criticized, and by some who would not be considered antiecumenical in principle.

Lutheranism. See LUTHERAN TRADITION IN AMERICA.

Lyman, Eugene William (1872-1948). Philosopher of religion and theologian. Raised in a family influenced by Horace Bushnell's* theology,* Lyman, through his own avid reading of Bushnell, Theodore Munger* and Washington Gladden,* as well as his study in Germany, became cemented in the liberalism* of the Social Gospel* that dominated turn-of-the-century American Protestant* thought.

Lyon, Mary (1797-1849). Founder of Mount Holyoke College. In 1835 Lyon helped found Wheaton Female Seminary in Norton, Massachusetts (now Wheaton College), and in 1836 she founded Mount Holyoke Female Seminary (Mount Holyoke College), which flourished under her inspired leadership. Mount Holyoke was to carry forward "the salvation of the world" by preparing women to take part in the creation of a Christian America.

M

Mabie, Henry Clay (1847-1918). Northern Baptist* pastor and missionary leader. In 1890 Mabie became home secretary of the American Baptist Missionary Union. In this capacity he traveled extensively to mission sites around the world. Mabie was also a prolific writer and apologist for the missionary cause. In matters of denominational* controversy, Mabie sympathized with the fundamentalists* against the modernists.*

Macartney, Clarence Edward Noble (1879-1957). Fundamentalist* Presbyterian* preacher. In 1922 Macartney led the conservative response to Harry Emerson Fosdick's* famous sermon "Shall the Fundamentalists Win?" A steadfast opponent of liberal* theology,* he supported the formation of Westminster Theological Seminary after the Princeton* reorganization in 1929.

MacGregor, James Drummond (1759-1830). Presbyterian* missionary to the Maritime Provinces. MacGregor was the first Presbyterian minister to visit Prince Edward Island (1791), the Miramichi area of New Brunswick (1797) and Cape Breton Island (1798). He was instrumental in forming the united secessionist Presbyterian Synod of Nova Scotia in 1817.

Machen, J(ohn) Gresham (1881-1937). Presbyterian* clergyman, New Testament scholar and educator. As a student at Princeton Theological Seminary,* Machen was greatly influenced by the teaching and scholarly model of Benjamin B. Warfield.* After advanced study in Germany, Machen returned to teach at Princeton. Machen's writings were marked by the careful conservative scholarship that had typified the Princeton tradition, and his views were given careful attention by liberals* and conservatives alike.

Machen was best known for championing the cause of orthodoxy in the fundamentalist-mod-ernist controversy.* The logic of Machen's opposition to liberalism led to confrontation both within Princeton Seminary and in the Presbyterian Church in the U.S.A. In 1929, when Princeton Seminary was reorganized to ensure a more inclusive theological spectrum, Machen and a core of conservative faculty members withdrew to found Westminster Theological Seminary at Philadelphia. Machen played a central role in founding a new denomination, the Presbyterian Church of America (later the Orthodox Presbyterian Church*).

Machray, Robert (1831-1904). Anglican* archbishop of Rupert's Land (which later became the provinces of Manitoba, Saskatchewan and Alberta). Under Machray's leadership, the church linked its expansion in the West to the denomination's* educational institutions.

Macintosh, Douglas Clyde (1877-1948). Baptist* theologian and educator. From his rural Canadian background, Macintosh emerged to become one of America's leading philosophical theologians. Early in his career he attempted an empirical* theology in response to the skepticism and historical relativism of his contemporaries. In several major books he created a theology based on empirically verifiable knowledge in combination with other emerging sciences.

Mack, Alexander (1679-1735). First Brethren* minister. In Germany, Mack emerged as the "teacher of the word" of an Anabaptist*/Pietist* community of eight persons founded in 1708. The congregation, with Mack as its leader, left Germany in 1720 for West Friesland, from where almost all members immigrated to Pennsylvania in 1729. There they joined an earlier (1719) emigration from Krefeld directed by Peter Becker.* At his death, Mack was a much-respected figure among the German-speaking element in Pennsylvania.

Mackay, John Alexander (1889-1983). Presbyterian* clergyman, missionary, ecumenist and educator. In 1916, as a missionary to Peru, Mackay founded the Anglo-Peruvian College and served as its principal (1916-1925). Later he served the YMCA* in South America (1925-1932), was a central figure in founding the World Council of Churches* (1948) and served as president of Princeton Theological Seminary* (1936-1959). At Princeton he was able to restore stability to a faculty that had recently undergone a struggle over fundamentalism* and the departure of the conservative element that formed Westminster Theological Seminary in 1929.

Mackie (Macky), Josias (John) (?-1716). Presbyterian* missionary in Virginia. One of the first Presbyterian ministers to come to America, Mackie was at work in Virginia by at least 1692. He was pastor of struggling dissenting churches along the Elizabeth River in Norfolk and Princess Anne Counties. He was probably the successor of Francis Makemie.*

Madison, James (1749-1812). First Protestant Episcopal* bishop of Virginia. Cousin to the future U.S. president of the same name, Madison during the Revolution* became president of William and Mary, a position he held until his death. His involvement in ecclesiastical business waned after 1800.

Madonna. Artistic representation of the mother Mary with her child Jesus, primarily through painting, sculpture, stained glass and medals. The Madonna theme responds to a yearning of some Christian believers for symbolic expression of sublime Christian truths that almost defy statement.

Magisterium. In the widest sense, the teaching authority of the whole church. In the Roman Catholic Church* since the nineteenth century, *magisterium* applies to the authority* of the pope and the college of bishops to teach on matters of faith and morals. Teaching authority is exercised (1) as doctrine* infallibly proclaimed and (2) as authoritative (noninfallible) teaching.

Magnalia Christi Americana. A history of the churches of New England written by Cotton Mather.* Mather, then minister of the Second Church (Old North), Boston, started to write the *Magna-*

lia in 1693 and had largely completed it by 1697. It was published in London in 1702. It remains one of the most valuable resources for New England's civil and ecclesiastical history.

Mahan, Asa (1799-1889). First president of Oberlin College.* Mahan accepted the presidency of Oberlin (1835-1850) on the condition that the school be integrated. He continually advocated a realistic equity for women and African-Americans at Oberlin, an attainable Christian perfection* and Scottish Common Sense* philosophy. Mahan's tactlessness and some faculty and community dissent led to his resignation. He became president of Cleveland University and later Adrian College.

Maier, Walter Arthur (1893-1950). Pioneer Lutheran* radio preacher. Ordained* by the Lutheran Church—Missouri Synod* in 1917, Maier taught Old Testament at Concordia Seminary beginning in 1922.

From 1935 until his death he was the regular speaker on *The Lutheran Hour.* This program eventually became the world's largest radio broadcast venture of its time, being aired on over 1,200 stations worldwide in thirty-six languages, with an estimated annual audience of some 700 million. Maier's messages were often characterized by denunciations of modernism,* communism and moral laxity.

Mainline Churches. The use of the term *mainline* to refer to churches appears to have emerged in the youth counterculture of the 1960s and from there passed into widespread usage by journalists, social analysts and church historians in the 1970s.

Today, it is not always clear what is meant by the phrase *mainline churches.* For some it means only those churches or denominations* most closely associated with tradition and convention, that is, the unofficial Protestant establishment (i.e., Congregationalists,* Presbyterians* and Episcopalians*). To these may be added the less traditional denominations, such as Baptists,* Methodists* and Disciples,* who in the nineteenth and twentieth centuries eventually found acceptance in socially prominent communities. More recently, a broader definition has included Roman Catholics* and Jewish congregations.

Many denominational leaders, as well as large segments of the clergy and laity in the older, generally acknowledged mainline denominations, have stood in a tradition largely shaped by theological liberalism.* They are noted for their ecumenism,* their philosophy of Christian nurture* and their interest in community, national and international affairs. Other churches, not defining themselves as mainline, have stressed the doctrine of personal salvation,* along with church growth* through personal evangelism.* The declining membership of most contemporary mainline churches has been credited to the lack of a clearly defined gospel and active personal witness.

With the rise of political conservatism in the 1980s, the older mainline churches, though continuing to exist, have ceased to be a dominant factor in American society. Americans at the close of the twentieth century may be witnessing the emergence of a new class of wealthy, socially prominent, evangelical/fundamentalist* "mainline" churches.

Major, Sarah Righter (1808-1884). Brethren* preacher. As a young woman, Sarah Righter felt a strong inward call to preach. In 1834, after some opportunities in local Brethren groups, she was forbidden to preach. She married Thomas Major in 1842, and the two held joint preaching missions in Ohio and Indiana, with Thomas commonly giving Sarah the more prominent role.

Major Orders. Catholic* term for a set of offices or orders within the Sacrament* of Holy Orders. Originating in the divisions of church leadership in the early church, the Catholic Church has come to recognize bishops, priests and deacons* as "major orders," or offices. Current Roman Catholic organization and doctrine regard the ministerial priesthood, as distinguished from the priesthood of all baptized* believers, as consisting of these three sacramental orders.

Makemie, Francis (c. 1658-1708). Colonial Presbyterian* missionary to America. Makemie served or founded churches on the eastern shore of Maryland and Virginia between 1692 and 1698, with Barbados as his base. In 1699 he was licensed to preach in Virginia.

During his lifetime he was Presbyterianism's chief exponent, a defender of its faith and liberties, a founder of congregations, and the chief organizer of the first American presbytery, the Presbytery of Philadelphia (1706).

Malone, John Walter (1857-1935). Evangelical* Quaker* educator, publisher, industrialist and philanthropist.* In 1892 Malone and his wife founded the Christian Workers Training School in Cleveland, known since 1956 as Malone College, now in Canton, Ohio. His interest in missions* led him to found an American Friends mission to India (1892) and to East Africa (1901).

Manifest Destiny. First used in 1845, the term *manifest destiny* conveyed the idea that the rightful destiny of the U.S. included imperialistic expansion. The idea certainly contributed to the war with Mexico, with the more ardent exponents envisioning American dominance from pole to pole.

Native Americans felt the pressure of Manifest Destiny as much as any group. Their resistance to the westward advance by the whites placed them in the role of obstructing progress. Hence, the very harsh measures which were employed to subdue them were justified because the end result would assure the triumph of the theory.

In the 1890s God was called upon to open the doors to "foreign mission fields," using the diplomatic and military forces of the U.S. government whenever necessary (*see* Spanish-American War).

Manly, Basil, Jr. (1825-1892). Southern Baptist* educator, preacher, organizer and hymn writer. In 1859 Manly composed an "Abstract of Principles" for the newly formed Southern Baptist Seminary. His effort reflects a moderate Calvinist* approach to Baptist doctrine. Manly also joined the seminary faculty as professor of Old Testament interpretation.

Manly, Basil, Sr. (1798-1868). Baptist* pastor, educator and Confederate statesman. Manly, a gifted preacher, was the second president of the University of Alabama (1837-1855). He was a strong supporter of the secessionist cause and a leader in the formation of the Southern Baptist Convention.*

Manning, James (1738-1791). Colonial Baptist* pastor and first president of Rhode Island College. In 1765 Manning founded the college (later Brown University*) to train Baptist ministers.

Manning represented Rhode Island at the Continental Congress (1785-1786) and was influential in the ratification of the constitution of the new nation.

Mardi Gras. A winter celebration marking the approach of Lent,* especially popular in New Orleans, Louisiana. Celebrated the Tuesday before Ash Wednesday,* the first day of Lent, a period of preparation for Easter,* *Mardi Gras* (French for "fat Tuesday") also designates the entire period between Epiphany* and Ash Wednesday.

Mardi Gras is usually associated with the vigorous celebrating in New Orleans and among the Cajuns in Southwest Louisiana.

Marechal, Ambrose (1764-1829). Third archbishop of Baltimore. In 1817 Marechal succeeded Leonard Neale as archbishop of Baltimore, with an ecclesiastical province encompassing the entire country.

Various problems made Marechal's tenure a stormy one. There were conflicts with the Jesuits* over Maryland property and ethnic tensions between French priests and Irish immigrants.* The archbishop concluded that one of the most pressing needs of the young American church was a native-born clergy.

Marian Devotions. Mary is honored among Roman Catholics* not only in the liturgy,* the church's official prayer,* but also in extraliturgical devotional* practices of individuals and groups. As forms of Christian worship,* Catholics believe that Marian devotions derive their origin and effectiveness from Christ, find complete expression in Christ and lead to the Father—through Christ and in the Spirit. Popular devotion to Mary has taken on many forms. The best-known form is the rosary,* a gospel-inspired meditation on central salvific events in Christ's life. Notable among other Marian devotions are novenas.*

Mariology. In post-Reformation Roman Catholic* theology,* Mariology emerged as the systematic study of Mary and, more precisely, as that part of theology treating her uniqueness. Today a preferable term is *theology of Mary*, which still highlights reflection on what Catholics understand to be her unique person, but always in light of the life, death and resurrection of her Son.

At the Council of Ephesus (431), the application to Mary of the title *theotokos* ("God-bearer") both underscored Christ's divinity and accentuated Mary's distinctiveness. In the Middle Ages, where Jesus was viewed as a stern and remote judge, Mary's role as a humane, approachable advocate of mercy came to the fore. The Reformers honored Mary precisely as a model of faith; but they expressed disgust with Marian devotional* practices, which they perceived as abuses.

Succeeding centuries brought intensification of Marian devotion among Catholics, with two long-standing Marian teachings ultimately being promulgated as dogmas: the Immaculate Conception* (1854) and the Assumption* (1950). Renewal in Catholic theology of the early twentieth century contributed to the Second Vatican Council's* finely balanced consideration of Mary, who stands in solidarity both with Christ and with his people.

See also MARIAN DEVOTIONS.

Marney, Carlyle (1916-1978). Southern Baptist* pastor. Marney was recognized as one of the great preachers of his day and was much in demand as a lecturer and conference speaker. Moving freely in wider ecumenical* circles, he exerted a great influence on progressive pastors within the Southern Baptist Convention, in spite of his becoming increasingly alienated from the denominational* hierarchy.

Maronite Catholics. Eastern Rite* Catholics* with origins in northern Syria. The Maronite Church traces its origins to the fourth century and to the monk Maron (d. 423). Centuries later, a community of Maronites developed in northern Syria, and persecution then led to their seeking refuge in the mountains of Lebanon.

The Diocese* of St. Maron (Brooklyn) includes many Maronites who have fled the political and economic turmoil in the Middle East.

Marquette, Jacques (1637-1675). Jesuit* missionary and explorer. As a missionary to New France from 1666, Marquette quickly became fluent in six Native American languages. He planted missions to the Algonquins (1668) and later also to the Ottawans, Hurons and Illinois. Marquette accompanied Louis Joliet* on the expedition that discovered the Mississippi River.

Popularized as a pioneer explorer, Marquette was a man of simple piety* who devoted his life to the evangelization and spiritual welfare of the Native Americans.

Marriage and Divorce. The Christian concept of marriage is not monolithic, though many Christians would agree that it is a relationship ordained by God from the creation, in which a man and a woman leave their parents to join in exclusive, monogamous union in order to carry out the will of the Creator (Gen 2:18). This union is for life—that is, until the death of one of the marriage partners dissolves the union, in which case most Christians would regard remarriage of the surviving partner as permissible. Theologically speaking, the role of marriage in the church is given special prominence, being given the status of a sacrament* or an ordinance.*

The New England Puritans,* who made up the first significant movement of European families to the New World, brought a Reformed* view of marriage with them. They thus set a strong cultural tradition in which marriage came to be regarded as both a civil and a Christian ordinance or sacrament.

With the rise of industrialization and urbanization in the late nineteenth century, women increasingly moved out of the home to participate in the work force and movements for social reform. Traditional family structures were inevitably altered, and male authority within the family was weakened. Marriage has increasingly become an egalitarian and voluntary relationship; with the relaxing of civil laws, divorce has become an acceptable alternative to continuing a relationship that no longer satisfies either or both parties.

The issue of divorce has taken a prominent place in church life. The sharp rise in the divorce rate among Americans, both churched and unchurched, has forced Christians to reexamine Scripture and tradition in order to understand the legitimate grounds for divorce and remarriage, and for the acceptance of divorced—and divorced and remarried—men and women into the church and its leadership.

Marsh, James (1794-1842). Congregational* educator. Marsh was president (1826-1833) of the University of Vermont, where he later served as professor of moral and intellectual philosophy (1833-1842). In Vermont, Marsh encountered the "new measures"* revivalism* of the Second Great Awakening* and became a strident critic of emotional excess in religious experience.* He sought to balance intense personal experience with the "deliberative aspects of religion."

Marshall, Andrew (?-1856). African-American Baptist* minister. Marshall succeeded his uncle, Andrew Bryan,* to the pulpit* of the First African Church in Savannah, Georgia (1813-1856), where

he developed a powerful and popular ministry. Marshall became a prosperous man and an astute leader among Southern African-American Baptists.

Marshall, Catherine Wood (1914-1983). Inspirational writer. In 1936 Catherine married Peter Marshall,* who became chaplain* of the U.S. Senate. When Peter died suddenly in 1949, Catherine published his sermons and prayers as *Mr. Jones, Meet the Master,* which became an instant bestseller.

In 1959 she married Leonard E. LeSourd, editor of *Guideposts* magazine, and became an editor of the magazine herself in 1961.

Marshall, Daniel (1706-1784). Separate Baptist* preacher and revivalist,* organizer of the first Baptist church in Georgia. In 1754 in Virginia, Marshall founded a Baptist church, where he was baptized and licensed to preach. He preached throughout southern Virginia and North Carolina and eventually established the first Baptist church in Kiokee, Georgia, in 1772. In 1784 Marshall moderated the first meeting of the Georgia Baptist Association, consisting of six churches.

Marshall, Peter (1902-1949). Presbyterian* minister, chaplain* of the U.S. Senate. In 1937 Marshall became pastor of the New York Avenue Presbyterian Church in Washington, D.C. With a growing reputation as a fine preacher, in 1947 he was elected chaplain of the U.S. Senate and soon became widely known for his brief and memorable prayers. His wife, Catherine Wood Marshall,* authored his bestselling biography, *A Man Called Peter* (1951).

Martin, T(homas) T(heodore) (1862-1939). Southern Baptist* evangelist. Martin was one of the most popular and influential Southern Baptist evangelists in the first third of the twentieth century. His full-time evangelistic ministry began in 1900, with most of his meetings held in secondhand Barnum and Bailey circus tents.

A strong fundamentalist* and antievolutionist (*see* Darwinian Evolution), Martin was a friend of William Jennings Bryan* and attended the Scopes Trial* in 1925.

Marty, Martin (1834-1896). Benedictine* abbot and missionary bishop. Marty was made bishop in South Dakota (1889) and Minnesota

(1895). He was by turn a charismatic religious superior, a church historian, a theologian and an innovative frontier bishop. As both pastor and political spokesperson, he tirelessly championed the cause of the Native American.

Maryknoll Missioners. *See* CATHOLIC FOREIGN MISSION SOCIETY OF AMERICA.

Mason, C(harles) H(arrison) (1866-1961). African-American Pentecostal* minister and founder of the Church of God in Christ. In 1895 Mason met Charles Price Jones,* with whom he conducted Holiness* conventions and formed a loose network of sympathetic congregations called the Church of God in Christ (*see* Churches of God).

After spending time at Azusa Street* in 1907, Mason became convinced that tongues* speech should evidence Spirit baptism. Jones disapproved of Mason's Pentecostal views, and the two parted company, with a majority of their followers supporting Mason. Mason retained the name *Church of God in Christ* and presided as bishop over a thriving constituency until his death in 1961. Mason was widely acclaimed within Pentecostalism for his spirituality.*

Mason, John Mitchell (1770-1829). Associate Reformed* minister and educator. In 1805 Mason established a biblical and theological school for training pastors of the Associate Reformed Synod, which was the prototype for the American seminary. He was its sole professor through its closing in 1821. Concurrently, he was a trustee and later provost (1811-1816) of Columbia College. He elevated its academic standards, enhanced its financial position, helped acquire the property for its present campus, and taught classics and apologetics.*

Mason, Lowell (1792-1872). Music educator, hymn writer and composer. In 1827 Mason became president of Boston's Handel and Haydn Society and published extensively. Following study in Europe, he returned to bring experimental music education to Boston schools, eventually influencing the entire city and all of the eastern U.S. His hymns include "When I Survey the Wondrous Cross" and "Nearer My God to Thee."

Mass, The. A term reflecting the Roman Catholic* understanding of the Eucharist,* or Lord's Supper, the Mass is the sacramental* thanksgiving at the heart of the church's existence, the memorial of Jesus' leave-taking and the sacrifice of Calvary.

The Mass especially has served as a memorial of Jesus' self-gift on the cross, through which God has redeemed humankind. Believers were to unite themselves with this self-gift, not as though the Mass were redoing the sacrifice of Calvary, but as though it bore on their present lives, as though they had become contemporary with it.

The traditional Catholic understanding of the consecration, as expressed at the Council of Trent, describes what happens in terms of transubstantiation:* while the elements—the loaf or wafer and the liquid in the chalice—remain bread and wine in appearance, their significance and ultimate being now are those of Christ, of whom believers partake in eating and drinking them. Modern Catholic theology* has stressed the shift in meaning and downplayed suggestions of the miraculous or magical.

See also LITURGY.

Mass Evangelism. The act of proclaiming the gospel to a large audience with the intention of converting large numbers of people. A mass evangelist is usually an itinerant* or visiting speaker who specializes in evangelistic ministry,* is gifted in expressing the gospel message in the language of the people and holds a series of meetings in one location before moving on. Mass evangelism, or "crusade evangelism," is a part of the broader Protestant* religious phenomenon known as revivalism.*

The phenomenon began in America with the Great Awakening* and the itinerant ministry of George Whitefield.* The next outstanding leader and innovator in mass evangelism was the nineteenth-century revivalist Charles Finney.* Other outstanding mass evangelists in American history have been Dwight L. Moody,* R. A. Torrey,* Billy Sunday* and Billy Graham.*

See also BILLY GRAHAM EVANGELISTIC ASSOCIATION.

Massachusetts Proposals. An attempt by Massachusetts clergy to revise Congregational* church government.* Written by Cotton Mather* in 1705, the proposals aimed to strengthen the authority* of ministers.* Though they were never implemented in Massachusetts, they did serve as the basis for the Saybrook Platform* in Connecticut.

Massanet, Damiàn (c. 1660-c. 1710). Franciscan* missionary to Texas. Arriving in Mexico in 1683, Massanet joined Alonso de Len's 1689 expedition to Texas. A Texas Indian chief requested Spanish missionaries, so in 1690 Massanet and three Franciscans built the first Spanish mission* in Texas.

Massee, J(asper) C(ortenus) (1871-1965). Baptist* pastor and evangelist. After several pastorates throughout the South and East, Massee served at Tremont Temple in Boston (1922-1929), where he witnessed a growth of almost 2,500 members. He later entered a Bible conference* and evangelistic ministry.

From 1920 to 1925 Massee was president of the Fundamentalist Fellowship* within the Northern Baptist Convention.

Masters, Victor Irvine (1867-1954). Southern Baptist* editor. From 1905 to 1942 Masters edited various Southern religious publications, including Kentucky's *Western Recorder* (1921-1942).

Throughout his editorial career, Masters was especially concerned about the socioeconomic and religious implications of the Catholic* presence, as well as the influx of immigrant* groups into America. In his editorials Masters warned Southern Baptists about the dangers of liberal* theology and the bureaucratization of their denomination.*

Mateer, Calvin Wilson (1836-1908). Pioneer Presbyterian* missionary to China. Sailing to China in 1863, Mateer spent his entire career in Shantung Province, North China, especially at Tengchow, where in the 1860s he established a boys' school which eventually became one of the best Christian colleges in nineteenth-century China.

Mather, Cotton (1663-1728). Puritan* minister and theologian. The son of Increase Mather,* Cotton was descended from a distinguished line of Puritan ministers and was exceptionally precocious, graduating from Harvard College* in 1678. He was pastor of the Second Church (Old North) in Boston from 1683 until his death.

Mather wrote on a vast array of subjects, ultimately publishing an incredible 469 works.

As a descendant of both the Mather and the Cotton families, Cotton Mather to some degree considered himself the preserver of a "priesthood" of New England pastoral leaders. Both his contemporaries and many historians have considered him to be overly pious, priggish and artificial at various junctures in his life. However, we are indebted to him for excellent insights on life in New England during the late seventeenth and early eighteenth centuries. He was a defender of the old ways of New England, but he nevertheless realized that New England was inevitably changing.

Mather, Increase (1639-1723). Puritan* minister, theologian and president of Harvard College.* The son of Richard Mather,* Increase was a delegate to the Half-Way Synod of 1662 (*see* Cambridge Platform), and in 1664 he became the teacher of the Second Church (Old North), Boston, where he remained until his death. He was elected president of Harvard in 1685 but was forced to resign in 1701.

Mather wrote 130 books and pamphlets covering a variety of subjects. He was a diligent opponent of Solomon Stoddard's* more liberal ways in western Massachusetts and was a defender of the older Congregational* way.

Increase married Maria Cotton, daughter of the distinguished John Cotton.* Their son, Cotton Mather,* carried on the family name as a distinguished Puritan leader in Boston.

Mather, Richard (1596-1669). Puritan* minister and defender of the congregational* form of church government. Immigrating to Boston in 1635, Mather in 1636 helped found the church of Dorchester, Massachusetts, where he was pastor until his death.

Mather is best known for his defense of the congregational form of government in the 1640s, being the main source of the Cambridge Platform* (1648).

Mather, Samuel (1706-1785). Congregational* minister. The son of Cotton Mather,* Samuel Mather was the last of the Mather family to occupy a Boston pulpit. He was pastor of the Second Congregational Church (1733-1741) and of the Tenth Congregational Society of Boston (1741-1785).

Mathews, Shailer (1863-1941). Baptist* educator, ecumenist* and spokesman for theological modernism.* Mathews taught at the University of Chicago Divinity School* (1894-1933), where he also was dean (1908-1933).

Mathews's *Faith of Modernism* (1924) was American liberalism's most widely read book in the 1920s. His starting point was "inherited orthodoxy,"* which, he believed, needed occasional, and even radical, restatement according to the latest scientific, historical and social standards.

See also CHICAGO SCHOOL OF THEOLOGY.

Matthews, Mark Allison (1867-1940). Fundamentalist* Presbyterian* minister and civic reformer. A Calvinist* premillennialist,* Matthews in 1917 founded the Bible Institute of Seattle. He founded the first church-owned and church-operated radio station in the country (KTW) and led in the founding of a major hospital. His pulpit pronouncements on social issues were wide ranging.

Matthews's Seattle congregation grew to become the largest Presbyterian church in the country (nine thousand members). Matthews combined in himself a personal pulpit flair, strong executive ability and a fundamentalist theology.

Mattson, Alvin Daniel (1895-1970). Lutheran* pastor and theologian. From 1932 until his retirement in 1967, Mattson was professor of Christian ethics at Augustana Seminary in Rock Island, Illinois. Mattson remained essentially orthodox* in his theology and became a strong advocate of the social application of the gospel.

Maundy Thursday. The designation given to the Thursday before Easter,* marked by special observances during Holy Week in many Christian traditions. The name is taken from the Latin words *mandatum novum* ("a new command") in John 13:34.

Maurin, Peter (Pierre Aristide) (1877-1949). Sidewalk philosopher and cofounder of the Catholic Worker movement.* Shortly before the Depression, Maurin underwent a conversion to Catholicism.* He now took no wages for his labor, only donations, and began to synthesize the writings of Catholic theologians, novelists and other thinkers into a program of radical change which he called the green revolution.

In 1932 he sought out Dorothy Day,* who was gradually won over to his program of radicalism based on an idealized view of medieval society. Together they founded the Catholic Worker.

Maxwell, L(eslie) E(arl) (1895-1984). Founder of Prairie Bible Institute. In 1922 Maxwell answered a call for help from some farmers on the Alberta prairie. These men wanted Bible instruction for themselves and their families, and Maxwell headed north to get a Bible school* founded. He stayed for the next sixty-two years, seeing Prairie Bible Institute in Three Hills, Alberta, become one of the largest and most influential Bible schools in the world.

Mayflower Compact. A civil compact signed in 1620 by Puritan* separatists* who were founding the Plymouth Colony in New England. It upholds total allegiance to King James I of Great Britain and acknowledges before God that the community has the right to enact laws and that the people must obey them.

Mayhew, Jonathan (1720-1766). Congregational* minister. Mayhew was descended from a family renowned for its Calvinist* missionary work among the Nantucket and Martha's Vineyard Indians. His Harvard* education, however, disposed him to favor Unitarian* and Arminian* views. In 1763-1764 he strenuously attacked Anglican* missionary efforts in New England.

His political Whiggism united with his Unitarianism to place him securely in the mainstream of eighteenth-century Dissenter opposition to centralized government and religious authority.

Mayhew, Thomas (c. 1620-1657). Congregational* missionary. Son of the original patentee and governor of Martha's Vineyard, Mayhew was ordained* pastor of the small English Puritan* congregation there in 1642. Quickly mastering the local Indian dialect, he began quietly evangelizing* individual Native Americans on the Vineyard in 1644 and set up a school in 1652.

Mays, Benjamin Elijah (1894-1984). African-American Baptist* minister, educator and racial leader. From 1934 to 1940 Mays was dean of Howard University School of Religion, and until 1967 president of Morehouse College. Mays, chairman of the Atlanta Board of Education (1970-1982), was an important influence on Martin Luther King Jr.*

Mazzuchelli, Samuel (1806-1864). Dominican* missionary to mid-America. One of the earliest Italian immigrants to the U.S., Samuel Mazzuchelli of Milano arrived in 1828 to answer the call for frontier missionaries. From 1830 to 1836 he traveled through the wilderness to reach Native Americans, fur traders and soldiers who guarded the American forts from Sault Ste. Marie to the Mississippi River. From 1836 to 1844 Mazzuchelli was assigned to the Upper Mississippi Valley, where he built Christian communities through preaching* and sacramental* ministry,* care of the sick and instruction.

McAlister, Robert Edward (1880-1953). Canadian Pentecostal* leader. One of the founders of the Pentecostal Assemblies of Canada* in 1919, McAlister was its first general secretary-treasurer until 1937 and the founding editor (1920-1937) of *The Pentecostal Testimony,* the denomination's official organ.

McAuley, Jeremiah (1839-1884). Evangelist and founder of New York's Water Street Mission.* While in prison, McAuley was converted* to faith in Christ. In 1872, eight years after his release, he founded the Helping Hand for Men Mission on New York's Lower East Side, in the Bowery district. One of the first city rescue missions,* this institution, renamed Water Street Mission* in 1876, became a model for similar facilities all over urban America.

McAvoy, Thomas Timothy (1903-1969). Catholic* historian. Assigned by his religious superiors in 1929 to organize the Catholic Archives of America at the University of Notre Dame, over the next forty years he supervised the cataloging and expansion of this collection. A cofounder of *Review of Politics,* McAvoy also taught history at Notre Dame from 1933.

McClain, Alva J. (1888-1968). Brethren* educator and theologian. Involved in the founding of the Brethren's Ashland (Ohio) Theological Seminary (1930), McClain spent several years there as professor and dean. Because of his strong advocacy of fundamentalist* views, he came into conflict with the school's administration and was dismissed in June 1937. The following October, Grace Theological Seminary opened in Akron, Ohio, as another Brethren institution, with McClain as president and professor of theology. The existence of the two seminaries helped polarize the Brethren Church, resulting in a 1939 division along Grace and Ashland lines.

McCloskey, John (1810-1885). First U.S. Catholic* cardinal and archbishop of the New York archdiocese. McCloskey was instrumental in the conversion to Roman Catholicism of many prominent Americans, including James Roosevelt Bayley,* Isaac Hecker* and Clarence Walworth.* He became archbishop of New York in May 1864.

McCloskey, William George (1823-1909). First rector of the North American College, Rome, and bishop of Louisville. After nine years as rector in Rome (1859-1868), he was appointed to Louisville, beginning a career (1868-1909) marked by authoritarian rule and widespread clerical discontent.

McCollough, Walter (1915-1991). Bishop of United House of Prayer for All People. By the 1950s McCollough was a follower of the flamboyant Charles Emmanuel ("Sweet Daddy") Grace* and was rising in the leadership of Grace's United House of Prayer for All People. When Grace died in 1960, McCollough succeeded him as bishop of the African-American denomination* of several hundred congregations and some three million members. Under McCollough's leadership the church moved closer to mainstream African-American Christianity and used its financial assets to develop social programs, including inner-city housing projects.

McComb, Samuel (1864-1938). Clergyman and pastoral counselor. In 1905 McComb, who had an interest in psychology, joined Elwood Worcester* in a new effort to provide counseling to troubled individuals using a combination of contemporary psychological knowledge, a medical understanding of mental illness and liberal* Protestant* theology.*

McConnell, Francis John (1871-1953). Methodist* bishop. In 1909 McConnell became president of DePauw University, leaving that post in 1912 when he was elected bishop. As bishop, he presided in Denver, Pittsburgh and New York (1912-1944). McConnell was active in ecumenical* affairs and was president of the Federal Council of Churches* (1928-1932). He also was president of the Methodist Federation for Social Service.

McCord, James I. (1919-1990). Presbyterian* minister, theological educator and ecumenical* leader. In 1959 McCord became president of Princeton Theological Seminary* following several years (1952-1959) as dean and professor of systematic theology* at Austin Seminary. His presidency at Princeton was marked by a substantial building of the seminary's endowment, library, faculty and student body. His concern for theology led to his founding the Center of Theological Inquiry in Princeton, an institution to which he devoted himself after retirement from the seminary in 1983. McCord was deeply involved in the ecumenical movement and was president of the World Alliance of Reformed Churches* from 1977 to 1982. In 1986 he received the Templeton Prize for Progress in Religion.

McCorkle, Samuel Eusebius (1746-1811). Presbyterian* minister and educator. As a trustee at the young University of North Carolina, McCorkle tried unsuccessfully to mold that school in the likeness of John Witherspoon's* College of New Jersey.* In the 1790s he published doctrinal works on deism,* Communion,* sabbath* observance, sacrificing and charity in order to raise funds for the university.

McCormick, Cyrus Hall (1809-1884). Presbyterian* philanthropist.* In 1831 McCormick invented the mechanical reaper, a machine which revolutionized farming in the American plains. A devout Old School* Presbyterian layman, McCormick used his wealth to fund educational enterprises, influencing Presbyterianism in both the North and South.

McCosh, James (1811-1894). Presbyterian* minister, philosopher and college president. Widely regarded as the last major voice of the philosophical realism of the Scottish Enlightenment, McCosh attempted throughout his diversified career as pastor, professor and educator to fuse the best modern thinking with a lively evangelical* faith.

McCosh's impact upon American Christianity became more direct after 1868, when he was appointed president of the College of New Jersey.* During his two-decade tenure (1868-1888) at Princeton,* he helped transform a fledgling, parochial college into a national university.

McCracken, Robert J(ames) (1904-1973). Baptist* preacher. After teaching theology and philosophy in Canada (1938-1946), McCracken succeeded Harry Emerson Fosdick* as minister of the Riverside Church, New York City, where he preached from 1946 to 1967. As a preacher, McCracken brought to the American pulpit the gift of classic Scottish oratory combined with an emphasis on the biblical text.

McCulloch, Thomas (1776-1843). Canadian Presbyterian* minister, educator and writer. In 1816 McCulloch established Pictou (Nova Scotia) Academy, soon recognized as one of the finest schools in British North America. A preeminent teacher, he was appointed the first principal of Dalhousie College in 1838.

McDaniel, George White (1875-1927). Southern Baptist* preacher and denominational* leader. McDaniel was president of the Southern Baptist Convention and the Baptist General Association of Virginia. In 1926 the Southern Baptist Convention approved the "McDaniel Statement," which repudiated the theory of evolution.*

McGarvey, John William (1829-1911). Church of Christ* minister and educator. In 1865 McGarvey became one of the founding faculty members of the College of the Bible in Lexington, Kentucky, serving as president from 1895 until his death.

When the teachings of higher criticism began to move into the Christian Churches, he used all the power of his teaching and writing to counter them. He wrote a number of significant books on biblical interpretation* as well as a weekly column on the topic.

McGary, Austin (1846-1928). Church of Christ* preacher and editor. McGary championed the position that baptism* is for remission of sins, which individuals being baptized must understand at the time or else the action is not valid. His major editorial opponent was David Lipscomb.*

McGavran, Donald A. (1897-1990). Founder of the church growth movement.* McGavran served as a missionary in India (1923-1954), where he studied the factors which led to church growth. He began to recommend a style of evangelism* which used the natural familial and social "bridges" existing within the cultural networks of each society.

In 1961 he established the Institute of Church Growth in Eugene, Oregon, and in 1965 he became the founding dean of the School of World Mission and Institute of Church Growth at Fuller Theological Seminary.*

McGee, J(ohn) Vernon (1904-1988). Radio evangelist. After serving Presbyterian* churches in the South and in California, McGee in 1949 became the pastor of an interdenominational congregation in Los Angeles. To increase church attendance, he began the widely received radio program *Through the Bible,* teaching the books of the Bible consecutively.

McGiffert, Arthur Cushman, Jr. (1892-1993). Congregational* theologian. Son of the well-known church historian Arthur C. McGiffert Sr.,* McGiffert spent several years in the pastorate (1920-1926) before becoming professor of theology at Chicago Theological Seminary (1926-1939). He was president of the Pacific School of Theology, Berkeley, California (1939-1945), and then president of Chicago Theological Seminary (1946-1958). McGiffert was instrumental in forming the Committee on American Principles and Fair Play to assist Japanese-Americans interned in U.S. camps during World War II. Among his published works are *Jonathan Edwards* (1932) and *Young Emerson Speaks* (1938).

McGiffert, Arthur Cushman, Sr. (1861-1933). Congregational* church historian and educator. In 1893 McGiffert succeeded Philip Schaff* at Union Theological Seminary,* New York. Denominational heresy* charges following publication of *A History of Christianity in the Apostolic Age* (1897) led McGiffert from the Presbyterians* to the Congregationalists in 1900.

McGiffert was president of Union Seminary from 1917 until 1926. His prominent position at Union Seminary enhanced his position as one of America's foremost advocates of theological liberalism.

McGlynn, Edward (1837-1900). Catholic* priest and social reformer. In 1866 McGlynn was appointed pastor of St. Stephen's, a working-class parish in New York City that included many who were poor, unskilled and unemployed. His ministry influenced him to become a well-known advocate of social and economic reform. He established an orphanage that cared for over five hundred children.

In 1870 he created a sensation when he attacked public aid to all religious institutions as a violation of the separation of church and state.*

McGready, James (c. 1758-1817). Presbyterian* revivalist* and father of the frontier camp meeting.* In North Carolina, McGready preached the wrath of God so vigorously that he ignited revival fires which drove penitents to faith in Jesus.

In 1796 he moved to southwestern Kentucky, preaching to three small congregations at Red River, Gasper River and Muddy River. In July 1800 McGready helped shape the course of American history. After an original revival at Red River, he decided to send out advance notice of the next Communion* service at the Gasper River church. When the word spread through the settlements, scores of pioneers headed in wagons and on horseback for Gasper River, expecting to witness the work of God. This was probably the first camp meeting in American history.

McGuffey, William Holmes (1800-1873). Professor of moral philosophy and author of readers for elementary schools. McGuffey, a licensed* Presbyterian* preacher, was president of Cincinnati College (1836-1839) and Ohio University, Athens (1839-1843).

McGuffey was best known as author of the Eclectic Readers. Published in six books from 1836 to 1857, they sold an astronomical 122 million copies and helped shape the nineteenth-century American mind. These books included simple moral exhortations to industry, honesty and loyalty, as well as warnings against strong drink and exhortations on sabbath keeping.

McGuire, George Alexander (1866-1934). Founder of the African Orthodox Church. By 1920 McGuire was active in Marcus Garvey's* United Negro Improvement Association. After a brief affiliation with the Reformed Episcopal Church,* McGuire decided to found a new denomination,* the African Orthodox Church, an all-black body with a polity* and ritual similar to Episcopalianism.

McIlvaine, Charles Pettit (1799-1873). Episcopal* bishop of Ohio. From 1820 to 1824 McIlvaine was rector of Christ Church, Georgetown, Washington, D.C. In 1824 John C. Calhoun, the secretary of war and an attendant at Christ Church, appointed McIlvaine chaplain* and professor of ethics at West Point, where under his leadership a revival* broke out. In 1832 he was consecrated the second bishop of Ohio, where he was president of Kenyon College and its theological seminary.

During his episcopate he was the leader of the evangelical* party in the Episcopal Church and an opponent of the Oxford movement (see Tractarianism).

McKelway, Alexander Jeffrey (1866-1918). Southern Presbyterian* progressive and political activist. As editor (1898-1905) of the *Presbyterian Standard,* McKelway developed an interest in social justice issues, particularly child labor reform. In 1909 he became a lobbyist for the National Child Labor Committee. He strongly supported Wilson* in the presidential campaigns of 1912 and 1916.

McKelway was one of the few Southern churchmen whose concerns matched those of the Social Gospel* advocates of the North.

McKendree, William (1757-1835). First American-born bishop in the Methodist* Episcopal Church and father of western Methodism. In 1801 McKendree moved to the Kentucky District of the newly formed Western Conference, where he did pioneer work, combining extraordinary gifts of lively preaching and solid administration. McKendree, in effect, domesticated the high enthusiasm of the frontier camp meeting* and harnessed it to the establishment of churches, circuits and districts throughout the conference.

In 1808 McKendree, commonly called the greatest successor of Francis Asbury,* became the third elected bishop for American Methodism.

McKinley, William (1843-1901). Methodist* churchman, lawyer and twenty-fifth U.S. president. McKinley served in the U.S. House of Representatives (1877-1883 and 1885-1891), where he became a powerful Republican leader and a national figure. With Marcus A. Hanna as his chief adviser, the popular McKinley successfully campaigned first for governor of Ohio (1891 and 1893) and later for president of the U.S. (1896 and 1900).

The strengthening and expansion of presidential power so characteristic of the twentieth century began during McKinley's presidency (1897-

1901). More important, he presided over the swift and decisive U.S. victory in the Spanish-American War* (1898).

McKinley's evangelical Christian faith undergirded his political philosophy and provided him with his basic worldview. His personal devoutness, his tender and patient care of his chronically invalid, epileptic wife, his public forgiveness of his assassin (a crazed anarchist named Leon Czolgosz), and the dignity of his lingering death made McKinley extremely popular among churchgoing Americans.

McLaurin, John Bates (1884-1952). Canadian Baptist* missionary. McLaurin was accepted in 1909 as a missionary in South India. There he exercised a remarkably effective ministry among Telugu-speaking people. McLaurin was one of Canada's best-known missionaries of the first half of the twentieth century.

McMaster, James Alphonsus (1820-1886). Catholic* editor and controversialist. After studying for the Episcopal* priesthood, McMaster eventually converted to Roman Catholicism. During the Civil War,* the paper he edited was banned by the U.S. postmaster as treasonable and seditious. His defense of the rights of American Catholic pastors earned him the opposition of many American bishops.*

McMaster, William (1811-1887). Canadian Baptist* philanthropist.* After immigrating to Canada from Ireland in 1833, McMaster became one of the wealthiest men in Toronto. He helped found Woodstock College, the first Baptist college in Ontario in 1860, and was even more involved in moving the theological department to Toronto in 1881. In 1887 the whole institution moved to Toronto and became McMaster University.

McNicholas, John Timothy (1877-1950). Catholic* archbishop of Cincinnati. In 1908 McNicholas was appointed to the head of the Holy Name Societies* and traveled extensively, building up the organization around the nation.

In 1925 he succeeded Archbishop Henry Moeller as the archbishop of Cincinnati. In his twenty-five-year administration, McNicholas was especially interested in promoting Catholic education on every level and served as president-general of the National Catholic Education Association (1946-1950).

McNicol, John (1869-1956). Canadian Christian educator. In 1902 McNicol began teaching at Toronto Bible Training School (later known as Ontario Bible College) and served as its principal from 1906 to 1946. He developed a remarkably broad-based support constituency for the institution.

McPherson, Aimee Semple (1890-1944). Pentecostal* evangelist and founder of the International Church of the Foursquare Gospel.* In 1908 McPherson embraced Pentecostalism and married Robert James Semple. After brief missionary service in China in 1910, Robert died. Early in 1911 Aimee returned to the U.S., and in February 1912 she married Harold McPherson.

Restless in the confines of her marriage and home, McPherson rediscovered her call to preach.* In 1915 she left her husband and for many years entered the world of itinerant* evangelism, in which she promulgated Pentecostal doctrine and practiced faith healing.* On January 1, 1923, she opened Angelus Temple, a five-thousand-seat church in Los Angeles. She dedicated it as the Church of the Foursquare Gospel. Her other ministries eventually included a radio station and a Bible institute.*

At the time of her death, her denomination* had some six hundred churches in the world, with a membership of twenty-two thousand. Her Bible institute had trained over three thousand pastors, missionaries and evangelists, many of whom were women.

McQuaid, Bernard John (1823-1909). Bishop of Rochester, educator. In the new Diocese* of Newark, McQuaid was the founding president of Seton Hall College and Seminary (1856). As bishop of Rochester, New York (1868-1909), he established sixty-nine parishes* and several welfare institutions.

Imaginative and forceful, McQuaid, as a progressive conservative, exercised a moderating influence on the American church of his day.

McQuilkin, Robert Crawford (1886-1952). President of Columbia Bible College and Bible conference* speaker. McQuilkin was one of the initiators of the Victorious Life Conferences (1913-1923; see Keswick Movement). McQuilkin became founding president of Columbia Bible School (1923-1952). Efforts to improve evangelical* education resulted in the Evangelical Teacher Training Association, with McQuilkin as president (1931-1941).

McQuilkin's role in promoting Victorious Life* teachings had a significant effect in shaping the spirituality* of a large sector of fundamentalism* and evangelicalism.

McTyeire, Holland Nimmons (1824-1889). Methodist* bishop and founding president of Vanderbilt University. After the Civil War* McTyeire was instrumental in reorganizing the Methodist Episcopal Church, South.

Through a family connection, McTyeire in 1873 persuaded Cornelius Vanderbilt to give $500,000 to create a university in Nashville aimed at healing sectional differences. McTyeire was president of the fledgling university until his death.

Meacham, Joseph (1741-1796). Shaker* leader. Meacham, an eloquent New Light* lay preacher, in 1780 embraced Mother Ann Lee's* message. Shortly after Lee's death, Meacham assumed leadership of the sect and promoted its expansion. Before his death, eleven other Shaker settlements had appeared.

Meade, William (1789-1862). Episcopal* bishop. Entering the ministry of the Episcopal Church in Virginia at the low point of its existence in 1811, Meade devoted his life to the revival of the church of his forefathers. A Spartan, circuit-riding,* missionary*-minded Episcopal evangelical* who was at once thoroughly Protestant* and loyally Anglican,* Meade placed a stamp that persists today on the Episcopal churches of Virginia.

Mears, Henrietta Cornella (1890-1963). Presbyterian* Bible teacher and pioneer in Christian education.* In 1928 Mears become director of Christian education at the Hollywood (Calif.) Presbyterian Church. Under her leadership the church's entire Sunday school* grew from 450 to more than 4,000 in less than three years. A highly respected Bible teacher, Mears had a powerful impact on college-age young men and is said to have encouraged about five hundred men to enter the ministry.

Meckelenburg, Jan van (Megapolensis, Johannes) (1603-1669). Dutch Reformed* Church cleric in New Netherland. In 1642 Meckelenburg and his family moved to present-day Albany, where he struggled to build a vibrant congregation among lower-class farmers and artisans. In 1649 he accepted the pastorate of New Amsterdam. He is best known for the defense of the historic principle of "religious uniformity in a civil commonwealth."

When the English fleet of conquest arrived in 1664, Meckelenburg prevailed on the fiery Peter Stuyvesant* to surrender, thus avoiding unnecessary bloodshed.

Megapolensis, Johannes. *See* MECKELENBURG, JAN VAN.

Melchite Catholics. Eastern Rite* Catholics* arising out of the patriarchates of Alexandria, Antioch or Jerusalem. In the countryside the liturgy* was celebrated in West Syriac or Aramaic, and in the cities in Greek. With the advent of Islam, Arabic gradually replaced Syriac.

Melchite dioceses* currently exist in Newton, Massachusetts, and in São Paulo, Brazil.

Membership, Church. *See* CHURCH MEMBERSHIP.

Memorial Day (Decoration Day). A legal holiday in the U.S., first celebrated on May 30, 1868, in the North, when members of the Grand Army of the Republic decorated the graves of Union soldiers who died in the Civil War.* Since World War I* it has become a day on which the U.S. honors the dead of all its wars.

Memorial Movement. A movement in the 1850s by evangelicals* within the Protestant Episcopal Church* resisting the introduction of Anglo-Catholicism* into the church. In 1853 William A. Muhlenberg* drew up a *Memorial* calling for (1) the extension of episcopal ordination* to nonepiscopal clergy who desired it; (2) the loosening of restrictions on "opinion, discipline,* and worship";* and (3) stronger ecumenical* ties with other Protestant denominations.*

Evangelical dissatisfaction led eventually to the formation of the Reformed Episcopal Church* (1873).

Men and Religion Forward Movement. An interdenominational campaign in the 1910s with a twofold goal: personal acceptance of Jesus Christ and enlistment in the program of Jesus Christ. Reaching 1.5 million people, the campaign attempted to make religion meaningful in the lives of men and boys.

Mendicant Orders. Religious communities, mainly Catholic,* emphasizing a vow of poverty. Mendicant orders include the Franciscans,* Dominicans,* Augustinians,* Carmelites and Servites. Mendicant priests, brothers and sisters mainly engage in preaching,* teaching, nursing and social work.

Mennonite Central Committee. The major North American relief, service and development agency of the Mennonites and Brethren in Christ.* The Mennonite Central Committee (MCC) was formed in 1920 as a unified North American response to the famine in Russia. The MCC carried on a massive relief program following World War II and in Vietnam (1976). Peacemaking, following the model and teaching of Jesus, has been a dynamic behind many MCC efforts.

See also ANABAPTIST TRADITION AND VISION; MENNONITE CHURCHES.

Mennonite Church/(Old) Mennonite Church. As a North American body, the Mennonite Church, frequently called the "Old" Mennonite Church (to be distinguished from Old Order Mennonites*), goes back to colonial times and the first major Mennonite immigration to Pennsylvania in 1683. Many waves of immigrations brought Mennonites first of all to southeast Pennsylvania and then, gradually, to almost every province and state of Canada and the U.S.

Throughout the nineteenth century, members of the Mennonite Church were bilingual, with German being their main language. By about 1890 English began to displace the German. After 1890 the spirit of evangelical* revivalism* and the missionary outreach of the Western world renewed Mennonite interests in urban as well as overseas missions.* Mennonite interest in higher education also began about this time.

Today the Mennonite Church is the oldest and largest of the several organized Mennonite groups in North America, with an adult membership of over 100,000 (with approximately 10 percent of that number in Canada and 90 percent in the U.S.).

Mennonite Churches. There are twenty organized church bodies in North America in the Anabaptist* "believers' church" or "historic peace church" tradition. Neither Catholic* nor Protestant,* this radical or left wing of the sixteenth-century Reformation stressed pacifism,* separation of church and state,* church membership* of believing adults and the conviction that ethics* are an essential part of the gospel of Jesus Christ. The Anabaptist tradition has been conveyed through the Mennonites,* Amish* and Hutterites.*

The Anabaptist or Mennonite family of churches in North America constitutes a mosaic of cultural backgrounds and styles. They are named after Menno Simons (c. 1496-1561), a Dutch Anabaptist leader. Anabaptist-Mennonite teachings emphasize the church as a body of believers who make mature decisions to commit themselves as a body to the discipline of the church. Mennonites believe that the state, ordained by God to maintain order in the world, has no authority in the realm of faith. Christians are to be disciples who follow the way of Jesus as revealed in Scripture, including the commands to reject violence and the oath, and to serve humanity in humility and love. In the modern era of nationalism and militarism, Mennonite refusal of military service has replaced rebaptism as a touchstone of identity and conflict with the world.

Mennonitism in North America has a bipolar ethnic-cultural shape. The larger pole consists of groups which originated in the Swiss and South German wings of the Anabaptist movement and immigrated in small groups to America from 1683 into the nineteenth century. Organized groups with the largest numbers of Swiss-background members are the "Old" Mennonite Church* (which includes many members of Amish background), the Old Order Amish* and the Brethren in Christ.*

A second pole of Mennonite culture in America consists of groups which originated in the Dutch and North German wings of the Anabaptist movement, many coming to North America via Russia. Groups with the largest numbers of Dutch-Russian background members include the Mennonite Brethren,* the Conference of Mennonites in Canada and the General Conference Mennonite Church.*

Most Mennonites in America have made more accommodations to North American society than have the Old Order groups. In the late nineteenth and the twentieth centuries, progressive Mennonites adopted the forms of church life and activity characteristic of evangelical* Protestant denominationalism.* One stage of this development was institutional, with Mennonites establishing overseas missions, publication boards, and schools and colleges. Another stage was theological, as Mennonite leaders sought to clarify and renew belief through historical study of Anabaptism.

In recent decades progressive Mennonites have expanded their work and witness through more than sixty inter-Mennonite organizations for a wide range of cooperative activities, including mutual aid, museums, relief sales, historical projects and disaster service. The Mennonite Central Committee,* founded after World War II* for international relief and service, has had a prominent role in this ecumenical* revival.

In 1984 a Mennonite world membership summary reported that there were 340,000 members in North America, or 47 percent of the world Mennonite total of 730,000.

See also ANABAPTIST TRADITION AND VISION; CHURCH OF GOD IN CHRIST, MENNONITE; FELLOWSHIP OF EVANGELICAL BIBLE CHURCHES; GENERAL CONFERENCE OF MENNONITE BRETHREN CHURCHES OF NORTH AMERICA; MENNONITE CHURCH; OLD ORDER MENNONITES.

Mercersburg Theology. The christocentric theological system developed after about 1836 at the German Reformed* seminary in Mercersburg, Pennsylvania, under the leadership of the theologian* John Williamson Nevin* and the church historian Philip Schaff.* Utilizing insights of the philosopher/psychologist Frederick A. Rauch,* Nevin and Schaff formulated a theological system based on the Incarnation and the continuation of the life of Christ in his church. This they hoped would be a corrective to the revivalism* and sectarianism* that prevailed in mid-nineteenth-century American Christianity.

Strongly influenced by the Romanticism,* idealism and Pietism* of the mediating (or evangelical*) school of German theology, they sought to make American Christianity more historical, more organic and churchly, more sacramental,* and more ecumenical.*

Meredith, Thomas (1795-1850). Pioneer Baptist* pastor, educator and denominational* leader in North Carolina. In North Carolina in 1819, Meredith emerged as a leading voice among Baptists and was one of the founders of the Baptist State Convention of North Carolina in 1830. He helped form Wake Forest Institute (now University).

Merit. As both a theological concept and a Roman Catholic* doctrine, merit refers to a supernatural value assigned by God to a believer's good act. This reward can be an increase of grace on earth or an increase of glory in heaven. The concept evolves from an adherence to God's promise of reward for progress in Christian living (see Rom 2:1-11; 2 Tim 4:7-8), not from any belief in the inherent value of human action. Accordingly, meritorious actions must be divinely oriented and prompted, freely willed and morally good. Protestant*-Catholic differences remain in the understanding of this concept.

Merritt, Timothy (1775-1845). Methodist* Holiness* author and editor. Merritt founded and edited the first Holiness periodical in America, the *Guide to Christian Perfection* (1839-1845), later known as the *Guide to Holiness.* Merritt was the first American Methodist to publish a sermon linking Christian perfection* with the baptism of the Spirit* (1821). He has some claim to being called the father of the American Holiness movement.

Merton, Thomas (1915-1968). Trappist* monk,* poet and spiritual writer. Deeply transformed by his conversion* in 1938, Merton entered a monastery near Bardstown, Kentucky, in 1941, beginning a strict monastic existence while pursuing what he considered his true vocation—writing. His spiritual autobiography, *The Seven Storey Mountain* (1948), which powerfully and popularly portrayed his conversion from worldliness to a life of contemplation, began his ascent to worldwide fame. Merton went on to write hundreds of articles, as well as books of poetry, works on the spiritual life, mysticism* and contemporary problems.

An eloquent exponent of nonviolence and justice, a formidable critic of American materialism and secularism,* and a sensitive spiritual writer and poet, Merton continues to have a significant impact on an elite, but ecumenical,* cross-section of religious readers in America.

Messianic Jews. *See* JEWISH CHRISTIANS.

Metaxakis, Meletios Emmanuel (1871-1935). Organizer of the American Greek Orthodox Church.* Elected metropolitan of Athens and primate of the Church of Greece in 1918, Metaxakis traveled to the U.S. in 1919 to organize the Greek

Orthodox parishes. In 1922 he established the Orthodox Archdiocese of North and South America.

Methodist Churches. Churches which acknowledge their origins in a revival* and reform movement begun by John Wesley* and his brother Charles in England in the eighteenth century.

In British North America, Methodism spread first through the efforts of migrating Methodists. In the 1760s the first congregations began to meet regularly in Virginia and New York, but growth was initially slow, not picking up until after the Revolutionary War.* Formal organization of an American Methodist church dates to the Christmas Conference* of 1784 in Baltimore, Maryland, when Francis Asbury* and Thomas Coke* were elected as the first two bishops.

By 1840 the Methodists had become the largest denomination* in America, outstripping the reigning colonial denominations—the Presbyterians,* Congregationalists* and Anglicans.* Methodists continued to outpace other Protestant* churches until the mid-twentieth century, numbering 5.7 million adherents in 1906 and over 8 million adherents in roughly 40,000 congregations in 1946. Today, North American Methodist bodies manifest a variety of emphases in polity (from episcopacy* to congregationalism*) and doctrine (from liberalism* to evangelicalism* and traditional to Holiness*) existing within the Wesleyan tradition,* a feature common to Methodism worldwide.

The largest North American Methodist body is the United Methodist Church* (8.8 million members), formed in 1968 by the merger of the Methodist Church with the Evangelical United Brethren Church. The African Methodist Episcopal Church* (3.5 million members) and the African Methodist Episcopal Zion Church* (1.2 million members) represent the major branches of African-American Methodism in America. The Christian Methodist Episcopal Church* (800,000 members) until 1954 was known as the Colored Methodist Episcopal Church.

The Primitive Methodist Church* is a very small evangelical body tracing its origins back to Connecticut-born Lorenzo Dow's* evangelistic efforts in England (1807). The Free Methodist Church of North America* (75,000 members) and the Wesleyan Church* (114,000 members) are smaller, more conservative bodies. Both the Free Methodists and Wesleyan Church are commonly known as Holiness churches because of their association with the Methodist Holiness revival of the nineteenth century.

As with the Pilgrim Holiness Church, a number of bodies, such as the Church of the Nazarene* (574,000 members), the Salvation Army* (446,000 members) and the Church of God* (Anderson, Indiana) (215,000 members), owe their existence to the Holiness movement within the Wesleyan tradition.

Many of the above bodies unite with other Methodist churches around the world in the World Methodist Council, which represents sixty-four member churches with fifty-four million adherents.

See also REVIVALISM, GERMAN-AMERICAN.

Metropolitan. An episcopal* title dating from the fourth century. In the early church, the title referred to the bishop of a large city whose authority* extended over an area corresponding to a civil province. In Greek Orthodox* churches the title denotes any bishop presiding over a diocese.*

Meyendorff, John (1926-1992). Orthodox* theologian and dean of St. Vladimir's Orthodox Theological Seminary. In the mid-1960s Meyendorff emerged as a leading clergyman in the Russian Orthodox Greek-Catholic Church of America. From 1967 to 1976 he served as chairman of the Faith and Order Commission of the World Council of Churches.* He also was editor of the Orthodox Church in America's monthly newspaper *Orthodox Church* (1965-1984).

Meyer, Albert Gregory (1903-1965). Cardinal archbishop of Chicago. In 1958 Meyer was designated archbishop of Chicago, and in 1959 was created a cardinal by Pope John XXIII.*

In Chicago Meyer met major urban problems head-on, forcefully condemning racial discrimination in a famous address entitled "The Mantle of Leadership" (1960). He threw the prestige of his office and the financial resources of the archdiocese behind the community-organizing activities of Saul Alinsky.

His most significant contribution came as one of the intellectual leaders and spokesmen for the American bishops at Vatican II,* where he took firm stands in favor of modern biblical exegesis and episcopal collegiality* and against anti-Semitism.

Meyer, F(rederick) B(rotherton) (1847-1929). Baptist* pastor, Bible conference* speaker and writer. In 1873 Meyer befriended Dwight L. Moody* and Ira D. Sankey* and helped them begin their English campaigns. This friendship resulted in Moody's inviting Meyer to America in 1891, the first of twelve trips. He spoke at the East Northfield Summer Conference for two weeks and proved to be so popular that he was asked to give postconference addresses. Even before coming to the U.S., Meyer's written works had received appreciative attention.

Meyer, Lucy Jane Rider (1849-1922). Social worker and pioneer of Methodist* deaconess* movement. In 1885 Meyer launched the Chicago Training School for City, Home and Foreign Missions, the center of her subsequent activities, which trained more than five thousand students for missions and social work.

Michaelius, Jonas (1577-?). Dutch Reformed* minister in New Netherland. Michaelius arrived in New Amsterdam in 1628, to become the first minister of the Dutch Reformed Church in America. Some fifty Walloon and Dutch communicants received the first administration of the Lord's Supper* in New Amsterdam.

Michel, Virgil George (1890-1938). Benedictine* leader of the liturgical movement.* Michel became the architect of the liturgical movement in the U.S. As attested by his extensive bibliography devoted to liturgy,* social action, economics, education, philosophy and the arts, Dom Virgil envisaged ultimately a synthesis of the theological movement, the liturgical movement and the apostolate.

Midtribulationism. *See* RAPTURE OF THE CHURCH.

Miles, William Henry (1828-1892). Black Methodist* bishop. Miles took part in the first General Conference of the Colored Methodist Episcopal Church* in 1870 and was elected one of its first two bishops. Miles was an enthusiastic supporter of the establishment of black colleges* such as Lane College in Jackson, Tennessee, and Paine Seminary in Augusta.

Miley, John (1813-1895). Methodist* minister and theologian. Miley developed a Methodist Arminian* theology. His *Atonement in Christ*

(1879) and two-volume *Systematic Theology* (1892, 1894) became standard texts for Methodist students of theology.

Millenarian Movements. Groups that expect a period of unprecedented peace and righteousness upon the earth, usually associated with the return of Christ. Some of these groups, commonly called by the term *postmillennial,** believe that the present age will be gradually transformed into the millennium through natural means, such as religious revival* and social reform.* Others, usually termed *premillennial,** believe that the golden age will come only after the present age is destroyed through supernatural means, such as the Second Coming of Christ.

Postmillennial Movements. From the beginning, Americans have been susceptible to millenarian hopes. Jonathan Edwards's* experience in the Great Awakening* led him to believe that the millennium was imminent and would begin in America. By the early nineteenth century, most evangelicals had adopted similar postmillennial views and used them to Christianize America and the world.

Postmillennial views were harder to maintain after the Civil War,* when mounting social, economic and religious crises made the arrival of the millennium seem less likely. However, postmillennial optimism and resolve can be detected in the Social Gospel movement,* which remained vital from the 1880s to World War I.*

Communities and Prophecies. Some groups— such as the Shakers* and the Mormons*—have been expressly established as harbingers of the comng millennium. Other millenarian groups— including the Millerites (*see* William Miller) and the Jehovah's Witnesses*—have become famous for their failed prophecies.

Dispensational Premillennialism. Given more to speculation about the "signs of the times" than date-setting are the dispensationalists,* whose teachings first came to America in the 1870s. In the twentieth century dispensationalists figured prominently in the rise of fundamentalism,* thanks especially to the Scofield Reference Bible* (1909). More recently dispensationalism has been popularized in the writings of Hal Lindsey, whose *Late Great Planet Earth* became a bestseller in the 1970s.

See also AMILLENNIALISM; APOCALYPTICISM; ESCHATOLOGY.

Millennial Church. *See* SHAKERS.

Millennial Dawnists. *See* JEHOVAH'S WITNESSES.

Miller, John Peter (1709-1796). Ephrata Society* leader. In 1735 Conrad Beissel* converted and rebaptized Miller and some of his parishioners to his mystical vision of the Christian life. After Beissel's death in 1768 Miller assumed Beissel's place within the community. Miller was less charismatic than his predecessor, and Ephrata's fortunes declined during his tenure.

Miller, Samuel (1769-1850). Old School* Presbyterian* minister. Elected moderator of the Presbyterian General Assembly* (1806), Miller was a founder of that denomination's* theological seminary at Princeton* (1812) and professor of ecclesiastical history and church government* there from 1813 until his death.

Miller, William (1782-1849). Baptist* lay preacher who predicted the Second Coming of Christ around the year 1843. In 1816 Miller was converted from his earlier deism* and began a systematic study of the Bible in an attempt to answer the challenges of skeptics. In 1818 he concluded that Christ would return around the year 1843, a date later identified specifically as October 22, 1844.

After the failure of this calculation, Miller said that the mistake might have resulted from a manmade error in Bible chronology. Until his death, however, Miller retained his faith in Christ's imminent return.

Estimates of Miller's following vary considerably, most ranging between 30,000 and 100,000. While many in the movement returned to their former churches after 1844, several adventist churches took form. Of these groups, the Seventh-day Adventists* became the largest and most widespread.

See also MILLENARIAN MOVEMENTS.

Mills, Benjamin Fay (1857-1916). Evangelist. In 1893 Mills began preaching a social gospel,* emphasizing the themes of brotherhood and the coming kingdom of God* and encouraging churches and individuals in their responsibility to transform society and its institutions. Mills was one of few evangelists in the nineteenth century who tried to combine the messages of personal salvation* and social responsibility. Though his revivals* were well attended, he found that many churches were reluctant to accept his twofold message. In later years Mills became a Unitarian,* and then a Presbyterian.*

Mills, Samuel John, Jr. (1783-1818). Promoter of foreign missions.* At Williams College, Massachusetts, Mills led the Haystack Prayer Meeting* (1806), which issued in the founding of the American Protestant* missionary movement.* In 1810 he helped form the American Board of Commissioners for Foreign Missions.*

Between 1812 and 1815 Mills undertook two missionary journeys through the South and Midwest, distributing Scriptures, preaching and collecting information. In 1816 he helped found the American Bible Society.*

Minister. As a noun, *minister* means an ordained* minister of the gospel; a member of the clergy, as distinct from the laity. The term is identified with the primitive church's offices of deacon,* elder* and bishop.

As a verb, *minister* means to proclaim the gospel; to engage in acts of Christian love and mercy, including visitation, physical assistance, prayer and spiritual counsel.

Ministerial Associations, Colonial. Regular meetings of the clergy for mutual edification and the resolution of church matters. By the late seventeenth century, Massachusetts clergymen formed scattered, unofficial associations that met by appointment several times a year. At these meetings, candidates were suggested for vacant pulpits, theological questions and current issues were debated, and conflicts within the churches were examined.

Ministerial Call. The divine call (vocation) to a person to be a priest or minister of the gospel, distinguishable from God's call of believers to salvation.* The term is most commonly used by presbyterial* and congregationally* organized churches in which the local body selects and calls its own pastor. Clergy "receive" and "answer" calls to specific ministries.

Ministerial Privilege. Rights or favors accorded clergy as part of their remuneration, in recognition of their role in society or by virtue of their responsibilities. As part of pastors' remuneration, churches often provide them with housing, fuel and sometimes furnishings. By the late twentieth century many privileges had been abandoned by a secular, pluralistic society.

Minister's Wife. Martin Luther's marriage to Katherine von Bora in 1525 created one of the Reformation's most important legacies, the Protestant* parsonage. In American Protestantism the role has evolved considerably, with the twentieth century bringing special stresses. Pressed by the social conservatism of the churches into a primarily domestic, companionate role, or pushed by the impetus of the women's movement into social and spiritual detachment from the congregation, ministers' wives have often struggled to establish themselves in viable public ministry.

Minor Orders. Lesser degrees of ministry within the Roman Catholic* Church, below the major orders* of bishop, priest and deacon.* While the minor orders (acolyte, exorcist, lector, porter and subdeacon) and their functions have varied somewhat, in recent centuries they have been ranks through which a man advanced to the priesthood.

Most recently, exorcism has been reserved for the clergy, and the orders of porter and subdeacon have been abolished. Laypeople have been encouraged to do the work of acolytes, lectors and porters.

Missiology, Protestant. The study of Christian mission. In the late nineteenth century, Europe (especially the Germans) sought to develop missiology in the university, by which it hoped to gain public recognition and theological respectability. Out of this approach came a methodological clarity and rigorous investigative discipline unmatched in North America. The ties with the university, however, left the study divorced from church life and practice.

In North America, impetus for the study of missions came from the pressure of student enthusiasm. In 1811 Samuel Mills* launched the student-centered Society of Inquiry on the Subject of Missions. By 1857 there were seventy such societies around the country, pressing universities and seminaries to give academic attention to their missions concerns. In 1886 the Student Volunteer Movement* (SVM) came into being, intensifying that pressure.

Missiology began to make a reluctant appearance in the seminary and university programs of study. Relegated to a place in the practical theology curriculum, however, missions often was the object of condescension by other faculty members working in the classic theological disciplines.

Mainline* denominational* seminaries and university programs now find interest in missions waning, due to a decline in theological certitude and a growing openness toward religious tolerance and pluralism. By contrast, evangelical seminaries have experienced growing interest in missiological studies and a solid increase in the number of missions lectureships. Fuller Theological Seminary's* School of World Mission, founded in 1965, is the clear leader with twelve full-time faculty and 755 students enrolled in 1986.

See also AMERICAN SOCIETY OF MISSIOLOGY; MISSIONS, EVANGELICAL FOREIGN; MISSIONS, PROTESTANT MAINLINE FOREIGN; MISSIONS, ROMAN CATHOLIC FOREIGN.

Missionary, Missioner. A person actively engaged in a mission, particularly one sent by a church to carry the gospel to those who have not heard the message of Jesus Christ. The so-called Great Commission of Jesus (Mt 28:19-20) provides the clearest direction for such a calling.

Missionary Baptists. Two types of Baptists* employ the term *missionary* in opposite ways. The first type promotes missions* solely through individual churches. Their most conservative branch is the American Baptist Association* (ABA). In contrast to the ABA, which has been caricatured as antimissionary, the second type cooperates in conventions which allow them to be involved in more comprehensive mission activities and diverse programs, such as the Southern Baptist Convention.*

Missionary Bishop. A bishop appointed to serve in an area not yet organized as a diocese.* The office was created in 1835 by the General Convention of the Protestant Episcopal Church.*

See also BOONE, WILLIAM JONES.

Missionary Movement, Women's. An American Protestant* movement in the late nineteenth and early twentieth centuries to form women's missionary* societies for the sending of single women to foreign mission fields.

The women's missionary movement ultimately sustained more than forty mission agencies, mobilized tens of thousands of women on the home front and sent thousands of women overseas during the late nineteenth and early twentieth centuries. The underlying impulse behind the women's missionary movement was the rejection of single women for missionary service by existing mission boards. The need for women to reach their "heathen" sisters was widely acknowledged, but missionary wives were generally too burdened with domestic duties to adequately meet the need.

Women thus banded together to form "female agencies" to send their sisters overseas. The first such organization was the Woman's Union Missionary Society, founded in 1861 by Sarah Doremus.* Other women's societies were soon formed along denominational* lines, with the Congregationalists* of New England being the first to take up the mantle (1869). Methodist* women were next to organize, and the Baptists* followed in 1870. In the decades that followed, a new women's mission society was formed on an average of one each year.

The most prominent leaders of the women's missionary movement on the national scene were Lucy Peabody* and Helen Barrett Montgomery.* Both worked tirelessly to promote the jubilee celebration in 1910, recognizing the five decades of women's missionary work.

In the decades following the 1910 jubilee, the women's missionary movement declined. Denominational boards had begun to readily accept single women missionaries, and there was considerable pressure for women's societies to merge with their "parent" boards. Women continued to have a vibrant interest in missions, but their focus was turned more and more to the new faith missions rather than to the mainline* denominational boards.

See also MISSIONS, EVANGELICAL FOREIGN; MISSIONS, PROTESTANT MAINLINE FOREIGN; MISSIONS, ROMAN CATHOLIC FOREIGN.

Missions, African-Americans and. African-Americans have been committed to the evangelization of Africa since the early nineteenth century. The earliest and most intensive denominational* expansion of African-American churches began in Liberia and Sierra Leone to provide organized churches for African-Americans who colonized West Africa. In 1815 Lott Cary* formed the Richmond African Baptist Missionary Society with William Crane, and by 1819 the American Colonization Society* and the Baptist Foreign Mission Board had accepted Lott Cary and Colin Teague as their first African-American workers.

Committed to the evangelization of African peoples wherever they lived, African-Americans sent missionaries to the Caribbean as well. In 1827, Scipio Bean began mission work in Haiti for the African Methodist Episcopal (AME) Church.*

All three major African-American denominations expanded their foreign missions in Africa and the Caribbean after the Civil War.* The AME Church established its first African mission in 1885 in Sierra Leone and now has foreign missions in South Africa, West Africa, the Caribbean, South America and India. The National Baptist* Convention now has missions in West Africa, Southern Africa, the Caribbean and South America. The African Methodist Episcopal Zion Church* (AMEZ) Foreign Mission Department was founded in 1875, with Rev. and Mrs. Andrew Cartwright starting Liberia missions in 1876. The Nigerian Conference, begun in 1930 by Rev. J. Drybauld Taylor, now has 1,104 places of worship* and over five hundred schools.

Missions, Evangelical Foreign. Historically, America's own founding was motivated by themes associated with world missions. Alexander Whitaker,* "Apostle to Virginia," reminded his readers in 1613 that they were planting the kingdom of God* in the New World.

Colonial Missions. This sense of divine destiny first crossed cultural barriers in the evangelization of Native Americans (see Missions to Native Americans). John Eliot,* known as the Apostle to the Indians, believed Native Americans had to "be civilized ere they could be Christianized." In keeping with that aim, he developed a mission strategy of gathering "praying Indians" into "praying towns,"* a model used widely throughout New England until the towns were largely destroyed in King Philip's War* (1675).

Revival and Mission. The Great Awakening* and the Second Awakening* transformed this situation. In the 1730s and 1740s, and again in the early nineteenth century, revival* fires swept through the churches of New England and the South. Out of the fire of the Awakenings, the growth of the Christian community, and the disestablishment of state religion came two missionary ideas that would draw the attention of the new nation to the world outside its borders. The first was church planting by larger ecclesiastical bodies.

The second idea was a growing sense of obligation of the American church toward the world. Increasingly, American interests turned beyond its shores. New boards began to emerge, with a growing focus on overseas ministry. The first was the American Board of Commissioners for Foreign Missions* (ABCFM), organized in 1810 through the appeal of Samuel Mills.*

"The Great Century" of American Missions. One hundred years later, by 1910, the U.S. and Canada were fast becoming the dominant world force in missions. Their Protestant* missionaries serving overseas totaled 7,219 (34 percent of the world total). The number of sending societies in the U.S. had grown from one in 1810 to ninety-six in 1910, with eleven closely associated organizations in Canada.

During the first half of the nineteenth century, India, Burma and Ceylon were the chief targets of American mission efforts overseas. Then followed Southeast Asia, West Africa, the southernmost tip of Africa, the Turkish empire and Hawaii. By the end of the century, China had become the major American field

Missionary motivation shifted during the nineteenth century. The earlier eschatological* theme of *gloria Dei* vanished. In its place, mission leaders like Rufus Anderson* of the ABCFM spoke of obedience to Christ's Great Commission (Mt 28:18-20).

In the late nineteenth and early twentieth centuries, still another motivation began to gain prominence. Fed by the rise of nationalism and a sense of America's Manifest Destiny,* liberal* writers like Horace Bushnell* spoke of America as "the brightest hope of the ages." At first associated with both liberal and evangelical Christians, this enthusiasm for Christian civilization's world conquest increasingly became a liberal theme. The Social Gospel* movement gave it theological backing.

The end of the nineteenth century saw the genesis of the Student Volunteer Movement* (SVM) in 1886. Soon carried to Great Britain and Europe, it became the most effective recruiting arm of the Western mission boards.

The Twentieth Century. By 1924, there were a reported 14,000 North American foreign missionaries, joined by 15,000 from Great Britain and Europe. The century was to become, in the language of Stephen Neill, "beyond question the American century." By 1992 there were 32,634 fully supported U.S. personnel overseas for a term of four years or more and 7,882 fully supported U.S. personnel overseas for terms ranging from two months to four years. For Canadian personnel these figures were 3,075 and 424 respectively.

In 1917 the Interdenominational Foreign Mission Association* (IFMA) was formed in the U.S. to accredit the evangelical character of these mission boards and provide limited cooperation among them, as was the Evangelical Foreign Missions Association* (EFMA), formed in 1945 as an affiliate of the National Association of Evangelicals.* The two agencies serve a total of over 17,000 missionaries from North America.

Since 1968 growth has plateaued within the IFMA and the EFMA. The four largest North American evangelical boards are not affiliated with either group—the Southern Baptist Convention* (3,500 career missionaries in 1992), Wycliffe Bible Translators* (over 3,000 in 1992), Youth With a Mission* (over 3,000 full-time and part-time personnel in 1992) and New Tribes Mission (1,837 in 1992).

North America's Pentecostal* churches and the charismatic* movement have had a growing impact on the evangelical foreign missions movement. Ignored by evangelicals until the 1970s, Pentecostals and charismatics have been increasingly accepted as part of the global evangelical movement.

See also MISSIOLOGY; MISSIONS, PROTESTANT MAINLINE FOREIGN; MISSIONS, ROMAN CATHOLIC FOREIGN.

Missions, Protestant Mainline Foreign. Rooted in earlier efforts to evangelize* Native American peoples of North America, the American Protestant missions movement was influenced by European initiatives and strongly motivated by the Second Great Awakening.* It began in the so-called Haystack Prayer Meeting* (1806), which led to the formation in 1810 of the American Board of Commissioners for Foreign Missions,* composed at first of Congregationalists.*

Nineteenth-Century Triumphs. By midcentury all of the churches which today would be considered mainline (Baptist,* Congregationalist, Episcopal,* Disciples of Christ,* Lutheran,* Methodist,* Presbyterian* and Reformed*) had their own mission boards.

In 1858 a new wave of revivals* began to sweep the U.S. (*see* Prayer Meeting Revival). New missionary societies were formed, many of them organized by women. Two other major developments were the establishment of the prototype of

interdenominational faith missions,* the China Inland Mission* (1865) and the Student Volunteer Movement* (1888).

Twentieth-Century Crises. Growth was now rapid. In 1900 American missionaries (including approximately 400 from Canada) numbered 4,891, making up 27 percent of the world's Protestant missionary force. Almost all were from the mainline churches. The total grew to 13,608 in 1925, making up 49 percent of the world's total.

The period between World War I* and World War II* brought new problems. Most seriously, the theological consensus which undergirded nineteenth-century missions began to crumble. The greatest challenge came from the Laymen's Foreign Missions Inquiry* report, *Rethinking Missions* (1932), which seemed to reject the uniqueness of Christ. Most executives and missionaries rejected that position and in their replies emphasized the finality of Jesus Christ. But the consensus was gone.

In the 1960s, as the churches became more aware of the problems in American society, the decline in mainline missions was accelerated. In contrast, the independent interdenominational missions and those of the newer evangelical* and Pentecostal* groups grew rapidly. The number of mainline missionaries fell to 6,800 in 1970 and to 2,600 in 1985, when there were 37,803 American Protestant missionaries.

Overall Achievements. Despite its weaknesses, the movement brought magnificent achievements. National churches now exist in nearly every nation in the world, many the result of American missions. Protestant churches are growing rapidly in most Latin American countries, and churches of every type are growing rapidly in most of sub-Saharan Africa. Medical and educational institutions have been established.

As the world missionary movement enters a new phase, the American mainline churches can look back and express gratitude for the achievements of this enterprise to which they have given so much. At the same time their future role is unclear. Can their traditional mission structures serve as adequate channels for the missionary service of the many within their ranks who still wish to obey the call to overseas mission?

See also MISSIONS, EVANGELICAL FOREIGN; MISSIONS, ROMAN CATHOLIC FOREIGN.

Missions, Roman Catholic Foreign. American Catholics* were serving in overseas missions before the U.S. was removed from the jurisdiction of the Sacred Congregation for the Evangelization of Peoples or for the Propagation of the Faith (Propaganda)* in 1908, but only after that can one refer to an American Catholic missionary movement.

The movement took two forms of expression: one of European origin and another of American origin. Older religious congregations of men (*see* Religious Orders, Catholic Men's), such as the Jesuits* and Franciscans,* came from Europe to the U.S., recruited personnel, sent some of them overseas, eventually developed American provinces and thus brought the direction of American overseas personnel under the direction of American superiors. Maryknoll, founded in 1911, was established as the Catholic Foreign Mission Society of America* under the auspices of the U.S. hierarchy. In subsequent decades it also provided a substantial number of overseas personnel.

American women who belonged to older European religious congregations (*see* Religious Orders, Women's) also served overseas even before 1908, and afterward followed the same pattern as the male congregations. The Maryknoll Sisters were founded in 1919 and soon began to provide the largest number of female personnel overseas.

There have been two major thrusts in the American Catholic missionary movement. The first came after World War I,* when over thirty mission territories were entrusted to the exclusive care of American missionaries, almost all of them in Asia. The second came after World War II,* when Americans saw themselves needing to perform a task which Europe could no longer perform. This thrust took them into South America and Africa.

Missions Conferences, Evangelical. Conferences convened to further the cause of the Christian world mission. Evangelical missions conferences take a variety of forms, but most can be categorized as either forums for discussing mission programs and policies or informative and inspirational meetings intended to enlist prayer and financial support, as well as to encourage new missionary candidates.

Local church missionary conferences are typically informative and inspirational. It has been estimated that roughly 10 percent of the churches in the U.S. have a missionary program that includes such a conference.

Perhaps the most famous ongoing evangelical missions conference is the Urbana Convention,* held triennially at the University of Illinois at Urbana since 1948. The total attendance at the 1987 convention was about 18,500. Since 1963 the Interdenominational Foreign Mission Association* and the Evangelical Foreign Mission Association* have sponsored joint triennial conferences.

See also MISSIONS, EVANGELICAL FOREIGN.

Missions to Alaska, Russian Orthodox. The initial introduction of the Orthodox* faith to the North American native population was the work of the Russian fur traders in the 1700s. When the first contingent of missionaries arrived in 1794, they found many of the indigenous people already baptized into the Orthodox faith. Gregorii Shelikov, founder of the Russian American Company, which was to control Alaska from 1799 to 1867, recruited the first missionaries, whose financial needs were to be met by the company.

At the time of the sale of Alaska (1867), there were about twelve thousand Orthodox Christians in forty-three communities. In 1872 the episcopal see was transferred to San Francisco. Support for the Alaskan Orthodox Church continued to come from Russia until 1917.

Missions to Native Americans, Protestant. Missions to Native Americans faced considerable difficulties, including the wide cultural and linguistic differences among the more than four hundred tribes, the persistence of the missionaries' own cultural biases and the pressures of a relentlessly expanding white population which often demonstrated little sympathy for either Native Americans or the missionary task.

The earliest Protestant effort was begun by Thomas Mayhew Jr.* among Native Americans on Martha's Vineyard in 1642. Other early workers in the Northeast included John Eliot,* John Sergeant, David Brainerd, and Eleazar Wheelock.*

The greatest advances, which came in the years after the War of 1812, were in part results of the Second Great Awakening.* The works in the Southeast and the Old Northwest began to show significant promise until the government began to push the program of Indian removal in the late 1820s, which had devastating effects upon the missionary enterprise. Yet by the mid-1830s, with the establishment of missions to Native Americans in Oregon's Willamette Valley (1834) and on the Northern Plains (1835), Protestant missions had expanded throughout the nation.

Twentieth-century missions to Native Americans have seen many new developments. A 1925 survey reported a Native American Christian community of 35,000. In 1979 there were over two thousand Native American congregations, representing over forty denominations* and many independent groups. The total Protestant community was estimated at 120,000.

Missions to North America, French. French colonization, whether in Acadia,* Canada, Louisiana or the West Indies, was almost immediately followed by the outreach to indigenous peoples that was believed to be its ultimate justification. The Jesuits,* for example, worked with the Hurons* of present Ontario from the 1620s. They had converted almost half of the Hurons by 1650, when Iroquois attacks wiped out both the mission and the nation. In 1642 the foundation of Montreal as a religious colony provided a base deep in Native American territory.

The Jesuits reached out to all accessible tribes, from Maine to the Upper Midwest and Canada. In 1725 they were made responsible for the Indian missions of Louisiana, and in the same period they accompanied exploring expeditions to the Canadian prairies. Meanwhile they had been joined by other groups as collaborators and sometimes competitors, including the Sulpicians,* the Franciscan* Recollects.

Despite this expansion, missionary outreach in the eighteenth century became more difficult both to sustain and to prosecute successfully. In France the Enlightenment* dampened religious zeal and discouraged missionary recruitment. On the frontier dissolute traders were a demoralizing influence, internecine warfare almost constant.

The story of French missions in North America, however, was by no means over. Priests fleeing revolutionary France preserved a fund of missionary experience and by the later 1800s were working from South Carolina to Alaska. Many missions were made possible by financial aid from the Society for the Propagation of the Faith.* That more than half of the native population of Canada embraced Roman Catholicism* is almost entirely the result of French missionary effort, and many missions in the U.S. can be traced to the same origin.
See also MISSIONS TO NORTH AMERICA, SPANISH.

Missions to North America, Spanish. Spain quickly harvested the fruit of Christopher Columbus's* 1492 landfall, dispatching conquistadors, soldiers, settlers and missionaries to secure the New World for the mother country. The most effective in establishing Spanish culture among the Native Americans were the missionaries—by and large Dominicans,* Franciscans* and Jesuits*—who everywhere accompanied the soldiers and established missions which converted,* Christianized and civilized the Native Americans who populated Latin and South America.

The first priests to enter what is today the U.S. were not missionaries but Catholic chaplains* who accompanied Hernando de Soto on his fruitless journey (1539-1540) from Florida to Louisiana. More permanent missionary endeavors took place between 1565 and 1769, as Spanish settlements appeared from the Atlantic coast across the Gulf states into the American Southwest and California.* Actual missions began with the establishment of St. Augustine, Florida (1565 or 1566), planted in response to abortive French settlements nearby. As in Florida, so in Texas the Spanish planted missions mainly in response to a French threat.

Spanish missions in present-day New Mexico and Arizona has a long history of Spanish military intrusion, Native American revolt, and continuing missionary presence by Franciscans and Jesuits. Successes were modest and often short-lived.

Prodded by Russian movement down the Pacific Coast in the eighteenth century, Spain sought to shore up its land claim to present-day California. In 1769 Father Junipero Serra* established Mission San Diego, the first of twenty-one missions which ultimately stretched up the coast to San Francisco. Under the missionaries' direction, California Indians settled into mission compounds, worked the fields and built the structures which typified the California missions. Some ninety thousand Native Americans were baptized* between 1769 and 1822, when the new nation of Mexico secularized the missions. As first Mexico, then the U.S., took control of California, the "Mission Indians" lost their lands and social structures which had become their way of life.

Despite two centuries of often-heroic missionary labors, from the Atlantic to the Pacific, little today remains of the Spanish missions in the U.S. Primarily because the Native Americans themselves were largely destroyed or removed by the voracious Anglo-American frontier, Spanish Catholicism left few traces on Native American peoples.

See also MISSIONS TO NORTH AMERICA, FRENCH; MISSIONS TO NATIVE AMERICANS, PROTESTANT.

Missions to the Slaves. Efforts to evangelize* enslaved African-Americans in the antebellum South. White Christian clergymen and philanthropic laymen* perennially expressed concern for the souls of slaves but often found slave owners unwilling to consider schemes for slave conversion,* instruction and worship.*

During the 1820s and 1830s Southern churchmen developed a strong biblical defense of slavery and pointed out its corollary: the Christian responsibility to bring slaves into the fold. Interest in missions to the slaves grew rapidly in the mid-1840s, following the North-South splits in the Methodist* and Baptist* churches (*see* Civil War and the Churches). These new denominations joined other Southern Protestants* in advocating the benefits of evangelizing slaves. Once masters were convinced that religion supported rather than disrupted slavery, white-sponsored missions spread westward from the established, tidewater plantation societies.

By 1861, the great majority of slaves were Christians. This diffuse mission was the only serious effort within the antebellum South to reform the slave system.

See also BLACK RELIGION.

Missions-Minded Church. A term often used among evangelicals* to refer to a local church's* or denomination's* commitment to the worldwide missionary* task. The degree of commitment is measured most objectively by the proportion of the budget which goes to missions.

Mitchell, Jonathan (1624-1668). New England Puritan* minister. Mitchell was the leading advocate of the Half-Way Covenant,* which he drafted in 1662. He argued that children of nonconfessing members in good standing could indeed be baptized.

Modernism, Catholic. The crisis over modernism in Roman Catholicism from approximately 1895 to 1910 was an attempt by alleged modernists to challenge the static character of Neo-Scholastic* theology* by introducing contemporary biblical scholarship and recent scientific developments into Catholicism, resulting in a less

absolutist outlook on Catholic dogma.* Modernism was condemned by the papal decree *Lamentabili* and the encyclical* *Pascendi* in 1907 and was brought to a halt by an antimodernist oath prescribed in 1910.

The complex roots of modernism included challenges to the Catholic Church to confront new philosophical movements, to reevaluate the essentialist metaphysics of Thomism,* to embrace evolutionary* theory in biology and to examine the church's changing role in the socio-political order. Modernists replaced the older Neo-Scholastic categories of thought with models of transcendence, immanence and experience. Modernism, like Americanism,* was not a disciplined movement or a specific heresy but rather a tendency or preference among liberal Catholics who claimed freedom of religious thought against the papal position that theological scholarship should be subject to the magisterium.*

Antimodernism led to a conservative reassertion of papal authority and narrow standards of orthodoxy.* In America, the combined effect of the Americanist and modernist crises was to end a short, enthusiastic spell in Catholic intellectualism and to push American Catholics into a period of intellectual retreat for the next half century until Vatican II.*

Modernism, Protestant. *See* LIBERALISM/MODERNISM, PROTESTANT.

Moe, Malla (1863-1953). Pioneer missionary to Swaziland. A missionary in southern Africa for fifty-four years with the Scandinavian Alliance Mission (now The Evangelical Alliance Mission*), Moe established dozens of churches, trained national pastors and served as an unauthorized bishop in her region.

Moffatt, James (1870-1944). Biblical scholar, church historian. Moffatt taught church history at Union Theological Seminary (New York)* (1927-1938). He is most widely remembered for his translation* of the Bible, designed to demonstrate graphically and simply to the layperson the contemporary scholarly understanding of the biblical text.

Moffett, Samuel Austin (1864-1939). Pioneer Presbyterian* missionary to northern Korea. Moffett arrived in Chemulpo, Korea, in 1890. By 1893 he had moved to Pyongyang, becoming, in effect, the first Protestant* missionary to take up residence in inland Korea.

In his forty-six years in Korea, Moffett co-founded Union Christian College (now Soong Jun University), founded the Presbyterian Theological Seminary and encouraged the young Korean Presbyterian Church to form its own mission board.

Monsignor. A form of address in the Roman Catholic Church* for all clerical officials of the papal retinue below the rank of cardinal, including titular or honorary officials.

The number of monsignors peaked at the time of the Second Vatican Council.* In the postconciliar era, the glamour of honorary titles has faded; only a few American bishops currently continue to recommend priests for these titular papal offices.

Montgomery, Carrie Judd (1858-1946). Pentecostal* minister and editor. Long interested in Holiness* teaching and divine healing, Montgomery published *Triumphs of Faith* (1881-1946), a monthly interdenominational magazine devoted to these topics.

In California, after working with the Salvation Army* and then identifying with Pentecostalism,* in 1917 she joined the Assemblies of God* and was issued credentials as an evangelist.

Montgomery, Helen Barrett (1861-1934). Biblical scholar and Baptist* denominational leader. Montgomery pioneered several leadership roles, serving as the first woman president of a religious denomination* (the Northern Baptist Convention, 1921) and the first woman to prepare a translation of the entire New Testament into English (1924). In Baptist life she promoted international missions by traveling abroad extensively with her colleague Lucy W. Peabody* and by helping to organize permanent support groups like the World Wide Guild and the World Day of Prayer.

Moody, Dale (1915-1992). Southern Baptist* theologian. Moody's career as a systematic theologian* was spent at Southern Baptist Theological Seminary,* where he received much of his initial theological training. But subsequent years found him studying under some of the leading theological figures of Europe and involved in numerous ecumenical endeavors. A gifted and engaging teacher of systematic theology and the Bible, Moody nevertheless sparked Southern Baptist controversy over the course of his teaching career. He is best known for his systematic theology, *The Word of Truth* (1981).

Moody, D(wight) L(yman) (1837-1899). Urban revivalist.* Converted* in Boston as a teenager, Moody moved to Chicago in 1856, where he became a successful shoe salesman. In 1858 he started a Sunday school in the Chicago slums and two years later quit his business to devote himself fully to his religious pursuits. In 1863 he expanded his Chicago Sunday school into the undenominational Illinois Street Church and in 1866 became president of the Chicago YMCA.*

In the following years, accompanied by his chorister Ira Sankey,* Moody preached to enormous crowds in the British Isles (1873-1875, 1881-1884) and also throughout the U.S. (1875-1879, 1884-1891). In 1889 he helped found a Bible institute in Chicago, which was renamed Moody Bible Institute after his death.

Moody brought a new level of sophistication and organization to urban* revivalism. Never a sensationalist, he was always modest and congenial; he looked and acted like the businessman he was. His sermons* were homey, engaging and sentimental, stressing the love of God over God's wrath.

Moody Bible Institute. An evangelical* training institution. Chicago's Moody Bible Institute has its roots in a Bible institute organized in 1889 that in 1900 was renamed after D. L. Moody.* The institute rather quickly became an influential organization in the religious world, partly because its objectives were practical and met a need for biblical training, and partly because of the influence of liberal* theology on the traditional seminaries.

The institute's first presidents, Reuben A. Torrey* and James M. Gray,* were both strong defenders of the authority* of Scripture in the wake of the theological liberalism then prevailing. Among other contributions to conservative Christianity, the institute has produced more missionaries than any other single school.

Moon, Charlotte ("Lottie") Diggs (1840-1912). Southern Baptist* missionary to China. In 1873 Moon sailed for China, where she initially taught in a children's school and later did evangelism and church planting. In 1889 her work in P'ing-tu was described as the Southern Baptist effort's "greatest evangelistic center in all China."

Her death from starvation on Christmas Eve 1912 has given impetus to the Lottie Moon Christmas Offering for Foreign Missions, which annually raises tens of millions of dollars.

Moon, Sun Myung. *See* UNIFICATION CHURCH.

Mooneyham, W. Stanley (1926-1991). Baptist* minister and relief agency administrator. Mooneyham was a National Association of Free Will Baptists* pastor (1949-1953) and denominational administrator (1953-1959) before taking an administrative position in the National Association of Evangelicals* (1959-1964) and working for the Billy Graham Evangelistic Association* (1964-1969). In 1969 he became president of World Vision International,* a Christian relief and development agency. His perspective on relief work is presented in his book *What Do You Say to a Hungry World?* (1975).

Moore, George Foot (1851-1931). Old Testament scholar. Moore was professor of Old Testament at Andover Theological Seminary* (1883-1902) and professor of the history of religion at Harvard* (1902-1928) until his retirement. His numerous publications gained him international recognition as a critical scholar in Hebrew and Old Testament. His work reflected German scholarship, which he was instrumental in introducing into America.

Moore, Joanna P. (1832-1916). Baptist* home missionary. Moore was a major figure in Baptist women's home missionary work; her efforts in establishing schools and missions around the South and enlisting black and white teachers and evangelists consistently enlarged the missionary society's vision and scope.

Moore, Richard Channing (1762-1841). Episcopal* bishop of Virginia. In 1814 the Diocese* of Virginia elected him its second bishop. Having languished since the Revolution,* the diocese prospered under his leadership. Churches were reestablished, and the Virginia Theological Seminary at Alexandria was founded in 1823. An evangelical* high churchman,* Moore stressed the divine origin of the church and its apostolic ministry, as well as justification* by grace and the necessity for revival.*

Moorehead, William Gallogly (1836-1914). Presbyterian* minister and educator. Moorehead, professor of New Testament (1873-1899) and president (1899-1914) of Xenia (Ohio) Theological Seminary, was prominent among American premillennialists.* He served as a long-time leader of the Niagara Conference* and was a frequent speaker at Bible institutes.*

Moral Majority. A conservative political group formed in 1979 by Baptist* pastor Jerry Falwell.* The Moral Majority was the most visible manifestation of the New Religious Right,* which seeks to root out secular humanism and restore Judeo-Christian* morality in society. The Moral Majority worked to educate and mobilize conservative citizens (mostly Christian) to elect moral candidates to office, to eliminate such evils as abortion* and pornography, and to influence a wide range of public policies through lobbying offices in Washington, D.C.

The group's impact was mixed. Although generally credited with registering two to three million new voters, the group was not a major factor in election outcomes. Media coverage was extensive, although usually unfavorable. In 1989 Falwell announced the dissolution of the Moral Majority, maintaining that the organization had fulfilled its goal of establishing the Religious Right within the public arena.

Moral Re-Armament. Movement to promote moral awareness and world peace. Founded by Frank Buchman* in 1938, the movement was to prevent war by promoting moral and spiritual awakening throughout the world. It is the direct successor to a worldwide crusade Buchman organized in 1921 called the Oxford Group movement, aimed to help individuals achieve dynamic religious experiences. Buchman renamed his movement and changed its purpose in response to the political and military tensions of the late 1930s.

Moral Theology. Roman Catholic* theologians have contrasted moral theology with dogmatic* theology. While dogmatic theology deals with teaching (an impersonal and abstract body of knowledge), moral theology deals with the goal of life and how it is to be achieved. Moral theology emphasizes the way a human being must live—with grace and virtue—in order to attain the presence of God, the proper end of every person's life.

Moravian Church in America. Popular name for two provinces of the Unitas Fratrum (Society of Brethren) in the U.S. and Canada. The first group of Moravians to settle in North America arrived in Savannah, Georgia, in 1735 under the leadership of Augustus G. Spangenberg.* The colony eventually located in Bethlehem, Pennsylvania, and grew with the German immigrations of the nineteenth century. In 1753 Spangenberg also began the Moravian settlement in Salem, North Carolina. Total membership in 1986 was 77,012.

Moravians. A Protestant* tradition with roots reaching back to the Unitas Fratrum (Society of Brethren). Founded by the followers of Jan Hus in 1457, the movement received protection in the 1720s by Count Nikolaus Ludwig von Zinzendorf* (1700-1760) in Lower Saxony. The group, which soon attracted other religious dissenters, was powerfully moved by the spirit of German Pietism.* Zinzendorf and his associate, Augustus Gottlieb Spangenberg,* were responsible for settlement of Moravians in the American colonies.

See also MORAVIAN CHURCH IN AMERICA.

Morehead, John Alfred (1867-1936). Lutheran international churchman. Morehead, president of Roanoke College in Salem, Virginia (1903-1920), was widely respected for his farsighted guidance of international church relief efforts after World War I.* He rallied churches in North America and Europe to form the Lutheran World Convention (Eisenach, 1923), a landmark in Lutheran history.

Morehouse, Henry Lyman (1834-1917). Baptist* minister and missionary statesman. Morehouse was correspondence secretary or field secretary of the American Baptist Home Mission Society from 1879 to 1917. He diligently sought to provide education for immigrants, Native Americans and African-Americans.

Morgan, G. Campbell (1863-1945). Expository* preacher. Although lacking in formal theological training, Morgan became one of the most famous preachers of his age in the English-speaking world by applying his remarkable intelligence to serious biblical study and wide reading.

Morgan came to prominence as the Bible teacher par excellence for the converts of Dwight L. Moody* and those who came to Christ in the revivals of 1904 to 1910. From 1917 to 1932 he gave himself almost entirely to North America.

Mormonism. A new religion founded in the nineteenth century by Joseph Smith.* Smith established the Church of Christ, which became the Church of Jesus Christ of Latter-day Saints, or Mormonism, in April 1830 in upstate New York, following the publication of *The Book of Mormon* in March 1830. Smith claimed to have derived the book from golden plates which he had discovered with the aid of the angel Moroni. Proclaiming himself a prophet, Smith gathered about him a following of devoted disciples.

In 1831 Kirtland, Ohio, became the first Holy City of Smith's new church. By 1838 the Kirtland community had suffered economic collapse, and Smith fled with others to Missouri and then to Nauvoo, Illinois. Smith's downfall in Nauvoo came as a result of his teachings and practice of polygamy, which had been exposed by a local newspaper. In jail in 1844 because of rioting which had destroyed the newspaper's offices, Smith was murdered by a lynch mob.

Following Smith's death, his disciples split into over twenty-five different groups. The largest group followed Brigham Young,* who in 1847 led the Mormons on their famous migration to the Salt Lake area of what would become the state of Utah (1850).

Branches of Mormonism. Today the largest group is the Utah Mormons based in Salt Lake City. At the end of 1986 there were 3.7 million Utah Mormons in North America and over 5.5 million worldwide. In 1890 the Utah Mormons officially abandoned polygamy on the advice of their president, Wilford Woodruff (1807-1898), in order to reach a political accommodation with the U.S. Government.

The other main branch of Mormonism is the smaller Reorganized Church of Jesus Christ of Latter-day Saints, with its headquarters in Independence, Missouri. This group was supported by Joseph Smith's legal wife, Emma, and legitimated its claims on the basis of lineal descent from Joseph Smith. In 1986 it had 205,025 members.

Mormon Beliefs and Practices. Utah Mormonism is an indigenous religious movement that incorporates American values of self-reliance, pragmatism, progress and democracy. *The Book of*

Mormon is fundamentally an early American romance based on the Bible, and its theology appears to be essentially Christian. Utah Mormon missionaries stress the importance of the Bible and *The Book of Mormon* as sources for their beliefs, downplaying the role of continuing revelation characteristic of their church. Yet in reality they read both the Bible and *The Book of Mormon* in light of later revelations given to Joseph Smith and successive prophets.

Structurally, Utah Mormon theology is held together by an evolutionary framework known as the doctrine of eternal progression. This belief is summed up by the phrase "As man is, God once was; as God is, man may become." Thus human destiny is to evolve to godhood through obedience to the laws and ordinances revealed to the Utah church.

From the beginning Christians have rejected Mormon claims to be a Christian church. Although most Mormons sincerely believe that they are Christians, the differences between the teachings of Utah Mormons and traditional Christianity are so great that it would more accurately be called a new religion.

Morris, Edward Dafydd (1825-1915). Presbyterian* pastor and educator. Morris taught church history and theology* at Lane Theological Seminary in Cincinnati, Ohio (1867-1897). An evangelical,* ecumenical,* New School Calvinist,* Morris worked hard to reunite the Old* and New Schools of the Presbyterian Church in the U.S.A.

Morris, Lelia Naylor (1862-1929). Camp meeting* hymn writer. Encouraged by H. L. Gilmore, Morris wrote over one thousand revival* hymns* and gospel song* tunes. Some of her more enduring hymns are "Jesus Is Coming to Earth Again" and "Nearer, Still Nearer."

Morris, Samuel (c. 1700-1770). Revival* leader in colonial Virginia. Around 1740 Morris began a reading ministry in his home that attracted some followers and engendered a small evangelical* awakening among them. In 1747 he helped obtain Samuel Davies* as pastor for his struggling congregation, thus helping bring the Great Awakening* into the South.

Morrison, Charles Clayton (1874-1966). Disciples of Christ* clergyman and editor of the *Christian Century.* In 1908 Morrison purchased and became editor of the *Christian Century,* a position he held until 1947. Morrison transformed the journal from a financially struggling Disciples of Christ magazine to a highly successful "undenominational" journal which spoke for a large segment of liberal* American Protestantism.* Leading liberals wrote for the *Century,* but Morrison maintained a firm grip on editorial policy.

Morrison, Henry Clay (1857-1942). Methodist* revival* preacher. From approximately 1890 to 1910, Morrison was a highly effective mass evangelist.* His ministry was extended through the *Pentecostal Herald,* which he founded about 1890, and in Asbury Theological Seminary, which he founded in 1923 during the first of his two terms as president of Asbury College in Wilmore, Kentucky (1910-1925; 1933-1948). Through these channels he furthered the cause of the Holiness movement,* rooted in the Wesleyan tradition.*

Morse, Jedidiah (1761-1826). Orthodox* Calvinist* opponent of Unitarianism.* While pastor of the First Congregational Church at Charlestown, Massachusetts (1789-1819), Morse became a persistent trinitarian opponent of the emerging Unitarian Congregationalists.* His efforts were frustrated when in 1805 the liberal party won the appointment of a Unitarian to fill the Hollis Chair of Divinity* at Harvard College.* Morse, along with Leonard Woods,* was then instrumental in establishing Andover Theological Seminary* in 1808.

Mother Angela. *See* GILLESPIE, ELIZA.

Mott, John Raleigh (1865-1955). Leader in student work, missions* and the ecumenical* movement. In 1888 Mott became college secretary of the YMCA* and also chairman of the joint committee which organized the Student Volunteer Movement for Foreign Missions.* He led in the formation of the World Student Christian Federation,* was one of the founders of the Foreign Missions Conference of North America* (1893) and led the planning for the Edinburgh Missionary Conference (1910).

Called the father of the World Council of Churches,* Mott participated in each of the movements that led to its formation. Widely honored as a symbol of hope and unity after World War II, he was one of the recipients of the Nobel Peace Prize in 1946.

Theologically Mott could be termed an ecumenical evangelical.* His spiritual formation was in a warm Methodist* piety* with an emphasis on perfectionist* holiness.* He was known as a man of prayer with a worldwide vision, a builder of organizations for unity and an outstanding fundraiser and administrator.

Mott, Lucretia Coffin (1793-1880). Quaker* minister and social reformer.* In Philadelphia, Mott became active in the Friends ministry and through her life and work was a forerunner of modern liberal Quakerism.

She is best remembered as a social reformer in the causes of abolition* and women's rights. By 1848 she, together with Elizabeth Cady Stanton,* had become active in the Women's Rights Convention at Seneca Falls, New York.

Mount Hermon One Hundred (1886). Nineteenth-century student mission* movement. In July 1886, Dwight L. Moody* sponsored a Bible study conference for leaders of collegiate chapters of the Young Men's Christian Association.* Held at Moody's Mount Hermon School in Northfield, Massachusetts, the conference led to exactly one hundred students' dedicating themselves to be foreign missionaries. The group toured colleges to enlist further support for missions, leading to the founding of the Student Volunteer Movement* (1888).

Mountain, Jacob (1749-1825). Anglican* bishop of Quebec. In 1793 Mountain became the first bishop of Quebec, a position which then encompassed the region later named Ontario. He was particularly critical of the Methodists,* whom he described as "ignorant Enthusiasts."

Mourner's Bench. In revival* meetings, a synonym for the "anxious bench" or altar,* the area at the front of a meeting place where persons went when responding to the altar call.* In churches or tabernacles, the mourner's bench was usually the first several rows at the front.

Mowat, Oliver (1820-1903). Premier of the province of Ontario and Presbyterian* layman. Mowat sat in the Parliament of the United Province of Canada (1857-1864) and, with Liberal leader George Brown, entered the Great Coalition of 1864. From 1872 until 1896 he was premier of Ontario. Never an "ultra-Protestant,"

Mowat tried to steer the Liberal Party away from its earlier anti-Catholic tendencies, instead stressing Protestant*-Catholic* cooperation.

Muhlenberg, Henry Melchior (1711-1787). Colonial Lutheran* minister and patriarch of American Lutheranism. Immigrating to Philadelphia in 1742, Muhlenberg set about the task of creating a stable Lutheran organization. The church Muhlenberg envisioned stood midway between orthodoxy* and pietism* and was adaptable to the American environment. To erect it he effectively disposed of two threats: the Moravians,* who wanted to create an interdenominational "Congregation of God in the Spirit"; and William Christoph Berkenmeyer,* who was determined to keep his New York Synod* (which included New Jersey) subservient to the church in Europe. Muhlenberg felt American Lutheranism* had to operate independently if it were to survive. He managed to bring rival Lutheran congregations under his control, establishing himself as the dominant Lutheran clergyman in America and making his ecclesiastical model normative.

In 1748 Muhlenberg created the Pennsylvania Ministerium* as the governing body of American Lutheranism. His liturgical schema insisted on conformity to a conservative, churchly liturgy,* thus preventing revivalism,* which Muhlenberg detested, from making inroads into the church.

Muhlenberg, John Peter Gabriel (1746-1807). Lutheran* clergyman, military officer and politician. The eldest son of Henry Melchior Muhlenberg,* John became a licensed* minister in Virginia. In June 1775 Muhlenberg dramatically left his parish to join the Patriots in the Revolutionary War.* After the war he served as vice president of Pennsylvania and three terms as a member of Congress.

Muhlenberg, William Augustus (1796-1877). Episcopal* clergyman and educator. In 1828 Muhlenberg opened the Flushing (N.Y.) Institute, which quickly became the basic pattern for the creation of church-related preparatory schools throughout the Episcopal Church. Muhlenberg's concern for deepening the spiritual life of his students led him to espouse a "Catholic Evangelicalism.*'"

In 1853 he was the leading figure in the Memorial movement,* which called on the House of Bishops* to grant greater liturgical* freedom to evangelicals in the Episcopal Church and to promote greater union with other Protestant* churches.

Mullins, Edgar Young (1860-1928). President of Southern Baptist Theological Seminary* and professor of theology.* After serving several pastorates, Mullins in 1899 was elected president of the Southern Baptist Theological Seminary in Louisville, Kentucky. As seminary president and professor, he was able to foster a new level of theological sophistication among Southern Baptist ministers. Thoroughly committed to the great verities of the Christian faith, his writings promoted moderate Baptist views.

As a Southern Baptist statesman Mullins led the denomination between the shoals of controversy over evolution* and the rise of the fundamentalist* movement. Under his leadership a revised version of the New Hampshire Confession of Faith* was adopted.

As a scholar, administrator and statesman Mullins was one of the most influential leaders among Southern Baptists in the twentieth century.

Mundelein, George William (1872-1939). Catholic* archbishop of Chicago and first American cardinal west of the Atlantic seaboard. In 1915 Mundelein was named third archbishop of Chicago, the youngest archbishop in America at the time. Mundelein was a consolidating bishop who centralized the administration of his archdiocese* and set it on a firm financial footing, while tying it more closely to Rome.

Munger, Theodore Thornton (1830-1910). Congregational* minister and theologian. Munger was pastor of the prestigious United Church on New Haven (Conn.) Green (1885-1900). Profoundly influenced by the progressive theologies of Horace Bushnell,* Munger became deeply involved during the 1880s in the liberalizing trend among American Protestant* theologians generally labeled the New Theology.* His *Freedom of Faith* (1883) is generally considered the manifesto of this movement.

Murphy, Edgar Gardner (1869-1913). Episcopal* priest and social reformer.* In 1900 Murphy planned a Conference on Race Relations that gained attention for its airing of diverse racial views. He helped form both Alabama (1901) and national (1904) child labor committees, and his lobbying aroused support for child-labor laws.

Murray, John (1741-1815). Early Universalist* minister and leader. Murray immigrated to America in 1770 and preached* as an itinerant* until 1779, when he became minister of a congregation in Gloucester, Massachusetts, the first Universalist group in America to sign a covenant and build a meetinghouse. Murray served as minister of the First Universalist Church of Boston from 1793 until his death in 1815.

Murray's doctrine of universal salvation readily coincided with the republican commitment to equality.

Murray, John (1898-1975). Presbyterian* theologian. Murray taught systematic theology* at Westminster Theological Seminary in Philadelphia (1930-1966). He combined a systematizing bent with superior exegetical gifts, fused by a deep piety.* Through his lecturing and numerous publications, he brought fresh exegetical depth to many areas of classic Reformed* theology.

Murray, John Courtney (1904-1967). Jesuit* theologian and expert on church-state* relations. Murray, professor of theology at Woodstock College (1937-1967), was one of the chief editors of the Jesuit journal *Theological Studies* (1941-1967). Murray's interest in ecumenism* and the problems of being Christian in a secular society led him to investigate church-state issues and the compatibility of Catholicism* with a secularized democratic* state professing religious freedom.

His views set him at odds with traditional Catholic teachings, as some Roman officials felt he was minimizing the claims of Catholicism and altering a centuries-old doctrine. Murray strongly believed that church teachings were historically and culturally conditioned, that they could evolve over time and that while certain teachings on church-state relations may have been proper at one time, they should no longer be considered the only approach.

Later, Murray was a chief architect of Vatican II's* "Declaration on Religious Freedom" (*Dignitatis Humanae*, 1965), which brought an important change in the church's traditional view.

Musical Instruments in Churches. Instrumental church music in the U.S. was slow to gain wide acceptance. Today's use of synthesizers, drums, guitars and prerecorded orchestras is a far development from the arguments in the colonies over the use of a pitch pipe to "set the tune" for unaccompanied psalm singing. In the early 1700s the Lutheran* Pietist* Justus Falckner* was one of the first in America to urge the use of organs in worship.* The Moravian* Pietists were the most notable early promoters of musical instruments in worship, accompanying their singing with flutes, trumpets, violins, horns and, later, organs. Except for a few denominations that retain the practice of unaccompanied singing (such as the noninstrumental Churches of Christ*), instruments now are unquestioned.

Myers, Cortland (1864-1941). Fundamentalist* Baptist* pastor. In 1918 Myers signed the call for the Philadelphia Prophetic Convention, where he decried German rational theology* and claimed it was a contributing factor to World War I.* Myers also warned of the dangers of foreign immigration to America.

Myland, David Wesley (1858-1943). Pentecostal* minister, evangelist and educator. Originally associated with the Methodist* Episcopal Church, Myland in 1890 joined the Christian and Missionary Alliance* but left it in 1912 when his theology had become more Pentecostal. He founded the Gibeah Bible School in Plainfield, Indiana, and the Ebenezer Bible Institute in Chicago. From 1920 to 1943, Myland pastored churches in Pennsylvania, Michigan and Ohio.

Mystical Body of Christ. Roman Catholic* term describing the relationship of Christ and the church.* In this metaphor, theologians have a way of tempering the more sociological descriptions of the church as a perfect visible society favored by the polemicists and apologists of the post-Reformation era.

Mysticism, Christian. Mysticism can be defined in general as an immediate link to the absolute. What this absolute is, and how one can have the link to it, varies from tradition to tradition.

Mysticism has not been a significant movement in American religion because of the pervasive influence of Reformed* Christianity, which tended to emphasize the place of Scripture in Christian piety,* and also because of a native American pragmatism. Examples of mysticism include the Quakers* as well as various branches of the Wesleyan Holiness movement.* In the twentieth century the Pentecostal* and charismatic* movements have oftentimes exemplified a mystical approach to Christianity, although this is not true in cases where a preoccupation with the gifts of the Spirit has replaced awareness of the Spirit's indwelling.

Nineteenth-century romanticism* as a whole influenced Catholic* piety by encouraging intuition and religious feelings as a means of apprehending God. This led to a renewal of mysticism among Catholics.

On the whole, mystical movements tend to deemphasize Scripture for the sake of private inner knowledge and thus tend to be incompatible with evangelicalism.* Nonetheless, insofar as Christian mysticism calls attention to the reality of the supernatural presence of the Holy Spirit in the life of the believer, one can look for its manifestation wherever there is genuine renewal in American Christianity.

N

Narrative Theology. A theological movement beginning in the 1970s. Narrative, or story, theology sees the Bible as the medium for metaphors. The emphasis is on the importance of narratives and the power of stories in human experience. Language is seen to have a shaping and participatory power which draws people into narratives in personal ways. The Bible's narrative genre gains authority by calling forth new visions of life and providing a central set of metaphors by which one's vision of life can be shaped. Narrative theologians and ethicists include Gabriel Fackre, Hans Frei,* Stanley Hauerwas and James McClendon.

Nation, Carry (or Carrie) Amelia Moore (1846-1911). Temperance* organizer and evangelist. Vehemently opposed to strong drink, in 1892 Nation became involved in the Women's Christian Temperance Union,* and by 1899 she was active in crusading against saloons. Convinced that her work was divinely commissioned by God, she became known as an extreme prohibitionist,* who waged war against liquor by singing hymns, quoting Scripture and smashing liquor bottles and saloon furnishings with her hatchet. An imposing presence, Nation stood nearly six feet tall and was unusually strong.

See also ALCOHOL, DRINKING OF.

National Association of Evangelicals. A voluntary fellowship of forty-eight (1995) member denominations* providing evangelical* identification for fifty thousand churches and over five million Christians. Formed in 1943 as a counterforce to both the Federal Council of Churches* and the American Council of Christian Churches,* the National Association of Evangelicals (NAE) adopted a seven-point doctrinal statement that has remained descriptive of evangelical faith. Numerous extensions of the NAE ministry were organized to address constituency concerns, including in 1943 the Office of Public Affairs, which represents evangelical interests in the nation's capital, in 1944 the National Religious Broadcasters* and the Chaplains Commission, and in 1945 the Evangelical Foreign Missions Association* and World Relief, the humanitarian* arm of the NAE.

National Baptist Evangelical Life and Soul-Saving Assembly of the United States of America. An independent organization founded in 1920 by Captain Allan Arthur Banks Sr. as an evangelical* and educational auxiliary of the National Baptist Convention of America, Unincorporated. In 1936 it declared itself independent. Never a denomination, it was a city mission engaged in evangelism, charity and relief work, with its greatest contribution being in the area of Bible correspondence courses. In 1952 it reported a membership of 70,843 and 644 churches. Upon the death of the founder the correspondence school was continued by Allan Arthur Banks Jr. and later by his widow, Victoria Banks, until her retirement.

National Baptists. Three predominantly African-American Baptist* denominations* have taken variations of the name *National Baptist,* as described below.

The National Baptist Convention of the United States of America, Inc. and the National Baptist Convention of America. Created in 1895 by the merger of three separate Baptist organizations, the National Baptist Convention of the United States of America, Inc., is the largest African-American denomination in America and the world. The first president was Elias C. Morris. In 1992 the convention numbered an estimated 8.2 million members in over 30,000 congregations. In 1915 the convention divided into two separate organizations following a dispute over the ownership of its National Baptist Publishing Board. R. H. Boyd led a group out of the convention that designated themselves the National Baptist Convention of America, Unincorporated. In 1987 this denomination claimed 3.5 million members.

The Progressive National Baptist Convention, Inc. This denomination emerged in 1961, following a five-year debate within the National Baptist Convention of the United States of America, Inc., over organizational policies. By 1991 the Progressive Convention had approximately 2.5 million members.

National Black Evangelical Association. Black evangelical* ecumenical* organization. Organized in 1973, the National Black Evangelical Association (NBEA) is generally conservative theologically, while political perspectives range from apolitical to nationalistic. Its purposes are twofold: to provide support and fellowship* for evangelicals involved in ministries* to urban* African-American communities, and to develop ministries embracing both social and spiritual concerns. Membership numbers approximately six hundred, divided roughly equally between clergy and laity.

National Campmeeting Association for the Promotion of Christian Holiness. *See* CHRISTIAN HOLINESS ASSOCIATION.

National Catholic Welfare Conference. A national coordinating body for American Catholicism.* The National Catholic Welfare Conference (NCWC) began its life as the National Catholic War Council in 1917, spearheaded by John J. Burke.* After the war the NCWC reorganized as a permanent welfare council. In 1966 the NCWC was replaced by the National Conference of Catholic Bishops* and the United States Catholic Conference.*

National Committee of Black Churchmen. *See* NATIONAL CONFERENCE OF BLACK CHRISTIANS.

National Committee of Negro Churchmen. *See* NATIONAL CONFERENCE OF BLACK CHRISTIANS.

National Conference of Black Christians. African-American ecumenical organization. The National Conference of Black Christians (NCBC) was formed by a group of radical African-American clergymen in 1966 in response to the hostile reaction of liberal* white clergy to the call for "black power." Its most important contributions

were in the development of black theology* under the leadership of Gayraud S. Wilmore.

The NCBC's most active years were from 1966 to 1972; since 1984 it has been inactive.

National Conference of Black Churchmen. *See* NATIONAL CONFERENCE OF BLACK CHRISTIANS.

National Conference of Catholic Bishops. Ecclesiastical organization of the U.S. Catholic bishops for the exercise of their joint pastoral ministry. Founded in 1966, the National Conference of Catholic Bishops (NCCB) is the ecclesiastical counterpart of the bishops' civil arm, the U.S. Catholic Conference.* The NCCB was founded to replace the National Catholic Welfare Conference* (1922-1966). The NCCB membership consists of every bishop and archbishop* in the U.S. and its territories and possessions.

National Conference of Christians and Jews. A nonprofit civic organization of individuals committed to the advancement of understanding, dignity and justice among peoples of various religious, racial and socioeconomic backgrounds. The conference began in 1928 as a campaign of good will, provoked originally by the campaign of hatred directed toward Catholic presidential nominee Alfred E. Smith* and by the hostility shown toward Catholics, Jews and African-Americans by the Ku Klux Klan. Its original purpose has remained unchanged: the elimination of prejudice and discrimination.

National Council of Catholic Men. A national federation of Catholic men's organizations. The National Catholic Welfare Conference* established the National Council of Catholic Men (NCCM) in 1920 to help promote Catholic* lay action through federating Catholic men's organizations at the parish,* diocesan* and national levels. In the 1960s approximately ten thousand men's societies with a total membership of about nine million were affiliated with the NCCM.

Recently, however, support for separate men's groups has been replaced by programs joining laymen and laywomen to address issues affecting not only Catholics but all persons. Since 1980 the NCCM has become dormant at the national level.

See also LAY MOVEMENT, MODERN CATHOLIC.

National Council of Catholic Women. A national federation of Catholic* laywomen's organizations. The National Council of Catholic Women (NCCW) is a federation of eight thousand Catholic Women's organizations from 123 dioceses* in the U.S. As a service agency, its programs extend from the parish* level to diocesan, state, national and international programs. The emergence of the NCCW after World War I* reflected the emerging Catholic middle class in America, as well as the general phenomenon of American women's organizations founded on a spiritual basis for social service.

Current programs include respite (assisting homebound elderly), a national drug and alcohol awareness day, an antipornography campaign, and evangelization* efforts at the parish and diocesan levels.

National Council of the Churches of Christ in the U.S.A. A cooperative ecumenical* agency representing thirty-three denominations.* The National Council of the Churches of Christ in the U.S.A. (NCCC), founded in 1950, was built on the cooperative foundations of the Evangelical Alliance* (1867) and the Federal Council of the Churches of Christ in America* (1908). Most of the member bodies are the so-called mainline churches,* with the majority of Christian churches in the U.S. remaining outside the NCCC, especially the Roman Catholic,* Southern Baptist* and Lutheran Church—Missouri Synod,* as well as many Pentecostal,* Holiness,* evangelical* and fundamentalist* churches.

Throughout its life the NCCC has sought to bring the implications of the gospel to the life and problems of the church and society. In recent decades the NCCC has suffered a decline in membership, which is generally attributed to the changing status of mainline churches in American culture.

See also ECUMENICAL MOVEMENT; ECUMENISM; NATIONAL ASSOCIATION OF EVANGELICALS; WORLD COUNCIL OF CHURCHES.

National Holiness Missionary Society. *See* WORLD GOSPEL MISSION.

National Liberal League. Nineteenth-century association established to combat government promotion of Christianity. A key figure in the organization of the league was Francis Ellingwood Abbot, a Unitarian*-turned-nonsectarian, who founded the league in 1869 to combat the conservative National Reform Association,* which

had as its goal a Christian preamble to the Constitution.

National Lutheran Council. A cooperative agency of eight Lutheran Churches* in the U.S. The council was formed by eight Lutheran Churches after their successful cooperation in ministry to servicemen during World War I.* In its early years the council was involved in relief efforts among European Lutherans distressed by war and postwar conditions. After World War II* the resettlement of refugees became a major emphasis.

National Reform Association. Association founded to restore the U.S. to its Christian* foundation. Reflecting nineteenth-century evangelical* convictions that the U.S. had a messianic national mission in the world, a group of conservative evangelical Christians founded the association in 1863. Their ultimate goal was to tie the republic and Christianity firmly together by means of a solid Christian preamble to the Constitution.

National Religious Broadcasters. Religious broadcasting in the U.S. began in 1921; its growth led to the founding of National Religious Broadcasters in 1944. The association was founded to defend freedom of access to the airwaves and to promote excellence in religious broadcasting. As of 1995 the number of full-time religious radio stations in the U.S. was 1,328, and the number of full-time religious television stations was 163. NRB organizational membership stands at 806.

See also ELECTRONIC CHURCH.

Nativism. A form of American nationalism. Nativism has been defined by historian J. Higham as an "intense opposition to an internal minority on the ground of its foreign (i.e., 'un-American') connections." Its most powerful strain is anti-Catholicism. Outbursts of anti-Catholic nativism have occurred in U.S. history whenever conditions of social and economic stress have conspired to arouse the deep-rooted suspicion that Catholicism is not compatible with American democratic institutions.

Three main waves of anti-Catholic nativism have surged through the land. Nativism in its prototypical form arose in response to the massive influx of European immigrants* from 1830 to 1860. The second wave emerged in the period of rapid growth, labor strife and economic difficulty during the decade of 1886-1896. The third wave, directed from rural areas against urban Catholic* political power and new immigrant groups, erupted sporadically between 1905 and 1930.

Nativism in general has tended to give patriotism a needlessly narrow cast and has probably led Catholics to an insufficiently critical embrace of American civil religion.*

Natural Law. Binding ethical* principles derived directly from an understanding of the world and particularly of human nature. Its main influence today stems from its expression by the Enlightenment* deists* who provided the intellectual basis for American constitutional democracy* and from its prominent role in Roman Catholic* theology* and ethics, especially Thomism.*

When the American Founding Fathers held it to be "self-evident" that all were created equal, they were in fact voicing the conclusions of a natural law theory. Within a Christian context, the starting point for understanding natural law may be in Romans 2:15, where the apostle Paul speaks of the Gentiles as having the law "written in their hearts, their consciences . . . bearing witness." This idea has become the background for Catholic thinkers such as Thomas Aquinas (1224-1274), who emphasize the reality and obligatory nature of this law.

Catholic natural law theory has made itself felt prominently in twentieth-century America in the context of bioethical discussions. The Vatican has decreed in various encyclicals* that natural law can be known by and is binding on all human beings.

Natural Theology. The attempt to discover truths about God by means of human reason or empirical observation, without recourse to supernatural revelation. Originating in ancient Greek philosophy, the concept was brought into Christian tradition as early as the second century. The enterprise presupposes (1) that certain aspects of God's self-disclosure are available to all (general revelation), having been etched in creation and/or in the structures of the human person; and (2) that humans have the ability to perceive this revelation.

Although attacked by Karl Barth* and de-emphasized by existentialist* theologies, natural theology continues to be prevalent among evangelicals* and Roman Catholics.*

Navigators, The. Evangelical* discipleship* ministry. In 1933 Dawson Trotman* and his wife, Lila, began an evangelistic outreach to sailors based at San Pedro, California. Trotman's energy, magnetism, directness of manner and love for people helped his ministry grow, and he enlisted a cadre of associates. By 1944 the Navigators had spread into all branches of the U.S. military.

The Navigators continue in their original purpose of discipling believers, having extended their outreach also to businesspeople as well as college students. By the early 1990s the organization was active in approximately seventy-five countries.

Nazarenes. See CHURCH OF THE NAZARENE.

Near East Relief. A national voluntary relief effort of the early twentieth century. A committee formed in 1915 to assist Christian Armenians expelled from the Ottoman Empire and famine victims in Syria was reorganized in 1919 and given a congressional charter as Near East Relief. After 1919 it aided Greek refugees from Asia Minor, those fleeing the Russian Revolution and disaster victims in Syria, Persia and the Caucasus.

Needham, George C. (1846-1902). Evangelist and Bible conference* leader. Coming to the U.S. in 1868, Needham made his home in Boston and considered A. J. Gordon* his pastor. He was a founder of the Niagara Bible Conference* and active in the early International Prophetic Conferences.

Neo-Conservative Catholicism. In the late 1960s and early 1970s, a host of new conservative movements arose in reaction to what was perceived as wrong-headed developments in American Catholicism* following Vatican II* (1962-1965). Neo-Conservative Catholics are primarily those intellectuals who are rooted in the liberal Catholic tradition but are disillusioned with post-Vatican II liberalism. They demand that Catholic theologians* be explicitly faithful to historical orthodoxy* and the authoritative magisterium.

Neo-Orthodoxy. Protestant* theological movement of the twentieth century. Neo-orthodoxy in America became an important force in the 1930s, when a number of theologians* became increasingly dissatisfied and disillusioned with the liberal* theology in which they had been trained. As the works of Europeans such as Karl Barth* and Emil Brunner* became known, their views came to have an increasing effect on American theologians and in mainline* American churches.

The Failure of Liberalism. The beginnings of American neo-orthodoxy can be traced to the 1930s, when the full effects of World War I,* coupled with the economic Depression in America, began to take their toll on American theologians. These events led them to question and reject the basic tenets of liberal theology. The Swiss theologian Karl Barth was led to reject liberal theology through his renewed study of Scripture, first expressed in his *Commentary on Romans* (1919; 2nd ed., 1922).

The Influence of Karl Barth. Barth, along with Rudolf Bultmann* and others, began what was known as dialectical, or crisis, theology. Directly opposing liberalism, they stressed the absolute contrast between the transcendent God and sinful humanity and emphasized God's initiative in revealing himself in Jesus Christ. For neo-orthodoxy the starting point of theology was God, as opposed to human experience, which marked the beginning for liberalism.

The American Movement. Throughout the 1930s, books and articles by liberal Protestants questioned the viability of liberalism. For many of that era the events of world history, characterized by social upheaval, political instabilities and economic disasters, called for a more realistic assessment of the relationship between God and humanity. Kierkegaard's* "infinite qualitative difference" between God and humanity was adopted by Barth and Brunner, who emphasized the "crisis" of the confrontation of a holy God with sinful humans. For them, God was the "Wholly Other" who revealed himself only in Jesus Christ, the Word of God. The Bible was the witness to God's revelation in Christ.

Neo-orthodoxy came to prominence in the wake of World War II.* During the 1940s and 1950s, neo-orthodoxy's realism was welcomed by many in mainline Protestant denominations.* As an alternative to liberalism and fundamentalism,* it offered a fresh means of hearing the gospel. Neo-orthodoxy was particularly strong in the Presbyterian Church in the U.S.A.*

However, as America moved into an era of progress and increasing prosperity in the decades following World War II, neo-orthodoxy began to wane as a dominant theological force. During the 1970s and 1980s process theology* and liberation theology* became major theological movements, gradually eclipsing the influence of neo-orthodoxy.

See also LIBERALISM/MODERNISM, PROTESTANT.

Neo-Thomism. A modern movement in philosophy and theology,* largely among Roman Catholic* thinkers, which applies the thought of St. Thomas Aquinas (1224-1274) to current issues.

There are two distinct trends in twentieth-century Neo-Thomism. One, revolving around Jacques Maritain (1882-1973) and Etienne Gilson (1884-1978), attempts to return to the thought of Aquinas himself as opposed to his later interpreters. The other tries not simply to repeat Aquinas's ideas but to philosophize the way he did, by creatively interacting with modern thought. Thus, thinkers such as Karl Rahner* and Bernard Lonergan* argue for discovering the need for God in the framework of the individual's subjective experience.

Nettleton, Asahel (1783-1844). Congregational* clergyman and conservative revivalist.* Nettleton's sober methods of revivalism stood in stark contrast to the progressive "new measures"* of Charles G. Finney.* Nettleton feared Finney's increasing power and attempted to protect New England from the sensationalism associated with the frontier revivals of the Second Great Awakening.* In 1833 Nettleton and other conservatives founded the Theological Institute of Connecticut (later renamed Hartford Theological Seminary) to combat "new measures" revivalism.

Nevin, John Williamson (1803-1886). Mercersburg* theologian and controversialist. In 1840 Nevin was called to Mercersburg Seminary of the German Reformed* Church. In 1843 he had burst upon the American theological scene with his critique of American "new measures"* revivalism,* *The Anxious Bench.* With the added stimulus brought by the coming of Philip Schaff* to Mercersburg in 1844, the work of Nevin and Mercersburg Seminary began to rise in prominence in the larger theological world of the U.S.

Nevin's most important contributions to theology and church life in America were his critique of the "sect spirit" and the excesses of revivalism, and his emphasis on the importance of tradition and the church. He was one of the most influential and controversial figures in the German Reformed Church in America.

Nevius, John Livingston (1829-1893). Presbyterian* missionary to China. Assigned to Ning Po, China, under the Presbyterian Mission Board, Nevius was there for several years (1854-1859) and then, after a brief period in Japan, spent terms in Shantung Province at Tungchow (1861-1864) and Chefoo (1871-1893).

Nevius objected to the conventional practice of missions boards paying national evangelists for their services. Rather, missionary churches should be self-supporting, self-propagating and self-governing units. Nevius's theories had an obvious influence on subsequent theories of church planting and growth.

New Age Movement. The 1980s in America witnessed a rising interest in the New Age movement (NAM), an umbrella term referring to a spiritual movement involving a variety of individuals, events, organizations, ideas and practices. The unifying essence of these manifold movements is a pantheistic and monistic worldview focused on the supposed unlimited powers of the unshackled self; its agenda is impelled by a messianic and millennial ideology (sometimes bolstered by astrological anticipations) of a New Age of peace, light and love soon to break forth. New Age influences can be found in areas as diverse as medicine, psychology, science, politics, business and education.

The NAM is both eclectic and syncretistic, drawing on sources as diverse as Vedanta Hinduism, assorted varieties of spiritism and avant-garde theories in quantum physics. It is best viewed not as a unified denomination,* sect,* cult* or conspiracy—although these factors are not lacking—but rather as a worldview shifting away from both monotheism and atheistic materialism and toward the "ancient wisdom" of various Eastern religions, pre-Christian Western religions, Christian heresies and the occult.

The most recent historical roots of the NAM in America are traced to the counterculture of the 1960s, when a variety of non-Christian spiritual gurus, swamis and yogis established themselves as alternatives to the "establishment" religions of Christianity and Judaism. Although by the late 1970s the cult explosion had lost much of its dynamism, the pantheistic/monistic worldview of the Eastern emissaries had taken root in the culture, and it began to play a significant part in American experience.

New Birth. An experience of Christian conversion* in which a person is born again,* being spiritually regenerated* by the work of the Holy Spirit. The term reflects the evangelical* emphasis on spiritual regeneration as the mark of a true Christian.*

The necessity of the new birth was the hallmark of George Whitefield's* preaching throughout the period 1740-1760, and largely through his influence it became the overarching theme of the revivalist* preaching of the Great Awakening.*

New Divinity. *See* New England Theology.

New England Theology (1750-1850). The pietist* revivals* in New England known as the Great Awakening* shattered the harmony of the established Congregational* churches of Massachusetts, Connecticut and New Hampshire, reawakening questions that had lain unresolved from the inception of the New England Way* in the seventeenth century

The most visible party to emerge within Congregationalism was the Edwardseans, or New Divinity Men—primarily Joseph Bellamy,* Samuel Hopkins* and Jonathan Edwards Jr.*—who took Jonathan Edwards* as their leader and mentor. Edwards was vitally concerned to formulate a Calvinistic* moral theology. He regarded the experimental* piety* of the revivals as a practical corollary to his efforts, leading him to embrace the pietistic strain of Congregational ecclesiology and to provide a series of justifications for closed Communion and diminished sacramental* efficacy.

The second major grouping in post-Awakening Congregationalism was Old Calvinism, or Old Lights,* which like Edwards wanted to preserve New England Calvinism, but more in terms of the pre-Awakening status quo than by means of revivals. They sharply repudiated Edwards's espousal of revivalism and his philosophical justifications for Calvinist theology. Ecclesiastically, they preferred parish* nurture by "use of the means" (sacraments,* preaching*) rather than immediate conversion* as the entrance to church membership.* Their most visible symbol was the perpetuation of the Half-Way Covenant.* This brought them into conflict with the New Divinity at every major point and sparked several major controversies.

Unitarianism* constituted a third major response within Congregationalism to the Awakening, in that the Awakening demonstrated to them the impracticality of Calvinism as a religion for enlightened thinkers. They embraced a liberalized Calvinism that deleted original sin* and the atonement, and added Arian or Socinian views of the person of Christ. The most important leaders of the Unitarians were Jonathan Mayhew* and, toward the end of his life, Charles Chauncy.*

New England Way. The unique system of church government* that evolved in Massachusetts Bay in the 1630s. By 1649 the central tenets of the New England Way were complete and codified in the Cambridge Platform.* Central to that system of government was the desire to create churches that were both "pure" in membership* and powerful in directing the outward governance of the New England towns.

Before joining a church, prospective members thus had to testify to a work of divine grace in their lives. Furthermore, the Puritans* established their churches as the law of the land, much like the Church of England.*

As a system of church government, the New England Way depended on a like-minded core of citizens. Such a way would have been impossible to institute in diverse Old World societies. But it was perfectly adapted to the circumstances of New World settlement in New England, and it survived intact throughout the colonial era.

New Evangelicalism. A movement among American conservative evangelicals* in the 1940s, 1950s and 1960s to reform fundamentalism* and restore evangelical Christianity's influence in modern life. Harold John Ockenga* was probably the first to coin the term *new evangelicalism* in 1948. Ockenga called this movement "progressive fundamentalism with a social message."

Besides Ockenga, Carl F. H. Henry* and Edward J. Carnell* at Fuller Seminary* were its leading proponents. The new evangelical intellectuals hoped to sweep away the stigma of fundamentalism and recapture the influence that their nineteenth-century ancestors had enjoyed. At the same time, they were committed to holding the fundamentalist line against liberal* theology.

New evangelical theology did resemble earlier fundamentalism. In particular, it made the inerrancy* of Scripture the keystone of orthodoxy.* By the late 1960s, the new evangelicalism began to break apart. Faced with either the disintegration of the movement or perhaps its takeover by

a growing "open evangelical" party, a group of conservatives, led by *Christianity Today** editor Harold Lindsell, made the inerrancy of the Bible the test of evangelical fidelity and waged open battle against the progressives. The result was further fragmentation.

The new evangelical pioneers, however, won some respect in the theological academy. They and their protégés produced a substantial body of biblical scholarship. The result has been a growing commitment to scholarship as kingdom work and a determination to confront the problems of the modern world.

New Hampshire Confession of Faith. A widely influential summary statement of Baptist* moderate Calvinism,* originally drafted in 1833. After 1850 the confession gained stature in the wider Baptist fellowship. It was disseminated by the publications of influential leaders, including J. Newton Brown, who had prepared the 1833 draft; the Landmark* Baptist James M. Pendleton;* and Edward T. Hiscox, author of a widely used Baptist manual.

In 1933 a group of conservative churches withdrew from the Northern Baptist Convention to form the General Association of Regular Baptists* and adopted a premillennial* version of the confession as their standard.

See also THE BAPTIST CHURCHES IN U.S.A.; BAPTISTS IN CANADA.

New Harmony. Site of Harmonist (1814-1824) and Owenite (1825-1827) utopian communities in southwest Indiana on the Wabash River. New Harmony was first the site of a utopian community founded by German separatists* led by Johann Georg Rapp.* The Rappite community practiced celibacy and a Christian communism. It disbanded in 1824.

Robert Owen,* a social reformer from Scotland, purchased New Harmony in 1825. He invited the general public to join his nonsectarian Community of Equality in which communal living, science and education would free their minds and bodies and become the foundation of a worldwide secular millennium. Communal living was abandoned in 1827.

See also MILLENARIAN MOVEMENTS.

New Haven Theology. A modified Calvinism* defined primarily by Nathaniel W. Taylor* and developed by the faculty of Yale's* Divinity

School from the early 1820s into the 1840s. Under the banner of "Calvinist orthodoxy," Taylor and his colleagues combined a rationalistic system based on God's moral government and a "reasonable" revivalism* that appealed to the "common sense" of Jacksonian America.

The New Haven theologians formally endorsed the "substance" of orthodox* Calvinist doctrine as found in the Westminster Confession* and Connecticut's Saybrook Platform,* but they discarded the "secondary doctrines" or "explanations" that had been attached to these articles of faith. Specifically, they rejected the explanation of depravity that described Adam's sin being imputed to all his descendants, for it robbed individuals of their status as moral agents, made God the author of sin and simply defied "common sense."

Although it is certain that individuals will choose to sin, at every moment they have "the power to the contrary." Similarly, they have the power to effect their own regeneration,* but lack the will to do so until the Holy Spirit makes its forceful appeal to their understandings.

New Lebanon Conferences. The meeting convoked in 1827 in New Lebanon, New York, for the purpose of obtaining a consensus on appropriate methods in Calvinistic* revivalism.* The occasion for the meeting was the denunciation by Asahel Nettleton* of the "new measures"* being introduced by Charles G. Finney.* The conference failed to restrain Finney's measures and signaled the decline of Nettleton's influence.

See also REVIVALISM, PROTESTANT.

New Lights. The term *New Light* emerged in New England during the Great Awakening* (1740-1743) to describe the evangelical* supporters of George Whitefield* and the mass revivals* he inspired. The New Light party of Congregational* ministers and churches was especially strong in the rural and frontier regions of New England. Jonathan Edwards* emerged as the preeminent champion of the New Light party. His two most famous students—Samuel Hopkins* and Joseph Bellamy*—absorbed his teaching and passed it on to their students, who in turn filled pulpits throughout Connecticut and western New England, ultimately informing a broad segment of what would eventually become the American "evangelical" tradition.

See also OLD LIGHTS.

New Lights (Canada). Followers of the revivalist* Henry Alline* in Nova Scotia. In 1776 Alline embarked on a lifetime of preaching and traveling throughout much of Nova Scotia and what later became New Brunswick, bringing his message of the necessity for a new birth* to the pre-Loyalist Yankees of the region. His itinerant* ministry and his writings, which proclaimed a somewhat idiosyncratic mixture of mysticism,* asceticism and anti-Calvinist theology,* exerted a profound effect on the religious life of the Maritimes and parts of northern New England.

New Measures. The style of revivalism* espoused by Charles G. Finney,* which highlighted the place of human effort in obeying divine laws to promote religious awakenings.* Finney used some highly criticized methods (or measures) to achieve results, including direct and often public pressure on individuals to make a decision, sustained prayer, women praying in mixed groups, encouragement of lay participation and the anxious bench.*

New Religious Right. The New Religious Right is a social, political and religious movement started in the late 1970s and reaching its peak during the early to mid-1980s. The core of the movement is a loose alliance of social and political groups that included most notably the Moral Majority,* led by Baptist* pastor Jerry Falwell.* Most supporters are fundamentalist* Christians with theologically and politically conservative views. The most important goal of the movement has been to attack the influences of secular humanism* in politics and society by restoring traditional moral views and lifestyles consistent with biblical prescriptions. Although the overall impact of the New Religious Right is the subject of widely varying interpretations, the most significant contributions have been the political mobilization of millions of conservative Christians and the inclusion of its major issues, such as abortion* and school prayer,* in the national political agenda.

The size of the movement is subject to various interpretations. At its peak, the Moral Majority numbered about four million, while Christian Voice, headed by Robert Grant, numbered 400,000, and the mailing list for Concerned Women for America, led by Beverly LaHaye, numbered approximately 100,000.

The historical roots of the New Religious Right lay in the emergence of fundamentalism in the

1920s as a reaction to the modernism* that swept through mainline* Protestantism.* The more recent stimulus for the movement lay in the perceptions of conservative fundamentalists that the U.S. was coming under the influence of liberal secularism, reflected in Supreme Court* decisions about prayer* and Bible reading in public schools and about abortion, in the political demands of feminists and homosexuals, and in the efforts by government agencies to regulate Christian day schools.*

The strength of the New Religious Right has come from the entrepreneurial leadership of individuals such as Falwell, Pat Robertson,* and Tim and Beverly LaHaye. In addition, the close ties with religious broadcasters (Falwell's *Old Time Gospel Hour,* Robertson's Christian Broadcasting Network and television program *700 Club*) have helped to reach an audience open to their conservative political and religious appeals.

Critics of the New Religious Right, led by Norman Lear's People for the American Way and the American Civil Liberties Union, have argued against this mixing of religion and politics, claiming that such use of political power to force sectarian morality on society is a violation of the separation of church and state.* They have perceived the movement as undermining the tolerant pluralism needed for democracy.

New School Presbyterians. New School Presbyterianism was the pro-revivalist version of nineteenth-century Presbyterianism* that had strong ties to New England Congregationalism* and for the middle third of the century existed as a separate denomination.* Its origins lay in the evangelical* awakening of the first third of the nineteenth century (*see* Second Great Awakening), especially enhanced by the Plan of Union* of 1801.

Growing apprehension among Old School Presbyterians* over the taint of heresy because of the close connections with New England paved the way for denominational schism in 1837-1838. Theological concerns particularly over the revisions of Calvinist* orthodoxy* made by Nathaniel Taylor* (*see* New Haven Theology) led to a series of heresy trials* and to the takeover by Old School partisans of the 1837 General Assembly. There they abrogated the Plan of Union, effectively removing the New School Presbyterians.

From 1837 until the reunion in 1869, New School Presbyterians existed as a separate denomination. During this time New Schoolers became more doctrinally vigilant, more distinctly Presbyterian and hence more narrowly denominational in their outlook. The experience of the Civil War* tended to reverse the parochial tendencies of the previous decades. The war also hastened Presbyterian reunion, as both sides realized that previous causes for separation had largely dissipated.

New School Presbyterianism is significant for understanding nineteenth-century American culture because it was so very typical of it. More typically American in character and spirit than Old School Presbyterians, New Schoolers combined a pietist*/revivalist* emphasis with the cultural mandate of making America a Christian nation.

See also REFORMED AND PRESBYTERIAN CHURCHES; REFORMED TRADITION IN AMERICA.

New Side Presbyterians. Revivalist* party within eighteenth-century Presbyterianism.* Conflict broke out in 1738 over the standing of candidates for ordination* graduated from the Log College,* a strongly pietistic* school operated by William Tennent.* Forced out of their synod, Tennent and the New Brunswick (N.J.) Presbytery organized their own so-called New Side jurisdiction, which was joined by the Presbytery of New York in 1745 to form the New Side Synod of New York.

Tennent later expressed regret for his actions, which opened the way to restoration of fellowship between the New Side and Old Side* synods in 1758. But the tension between the confessional* and Pietist factions in the Presbyterian Church remained apparent and surfaced again in the New School*-Old School* schism of 1837.

See also OLD SIDE PRESBYTERIANS.

New Theology. *See* EVANGELICAL LIBERALISM.

New York Bible Society. An early nondenominational society established for the local publication and distribution of Scripture. Founded in 1809, the New York Bible Society (NYBS) aimed to publish and distribute the Bible in the languages used in and about the city and the harbor of New York. In its prime, the NYBS distributed more than a million copies of Scripture in some seventy different languages annually.

With the publication of the New International Version (1978), the NYBS gave birth to the International Bible Society.*

New York Missionary Society. Interdenominational voluntary society* dedicated to the evangelism* of the American frontier.* Founded in 1796 by New York Presbyterian,* Baptist* and Dutch Reformed* clergy, the New York Missionary Society was the first interdenominational missionary* association established in a new era of American benevolent activity. Its mission was concentrated on Native Americans.

In 1822 the society merged with other New York home-missionary societies into the United Domestic Missionary Society.

Newcomer, Christian (1749-1830). Missionary bishop of the Church of the United Brethren in Christ. Becoming a full-time itinerant* in 1777, Newcomer established circuits across the Allegheny Mountains in the Midwest and Upper South. A staunch opponent of slavery, he provided moral guidance to the rapidly expanding United Brethren during the antebellum years.

Newell, Bertha Payne (1867-1953). Educator and social reformer. In North Carolina Newell was active in various agencies of the Methodist* Episcopal Church, South, as well as in the Federal Council of Churches* department of race relations (1927-1935) and department of social service (1929-1935) and the North Carolina Interracial Commission.

Newell, Harriet Atwood (1793-1812). Pioneer missionary to India. In February 1812 Harriet set sail with her husband of ten days and with Adoniram* and Ann* Judson. She gave birth prematurely at sea, lost the baby, and died in November, the first American missionary to die in service on a foreign field.

Newman, Albert Henry (1852-1933). Baptist* church historian and educator. Newman taught at what became McMaster University in Toronto (1881-1901), Baylor University (1901-1908) and Southwestern Baptist Theological Seminary* (1908-1913). He was one of the premier church historians of the late nineteenth century and one of a few Baptist educators who rose above regional politics and served in Northern, Southern and Canadian institutions.

Newman Movement. A Catholic* student ministry movement inspired by the life and writings of John Henry Newman (1801-1890) to provide pastoral care and religious education on non-Catholic college and university campuses. In the first phase (1883-1908), the movement received strong leadership from bishops. The second phase (1908-1962) emphasized student organizations. Finally, since 1962 it has followed a diocesan-centered approach.

Newton, Joseph Fort (1867-1950). Liberal* Protestant* preacher, writer, ecumenist* and mystic.* Newton was a curious combination of diverse ideals and ecclesiological practices. A popular preacher, he was widely known for his homiletic skills. Largely self-educated, he was a prolific writer on various historical, theological and political subjects. A self-styled mystic, his concern for direct encounter with the Divine provided continuity throughout a diverse denominational pilgrimage.

Niagara Conferences. A series of summer conferences that served as the progenitor of Bible and prophecy conferences* in the U.S. and Canada. Organized in the late 1860s, the meetings were first opened to the public in the mid-1870s. After being held at a variety of locations in the northern U.S., this interdenominational conference found a home at Niagara-on-the-Lake, Ontario, where it thrived from 1883 through 1897. After 1897 controversy over the rapture* of the church sent the conference into rapid decline. The final meeting was held in 1900.

Niebuhr, H(elmut) Richard (1894-1962). Protestant* theologian. Niebuhr, professor of Christian ethics at Yale* Divinity School from 1931 until his death, had a lifelong concern for the relationship of the church and the modern world. He analyzed the sociological and historical roots of denominational* divisions in *The Social Sources of Denominationalism* (1929). He studied the influence of the idea of the kingdom of God* on American culture in *The Kingdom of God in America* (1937). And his typology of church/world interaction in *Christ and Culture* (1951) has become a classic.

Niebuhr's theological work centered on questions of unity and diversity, the shape of knowledge of objective truth in a relativistic framework and the nature of faith in modern life. Influenced by Jonathan Edwards,* William James,* Josiah Royce* and George Herbert Mead as well as Karl Barth,* Paul Tillich,* Albrecht Ritschl and Ernst

Troeltsch, Niebuhr developed a crosscultural theology that addressed the issues of his day: the fundamentalist-modernist debate,* World War II* and the cold war era.

Niebuhr, (Karl Paul) Reinhold (1892-1971). Theologian and ethicist. After pastoring a church in Detroit for thirteen years, Niebuhr moved to Union Theological Seminary* in New York, where he taught from 1928 to 1960. During his years at Union, Niebuhr wrote several significant books, including his highly influential *Moral Man and Immoral Society* (1932). He was the founder and editor (1941-1966) of *Christianity and Crisis,* a magazine bringing religion to bear on critical social issues.

Theologically, Niebuhr was deeply influenced by Social Gospel* liberalism,* but his theological reflection and pastoral experience in Detroit transformed his optimism into a "Christian realism." Increasingly pessimistic regarding human possibilities, Niebuhr began to see the hope of the world in the coming kingdom of God* which stands in judgment over all human endeavors and achievements.

Niebuhr is best understood as an apologetic theologian who sought to validate the claims of the Christian faith to the secular world. His apologetics proceeded by exposing the contradictions in human existence and showing that only the love of the cross, which represents the divine forgiveness, can be the answer to human sin and despair.

See also NIEBUHR, HELMUT RICHARD.

Niles, Samuel (1674-1762). Old Light* Congregational* minister. After ten years of missionary work in Rhode Island, Niles was called to the South Church of Braintree, Massachusetts, where he remained until his death. Obstinate by nature, Niles took an active part in the religious controversies of his day.

Nixon, Richard Milhous (1913-1994). Thirty-seventh U.S. president. Nixon's faith was essentially that of a generalized Protestantism,* with a decided emphasis on civil religion.* His spiritual counselor was evangelist Billy Graham,* whose early relationship with him lasted even after Nixon's fall from power. This endeared Nixon to the evangelical community, which firmly supported his presidential bids in 1960, 1968 and 1972. However, the Watergate tapes revealed his religi-

osity to be much less than his evangelical supporters had supposed, and eventually they reluctantly turned from him.

Nominal Christian. A term describing those who are Christian in name only, often used in a pejorative sense. The term often operates as a critique of Christians outside any given group who appear to be superficial in their commitment to the Christian faith.

Norelius, Eric (1833-1916). Pioneer Swedish Lutheran* minister. In 1860, with his bride and much of an Indiana Swedish group, Norelius moved to Minnesota, where he organized several congregations, serving these until his retirement in 1915. In Minnesota he also founded St. Ansgar Academy (1865), which became today's Gustavus Adolphus College. Norelius was the youngest of the founding fathers of the Evangelical Lutheran Augustana Church (Synod) and the only one of them educated and ordained on this side of the Atlantic.

Norris, J. Frank (1877-1952). Fundamentalist* Baptist* minister. Norris served as pastor of First Baptist Church in Fort Worth, Texas (1909-1952), and in later years served simultaneously as pastor of Temple Baptist in Detroit, Michigan (1935-1948), commuting by air between the two churches. Both were large congregations for their day (memberships of 15,000 and 10,000 respectively) and were built around Norris's forceful personality, sensational tactics, soul-winning* fervor and conservative theological and political views.

Exposing sin,* criticizing the Southern Baptist Convention* and promoting the fundamentalist cause, Norris became known by many of his fellow Baptist ministers for his independent spirit and acrimonious behavior. He was known also for his anti-Catholic convictions.

North, Frank Mason (1850-1935). Methodist Episcopal* minister and ecumenist.* For nineteen years (1873-1892) North served in various pastorates of the Methodist Episcopal Church (*see* Methodist Churches) in the New York area. For two decades he also directed a network of metropolitan missions.* He helped draft the Federal Council's* historic "Social Creed of the Churches."*

North American Baptist Conference. A small Baptist* denomination* with German ethnic background. The roots of the North American Baptist Conference lie in the nineteenth century in the concern felt by European and North American Christians for the spiritual welfare of German immigrants* to the U.S. and Canada. As a result, German-speaking Baptist congregations were founded in the East, Midwest and Province of Ontario. In 1865 the General Conference of German Baptist Churches in North America was formed, the forerunner of the current triennial meeting.

See also THE BAPTIST CHURCHES IN U.S.A.; IMMIGRATION AND ETHNICITY, PROTESTANT.

North American Christian Convention. The annual national convention of the Christian Churches/Churches of Christ,* first held in 1927. This convention has become the major assembly point for Christian Churches/Churches of Christ, who currently number about one million in total membership. Approximately twenty thousand people attend each year.

North American College, The Pontifical. A church residence in Rome, Italy, for American Catholic* secular priests and seminarians attending the Roman theological universities. Founded in 1859 by Pope Pius IX,* it is managed by the U.S. bishops. In 1953 a new facility was dedicated within Vatican City.

Northern Baptist Convention. *See* AMERICAN BAPTIST CHURCHES IN THE U.S.A.

Northfield Conferences. A series of summer conferences founded by Dwight L. Moody* and held in Moody's hometown of Northfield, Massachusetts. Established in 1880, the conferences emphasized the power of the Holy Spirit to lead believers toward a sanctified life. At the first student conference, in 1886, one hundred students pledged themselves to work on the foreign mission field (*see* Mount Hermon One Hundred).

The 1880s and 1890s were the heyday of the Northfield Conferences.

Norton, Andrews (1786-1853). Unitarian* theologian. After serving as professor of sacred literature at Harvard* (1819-1830), Norton devoted himself to full-time study and writing. He rejected trinitarian orthodoxy* and was one of the leaders in the founding of the American Unitarian Association* in 1825.

While espousing a liberal* theology, Norton retained confidence in the historicity and authority of Scripture. For his efforts in maintaining a conservative Unitarianism, Norton became known as the pope of Unitarianism.

Norton, John (1606-1663). New England Puritan* minister. Arriving in Plymouth in 1635, Norton shortly thereafter moved to Massachusetts Bay. He quickly assumed a position of leadership in the young colony, playing an important part in the antinomian controversy* and in drawing up the famous Cambridge Platform* of 1648.

Notre Dame, University of. Catholic* university. Founded in 1842 by Edward F. Sorin,* the University of Notre Dame du Lac was the first Catholic school in the country with programs in law (1869) and engineering (1873).

Besides instructional programs through the doctoral level, Notre Dame currently sponsors a wide range of research institutes. These, along with its athletic and educational programs, have made it arguably the best-known Catholic university in America.

Novena. A Catholic* devotional practice of nine successive days of prayer* to obtain some special grace, modeled on the reputed nine days of prayer before Pentecost (Acts 1:13-14).

Novice. A candidate for the religious life as lived within a particular institute. A period of testing and formation, usually lasting at least a year, is required before admission of a candidate to full membership within the institute.

Noyes, John Humphrey (1811-1886). Perfectionist* and founder of the Oneida Community (1848-1881). Noyes developed a variety of radical theological and social theories rooted in perfectionism, revivalism,* millennialism,* the Unitarian* socialism of Brook Farm* and eugenics. In 1844 he established a "biblical communism" at Putney, Vermont, for his disciples. In 1846 the group began its notorious practice of sharing mates, or "complex marriage."

Noyes moved his disciples to Oneida, New York, in 1848, after being indicted on adultery charges. There more than three hundred Oneida perfectionists lived communally and prospered economically. By 1879 pending legal action had caused Noyes to flee to Canada, from which he never returned.

See also MILLENARIAN MOVEMENTS.

Nun. A popular term referring to any Catholic* or Anglican* woman who is a vowed member of a religious community. Unlike sisters,* nuns do not engage in active works of charity.

See also RELIGIOUS ORDERS, WOMEN'S.

Oakes, Urian (c. 1631-1681). Puritan* minister, poet and president of Harvard College.* Oakes came to New England in 1640 and then in 1671, when he was called to the ministry of the Cambridge, Massachusetts, church. In 1675 he became acting president of Harvard College and in 1680 was elected president. He is perhaps best remembered for his one published poem, the "Elegie" on Thomas Shepard.*

Oberholtzer, John H. (1809-1895). Mennonite* minister and a founder of the General Conference Mennonite Church.* Oberholtzer's attempts to initiate change led to the so-called Oberholtzer schism of 1847. After 1860 this group was known as the Eastern District Conference of the General Conference Mennonite Church.

Oberlin College. An educational institution with roots in nineteenth-century evangelicalism.* John J. Shipherd opened the school in 1833 and in 1835 attracted a group known as the Lane Rebels. They brought to the school an intense crusading spirit of reform unmatched in American educational history. Oberlin also promoted women's rights, pioneering in awarding degrees to both white and African-American women.

After the presidency of Charles Finney* (1851-1866), Oberlin continued its social reform emphasis, but the motivation for it gradually changed from evangelical and Holiness* theology* to the newly developing liberal* Protestant* theology.

Oberlin Theology. The doctrine* of holiness* associated with Oberlin College* during the nineteenth century. "Oberlin perfectionism,*" the teaching that holiness consists primarily of the perfection of the will and is available to every Christian after conversion,* became associated with Oberlin primarily through the influence of Asa Mahan* and Charles G. Finney.*

Mahan, the first president of the college, was committed to a doctrine of perfectionism, which he described as holiness or the baptism of the Holy Spirit.*

Finney began his association with Oberlin College in 1835 as professor of theology* and was the president of Oberlin from 1851 to 1866. Like Mahan, Finney emphasized holiness as voluntary conformity of the human will to the will of God.

Unlike those who advocated a private holiness, Oberlin theology was associated with social reform. Oberlin College was in the forefront of the antislavery struggle, and under Finney's influence it became a hotbed of social reform and Christian activism.

Oblate Sisters of Providence. The first congregation of African-American Catholic religious women. In the 1790s, out of a desire to provide an education for their children, several African-American women began a school near St. Mary's Seminary, Baltimore. The Sulpician* priest James Hector Joubert (1777-1843) helped form them into a religious community. The school flourished and became a center of worship* for the Baltimore African-American community until the death of Joubert.

Obookiah (Opukahaia), Henry (1792-1818). Hawaiian Christian and inspiration for the American Board's Sandwich Islands Mission. Taken as a teenage orphan from Honolulu to New Haven, Obookiah in 1816 became affiliated with the American Board of Commissioners for Foreign Missions* and became an effective advocate for foreign missions.

O'Brien, John Anthony (1893-1980). Catholic* apologist* and journalist. O'Brien was an extremely effective chaplain* to Catholic students at the University of Illinois (1918-1940). Responsible for some forty-five books, O'Brien saw his best-known work, *The Faith of Millions* (1938), eventually published in ten languages.

Occasional Sermon. Sermons delivered at times other than regularly scheduled Sunday sermons. New England preachers continued the English practice of delivering sermons on special occasions, such as election days, days of thanksgiving, or after natural disasters.

Occom, Samson (1723-1792). Native American evangelist. A Mohegan Indian converted to Christianity about 1740 during the Great Awakening,* Occom received ordination* in 1759 as a Presbyterian* minister. He became an influential preacher and tribal leader among Native Americans in the Northeast, traveling widely in southern New England and New York.

Occultism. The word *occult* refers to those practices and beliefs dealing with supernatural influences, agencies or phenomena which are concealed or hidden from the masses and available only to "the initiated." The occult is best understood as religion, since its subject matter lies in the realm of the paranormal and the supernatural and because its main goals pertain to the discovery of "ultimate meaning." Most scholars include under the rubric of the occult such phenomena as clairvoyance, telepathy, precognition, divination, necromancy, astrology, spiritualism and mediumship, palmistry, tarot card reading, numerology, crystal gazing, poltergeist activity, vampirism, voodoo, shamanism, Satanism, demonology, exorcism, witchcraft, mysticism,* faith healing,* and the New Age movement.*

Western civilization has experienced two major outbreaks of occult activity: first in the Renaissance era and again in the twentieth century. Christians historically have distrusted and avoided the occult because of explicit biblical teachings and warnings.

See also SALEM WITCH TRIAL.

Ockenga, Harold John (1905-1985). Congregational* minister and new evangelical* organizational leader. At Boston's Park Street Congregational Church (1936-1969), Ockenga's organizational gifts and scholarly preaching* made the church thrive and brought him leadership opportunities among evangelicals in New England and throughout the country.

In the early 1940s he was instrumental in founding the National Association of Evangelicals.* In 1947 he became founding president of Fuller Theological Seminary,* which he helped establish as the leading scholarly institution of the "new evangelical" movement. As one of the organizers in the founding of *Christianity Today*￼* in 1956, Ockenga helped provide the new evangelical movement with a national voice.

Ockenga left Park Street Church to become president of Gordon College and Divinity School. He later presided over the newly merged Gordon-Conwell Theological Seminary from 1970 until 1979.

O'Connell, Denis Joseph (1849-1927). Strategist and Roman agent for the American Catholic liberal party of bishops in the late nineteenth century. Allied with such American liberal prelates as James Gibbons,* John Ireland* and John Keane,* O'Connell sought greater control of church affairs by American leadership and a full participation by American Catholics in the institutions of national life, including the public schools.

O'Connell, William Henry (1859-1944). Cardinal of Boston. In 1906 O'Connell became coadjutor bishop of Boston, with the right of succession, becoming archbishop the following year. In 1911, at an unusually young age, he was made a cardinal.

For a quarter of a century O'Connell was the dominant figure in the American Catholic hierarchy, a status achieved by both his strong personality and his close Vatican connections. Considered autocratic by many, he had a firm sense of episcopal* authority.*

Cardinal O'Connell was a cultured man who played and composed music. He was also a lover of art and a great builder of churches.

O'Connor, Flannery (1925-1964). Catholic* Southern fiction writer. A master of short fiction and a superb regionalist, Flannery O'Connor lived most of her life in Milledgeville, Georgia. In her two novels, *Wise Blood* (1952) and *The Violent Bear It Away* (1960), and in her short stories, especially "A Good Man Is Hard to Find" (1955) and "Everything That Rises Must Converge" (published posthumously in 1965), O'Connor's vision of the human predicament is carefully delineated.

A staunch apologist* for the Christian faith, she nevertheless struck out at facile formulations but

[247]

nearly always found a supernatural grace operating in the midst of horror and degradation.

Oglethorpe, James Edward (1696-1785). English philanthropist* and colonizer. Oglethorpe raised the capital to create a colony (Georgia) to which English poor could be sent as an alternative to debtors' prison. George II approved a charter (1732), and Oglethorpe sailed with the first ship of settlers, arriving in 1733. He spent most of the next ten years as resident governor of the colony, which he managed to shape along more humane lines than the existing colonies had been.

O'Gorman, Thomas (1843-1921). Catholic* bishop of Sioux Falls, South Dakota. O'Gorman taught English, French, dogmatic theology and modern church history at the Catholic University of America,* where he actively supported the liberal policies of Americanists* during the controversies of late nineteenth-century American Catholicism.

O'Hara, Edwin Vincent (1881-1956). Catholic* archbishop and rural sociologist. When an Oregon school bill requiring attendance in the public schools was passed, O'Hara led the legal fight against it until it was declared unconstitutional by the U.S. Supreme Court.* While O'Hara was bishop of Great Falls, Montana, he formed the Confraternity of Christian Doctrine,* which later expanded into a national confraternity. A leading American proponent of the use of the vernacular in the liturgy,* O'Hara was largely responsible for the first approved English ritual that came out in 1954.

O'Hara, John Francis (1888-1960). Educator and cardinal archbishop of Philadelphia. O'Hara became bishop of Philadelphia in 1951 and in 1958 was named a cardinal. He developed Philadelphia's parochial* school system by building over sixty new schools and promoting education for the mentally retarded.

O'Kelly, James (1757-1826). Methodist* minister and leader of the O'Kelly schism.* For several years O'Kelly was presiding elder of the South Virginia district, during which time he became enamored with the independent spirit of the Republic and the themes of freedom and equality. This led him to a confrontation with the church

hierarchy in 1792, during the first General Conference of the Methodist Episcopal Church. O'Kelly's resolution was defeated, and he subsequently led eight thousand members in withdrawing to form the Republican Methodist Church.

O'Kelly Schism. A schism named for Methodist* preacher James O'Kelly,* whose attempt to restrict the authority* of bishops caused the first major division in the American Methodist Church. Becoming alarmed at the increasing authority of Bishop Francis Asbury,* O'Kelly tried unsuccessfully in the 1792 General Conference* to have ministerial appointments made more democratically. He then withdrew from the Methodist Episcopal Church, forming the Republican Methodist Church. The schism had the lasting effects of solidifying the power of the bishops.

Old Calvinists. *See* NEW ENGLAND THEOLOGY.

Old Lights. The term *Old Light* emerged in New England during the Great Awakening* (1740-1743) to describe the socially and theologically conservative opponents of George Whitefield* and the mass revivals* he inspired. Old Lights denied that the Great Awakening was a work of God, claiming instead that it destroyed the peace and unity of the church by pitting enthusiastic laypeople and itinerant* preachers against the established clergy of New England.

The Old Light clergy could be found throughout New England but were especially strong around Boston, where they were led by the clergyman Charles Chauncy.* The faculties of Harvard* and Yale* also were strongly opposed to Whitefield and the revivals.

Old Order Mennonites. A broad term referring to independent conservative Mennonite* bodies that separated from the Mennonite Church in a series of schisms from 1872 to 1901. Old Order Mennonites can be classified as (1) more progressive and (2) more conservative. In general, the progressive groups conduct their worship* services in English and drive cars; they are also free to use modern inventions such as the telephone. The more conservative groups often conduct their services in Pennsylvania German and drive horses and buggies. Old Order Mennonites number under twenty thousand members in approximately one hundred churches.

Old Order River Brethren. A small Brethren* denomination.* The Old Order River Brethren withdrew from the larger River Brethren Church (now Brethren in Christ*) in the 1850s in order to maintain conservative standards. First identified as a separate group in York County, Pennsylvania, they became known by some as "Yorker Brethren." In the twentieth century they have centered in Franklin County and Lancaster County, Pennsylvania, and Dallas County, Iowa.

Old School Presbyterians. During the 1730s and 1740s Presbyterians* suffered internal divisions over questions regarding the theological legitimacy and ecclesiastical propriety of the Great Awakening.* Under the leadership of Gilbert Tennent,* "New Side"* Presbyterians labored to advance the Awakening, against the objections of "Old Side"* traditionalists. By 1758 a rapprochement had been reached that favored the New Side party, who had managed to install a series of pro-Awakeners in the presidency of the fledgling College of New Jersey* at Princeton, New Jersey.

A shift away from the New Side occurred under Archibald Alexander,* who in 1812 became the first professor at Princeton Theological Seminary.* Alexander formed a distinct version of Presbyterian theology that found its genesis in older, European formulations of Calvinism.* Demanding strict adherence to the Westminster Confession of Faith,* Alexander formed what became known as the Old School theology.* Under Alexander's direction, and through the efforts of his colleague Charles Hodge,* Princeton Seminary became the intellectual center of Old School Presbyterianism. It criticized the revival* tactics of the Second Great Awakening* as well as the "New Haven" theology* of Lyman Beecher* and Nathaniel W. Taylor.*

The tumultuous slavery issue led ultimately to the division of both the New School* (1857) and the Old School (1861). The New School—Old School schism in the North was healed during the period 1868-1870, while Presbyterians in the South reunited in 1864.

See also PRINCETON THEOLOGY; SCOTTISH PRESBYTERIANS IN AMERICA.

Old Side Presbyterians. Conservative party within eighteenth-century Presbyterians.* In the early 1700s the Presbyterian churches of Scotch and Scotch-Irish immigrants* often had as ministers graduates of New England colleges, who tended to import notions of pietist* evangelicalism* and who held rather loosely to the political tenets of the Westminster Confession.*

This challenge to traditional Presbyterian order was exacerbated after 1735 by William Tennent* and his pietist "Log College."* The censure of "New Side" Tennent and a New Jersey presbytery by the "Old Side" Scottish and Scotch-Irish clergy* led to a protracted pamphlet war. The two parties were eventually reunited in 1758.

Old Side principles continued to command significant loyalty within Presbyterian education and played a key role in the Old School*—New School* schism of 1837.

See also GREAT AWAKENING.

Olney, Thomas (?-1682). Colonial Baptist* leader. Olney followed Roger Williams* to Providence, Rhode Island, in 1638 and joined him at the first Baptist church established in America. When Williams stepped down as pastor, Olney replaced him.

OMF. *See* OVERSEAS MISSIONARY FELLOWSHIP.

OMS International, Inc. A nondenominational mission* agency in the Wesleyan* tradition. OMS International, originally known as the Oriental Missionary Society, was founded in 1901 by Charles E. and Lettie B. Cowman,* who launched out on their own for missionary service in Japan. From Japan the mission expanded to Korea, China and India, and today ministers in Asia, Latin America, Europe and the Caribbean.

Onderdonk, Benjamin Tredwell (1791-1861). Episcopal* bishop of New York. Onderdonk, professor of ecclesiastical polity and law (1821-1861) at the General Theological Seminary, New York, was consecrated the fourth bishop of New York in 1830. In 1845 he was removed from office on charges of immorality. Along with his brother Henry Ustick Onderdonk,* Benjamin was a high churchman* and an aggressive supporter of the Oxford movement.*

Onderdonk, Henry Ustick (1789-1858). Episcopal* bishop of Pennsylvania. Onderdonk, following his younger brother Benjamin Tredwell Onderdonk,* studied for the ministry* under Bishop John Henry Hobart* of New York. In 1836 he became the second bishop of Pennsylvania.

Onderdonk was subject to a chronic intestinal disorder, and he became addicted to the brandy he used to relieve his pain. He was suspended from his office in 1844, but then was reinstated in 1856.

Oneida Community. *See* NOYES, JOHN HUMPHREY.

Open and Institutional Church League, The. An interdenominational agency promoting broad access to churches. Founded in 1894 at the Madison Avenue Presbyterian Church in New York City, the league sought to promote the practice of opening church buildings to all worshipers (not just those who paid pew rents) and encouraging congregational programs of Christian social service that would bring Christian teachings and practice to everyday life.

Opus Dei. A Catholic* organization nurturing lay spirituality.* Founded in 1928 by Josemaría Escrivá de Balaguer (1902-1975), a young Spanish priest,* Opus Dei later spread throughout Europe and beyond, including to the U.S. in 1949.

Opus Dei centers offer spiritual direction and a program based on prayer and active appreciation for the sacraments* as the catalyst for putting Christian ideals into practice in everyday life.

Order of Cistercians of the Strict Observance. *See* TRAPPISTS.

Ordination. The setting apart of some members by a church for ministerial or priestly leadership, usually by laying on of hands* and invocation of the Holy Spirit. It is considered a sacrament* in Catholic* and Eastern Orthodox* theology.* Ordination usually requires both a spiritual call from God and an ecclesiastical call, including the fulfillment of standards of training, doctrinal conformity and other institutional requirements. Roman Catholic, Eastern Orthodox and most conservative Protestant* churches ordain men only, while the ordination of women* in liberal and some Holiness* and Pentecostal* churches began within the last century.

In Baptist* and other groups with radical congregational* polity,* ordination is administered by the local church. In presbyterial* denominations* the regional body examines candidates and exercises authority to ordain. In episcopally* organized churches such as the Methodist,* Episcopal,* Lutheran,* Roman Catholic and Eastern Orthodox, the bishop is required to administer the rite.

Ordination of Women. Women have played an active and varied role as laypeople within the church since colonial days—and some women were ordained* by the mid-nineteenth century—but the general movement for the ordination of women in the American churches is a more recent development.

In America, although women preachers were common among the Quakers,* early Methodists* and Free Will Baptists,* not until 1853 was the first woman (Antoinette Brown Blackwell*) officially ordained. The Unitarians,* Christian Church (Disciples),* Wesleyan Methodist Church and Pilgrim Holiness Church (*see* Wesleyan Church), Salvation Army* and others ordained women in the nineteenth century.

Among mainline* denominations,* women have been permitted to be ordained by the United Church of Canada* (1936), the Methodists (1954), the Presbyterian Church in the U.S.A.* (1956), the Presbyterian Church in the U.S.* (1964), the American Lutheran Church* and the Lutheran Church in America* (1970), and the Episcopal Church* (1976).

The Southern Baptist Convention* is on record as opposing the practice, as are most modern fundamentalist* churches and denominations and the Roman Catholic* and Orthodox* churches.

O'Reilly, John Boyle (1844-1890). Catholic* newspaper editor. In 1870 O'Reilly obtained a job with the *Boston Pilot* as a reporter and editorial writer. Within a few months he advanced to editor and eventually became a respected journalist and poet in the U.S., especially among Irish-Americans. He favored the Democratic Party, championed social reform, advocated westward migration in order to alleviate labor problems and attacked prejudice against Native Americans, Jews and African-Americans.

Orr, James (1844-1913). Scottish theologian and apologist for orthodoxy.* Orr, professor of apologetics* and theology* at United Free Church College, Glasgow (1901-1913), became recognized as an expert in German philosophy and theology and as an orthodox opponent of modernism.*

Orr was one of a small number of British theologians invited to participate in *The Fundamen-*

*tals** project (1910-1915). His work made significant contributions to the issues and structures of the fundamentalist apologetic in the U.S.

Orthodox Presbyterian Church. A small Presbyterian* denomination* with roots in the fundamentalist-modernist controversy.* The Orthodox Presbyterian Church (OPC) was founded in 1936 in the aftermath of the 1929 exodus from Princeton Theological Seminary,* led by J. Gresham Machen.* Since its inception, the OPC has been best known for its vigorous affirmation of the truths of historic Christianity and Reformed* orthodoxy* as they are expressed in the Westminster Confession of Faith* and catechisms.*

Orthodox Tradition. Since the time of Augustine in the West and the Cappadocian fathers in the East, Orthodox Christianity has understood and celebrated the Christian faith in a manner which is distinctive: sometimes complementary to the Christian West and sometimes dramatically opposed to the Christian West.

The Orthodox in America have a strong sense of unity with the Orthodox in other parts of the world and claim that they live in continuity with those who have shared the same faith since the time of the apostles. While the Orthodox will frequently speak of "Greek Orthodoxy"* or "Russian Orthodoxy,"* these designations generally refer to historic expressions of a particular liturgical,* spiritual* or theological nature and do not imply different doctrinal understandings.

Orthodox. By using the term *orthodox,* Orthodox Christians recognize two very important and interrelated affirmations describing their church and their faith. First, *orthodox* means "true glory." Orthodox believe that the glorification of God, especially as expressed in praise and thanksgiving, is the fundamental response both of each believer and of the church to his mighty acts. The central expression of community worship* for the Orthodox is the Eucharist.*

The second meaning of *orthodox* is "true doctrine." The Orthodox believe that under the guidance of the Holy Spirit, the church has proclaimed, preserved and taught the authentic Christian faith free from addition, diminution or distortion since the time of the apostles.

God: Unknown and Known. The Orthodox understanding of God and the human person is rooted in divine revelation. Since God is impenetrable mystery and wholly beyond the reach of the human mind, the limited knowledge we have of God comes not chiefly from our human speculation but from God's having chosen to reveal himself to us. Although God in his *essence* remains forever beyond our understanding, in his *energies* or *activities* he is knowable in a deeply experiential manner within the context of the faith community.

Jesus Christ. The Incarnation of God the Son in fulfillment of the will of the Father and through the power of the Holy Spirit is the very core event of the divine revelation. In Jesus Christ divinity is united with humanity in such a way that both maintain their own characteristics while being brought together in a single person, the God-man. In his healings and exorcisms, and especially through his own death and resurrection, Christ proclaims the ultimate victory of God over every force of evil.

The Human Person: The Icon of God. According to the Orthodox perspective, the whole purpose of the Incarnation of the Son of God is to restore the human person and the entire creation to fellowship with God. While the Orthodox recognize the tragic character of humankind's fall through an act of disobedience, the emphasis is always on the love and mercy of God, who could not abandon those whom he created in love.

The Orthodox understand salvation as (1) sharing, or fellowship with the triune God; (2) ecclesial, or occurring within the fellowship of the church; and (3) cosmic, with the entire created world participating in the restoration accomplished in and through the Incarnation.

Tradition and Scripture. Sacred tradition is the body of fundamental faith affirmations which have been handed down through the life of the church under the guidance of the Spirit from the time of the apostles. Within the context of the believing community, these faith affirmations express themselves especially in the lives of faithful men and women, in the prayers of the church, in the teachings of the fathers, in the decisions of the seven ecumenical councils and in the Scriptures.

Councils and Creed. Only when the fundamental truths of the faith have been seriously threatened by false teachings has the church acted to express formally an article of faith. The seven ecumenical councils did not create new doctrines but proclaimed in a particular place and in a particular manner what the church has always believed. The decisions of these councils thus must be received by the whole body of the church.

Christian Divisions. In the Middle Ages serious doctrinal questions, complicated by political and cultural differences, led to the gradual separation of Eastern churches centered in Constantinople and the Western churches centered in Rome. The Orthodox have always recognized the tragic character of Christian division and have been active in efforts to achieve unity through greater mutual understanding and agreement in doctrine.

Orthodox Tradition in American Experience. Two significant events led directly to the formal establishment of Orthodox Christianity in North America. The first was the mission in Alaska* begun in 1794 under the direction of the Church of Russia. The second was the massive immigration of Orthodox, especially from Greece, Asia Minor, Russia, the Balkans and the Middle East, which took place especially in the late nineteenth and early twentieth centuries.

The Orthodox in America number about five million, with the Greek Orthodox Archdiocese being the largest jurisdiction. In due course, it is expected that the various jurisdictions will be united into a single autocephalous* church which will be officially recognized as such by the ecumenical patriarchate and the other autocephalous Orthodox churches.

See also ARMENIAN CHURCH; PIETY: POPULAR ORTHODOX; SPIRITUALITY: ORTHODOX; SYRIAN ORTHODOX CHURCH OF ANTIOCH.

Orthodoxy. Theological beliefs judged to be essential to Christian truth. The term *orthodoxy* literally means "right opinion" and has come to refer to established beliefs or doctrines. In traditional Christianity the basis for orthodoxy is divine revelation, particularly in the Bible. Christian confessions attribute varying amounts of authority to tradition, with Roman Catholics* seeing it as a further expression of revelation and Protestants* denying it direct authority, though usually agreeing that many traditional doctrinal formulations are biblically accurate.

Otey, James Hervey (1800-1863). Episcopal* bishop. When Otey was consecrated* bishop of Tennessee in 1834, the tiny diocese* consisted of only two hundred communicants. By 1860, in spite of years of energetic effort, the diocese had increased to only about 1,500 communicants. Tolerant of other denominations,* Otey once declared that he was neither high* nor low* church.

He helped to found seven schools, including the University of the South.

Otterbein, (Philip) William (1726-1813). German Reformed* pastor, cofounder and bishop of the United Brethren in Christ.* Arriving in the colonies in 1752, Otterbein served a series of German Reformed congregations, with his last pastorate in Baltimore (1774-1813).

Otterbein met the Mennonite* evangelist Martin Boehm,* and the two engaged in preaching tours together. Out of their joint endeavors came the United Brethren in Christ in 1789. At the newly formed group's first conference, both Otterbein and Boehm were elected bishops (1800).

See also REVIVALISM, GERMAN-AMERICAN.

Outler, Albert Cook (1908-1989). Methodist* theologian. A noted scholar in historical theology and active in the Faith and Order movement, Outler gained stature as an ecumenical* theologian who interpreted John Wesley* as a significant practical theologian with catholic breadth as well as evangelical* fervor. He placed considerable emphasis on the influence of patristic theologians upon Wesley, particularly in Wesley's doctrine* of soteriology.

Overseas Missionary Fellowship. An interdenominational and international faith mission.* The Overseas Missionary Fellowship (OMF) was founded in England as the China Inland Mission (CIM) in 1865 by James Hudson Taylor. A distinctive of the mission from the very beginning was a financial policy based on prayer to God without any public or private solicitation of funds.

When missionaries were forced to leave China in the early 1950s, the mission expanded to other countries of East Asia. In 1964 the mission became fully international, opening its doors to members of any race. Currently, about one-tenth of the one thousand members are from Asian backgrounds.

Owen, Robert (1771-1858). British industrialist, social reformer and communitarian. At New Harmony,* Indiana (1825-1827), Owen experimented with education, science and communal living as means to create a model Community of Equality. Such communities replicated worldwide were to produce the New Moral World.

Oxford Movement. *See* TRACTARIANISM.

Oxnam, Garfield Bromley (1891-1963). Methodist* bishop, ecumenical* leader and advocate of social reform. Oxnam was president of DePauw University in Greencastle, Indiana (1928-1936), and then bishop in Omaha, Boston, New York and Washington, D.C. (1936-1960). Devoted to the movement for Protestant* unity, Oxnam served as the president of the Federal Council of Churches* (1944-1946), as an officer at the founding of the National Council of Churches* (1950) and as a president of the World Council of Churches* (1948-1957).

Ozman, Agnes. *See* LABERGE, AGNES N. OZMAN.

P

Pacem in Terris. 1963 papal encyclical* on peace. When Pope John XXIII* was elected to the papacy* in 1958, the just-war doctrine was viewed as the normative position for Roman Catholics,* and there was no proscription against war in any of the church's teachings. In *Pacem in Terris* (Peace on Earth), Pope John XXIII moved in a pacifist* direction and repudiated war in the modern world. By repudiating the suitability of war as a means of restoring violated rights, he brought into question the theory of the just war.

See also PEACE MOVEMENT, CATHOLIC.

Pacific Garden Mission. Evangelical* rescue mission* in Chicago. Founded in 1877 by Sarah Dunn Clarke* and her husband, the mission opened amid brothels, saloons and gambling halls. In 1922 the mission moved to its current location on State Street. In the World War II* era several new ministries were begun under Superintendent Harry George Saunier (1902-). After the war, the mission began a radio broadcast known today as *Unshackled.*

One of the most celebrated of the urban rescue missions in America, the Pacific Garden Mission has served as a model to many similar ministries across North America.

Padilla, Juan De (c. 1500-c. 1544). Franciscan* missionary and martyr. In New Spain from around 1528, Padilla sought to protect natives from exploitation and made many missionary journeys to reach them. In 1542 he and a few companions established a mission at "Quivira," in what is now Kansas. The Native Americans nearby treated him well, but when he sought to do missionary work among a neighboring tribe, the Quiviras killed him.

Page, Kirby (1890-1957). Disciples of Christ* minister, pacifist* and social activist. Page edited *The World Tomorrow* (1926-1934), a pacifist jour-

nal, and helped organize the Fellowship for a Christian Social Order* (1922), serving as its executive secretary. An ardent pacifist and socialist,* he believed that the teachings of Jesus must lead to a nonviolent, cooperative social order.

Paine, Robert Treat (1731-1814). Massachusetts politician and jurist. As attorney general of Massachusetts (1777-1790), Paine engaged in a protracted effort to prop up the state's tottering religious order, prosecuting a series of cases concerning nonpayment of taxes assessed for the support of established* parish* clergy.

Paine, Solomon (c. 1700-1754). Separate* Congregational* minister. Paine, a leading speaker for strict Calvinistic* Congregationalism, helped to organize the colony's first Separate Congregational church, at Canterbury, in 1744. Paine opposed equally the Congregational religious establishment and its nascent Baptist* critics.

Paine, Thomas (1737-1809). Deist* and pamphleteer during the American and French Revolutions. Although Paine did not have an original mind, his pamphlets pioneered in simplifying complex issues for a mass audience. His best-remembered American pamphlet was *Common Sense.* Writing in early 1776, he summed up in clear language the best arguments for independence from Britain at a time when few were so bold as to advocate such a radical step.

By the time the French Revolution broke out in 1789, Paine was in England attacking aristocratic and monarchical privilege. Later, in France, he condemned the church. Such ideas, expressed in Paine's soul-stirring language, caused a sensation in these two countries.

Palm Sunday. The Sunday* before Easter,* celebrating Christ's entry into Jerusalem. A procession with palm branches down the Mount of Olives is reported at Jerusalem for this day in A.D. 383 by the pilgrim Egeria, and the custom spread slowly from there to Spain, Gaul and eventually Rome.

Palmer, Benjamin Morgan (1818-1902). Southern Presbyterian* pastor. Palmer helped found the *Southern Presbyterian Review* in 1847 and thereafter was an editor and frequent contributor. In 1856 he became the minister of the First Presbyterian Church of New Orleans, a position he held for more than forty-five years.

Perhaps the most outstanding Southern pulpit orator during the years from 1850 to 1900, Palmer influenced Southern views of slavery, abolition,* the North, secession and many other matters.

Palmer, Elihu (1764-1806). Deist* preacher. After earlier service as a Presbyterian* minister, Palmer founded a deist society in New York City. His religious views evolved into a militant, anti-Christian deism. He attacked the Bible as immoral and claimed that Moses, Mohammed and Jesus were all impostors—even murderers, in principle if not in fact. Joining his own form of natural religion and rationalism with ardent republicanism, Palmer's goal was the overthrow of both superstition and tyranny.

Palmer, Paul (?-c. 1750). Colonial Baptist* preacher. After preaching for several years, Palmer organized the first Baptist church in North Carolina in 1727. Arminian* in doctrine, he was a major leader of the early General Baptists* in America.

Palmer, Phoebe Worrall (1807-1874). Methodist* lay revivalist,* feminist,* humanitarian and editor. By 1835 Palmer was active in a "Tuesday Meeting for the Promotion of Holiness" at the home of her sister Sarah Worrall Lankford (Palmer*), where she began to develop and popularize her modified version of John Wesley's* perfectionism,* or "entire sanctification."* Her theology was adopted by Holiness* denominations as well as by the Salvation Army* and the Keswick movement* in England.

In addition, Palmer popularized the idea that Pentecostal Spirit baptism* was available to every believer. This emphasis helped pave the way for the later emergence of the Pentecostal* and charismatic* movements in America. Her ministry helped reintroduce the concept of lay ministry to the church and touch off the awakening of 1858 (*see* Prayer Meeting Revival).

See also HOLINESS MOVEMENT.

Palmer, Sarah Worrall Lankford (1806-1896). Methodist* laywoman. In 1835 Palmer established the "Tuesday Meeting for the Promotion of Holiness" in her New York home. Led by her and her younger sister, Phoebe Worrall Palmer,* this meeting continued weekly for more than fifty years.

Palmyra Manifesto (1865). A call for reorganization of Southern Methodism* following the Civil War.* Stemming from a meeting in June 1865 in Palmyra, Missouri, the manifesto disavowed the slave issue as the only question separating Northern and Southern Methodism. It asserted the integrity of the Methodist Episcopal Church, South, and urged that this integrity be preserved.

Papacy and U.S. Catholics. Republican ideas during the American Revolution* led to demands by U.S. Catholics for recognition as "an ordinary national church" in union with Rome but picking its own leaders and managing its own affairs. Nineteenth-century immigration* diluted American Catholic national unity at the same time as events in Europe brought about a highly centralized church centered on a monarchical pope. Papal condemnation in 1907 of Catholic modernism* brought in its wake increased Roman supervision of doctrinal* teaching and church discipline.*

Between the world wars and into the 1950s, American Catholics were known for unquestioning loyalty to the pope. Vatican II* brought changes, with debate among bishops and theologians* spreading to priests and people.

See also AMERICANISM; CONCILIAR TRADITION, AMERICAN; VATICAN-U.S. CATHOLIC CHURCH RELATIONS.

Papal Infallibility. A Roman Catholic* term referring to the pope's share in the general grace that preserves the church from error. The First Vatican Council* (1870) formally defined the pope's role and share in infallibility. Present-day Catholic theologians generally teach that the pope is preserved from error when teaching in union with the entire episcopate, in union with a General Council or alone ex cathedra (formally) on matters of faith and morals.

See also MAGISTERIUM.

Papal Nuncio/Pro Nuncio. An envoy accredited as the pope's ambassador to the civil government of a particular country. The nuncio or pro nuncio is distinguished from an apostolic delegate,* who is a papal representative with an exclusively religious mission to the Catholic church in a particular country.

Parachurch Groups (Voluntary Societies). Voluntary, not-for-profit associations of Christians working outside denominational* control to achieve some specific ministry* or social service.

Voluntary Societies and the Churches. In mainline* Protestant* denominations, coalitions of liberal* Christians have usually not assumed the form of parachurch organizations because they have had no need to raise money directly from church members.

Among evangelical* Christians, however, parachurch organizations have become the primary means of cooperative endeavor. The Billy Graham Evangelistic Association,* for example, has its own board of directors, which oversees an annual budget running into millions of dollars. Literally thousands of other groups are in operation, often as "one-man" operations.

Evangelicals and Parachurch Structures. Extensive evangelical employment of parachurch structures in modern times is traceable to the vision of William Carey, the pioneer in modern foreign missions. He proposed forming a company of serious-minded Christians, laymen and ministers, who would collect and sift information and find funds and suitable missionaries to send to foreign lands.

The voluntary society, as it was often called, transformed nineteenth-century Christianity. It effectively bypassed established church doctrines and denominational structures, allowing people from different denominations to work together for defined purposes without raising the troublesome questions of dogma* or polity.* It also altered the power base of the churches by encouraging lay leadership among both men and women.

Later, during the 1920s when the fundamentalist-modernist controversies* took place in the major denominations, conservative evangelicals came to rely even more heavily on parachurch agencies, which became channels for dissent and for alternative activities.

Significant Questions. Is it wise to continue the proliferation of parachurch groups in U.S. evangelicalism? Do they simply reflect an American frontier spirit of self-reliance and individualism that prefers to start a new work rather than join an organization already in existence?

Widespread questions about the financial practices of parachurch agencies led in the late 1970s to the formation of the Evangelical Council for Financial Accountability. Some—but not all—groups have brought their practices in line with the council's standards.

Parham, Charles Fox (1873-1929). Founder of the Apostolic Faith movement and one of the founders of the modern Pentecostal movement.* In 1900 Parham founded the Bethel Bible School, near Topeka, Kansas, where he come to his lifelong conviction that the initial evidence of the baptism with the Holy Spirit was speaking in tongues.* In 1901 a student named Agnes N. Ozman* prayed for the experience and began speaking in tongues. Soon the other students and Parham himself were also practicing tongues-speech. Within seven years his loosely organized "Apostolic Faith Missions" had spread throughout the Lower Midwest, attracting some 25,000 followers.

In 1905 Parham opened a Bible school in Houston, Texas, which trained William Joseph Seymour,* who became the leader of the 1906 Azusa Street revival.*

Parish. An ecclesiastical territory over which a pastor presides, in which usually one church exists and to which Christians living within that territory automatically belong. Used originally to refer to the district under the jurisdiction of a bishop, it was eventually applied to subdivisions in a diocese.* Usually one church and pastor served the Christians of the parish. Besides its religious functions, the parish often has become a center for recreation, charitable activities, political involvement and education.

Parish Council. A consultative body composed of the clergy and lay representatives of a local congregation for the purpose of fostering parochial activity. Although not mandated by Roman Catholic canon law,* it is quite common in the U.S. and Canada.

Parish Mission. A movement in the Roman Catholic Church* to cultivate religious devotion in the local parish.* The parish mission began after the Council of Trent to strengthen the faith of practicing Catholics and to win back those lost to Protestantism.*

It was well suited for nineteenth-century American Catholicism, spreading rapidly after 1830. Catholics resorted to persuasion instead of coercion to revive the parish and to spread a popular piety* known as "devotional Catholicism." The modern charismatic movement* in American Catholicism is a contemporary example of the parish mission at work.

Park, Edwards Amasa (1808-1900). Congregational* minister and theologian. Park taught at Andover Seminary from 1836 to 1880. He identified himself with Jonathan Edwards,* and especially that strand of Edwardsean theology represented by the "Exercisers" among the New Divinity* Men and (as he believed) by Nathaniel W. Taylor.*

He bitterly resisted the introduction of German biblical criticism and philosophy to Andover in the 1860s and 1870s, but upon retirement in 1880, he was unable to prevent Andover from falling into the hands of the "Progressive Orthodoxy."*

Parker, Daniel (1781-1844). Baptist* preacher, antimission* leader, founder of the Two-Seed-in-the-Spirit Predestinarian Baptists. Parker staunchly opposed missionary societies and schemes not under church control, although he was not opposed to itinerant* preaching. His efforts touched Baptists in several states and resulted in the formation of a small antimission denomination.

A man of great energy, natural ability and uncommon resourcefulness, Parker was vigorous in the pulpit in denouncing the society method of denominational organization and caused much dissension among Baptists on the frontier.

Parker, Horatio William (1863-1919). Composer, organist and music educator. Parker taught at the National Conservatory of Music and also was a popular professor at Yale* (1894-1919), teaching such notables as Charles Ives. His international honors included guest-conducting in many European cities. Parker was the most distinguished American composer of church music of his time.

Parker, Isaac (1768-1830). Massachusetts politician and jurist. Parker served on the Massachu-

setts Supreme Judicial Court (1806-1830), from 1814 as chief justice. A staunch Unitarian,* Parker strove to preserve at least a vestigial religious establishment.*

See also DEDHAM DECISION.

Parker, Theodore (1810-1860). Unitarian* minister and radical theologian of New England transcendentalism.* A man of prodigious learning and probing intellect, Parker flowed with some of the deeper philosophical currents of his day. Parker's theology was influenced by close contact with German idealistic philosophy and the emerging higher criticism.

Parker lived out his ethical beliefs with great integrity. He was a courageous reformer who did not hesitate to speak from his convictions. A leading spokesman of the antislavery movement,* he saw slavery as a crime against nature. Ethically and theologically, he anticipated the style and limitations of the Social Gospel.*

Parochial Schools, Roman Catholic. Parish-supported Catholic, usually elementary, schools. Catholic schools began to increase in the 1840s. Their growth was spurred by conflicts over curriculum, textbooks, teachers and policymakers, which Catholic leaders viewed as being dominated by a pan-Protestantism. From 1870 to 1920 the growth of the secular public school, coupled with heavy Catholic immigration,* contributed to the increase of Catholic parochial schools, which were founded on ethnic* as well as religious bases.

Events of the 1960s produced substantial change in the Catholic parochial education. Beset by spiraling financial costs, a widely doubted rationale, teacher strikes, uncertain support from clergy and a sizable population that was moving to the suburbs, Catholic parochial schools reached a low point in the 1970s. They survived, but still face the challenges of serving the urban poor, avoiding elitism, finding adequate financing and maintaining their uniqueness as religious institutions.

See also SCHOOLS, PROTESTANT DAY.

Parrish, Sarah Rebecca (1869-1952). First woman missionary medical doctor in the Philippines. Arriving in the Philippines in 1906 under the Methodist* Episcopal Woman's Foreign Missionary Society, Parrish established the still-functioning Mary Johnston Hospital in Tondo, Manila.

Here she maintained high medical standards and also was involved actively in evangelism.*

Parsons, Henry Martyn (1828-1913). Canadian millenarian leader. Parsons was pastor of Knox Presbyterian Church in Toronto from 1880 until his death. Prominent in the millenarian movement, Parsons was a long-time leader of the Niagara Conferences.* He helped organize the 1885 Niagara Prophecy Conference, a crucial event for the spread of premillennialism* in Canada.

Particular Baptists. Calvinistic* Baptists* with origins in English Puritanism.* English Particular Baptists, following the Calvinistic doctrine of predestination,* believed that God redeemed only "particular" individuals. This opposed the Arminian* concept of "general" redemption held by General Baptists* and many Anglicans.* A revision of a confession issued in the 1680s by Particular Baptists in London (known in the U.S. as Regular Baptists*) became the first widely used Baptist confession in America.

Passavant, William Alfred (1821-1894). Lutheran* minister, editor and leading promoter of Lutheran home missions* and institutions of mercy. In the late 1840s, chiefly under the influence of Charles Porterfield Krauth,* Passavant espoused the trend toward "old Lutheranism," a conservative movement which found its norms in Lutheran orthodoxy.*

Passavant was a strong influence in the slow process of transforming Lutherans (particularly the nineteenth-century arrivals) from their defensive immigrant mentality into "a worshiping, witnessing, working church." He promoted and exemplified a Lutheranism committed to nurturing a devout Christian life, aggressive outreach through evangelism* and humanitarian service, and responsible citizenship in American and Canadian society.

Pastor. A term describing the relationship between a minister and his or her congregation. The term has come to describe the relationship between minister and congregation as that between shepherd and flock—one that entails caring, loving and giving. The term is most frequently used by Protestants* in referring to their minister (sometimes as a synonym for *Reverend,* and as a form of address); many Roman Catholics* use it for parish priests.

Patrick, Mary Mills (1850-1940). Missionary educator in Turkey. Patrick was sent to Turkey in 1871 by the American Board of Commissioners for Foreign Missions.* She taught in an Armenian girls school and was founder and first president of the American College for Girls at Constantinople.

Patterson, Frederic William (1877-1966). Canadian Baptist* leader and university president. In 1922 Patterson was appointed president of Acadia University, in Wolfville, Nova Scotia, serving there until 1948. During his presidency Acadia's enrollment expanded from 307 to 890.

Patton, Francis Landey (1843-1932). Presbyterian* clergyman, educator and theologian. Hired by Princeton Theological Seminary* in 1881 as professor in apologetics, Patton in 1883 took on the additional task of lecturing on ethics* at the College of New Jersey.* His career took an unexpected turn when the college chose him to follow James McCosh* as the president of the institution in 1888. Patton successfully restructured the college to become Princeton University in 1896.

Pauck, Wilhelm (1901-1981). Theologian and church historian. Arriving in the U.S. in 1925, Pauck taught at several institutions, including the University of Chicago Divinity School* (1939-1945), Union Theological Seminary* (New York) (1945-1967), Vanderbilt University (1967-1972) and Stanford University (1972-1981).

Pauck maintained the abiding values of liberal* theology. As a church historian, he produced significant studies on the Reformation and the development of Protestant* theology.

Paul VI (1897-1978). Pope from 1963 to 1978. Upon election as pope, Paul VI pledged to bring the work of the Second Vatican Council* to completion. At the end he promulgated all the Vatican documents, including the Declaration on Religious Freedom, sponsored by the American bishops.

The church revolution he made possible erupted within the American church, transforming its liturgy,* self-identity, practices and priesthood. His encyclicals* commending caution provoked antagonism.

Paulists. *See* CONGREGATION OF THE MISSIONARY SOCIETY OF ST. PAUL THE APOSTLE.

PAX. *See* PEACE MOVEMENT, CATHOLIC.

Pax Christi. *See* PEACE MOVEMENT, CATHOLIC.

Paxson, Stephen (1837-1881). American Sunday School Union* missionary. Paxson, as a newly converted, thirty-year-old Illinois farmer, began to organize Sunday schools in his spare time. He eventually became a missionary with the American Sunday School Union and continued to travel throughout Illinois and adjoining states, teaching, counseling, preaching, organizing and distributing tracts, books, Bibles and other materials. In his years of labor he was credited with founding 1,314 new Sunday schools.

Payne, Daniel Alexander (1811-1893). African Methodist Episcopal* bishop, educator and church historian. In 1843 Payne was appointed a minister in the African Methodist Episcopal (AME) Church and in 1852 became a bishop. For twelve years thereafter he traveled around the country, establishing schools and otherwise promoting education among illiterate African-Americans.

In 1863 he purchased Wilberforce University in Ohio, becoming the first president of a African-American institution of higher learning in the U.S. (*see* Black Colleges). He served in that capacity until 1876.

Peabody, Andrew Preston (1811-1893). Unitarian* minister and educator. In 1853 Peabody began editing the *North American Review,* considered by many the finest scholarly journal of its time. In 1860 he was appointed professor of Christian Morals at Harvard* and later served twice as acting president of the college.

Peabody, Francis Greenwood (1847-1936). Unitarian* minister and professor of social ethics* at Harvard* Divinity School. Peabody taught at the school from 1880 to 1913. As a clergyman* Peabody observed that moral problems arose from social contexts. He taught that the minister was the natural leader for social reform and believed that the minister should mediate class conflicts and advise community charities. A theological liberal,* Peabody was influenced by the thought of Friedrich Schleiermacher (1768-1834).

Peabody, Lucy Whitehead McGill (1861-1949). Baptist* missionary and denominational* leader. After missionary service in India, Peabody became a roving ambassador for missionary endeavor, particularly women's work. In 1913, she and Helen Barrett Montgomery* made an extensive tour of mission fields in India, China and Japan, out of which grew study guides on mission work, new funds for overseas women's colleges and a proposal for a World Day of Prayer, which began as a vigil involving over seventy countries.

Peace Churches. A name first used in 1935 to refer to the Mennonites,* Friends* (Quakers) and Brethren,* who share a witness against war. Their nonresistant views have led them to cooperate in programs of reconstruction, relief and social justice. They were originally brought into contact with one another when Mennonites and Brethren settled in the Quaker colony of Pennsylvania. The influence of the Friends on the other two sects is apparent in their plain dress, simple style of meeting places and church organization.

Peace Movement, Catholic. Before the 1960s Catholics* did not play a leading role in the American peace movement. The Roman Catholic Church was predominantly a conservative and patriotic body whose hierarchy sanctified the doctrine of a just war in its official church teaching and imposed it on a largely compliant laity.

Early American Catholic organizations challenging the church's position were the Catholic Association for International Peace (1928), founded by John A. Ryan;* the Catholic Worker* (1933), cofounded by Dorothy Day;* PAX, formed on the eve of World War II;* and the Catholic Peace Fellowship (1964), mainly started by the brothers Daniel and Philip Berrigan. From 1928 to the 1960s Catholics had moved from a marginal status in the American peace movement to a position of central importance.

The Catholic peace movement of the 1960s coincided with two of the major forces of the century: Vatican II* and Vietnam. During the course of Vatican II, Pope John XXIII* issued his encyclical on peace, *Pacem in Terris.* With the involvement of the United States in Vietnam underway, the impact of Vatican II was decisive in challenging Catholics with the issue of positive peacemaking.

For the first time in U.S. history, the Catholic hierarchy declared that conscientious objectors, even selective conscientious objectors, have a basis for their position in modern Catholic teaching.

Finally, in November 1971 the U.S. bishops condemned the war in Vietnam as unjust.

Pax Christi, formed in 1975, was an important peace organization, primarily pacifist in orientation.

The conversion of the American Catholic church into a force for peace is nowhere more clearly seen than in the direction taken by the National Conference of Catholic Bishops* (NCCB) since 1970. The bishops' 1983 pastoral letter *The Challenge of Peace,* for the first time in American Catholic history, proclaimed pacifism and active nonviolence as means of Christian action as legitimate as military defense in the service of the nation.

Peale, Norman Vincent (1898-1993). Reformed Church of America* minister and promoter of positive thinking. In 1932 Peale accepted a call to Marble Collegiate Church in New York City, where he spent the remainder of his career. Peale's message has been a combination of psychological themes and therapeutic prescriptions drawn from his understanding of Scripture and cast in simple principles expressed in everyday language.

His most famous book appeared in 1952—*The Power of Positive Thinking*—and within weeks was at the top of the *New York Times* bestseller list, where it stayed for about three years. The phenomenal success of the book brought Peale to national prominence. With numerous speaking engagements, a syndicated newspaper column and a broadening radio audience, his name became synonymous with the phrase *positive thinking.*

Arguably, the post-World War II economic affluence and the accompanying anxieties of modern urban living contributed to build a religious atmosphere primed to receive a gospel promising confident living and peace of mind. But whatever the reasons for his success, Peale became one of the most prominent religious figures of the postwar decades.

Peck, E(dmund) J(ames) (1850-1924). Anglican* missionary to the Canadian Inuit. In 1885 Peck reached the Inuit at Fort Chimo on Ungava Bay, where he established a Christian community that flourished without missionary visitation for over fifteen years. A prolific writer, Peck is remembered especially for his *Eskimo Dictionary.*

Peck, George (1797-1876). Methodist* minister, educator, editor and author. In 1818 Peck became a member of Genesee Conference, New York, beginning a career of nearly six decades in seventeen pastorates, as a presiding elder,* as the denominational book agent and as editor of religious publications. He wrote on the topics of Christian perfection,* Universalism* and the nature of authority.*

Peck, John Mason (1789-1858). Baptist* missionary to the Missouri Territory, journalist and educator. Appointed to the St. Louis area in 1817, Peck preached,* formed churches, organized Sunday schools,* taught school, formed women's "mite societies" to sponsor mission work, and distributed Bibles and religious literature. In 1827 he founded Rock Springs Seminary, one of the earliest schools west of the Mississippi. In 1829 Peck launched *The Pioneer,* the first of several papers he sponsored in the West.

Peloubet, Francis Nathan (1831-1920). Congregational* minister, Sunday-school* lesson writer and Bible commentator. In 1875 Peloubet began editing *Select Notes on the International Sunday School Lessons,* intended for Sunday-school teachers and advanced students and published annually. He continued in this work for forty-five years (1875-1920).

Pemberton, Ebenezer (1704-1777). Congregational* clergyman. Pemberton preached* in a New York Presbyterian church (1727-1753) and then assumed the pastorate of Boston's Middle Street Church. His friendship with royalist governor Thomas Hutchinson damaged his reputation.

Penance, Sacrament of. The approved name for the sacrament* which Roman Catholics* have popularly called "confession,"* the ritual expression of a repentant heart. The Catholic Church teaches that persons who have sinned after the first forgiveness of sins* through baptism* are to openly acknowledge subsequent sins. They are to receive guidance from a priest, ask for and receive forgiveness and perform some penance. The sacrament is normally required before being admitted to the Lord's Table.

Pendleton, James Madison (1811-1891). Baptist* pastor, professor and journalist. In 1837 Pendleton became pastor of First Baptist Church,

Bowling Green, Kentucky. There he remained until 1857 when he became professor of theology at Union University, Murfreesboro, Tennessee. The following year he became a joint editor of the *Tennessee Baptist.*

· Pendleton, along with A. C. Dayton and James Robinson Graves,* made up the "Great Triumvirate" of a Baptist ecclesiological movement known as Landmarkism.*

Penn, William (1644-1718). Quaker* statesman and founder of Pennsylvania. Penn was the Quakers' leader after their first two decades of radical witness and world challenge under George Fox.* His attitudes to social reform and responsibility have characterized most Quakers to the present day.

Penn's trust in truth and human conscience undergirded his second major life work, as advocate of religious toleration.* He wrote tracts such as *The Great Case of Liberty of Conscience* (1670).

Charles II opened for Penn his third career as the founder of colonies. In 1674 Penn had helped to buy and settle the West and later East New Jersey colonies. Then in 1688 Charles II granted the larger, richer Pennsylvania territory across the Delaware. Penn proclaimed equal legal rights there for the Delaware Indians and toleration not only for Quakers but for persecuted Germans such as Mennonites. Penn resided in Pennsylvania during 1682-1684 and 1699-1701.

Pennington, J(ames) W(illiam) C(harles) (1809-1870). African-American Presbyterian* minister. Pennington served congregations in New York and Connecticut (1838-1855). A skilled and popular lecturer and preacher, Pennington gave addresses in London, Paris and Brussels. He was active in the abolitionist* and Negro Convention movements.

Pennsylvania, University of. A secular university with origins in colonial Anglicanism.* This educational institution traces its origins to a 1740 gathering to erect a charity school in response to the preaching of George Whitefield.* By 1749 this group, which now included Benjamin Franklin, had evolved into the board of trustees of a nonsectarian academy.

In 1872 the university moved to its present location in West Philadelphia. A wide variety of programs offer both undergraduate and graduate education.

Pentecost. An annual commemoration of the descent of the Holy Spirit. The word *Pentecost* is derived from the Greek name for the festival, literally meaning "fiftieth [day]"—the length of time after the feast of Passover when the wheat harvest was celebrated. In the early centuries of the church, the celebration of Pentecost was the fifty days following the Pasch, or Easter.*

Pentecostal Assemblies of Canada. The largest Pentecostal* denomination* in Canada. The Pentecostal movement sprang up in Canada from 1906, with R. E. McAlister going to the Azusa Street* meetings in Los Angeles and returning with the Pentecostal message to the receptive Ottawa Valley, with its Holiness heritage. As the movement spread and some kind of organization became necessary, the Pentecostal Assemblies of Canada was chartered in 1919.

The Assemblies have become the fastest-growing form of Canadian Christianity, with the total number of members and active nonmembers by the early 1900s being 195,000, with about 34,000 more belonging to the Pentecostal Assemblies of Newfoundland.

Pentecostal Churches. The Pentecostal movement* that emerged in 1901 has spawned some three hundred distinct American denominations,* with most adherents belonging to one of the seven denominations surveyed here. While these share roots in the early twentieth-century revival, they differ in significant ways in polity,* doctrinal emphasis, racial composition, social class and regional appeal.

All classical Pentecostals have in common at least one conviction: conversion* to Christ should be followed by another intense experience of Spirit baptism.* This baptism, classical Pentecostals insist, should be evidenced by tongues speech.* Spirit-filled believers then expect to manifest one or more of the nine gifts of the Spirit listed in 1 Corinthians 12 and 14. The older Pentecostal denominations generally also affirm divine healing* and subscribe to a premillennial* eschatology.*

*Church of God (Cleveland).** This body traces its roots to the formation of the Christian Union, a small Restorationist* come-outist congregation formed in the mountains of western North Carolina in 1886. The church is part of the Holiness family of Pentecostal denominations. It affirms the necessity of two crisis works of grace: conversion and sanctification.* It expects believers to have a third experience: an enduement with power, or baptism with the Holy Spirit, evidenced by tongues speech. In 1992 the denomination reported 672,000 members in the U.S. and 6,700 in Canada.

*International Pentecostal Holiness Church.** This Holiness-Pentecostal denomination also traces its roots to the Holiness revivals* of the late nineteenth century, being created by the amalgamation of several Holiness associations* whose constituencies were based in North and South Carolina. In 1990 the church reported 131,674 members in the U.S.

*Church of God in Christ.** This church also emerged from the Holiness movement of the 1890s, being formed as a result of the activities of two African-American Baptists, Charles Price Jones* and Charles Mason.* Mason accepted the teaching that tongues speech would always evidence the baptism with the Holy Spirit. Jones, who agreed that the experience was necessary, disagreed over evidential tongues, and the two parted company. Mason retained the name Church of God in Christ and remained its bishop until his death in 1961. By some disputed figures (5.5 million members in 1991), this group is the largest American Pentecostal denomination.

*Assemblies of God.** This group traces its origins to a 1914 camp meeting* in Hot Springs, Arkansas, which led ultimately to a denomination combining aspects of congregational* and presbyterian* polity. It was the first, and has always been the largest, non-Wesleyan Pentecostal denomination. The Assemblies of God has historically been predominantly white, although it has growing Hispanic* and Korean constituencies. In 1991 the denomination numbered over 2.25 million members in the U.S. It is the largest classic Pentecostal denomination in the world (over 13 million members in 1985).

Pentecostal Assemblies of the World. The first influential "oneness" denomination, the Pentecostal Assemblies of the World attracted many of those who left the Assemblies of God in a heated doctrinal dispute in 1916. The Assemblies today is African-American and non-Holiness, with its polity resembling that of Methodism. In 1989 the church reported a worldwide membership of 500,000.

*United Pentecostal Church, International.** White oneness Pentecostals withdrew from the Pentecostal Assemblies of the World in 1924 and formed an organization later called the United Pentecostal Church. Excluded from trinitarian organizations, the church has developed in relative isolation from other Pentecostal denominations. In late 1992 the denomination reported a membership of approximately 550,000 members in the U.S. and Canada.

*International Church of the Foursquare Gospel.** This body is the only sizable Pentecostal denomination that developed out of the ministry of a single charismatic individual. Aimee Semple McPherson,* the denomination's founder, was a gifted though controversial figure throughout her career as a religious leader. The church, which is non-Holiness and trinitarian, resembles the Assemblies of God in doctrine and practice. In 1992 the church reported about 205,000 members in the U.S.

Pentecostal Fellowship of North America. A fellowship of Pentecostal organizations. The Pentecostal Fellowship of North America was founded in 1948. Fellowship,* rather than amalgamation of denominations, was the purpose of the association, to which twenty-four Pentecostal organizations belonged. The Fellowship was disbanded in October 1994 in favor of forming a racially inclusive organization.

Pentecostal Movement. A twentieth-century Christian movement emphasizing a postconversion experience of Spirit baptism* evidenced by speaking in tongues.* Once considered a glossolalic aberrant within Holiness* revivalism,* the Pentecostal movement has emerged as perhaps the single most significant development in twentieth-century Christianity. In contrast to the stigmatization of early adherents, contemporary Pentecostals bask in the light of a modern-day success story. Glittering "super churches," political clout and renowned (and sometimes notorious) media evangelists now adorn a burgeoning movement that defies categorization and confounds census takers. No one knows just how large the movement is, nor is there agreement even on who should be included in its ranks. The latest estimates suggest over 30 million adherents in the U.S., with over 450 million worldwide.

Pentecostalism is sometimes divided into two branches: "classic Pentecostalism," indicating the movement's historic bodies; and "neo-Pentecostalism," or the charismatic* renewal, indicating more recent forms of Pentecostalism especially among the mainline* churches. Although few generalizations can span the vast body of contemporary Pentecostalism, threads of continuity can be seen in a frank openness to supernatural gifts in a natural world, in the presupposition of an intimately involved and personal deity, and in a simple and faithful biblicism.

Beginnings. The origins of the Pentecostal movement lie in the ministry of an itinerant* Holiness evangelist and faith healer, Charles F. Parham.* An experience of glossolalic baptism in 1901 convinced Parham that glossolalia was the "initial, physical evidence" of baptism in the Spirit, its inevitable accompaniment. This belief became the doctrinal hallmark of the Pentecostal movement.

Parham influenced a young African-American Holiness minister named William J. Seymour,* whose ministry in Los Angeles sparked the epochal Azusa Street revival* in 1906.

Beliefs and Practices. The concept of Spirit baptism was familiar to Holiness revivalism, and glossolalia was not unknown. What distinguished the Pentecostals from the Holiness mainstream was their insistence that glossolalia was the normative and necessary sign of Spirit baptism.

Pentecostal doctrine soon consolidated around the "four-square gospel" (see Rev 21:16), the cornerstones of which were personal salvation* through faith in Jesus Christ, divine healing, the soon Second Coming of Christ, and Spirit baptism with the evidence of tongues. The movement's theological center lay in the first article and was expressed in a deeply pietistic, even mystical, devotion to Jesus Christ.

Worship. The fundamental precept of Pentecostal worship was that the Holy Spirit alone should direct the order and conduct of a service. Prepared speeches, rehearsal and formality were censured as hindrances to the free operation of the Spirit. Services were subject at any moment to outbursts of glossolalia or other charismatic phenomena.

Because of such persuasions, early Pentecostalism was a preeminently participatory religion. Testimony,* song, sermon,* prophecy, prayer,* divine healing and glossolalic utterance were the potential domain of anyone present, and not the restricted privilege of a designated few.

Social Factors. Recent studies suggest that most early Pentecostals were drawn from the blue-collar working class, not from the ranks of the truly disinherited. Nevertheless, the movement clearly thrived among the poor and marginalized members of society.

Racial diversity was another trademark of early Pentecostalism, one that directly challenged prevailing societal norms. The West Coast missions in particular were known for a veritable smorgasbord of ethnic identities. Pressures to segregate took their toll within a few decades, however, and most of Pentecostalism today is segregated.

Another noteworthy aspect of Pentecostalism consists in the role it has traditionally afforded women. Some of the movement's most prominent leaders have been women, indicating that Pentecostal churches clearly do not expect women to remain silent. Pentecostals rarely endorse the current feminist agenda, however, and the role of women in leadership, while allowed, has been viewed with ambivalence.

Controversy and Schism. In its short history, the Pentecostal-charismatic movement has spawned as many as three hundred denominations and organizations in the U.S. alone, many of these because of schism. By 1910 a dispute of long-standing significance had erupted over the doctrine of sanctification, with William H. Durham* preaching a non-Wesleyan, or "Reformed,"* view of sanctification (as an outward process expressing a completed, inward reality), in contrast to the Holiness view of sanctification (as a distinct, second work) of most of the early Pentecostals.

An even more bitter controversy arose over the doctrine of the Trinity. At a camp meeting* in 1913, the apostolic baptismal formula "in Jesus' name" was used as a basis for arguing that the "name" of the Father, Son and Spirit is *Jesus.* This led to a Jesus-Unitarian theology, dubbed "Jesus-Only," "oneness" or "Jesus-Name" doctrine, which initiated what has become Pentecostalism's most deeply entrenched division.

Organization. Early Pentecostal pioneers had taken pride in their movement's lack of ecclesiastical vestments, although practical concerns led Charles Parham to appoint rudimentary offices and to form an "association" among the congregations sympathetic to his message. The most significant step toward formal organization, however, occurred when the Assemblies of God* emerged from a conference in 1914. The Assemblies soon after published a "Statement of Fundamental Truths," which clearly affirmed the doctrine of the Trinity.

After the Assemblies of God, other groups organized themselves for a variety of reasons. Thousands of independent Pentecostal congregations, however, still shun traditional modes of affiliation.

Growth and Expansion. The history of Pentecostalism has been interspersed with periods of explosive numerical growth. The reasons for this growth are certainly complex but are related to a zeal for missions and personal evangelism virtually unmatched in twentieth-century Christianity.

The medium of print has also been instrumental in the growth of Pentecostalism, as have popular mass evangelists and faith healers.

A controversial offshoot of the faith-healing tradition is the "faith movement,"* identified by what its critics term the "name it and claim it" doctrine. Built on the idea of "positive confession," apparently first developed by E. W. Kenyon,* the movement's chief leaders currently are Kenneth Copeland and Kenneth Hagin.

The spread of Pentecostalism into the mainline denominations, known as the charismatic renewal (*see* Charismatic Movement), is one of the most remarkable and influential developments in recent church history. This new direction for Pentecostalism was signaled in 1951 with the formation of the Full Gospel Business Men's Fellowship, International (FGBMFI).* Also, David Du Plessis* was beginning his rise to prominence as a Pentecostal emissary to the ecumenical* world. Most important, in 1959 Episcopal* rector Dennis Bennett received his baptism in the Spirit, which is generally viewed as the beginning of the charismatic movement. By the mid-1960s the movement had crossed into the Catholic Church.*

Even decidedly noncharismatic bodies have seen fit to place new emphasis on spiritual gifts, evangelism, personal salvation and enthusiasm in worship because of the Pentecostal-charismatic presence. In this respect Pentecostalism has changed the face of American Christianity.

Pentecostal World Conference. A loosely organized fellowship of Pentecostal* groups throughout the world. Although preliminary meetings had been held earlier, not until after World War II* did an international conference become a reality. A contributing factor in calling the meeting was to offer cooperative aid to victims of the war. A second purpose was to work together "in spreading the full Gospel testimony in every country."

Perfectionism. The doctrine that holiness* or perfect love, brought about by the grace of God through faith, is attainable by every Christian in this life and sets believers free from willful sin.* This doctrine grew out of the teaching of John Wesley,* who believed that the clear teaching of Scripture was that spiritual growth after conversion* culminates in a second work of grace wrought instantaneously in the heart of the believer. By this work the believer is filled with perfect love. Wesley taught that this perfect love was Christian perfection rather than human perfection, and that the Christian in this life would never be free from temptation, physical ailment or a multitude of cares.

Such perfectionist doctrine found its way into numerous groups in America outside the Methodist Church. It was associated with the Oberlin theology* of Asa Mahan* and Charles G. Finney,* who taught a doctrine of perfectionism made possible by the baptism of the Holy Spirit, which empowered and perfected the will of the believer to act in conformity with the will of God.

Some groups, such as the Wesleyan Methodist Connection (1843) and the Free Methodist Church* (1860), withdrew from the Methodist Episcopal Church, perceiving a declining interest among Methodists in the doctrine. Other denominations that maintained a doctrine of sanctification characterized by perfectionism included the Salvation Army,* beginning in England in 1865, and the Church of the Nazarene* (1908).

Perkins, William (1558-1602). English Reformed* theologian. Perkins was Cambridge University's most popular preacher of the day, as scholars and townspeople alike flocked to hear his reasoned and passionate sermons. His "practical divinity" analyzed and preached a psychology of conversion upon which the ministry of New England's first generation was closely modeled.

The Puritanism* which Perkins helped delineate was an experiential form of religion based on the primacy of God's action (as opposed to human effort) in salvation.*

Permanent Deacon. In the Patristic period the office of deacon was normally held for life, or permanent. Since Vatican II* the Catholic* Church has given extensive consideration to the office of deacon, and permanent deacons have become widely recognized, as they are also in the Eastern Orthodox* and Episcopal* Churches.

Perry, Harold R. (1916-1991). Auxiliary Roman Catholic* bishop of New Orleans. Perry in 1944 became the twenty-sixth African-American to be ordained a priest in the Roman Catholic Church. He served in parishes in his native Louisiana as well as in Arkansas and Mississippi and was an active leader in the church. In 1965 he was appointed auxiliary bishop of New Orleans, the first African-American bishop to be appointed in the twentieth century and the second, after James A. Healey,* in American history. At the time of Perry's appointment there were 150,000 African-American Catholics in Louisiana with some 50,000 in the archdiocese of New Orleans.

Perseverance of the Saints. *See* ETERNAL SECURITY.

Peter, Johann Friederich (John Frederick) (1746-1813). Moravian* minister and composer. Peter was diarist and pastor at Bethlehem, Pennsylvania (1770-1786), and then in other churches in New Jersey, Pennsylvania, Maryland and North Carolina. He was the primary force in the musical development of each of these communities.

Peter's work exemplifies the important musical contribution the Moravians made to American religious life.

Peters, George Nathaniel Henry (1825-1909). Lutheran* minister and biblical scholar. Profoundly influenced by the "American Lutheranism" of Samuel Simon Schmucker,* Peters served various congregations in Ohio. As a writer, his major work was *The Theocratic Kingdom* (3 vols., 1883; repr. 1957), a masterful study of eschatology.*

Pettingill, William Leroy (1866-1950). Fundamentalist* Bible teacher, author and cofounder of the Philadelphia School of the Bible. In 1914 Pettingill assisted in founding Philadelphia School of the Bible and was dean (1914-1928) under its president, C. I. Scofield.* He was a tireless promoter of dispensational* premillennialism.*

Pew, John Howard (1882-1971). Industrialist, Christian layman and philanthropist.* President of the Sun Oil Company from 1912 to 1947, Pew was a strong supporter of Christian and independent education. His most significant religious role was in funding a number of Presbyterian,*

fundamentalist* and evangelical* causes, where his primary interest was in maintaining conservative Christianity and free enterprise in American society.

Pew Rents. An annual fee that determined seating in a meetinghouse. Nearness to the pulpit was typically determined by how much a family had contributed to the building of a new meetinghouse or by how much parishioners had given to the annual ministerial rate.

Philadelphia Baptist Association. Oldest surviving Baptist* association in America. Formed in 1707, by the 1750s the association extended from New England to the South and heavily influenced Baptists in America through its confession,* moderate Calvinist* theology,* organizational pattern and missionary zeal.

Philadelphia College and Academy. *See* PENNSYLVANIA, UNIVERSITY OF.

Philanthropy, Christian. Christianity inherited from Judaism its concern for the poor, the widow, the orphan and the stranger. Jesus' teaching and example raised charity to new intensity, with the cross becoming the supreme example of self-giving.

The Puritan* conscience, while it drove people to labor, also pointed to the dangers of riches and stressed community responsibility. This intensified benevolent giving.

In the nineteenth century the Civil War* and then Reconstruction stimulated the rise of large philanthropic organizations which came to the aid of Union soldiers and their families and then the freed slaves.

In America, wealthy industrialists and businessmen have made large contributions to various Christian causes and institutions, as have organizations such as American Friends Service Committee,* Church World Service,* Catholic Relief Services and World Vision, International.*

Phillips, W(illiam) T(homas) (1893-1973). African-American oneness Pentecostal* preacher and founding bishop of the Apostolic Overcoming Holy Church of God. Phillips, the sole bishop of his church for fifty-seven years, practiced divine healing,* foot washing,* holy dancing and water baptism* in the name of "Jesus only."

Philosophical Theology. The discipline of thought which attempts to demonstrate truths of God and religion by means of philosophical methodology. Philosophical theology does not seek to correlate revealed truths as does dogmatic or systematic theology.* Instead, it relies on a rational exploration of the issues.

Philosophical theology began with the pre-Socratic philosophers and continued throughout the Middle Ages under the aegis of natural theology. As the world of thought moved into the modern period, philosophical theology remained an important enterprise, although conclusions reached were often more negative.

Some of the more significant issues frequently addressed by philosophical theology are (1) the relationship between faith and reason; (2) the meaningfulness of religious language; (3) the validity of religious experience; (4) the existence of God; (5) the nature of God; (6) the possibility of divine revelation; (7) the rational tenability of the Incarnation; (8) the compatibility of evil with the existence of an all-good and all-powerful God; (9) the possibility of miracles; and (10) the religious basis for ethics.

Philpott, Peter Wiley (1865-1957). Fundamentalist* pastor and preacher. Philpott is best remembered as the founding minister and leader of the Philpott Tabernacle, in Hamilton, Ontario (1896-1922), a nondenominational congregation that grew to over 1,700 members. Later he held pastorates at Moody Memorial Church in Chicago (1922-1929) and Church of the Open Door in Los Angeles (1929-1934).

See also ASSOCIATED GOSPEL CHURCHES.

Pickett, Jarrel Waskom (1890-1981). Methodist* missionary to India. In 1910 Pickett sailed for India, where he served with distinction for the next forty-six years as pastor, evangelist, superintendent,* editor of the *Indian Witness* and bishop (1935-1956).

Pidgeon, George Campbell (1872-1971). Canadian church leader. Pidgeon's great ministry was at Bloor Street Church, Toronto, where he served from 1915 until 1948. He was chosen as moderator of the Presbyterian* General Assembly* in 1925, when he also became moderator of the newly formed United Church of Canada.*

Pidgeon was conservative in theology,* stressed the element of personal decision, embodied piety,* gave leadership in movements of moral reform and sought cooperation among the churches.

Pieper, Franz August Otto (1852-1931). Lutheran Church—Missouri Synod* theologian. Pieper served as president of Concordia Seminary (1887-1931) and as president of the Lutheran Church—Missouri Synod (1899-1911). Pieper ably defended the verbal inspiration of the Scriptures, the vicarious atonement* of Christ and justification* through faith. He opposed every doctrinal compromise.

Piepkorn, Arthur Carl (1907-1973). Lutheran* theologian. Piepkorn became distinguished as Concordia Seminary's erudite professor of systematic theology* (1951-1973), becoming known as a perceptive thinker and stimulating teacher.

A consultant to the Federal, later National Council of Churches* department of worship and the arts (1947-1960), he was much in demand for his breadth of learning and his evangelical* commitment. He also became a key member of the Lutheran-Roman Catholic dialogue* (1965-1973).

Pierce, Lovick (1785-1879). Methodist* minister and presiding elder. In 1809 Francis Asbury* appointed Pierce as presiding elder of the Oconee District in Georgia. Elected to the first delegated Methodist General Conference in 1812, Pierce served as a delegate to every general conference between 1824 and his death in 1879. During the War of 1812, Pierce was a chaplain* at Savannah.

After the Civil War* the elderly Pierce was elected to head the fraternal delegation for the Methodist Episcopal Church, South, to the General Conference of the Northern Church.

Pierce, Robert ("Bob") Willard (1914-1976). Evangelist and founder of World Vision International.* In light of the human suffering and need he witnessed in Asia after World War II,* Pierce founded World Vision International (1950), which supported orphanages, hospitals, national pastors and missionaries. After resigning from World Vision in 1967, he later founded Samaritan's Purse, devoted to raising money for evangelism and relief in Asia.

Pierson, Abraham (c. 1645-1707). Congregational* minister and educator. Pierson was the pastor of churches in New Jersey and Connecticut. He was critical of directions taken by Harvard* and become involved in the founding (1701) and early leadership of the Collegiate School in the Colony of Connecticut, later known as Yale College.* Pierson was the school's first rector.

Pierson, A(rthur) T(appan) (1837-1911). Presbyterian* minister, mission theorist and Bible expositor. In 1886 Pierson wrote *The Crisis of Missions,* a bestselling book that vividly put the issue of missions before the American people. He helped to found the Africa Inland Mission.* In 1893 he succeeded A. J. Gordon* as president of Gordon's Missionary Training School, now known as Gordon College.

Pierson's greatest theoretical contribution to missions stemmed from his premillennialism.* He did not believe that the world would be converted before Christ returned, but that world evangelization was a prerequisite to his return. For Pierson, the motivating force of the Student Volunteer Movement* watchword (which was credited to him)—"the evangelization of the world in this generation"—was its implicit belief that Christ would return once world evangelization was complete.

Pierson was the leading American spokesman for foreign missions in the late nineteenth century. Under his influence men such as John Mott,* Robert Speer,* Samuel Zwemer* and Henry Frost* were propelled into work for foreign missions.

Pietism. Pietism is gradually coming to be seen as a clearly discernible religious movement which has left few aspects of world Protestantism* untouched. The term itself seems to have been used first in 1674 in reference to the followers of the Lutheran* pastor Philipp Jakob Spener (1635-1705) at Frankfurt am Main, Germany. Gradually, however, historians with a primary interest in religion as it is lived felt the need to expand the concept to include developments in other Protestant circles which appear to parallel Spener's preoccupation with biblical piety.

Continental Pietism. Pietism as it is now widely understood has its roots both in the magisterial and radical phases of the Reformation, as well as in the emphasis on "godliness" of many Puritans.*

In general terms Pietism represents a reaction against the lack of religious fervor, the moral laxity, the tendency toward cultural accommodation and the interconfessional bickering of the representatives of orthodoxy* within the established Protestant communions. In time Pietism influenced every facet of Protestantism—its theology,* its hymnody,* its worship* and its church life. It encouraged the devotional* study of the Bible in the churches as well as in the homes; it stimulated church attendance, awakened the desire to establish charitable and educational institutions, created an awareness of the need for both domestic and foreign missions,* held out the hope for ecumenical* relations and opened the way for lay participation in the life of the churches. Against this background its impact upon Protestantism in colonial America becomes apparent.

New World Pietism. From about 1710 to the time of the American Revolution, succeeding waves of German immigrants* swelled the ranks of American settlers, many of them having had a Lutheran background. Because of the paucity of competent Lutheran clergymen various appeals were made to charitable societies in the home country and in Britain to supply them. The most generous response to these appeals came from Halle, the academic center of Pietism in Germany. Halle-trained pastors soon outnumbered by far their anti-Pietist colleagues. In 1748 they controlled the synod.*

In 1720 Theodorus J. Frelinghuysen,* a confirmed Pietist, arrived in America and presently took up his work in the Raritan Valley of New Jersey. Under his fervent preaching a revival* broke out which attracted the Tennents—William Sr.* and his son Gilbert.* This fused the Pietist impulse with Puritanism.

In one way or another Pietism appears to have influenced most if not all Protestant groups in America, though the specific lines of development are only beginning to emerge. Whether it was Pietism or Puritanism which dominantly shaped Protestant church life in North America, future historians will have to decide.

See also FREE CHURCH TRADITION IN AMERICA.

Piety: Popular Catholic. Indigenous or extra-sacramental religious behavior of Catholics. In addition to the normal Sunday* Eucharistic* worship* and the sacramental* rituals which generally signified major transitions in life, Catholics in the Middles Ages engaged in numerous devotions* and prayer* forms, generally the product of individual or group zeal. Much of this activity was carried to colonial America.

The influence of the Enlightenment* cooled Catholic devotionalism, at least along the eastern seaboard, and thus in the period just before and shortly after the American Revolution, a rather plain Catholic religiosity, focused on Sunday and especially the Mass,* existed and was suitably housed in neoclassic churches with clear glass windows and only a crucifix* and two statues or pictures of saints as interior decoration.

This situation was radically altered, however, as a result of the Romantic* revolt which seems to have begun among American Catholics in the 1830s. An elaborate devotional revolution followed which not only altered architecture,* making Gothic popular again, but now included multiple devotions, with a corresponding expansion of prayer books, hymnals* and even churches. This Romantic Catholicism lasted for well over a century.

Vatican II,* emphasizing the Catholic liturgy,* a more personal Christian faith and concern for a better world, had the effect of significantly diminishing the devotional side of Catholic religiosity. Since much of the domestic religiosity emphasized routine prayer, devotionalism and world-denying fasting,* it declined after the council also.

Piety: Popular Orthodox. Orthodox piety is a way of living and thinking marked by fidelity to liturgical, moral and devotional practices of the Orthodox Church* reaching back to apostolic times, such as almsgiving, prayer* and fasting (Mt 6:2-18).

Orthodox piety is distinctly corporate and liturgical* insofar as Orthodox life is practically dominated by corporate participation in the sacraments* and in numerous other liturgical services. The entire church year* features established cycles of feasts and fasting periods, together with their related universal or local customs. The personal life of an Orthodox reflects this liturgical and ecclesial spirit through daily prayer before icons,* use of candles and incense, and other activities.

In the new urban American milieu, especially among the third and fourth generations of American-born Orthodox, a gradual dissolution of Orthodox piety is occurring due to acculturation—including secularism, work patterns and a weakening of the ethnic community.

Piety: Popular Protestant. Popular piety involves certain inner religious experiences* and outward observances which contribute to spiritual growth. Pietists of the seventeenth century urged all Christians to move beyond the dogma* and ritual of the church to a personal experience of God through conversion,* Bible study,* prayer* and virtuous living. Classic Pietism fostered spirituality* through small groups gathered for devotional confession, prayer, fellowship and study of Scripture. Much Protestant piety continues to be nurtured in small groups.

Private devotion to God became public through collective services of worship,* preaching* and evangelism.* Lutheran,* Episcopalian* and other more liturgical traditions provide opportunities for Christians to articulate and enact personal piety through the order and dignity of common prayer, litany* and sacrament.* In the free church tradition,* popular piety was influenced by the spontaneity of the revivalistic* tradition and the camp-meeting* experience.

See also SPIRITUALITY, PROTESTANT.

Pike, James Albert (1913-1969). Episcopal* bishop of California. After serving as bishop of California (1958-1966), Pike became theologian-in-residence at the Center for the Study of Democratic Institutions in Santa Barbara.

From 1960 on, Pike struggled to relate the gospel to modern realities; in the process, he departed from orthodoxy,* denying the historical virgin birth and challenging the doctrine of the Trinity. In 1966 Pike was censured by the House of Bishops* for his "caricatures of treasured symbols" and "cheap vulgarizations of great expressions of the faith." Following his son's suicide in February 1966, Pike ventured into spiritualism.

See also BLAKE-PIKE UNITY PROPOSAL.

Pilgrim Holiness Church. See WESLEYAN CHURCH.

Pilgrims. Plymouth colonizers and American saints. The original Pilgrims were members of a Separatist* group that in 1620 arrived in Plymouth from England, via Holland. William Bradford,* the first governor of the colony, kept a detailed history that has since become a classic of American literature.

Especially with Abraham Lincoln's* 1863 declaration of a national Thanksgiving Day,* the Pilgrims ceased to be merely regional heroes and became national symbols of American principles and values.

Pioneer Clubs. International nondenominational weekday club and camping program for young people. Begun in 1939 as the Girls' Guild and later renamed Pioneer Girls, the program expanded in 1981 to include Pioneer Boys, and the club's name was changed to Pioneer Clubs.

The program integrates spiritual and personal development and emphasizes evangelism and discipleship by giving young people from kindergarten through twelfth grade opportunities to learn new skills, make friends with peers and adults, and develop Christian values. Over eighty denominations* sponsor the weekday club program in the U.S.

Pioneer Girls. See PIONEER CLUBS.

Piper, Otto A. (1891-1981). Presbyterian* theologian. Piper was born in Germany and studied theology in Germany and France. His teaching career took him from Göttingen (1920-1930) to Münster (1930-1933), but under the Nazis he was forced to leave Germany. After a brief period of teaching in Wales (1934-1937), Piper moved to Princeton Theological Seminary,* where he remained from 1937 until 1981. Among his published works are *God in History* (1939) and *The Biblical View of Sex and Marriage* (1959).

Pitt, Robert Healey (1853-1937). Southern Baptist* pastor and editor. While he was pastor in Richmond, Virginia, Pitt began his career at the *Religious Herald.* Pitt's editorials won him acclaim for his progressive social views and for his staunch defense of religious liberty. In the 1920s, when fundamentalists* within the Southern Baptist Convention were advocating a more firm expression of doctrinal orthodoxy* within educational institutions, Pitt advised mutual respect and tolerance among differing Baptists.

Pius IX (1792-1878). Pope from 1846 to 1878. Pius IX's pontificate was the longest in history and among the more controversial. As pope, his major project for America was the organization and spirituality of the church. He created new dioceses,* named Archbishop James Gibbons* as the first American apostolic delegate* and encouraged the creation of colleges and parochial schools.* Nevertheless, the distance between him and the American church widened.

Pius X (1835-1914). Pope from 1903 to 1914.

During his pontificate, close to five million Catholic immigrants* to the U.S. consolidated the Roman Catholic Church's standing as the largest denomination.* The desperate economic conditions of the immigrants helped stimulate the pope to promote the rights of laboring people.

The pope's encyclical *Pascendi Dominici Gregis* (1907) effectively established Roman-oriented domination of Catholic intellectual life for two generations.

Pius XI (1857-1939). Pope from 1922 to 1939. His impact on the U.S. included his emphasis on education for the priesthood. His many social statements were extraordinarily influential, especially *Quadragesimo Anno* (1931), which criticized both capitalism and socialism* and advocated a Christian reconstruction of society. The encyclical probably played a role in the massive Catholic votes behind Franklin Delano Roosevelt and the New Deal.

Pius XII (1876-1958). Pope from 1939 to 1958. He had the major responsibility for handling or defining Vatican relations with the Hitler government before and during World War II.* He has received thorough criticism for not doing enough for the Jews, an issue perennially debated. The American Catholic Church doubled in size again during his pontificate, making it by far the largest church in the country. He gave approval to Catholic discussion with the Protestant* ecumenical movement.*

Plan of Union. Congregational*-Presbyterian* alliance. Sealed in 1801, the plan formally united Presbyterians and Connecticut Congregationalists in efforts to evangelize* the western frontier. Close ties that had existed among the two groups for at least thirty-five years finally culminated in this plan designed to foster joint action rather than needless conflict in the home missionary* enterprise.

When Old Schoolers* gained control of the Presbyterian General Assembly in 1837 (*see* Auburn Declaration), they revoked the Plan of Union, as did Congregationalists at the Albany Convention of 1852.

Plessis, Joseph Octave (1763-1825). Roman Catholic* bishop of Quebec. Plessis's administrative abilities and political instincts combined to make him Quebec's most influential Catholic leader in the early nineteenth century.

Plockhoy, Pieter Cornelisz (c. 1620-c. 1700). Mennonite* religious and social reformer. Plockhoy was concerned with the establishment of ideal communities in North America and appealed in part to the example of the sixteenth-century Moravian* Anabaptists* and Hutterites* to support his theories.

Plymouth (Christian) Brethren. An independent, nondenominational, evangelical* movement. Dissatisfied with the spiritual dryness of many British churches in the early nineteenth century, Christians of various groups gathered in a simple, "New Testament" pattern. With centers in Dublin and Plymouth, the (Christian) Brethren developed into a separate movement by the 1830s but then split in the 1840s over church discipline. The two predominant groups are the "Exclusives" and the "Opens."
See also DARBY, JOHN NELSON.

Pocket Testament League. A nondenominational organization seeking to evangelize* through distributing the written Word of God. The inspiration for the founding of the league came from a thirteen-year-old British girl who made it a practice to read the Bible every day. Charles M. Alexander* and J. Wilbur Chapman* launched the organization on its worldwide mission in 1908. Today the ministry* of the Pocket Testament League encircles the globe.

Political Theology. The term *political theology* began to be used in the 1960s by theologians who were committed to establishing explicit connections between theology* and politics. The primary impetus for these efforts came from Germany and Latin America, where the lessons learned during the struggle against Nazism took shape in the "theology of hope," and the question of the church's role in revolutionary settings stimulated the development of "liberation theology."* The representatives of these schools of thought have meant to highlight the ways in which theology always is political in nature, even when it claims to be "apolitical."

The political scope of the gospel has been recognized by a number of important strains within the evangelical tradition. New England Puritanism* was systematically political in its theologizing. The Puritans insisted that the righteous ordering of public life was an essential part of obedience to the conditions of the divine covenant.* The theocratic* vision of New England has been revived by the New Right* of the 1970s and 1980s.

Traditional Roman Catholicism* has also actively pursued questions of political theology; political instruction has been viewed as an important dimension of the church's teaching office, or magisterium.* The West German Catholic theologian Johann Baptist Metz has been the most prominent international proponent of political theology and was largely responsible for reviving the term in the 1960s.

Polity. *See* CHURCH GOVERNMENT.

Polk, Leonidas (1806-1864). Episcopal* bishop. Polk, a cousin of President James K. Polk, was elected missionary bishop* of the Southwest in 1838. The jurisdiction—which embraced five states—proved impossible to supervise, and in 1841 Polk was glad to accept election as first bishop of Louisiana. Polk's special concern for the conversion and religious instruction of slaves caused African-American communicants to outnumber whites.

In 1856 Polk began planning and raising funds for a great Episcopal university that would rival Harvard* and Yale* and dissuade young Southerners from attending Northern colleges. In 1860 Polk laid the cornerstone of the University of the South in the mountain town of Sewanee, Tennessee.

At the outbreak of the Civil War,* Jefferson Davis offered a military commission to Polk, a graduate of West Point. He accepted a commission as a major general, serving until he was killed by a cannonball in June 1864. Ironically, he is better remembered for his death while serving the Confederacy than for his humanitarian efforts with Louisiana's African-Americans and his plans for the gradual removal of slavery from his native South.

Pontifical Biblical Commission. A committee named to help the pope guide Catholic* biblical studies. The commission was created by Pope Leo XIII* in 1902 in an atmosphere colored by fears of modernism.* Since the issuance of Pope Pius XII's* encyclical* *Divino Afflante Spiritu** (1947), Catholic scholars have had the liberty to employ the findings of new methods of biblical research.

Pope. See PAPACY AND UNITED STATES CATHOLICS.

Pope, Liston (1909-1974). Congregational* minister, educator and sociologist. Pope taught at Yale and was dean of its divinity school from 1949 to 1962. He combined a deep interest in sociology with concern for the role of religion in relation to problems confronting American life. Active in the World Council of Churches,* he frequently traveled and spoke in support of worldwide unity among Protestant* denominations* and with the Catholic Church.*

Pope, William Burt (1822-1903). Methodist* theologian. While teaching theology in England, Pope published his three-volume *Compendium of Christian Theology* (1875-1876). It long served as a standard theology for Methodists on both sides of the Atlantic.

Porter, Frank Chamberlain (1859-1946). Biblical scholar. Porter, who taught at Yale* from 1889 until his retirement in 1927, valued the historical-critical method and opposed the Princeton theology.* For Porter, a romanticist, the Bible had a poetic character with spiritual truths and a sense of wonder which illumines the soul.

Porter, Noah (1811-1892). Congregational* minister, scholar and president of Yale.* In 1846 Porter began teaching at Yale and then served as its president from 1871 until 1886. Porter spent most of his career in teaching ethics* and philosophy, always warmly and with a strongly evangelical* bent. Recognizing that graduates were turning away from the ministry to secular professions, he sought to accommodate that development by replacing the inculcation of orthodox doctrine in the college with the building of "Christian character."

Portland Deliverance. A statement by the 1892 General Assembly* of the Presbyterian Church (U.S.A.)* in Portland, Oregon, requiring ministers to subscribe to a strict understanding of the inspiration and authority* of the Bible. Conservatives adopted this position to thwart efforts by theological moderates to revise the Westminster Confession.*

Positive Thinking. The general belief that optimistic thought can bring beneficial results. The immigrant* experience itself was a major source of optimism. Puritan* theology* carried a post-millennial* theme, an optimistic note that was emphasized during the revivals* of the First and Second Great Awakenings.* The Arminian* theology that triumphed in these revivals explicitly encouraged human effort to transform one's will.

In the twentieth century, Norman Vincent Peale's* bestseller *The Power of Positive Thinking* (1952) reclaimed the techniques of self-improvement as an aspect of conventional Protestant piety,* an aspect that is now identified with the television ministry of Robert Schuller's* *Hour of Power.*

Postmillennialism. The belief that the return of Christ will take place after the millennium, which may be a literal period of peace and prosperity or else a symbolic representation of the final triumph of the gospel.

The classic expression of postmillennialism is found in the work of the Anglican* commentator Daniel Whitby (1638-1726), whose view was adopted by Jonathan Edwards* and the leaders of the Protestant* missionary movement* during the nineteenth and early twentieth centuries.

Posttribulationism. See RAPTURE OF THE CHURCH.

Praise the Lord. A verbal exclamation of praise that God has acted in a special way, used primarily by Christians of an evangelical* or charismatic* persuasion.

Prayer. Communication with God, usually in verbal form. All Christian traditions find precedent for private and corporate prayer in the Hebrew Scriptures and the New Testament. Christians through the centuries have found private prayer to be an essential aspect of their spiritual life, as a means of both expressing themselves to God and experiencing his presence. Private and public prayer may be extemporaneous, recited or read from a prayer book. Scripture may also be used as a form of prayer or in contemplative or meditative prayer.

The most prominent setting for prayer is public worship. Depending on the tradition, this prayer may follow a set liturgical form, be led by the minister with responses from the congregation, or be extemporaneous. Prayer may take one of several different attitudes or may combine any number of these into a single occasion of prayer: adoration, confession, intercession, petition or thanksgiving.

See also PRAYER BREAKFASTS; PRAYER MEETING; SPIR-
ITUALITY.

Prayer Breakfasts. Periodic morning prayer*
gatherings of laypeople, frequently including political figures. Originated in Seattle (1935) by
Methodist* minister Abraham Vereide (d. 1969),
prayer breakfasts spread quickly to other cities.
The first national prayer breakfast, held in 1953,
was attended by President Eisenhower.* Since
then, presidents have generally attended.

Prayer Cloths. A method of prayer used primarily by charismatics* and Pentecostals,* especially
for physical healing.* The biblical basis for the
practice is Acts 19:11-12, which is used to support
the belief that God desires to work similar miracles today.

Prayer in Public Schools. The issue of prayer
in public schools is framed by the First Amendment to the U.S. Constitution (1791): "Congress
shall make no law respecting an establishment of
religion, or prohibiting the free exercise thereof . . ." This statement of freedom of religion
must be interpreted today within the context of
a pluralistic* society with a system of public education rooted in religious convictions.

By 1800 seven of sixteen states had enacted
legislation providing for public education. Some
of those states required religious practices in
their schools, and others permitted them. By the
end of the nineteenth century, prayer in public
schools had been banned in six states, yet after
1910 twelve states required religious exercises in
the public schools.

In 1962 and 1963, in *Engel v. Vitale, Abington
v. Schempp* and *Murray v. Curlett,* the U.S. Supreme Court ruled that school-sponsored prayer
(including use of the Lord's Prayer) and devotional Bible reading were unconstitutional, decisions that set the precedent for the relationship
of prayer and public education today. The study
of the Bible as literature, the academic teaching
of religion and voluntary prayers, however, are
acceptable in the public schools.

Prayer Meeting. A meeting convened for the
sake of prayer.* Prayer meetings are mentioned
occasionally before 1800, but they were popularized particularly by Charles G. Finney* and
Dwight L. Moody.* By the turn of the century,
prayer meetings or midweek services became

common in Protestant* churches with evangelistic* legacies.

Prayer Meeting Revival (1857-1859). A revival originating in noon prayer meetings* begun
by Jeremiah Lanphier in September 1857, in the
Dutch Reformed* Church on Fulton Street in New
York City. The movement soon spread to other
cities around the nation and around the world.

In geographic and numerical extent, in fact, the
Revival of 1857-1859 has probably never been
equaled. Estimates range up to one million or
more converts in the U.S., with another million in
Great Britain and Ireland.
See also REVIVALISM, PROTESTANT.

Praying Indian Towns. Towns of settled,
Christian Native Americans in colonial Massachusetts. Missionary John Eliot* saw the advantage of
locating the new converts in separate towns, with
the first at Natick, in 1651. By 1674 there were
some 2,500 converted Native Americans, settled
in fourteen such towns.

Preacher. A person, usually of the ordained*
clergy,* who regularly preaches sermons. The
term usually refers to an ordained minister* of
nonliturgical religious groups in which preaching
is the clergy's primary public function.

Predestination. In its normal and proper sense,
the term refers to the foreordination of moral
agents to their eternal ends. That is, the knowledge and choice, made by God before time began, of angels and men as to their final blessedness with God or damnation apart from him.

The doctrine was formulated by Augustine in
his controversies with Pelagius (405-418). Augustine held that all persons were predestined either
to belief or to unbelief, whereas Pelagius considered election* to refer simply to God's foreknowledge of who would believe. The later dispute between Calvinism* and Arminianism*
(1603-1619) was essentially the same.

In American church traditions, there is a broad
spectrum of belief about this doctrine. While Catholicism* has embraced a range of views on the
question, for Protestant* churches an understanding or denial of the doctrine has frequently
formed an important part of their self-identity.
Two views affirm both God's foreknowledge and
his choice in predestination: Dortian, or Extreme,
Calvinism and moderate Calvinism. Two views

define predestination as foreknowledge only: Wesleyan Arminianism and Arminianism. Two views deny that God chooses individuals: Socinianism, or old Unitarianism,* and Barthianism, or neo-orthodoxy.*

Premillennialism. This is the belief that there will be a 1,000-year reign of Christ on earth at the end of the present age. This teaching is based on Revelation 20:1-10, elaborated by certain Old Testament texts, such as Isaiah 55—66, which teach that there will be a time of justice, peace and righteousness on earth. In the twentieth century, premillennialism has been identified with dispensationalism,* although the two do not necessarily imply each other.

Presbyterian Church in America. A conservative Presbyterian* denomination,* organized in December 1973 as the National Presbyterian Church. The present name dates from the second General Assembly* (1974). The denomination had its origin in the "continuing church" movement, a conservative effort in the Presbyterian Church in the U.S.* (the "Southern Presbyterian" Church) opposed to the denomination's perceived departures from historic doctrines, its membership in the National* and World Councils of Churches* and to social and political pronouncements by church bodies.

Some independent churches and presbyteries,* as well as congregations from other denominations, have joined the denomination. The denomination was augmented in 1982 by reception of the Reformed Presbyterian Church, Evangelical Synod.* The Presbyterian Church in America is now a national church, the second-largest Presbyterian denomination in the U.S. In 1992 there were 1,212 churches with 194,825 members.

See also PRESBYTERIAN CHURCH IN THE UNITED STATES; REFORMED AND PRESBYTERIAN CHURCHES.

Presbyterian Church in Canada. Canada's major Presbyterian denomination.* Canadian Presbyterianism arose first in Nova Scotia in the mid-eighteenth century. It followed the patterns of migration from the U.S. and the United Kingdom, but the predominant numbers and influence came from the Church of Scotland. In 1875 the major Presbyterian bodies in Canada united to form the Presbyterian Church in Canada, a denomination independent of, if still in contact with, the Scottish church.

Fifty years later, the formation of the United Church of Canada* split the Presbyterian church into two groups: the larger one went into union* with the major Methodist* and Congregational* bodies, while about a third remained as "continuing" Presbyterians.

Canadian Presbyterians have a long heritage of distinguished work in missions,* theology and social ministry. Once the largest Protestant denomination in Canada, like the other mainline Canadian churches the Presbyterian Church has lost members steadily since the early 1960s. In the 1992 it claimed over 998 churches and an inclusive membership of 233,335.

Presbyterian Church in the United States. Commonly known as the Southern Presbyterian Church, a Reformed* denomination, formed from the Presbyterian Church in the Confederate States of America (1861-1866) and Presbyterians who had belonged to border synods* of the Old School* branch of the Presbyterian Church in the U.S.A.

During much of its existence, the PCUS stood for a doctrine of "the spirituality of the church," contending that corporate involvement in social and political issues was inappropriate. Beginning in the 1930s, however, the assemblies began to speak and act more widely on issues affecting the larger society.

Growing in numbers from 80,000 members in 1869 to more than 1 million in 1962, the PCUS began to decline, in part from the withdrawal of dissidents who formed the Presbyterian Church in America* in 1973. The PCUS joined with the United Presbyterian Church in the U.S.A.* in 1983 to form the Presbyterian Church (U.S.A.).*

See also REFORMED AND PRESBYTERIAN CHURCHES; REFORMED TRADITION IN AMERICA.

Presbyterian Church (U.S.A.). A mainline* Presbyterian denomination formed from 1983 to 1987 by the union of the United Presbyterian Church in the United States of America (UPCUSA)* and the Presbyterian Church in the United States (PCUS),* also known as the Southern Presbyterian Church.

The present-day Presbyterian Church (U.S.A.) (PCUSA) can trace its roots back to 1788 and the formation of the Presbyterian General Assembly.* In the 1830s, disputes in the Presbyterian Church in the U.S.A. (PC-USA) about theology, relations with other Christian bodies, and reform* methods regarding slavery* led to another split—into Old School* and New School* assemblies. The Old School in the South became the Presbyterian Church in the Confederate States of America, later taking the name Presbyterian Church in the U.S. (PCUS) in 1866. After the Civil War, Old and New School assemblies in the North reunited into one denomination, the PC-USA (1870).

The PC-USA, more than other Reformed* denominations, was the scene of struggles between fundamentalists* and so-called modernists.*

In the 1970s, a number of conservative members and congregations left the PCUS to join the newly formed Presbyterian Church in America.* Their departure enabled the PCUS to join with the UPCUSA to form the Presbyterian Church (U.S.A.) in June 1983. In 1992 the PCUSA reported 11,456 congregations with a membership of 2.8 million.

See also CIVIL WAR AND THE CHURCHES; REFORMED AND PRESBYTERIAN CHURCHES; REFORMED TRADITION.

Presbytery. The legislative and judicial body of a geographic district in Presbyterian* church government.* A district, or presbytery, is made up of a given number of congregations. Issues concerning the churches within a district are referred to the presbytery.

See also CHURCH GOVERNMENT: PRESBYTERIAN.

Press, Catholic. As of 1994 a total of 647 Catholic newspapers, magazines, newsletters and other periodicals had a combined circulation of 26.8 million in the U.S. and Canada.

The Irish-born Bishop John England,* of Charleston, South Carolina, is regarded as the founder of the Catholic press in the U.S. His *U.S. Catholic Miscellany* (1827-1861) served as something of a national Catholic paper. With several title changes, the *Boston Pilot* (1829-) is considered the oldest of the U.S. Catholic newspapers.

In the period from 1900 through World War II,* the U.S. Catholic press evolved into the character that has endured into the present. It is multifaceted and controlled and operated by the church. The independent publications once common in the nineteenth century have become a rarity. Official diocesan newspapers have predominated, helped by the National Catholic News Service, which began in 1920. Following World War II, a notable growth in professionalization began in the Catholic press.

The *Catholic Digest,* founded on the model of the *Reader's Digest* in the 1930s, is the most widely circulated Catholic publication today. One generally finds a progressive viewpoint in *America, Commonweal* and the *National Catholic Reporter,* and a cautious-to-conservative viewpoint in *Our Sunday Visitor,* the *National Catholic Register* and especially *The Wanderer.*

The history of the Catholic press in Canada begins in 1806 when *Le Canadien* appeared in Quebec. The first English diocesan weekly was begun in 1826 by Bishop Alexander MacDonell, who brought it to his Kingston diocese* in 1830 and gave it the title of the *Catholic.* Most Catholic publications, however, date from the late nineteenth century and even more from the early twentieth century. Canada's first chain of diocesan newspapers, the *Canadian Register,* was founded in 1941, when the archbishops of Ontario amalgamated five diocesan weeklies.

Press, Protestant. The actual birth of the Protestant religious press in America came during the Second Great Awakening* of the early nineteenth century. For example, in 1800 the *Connecticut Evangelical Magazine* began publication, reporting on and encouraging the revivals in New England.

On the advancing western edge of the new nation, Protestant denominations were faced with the breakdown of established religion and the challenge of an ever-expanding frontier. In this new setting the Methodists,* Baptists* and Disciples of Christ* mobilized itinerant* preachers who moved from community to community, evangelizing* and ministering as they went. But these efforts were unable to provide ongoing instruction in the faith and instill a sense of belonging to a larger body of kindred spirits. This missionary and pastoral need was met by the rise of the religious press.

The Restoration movement* in particular found journalism to be an effective tool for growth. Alexander Campbell,* the principal leader of the movement, edited first the *Christian Baptist* (1823-1830) and then the *Millennial Harbinger* (1830-1866). Denominational organs are a part of nearly every religious body in America, making them the most common form of religious journalism.

A further impetus to publish was the rise of the nineteenth-century voluntary religious societies, each addressing itself to a particular goal or cause. These special-interest groups stood outside the established denominational structures and could not depend on denominational organs to reach or expand their constituencies.

The Holiness movement* utilized the printed word in spreading its message and method of spirituality.* Phoebe Palmer,* for example, a leading figure in the early years of the Holiness movement, disseminated her ideas through her books and her widely circulated magazine *Guide to Holiness* (1864-1874).

As with the Holiness movement, the Pentecostal movement* came to rely on periodicals to inform, instruct and inspire what was soon to become a far-flung movement. The offspring of the Pentecostal movement, the charismatic movement,* has been nourished and informed by a variety of publications, including Stephen Strang's *Charisma* (1975-), which in 1987 merged with *Christian Life* to become *Charisma and Christian Life* (circ. 225,000).

Within the mainline* Protestant sector, the outstanding religious journal in the twentieth century has been the *Christian Century* (circ. 35,000). Beginning in 1884 as the *Christian Oracle,* the journal achieved prominence under the editorship (1908-1947) of Charles Clayton Morrison.*

The leading periodical of evangelical opinion during the latter half of the twentieth century has been *Christianity Today* (CT), launched in 1956 largely at the initiative of Billy Graham* and his father-in-law, L. Nelson Bell.* Now with a circulation of 192,000, CT fosters a broad evangelical engagement with culture and society, though it has generally taken a conservative political stance.

Far more popular in its appeal, *Guideposts,* started in 1946 by Norman Vincent Peale* and featuring the religious faith of celebrities and ordinary laypeople, by 1975 claimed to have more paying subscribers (3.1 million) than any other inspirational magazine in the world.

Preston, John (1587-1628). English Reformed* theologian influential among New England Puritans.* In England, Preston devoted most of his time to preaching and advanced from one prominent post to another. In 1622 he became master of Emmanuel College, Cambridge, training ground of early New England pastors. Huge crowds gathered to hear him, prompting limiting of access to his sermons and the enlargement of chapel buildings. His published sermons went through numerous editions and were on the shelves of New England pastors.

Preston, Thomas Scott (1824-1891). Catholic* priest and apologist.* After studying for the Episcopal* priesthood, Preston in 1849 was received in the Catholic Church. In 1853 he was appointed secretary to Archbishop John Hughes* and in 1855 diocesan chancellor. Preston achieved distinction as an apologist and lecturer for Roman Catholicism.

Presuppositionalism. A term describing a particular approach to philosophy and theology. Presuppositionalism argues that all systems of knowledge are founded on unprovable assumptions about God, human nature and reality. Theoretical thought must therefore begin with a conscious appraisal of these assumptions.

Among Christians, presuppositionalism began in the 1930s through the efforts of two Calvinist* thinkers, Herman Dooyeweerd* and Cornelius Van Til.*

Pretribulationism. See RAPTURE OF THE CHURCH.

Preus, Jacob Aal Ottesen (1920-1994). Lutheran Church—Missouri Synod* educator and leader. In 1958 Preus became professor of New Testament at Concordia Theological Seminary, Springfield, Missouri. He quickly rose to leadership within the denomination and became president of the seminary in 1962. In 1969 Preus was elected president of the Synod, leading the conservatives who had grown concerned over the inroads of liberal theology and biblical criticism within their denomination. In 1972-1974 Preus led a struggle to rid the Synod of liberalism. Preus became a respected figure in other conservative Protestant denominations and institutions who identified with his stand for confessional orthodoxy. Preus remained president of the Synod until 1981 and then returned to teach at Concordia Theological Seminary.

Price, Charles Sydney (c. 1880-1947). Healing* revivalist.* After earlier ministry among the Methodists* and Congregationalists,* Price in 1920 became a Pentecostal,* receiving the Spirit baptism* under Aimee Semple McPherson's* preaching. In 1922 he launched a successful independent national, and ultimately worldwide, healing ministry. In 1925 he began publishing *Golden Grain,* an excellent source for studying healing revivalism.

Price, Joseph Charles (1854-1893). African-American clergyman, educator and civil rights* advocate. While lecturing in England, Price obtained $10,000 in pledges for what became Livingstone College, incorporated in 1885 in North Carolina. Under his leadership, Livingstone became one of the important liberal arts colleges for Southern African-Americans. Price also campaigned actively for Prohibition* and civil rights.

Priest. *See* HOLY ORDERS.

Priesthood of Believers. A Protestant* principle stating that each believer has immediate access to God through the one mediator, Jesus Christ. This great principle of the sixteenth-century Protestant Reformation helped cut through the tangles of medieval Catholicism* that tended to place barriers between the individual Christian and God. The implications of the principle were that no priest was necessary, no saints,* no Blessed Virgin Mary,* to intercede for the ordinary believer.

Transported to the American environment, without bishoprics and generally established churches, the priesthood of all believers provided a basis for greater lay influence than had characterized European Christianity.

Priestley, Joseph (1733-1804). Noted English scientist, philosopher and Unitarian* minister. Although Priestley was engaged as pastor by a succession of congregations, his iconoclastic doctrinal views, along with his hot temper and tendency to stammer, led to repeated difficulties. A diligent experimental scientist, Priestley is best remembered today for his discovery of oxygen in 1774.

Priestley's outspoken defense of the French Revolution incited a mob to torch his chapel* and sack his home in 1791. This assault precipitated Priestley's eventual decision to immigrate to America. Here he was ultimately judged irrelevant by American Christians drawn to the rationalism* of Scottish Common Sense philosophy* and caught up in the fervor of the Second Great Awakening.*

Priests of St. Sulpice. *See* SULPICIANS.

Primitive Baptists. Baptist* churches and associations generally characterized by rigid predestinarianism and a desire to recapture the original faith and order of the New Testament apostles. Emerging in the early nineteenth century, these Baptists used Particular Baptist* confessions to develop a rigid Calvinism* and an opposition to organized missions.* Most Primitive Baptists oppose church auxiliaries not found in Scripture, such as Bible and tract societies,* seminaries and Sunday schools.*

Primitivism. The impulse to restore the primitive or original order of things as revealed in Scripture,* free from the accretions of church history and tradition. The New England Puritan* ideal was to establish the "original," "primitive" or "ancient" order and doctrine in their Congregational* life and worship.* Methodism* was a movement self-consciously pursuing John Wesley's* ideal of restoring apostolic Christianity.

The most outstanding examples of primitivism are the religious traditions indigenous to America, such as the Churches of Christ* and Pentecostalism.* The Churches of Christ began in the early nineteenth century as a quest for Christian unity based not on creeds* but on the essential truths of Christianity as expressed in the New Testament. Pentecostalism has expressed primitivism in its claims to a twentieth-century restoration of first-century apostolic power and order.

Prince, Thomas (1687-1758). Congregational* minister and historian. Prince, pastor at Boston's Third Church (Old South) from 1718 until his death, quickly emerged as a central figure in eighteenth-century New England's religious and political history.

During the Great Awakening* of the 1740s he was a New Light* and engaged in friendly controversy with the revival's leading opponent, Charles Chauncy.* He was among those who invited evangelist George Whitefield* to preach in Boston.

Princeton Theological Seminary. Presbyterian* seminary. Princeton Theological Seminary was established in 1812 by the Presbyterian Church as a ministerial training institution located adjacent to the College of New Jersey (*see* Princeton University). Princeton was one of the first seminaries to be founded in the U.S. and was formative in the shaping of theological seminary curriculum. It was a center of Presbyterian theology throughout the nineteenth century (*see* Princeton Theology) and has continued through the twentieth century as the flagship seminary of the Presbyterian Church (U.S.A.).* It was at the center of the fundamentalist-modernist controversy* in the late 1920s when the seminary was reorganized to ensure an inclusive spectrum of theology and several of its conservative theologians, including J. Gresham Machen,* departed. The roster of notable Princeton scholars and theologians includes Archibald Alexander,* Charles Hodge,* Archibald A. Hodge,* B. B. Warfield,* J. Gresham Machen, Otto A. Piper,* Lefferts A. Loetscher,* John A. Mackay,* Hugh T. Kerr* and contemporary New Testament scholars Bruce M. Metzger, J. Christiaan Beker and James H. Charlesworth. In 1983 Thomas W. Gillespie became president, succeeding James I. McCord.* In 1991 the seminary enrolled 784 students.

Princeton Theology. A Presbyterian* and Reformed* theological tradition developed at Princeton Theological Seminary. American Presbyterianism's most dominant theology* was propagated at Princeton Seminary from its founding in 1812 until its reorganization in 1921.

For over a century Princeton was the domain of prominent professors—Archibald Alexander,* Charles Hodge,* Archibald A. Hodge,* Benjamin B. Warfield* and J. Gresham Machen*—who taught a demanding theological curriculum to over six thousand students, defended Reformed interpretations of Scripture and laid intellectual and spiritual foundations for twentieth-century evangelicalism.*

Princeton's theologians advocated a Reformed confessionalism.* They taught that human depravity resulted from a historical fall and that the imputation of Adam's sin* resulted in a fallen race which could only be saved by Christ's sacrificial atonement.* God worked out his plan of covenantal redemption through election* and predestination.* While they displayed little sensitivity to historical conditions shaping doctrines and to the necessity of contextualizing faith for each generation, they were committed to retaining the Reformed biblical worldview as foundational for all Christian teaching.

As modern theologians mounted hostile attacks against orthodoxy,* each Princeton generation responded by refining its predecessors' view of Scripture. After Alexander defended the Bible* against deism* and Charles Hodge met the first onslaught of European biblical criticism, A. A. Hodge and Warfield taught that God's verbal and plenary inspiration produced a Scripture inerrant* in the original autographs.

Princeton University. Educational institution with roots in colonial Presbyterianism.* Princeton was probably the first truly national college in America and from the late eighteenth century through the nineteenth century perhaps the most influential educational institution in shaping Christian thought in the New World. Founded in 1746 by New Light* Presbyterians and relocated in Princeton in 1756, it quickly attracted students from all regions of the country and gained a reputation for training leaders for public life.

Princeton Theological Seminary opened in 1812 as one of the first graduate schools of theology in America. Princeton theology* was one of the most influential theological systems then promoted in America.

Prior/Prioress. The male and female leaders of a religious house (priory) of men or women who have taken either simple or solemn vows. Most of these communities are Catholic;* some are Anglican.*

Prison Fellowship Ministries. A parachurch* organization dedicated to encouraging and assisting the church in its volunteer ministry to prisoners, former prisoners and their families. In 1976 Charles Colson, former special counsel to President Nixon,* started Prison Fellowship Ministries in response to the spiritual and emotional needs evident during his Watergate-related prison term.

In 1979 Prison Fellowship International was begun as an international association of prison ministries, each operating under its own national board of directors.

Prison Ministries. Lay and ordained* ministries* to prisoners, former prisoners and their families. Although the church spearheaded many nineteenth-century social reforms, ministry to prisoners was relatively quiet and local until after World War II,* when several large denominations* placed chaplains in selected institutions. Ray Hoekstra established International Prison Ministries, which has met a need for free distribution of Bibles and Christian literature in prisons.

The 1970s ushered in a new era for the church, as America's jails and prisons were more generally viewed as a mission field. In 1972 Bill Glass founded the Bill Glass Prison Ministry, emphasizing crusade evangelism, and in 1976 Charles Colson founded Prison Fellowship Ministries,* whose array of programs support local churches in their ministry to prisoners, former prisoners and their families.

Prison Reform, Christians and. Prison reform movements in America have been marked by individuals whose Christian commitment has motivated them to develop, articulate and popularize innovations in the sanctioning of offenders.

The first use of imprisonment as punishment was the penitentiary, inaugurated in 1790 in Philadelphia and inspired by Quaker* beliefs. The "Auburn system" was pioneered in the 1820s by Louis Dwight, who argued that reform came through revival,* religious training and strictly supervised work performed in silence with other inmates. In 1870, Zebulon Brockway, who had been converted during Charles Finney's* revivals, joined with other prison leaders in beginning the reformatory movement.

In recent decades, major Christian denominations* and organizations have advocated alternative sanctions to prison, such as restitution and community service.

See also PRISON MINISTRIES.

Pro Nuncio. *See* PAPAL NUNCIO.

Process Theology. As a theological movement, process theology began to receive attention after World War II and has had its primary influence in the U.S. The two most influential process philosophers have been Alfred North Whitehead (1861-1947) and Charles Hartshorne (1897-).

Several recurring themes identify process thought. The first motif is radical *empiricism.* The empiricism of process thought is radical because the process thinker can find no reason to limit experience to sense perception. And it is also radical because the process thinker can find no reason to assume that all genuine experience must be conscious. Process thinkers maintain that all life, including human life with its religious intuitions, rests on primitive, presensual and preconscious experience, out of which the capacity for sense perception and consciousness emerges.

The second central motif of process thought is *relationalism,* which affirms that we directly experience not only things but relations between

those things. For example, process thought holds that we directly experience causation and that the very identities of the things related consist, at least in part, in their relationships. If relationships such as causality may be directly experienced at the presensual and preconscious level, then it is at least possible that we can directly experience God's working in our lives.

Process thought takes its name from the third primary motif, which is *process.* Time, history, change, coming to be, enduring and perishing are among the most important items we can directly experience. Process thought accepts the evolutionary motifs of recent biology and physics, the modern sense of the importance of our past in shaping our present identity, as well as the deep sense of historical movement under God's guidance which permeates the Bible.

These three motifs lead to the fourth central motif of process thought: the basic units in our world are *events.* Even entities such as rocks or persons may be considered to be ultimately composed of events. It is important to note that the identity of an event (and thus of any "entity" whatsoever) consists, at least in part, in its relationships.

While most process theologians have concentrated on rethinking the category of God, some theologians have also tried to provide process perspectives on other Christian topics, particularly Christology,* ethics,* love, humanity and the church. Best known among contemporary North American process theologians working in these areas is John B. Cobb Jr. (1925-).

In the 1980s process theology continued to grow in importance and acceptance among mainline* Protestants* in the U.S. Its continued influence poses a challenge to evangelical* theologians, both as they seek to provide convincing rebuttals to its many subbiblical claims and as they consider other process themes which may provide a bridge from genuinely biblical perspectives to contemporary ways of experiencing the world.

Professional Ministry. Ministry distinguished from the ministry of all believers, not only by ordination,* but by training and employment by a church or religious agency. While ordination sets clergy apart, the secular concept of "profession" links ministry with other occupations. In colonial days it was, with law and medicine, among the learned professions. Proficiency in theology* and ancient languages, plus spiritual vocation,* were the criteria for entry into the profession. The need to train ministers motivated founding of colleges.

Progressive Orthodoxy. *See* EVANGELICAL LIBERALISM.

Prohibition Movement (1920-1933). The movement to outlaw the manufacture and sale of alcoholic* beverages by Constitutional amendment, which was part of the early twentieth-century Progressive movement for social reform. The Eighteenth Amendment banned the manufacture, sale or transport of intoxicants, beginning in 1920. Alcoholic consumption declined initially, though a growing illegal liquor traffic aided the growth of organized crime. The Twenty-first Amendment repealed Prohibition in 1933, returning liquor regulation to the states.

Propaganda. *See* SACRED CONGREGATION FOR THE EVANGELIZATION OF PEOPLES OR FOR THE PROPAGATION OF THE FAITH (PROPAGANDA).

Propagation of the Faith. *See* SACRED CONGREGATION FOR THE EVANGELIZATION OF PEOPLES OR FOR THE PROPAGATION OF THE FAITH (PROPAGANDA).

Prophecy, Gift of. A gift of the Holy Spirit; an inspired utterance in vernacular language. The gift of prophecy has been claimed by Christians throughout the centuries. In the postapostolic church, the gift was widely recognized as a genuine manifestation of the Spirit, being practiced by the orthodox as well as the Montanists and Gnostic groups.

In the modern era, the birth of the Pentecostal* movement began to bring the gift of prophecy once again to the church's attention. With the wider acceptance of Pentecostalism and the growth of the charismatic* movement in mainline* churches, the gift has earned wider acceptance. Pentecostals and charismatics claim that the gift of prophecy did not cease with the apostolic church and the closing of the biblical canon. They believe that the gift operates under the same conditions as it did in the days of the apostles and should be regulated by principles set forth in the New Testament.

Prophetic Conferences. *See* BIBLE AND PROPHETIC CONFERENCE MOVEMENT.

Protestant, Protestantism. The term *Protestant* emerged in the early years of the Reformation of the sixteenth century. In a general sense the term refers to all groups who have separated from the Roman Catholic* Church since the Reformation, including those in the Reformed,* Lutheran,* Anglican,* Anabaptist,* Baptist* and Methodist* traditions and a host of smaller groups.

The one belief which serves both as a common denominator and as a driving force for all Protestants is the priesthood of all believers.* This belief has led to revitalizing new approaches to the formulation of doctrine and ethics,* as well as to the practice of worship,* missions,* theological education* and hymnody.*

Protestant Episcopal Church in the U.S.A. Alternately called the Episcopal Church, the Protestant Episcopal Church in the U.S.A. is a member of the worldwide fellowship of Anglican Churches.* The Episcopal Church began in America as an extension of the Church of England and under its jurisdiction. By the end of the colonial period, Anglican churches were to be found in all thirteen colonies.

During the American Revolution, the church went through a severe crisis. In the end those colonies where Anglicanism had become the legally established religion (Virginia, Maryland, Georgia, North Carolina, South Carolina and certain counties of New York) were forced to revoke this status of the church.

After the Revolution the church gathered its forces to create a denomination* independent and autonomous of the Church of England. The first general convention met in Philadelphia in 1785 and took preliminary steps toward the establishment of a duly recognized denomination. By 1789 the first bishops had been consecrated and a revised version of the Book of Common Prayer* authorized.

During the nineteenth century the Episcopal Church expanded with the growth and development of the U.S. Missionary* work, carried out by missionary bishops and priests, extended into the Midwest, the South and the Southwest. Unlike other major American denominations, while the Civil War* separated Episcopalians into Northern and Southern factions, they quietly resumed full relations when the war ended.

From 1955 to 1965 the Episcopal Church enjoyed a 20 percent gain in membership, followed by a more than 16 percent loss in the decade

1965-1975. In 1991 the inclusive membership was a reported 2.5 million (1985).

See also ANGLICAN CHURCH OF CANADA; ANGLICAN COMMUNION; ANGLICANISM.

Protestant Reformed Churches in America, The. Reformed denomination. The Protestant Reformed Churches in America was formed in 1925 by three consistories and their pastors. These three ministers of the Christian Reformed Church had refused to sign a doctrinal statement that had been adopted by the denomination. The unacceptable statement maintained that in addition to God's particular, saving grace that is given to the elect alone, there is a "common grace" that is extended to all people, restraining sin, enabling good and expressing God's desire to save all who hear the gospel. In 1994 the denomination numbered approximately 6,300 members in twenty-four congregations distributed across the United States and two in Canada.

Protestant Work Ethic. The thesis that there is an affinity between early modern capitalism and Calvinism.* The concept of the Protestant work ethic originated in a study by the German sociologist Max Weber, *The Protestant Ethic and the Spirit of Capitalism* (1904-1905). Weber's thesis, which has failed to gain general acceptance, held that Calvinism (as distinct from Catholicism,* Lutheranism* and Anglicanism*) inculcated in its followers an austere outlook on life which systematically suppressed the pursuit of pleasure and encouraged hard work, which in turn led to savings, or capital.

Protestant-Catholic Relations, Contemporary. Since the 1960s relations have moved beyond previous mutual hostility to a new spirit of mutual respect. This is based not only on the common recognition of a partially shared Christian life through faith in Christ, the Bible and baptism* but also on candor about honest differences. The election of the first Catholic president, John F. Kennedy,* in 1960 signaled a diminishing of hostilities. But it was the U.S. response to the Second Vatican Council* that revolutionized Protestant-Catholic relations. Vatican II's "Decree on Ecumenism" brought Catholics into the ecumenical movement.*

The Catholic Charismatic* Renewal, begun in the U.S. in 1967, serves as a bridge between Catholics and evangelicals. Through the efforts of committed individuals and such bodies as Ann Arbor's Center for Pastoral Renewal, considerable exchange and mutual understanding has taken place between Catholics and evangelicals, who, taken together, make up more than half of the U.S. population.

In March 1994 an ad hoc group of prominent evangelicals and conservative Catholics, led by Charles Colson and Richard John Neuhaus, signed a declaration of common understanding that received widespread media attention.

See also ECUMENISM; LUTHERAN-CATHOLIC DIALOGUE; NATIVISM.

Protracted Meeting. *See* FINNEY, CHARLES GRANDISON; REVIVALISM, PROTESTANT.

Provoost, Samuel (1742-1815). Episcopal* bishop of New York. Provoost was an assistant minister at Trinity Parish in New York from 1766 to 1771, when he resigned because of his support of the American colonies. After thirteen years spent in farming and reading, he was elected rector of Trinity Parish in 1784.

Provoost later became chaplain* to the Continental Congress (1785), the first Episcopal bishop of New York (1786) and chaplain of the U.S. Senate (1789). During these years he was an opponent of Samuel Seabury,* first bishop of the Episcopal Church, especially of Seabury's emphasis on episcopal prerogatives. From 1792 to 1795 he was presiding bishop of the Episcopal Church.

Provost. A title of certain ecclesiastical and academic officers. It denotes an officer of a cathedral* chapter with duties similar to those of a dean.

Public Education, Religion and. The subject of religion and public education has long been a critical issue in American church-state* relations. As the pattern of the state church gave way to disestablishment and pluralism* in the New World, so the free, secular public school gradually emerged and in time supplanted the sectarian school that dominated during the colonial era and the early decades of the new republic.

Battles involving the establishment clause and the free-exercise Clause of the First Amendment* have been repeatedly waged over religion and the public schools. Religion in the public schools has been adjudicated on the basis that public schools are necessarily subject to public control and public policy by virtue of the fact that they are tax supported and therefore must be governed by the establishment clause of the First Amendment, even if a given program of religion is maintained on a "voluntary" basis. That the Supreme Court's most far-reaching decisions on church and state should have to do with the public schools has been noted as both historically significant and judicially appropriate, since the role played by the public schools is crucial to this nation's being a secular state and a free and pluralistic society.

See also SUPREME COURT DECISIONS ON RELIGIOUS ISSUES.

Pulpit Exchange/Pulpit Supply. The practice of allowing a minister other than the regular preacher of a church to deliver the sermon.*

Punshon, William Morley (1824-1881). Methodist* minister. Arriving in Canada from England in 1868, Punshon was regarded as the leader of the Canadian Wesleyan Methodists. Before returning to England in 1873, he oversaw the building of Toronto's Metropolitan Church.

Purcell, John Baptist (1800-1883). Archbishop of Cincinnati. Purcell was an active and energetic bishop who capably directed the growth and development of a major midwestern diocese* (1833-1860). His work among the Catholics involved a building of the archdiocesan infrastructure, with the establishment of parishes,* schools, a cathedral* and a seminary. He actively crusaded against the anti-Catholic propagandists, forthrightly debating Alexander Campbell.*

His strong support of the Union cause during the Civil War* and his call for the emancipation* of slaves engendered controversy but also distinguished him as a leader of the Northern American bishops.

Purgatory. The place, state or condition of departed Christian souls in which they undergo purifying suffering before entering heaven. The Roman Catholic* doctrine of purgatory, while finding some support in apocryphal and biblical texts (e.g., 2 Macc 12:39-45; Mt 5:26; 12:32; 1 Cor 3:11-15), relies chiefly on church tradition for its authority and content. By Augustine's time the doctrine was widely, if vaguely, understood and taught.

Eastern Orthodox* churches, while agreeing on the existence of purgatory, view it in terms of maturation rather than paying a debt.

Puritanism. Of all the religious movements that helped shape early American culture, none was more important than Puritanism. Originally the term appeared in sixteenth-century England as a pejorative one aimed at those reformers who wanted to "purify" the Church of England in more Reformed* Protestant* ways.

Of all the teachings of the English Puritans, none was more important than that of sola scriptura.* In contrast to Roman Catholics* and Anglicans,* who emphasized the authority* of tradition alongside the Bible, and in contrast to more radical Puritans, who emphasized an ongoing special revelation through visions or inner lights, the New England Puritans insisted that Scripture alone was a sufficient and all-encompassing guide for all aspects of life and faith relative to this world and the world to come.

The differences that separated Puritans and Anglicans over sola scriptura and the place of tradition soon extended to further questions of worship.* The Puritan rejection of tradition as an authoritative guide to faith implied a radical redefinition of worship away from the highly ritualized and costumed worship of the Church of England toward simpler forms that eventually rejected liturgy* altogether.

Between 1620 and 1640 New England absorbed a "Great Migration" of twenty thousand men, women and children. The overwhelming majority of these settlers were Puritans, among whom two strains predominated. One, arriving with the Mayflower in 1620, were "Separatists" who settled Plymouth Colony under the governorship of William Bradford.* This group of "Pilgrims"* has been romanticized in American history, but in fact they were the most radical, unpopular Puritan faction of their age. The other more numerous and powerful strain of Congregationalists* was the nonseparating Puritans who settled in and around Boston, Hartford and New Haven. This group has often been vilified in American history and national mythology, while in fact they were the more moderate strain of accommodative Congregationalists who refused to give up on the Church of England and worked instead to reform it.

In many respects the Puritans continued to cast a long shadow on New England society long after the seventeenth century, through their emphasis on sola scriptura, lay rule, education, plain speaking and the household of faith. Through their voluminous writings and testimonies, they have continued to influence generations of Americans.

Q

Quadragesimo Anno. Papal encyclical* on social reconstruction. Issued in 1931, forty years after Leo XIII's *Rerum Novarum,** Pius XI* wrote his encyclical *On the Reconstruction of the Social Order* to develop Leo XIII's teachings. Pius claimed the right to speak to the moral dimensions of the socioeconomic conditions. People should defend their economic rights and aid one another materially and spiritually through associations. They can even, as did American Catholics, separate these goals and join religiously neutral unions.

Quakers. *See* FRIENDS, THE RELIGIOUS SOCIETY OF (QUAKERS).

Quebec Act (1774). An act of the British Parliament extending religious toleration to the Roman Catholic* majority in the colony, which had been wrested from the French crown in the previous decade. The policy of assimilation under the British Royal Proclamation of 1763 was unsuccessful, and the rising unrest in the American colonies to the south required pacifying the predominately French population. The measures taken were political, cultural and religious.

Queens College. *See* RUTGERS UNIVERSITY.

Quietism. A term principally applied to one of the extreme forms of Roman Catholic* mysticism* popular in the seventeenth and eighteenth centuries, mainly in Spain, France and Italy.

Quietism emphasized the cleansing of the interior life. It was a meditative, passive, nonactive way of life intended to bring one into perfect rest with God.

Quimby, Phineas P(arkhurst) (1802-1866). Mentalist who transformed magnetic healing (similar to today's hypnotism) into mind cure. Although Quimby practiced healing for less than two decades, he exerted an important influence on the birth of both spiritual healing and mind cure in America. His patients included Mary Baker Eddy,* founder of Christian Science.*

Quintard, Charles Todd (1824-1898). Second Protestant Episcopal* bishop of Tennessee. Quintard became bishop in 1865, after serving as chaplain* and surgeon of the 1st Tennessee Regiment during the Civil War.* His episcopate was characterized theologically by sympathy with the Oxford* and Ritualist movements, and administratively by efforts to rebuild war-damaged church properties and to educate Episcopal clergy* in the South.

Quitman, Frederick Henry (1760-1832). Lutheran* minister and theologian. From 1795 until his retirement in 1825, Quitman pastored congregations in and near Rhinebeck, New York. He was the leading theologian of the generation between the Pietism* of Henry Melchoir Muhlenberg* and the evangelicalism* of Samuel Simon Schmucker.*

R

Rader, Paul Daniel (1879-1938). Christian and Missionary Alliance* evangelist, pastor and leader. From 1915 to 1921, Rader ministered in the Moody Church, Chicago. He was elected vice president of the Christian and Missionary Alliance (CMA) and, upon the death of its founder in 1919, became president, a position he held until 1924. In 1922 he began the Chicago Gospel Tabernacle.

Rader later left the CMA and went on to organize the Christian World Couriers, a missionary organization, with Oswald J. Smith* as the Canadian director.

Radical Catholicism. The radical gospel—the demand of Christ that his followers give themselves unconditionally to their neighbors in need—has long been honored as an ethical ideal. What distinguishes radical gospel movements from individual works of self-sacrificial charity and from institutionalized forms of apostolic service (priesthood,* sisterhood*) is their attempt to make this ideal the foundation of a functioning social order.

Radical Catholicism has existed in the U.S. since 1933, when Dorothy Day* and Peter Maurin* founded the Catholic Worker movement.* Day and Maurin advocated a social program featuring service to one's immediate neighbors, satisfying and socially useful labor, a rejection of all forms of violence and coercion, and a personal detachment from material goods through the practice of voluntary poverty.

In the 1960s the radical social activism of Catholic priests Daniel and Philip Berrigan and others in the Catholic Left attracted widespread public notice and underscored this element of social, political and religious extremism in Roman Catholicism. Other Catholic intellectuals of the Left, including the popular author and Trappist* monk Thomas Merton,* supported such acts of protest.

See also PEACE MOVEMENT, CATHOLIC.

Rahner, Karl (1904-1984). German Catholic* theologian. In his career as a prolific writer and lecturer, Rahner covered the gamut of Catholic doctrinal theology* and spirituality.* He was probably the most influential Catholic thinker of his era. His most significant work is found in his twenty-volume *Theological Investigations* (1961-1981) and *Foundations of Christian Faith* (1978).

He has been revered in the U.S. for championing a church free of Roman legalism and for his spiritual writings, which center on the divine mystery.

Railton, George Scott (1849-1913). The first officer officially to begin the work of the Salvation Army in America.* Railton was a tireless evangelist, an advocate of the Wesleyan doctrine of holiness,* and a lifelong friend of both William* and Catherine* Booth. In 1880 Railton and seven women arrived in New York City and soon had started ten corps (churches) and two hundred weekly meetings.

Ramism. A method of logical analysis based on dichotomies. Based on the writings of the French Reformed* philosopher Petrus Ramus (1515-1572), Ramism proceeded by dividing a subject into two parts, dividing each of these two into two more, and so on. William Ames* was a thoroughgoing Ramist.

Ramm, Bernard (1916-1992). Evangelical* theologian. Ramm attended Eastern Baptist Theological Seminary* and pursued graduate study in philosophy at the University of Southern California. He taught at a number of institutions, but spent much of his career (1959-1974, 1978-1986) at American Baptist Seminary of the West* (formerly California Baptist Theological Seminary). Ramm was an important theologian in the post-World War II era of evangelicalism and represented the irenic spirit of an emerging new evangelical* theology that was ecumenically* aware and engaged with many of the intellectual issues of its day. His breadth of interests are evident in a selection of titles from his numerous books: *Protestant Biblical Interpretation* (1950); *Types of Apologetic Systems* (1953); *The Christian View of Science and Scripture* (1954); *After Fundamentalism: The Future of Evangelical Theology* (1983) and *An Evangelical Christology: Ecumenic and Historic* (1985).

Ramsey, Paul (1913-1988). Ethicist. A Methodist,* Ramsey began his teaching career at Garrett Biblical Institute, Evanston, Illinois, but in 1946 moved to Princeton University* where he taught in the department of religion for the remainder of his career. Ramsey was known as a leading Christian ethicist who tackled the difficult issues of his age with rigor and faithfulness to the Christian tradition. In the 1970s he did pioneering work in biomedical ethics, contributing a celebrated volume to the field, *Ethics at the Edges of Life: Medical and Legal Intersections* (1977). His interest in political ethics found expression in *The Just War: Force and Political Responsibility* (1968). In addition to these and other works, he edited two volumes in the Yale edition of the collected works of Jonathan Edwards.*

Randall, Benjamin (1749-1808). Founder of New England branch of Free Will Baptists.* In 1776 Randall joined the Baptists* and soon embarked on an itinerant* evangelistic* ministry. Resisting the strict Calvinistic* Baptist emphasis on predestination,* he broke from the Regular Baptists* in 1779, and in 1780 began forming churches in New England that eventually took the name *Free Will Baptist* to emphasize their belief that any person is free to believe in Jesus Christ.

Rankin, Milledge Theron (1894-1953). Southern Baptist* missionary and missions* leader. A long-time missionary to China (1921-1935), Rankin was elected secretary for the Orient (1935-1944). From 1945 to 1953 he served as executive secretary of the Southern Baptists' Foreign Mission Board, which flourished under his leadership.

Rapp, Johann Georg (1757-1847). Pietist* leader, mystic* and founder of the Harmony Society.* Rapp, with several hundred followers from Germany, formed the Harmony Society in western Pennsylvania in 1805. The society practiced communitarian living and celibacy (after 1807). "Father" Rapp's strict spiritual leadership enabled the Harmonists to flourish. Later the group moved to found New Harmony,* Indiana (1819), and Economy, Pennsylvania (1824). Communal ties were dissolved in 1905.

Rapture of the Church. A phrase premillennialists* use to refer to the "catching up" (from Latin *rapio*) of the church to be with Christ at his Second Coming. All premillennialists trace the doctrine to the same passage (1 Thess 4:15-17) but disagree on when it will occur in relation to the tribulation period. Historically, premillennialists have divided over whether the rapture will happen before, during or after the tribulation.

Pretribulationism, which is nearly identical with dispensationalism,* argues that the rapture will occur before the tribulation. It was John Nelson Darby* in about 1830 who first divided the Second Coming into two stages: Christ's coming *for* his saints before the tribulation (the rapture) and his coming *with* his saints after it (the Second Coming per se).

Midtribulationism, an alternative view, contends that the church will be raptured halfway through the tribulation. This view became popular among a relatively small number of premillennialists after World War II.

Posttribulationism, which appears to be the oldest premillennialist view, holds that the rapture and the Second Coming of Christ will occur at the same time, at the end of the tribulation. Though eclipsed by pretribulationism before World War I, this view has gained many followers since World War II.

See also ESCHATOLOGY.

Ratcliffe, Robert (fl. 1680s). The first Anglican* minister in New England. Ratcliffe was a major contributor to the establishment of Anglicanism in New England. Arriving in Boston in 1686, he became the first minister of King's Chapel.

Rauch, Frederick Augustus (1806-1841). German Reformed* educator. In 1836 Rauch became the president of Marshall College in Pennsylvania. As a teacher, Rauch was the first to popularize the philosophical idealism of G. W. F. Hegel (1770-1831) in the U.S. Although Rauch showed little interest in the Mercersburg* theological themes, his philosophical idealism and profound historical consciousness provided a substantial theoretical foundation for the work of John W. Nevin.*

Rauschenbusch, Walter (1861-1918). Prophet and theologian of the Social Gospel.* As a pastor in New York City, Rauschenbusch encountered the human effects of poverty, unemployment, insecurity, malnutrition, disease and crime. Becoming active in social-reform work, he sought in biblical and theological teachings for resources to counter the individualistic, laissez-faire social philosophies and practices then so rampant. In the doctrine of the kingdom of God,* particularly as emphasized by Albrecht Ritschl (1822-1889), he found clues for understanding Jesus' teachings and for bringing his evangelical* faith, scholarly interests and social concerns together.

In 1907 his book *Christianity and the Social Crisis,* written "to discharge a debt" to the working people among whom he had ministered, became a bestseller and made him in great demand as speaker and author.

Ravenscroft, John Stark (1772-1830). Episcopal* bishop. In 1823 Ravenscroft was elected bishop of the tiny and disorganized Episcopal Church of North Carolina. A Hobartian* high churchman* of striking personality, Ravenscroft emphasized the apostolic character and distinctive teachings of the Episcopal Church. At his death Ravenscroft had united the diocese* and made it more distinctively Anglican.*

Rayburn, James C., Jr. (1909-1970). Founder of Young Life.* In Texas, with financial support from Herbert J. Taylor,* Rayburn started Young Life Ministries (1941) and *Young Life* magazine. Star Ranch, started in 1946 near Colorado Springs, added to his highly pragmatic ministry to youth.*

RBMU International. Nondenominational foreign missionary agency. This faith mission* traces its roots to the East London Institute for Home and Foreign Missions (Harley College), founded in 1873 by Irish evangelist H. Grattan Guinness. In 1900 its name became Regions Beyond Missionary Union. In 1979 the American, Australian and Canadian Councils of the mission formed RBMU International, while the British Council retained its older name.

Reagan, Ronald Wilson (1911-). Fortieth U.S. president. First emerging as a national figure in the 1964 Goldwater campaign, Reagan was elected governor of California in 1966. During the late 1970s the New Religious Right,* delighted with the way he mixed conservative politics with an affirmation of evangelical* beliefs, adopted him as one of their own and avidly promoted his successful presidential campaigns in 1980 and 1984.

Reagan espoused a civil religion* which included faith in America's divine chosenness, his country's spiritual nature and the importance of religion in general to maintain a healthy national existence and to combat communism.

Rebaptism. The performing again of the sacrament* or ordinance* of baptism, considered to have been valid by one Christian body but invalid by the body administering the rebaptism. Technically, *rebaptism* is a misnomer, since Christians practice a single baptism. Hence, rebaptism relates to debate over what constitutes a valid sacrament or ordinance.

During the sixteenth-century Reformation, radical reformers began to question and eventually deny the efficacy of baptisms performed in Catholic and state churches and so rebaptized believers.

In North America most evangelical* and believers' churches rebaptize if they determine that personal faith was absent at the time a previous sacrament/ordinance was received.

Reconciliation, Sacrament of. *See* PENANCE, SACRAMENT OF.

Reconstructionism, Christian. A fundamentalist*-evangelical* movement, dating from the early 1960s, intent on reconstructing society along lines explicitly set forth in Old Testament law. Leaders include the acknowledged patriarch of the movement, Rousas John Rushdoony; theologian Greg Bahnsen; and economist Gary North. Three foundational ideas underlie the Reconstructionist agenda: (1) a presuppositional* apologetic;* (2) a belief that Old Testament law applies today, in "exhaustive" and "minutial" detail; and (3) postmillennialism.*

By the late 1980s Reconstructionism (also known as theonomy) had gained a following among independent Baptist,* separatist Presbyterian* and some charismatic* circles—most notably those within the faith movement.*

Rector. A priest* who is placed in charge of a

church or parish.* The term is commonly used among Episcopalians,* less frequently by Roman Catholics.*

Redemptorists. A Roman Catholic* community of priests and lay brothers dedicated to proclaiming the Word of God by means of missions,* retreats* and novenas,* as well as the administration of parishes.* Founded in Italy in 1732, Redemptorists first came to North America in the early 1830s. At first they worked primarily among immigrants* from Germany, France and Bohemia; later, in World War II, they served as chaplains.*

Reed, Luther D(otterer) (1873-1972). Lutheran* liturgist.* At Lutheran Theological Seminary (Philadelphia), Reed was professor of liturgics and church art (1910-1939) and president (1939-1945). He was a leader of Lutheran liturgical renewal.

Rees, Paul Stromberg (1900-1991). Minister, evangelist and author. Rees became well known as pastor of First Covenant in Minneapolis, Minnesota (1938-1958). In the broader evangelical world he was vice president of World Evangelical Fellowship* (1950-1955), vice president of World Vision* (1958-1975) and editor of *World Vision Magazine* (1964-1972).

Reform Movements. Movements for the spiritual renewal of the church and of its mission. Three periods of reform stand out in American religious history: (1) the early to mid-nineteenth century, dominated by the question of slavery but marked by a host of other reform efforts as well; (2) the late nineteenth and early twentieth centuries, with the Social Gospel* and related responses to the problems of the emerging urban-industrial America; and (3) the decades after World War II,* with multifaceted efforts for the renewal of the church.

Spiritual Revival and Societal Reform. Coinciding with the Second Great Awakening* in the early nineteenth century was a remarkable explosion of energies centered on humane causes. Reflecting a belief that society could be changed and an unwillingness to accept the injustices of the existing social order, Americans organized scores of reform societies in areas such as women's rights,* antislavery,* sabbath* observance, temperance,* peace,* missions* and prison reform.*

By the 1830s Charles G. Finney* was giving energetic support to the efforts of the various societies, including the antislavery movement, which came to overshadow all other reform efforts.

Urban Poverty and Urban Missions. The decades following the Civil War produced striking changes in American life, including an accelerating shift from a rural-agricultural to an urban-industrial social and economic order. The poverty and related miseries generated by that transition were intensified by a growing tide of immigrants, many of whom settled in the already-troubled cities. Only gradually did the nation awaken to the new poverty and its causes.

Among those who responded early were an increasing number of missionaries who entered the slums of virtually every American city with an evangelistic* witness that was soon augmented by practical assistance. Among the largest and best-known of the organizations then operating in American cities was the Salvation Army.*

Industrial Reality and Social Gospel. The most well-known facet of the response to the developing urban crisis of the late nineteenth century came to be known as the Social Gospel. This began to take shape during the 1870s and 1880s in response to the first of a series of industrial crises, and in the preaching* of a growing number of Protestant* clergy, including Washington Gladden,* Josiah Strong* and, after 1890, Walter Rauschenbusch.*

Although the Social Gospel continued into the 1930s, it was increasingly undermined by a growing isolationist and reactionary national temper, and by the gradual decline of liberal theology in the mainline* churches.

Social Action and Church Renewal in the Late Twentieth Century. The fading of the Social Gospel movement did not mean the death of its central emphasis on applying Christian principles to social problems and to human need. In the Civil Rights,* antiwar and feminist* movements of recent decades, and in the social stance of the National* and World* councils of churches, some see continuity with the Social Gospel. Evangelicals have returned, meanwhile, to the social concern and action that had characterized them until at least World War I.* In both cases the ongoing social Christianity appears to be less marked by utopianism and narrowly industrial concerns and more by social action than was the Social Gospel itself.

See also ABOLITION AND THE CHURCHES; PROHIBITION MOVEMENT; RENEWAL MOVEMENTS, PROTESTANT; URBAN CHURCHES AND MINISTRIES; WOMEN'S SUFFRAGE MOVEMENT.

Reformed and Presbyterian Churches. The diverse assortment of Presbyterian and Reformed denominations* in the U.S. and Canada all trace their roots to the Calvinist* branch of the Protestant Reformation in the sixteenth century.

The doctrines that are usually associated most directly with Calvinism—predestination* and election*—revolve around the twin themes of divine sovereignty and human depravity. But these Calvinist teachings are not the exclusive property of a specific family of denominations. What is unique to the Reformed and Presbyterian churches is their traditional insistence that Calvinist soteriology is logically linked to a Reformed ecclesiology: divine election is an election to participation in the life and mission of the redeemed people, the church of Jesus Christ. Reformed-Presbyterian Christians have thus been intensely interested in questions of "order" in general and "church order" in particular.

Basic to the presbyterian scheme of church governance is the understanding that ecclesial authority* resides primarily in the local presbytery* or consistory. Here the central "ruling" office is that of elder.* The elders are elected by congregational vote, and they in turn send delegations of local officeholders to broader assemblies, usually called presbyteries and general assemblies* by Presbyterians, and classes (plural of classis*) and synods* by the Reformed.

Debates over the acceptability of the emphases associated with the Great Awakening* led to a long-standing argument between Old Side* and New Side* Presbyterians, with the former resisting the more emotional and less doctrinally stringent emphases of revivalism,* and the latter advocating openness to these developments. Some of the same issues characterized the debate that began in the early nineteenth century between the Old School* and the New School* Presbyterians. These controversies were accentuated by the later debate over slavery and by regionalist impulses which were reinforced by the War between the States. The result was a major split in 1861 between the Northern and Southern Presbyterian churches.

The second half of the twentieth century has seen some realignment of relationships, especially among Presbyterians. A rather large new denomination was formed when a group of congregations began separating from the Southern church in early 1970, in protest against what were perceived as liberal trends in doctrine and social advocacy. Adopting the name Presbyterian Church in America,* this denomination soon absorbed a number of Northern congregations, as well as the churches belonging to the Reformed Presbyterian Church—Evangelical Synod.

After more than a century of separation, the major Northern and Southern Presbyterian denominations were reunited in June 1983 to form the Presbyterian Church (USA).* This reunited denomination is the largest and most inclusive Reformed-Presbyterian body on the continent, although it has been experiencing some decline in total membership in recent years.

See also REFORMED TRADITION IN AMERICA.

Reformed Church in America. The Reformed Church in America has its origin in the formation of a Dutch Reformed congregation on Manhattan Island by Jonas Michaelius* in 1628. Although Dutch settlers virtually ceased coming to America after the Netherlands lost control of New Netherland to the English in 1664, a goodly number of congregations took root in New York and New Jersey. The American Revolution and the independence of the thirteen colonies eventually led to the independence of the Dutch church and their organization into a distinct body in 1792.

Beginning in 1847 a new surge of Dutch and German Reformed immigrants* moved into the Midwest under the leadership of Albertus C. Van Raalte and settled in western Michigan. Another group of settlers under the direction of Hendrik P. Scholte went to Pella, Iowa. Most of these new settlers had been members of the "Afscheiding," or separatist,* movement, which seceded from the state church of the Netherlands in 1834. Strongly orthodox* and pious, the newcomers immediately formed congregations. Under Van Raalte's effective leadership, separatists were encouraged to unite with the old Dutch church in the East. The classis of Holland (Mich.) was accepted into the Dutch Reformed Church in 1850.

The separatist spirit which many Afscheiding settlers brought to America became evident in 1857 when some members showed their dislike of the union of 1850 by seceding and forming the Christian Reformed Church.* This same separatist spirit successfully blocked all merger attempts of the Reformed Church after 1850. In 1867 the church dropped the word *Dutch* from its title and began to call itself the Reformed Church in America.

In 1992 the denomination reported 190,400 full communicant members in 927 churches.

See also REFORMED AND PRESBYTERIAN CHURCHES; REFORMED TRADITION IN AMERICA.

Reformed Church in the U.S., Eureka Classis. German Reformed denomination. The classis was organized in 1911 in the Northwest Synod of the (German) Reformed Church in the United States. The history of the denomination extends back to German Reformed congregations formed in the Great Lakes area in the 1850s and the Northwest Synod organized in 1867. The Eureka Classis was a nongeographical association of conservative churches with its theological center in the Mission House in Sheboygan and united in allegiance to the Heidelberg Catechism. In 1934, when the rest of the Reformed Church merged with the Evangelical Synod of North America, the Eureka Classis, committed to confessional faithfulness and opposed to liberalism within the Evangelical Synod, did not merge and claimed to be the "legally constituted Reformed Church in the United States." In 1992 the Eureka Classis claimed 3,200 communicant members in thirty-seven churches.

Reformed Episcopal Church. An evangelical* Episcopal church organized in 1873 by Bishop George David Cummins* of Kentucky. A *Declaration of Principles* (condemning transubstantiation* in the Eucharist,* moral regeneration in baptism* and the exclusive validity of episcopal government*) was issued by Cummins and remains the founding document of the church. By 1876, the Reformed Episcopal Church comprised seven jurisdictions in the U.S. and Canada. In 1990 there were approximately six thousand members in eighty-three congregations in its three synods.*

See also ANGLICAN CHURCHES IN AMERICA; ANGLICANISM.

Reformed Presbyterian Church, Evangelical Synod. A conservative denomination existing from 1965 to 1982, the result of a blending of dissenting American Presbyterians (the Bible Presbyterian Church, renamed after 1961 the Evangelical Presbyterian Church) and former

Scottish Covenanters (the Reformed Presbyterian Church in North America, General Synod*). The denomination, which included J. Oliver Buswell Jr.* and Francis Schaeffer,* stressed national and international missionary efforts and emphasized local church autonomy and individual conscience. In 1982 it merged with the Presbyterian Church in America.*

Reformed Presbyterian Church in North America, General Synod. A Reformed* denomination* with roots in Scottish Presbyterianism* that in 1965 was absorbed into the Reformed Presbyterian Church, Evangelical Synod.* Although deriving mainly from dissenting Scottish Covenanters coming to America in the 1700s, this denomination officially began in 1833. It split off then from the Reformed Presbytery (established in 1774), disagreeing with the presbytery's position that members should not participate in government.

Reformed Presbyterian Church of North America, Covenanter Synod. Reformed* denomination* of Scottish Presbyterian* descent. The denomination traces its roots to the dissenters to the Revolution Settlement of 1689-1692 in the Church of Scotland who met in societies until their organization as a denomination in 1743. Some of these dissenters migrated to America, and their first organized congregation in North America was formed in Pennsylvania in 1742-1743. A Reformed Presbytery was formed in 1774 but soon dissolved in 1782. The Reformed Presbytery of the United States of North America was formed in 1798 and the Synod of the Reformed Presbyterian Church was constituted in 1809. In 1833 the denomination divided over the issue of whether or not members should be allowed to participate in civil government, with the Reformed Presbyterian Church, General Synod, taking the moderate view of participation and the Reformed Presbyterian Church of North America maintaining the traditionalist stance, a position it still maintains. The Reformed Presbyterian Church of North America adheres to the Westminster standards, sings the Psalms exclusively in worship, without musical accompaniment, and is characterized by its theological emphasis on covenantal theology. In 1992 the denomination numbered 5,469 baptized and communicant members in seventy-one congregations.

Reformed Tradition in America. The Reformed tradition has played a prominent role within American Christianity and has significantly affected both religious and cultural development in the U.S. Its general principles, such as the Protestant* work ethic* and the sovereignty of God, have helped to shape the American character and ethos; its specific tenets, such as total depravity, limited atonement* and perseverance of the saints, have powerfully influenced American theological understanding. The roots of the Reformed tradition lie in John Calvin's (1509-1564) *Institutes of the Christian Religion* (1st ed., 1536), which expounded the central features of Reformed theology and helped shape its subsequent development, including the rise of Puritanism* in England.

The Reformed Tradition in the New World. Most immigrants to the colonies during the first 150 years following the Puritan settlements at Plymouth and Massachusetts Bay in the 1620s were Reformed Christians from various denominational backgrounds. During these years hundreds of thousands of Dutch, German, Hungarian and Swiss Reformed, as well as French Huguenots,* streamed to the colonies. Different views of church organization divided English Puritans into Congregationalists* and Presbyterians.* These groups, along with Scottish and Scotch-Irish Presbyterians,* came to America in increasing numbers in the years between 1650 and the American Revolution.*

The Reformed Tradition and the Great Awakening. Reformed Christians contributed significantly to the First Great Awakening* of the 1730s and 1740s, which helped to stamp evangelical* Christian convictions and mores upon the colonies. Spreading from Georgia to Massachusetts, this revival* flowered especially among three Reformed communities: the Dutch Reformed, Congregationalists and Presbyterians.

Reformed Denominations in the Eighteenth Century. Most Reformed denominations grew rapidly during the eighteenth century. Extensive immigration of Scotch-Irish increased the number and vitality of Presbyterians who settled primarily in the Middle Colonies. From its founding in America in 1706, the Presbyterian Church embraced two traditions: the Scotch-Irish and Scottish desired precise theological formulations and orderly church government,* while the English and Welsh emphasized religious experience and adaptability. Twice the tension between these

two elements produced schisms in the denomination—in the Old Side*/New Side* division of 1741-1758 and the Old School*/New School* division of 1837-1869. Yet most of the time the communion was able to hold together those committed to Pietist* revivalism and those devoted to doctrinalist confessionalism.*

Other active Reformed denominations included the German Reformed Church, most Baptists* (especially the Philadelphia Baptist Association*), Congregationalists and the Reformed Church of America.*

The Reformed Tradition and the American Revolution. The teachings of the Reformed tradition helped to inspire the American Revolution, and many proponents of Reformed theology supported the Patriot cause. While revolutionary leaders generally did not appeal directly to the Scriptures or to their religious heritage to justify their revolt against England, Reformed convictions about covenants, history, human nature, and the connection between freedom and virtue helped to reinforce Whig arguments.

In the years following the Revolutionary War, Reformed commitments to the doctrines such as total depravity, unconditional election* and limited atonement seemed to many Americans to deny human freedom and responsibility and contradict America's democratic* principles. Whereas in 1776 about 85 percent of the colonists were affiliated with Reformed denominations, by 1850 some 70 percent of Protestant church members were Baptists or Methodists.

The Reformed Tradition and the Second Awakening. The predominant theology of this Awakening, as it was proclaimed by revivalist Charles G. Finney,* was more Arminian* than Calvinist in nature. Stressing the individual's right and ability to choose salvation, Finney promoted his "new measures"* rather than awaiting what Calvinists regarded as God's sovereign and surprising work in conversion.

The Rise of Four Reformed Schools, 1850-1930. While adherence to the Reformed faith declined between 1850 and 1930, four Reformed schools or emphases took shape during these years that are still influential within American Christianity today: (1) the Princeton theology* of Archibald Alexander,* Charles Hodge, A. A. Hodge* and B. B. Warfield;* (2) the Dutch Calvinism of the Reformed Church of America* and the Christian Reformed Church;* (3) the Southern tradition, expressed in the Presbyterian Church in the United States;* and (4) the Westminster School, led by J. Gresham Machen* and the former Orthodox Presbyterian Church.*

The Continuing Legacy. There are today eighteen Presbyterian, Reformed and Congregationalist denominations in America with a combined membership of about six million. Substantial numbers of Episcopalians,* Baptists and members of independent churches also espouse Reformed theological convictions. In addition, the influence of the Reformed tradition is strong within the evangelical community because of the role Reformed and Reformed-oriented seminaries (most notably Calvin, Westminster, Biblical, Covenant, Reformed, Gordon-Conwell, Trinity and Fuller*) have played in training evangelical leaders.

Reforming Synod (1679). A meeting of Massachusetts clergy to define and offer solutions to religious declension. By 1679 the elders* of Massachusetts Bay were convinced that contention, pride and a "dying interest in religion" had provoked the Lord to bring his judgments on New England. A formal synod* met to identify the offenses against God and propose means of reform.

Regeneration. The Bible uses terms like *new birth,* *being born again,* *being a new creature* and *having a renewed mind* to describe the process of spiritual renovation whereby the image of God is restored within fallen people who have become Christians. Thus *regeneration, renovation* and *conversion** are often used as synonyms in the Protestant* tradition. While Christians generally agree on what regeneration ultimately implies, they tend to disagree over how it takes place.

Reflecting the New Testament conjunction of "the washing of rebirth" with "renewal by the Holy Spirit" (Tit 3:5), the church fathers and the Catholic* tradition have associated regeneration with the sacrament* of Christian baptism.* Protestants, in contrast, typically identify regeneration as the inward renewal beginning with justification* by faith and continuing through the process of sanctification.

Revivalism* profoundly shaped Protestant concepts of regeneration by emphasizing individual personal religious experience over baptism and the nurturing community. Through the revivals *conversion,* or a *personal decision for Christ,* became synonyms for *regeneration.*

Regeneration has played a central role in the message of popular urban evangelists since the Civil War.* Dwight L. Moody* emphasized "ruin by sin, redemption by Christ, regeneration by the Holy Spirit" and looked for instantaneous conversions. Billy Graham's* *How to Be Born Again* (1977) uses *regeneration* and *conversion* as synonyms for describing the presence of Christ or the Holy Spirit in the motivational center of a person and makes no reference to baptism or the role of the church in that transformation.

See also SALVATION.

Regions Beyond Missionary Union. *See* RBMU INTERNATIONAL.

Regular Baptists. Calvinistic* Baptists* opposed to the emotionalism and evangelistic* invitations of the Great Awakening.* In contrast to revivalistic Separate Baptists,* Regular Baptists were more urbane and more orderly in worship.* By 1800 most Regulars and Separates had merged on the basis of the Philadelphia Confession (1742).

Today Regular Baptists comprise a cultural-religious movement that preserves rural folkways through monthly worship, community gatherings and annual association fellowship.

Relation. *See* CONVERSION NARRATIVES.

Relational Theology. A recent, largely American theology* stressing the centrality of interpersonal relationships. Unlike traditional orthodoxy,* which emphasizes God's great transactions for humanity, such as the Incarnation, the Cross and the Resurrection, relational theology places emphasis on persons and the quality of their relationships. Numbers of American evangelicals adopted the emphasis in the 1970s.

Religionless Christianity. The term *religionless Christianity* is most closely associated with Dietrich Bonhoeffer* and his *Letters and Papers from Prison* (1953; enlarged, 1971). In the 1960s some theologians used Bonhoeffer's phrase to construct secular theologies that focused strongly on the present world.

Religious Education. *See* CHRISTIAN EDUCATION.

Religious Freedom. Virginia's state constitution (1776) was the first to mandate religious freedom, and it became a model for the Federal Constitution. The First Amendment* to the Constitution provided the legal means, however, for every citizen to be free of state interference in the practice of personal religious beliefs and also guarantees all citizens the "free exercise" of their religious beliefs.

See also CHURCH AND STATE, SEPARATION OF.

Religious Liberty. See RELIGIOUS FREEDOM.

Religious Orders, Catholic Men's. *Religious order* is a term often loosely used in reference to groups of men or women, usually Roman Catholic,* committed to a particular religious life. Religious, or members of a religious order, are those who have taken the traditional vows of poverty, chastity and obedience.

Growth in the number of religious continued steadily in the early twentieth century, rising to a peak in the years 1945 to 1965. After the Second Vatican Council,* with its emphasis on the role of the laity, and after the sexual revolution in the U.S., vocations to the religious life fell sharply among men and very sharply among women. Unless the vocation crisis abates, religious orders seem destined to play a decreasing role in American Catholicism.

Currently there are 109 religious orders for clerics* and 28 orders for lay brothers serving the Catholic Church in the U.S. Aside from small orders which are confined to a single diocese* and answer to its bishop, all orders come under papal control through the Sacred Congregation of Religious, one of the administrative divisions of the papal curia.

The largest single order in the U.S. is the Society of Jesus (or Jesuits). In 1986 there were over 4,000 American Jesuits in ten provinces. More numerous still are the Franciscans,* but they are divided into three separate families or orders: the Order of Friars Minor, the Conventuals and the Capuchins.

The greatest contribution of the religious orders to the American Catholic Church is a network of Catholic universities; there is nothing comparable elsewhere in the Catholic Church or in Catholic history. The Jesuits alone established nineteen universities, including Georgetown, Fordham and Boston College. After education, the most important ministries for male religious are foreign missions,* giving retreats,* publishing religious magazines and journals (*see* Press, Catholic), and working in hospitals and nursing homes.

The friars* and Jesuits have been active in Canada since the earliest French settlements. Most of the larger orders found in the U.S. are also represented in Canada. Often religious orders in Canada are divided on linguistic lines, with one province or jurisdiction for French speakers, another for English speakers.

See also RELIGIOUS ORDERS, PROTESTANT; RELIGIOUS ORDERS, WOMEN'S.

Religious Orders, Protestant. Protestant* religious communities, which had declined after the Reformation, reappeared in the seventeenth century through the influence of Pietism.* The first influential community in the U.S. was the Ephrata* cloister (1732) in Lancaster County, Pennsylvania. The earliest sisterhood was formed within the Episcopal Church* in 1852. The first regular order for men was established in 1872. Today there are forty-six Episcopal or Anglican* religious communities for men and women in North America.

During the late nineteenth century, orders of deaconesses* were also established in many Protestant denominations.* Between 1870 and 1900 over 140 deaconess houses were organized by Lutherans,* Episcopalians,* Methodists,* Presbyterians* and others.

Since 1945 there has been a new flowering of community life within American Protestantism, both traditional and experimental in nature. Many of these communities have been influenced by contemporary liturgical* and ecumenical* movements.

Religious Orders, Women's. Women's communities with a religious orientation, often with recognized ecclesiastical status and/or vows of poverty, chastity and obedience, have been a feature of Christianity in North America for most of its history, particularly in the Roman Catholic* tradition. There are also Protestant* sisterhoods, including Episcopal* sisters, Lutheran,* Mennonite* and Methodist* deaconesses,* and Orthodox* nuns in North America.

From 1693 nuns were present in Canada; the Ursuline* convent established in French New Orleans in 1727 was the first religious community of women in the present-day U.S. Lacking any institutions for education, health care and social work, the Catholic Church in America looked to new religious foundations to meet this need. In many frontier situations, sisters provided the only educational or care-giving institutions there were.

The chief work of sisters in the U.S. has been education—at first in boarding academies accompanied by a free school. Later, they staffed parochial schools,* forming the largest private system of religious education in the world. The second involvement numerically of sisters is health care. Among the only trained nurses in the country, sisters were called into duty in both the Civil War and Spanish-American War.

A renewed ecclesiology, coupled with experience in missionary situations and high levels of theological and professional education, has affected sisters' former emphasis on separation from the world. Directed by the Second Vatican Council* to adapt to modern conditions and reexamine the spirit of their founders, Catholic women religious, who in 1994 numbered over 94,000 in the U.S., have developed an increasing social consciousness and are in the process of redefining their role in view of a changing church and society.

Renewal Movements, Catholic. Catholics view renewal as essential to the church in every age. It refers not to starting something new but to making something old new again or like new. It is a return to faithfulness to what Christ has established. Catholics believe that authentic renewal is not a human project but an ongoing and necessary work of the Holy Spirit.

The history of the Catholic Church* includes many movements of renewal, including the monastic movement (fourth century onward), the Cluniac and Cistercian renewals of monastic life (tenth and eleventh centuries), the mendicant movement giving rise to the Franciscan* and Dominican* orders (twelfth century), the reforms of the Council of Trent (sixteenth century onward), Catholic revivalism* in America (nineteenth century) and the recent wave of Catholic renewal ushered in by the Second Vatican Council.*

After the Second Vatican Council, many renewal movements and groups that promise to be successful have emerged within the Catholic Church, including Cursillo,* Focolare, Communion and Liberation, Marriage Encounter,* parish renewal programs, and the Catholic charismatic* renewal. In 1975 Pope Paul VI* gave his approval to the charismatic movement, and Pope John Paul II* has also encouraged the movement.

See also LAY MOVEMENT, MODERN CATHOLIC.

Renewal Movements, Protestant. Movements, usually within larger Protestant* denominations,* seeking to revitalize the church or denomination in some specific way. Such movements are usually concerned with theology* or mission.* Since the 1920s, when modernity impacted most American denominations, movements for revitalization within Protestant circles have usually been concerned with "evangelical" renewal, a combination of theology and mission.

In the 1960s and 1970s, however, movements pressing for renewed commitment to the authority of Scripture or evangelism* tended to remain within the mainline* denominations. Renewal efforts within the Episcopal Church,* for example, have been diverse and have included initiatives by Anglo-Catholics,* evangelicals* and charismatics.*

Republican Methodists. *See* O'KELLY SCHISM.

Rerum Novarum. Papal encyclical* outlining Catholic* social principles. Issued in 1891 by Leo XIII,* *Rerum Novarum* was a response to the growing social movement within the Catholic Church. Though not the sole or even most significant impetus for the encyclical, events in the U.S. had attracted the attention of the papacy and invited a response. The encyclical upheld the natural right of private property and rejected socialism, affirmed the principle of a just wage and the efforts of workers to seek wage settlements and organize labor unions, and emphasized the role of the church in social issues, both in practicing charity and upholding justice.

Rescue Mission Movement. The spread of urban missions* designed to present the gospel and offer food and lodging to street people. During the late nineteenth century, the forces of immigration,* industrialization and urbanization brought unprecedented change to America. Some people were left homeless and helpless in the wake of these changes, and poverty became a national problem, especially in cities.

A few sensitive evangelicals looked at this street-people phenomenon and saw it as an opportunity. Reaching out to these hurting people, they provided them with meals, temporary lodging and secondhand clothing. They not only met immediate physical needs but took the opportunity to preach the gospel of Jesus Christ.

Early leaders in such ministries (and all still

active in it) were Jerry McAuley's* Water Street Mission* (1872) in New York City, Rachel Bradley's Olive Branch Mission (1872) in Chicago and Sarah Dunn Clarke's* Pacific Garden Mission* (1877) in Chicago.

See also URBAN CHURCHES AND MINISTRIES.

Restitutionism. See PRIMITIVISM.

Restoration Movement. A religious movement, beginning about 1800, to reform the churches by restoring New Testament teaching about the church. Two basic thrusts mark the beginnings of this movement: a commitment to the practice of Christian unity and a commitment to the authority* of the Bible as the only guidebook for the faith and practice of the church.

Origins. Restoration movement sources include James O'Kelly* in the Southern states, and Abner Jones* and Elias Smith in New England. By 1811 the two groups had formed a union.

In 1803 Barton W. Stone* and several other clergy in Kentucky left the Presbyterians* and formed their own group, calling themselves simply Christians. When Stone met members of the Jones-Smith movement in 1826, they united in fellowship with them.

Thomas Campbell,* a Presbyterian minister from Northern Ireland, came to the U.S. in 1807. He soon left his denomination to function as an independent minister, coining the slogan "Where the Bible speaks, we speak; where it is silent, we are silent." He became committed to the principles of Christian unity and exclusive biblical authority. That same year his son, Alexander Campbell,* joined him from Northern Ireland and soon became the major voice in the Campbellite movement. The Campbells emphasized baptism by immersion "for remission of sins." Their churches also developed a uniform practice of weekly observance of the Lord's Supper.*

Development. In 1831 followers of Stone and of the Campbells joined forces in central Kentucky. However, about half of Stone's movement of Christians distrusted the Campbells' emphasis on baptism for remission of sins and refused to follow their leader into the union with the "Campbellites." Instead, they remained united with the Smith-Jones movement in New England and the Christian Connection.*

Division. In the mid-1800s, differences arose over the use of missionary societies and over the use of instrumental music* to accompany congregational singing in worship.* In 1906 the U.S. Census Bureau began to list the noninstrumental Churches of Christ* separately from the Christian Churches, or the Disciples of Christ.*

A second problem emerged in the late nineteenth century with the impact of theological liberalism.* As liberals became more prominent in the movement, conservatives felt betrayed and in 1927 developed their own convention, the North American Christian Convention.* Thus a further division developed between the independent Christian Churches* and the Disciples of Christ, with the latter oriented toward liberalism.

Current Status. The noninstrumental churches today number somewhat under two million members, while the other two groups, the Independent Christian Church* and Disciples of Christ, number just over one million each, for a cumulative total of about four million members.

Restorationism. See PRIMITIVISM.

Retreats, Religious. Times of withdrawal from the normal affairs of life to cultivate a deepened personal relationship with God. Christians find precedence for retreats in Jesus' own practice of withdrawing, either privately or with his disciples, for prayer and spiritual renewal. Spiritual-life retreats vary greatly—they may be private or corporate, silent or dialogic, guided or unguided, long or short.

The retreat movement has a long history in the Roman Catholic Church,* going back to St. Ignatius in the sixteenth century, and in the Church of England,* going back to its first retreats in 1856. Since World War II* retreats have flourished among many Protestant* groups as one of many important renewal* movements growing out of that period. In the U.S. there may now be as many as one thousand retreat centers or places used for spiritual-life retreats.

Reu, J(ohann) M(ichael) (1869-1943). Lutheran* pastor, theologian and churchman. From 1899 until his death, Reu served at Wartburg Seminary, in Dubuque, Iowa, where he taught dogmatics,* homiletics,* catechetics,* exegesis* and other subjects. He authored numerous works in German and English, including *The Augsburg Confession* (1930). *

Revell, Fleming Hewitt (1849-1931). Protestant* publisher. At the encouragement of his brother-in-law Dwight L. Moody,* Revell began publishing religious literature. By 1890 the Fleming H. Revell Company was one of the largest publishers of religious literature in America. He was influential in publishing many premillennialist* and fundamentalist* authors.

Revels, Hiram Rhoades (1822-1901). African-American Methodist* minister* politician and educator. During the Civil War,* Revels recruited for African-American regiments, served as a chaplain and helped set up Freedmen's Bureau schools in Mississippi. During Reconstruction, Revels advanced from local political roles in Mississippi to become the first of his race to serve in the U.S. Senate (January 1870 to March 1871).

Revivalism, Catholic. In the first half of the nineteenth century, revivals of religion became a permanent fixture in the U.S. Revivals of religion were not an exclusively Protestant* phenomenon in nineteenth-century America, however, for Roman Catholics* also were involved in religious revivals, known at that time as parish missions.*

The Catholic revival originated in sixteenth-century Europe, the era of the Reformation, when the church was attempting to renew the piety* of the people. After a period of decline, parish missions again became popular in the 1830s. When Catholic priests immigrated to the U.S., they brought with them the idea of the parish mission.

Like Protestant revivals, parish missions were a technique used in the evangelization of the people. They were ideally suited for the immigrant Catholic community in the antebellum period because this community was, as far as the clergy was concerned, in dire need of religious conversion. The parish mission movement peaked in the late nineteenth century, lost momentum in the twentieth century and disappeared in the post-World War II era. In the 1970s and 1980s, a new form of the parish mission, now referred to as a revival, came into vogue with its goal being much the same as in prior centuries—the evangelization of the people.

Revivalism, German-American. Beginning in the late seventeenth and early eighteenth centuries, large numbers of Germans immigrated* to the American Middle Colonies. Their formal religious identity was either Lutheran* or Reformed,* though a significant number were sectarian Christians representing the Mennonites* and other groups.

The impact of New England's Great Awakening* rippled through the German communities in the years following the revival,* although in general the spiritual life of these German-Americans was at a low ebb in the decades preceding and during the American Revolution.*

In 1726 Philip William Otterbein* arrived in Pennsylvania. A German Reformed missionary, he became the leader of the revivalist wing of his church and, with Mennonite Martin Boehm,* cofounder of the first indigenous German-American revivalist denomination, the Church of the United Brethren in Christ.*

For the most part, Lutherans, German Reformed and Mennonites resisted nineteenth-century revivalism. The major fruit of German-American revivalism, the Evangelicals and the United Brethren, were largely assimilated into American culture during the early twentieth century prior to their union with each other in 1946 and the United Methodist Church* in 1968.

Revivalism, Protestant. Revivalism is the movement that promotes periodic spiritual intensity in church life, during which the unconverted come to Christ and the converted* are shaken out of their spiritual lethargy. Often leading to social and moral reform* activities, revivalism was one of the chief characteristics of American Protestantism in the eighteenth and nineteenth centuries and still retains a powerful influence in many quarters. Unevenly distributed among the denominations,* revivalism has been strongest in Baptist,* Methodist,* Holiness* and Pentecostal* groups and weakest among Lutherans* and Episcopalians.* Theologically, it has been closer to conservative evangelicalism* and fundamentalism* than to liberalism.*

The Beginnings of Revivalism. Many people played important roles in the Great Awakening* of the 1730s and 1740s, including Theodore Frelinghuysen,* the Tennent family—William Sr.* and his four sons, most notably Gilbert,* and Jonathan Edwards.* The Awakening reached its zenith in the 1740s with the preaching tours of George Whitefield.*

The effects of the Great Awakening were clear enough. Belief in awakenings became the commonly held legacy of the movement, based largely on Edwards's apologetic work and on the experience in scores of churches. Detractors also came to the fore, producing Old* (anti-revival) and New* (pro-revival) Lights, indicative of the dividing effects that revivalism was always to have among American Protestants.

Revivalism Reaches Maturity. Instances of revival occurred throughout the revolutionary generation, with strong local expressions at times, but the Second Awakening* is usually dated from 1800, with the appearance of the camp meeting.* Begun by Presbyterians and Baptists as well as Methodists, the camp meeting became an almost exclusive Methodist domain after 1810.

New England revivalism was more sedate than its western counterpart, producing debate on the nature of revivals that was settled, but never fully resolved, by the career of Charles G. Finney.* Finney, believing that the crucial component in human nature was the will, developed his "new measures"* to foster the making of decisions. From the time of Finney on, most advocates of revivalism have believed that revival can be "worked up," that it is not simply "sent down" from God.

The move of revivalism to the urban center was embodied in the Awakening of 1857-1858, during which perhaps a million members were added to church rolls.

Revivalism in the Modern Era. After the Awakening of 1857-1858, it is difficult to find instances of general awakening. But revivalism continued in the years following, and some of the most noteworthy names in revival history made their appearance.

Dwight L. Moody* was the premier revivalist in the last third of the nineteenth century. His simple and low-key approach was heard by millions in many citywide campaigns. Billy Sunday* was a flamboyant revivalist of the Progressive Era, whose greatest effort was his New York meeting in 1917. Billy Graham* came on the national scene in the late 1940s. Initially representing fundamentalism, Graham eventually aligned himself with the more culturally affirming neo-evangelicalism, thereby bringing revivalism back to a more central place in American life.

Characteristics of Revivalism. Revivalism has undergone theological change over the years, moving from a rather strong Calvinism* in the Great Awakening to the "Calvinized Arminianism"* of the last two centuries. Interestingly enough, opposition to revivalism has come from both the conservative side—for example, Charles Hodge* and some of the nineteenth-century Princetonians*—and the liberal side of the theological spectrum.

Social and moral reform are intimately tied to revivalism, reaching a peak of influence in the "benevolent empire" of reform societies in the antebellum era. Revivalism also gave support to the lay, student and faith mission* movements of the nineteenth and early twentieth centuries.

Revolution, American. *See* AMERICAN REVOLUTION, CHRISTIANITY AND THE.

Rice, ("Father") David (1733-1816). Presbyterian* minister, antirevivalist and abolitionist* leader. Rice initiated higher education in Kentucky, working with members of his extended family and with close friends. The Transylvania Seminary (later Transylvania University) was begun in his house. "Father" Rice firmly opposed both slavery and revivals.*

Rice, John Holt (1777-1831). Presbyterian* minister and educator. With others, Rice founded the Virginia Bible Society in 1813 and the American Bible Society* in 1816. In 1824 he became president of the Theological Seminary at Hampden-Sydney (later Union Theological Seminary in Virginia).

Rice mixed Calvinism* with humane care for those who differed in Christian conviction. His lobbying for Presbyterian missions* led in part to the forming of the Board of World Missions by the denomination.

Rice, John R. (1895-1980). Baptist* fundamentalist,* evangelist, editor and controversialist. In 1934 Rice founded *Sword of the Lord,* a periodical promoting fundamentalist theology and attacking modernism* and liberalism.* He was well known for his polemical response to Catholicism,* communism* and the civil rights movement.*

Rice, Luther (1783-1836). Baptist* denominational* leader, promoter of missions* and education. Embarking for India in 1812 as a Congregationalist,* Rice became convinced of Baptist views and in 1813 returned to the U.S., where he began to stir up Baptist interest in missions. His extensive travels and enthusiastic preaching resulted in the formation in 1814 of an organization known as the Triennial Convention.* Rice's missionary vision led him to advocate the founding of Baptist colleges, beginning in 1821 with Columbian College in Washington, D.C.

Richard, Gabriel (1767-1832). Catholic* educator and missionary. After the Detroit fire of 1805, Richard was the sole priest there, building up St. Anne's Parish and helping with the development of the new Michigan Territory. In 1824 he won election to Congress, the only priest before the twentieth century to have a seat in the House of Representatives.

Richards, George Warren (1869-1955). Reformed* theologian and educator. Richards joined the faculty of the Theological Seminary of the Reformed Church in the U.S. at Lancaster, Pennsylvania, in 1899 and became its president (1920-1937). Richards was an exponent of Barthian, or neo-orthodox,* theology, which he considered to be an alternative to both liberalism* and fundamentalism.*

Rigdon, Sidney (1793-1876). Early Mormon* leader. After serving as a Baptist* minister, Rigdon worked with Alexander Campbell* throughout the 1820s. In 1830 Rigdon was one of the earliest converts to Mormonism, soon becoming a spokesman for Joseph Smith* and an ardent evangelist for the Mormon Church. Upon Smith's death in 1844, Rigdon considered himself a serious claimant to the leadership of the church.

Riggs, Stephen Return (1812-1883). Missionary and linguist among the Dakota Indians. In 1837 Riggs was sent by the American Board of Commissioners for Foreign Missions* to the Lac Qui Parle mission near Fort Snelling, Minnesota, where he worked until the outbreak of the Sioux Wars in 1862. By 1880 he had translated the entire Bible into Dakota.

Right to Life. A movement opposed to the taking of innocent human life at any time from conception to natural death. Arising as a reaction to the movement for liberalized abortion,* the first permanent group was founded in New York in 1966. From early on, however, Right to Life groups were concerned with the question of euthanasia as well and came to devote more of their energies to this subject during the 1980s. Initially predominantly Roman Catholic,* the movement gained many evangelical* Protestants* in the later 1970s.

Riley, William Bell (1861-1947). Baptist* pastor and fundamentalist* leader. In 1897 Riley became pastor of the First Baptist Church of Minneapolis. After only a short time in the Twin Cities area, he founded the Northwestern Bible and Missionary Training School. In 1935 he established Northwestern Evangelical Seminary and in 1944 Northwestern College. Riley was an active participant in the fundamentalist-modernist controversy,* developing a powerful regional fundamentalist network.

Rimmer, Harry (1890-1952). Presbyterian minister and Christian apologist. In 1920 Rimmer started the Research Science Bureau, Inc., in Denver, Colorado, through which he brought forward scientific evidence in support of the authenticity of the Bible. He undertook archaeological expeditions, studied manuscripts in British and Egyptian museums and lectured widely on the harmony of science and Scripture.

Ripley, George (1802-1880). Transcendentalist,* editor, literary critic and reformer. In 1836 the first meeting of the Transcendental Club was held in Ripley's home, and when that group first began publishing *The Dial* in 1840, he assisted in writing and editing it. In 1841 Ripley established Brook Farm,* a farming cooperative near Boston. When the farm dissolved in 1847, Ripley next began a long career in journalism, exerting significant influence on the American public's opinion of new writers such as Nathaniel Hawthorne* and Charles Darwin.

Ritter, Joseph Elmer (1892-1967). Cardinal of St. Louis. After becoming the first archbishop of Indianapolis in 1944, Ritter was transferred to St. Louis in 1946. There he quickly established the character of his episcopacy by ordering the racial desegregation of all Catholic schools and parishes.* During the 1950s Ritter quietly encouraged newer movements within the church, such as greater lay participation in the liturgy,* and especially the cause of racial justice. He was made a cardinal by Pope John XXIII* in 1960 and was one of the leading American delegates to the Second Vatican Council.*

Roberts, Benjamin Titus (1823-1893). Founder of the Free Methodist Church.* In 1860 Roberts and others founded the Free Methodist Church. He was general superintendent* and vigorously promoted abolition* as well as the Wesleyan* doctrine of entire sanctification.*

Robertson, Archibald Thomas (1863-1934). Southern Baptist* Greek scholar, professor of New Testament and author. Robertson became the most widely respected Southern Baptist scholar of his time. His *Grammar of the Greek New Testament in the Light of Historical Research* (1914) established him as the foremost New Testament Greek scholar of his day. He authored forty-four other books, including four grammars and fourteen commentaries.

Robertson, James (1839-1902). Presbyterian* missions* leader in Canada. In 1881 Robertson became superintendent of Presbyterian missions on the prairies. During his tenure the denominational presence increased from 4 to over 140 established churches, in addition to 226 mission charges.

Robinson, Edward (1794-1863). Biblical scholar and geographer. Robinson taught at Andover Seminary* and, from 1837, Union Theological Seminary,* New York. After a three-month expedition to Palestine, Sinai and southern Syria, he wrote *Biblical Researches in Palestine, Mount Sinai, and Arabia Petraea* (3 vols., 1841). This work established him as the foremost historical geographer of the Holy Land. Two subsequent expeditions to Palestine in 1852 and 1856 led to further published results.

Robinson, John (1575-1625). English separatist* minister. Robinson became the minister of an English separatist group that immigrated to the Netherlands in 1608 in search of freedom. In 1620 part of this group immigrated on the *Mayflower* to Plymouth in New England. Robinson stayed behind with the larger portion, but his standing as the pastor of the American Pilgrims gives him a place in American history.

Robinson was one of the most creative theologians* of Separatism, a forerunner of Congregationalism.*

Robinson, Stuart (1814-1881). Southern Presbyterian* minister. A gifted preacher, Robinson was an ardent defender of Old School* Presbyterianism. He was also a strong proponent of the distinctive Southern Presbyterian doctrine of the "spirituality of the church," which asserted that the church should deal only with spiritual matters and avoid all political statements.

In 1869 he led the majority of the Synod of Kentucky out of the Northern church and into the Southern church.

Robinson, William (?-1746). Presbyterian* evangelist to Virginia and North Carolina. After being ordained* to the Presbyterian ministry in 1741, Robinson embarked as an evangelist to Presbyterian settlements in Virginia and North Carolina. The success of his southern missionary journey in 1743 paved the way for an extensive Presbyterian revival* in Virginia and the larger work, beginning there in 1747, of his former pupil Samuel Davies.*

Rodeheaver, Homer Alvan (1880-1955). Song leader for Billy Sunday,* music publisher and hymn* tune composer. From 1910 to 1930, Rodeheaver served as Billy Sunday's song leader. In that role, as well as through his instructional books, he established the enduring style of evangelistic* song leading.

Rodgers, James Burton (1865-1944). First regularly appointed permanent Protestant* missionary to the Philippines. From his arrival in Manila in 1899 until his retirement in 1935, Rodgers participated actively in evangelistic,* educational and ecumenical* ministries. In addition to serving as head of the Presbyterian* mission, Rodgers played instrumental roles in the founding of the Evangelical Union (1901), Union Theological Seminary, Manila (1907), and the United Evangelical Church (1929).

Roman Catholicism. Roman Catholicism arrived in what is now the U.S. with sixteenth- and seventeenth-century Spanish and French explorers (*see* Missions to North America).

Catholics in the South and Southwest. The first permanent settlement in the continental U.S. was at St. Augustine, Florida, in 1565. Spanish missions ended, however, when Florida became British in 1763. Twentieth-century Catholic growth in this region owes much to the influx of retired people from northern states and Canada and to immigrants and refugees from Latin America and the Caribbean.

In the Southwest, Spanish Catholic influence remains strong in New Mexico and Arizona. In California in the latter half of the eighteenth century, the Spanish established a chain of twenty-one missions from San Diego to San Francisco Solano.

Catholics in the North. Establishment of Catholicism in American sections of the old French empire came after the American Revolution* as settlers moved across the Appalachians and into the Ohio and Mississippi Valleys. Cincinnati, St. Louis, Chicago and Milwaukee became major Catholic centers.

Formal church structure in the future U.S. began with Maryland, founded in 1634 by a Catholic, Lord Baltimore (*see* Colonial Catholicism).

Catholic congregations developed during the Revolution in East Coast cities; the Middle Atlantic states waited until the inflow of nineteenth-century immigrants to develop substantial communities. There were few colonial Catholics in New England.

Catholics and the New Republic. In 1776 American Catholics numbered about 25,000, or 1 percent of the population of English America. In 1784 Rome named John Carroll* "superior of the missions." He was elected bishop of Baltimore in 1789 and became archbishop* there in 1808.

A more diversified post-Revolution Catholic population and the free republican air of the new nation brought national rivalries to a head, and frequent conflicts arose over the role in church management of bishops, clergy and lay trustees (*see* Trusteeism). As a result the authority of the bishops was strengthened at the expense of both local clergy and laity.

Catholics and Nineteenth-Century Immigration. Between 1820 and 1920, ten million Catholics arrived from Europe (*see* Immigration and Ethnicity, Catholic). In terms of numbers, the Roman Catholic Church was the largest in the country by 1850, but it lived in a culture that was Protestant* and evangelical* and in which there was a strong measure of antiforeign and anti-Catholic feeling (*see* Nativism). One result of nineteenth-century Catholic isolationism was a heavy investment of financial and personnel resources in schools (*see* Parochial Schools, Roman Catholic), hospitals and other institutions.

Catholics and Americanization. The turn of the century saw internal conflict among American Roman Catholics over the pace and extent of the church's Americanization. Americanists* praised separation of church and state* and championed primitive unions like the Knights of Labor.* Papal letters in 1895 and 1899 dampened their enthusiasms (*see* Longinqua Oceani; Testem Benevolentiae).

The 1930s witnessed rising Catholic influence in labor circles, and radical movements like the personalist, communitarian Catholic Worker* movement flourished. Most American Catholics were supporters of Franklin D. Roosevelt, who reciprocated by appointing Catholics to public office in record numbers.

Catholics and the Postwar Era. Postwar Catholics shared in the socioeconomic upswing, the move to the suburbs and the religious revival of the 1950s. After the Second Vatican Council* (1962-1965), which was a catalyst for extensive change, a sharper ideological spectrum has emerged. While most American Catholics are religiously centrist, there is greater liberalism in ethical areas and in judging what is, or is not, sinful—and more reliance on individual conscience instead of unquestioning obedience to church directives.

A third age of Catholicism in the U.S. is developing, following the colonial and federal periods. American Roman Catholics now find themselves better integrated into the national life and less defensive about their religion. But a structure and style for the third age are still being worked out.

Romanticism, Catholic (1840-1888). Catholic Romanticism refers to a movement in apologetic* literature and religious piety* that emphasized divine immanence in creation, history, tradition and the church, as well as the role of intuition and religious feelings in apprehending the divine.

Romanticism had its origins in late eighteenth-century European thought and had little impact upon American sensibilities and patterns of thought until the 1840s. From the 1840s until the death of Isaac Thomas Hecker* (1888), a few Catholic apologists (e.g., John Hughes,* Martin John Spalding,* Orestes Brownson,* Isaac Hecker*) appropriated elements of Romanticism in their accounts of Catholic life and thought. The revival of American Catholic piety during the 1840s also manifested the Romantic temperament.

See also AMERICANISM; ENLIGHTENMENT CATHOLICISM; PIETY, POPULAR CATHOLIC; ROMANTICISM, PROTESTANT.

Romanticism, Protestant (1836-1860). *Romanticism* is the name commonly applied to Western intellectual history of the first half of the nineteenth century. It stressed the importance of human feelings, intuition and emotion and was expressed in numerous disciplines, including literature, art, music, philosophy and religion. The term is vague, and interpreters frequently call it a mood or outlook rather than a system of thought. In the religious arena it created no American denomination,* but it did provide an ethos for important new ways of understanding Christian faith.

The Romantic Movement. In Europe, romanticism followed the Enlightenment* (1750-1800) and preceded the era of realism (1860-1900). Romantic notions were advocated by a cluster of creative European thinkers, and Americans such as Ralph Waldo Emerson* and James Marsh* helped to transmit European romanticism into the fabric of American culture.

Romanticism was very diverse, but several characteristic themes recur. Feelings and intuition were central to romantic understanding, as expressed so clearly by Jean-Jacques Rousseau (1712-1778), often considered the founder of romanticism. Closely allied with the significance placed on feeling was the romantic emphasis on individual freedom and expression. Romantics also reveled in the remote and exotic, found truth in remote cultures and embraced the nonrational aspects of human experience.

Romanticism and American Protestantism. Christian thought was deeply influenced by romanticism. The leading Protestant theologian in the era of romanticism was Friedrich Schleiermacher, who wrote that religion is not primarily a matter of doctrinal orthodoxy,* nor is it primarily right behavior. Instead, he urged that the essence of religion comes from the heart: it is a feeling and an intuition of absolute dependence on God.

The romantic impulse spawned important Catholic* movements within American Protestantism. The Oxford, or Tractarian, movement* defended the Anglican Church* as a true church and understood the sacraments* to be a means of grace.

Another highly significant dimension of romantic religion was the theological work of Horace Bushnell,* who was deeply influenced by Coleridge and Schleiermacher. Bushnell sought to reshape theology so that the gospel would speak to his urban congregation, which believed in self-improvement and reform and was affronted by orthodox Calvinism.* Bushnell's reconstruction laid the basis for liberal* Protestant thought in America.

Recognizing the plurality of theologies and denominations, Bushnell believed that comprehensiveness was a useful approach for theology: one should be open to insights from many traditions, since no one theology possessed all truth. Bushnell, whose influence on American Protestantism was enormous, has been called the father of American religious liberalism.

Roots, Logan Herbert (1870-1945). Episcopal* missionary and bishop of Hankow, China. Roots spent his entire China career (1896-1938) in the cities of Hankow and Wuchang. In the 1910s and 1920s he was a leader in the ecumenical movement* in China.

Rosary. The term derives from *rosarium,* meaning "rose garden." It commonly refers to a set of beads divided into five sets of ten separated by single beads. The rosary is used as a counter of prayers and, as such, bears a general resemblance to the prayer beads of Buddhists and Muslims or the "rope" or "cord" used by Eastern Orthodox* Christians for the recitation of the Jesus Prayer. In the Roman Catholic* Church, the rosary is a devotion* in honor of the Virgin Mary.*

See also PIETY, POPULAR CATHOLIC.

Royce, Josiah (1855-1916). Harvard* idealist philosopher. From 1882 until his death, Royce was part of a distinguished faculty of Harvard philosophers which included William James.* Out of his use of logic to explore the meaning of religious ideas and values, Royce evolved a system of absolute idealism, based on the premise that individual experience was part of and validated by a universal consciousness.

Though Royce rejected the evangelical* Christianity of his parents, religious questions shaped his philosophy. As philosophical pragmatism gained prestige, Royce wrote increasingly on applied ethics.* His argument that human salvation* depended on individual loyalty to a universal "beloved" community dominated his last works.

Rozhdestvensky, Platon Porphyry (1866-1934). Russian Orthodox* metropolitan*-archbishop in America. In 1907 Rozhdestvensky replaced Archbishop Tikhon* in the U.S., serving until 1914. After service in Russia, he returned to America in 1922 and was subsequently reappointed head of the North American archdiocese.

Rozhdestvensky's church became independent in 1924; in 1970 its name was changed to the Orthodox Church in America.

Ruffner, Henry (1789-1861). Presbyterian* minister and educator. After serving in a number of pastorates in Virginia, Ruffner went to Washington College (Lexington, Va.) to teach. Over a thirty-year period he served twelve years as president (1836-1848) and taught nearly every subject offered by the college. He wrote a valuable antislavery pamphlet that detailed the system's evils and recommended gradual emancipation.

Russell, Charles Taze (1852-1916). Founder of the Watch Tower Bible and Tract Society.* Russell started Bible study* groups (later known as Russellites or Millennial Dawnists) in which he rejected the Trinity, the resurrection of Christ and other traditional Christian doctrines. In 1884 he founded the Watch Tower Bible and Tract Society.

By the time of his death he was the head of a worldwide network of loosely associated groups of Bible students, the majority of whom became Jehovah's Witnesses* under the leadership of J. F. Rutherford.*

Russell, Howard Hyde (1855-1946). Congregational* clergyman and founder of the Anti-Saloon League.* In 1893 Russell helped organize the Ohio Anti-Saloon League, which he effectively served as superintendent from 1893 to 1897. The "Ohio model" attracted national attention and a national league, later named the Anti-Saloon League of America, was formed in 1895, with Russell serving as general superintendent (1895-1903). He organized state leagues in thirty-six states. His implementation of the techniques and tactics pioneered in Ohio made the Anti-Saloon League the dominant organization in the national Prohibition movement.*

Russian Orthodox Church in America. This label applies to three church organizations in North America. The most widespread one, known officially as the Orthodox Church in America (600,000 members in 1992), originated around 1800 in missionary work by Russian priests in Alaska. The two other Russian Orthodox churches in North America are the Russian Orthodox Church Outside of Russia (100,000 members in 1988) and the Patriarchal Russian Orthodox Church in the U.S.A. (10,000 members).

See also MISSIONS TO ALASKA, RUSSIAN ORTHODOX; ORTHODOX TRADITION.

Rutgers University. Institution of higher education with origins in the Dutch Reformed* Church. Formerly called Queens College, the institution was chartered in New Jersey in 1766. In 1825 the school received a $5,000 gift from Colonel Henry Rutgers, whose name it bore from that year on. Control by the Reformed Church waned during the last half of the century, especially after Rutgers became New Jersey's Land Grant institution in 1862. In 1956 the charter was amended to give the state formal control.

Rutherford, Joseph Franklin "Judge" (1869-1942). Leader of the Watch Tower Bible and Tract Society* and true founder of the Jehovah's Witnesses* theocratic* organization. Rutherford joined C. T. Russell's* Bible students in 1906 and, after Russell's death in 1916, became president of Jehovah's Witnesses (this title dates to 1931). Under his leadership (1917-1942) the loose and undogmatic organization of Bible Students was gradually reorganized and turned into a highly disciplined, dogmatic bureaucracy.

Ryan, John Augustine (1869-1945). Catholic* priest and social theorist. In 1920 Ryan was appointed director of the Social Action Department of the newly organized National Catholic Welfare Council,* a position he held until his death. Ryan decisively influenced Catholic theory and practice concerning social, political and economic issues.

His involvement with such organizations as the Federal Council of Churches* and the American Civil Liberties Union also did much to break down stereotypes of Catholics as conservative and aloof from contemporary life.

Ryerson, Adolphus Egerton (1803-1882). Canadian Methodist* leader and educator. Ryerson argued for a British-style Christian nation, without an established church and with full religious liberty. In 1829 he was appointed first editor of the Methodist newspaper *Christian Guardian* and for a decade was the Methodist spokesman on all major public issues. He was the founding superintendent of the Ontario public school system, which he developed and administered brilliantly for several decades.

S

Sabbatarianism. The rigid and scrupulous observance of the sabbath as a divinely ordained day of rest. Its most rigorous form arose out of the Scottish and English Reformation and was transferred to the New World by the Puritans.*

In the colonies the first generation of Puritans imposed severe penalties for violations of the sabbath. Contemporary Sunday restrictions and so-called blue laws in various states reflect its long-term impact upon American society.

See also LORD'S DAY ACT.

Sabbath. *See* SABBATARIANISM.

Sacramentals. Predominantly a Catholic* term for sacred signs signifying spiritual effects obtained by the intercession of the church. Each of the sacraments* is surrounded by subsidiary actions and signs meant to enrich the believer's participation in the sacraments.

Sacramentary. The liturgical* book of the Roman Catholic Church* containing all the Mass* texts required for the celebrant at Mass, exclusive of the readings and chants reserved to other ministers and singers.

Sacraments and Ordinances. Catholics* in America have affirmed seven sacraments (baptism,* confirmation,* the Eucharist,* penance,* extreme unction,* ordination* and matrimony), which, in accord with the Council of Trent (1545-1563), are defined as efficacious means of grace. Eastern Orthodox* Christians have accepted the same seven sacraments, though some Orthodox theologians have emphasized that other "holy acts" also possess a sacramental character. Protestants* have accepted only the sacraments of baptism and the Lord's Supper,* with Baptists* and heirs of the Continental Anabaptist* traditions preferring to designate the rites as *ordinances,* performed because Jesus ordained their use, rather than as means of grace.

Early Sacramental Debates. As early as the 1650s sacramental issues divided New England Puritans.* A 1662 synod* in Boston finally decided that baptized but unconverted members could present their children for baptism, though neither they nor their children could receive the Lord's Supper without offering a credible narration* of their conversion.* Opponents derided this Half-Way Covenant.* But the Lord's Supper also became the subject of renewed controversy when Solomon Stoddard* of Northampton defined it as a "converting ordinance" that could move the hearts of the unconverted.

Sacraments and Revivalism. Revivalism tended to diminish interest in traditional sacramental doctrines and liturgies.* The revivalist ethos and the yearning to recover primitive biblical patterns also encouraged various innovative baptismal doctrines on the part of Alexander Campbell,* Joseph Smith* and the Landmarkers.*

The flowering of nineteenth-century sacramental thought and piety, however, came from groups uncomfortable with revivalism such as the Tractarians* and the confessional Lutherans, led by Charles Porterfield Krauth.*

Sacraments in the Twentieth Century. Besides being the focus of debates, the sacraments have also served as means of renewal* and symbols of unity. Virgil Michel's* journal *Worship* encouraged the emphasis in the Catholic liturgical movement* on lay participation in the Eucharist, an emphasis confirmed by Vatican II.*

A growing Protestant interest in sacramental liturgy found expression in a new Presbyterian Book of Common Worship in 1946 and in a decision by Episcopalians* three years later gradually to revise their Book of Common Prayer.* After 1964 several denominations prepared new sacramental liturgies that recovered traditions from both the Reformation and earlier Christian worship.

Sacred. A term referring to the quality of otherness or holiness.* The term *sacred* refers to objects, places, times and events that are holy or religious in nature. Such sacred categories are usually distinguished in opposition to objects that are profane or ordinary (lacking in holy qualities). In addition, the term *sacred* can refer to a perception of reality—how one views the world. In the Christian tradition, rituals (e.g., regular Sunday* worship*) and ritualistic sites (e.g., churches) define the idea of the sacred.

Sacred Congregation for the Evangelization of Peoples or for the Propagation of the Faith (Propaganda). A Roman curial congregation coordinating the missionary activity of the Catholic Church.* The congregation was established in 1622 by Gregory XV to take control of the missionary work then languishing under the Spanish and Portuguese patronages. The Propaganda developed under the popes of the nineteenth and twentieth centuries.

See also MISSIONS, ROMAN CATHOLIC FOREIGN.

Sacred Congregations. Administrative bodies in the Catholic Church* that the pope uses to implement his judicial, legislative and executive office as head of the church. Their specific powers are set out in the Code of Canon Law.* These congregations constitute the Roman or papal curia.

Sacred Heart of Jesus. A theology, popular devotion and official liturgical feast. The theology and devotion of the sacred heart is primarily based on two New Testament texts: John 7:37-38 and John 19:34. In the Middle Ages the wounded heart of Jesus was understood not so much as the source of grace as it was the explicit, direct object of personal devotion.

The entire complex of the Sacred Heart emphasizes the incarnational principle of Christianity—that the love of God for the world is truly present in the historical heart of Jesus.

See also PIETY, POPULAR CATHOLIC.

St. Vincent de Paul. *See* SOCIETY OF ST. VINCENT DE PAUL.

Saints, Cult of the. In the Catholic tradition the term *saints* may refer to (1) the comparatively few well-known or canonized* deceased holy ones; (2) the many deceased holy ones celebrat-

ed on the feast of "All Saints"; or (3) the many living, faithful believers in Christ. The *cult of the saints* is a broad term for various kinds of honor directed by the third group toward the first group especially, and less often toward the second.

The practice has three main aspects: veneration, or giving honor to the saints; invocation, or praying* for their intercession with God; and imitation, or acting on their inspiration and example. The cult of the saints is based theologically on the doctrine of the communion of saints,* which asserts a bond of unity among all those who live in Christ, including even those whose lives on earth are ended.

St.-Vallier, Jean Baptiste de la Croix de Chevières de (1653-1727). Second bishop of Quebec. Consecrated bishop in 1688, St.-Vallier was in constant conflict with the civil authorities and the Jesuits over ecclesiastical jurisdiction and the moral tone of the colony. Through his piety,* untiring service to the poor and breadth of legislation, St.-Vallier helped greatly in establishing the Catholic Church* in North America.

Salem Witch Trial. The infamous Salem witch trial of 1692 was precipitated by several young girls who, when caught gazing into a crystal ball, claimed that they had been assaulted by witches. The parents believed their charges and began searching for the witches in their midst. The local pastor, Samuel Parris, heightened tensions by suggesting that the witches might even be found in his own church. Before the panic subsided and the neighboring ministers intervened to bring a halt to the judicial proceedings, over 150 suspected witches had been imprisoned and 19 hanged.

Salvation. In biblical usage *salvation* describes the full range of divine activity in physical and spiritual deliverance—past, present and future. It includes and integrates other more specific terms such as *justification,* redemption, reconciliation, regeneration,* sanctification* and the final eschatological* deliverance from death and judgment and into the life to come.

Among Roman Catholics* salvation is linked to the sacramental* ministries of the church and the purifying effects of purgatory.* In churches of the Reformed tradition,* like the New England Puritans,* salvation was connected to covenant theology,* eternal predestination* and election.* Under this formulation *predestination* describes

God's decree by which he chooses individuals to be included in the community of the elect, while *election* describes an effectual divine calling of irresistible grace that irrevocably joins Christians to Christ. In churches of the Wesleyan*-Arminian* tradition, salvation is considered to be conditional, since it could be lost through faithlessness, and justification is inextricably linked to sanctification or holiness.*

The extent of salvation has been the subject of periodic controversy. New England liberals attacked the Calvinistic doctrines of original sin and election in the mid-eighteenth century. And Charles Chauncy,* minister of Boston's First Church, argued against the doctrine of eternal damnation, maintaining a universalism* in which all humanity would eventually be redeemed.

Most evangelicals* continue to emphasize the personal aspects of salvation, often echoing themes shaped by revivalism in the evangelical, Arminian tradition. A few evangelicals, reflecting on the themes of liberation theology* and the biblical basis for a more holistic view of salvation, have sought to define salvation in more comprehensive terms.

See also ETERNAL SECURITY.

Salvation Army, The. Holiness* denomination.* The mission that became the Salvation Army was established in 1865 in the slums of London by William Booth* and his wife, Catherine. The mission was given its present military form in 1878, after which its spread throughout Britain and overseas was very rapid. The Army's official missionaries "opened fire" on the U.S. in March 1880, and on Canada in July 1882.

Beginning in 1890, all Salvationists have been required to accept and sign the Army's "Articles of War," which pledge its members to evangelistic fervor and to a disciplined lifestyle in support of "Salvation* warfare," which since Victorian times has meant a wide range of energetic activities designed to save souls and relieve human suffering.

The organization currently operates in eighty-seven countries, but the branches in English-speaking countries are particularly strong. The American Salvation Army is by far the largest, with 5,241 officers and 133,214 full adult members reported in the U.S. in 1992, and 2,098 officers and 24,597 full adult members in Canada.

Salzburgers. Members of a colony of Lutheran* refugees from Austria who settled in colonial Georgia. In 1731 some twenty thousand Lutherans were driven out of Salzburg amid much suffering. Most were resettled in Prussia, but with help from the Society for Promoting Christian Knowledge (SPCK),* some three hundred emigrants were sent between 1734 and 1741 to the newly founded colony of Georgia. After initial difficulties, the colonies of Lutheran exiles prospered until the Revolutionary War* era.

Sampey, John Richard (1863-1946). President of Southern Baptist Theological Seminary* and professor of Old Testament and Hebrew. Sampey entered Southern Baptist Theological Seminary in 1882 to prepare for foreign missionary* service but was persuaded to remain and teach at the seminary upon his graduation in 1885. In 1928 he became president, serving until 1942.

Sampey served on the International Sunday School Lesson Committee for forty-six years. He also was a cofounder of the Baptist World Alliance.*

Sanctification. To make or be made holy. In biblical theology and religion, objects, occasions, places and persons are sanctified or set apart for sacred use. Sanctification is the act or process by which they are made to correspond with God's holiness. In the context of personal redemption as it is set forth in the New Testament, sanctification is the process by which believers are made holy.

Protestants* have understood sanctification as distinguishable from, and logically subsequent to, justification,* whereas Catholics have used the term *justification* to refer to both the event (*justification* in Protestant terminology) and the process (*sanctification* in Protestant terminology). The Catholic tradition has produced many outstanding examples of men and women who have sought after holiness with methods and understanding that invite comparison with later Protestant proponents of sanctification. Eastern Orthodoxy has also spoken of the pursuit of holiness, placing a distinctive emphasis on the attainment of the "divine nature" (see 2 Pet 1:4), or likeness of God (*see* Spirituality). But no tradition of spirituality in America has placed more emphasis on the term *sanctification,* nor thereby had more influence on American religion, than evangelicalism.*

Among evangelicals, the Wesleyan,* or Methodist,* tradition has been the most vocal in promoting its doctrine of sanctification. Wesley believed that sanctification culminated in the dramatic experience of a second work of grace, given by God and appropriated by faith, whereby the believer attained Christian perfection,* manifested in "perfect love."

Concern for holy living became a central theme of the camp meetings* and revivals* that characterized so much of the religious life of the nineteenth-century American frontier.* Instrumental in providing a theological rationale for this revivalism were Charles Finney* and Asa Mahan* of Oberlin College.*

By the 1870s this Holiness movement* had made significant inroads into evangelical Christianity. The Keswick movement* further developed themes of Holiness in both England and the U.S.

The Pentecostal movement,* arising around the turn of the century, grew out of the Holiness movement. Early Pentecostals, in speaking of the baptism of the Holy Spirit, described the experience as a third step in the two-step Wesleyan formula of salvation and sanctification.

See also HIGHER CHRISTIAN LIFE; OBERLIN THEOLOGY; SECOND BLESSING; VICTORIOUS CHRISTIAN LIFE.

Sanctuary Movement. A network for illegally transporting refugees from Central America into the U.S. and assisting them in establishing themselves. John Fife, a Presbyterian* minister in Tucson, Arizona, and Jim Corbett, a Quaker* and a retired rancher, originated the idea of a national sanctuary movement. Fife's church and five congregations on the east side of San Francisco Bay were the first to declare themselves publicly as sanctuary churches in 1982. By 1986 the movement had grown to include over three hundred sanctuary churches or synagogues, twenty-two sanctuary cities and a sanctuary state, New Mexico.

Sandeman, Robert (1718-1771). Founder of Sandemanian churches in New England. Sandeman, who immigrated to the U.S. in 1764, argued that the state had no authority over the church and urged a restoration of primitive* Christianity. "Sandemanian" congregations were soon established in Massachusetts, New Hampshire and Connecticut, and controversies arose with both Baptists* and Congregationalists.* By 1900 no

Sandemanian churches remained in the U.S.

Sandemanians. *See* SANDEMAN, ROBERT.

Sandford, Frank (1862-1948). Founder and leader of Kingdom, Inc. In the 1890s Sandford, a minister and evangelist, founded Shiloh, a residential Christian community in Durham, Maine. In 1901 Sandford became convinced that he was the Elijah of Revelation 11 and proceeded to establish the Kingdom (incorporated 1904), over which he held temporal authority as "David." Sandford's autocratic rule at Shiloh led to opposition from within and without the community, and in 1903 he was tried, convicted and fined for cruelty to children. In 1906 he purchased two ships and began a series of missionary tours with the intention of establishing the Kingdom in Jerusalem. In 1911 he was indicted and convicted of manslaughter of crew members and served a ten-year prison sentence. After his release in 1921 he resumed control of Shiloh until the community was disbanded in 1923.

Sanford, Elias Benjamin (1843-1932). Congregational* minister and ecumenical* leader. Beginning in 1895 Sanford was the key organizational figure in a series of bodies leading to creation in 1908 of the Federal Council of the Churches.* A steady vision of denominational* federation, rather than organic union, and skill at gaining confidence and support from people he deemed critical to success characterized Sanford's unique contribution to Protestant* ecumenicity.

Sankey, Ira David (1840-1908). Singing evangelist and associate of Dwight L. Moody.* In 1870 Moody heard Sankey sing at a YMCA* convention in Indianapolis and recruited him for evangelistic work in Chicago. For the next twenty-five years, Sankey was an indispensable part of Moody's revivalistic* work. During Moody's first tour of Great Britain (1873-1875), Sankey contributed significantly to Moody's success.

Sankey is generally credited with popularizing the "gospel hymn"* and making that musical style a crucial part of modern revivalism.

Satolli, Francesco (1839-1910). Catholic* cardinal and first apostolic delegate* to the U.S. Satolli was a major force in the general renewal of serious scholarship in the Roman Catholic Church. He visited the U.S. as a papal representative in 1889 and in 1892. He became a permanent delegate to the U.S. in 1893, only after the American Catholic hierarchy became deeply divided over questions of educational policy and ethnic representation.

Savage, Mary (fl. 1790s). Freewill Baptist* preacher. Savage joined the Freewill Baptists and began preaching the gospel in 1791. Though she only served as a minister for about a year, she is credited with being the first Baptist woman preacher.

Sawdust Trail. In the late nineteenth century, lumbermen in the Pacific Northwest used trails of sawdust to find their way back to camp. Applied to evangelistic* meetings first by Billy Sunday* in 1910, *sawdust trail* became a metaphor for finding one's way to God.

Saybrook Platform. Congregational* platform of church discipline.* In response to a perceived decline in lay piety and the failure of councils to settle an increasing number of church disputes, Connecticut's General Court authorized and summoned a synod* in Saybrook in 1708 to revise the system of church discipline. The most important point of the platform it prepared called for establishing consociations made up of lay and clerical representatives that would offer binding judgments on disputes arising within local churches.

Sayle, William (?-1671). Puritan* governor of Bermuda and South Carolina. Although Sayles's real influence was limited, he was significant as a visionary and fiery Calvinist* whose politics, like those of his occasional contacts in New England, were tied to his Puritan hopes for an experimental society in the New World.

Scandinavian Alliance Mission. *See* EVANGELICAL ALLIANCE MISSION, THE.

Scanlan, Patrick F. ("Pat") (1894-1983). Catholic* journalist. Scanlan was the long-time editor of the *Brooklyn Tablet* (1917-1968). In 1924 he became the youngest president of the Catholic Press Association, and as his career continued, he was widely regarded as the dean of the Catholic press* in the U.S. A fierce opponent of communism,* he was much admired by Cardinals Spellman,* O'Hara* and McIntyre.

Scarborough, L(ee) R(utland) (1870-1945). Southern Baptist* denominational* leader and seminary president. In 1908 Scarborough was appointed to the department of evangelism* in the newly organized Southwestern Baptist Theological Seminary* in Fort Worth, Texas, and later served as president (1914-1942). He also was active in the Baptist World Alliance.*

Schaeffer, Francis August (1912-1984). Evangelical* missionary and apologist.* In 1938 Schaeffer became the first ordained* minister of the Bible Presbyterian Church and subsequently pastored churches in Pennsylvania and Missouri.

In 1948 Schaeffer and his wife, Edith, moved to Switzerland, serving under the Independent Board for Presbyterian Foreign Missions. In 1955 Schaeffer founded L'Abri, an international study center and caring community in the Swiss Alps, where he offered an analysis of modern thought and a critique of secular culture from a Christian perspective. Over the years thousands of students and other seekers stayed with the Schaeffers, and through prayer, study and conversation many of them came to Christian faith.

The ministry was greatly extended through Schaeffer's writings, and by the 1970s he was widely regarded among American evangelicals as a preeminent apologist for the faith. Schaeffer's twenty-four books have sold over three million copies in more than twenty languages. Two film series based on his books were widely viewed in churches.

Schaff, Philip (1819-1893). German Reformed* church historian and ecumenist.* Schaff came to the U.S. in 1844 to teach at the newly organized German Reformed Seminary at Mercersburg,* Pennsylvania, where he began a career of nearly a half-century of scholarship at the forefront of the study of church history. In 1870 he accepted a professorship at Union Theological Seminary* in New York, where he remained until his death.

Schaff founded the American Society of Church History in 1888 and served as president of that organization until his death. His first major work in America was *The Principle of Protestantism* (1845), which brought upon Schaff charges of heresy* and Romanism. In it he traced the development of the Christian church through history and emphasized the value of the church in every age. In 1858 Schaff published the first volume of his most ambitious work, his *History of the Christian Church,* which ultimately grew to eight volumes. In 1877 the first edition of Schaff's three-volume *Creeds of Christendom* appeared. The *Schaff-Herzog Encyclopedia of Religious Knowledge* was published in three volumes (1882-1884). Inspiring all of his prodigious labors was Schaff's ultimate goal to heal the wounds caused by divisions in the church.

Scherer, Paul Ehrmann (1892-1969). Lutheran* preacher and homiletics* professor. In 1920 Scherer was called to be pastor of the Evangelical Lutheran Church of the Holy Trinity, on Central Park West in New York City.

Scherer became a prominent national figure during his years in New York. From 1932 to 1945 he was the vacation replacement preacher for Harry Emerson Fosdick* on the network radio broadcast *Sunday Vespers.*

Schlatter, Michael (1718-1790). Colonial German Reformed* leader. Impressed by his gifts, the classis* of Amsterdam dispatched Schlatter to America with instructions which amounted to the task of overseeing the German Reformed congregations in the American colonies. After strenuous efforts, he succeeded in organizing the so-called coetus in 1747, consisting of four ordained ministers and twenty-eight elders who together represented twelve of the thirteen German Reformed congregations. His ministry and leadership were strategic in the organization and growth of the German Reformed churches in Pennsylvania.

Schmemann, Alexander (1921-1983). Orthodox* theologian and dean of St. Vladimir's Theological Seminary. Becoming dean of St. Vladimir's in 1962, Schmemann oversaw the school's growth into a pan-Orthodox institution serving most of the jurisdictions in America. As one of the most popular and charismatic Orthodox speakers and writers of the 1960s and 1970s, he traveled widely, championing liturgical* and Eucharistic* renewal in U.S. Orthodox churches.

Schmucker, Samuel Simon (1799-1873). Lutheran* theologian and educator. Schmucker was the first president and professor of Gettysburg Seminary, serving from 1826 until his retirement in 1864. Opposed to the rationalism* of the Enlightenment,* Schmucker urged a return to the

evangelicalism* of the Reformation. He envisioned a Protestant* consensus based on the common-core convictions of the Reformers.

A product of German Pietism* and American Puritanism,* Samuel Simon Schmucker was the preeminent Lutheran educator and theologian of the mid-nineteenth century.

Schools, Protestant Day. Since the mid-1960s, fundamentalist* and evangelical* Protestants* and their churches, few of which are affiliated with mainline* denominations,* have been founding so-called Christian day schools or fundamentalist academies at a remarkable rate. Some ten thousand of these schools have been established, with a cumulative current enrollment of approximately one million students (kindergarten through twelfth grade). These independent institutions, which emphasize the Bible, moral absolutes, spiritual growth, mastery of basic subject matter and varying degrees of separation from contemporary culture, currently account for more than two-thirds of the Protestant day schools in the U.S., and their enrollment amounts to one-fifth of the total number of students in private schools.

By the 1960s the evangelical strain in America's civil religion* had been largely superseded by the more secularistic Enlightenment* theme, a factor that perhaps helps explain the rapid growth of Christian day schools among evangelical Protestants.

See also PRAYER IN PUBLIC SCHOOLS.

Schwenkfelders (The Schwenkfelder Church). Followers of the sixteenth-century spiritualist reformer, Caspar Schwenckfeld von Ossig (1489-1561). Schwenckfeld initially embraced the Lutheran* Reformation but eventually broke with his friend Luther and other reformers, primarily over Christology* and the nature of the Lord's Supper.* Although Schwenckfeld did not wish to organize a church, small, informal conventicles developed, one eventually finding refuge in colonial Pennsylvania (1734).

Scofield, C(yrus) I(ngerson) (1843-1921). Bible conference* speaker and defender of dispensational* premillennialism.* While in his late thirties, Scofield experienced an evangelical* conversion.* Soon becoming active in ministry, he served as the pastor of a Congregational* church in Dallas (1882-1895), founded the Central American Mission (1890) and wrote *Rightly Dividing the Word of Truth* (1888), which established him as a leading defender of dispensational premillennialism.

In 1895 Scofield left Dallas for Northfield, Massachusetts, where he became involved in the Northfield conferences,* having already become a regular participant in the Niagara conferences.* In 1909 his Scofield Reference Bible* was published by Oxford University Press, which soon became the most widely received defense of dispensational premillennialism. In 1914, with Lewis S. Chafer,* he founded the Philadelphia School of the Bible.

Scofield's influence on the evangelical*/fundamentalist* movement of the early twentieth century was enormous. Not only did he contribute to the infrastructure of evangelical societies, but his writings defined that segment known as dispensational premillennialism.

Scofield Reference Bible. A highly influential study Bible providing a dispensational* premillennialist* interpretation of Scripture. The Scofield Reference Bible was edited by C. I. Scofield,* a lawyer and Congregational* minister. The work was published in 1909 by Oxford University Press, expanded in 1917 and revised in 1967. Scofield believed that the Bible, when interpreted literally, was clear in its divisions and plans for Jews, Gentiles and the church. For example, he argued that the division of law and grace was so distinct "that Scripture never, in any dispensation, mingles these two principles."

Scopes Trial. The trial of John T. Scopes in 1925 in Dayton, Tennessee, for teaching the biological evolution of humans. With the backing of the American Civil Liberties Union, Scopes confessed to having taught the banned views. At his trial the ACLU defense team was led by famed trial lawyer and religious skeptic Clarence Darrow. The fundamentalists* countered with William Jennings Bryan.*

The highlight of the trial was Darrow's cross-examination of Bryan as an expert on the Bible. Bryan's difficulties at answering some of Darrow's village-atheist questions made him vulnerable to further press ridicule. Scopes was convicted, but his conviction was reversed on a technicality by a higher Tennessee court. Bryan died in Dayton a few days after the trial, and the press declared a rout of fundamentalism, an image that has long stuck in the popular imagination.

See also CREATION SCIENCE; DARWINIAN EVOLUTION AND THE AMERICAN CHURCHES.

Scott, Orange (1800-1847). Methodist* minister, abolitionist* and founder of the Wesleyan Methodist Church.* Scott became a successful revival* preacher and a widely known presiding elder* within the Methodist Episcopal Church.* However, his open support of the antislavery movement caused his popular support to diminish.

In the General Conference of 1840 his delegation failed to restore the early Wesleyan doctrine opposing slavery to the *Discipline* of the Methodist Church. Consequently, he withdrew from the Methodist Episcopal Church in 1842 and became the first president of the Wesleyan Methodist Church.

Scott, Peter Cameron (1867-1896). Founder of the Africa Inland Mission.* Scott had the vision of a chain of mission stations stretching from eastern to central Africa. In 1895 he and his first missionary party sailed for East Africa, where he died the following year.

Scott, Walter (1796-1861). Early leader of the Restoration movement.* In 1821 Scott met Alexander Campbell,* a man in whom he recognized a kindred spirit. In 1826 Scott moved to Ohio to open an academy and that same year began attending the meeting of the Mahoning Baptist Association. Later Scott became an evangelist for the association. Known for his dynamic speaking ability, Scott never missed an opportunity to preach* and evangelize and is said to have converted over a thousand persons a year for over a period of three decades.

For his forty years of service and leadership, Scott is recognized as one of the founding fathers of the Restoration movement.

Scottish Presbyterians in America. While English Puritan* immigration* to New England in the early seventeenth century gave American Presbyterianism* its earliest churches, the influx of Scottish and Scotch-Irish immigration rapidly changed the shape of the colonial church. Tensions surfaced after 1700 as New England Puritan-style Presbyterians were quickly outnumbered by the Scotch-Irish, who generally held stricter conceptions of Presbyterian church government* and subscription to the Westminster Confession.* A compromise was effected between the two groups with the approval of the Adopting Act* of 1729.

Divisions in Presbyterian groups in Scotland were perpetuated in America, including those representing the Covenanter and Seceder traditions.

Scottish Realism. Eighteenth-century Scottish philosophy influential in nineteenth-century American Protestantism.* Common Sense philosophy, or Scottish Realism, was the most influential intellectual tradition shaping American Protestantism between the late 1700s and the Civil War.*

Within America, Scottish Realism first gained prominence at the College of New Jersey* during the presidency of John Witherspoon.* Overall, Scottish Realism imparted to nineteenth-century Protestants a supreme confidence in their abilities to apprehend and defend the truth.

See also PRINCETON THEOLOGY.

Scroggie, William Graham (1877-1958). Scottish minister and author. Scroggie held pastorates at London, Halifax, Sunderland and Edinburgh. From 1933 to 1937 he traveled to North America and worldwide as an evangelist and Bible teacher, promoting the themes of the Keswick* deeper life movement.

Scudder, Ida Sophia (1870-1959). Raised in India, Scudder was the daughter of Dr. John Scudder, one of a long line of Scudder medical missionaries to India who served under the Reformed Church in America.* She established a medical complex at Vellore which included a clinic, a hospital and the Christian Medical School (1918).

Scudder, John, Sr. (1793-1855). Medical missionary to Ceylon and India. Scudder was the first American foreign medical missionary, leaving for Ceylon in 1819 under the American Board of Commissioners for Foreign Missions.* There he founded a hospital and several schools. In 1835 Scudder moved to Madras, India, where he established one of the first medical missions in India.

See also SCUDDER, IDA SOPHIA.

Seabury, Samuel (1729-1796). First bishop of the American Episcopal Church.* Seabury gained notoriety for his writings (under the pseudonym A. W. Farmer) opposing American independence.

After failing to gain consecration in England as a bishop in 1783, Seabury was consecrated in 1784 by Scottish bishops. Not until 1789 were Seabury and the Connecticut church fully integrated into the organization of the Episcopal Church. For the rest of his ministry Seabury worked at organizing the Episcopal Church in both Connecticut and Rhode Island.

Seamands, Earl Arnett (1891-1984). Methodist* missionary to India. Seamands served with distinction in the South India Annual Conference as engineer, pastor, evangelist and superintendent from 1919 until his retirement in 1957. There he was responsible for the construction of over 175 churches.

Second Blessing. A term used primarily in Holiness* groups for the sanctification* experience. Looking back to John Wesley,* proponents teach that believers can and should seek a second spiritual experience after being converted.* In Holiness circles it is common for believers to point to a time they were converted and a time they were sanctified (or received the "second blessing").

See also PERFECTIONISM; SANCTIFICATION.

Second Great Awakening. The term *Second Great Awakening* refers to a diverse series of religious revivals* that took place in the U.S. beginning in the latter years of the eighteenth century. As in the Great Awakening* of the 1730s and 1740s, Protestant* activists mounted aggressive evangelistic* campaigns intended to offer salvation* to the unchurched, convince skeptics of the truths of Christian faith and extend the effects of Christianity over the nation.

The two Awakenings differed in their scope and their theology. The first was largely confined to New England and the Middle Colonies, whereas the Second Awakening knew hardly any boundaries. In the First Awakening, George Whitefield* and Jonathan Edwards* preached a distinctly Calvinistic* gospel; in contrast, many ministers of the Second Awakening leaned decisively toward theological Arminianism.*

Revivalism on the American Frontier. Beginning in 1800, camp meetings* became prominent. In 1801 Barton Stone* led the famous revival in Cane Ridge,* Kentucky, which lasted nearly a week and may have included as many as twenty-five thousand participants. Methodist* and Baptist* circuit riders* traversed the South and Southwest, building hundreds of churches and several new denominations.

The New England Phase of the Second Awakening. Timothy Dwight* at Yale,* Lyman Beecher* and Asahel Nettleton* played key roles. Beecher and Nettleton originally opposed Charles Finney,* wanting to protect New England from unchecked enthusiasm. To Nettleton's dismay, however, Beecher abandoned his opposition to Finney and the frontier evangelists and embraced the new revivalism at the New Lebanon Conference* of 1827.

"The Burned-Over District." Over the course of several years Finney refined a set of "new measures" explicitly designed to win Christian converts. Finney's work, centered in upstate New York, was not confined to evangelism alone. Under his and others' leadership, abolition* leagues, temperance* societies, missionary* programs and a host of other voluntary* organizations were formed in an effort to bring the salutary effects of Christian faith to citizens in antebellum America.

See also FRONTIER RELIGION; GREAT AWAKENING; REVIVALISM.

Sect. Sociologically, a minority religious group previously tied to another, more churchly, religious organization. Sects are characterized by strong allegiance to the group and its teachings, a protest orientation, strict adherence to standards and a tendency to be antisacerdotal.

See also CULT.

Secular Clergy. A term for ordained* Catholic* priests not belonging to a religious order,* society or congregation. The designation *secular* emphasizes that the service rendered is in the world.

Secular Humanism. A nontheistic worldview based on the belief that humanity is of ultimate importance. Humanism usually refers to a philosophy that emphasizes the importance of humanity in this life. There long have been Christians and other theistic humanists. Secular humanism is distinguished from these views in its atheism or agnosticism, hence leaving the development of humanity as the ultimate value. Such views, although anticipated by Enlightenment* skeptics (who nonetheless were mostly deists*), became common only after the mid-nineteenth century.

Secular humanists typically have emphasized the values of human freedom, especially freedom from restrictive or irrational religious traditions, and for educated inquiry leading to development of human potentials, rationally based values and a just society.

Secularism, Secularization. *Secularism* denotes a religious commitment to this world, or anything within it, as ultimate. *Secularization* refers to a transformation of the way in which a people's traditional religion relates to their social and intellectual life.

In North America, *secularism* indicates that people have taken the affairs and things of the world as the basis and goal of life and that they are indifferent, or opposed, to the message and ministrations of the church. The secularist ethos appears most prominently in the public school systems, the megacorporations and the entertainment media of the U.S. and Canada.

Secularization sometimes means the process which is turning a Christian society into a merely secular society. Beginning in the 1950s, countless voices noted a monumental shift in the U.S. and Canada toward the marginalization of the church and of Christian ethics* in economic, educational and political affairs.

Seiss, Joseph Augustus (1823-1904). Lutheran* minister and author. Seiss was pastor of St. John's Church in Philadelphia (1858-1874), then the largest English-speaking Lutheran congregation in America. In 1874 he founded the Church of the Holy Communion, Philadelphia, pastoring it thirty years until his death in 1904.

Selyns (Selijns), Henricus (1636-1701). Dutch Reformed* minister in New York. Selyns served two tours of duty in New York, first as minister to the Dutch churches on Long Island (1660-1664) and then as senior minister in New York City (1682-1701). Selyns corresponded frequently with Cotton Mather* in New England.

Seminary, Catholic Diocesan. The Council of Trent (1545-1565) framed legislation in 1563 creating the seminary to provide a program for training diocesan, or secular, priests under the authority* of the bishop of the diocese.* The first Catholic seminary in the U.S. was established at Baltimore in 1791 by priests of the Society of St. Sulpice (Sulpicians).*

Up to the 1880s the American Catholic community had depended heavily on immigrant priests, despite local seminary activities. The desire to create a clergy from the American-born sons of Catholic immigrants* and to improve the standards of seminary training were major concerns of the American bishops at the Third Plenary Council of Baltimore* (1884). The bishops established a graduate school, at first offering theology only to priests, which opened in 1889 at Washington, D.C., as the Catholic University of America.*

The locus of authority for seminaries shifted in the early twentieth century when the Holy See embarked on a policy of imposing greater control on Catholic life to meet the challenges of modernity. This control was demonstrated in the condemnation of theological modernism* in 1907 and the imposition of an oath against modernism on seminary faculties in 1910.

Vatican II* was a turning point for the Catholic seminary. The council's "Decree on Priestly Formation" directed each national hierarchy to devise its own program of seminary education within broad guidelines. After consultation with seminary educators, the American bishops issued in 1971 their *Program of Priestly Formation* to guide diocesan seminaries and the seminaries of religious orders, the reforms of which conform the seminary to contemporary professional practices. The program introduced pastoral field education and ecumenical* activities that were new to the Catholic seminary.

See also EDUCATION, PROTESTANT THEOLOGICAL.

Seminary, Protestant. *See* EDUCATION, PROTESTANT THEOLOGICAL.

Semple, Robert Baylor (1769-1831). Baptist* minister and denominational leader. Deeply committed to missions, education and denominational service, Semple was active in several societies devoted to these ends, and in 1814 he participated in the founding of the Triennial Convention,* the first national organization of Baptists. He served as its president from 1820 to 1831.

SEND International. A nondenominational evangelical* foreign missionary agency. During World War II* some Christians among U.S. military personnel stationed in the Pacific caught an ambitious vision for the evangelization of Asia. After the war this led to witnessing campaigns in the Philippines and Japan and, in 1947, to the establishing of the Far Eastern Gospel Crusade

(FEGC).

In 1971 Central Alaskan Missions merged with FEGC, which changed its name in 1981 to SEND International.

Seneca Falls Woman's Rights Convention (July 19-20, 1848). A convention held to discuss the social, civil and religious rights of women. In 1840 Elizabeth Cady Stanton* and Lucretia Mott* agreed on the need for a woman's rights convention, which they helped organize in 1848. Three hundred persons met at Seneca Falls, New York, to discuss eighteen grievances modeled on the Declaration of Independence. Over a hundred persons signed the documents, thus inaugurating the woman's rights movement in the U.S.

Separate Baptists. Baptists* originating among the pro-revivalists of the Great Awakening.* During the Great Awakening many Baptist churches split into revivalistic* (Separate) and antirevivalistic (Regular*) factions. The first identifiable Separate Baptist church resulted from such a schism (1743) in Boston. Many revivalistic New Light* Congregationalists also became Separate Baptists.

Highly evangelistic* and moderately Calvinistic,* Separate Baptists allowed women to preach and disdained a learned or paid ministry and confessionalism.*

Separates. A Congregational* separatist movement especially prominent in New England during the period 1735-1750. The Separates were strict Congregationalists who desired to return to the original New England ideals of the seventeenth century. Standing for spontaneous, zealous piety,* they maintained that the established New England Congregational churches—clergy and members—were formal, cold and dead. Over one hundred congregations were formed in New England as a result of splits from the established churches.

Separatism. Separatism has been a dominant theme of American fundamentalists* in the twentieth century. During the fundamentalist-modernist controversy* of the early decades, the question of separatism came to the fore, especially as it related to the apparent growth of apostasy in mainline* denominations.* Apostasy was defined as the conscious denial of key biblical truths (e.g., the deity of Christ). Fundamentalists argued for the need to separate from theological liberals* and worldly living.

Serra, Junipero (1713-1784). Franciscan* missionary to Mexico and the Southwest. Serra served in Mexico from 1750 until 1767. In 1767 he was appointed *presidente* for Baja California. He joined an expedition to Alta (present-day) California, which in 1769 established Mission San Diego. In a region he described as a veritable paradise, he oversaw construction of mission compounds, helped plant flourishing fields around them and saw some six thousand Native Americans baptized.*

See also MISSIONS TO NORTH AMERICA, SPANISH.

Session. Presbyterian* decision-making body at the congregational level, composed of the minister(s) and lay elders* of a local congregation.

See also CHURCH GOVERNMENT: PRESBYTERIAN; PRESBYTERY.

Seton, Elizabeth Ann Bayley (1774-1821). Founder of a religious community and Roman Catholic saint. In 1808, at the urging of William Valentine Du Bourg,* Seton opened a girls' school in Baltimore. There she began one of the first American religious communities, the Sisters of Charity* of St. Joseph, professing vows in 1809. Mother Seton and her companions moved that year to Emmitsburg, where the new community opened schools, nursed the sick and assisted the needy. She later sent sisters to Philadelphia and New York. She was canonized, the first American-born saint, in 1975.

See also RELIGIOUS ORDERS, WOMEN'S.

Settlement House Movement. An urban social reform movement of the late nineteenth and early twentieth centuries. The first settlement house, Toynbee Hall, was established in 1884 in London when Samuel Augustus Barnett, the vicar of St. Jude's Parish (Anglican), invited several university students to "settle" and live among the poor of East London. The idea was transferred to New York in 1886. In 1889 Jane Addams* visited Toynbee Hall and, with her friend Ellen Gates Starr,* returned to Chicago, where they established Hull House as a social settlement house after the British model.

In 1891 there were only six settlements in the U.S., but by 1910 the number had grown to over four hundred.

Seventh-day Adventists. Christian denomination* originating in the U.S. which emphasizes Saturday as the sabbath* and the imminent Second Coming of Christ. Seventh-day Adventism arose out of the nineteenth-century Millerite movement, which had predicted Christ's Second Coming about 1843-1844. Through the work of James and Ellen White* and Joseph Bates, a small group coalesced in the Northeast around what became distinctive Adventist doctrines.

In 1860 the name *Seventh-day Adventist* was chosen, and a year later the Michigan churches formed a conference. By 1900 there were missionaries on every continent, creating educational, publishing and medical institutions.

In the twentieth century, the primary growth of Seventh-day Adventism has been outside the U.S., although Americans have continued to maintain primary influence within the church. In 1985, out of a worldwide membership of 4.6 million, the U.S. accounted for over 640,000 members.

Seventh-Day Baptists. Baptists* differing from mainstream seventeenth-century Baptists primarily in their strict sabbath* observance. Their first known congregation was Mill Yard Church, London (1653). The earliest American church emerged in 1671 when Stephen Mumford and seven Sabbatarians left the Newport (R.I.) Baptist Church. Initial centers of growth were Rhode Island, Philadelphia and New Jersey. During the nineteenth century they lost many members to the Seventh-day Adventists.*

Sewall, Samuel (1652-1730). Colonial politician and magistrate. Sewall served on the Governor's Council of the Commonwealth of Massachusetts (1691-1725). In 1718 he was appointed chief justice of the Superior Court of Massachusetts. For many years he was secretary and treasurer of the Society for the Propagation of the Gospel in New England.*

Seybert, John (1791-1860). First constitutional bishop of the Evangelical Church. Converted* at an Evangelical Church camp meeting* in 1810, Seybert soon became an itinerant* preacher in Pennsylvania and Ohio. In 1839 he was elected bishop, the first Evangelical leader to hold that post since the death of the founder, Jacob Albright,* who died in 1808, prior to the constitutional organization of the denomination.

See also REVIVALISM, GERMAN-AMERICAN.

Seymour, Richard (fl. c. 1600). Anglican* priest. The first practical attempt to establish an English Colony on the coast of Maine was made by the Plymouth Company in 1607 (the year of Jamestown's settlement). Seymour, the first Episcopal* priest known to have ministered in New England, led the settlers in worship.

Seymour, William Joseph (1870-1922). Pentecostal* leader. After meeting Charles Parham* in Houston, Seymour embraced Pentecostal teaching. In 1906 he began preaching in a black Holiness* mission in Los Angeles but was removed when he taught that tongues* speech always evidences Spirit baptism. He continued with cottage meetings, and then large interracial crowds forced the moving of the services to 312 Azusa Street.*

Seymour's activities in Los Angeles between 1906 and 1909 effectively launched American Pentecostalism.

Shakers. Millenarian* communal society. The Shakers (officially, the United Society of Believers in Christ's Second Appearing, or Millennial Church) originated in England as a loose union of enthusiasts under the leadership of Quakers* Jane and James Wardley. The group did not fare well until visionary member Ann Lee* led a band of eight Shakers from Manchester to New York in 1774. After initial persecution and financial difficulty, the group organized as a community, gained members through missionary* efforts, grew and prospered.

The Shakers are most remembered for their functional and gracefully simple furniture and handicrafts, and the lively Shaker worship,* which included original hymns* and dances. Shaker lifestyle was simple, efficient and regulated, but not austere.

Some nineteen communities were formed, from Maine to Florida and west to Indiana and Kentucky. At its height, there may have been five thousand members.

Sharing. A verbal expression of ideas or experiences directly related to some aspect of the Christian life. In contemporary evangelical* usage, the term refers to what God has said or done, to what he is doing or to what believers wish him to do. For example, Christians may share the gospel, share their testimonies, share in Bible study* or share prayer requests.

See also RELATIONAL THEOLOGY.

Shaw, Anna Howard (1847-1919). Methodist* minister and suffragist.* Shaw was licensed* to preach* by the Methodist Church and did so for a living while attending Albion College and Boston University's School of Theology. In 1880 she was ordained by the Methodist Protestants. She was a successful lecturer for the suffrage movement.

Shaw, Knowles (1834-1878). Christian Church (Disciples of Christ)* evangelist. By the early 1860s Shaw had become known throughout the frontier, from Michigan to Texas, as the Singing Evangelist. Before each service he played the organ for a half hour and sang gospel hymns.* His methods heralded a new style of evangelism* later embellished by Billy Sunday.*

Shedd, William Greenough Thayer (1820-1894). Calvinist* theologian and church historian. The greater part of Shedd's career was devoted to teaching, including at Union Theological Seminary* (New York) from 1863 to 1891. One of the eminent theologians of his era, Shedd exhibited literary gifts, historical interests and a speculative spirit in his many works. As an Old School Presbyterian,* he opposed any revision of the Westminster* Standards and remained a great advocate of Baconianism and its inductive reasoning.

Sheen, Fulton J. (1895-1979). Roman Catholic archbishop, preacher and author. Sheen taught theology and philosophy at the Catholic University of America* from 1926 until 1950. During these years, Sheen attracted widespread attention and won a national reputation as an eloquent and dynamic orator and preacher. He became a pioneer of the electronic church* as the featured speaker on NBC radio network's *Catholic Hour Broadcasts.* His radio audience was estimated at four million listeners. For decades, Sheen was prominent as an outspoken opponent of Marxism, speaking often of the crisis of the times and the worldwide struggle between the forces of communism* and Christianity. His television program, *Life Is Worth Living* (1951-1957), reached approximately thirty million viewers each week on the ABC network.

The key to his legendary success on radio and television was his appeal to Americans of all faiths, Catholic and non-Catholic alike. His talks were a blend of common sense, patriotism and

Christian ethics. Having dedicated his life to "working out a Christian response to the challenge of the times," he succeeded admirably as the greatest evangelist in the history of the Catholic Church in the U.S.

Sheil, Bernard James (1886-1969). Auxiliary bishop of Chicago, founder of the Catholic Youth Organization.* Sheil founded the Catholic Youth Organization in 1930. He was active also in the organization of CIO industrial unions, the formation of the Back of the Yards Neighborhood Council and the fostering of interracial harmony.

Sheldon, Charles Monroe (1857-1946). Congregational* minister and Social Gospel* reformer. In 1899 Sheldon accepted what turned out to be a lifelong call to the newly formed Central Congregational Church in Topeka, Kansas. A tireless pastor and reformer, Sheldon strove throughout his life to improve the living and working conditions of others.

Sheldon was a folk theologian who focused on the person and work of Jesus, frequently using the medium of story. He is best known as an author of some fifty books and hundreds of articles in religious and secular periodicals as well as poems, hymns* and plays. His most famous work is the bestseller *In His Steps* (1897).

Shepard, Thomas (1605-1649). Puritan* minister. In 1636 Shepard accepted a call to be pastor of the church at Newtown (Cambridge), where his ministry flourished. He was a participant in the founding of Harvard College* at Cambridge in 1636 and took a keen interest in efforts to evangelize Native Americans, particularly the missionary* work of his friend John Eliot.*

Shepard was one of the most accomplished preachers among the first-generation New England Puritans.

Shepherding Movement (Discipleship Movement). A movement, primarily within charismatic* Christianity, emphasizing strict discipleship* and submission to church leaders. It received its initial impetus in 1970 from four prominent Florida charismatics—Derek Prince, Don Basham, Bob Mumford and Charles Simpson—who felt a need for greater accountability among Christians. They encouraged dozens of churches to affiliate with their Christian Growth Ministries and adopt their pyramidlike structure.

Abuses quickly appeared, which eventually led to the four founding teachers' dissolving their covenant with one another in 1986.

Sherrill, Lewis Joseph (1882-1957). Presbyterian* professor of Christian education. Sherrill taught at the Presbyterian Theological Seminary of Kentucky (Louisville) (1925-1950) and Union Theological Seminary,* New York (1950-1957). Emphasizing the value of Christian nurture, he developed a view of Christian education which moved away from evangelical* revivalism.*

Shields, T(homas) T(odhunter) (1873-1955). Canadian Baptist* pastor and fundamentalist* leader. In 1910 Shields became pastor of the largest Baptist church in Canada at the time, Jarvis Street in Toronto. Shields served there for the rest of his life, developing a reputation as the Canadian Spurgeon.

He is best known for his leadership of fundamentalists in the Baptist Convention of Ontario and Quebec, who resisted (largely unsuccessfully) the appointment of theological liberals* at the denomination's McMastor University.

See also BAPTIST CHURCHES IN CANADA.

Shiloh. *See* Sandford, Frank.

Shinn, Asa (1781-1853). Methodist* preacher, theologian and ecclesiastical reformer. A self-educated man, Shinn is remembered as a powerful orator and a writer whose work reveals a keen mind. His *Essay on the Plan of Salvation* (1813) was the first systematic theology* written by an American Methodist. Shinn is most famous for his role in the reform movement that resulted in the formation of the Methodist Protestant Church (1830).

Shoemaker, Samuel M(oor) (1893-1963). Episcopal* clergyman. Shoemaker became rector of Calvary Episcopal Church in New York (1925-1952). His ministry there was marked by a social conscience leading to establishment of the Calvary House in New York and its mission to down-and-outers and alcoholics. Shoemaker assisted the founders of Alcoholics Anonymous in formulating their Twelve Steps. Later he was rector of Calvary Episcopal Church, Pittsburgh (1952-1962).

Shuler, Robert Pierce (1880-1965). Fundamentalist* Methodist* minister and radio preacher. Shuler pastored several churches in Virginia and Tennessee until 1906, when he moved to Texas. There he pastored until 1920, when he moved to Trinity Methodist Church in Los Angeles. Witty and contentious, Shuler saw the church grow to five thousand members in the 1930s. Shuler was perhaps the strongest voice for fundamentalism within Methodism and strongly opposed the union of the Southern and Northern Methodist Churches.

Shuster, George Nathan (1894-1977). Catholic* author, editor and educator. Among the highlights of Shuster's career were his stints as professor of English at Notre Dame until 1924; his writing for and then editing of *Commonweal* until 1937; and his service as president of Hunter College, New York (1940-1961). A man of intellectual vigor, courtesy and principle, Shuster authored twenty-one books on literature, politics, education and religion.

Sign of the Cross. A devotional* or liturgical* gesture tracing the cross. While the sign was originally restricted to the forehead, the large sign of the cross made on forehead, breast and shoulders seems to have been introduced into the monasteries in the tenth century. Currently in the West the crossing of the chest is from left to right, and from right to left in the Eastern church.

Silliman, Benjamin (1779-1864). Yale* scientist. Converted* in the Yale College revival* of 1802, Silliman was recruited by Timothy Dwight* to develop the "doxological" aspects of science and thereby counter the perceived threat of French scientific infidelity. Silliman, widely regarded as the dean of antebellum American science, taught geology, chemistry and mineralogy at Yale for decades.

SIM International. Evangelical* foreign mission* agency. SIM International was formed in 1982 in a merger of the Sudan Interior Mission (SIM, founded in 1893) and the Andes Evangelical Mission (originally the Bolivian Indian Mission [BIM]), founded in 1907. The SIM came into being in response to the need of unevangelized millions who lived some distance away from the more easily accessible coastal regions of Africa. The BIM arose from a burden for the Indian peoples of the Andes.

From difficult physical beginnings on two con-

tinents, SIM International unites today some nine thousand congregations in twenty-one countries, with a total church community approaching four and a half million persons. Mission membership in 1995 numbered 1,899 full-time persons from at least twenty-three countries, 1,305 from the U.S. and Canada.

Simonton, Ashbel Green (1833-1867). Presbyterian* missionary to Brazil. Simonton traveled to Brazil under the Presbyterian Board of Foreign Missions in 1859. Settling in Rio de Janeiro, he founded the first Presbyterian church, presbytery and Protestant seminary in that country.

Simpson, A(lbert) B(enjamin) (1843-1919). Preacher, hymn writer and founder of the Christian and Missionary Alliance.* In 1881, when pastor of a Presbyterian church in New York City, he experienced physical healing* from a weakened heart, received baptism* by immersion and resigned his church. In 1882 he began training classes for workers in his new Gospel Tabernacle.* The next year his congregation incorporated, formed their own missionary society and began the New York Missionary Training College (now Nyack College and Alliance Theological Seminary).

In 1887 Simpson organized the Christian Alliance and the Evangelical Missionary Alliance at the Methodist* Campgrounds in Old Orchard, Maine. The two alliances joined in 1897 to form the Christian and Missionary Alliance.

Simpson authored over 175 hymns, including "Yesterday, Today, Forever" and "What Will You Do with Jesus?"

Simpson, Matthew (1811-1884). Bishop of the Methodist Episcopal Church.* Simpson was deeply involved in the bitter conflicts between Methodists regarding abolition.* An ardent opponent of slavery, he sought to repudiate the Plan of Separation, by which the Northern and Southern churches had agreed to divide constituencies and assets in 1844, and his aggressive onslaughts on slavery after 1848, as editor of the *Western Christian Advocate,* spread his fame widely.

Sin. Theologians differ over whether sin should be defined as a human privation of good or as purposeful disobedience of God's holy law, but orthodox* theologians are agreed that sin is the human condition that separates humanity from

God, who is holy. The reality of sin is one of the basic foundations of biblical Christianity, and the doctrine of sin has played an important role in defining each of the major theological traditions of Christianity.

Both Catholics* and Protestants* have traditionally maintained some form of a doctrine of original sin—the state of sin that has pervaded humanity since the Fall. Catholic theologians have generally followed Augustine in understanding original sin to be a "privation of good" or the loss of sanctifying grace. The Protestant Reformers, in contrast, spoke of sin as a perversity encompassing human nature in its entirety, including the mind and will.

Augustinian Views. In American theology, the most notable discussions of sin have taken place in the Reformed tradition. Within both the Lutheran* and Reformed* traditions, many theologians have built on the Augustinian tradition and adopted a view of the consequences of Adam's first sin that may be termed *immediate* or *antecedent imputation.* The essence of this view is that all people are born already under God's wrath, that their lack of original righteousness results in inherent sin in which all human capacities are corrupted, and that sinful actions, being a result of those corrupted faculties, are not the ground for condemnation.

Arminian Views. Theologians within the Arminian* tradition took their cue neither from Augustine or Placaeus, but from John Wesley* and Isaac Watts (1674-1748). The "prince of Wesleyan* theologians," Richard Watson (1781-1833), provides a paradigm for understanding this perspective. Watson advocated a view of the consequences of Adam's first sin known as *deprivation* or *liability.* In essence, Watson perceived the result of Adam's sin, not as imputed guilt and inherent corruption, but simply as a lack of original righteousness. This original deprived state inevitably leads to voluntary depravity because preventative assistance was removed in Adam.

Modern Views. In the twentieth century the concept of sin has been radically reinterpreted. The current theological consensus seems more in harmony with Augustine's fifth-century opponent Pelagius than with any other source. Pelagius suggested that the relationship between Adam and his progeny was neither organic nor negative; it was environmental, sociological and psychological. The injury of Adam's sin to the race was mere-

ly that it set a bad example or precedent that humans have emulated.

Sinclair, Upton Beall (1878-1968). American writer and advocate of reform. Sinclair's novel *The Jungle* (1906) brought national acclaim for its exposé of Chicago machine politics and the unsanitary processing of meat products. His thoughts on religion were expressed in *The Profits of Religion* (1918), Sinclair's manifesto on the evils of the institutional church, which he believed the rich and powerful had turned into a haven of privilege and hypocrisy.

Sister. A woman who publicly professes simple vows or promises, usually obedience, chastity and poverty, in a religious community of women. Most congregations of sisters are Catholic.*

Sisters of Charity. This title includes numerous Catholic sisterhoods of diverse origin, many of whom follow the tradition of St. Vincent de Paul. Presently, the Daughters of Charity of St. Vincent de Paul include a worldwide membership of more than thirty-two thousand.

Many women's congregations in the U.S. are called Sisters of Charity. The first, the Sisters of Charity of St. Joseph, was founded by Elizabeth Ann Seton* in 1809 at Emmitsburg, Maryland. By 1830 they were in Philadelphia, New York, Baltimore, Boston and St. Louis, where they pioneered in education, health care and social service.

Sisters of Mercy. Roman Catholic* congregations of women religious.* The title *Sisters of Mercy* (RSM) includes all those communities of women religious who trace their lineage from, and claim as their founder, Catherine Elizabeth McAuley, whose Institute of Mercy opened in Dublin, Ireland, in 1831. Historically involved in education, health care and various forms of social work, in 1847 Sisters of Mercy established the first permanent hospital west of the Allegheny Mountains in Pittsburgh.

Six-Principle Baptists. An Arminian* Baptist tradition maintaining the ordinance* of the laying on of hands.* Six-Principle (from the six points of Heb 6:1-2) Baptists appeared at an early date as minorities among the first Baptist churches in America—Providence and Newport—most of whose members were Calvinistic.* By 1652 they had become the majority at Providence. By the

1670s several Rhode Island Six-Principle churches had formed what perhaps was the first Baptist association in America.

Skelton, Samuel (1584-1634). First pastor of the Congregational* church of Salem, Massachusetts. An organizer of the Massachusetts Bay Company, Skelton and his family helped lead the first settlement in 1629. He and Salem colleague Francis Higginson,* who became the church's teacher, organized the church strictly along Congregational lines.

Skinner, Tom (1942-1994). Evangelist and African-American evangelical leader. During his teen years Skinner, the son of a Baptist* minister in New York City, led a double life of youth leader in church and gang leader on the streets of Harlem. After a dramatic conversion experience Skinner left the gang and began to evangelize on the streets of Harlem. He was ordained in 1959 by the National Baptists.* In 1961 he was instrumental in forming the Harlem Evangelistic Association, and in 1964 he started a radio ministry and Tom Skinner Radio Crusades, Inc., which eventually became Tom Skinner Associates. By the time of his death he was a widely known evangelist, speaker, writer and leader of African-American evangelicals. Among his books are his autobiography, *Black and Free* (1968), and *How Black Is the Gospel?* (1970).

Slattery, Charles Lewis (1867-1930). Episcopal* bishop. Slattery served churches in Minnesota (1896-1907), Massachusetts (1907-1910) and New York (1910-1922). In 1927 he became bishop of Massachusetts. He was a sensitive pastor and an outstanding scholar.

Slattery, John Richard (1851-1926). Catholic missionary to Southern African-Americans and modernist.* Slattery was rector of St. Joseph's Seminary in Baltimore (1888-1902), which he founded to train priests for the African-American missions in the U.S. He published widely on the "Negro question" and came to be recognized as the leading Catholic spokesperson on it, refusing to separate evangelization from the overall amelioration of African-Americans.

The Vatican's 1899 censure of Americanism,* added to his disillusionment with church support for the missions, precipitated a religious crisis from which he never recovered.

Slavic Gospel Association. An evangelical* mission agency ministering to Russians and Russian immigrants. Initially called the Russian Gospel Association, the Slavic Gospel Association was organized in 1934 by Peter Deyneka Sr. to evangelize* Russian-Slavic émigrés and minister to the church in Russia. By the mid-1980s Slavic Gospel Association personnel were broadcasting on ten international radio stations.

Small, Albion Woodbury (1854-1926). Professor of sociology. When the University of Chicago was founded in 1892, Small was invited to head the sociology department, one of the first in the country. His understanding of social science was informed by his religious beliefs.

Smalley, John (1734-1820). New Divinity* Congregational* minister. In 1757 Smalley became pastor of the Congregational church at New Britain, Connecticut, a position he held for sixty-three years. Smalley exerted a wide influence through his writings and the training of theological students in his home, one of whom was Nathanael Emmons.*

Smith, Alfred Emanuel (1873-1944). Governor of New York and first Roman Catholic* presidential nominee. After being elected four times as governor of New York, Smith was chosen in 1928 as the Democratic nominee for president. His religious affiliation, opposition to the Eighteenth Amendment, and urban and immigrant origins alarmed many Protestants,* supporters of Prohibition, and rural and small-town dwellers, and he eventually lost the election decisively.

Smith was a "devoutly pious" Catholic, almost childlike in his faith, who believed strongly in the separation of church and state.*

Smith, Amanda Berry (1837-1915). African-American evangelist and missionary to India and Africa. From 1870, Smith was a full-time evangelist and a familiar figure on the Holiness* camp meeting* circuit. She then was a missionary to India (1879-1881) and Liberia (1882-1889). Returning to the U.S. in 1890, she preached on the east coast and then, beginning in 1895, devoted herself to an orphanage she founded in Chicago.

Smith, Benjamin Mosby (1811-1893). Presbyterian* seminary professor, church statesman and advocate of public education. A person of irenic disposition and blessed with personal charm, Smith was a moderate among Southern Presbyterians during Reconstruction, willing to discuss reconciliation with the North, but not on terms which would require Southern apology.

From 1871 to 1882 Smith was superintendent of public education in Prince Edward County, Virginia.

Smith, Gerald Birney (1868-1929). Liberal* theologian. Smith taught at the University of Chicago* Divinity School from 1900 until his death. Deeply influenced by Albrecht Ritschl (1822-1889) and Wilhelm Herrmann (1846-1922), Smith was a theological liberal who emphasized the centrality of human experience and was critical of authoritarianism of any sort. He developed what he called empirical theology.*

Smith, Gerald L. K. (1898-1976). Disciples of Christ* minister, politician and nativist.* Smith became a major figure in the fundamentalist* far-right movement during the 1940s and 1950s. Most of Smith's early political rhetoric was aimed at President Roosevelt's New Deal. After World War II,* Smith increasingly alienated himself from mainstream American politics and expressed a paternalistic segregationism, along with an explicit anti-Semitism.

Smith, Hannah Whitall (1832-1911). Holiness* writer and speaker. Hannah married Robert Pearsall Smith* in 1851, and during the 1858 urban prayer meeting revivals,* she and her husband committed their lives to God. Some years later Robert experienced an emotional "baptism of the Holy Spirit";* Hannah had a similar experience in 1867.

The Smiths held meetings promoting Holiness in the U.S., and from 1873 to 1874 they were popular speakers at Holiness meetings in England, the immediate predecessors to the Keswick conferences.* Hannah's *Christian's Secret of a Happy Life* (1875) was influential in its time and remains a popular devotional guide today.

See also HIGHER CHRISTIAN LIFE; SANCTIFICATION.

Smith, Henry Boynton (1815-1877). New School* Presbyterian* theologian and historian. From 1850 to 1874 Smith taught church history and systematic theology at Union Theological Seminary* in New York City. He exercised his greatest influence through his efforts to reconcile the principles of Edwardsean theology and German-inspired philosophy for an American audience. As a theologian, he disagreed sharply with Horace Bushnell's* dismissal of theology as an enterprise irrelevant to faith.

Smith, Henry Preserved (1847-1927). Presbyterian* minister, Old Testament scholar and educator. Smith was professor of Old Testament at Lane Theological Seminary in Cincinnati (1877-1893). His scholarship led him to accept critical conclusions about the Old Testament which many conservatives in the Presbyterian Church (U.S.A.) regarded as an attack upon the infallibility of the Bible. He ultimately was tried for heresy,* found guilty of denying the verbal inspiration and inerrancy* of the Bible, and suspended from the ministry (1892). In 1915 he became librarian at New York's Union Theological Seminary.*

Smith, Hezekiah (1737-1805). Baptist* pastor. Smith was influential in the founding of Rhode Island College, which later became Brown University.* In 1766 he became pastor of a Baptist church in Haverhill, Massachusetts, which he served for forty years. He became a leader of Baptists in the region and a strong proponent of missionary* endeavors, including leadership in establishing eighty-six new churches.

Smith, John "Raccoon" (1784-1868). Kentucky farmer and early Restoration movement* preacher. Influenced by an encounter with Alexander Campbell* in 1824, Smith resolved to "preach the Ancient Gospel" and became a Baptist* farmer-preacher in Kentucky. Smith was present at the 1831 Christmas meeting in Georgetown, Kentucky, when the Stone and Campbellite movements merged.

Smith, Joseph, Jr. (1805-1844). Founder of the Church of Jesus Christ of Latter-day Saints. In Palmyra, New York, part of the famous "burned-over district,"* Smith claimed to encounter God the Father and Jesus Christ in human form, who commissioned him to restore the "true church" and "lost priesthood" to earth. He also said an angel, Moroni, showed him an ancient book, which he translated using magical stones and published in 1830 as *The Book of Mormon.*

In April 1830 he founded his new church, and his followers became known as Mormons.* In

1832 local hostility forced him and his followers to move to Kirkland, Ohio, and then in 1838 to Nauvoo, Illinois. In 1844 his practice of polygamy led to his arrest and murder. His death provided his church with a martyr and created the basis for the transformation of an American folk religion into a world faith.

Smith, Joseph Henry (1855-1946). Methodist* evangelist and theologian. Smith was inspired by William Taylor's* "faith missions" and went to Georgia (1875-1881) as a missionary. He joined the National Campmeeting Association for the Promotion of Holiness* in 1883 and served as an evangelist by conference appointment from 1902 to 1923.

Smith, Oswald J(effrey) (1889-1986). Pastor and missionary statesman. In 1928 Smith began "The People's Church," a large independent mission-oriented church in downtown Toronto. A powerful preacher, Smith was a leading figure in Canadian fundamentalism* and wrote thirty-five books.

Smith, Robert Pearsall (1827-1899). Holiness* evangelist and writer. In 1851 Robert married Hannah Whitall,* with whom he served as popular exponent of the "higher Christian life" movement. Although it was Mrs. Smith who first testified to a personal faith and wrote about it in *The Christian's Secret of a Happy Life* (1875), Robert eventually "claimed the blessing" himself during a camp meeting* at Vineland, New Jersey. Smith's greatest contribution to the revival* movement was his involvement in Holiness and revival meetings in England, Germany, France and Switzerland.

Smith later suffered a nervous breakdown, and after 1876 neither he nor his wife was further involved in revivals.

Smith, Rodney ("Gipsy") (1860-1947). British evangelist. In 1876 Smith was converted to evangelical* Christianity and publicly confessed Christ at a Primitive Methodist chapel. Feeling called to the ministry, he soon began preaching, becoming known as Gipsy Smith. In 1889 he made the first of approximately fifty trips to the U.S., during which he held evangelistic meetings in major churches and assembly halls.

Smith, Samuel Stanhope (1750-1819). Pres-

byterian* minister and educator. Smith was educated at the College of New Jersey (Princeton University*) and studied for the ministry under the college's president, John Witherspoon.* After ministering in Virginia and helping to found Hampden-Sydney Academy, Smith returned to Princeton in 1779 to join its faculty as professor of moral philosophy. Smith helped rebuild the college after the Revolutionary War and succeeded Witherspoon as president of the college in 1795. Smith was a leading proponent of Scottish common sense realism.* His emphasis on scientific inquiry and moral philosophy, as well as his progressive approach to Presbyterian theology,* aroused the suspicion and controversy that led to his resignation from Princeton in 1812.

Smith, Wilbur M(oorehead) (1894-1976). Presbyterian* fundamentalist* educator. From 1937 to 1947, Smith taught at the Moody Bible Institute. In 1947 he helped design Fuller Theological Seminary* and then joined its faculty.

Smith was a very popular Bible lecturer and a tireless author. He wrote over two dozen books, several hundred short magazine pieces and pamphlets, and thirty-eight annual volumes (1934-1971) of *Peloubet's* Select Notes on the International Bible Lessons for Christian Living*.

Smith, William (1727-1803). Anglican* minister and educator. In 1755 Smith became provost of a newly created college, Academy and Charitable School of Philadelphia, the forerunner of the University of Pennsylvania,* to which he gave twenty-five years of distinguished service. Smith was an ardent Anglican minister who played an important part in the establishment of the Protestant Episcopal Church.*

Smyth, Newman (1843-1925). Congregational* minister and theologian. Smyth became an early proponent of the New Theology* and in books such as *The Religious Feeling* (1877) and *Orthodox Theology Today* (1881) argued that the new approach could better respond to the modern era than the older New England theology. He labored in vain for the union of the Congregational and Episcopal* churches.

See also MUNGER, THEODORE THORNTON.

Smyth, Thomas (1808-1873). Southern Presbyterian* minister. Ordained* in 1831, Smyth became pastor of Second Presbyterian Church,

Charleston, South Carolina, where he remained the rest of his life. He was famous as a scholarly pastor, amassing one of the largest private collections of theological books in the U.S.

Snake Handling. The religious practice of handling deadly vipers as a demonstration of special anointing by God. The practice (supported by reference to Mk 16:18) is today largely limited to particular Pentecostal* churches in the rural Appalachian region. Snake handling first made its appearance among Pentecostals in about 1913. By the late 1930s it was widely practiced and had moved into some midwestern states. Considered a public hazard, between 1936 and 1953 it was prohibited by law in Alabama, Georgia, Kentucky, North Carolina, Virginia and Tennessee.

Social Creed of the Churches. A social manifesto principally subscribed to by mainline* American churches. Developing from a statement adopted at the first meeting of the Federal Council of Churches* (1908) and accepted by several Protestant* denominations* and the YMCA* and YWCA,* the Social Creed is a classic statement of the goals of the Social Gospel.*

Social Ethics. *Social ethics* is typically contrasted with *personal ethics* as a way of marking off two complementary areas of ethical concern. The distinction is a useful one, even though it is sometimes difficult to draw clear boundary lines between the two areas of investigation. Abortion* is certainly a social issue; but it is also an intensely personal matter for many women. Phenomena such as gambling, pornography, racial prejudice and the use of sexist language have a similar status; each can be viewed as an item that is both personal and social in nature. The two areas are found on a spectrum of moral deliberation, and they shade into each other. But a topic can be said to fall properly within the domain of social ethics if it deals with issues of moral value—rightness, goodness, virtue—as they arise in group or institutional contexts. Thus, when a question about sexual behavior or race relations is considered from the perspective of social policy, or when it is viewed in a group or institutional context, it has clearly become an appropriate topic for social ethics.

Social ethics in North America is a vitally important area of discussion for the Christian community, one that has increasingly become a matter of dialogue with the traditions of the past and with contemporary Christians who represent a variety of theological persuasions and cultural contexts. In this setting many central theological concerns of the past continue to be of pressing importance, even though they may appear in new forms in these newer situations. The issue of where the ultimate authority resides in moral decision-making will always loom large for those Christians who seek to know and to do the will of the biblical God in all of life, including the complex spheres of social interaction.

See also BIOETHICS; EUTHANASIA; PACEM IN TERRIS; PACIFISM; PEACE MOVEMENT, CATHOLIC; POLITICAL THEOLOGY; QUADRAGESIMO ANNO; RERUM NOVARUM; SOCIAL GOSPEL MOVEMENT.

Social Gospel Movement. The term *Social Gospel* came into prominence only at the beginning of the twentieth century, when it was used primarily to refer to a movement among North American Protestants* to relate biblical and theological insights to the need for social reform.

Early leading figures in the emergence of social Christianity in the U.S. included such ministers as Washington Gladden,* Josiah Strong* and Charles M. Sheldon* and also prominent members of the laity such as Richard T. Ely* and Jane Addams.* By the turn of the century the term *Social Gospel* became especially attached to the more moderate, reformist elements in the churches, most of which were influenced by liberal* theology and progressive social thought. The outstanding prophet of the movement became Walter Rauschenbusch,* whose book *Christianity and the Social Crisis* (1907) thrust both him and the Social Gospel into national prominence.

In the prewar years it became a highly visible, controversial movement that gained considerable influence, especially in Congregational,* Episcopal,* Baptist,* Methodist* and Presbyterian* churches. The Social Gospel called for cooperation among the churches; its influence was strong in the formation of the Federal Council of the Churches of Christ in America* in 1908.

Theologically, Social Gospel leaders looked to the historical Jesus, believing he could be known through biblical scholarship and declaring that his principles were reliable guides for personal and social life in any age. At the center of his teaching they identified the doctrine of the kingdom of God,* which they interpreted as a historical possibility that would soon come to earth in some fullness, bringing with it social harmony and ending gross injustices.

In Canada, the Social Gospel became a significant movement which combined indigenous as well as British and American influences. The Canadian movement actually had a wider impact on the numerically much smaller nation than did its sister movement in the U.S. No major Protestant body escaped its impact, and its political influence was more direct.

After World War I* the optimism that had characterized the early thrust of the Social Gospel began to fade. Its liberal theological basis was challenged both by conservatives who stressed the premillennialist* interpretation of the kingdom of God* and by neo-orthodox* realists who criticized it as overly idealistic and naive. Yet it remained an important force in many denominations and in interdenominational movements until midcentury and beyond.

Socialism, Christian. During the latter half of the nineteenth century, a contemporary form of Christian socialism appeared in the Christian Labor Union* (1872-1878) and in such diverse personalities as Washington Gladden,* William Dwight Porter Bliss* and Frances Willard.*

In the first two decades of the twentieth century, socialism reached the peak of its popularity in the U.S. in the presidential campaigns of Eugene Debs. Christian socialism died during the 1920s, only to be revived by Reinhold Niebuhr* in the Fellowship of Socialist Christians* (1931-1948) and its periodical, *Radical Religion*. In Canada, where the New Democratic Party provides a more prominent socialist presence, Christian socialism has been an even more significant factor. The opposition of the Catholic Church* to socialism, also prominent in the U.S., has evaporated in recent years as statements of the Socialist International and the Vatican* have become more and more similar.

Society for Propagating the Gospel Among the Indians and Others in North America. Missionary* society. Founded in Boston in 1787, the society is the oldest continuing missionary organization in the Americas, though in recent times its emphasis has shifted more to educational endeavors. Its primary function has been to act as a supporting agency for missionary and educational works among Native Americans, but it has also aided works among other disadvantaged or unchurched peoples in America.

See also MISSIONS TO NATIVE AMERICANS, PROTESTANT.

Society for the Promotion of Christian Knowledge. An Anglican* missionary* society supplying libraries for clergy and parishes* overseas. English evangelizing in the colonies began early, with the founding of the Society for the Propagation of the Gospel in New England* (1649).

In 1696 Thomas Bray* was appointed as commissary to Maryland, an office designed to promote the church in the colonies. Bray founded the Society for the Promotion of Christian Knowledge to publish and distribute significant theological works. The society continues its work in the late twentieth century.

Society for the Propagation of the Gospel in Foreign Parts. Anglican* missionary* society. The Society for the Propagation of the Gospel was founded in 1701 by Thomas Bray* to achieve two objectives: (1) supply a well-qualified ministry for Anglican parishes* in the English colonies and (2) provide the vanguard of the Anglican outreach to Native Americans. During the eighteenth century the society was active in the North American colonies, admirably supporting the Anglican cause and establishing some three hundred new churches.

Society for the Propagation of the Gospel in New England. A colonial mission* agency. In 1649 the English Parliament chartered the Society for the Promoting and Propagating the Gospel of Jesus Christ in New England, which was the first formal overseas Christian mission agency. A handful of American Puritan* evangelists relied on the support of the society, the most notable being John Eliot,* whose expansive views of Christianizing Native Americans prevailed.

At the time of the Revolution, the mission channeled its resources into reaching Native Americans in Canada, where it still supports the education of Native Americans.

Society of Biblical Literature, The. A North American association of biblical scholars. At the society's founding in 1880, there were thirty-two male charter members, mostly professors; all were Protestants* from the Northeast. By the turn of the century, Jews, Catholics* and women had been inducted. Papers at the annual meetings, later published in the *Journal of Biblical Literature,* focus on philology, exegesis, archaeology, text and translation, and literary criticism. In 1994 there were approximately six thousand members from over eighty countries.

Society of Jesus. Catholic religious order.* The Society of Jesus, better known as the Jesuits, is the largest Roman Catholic* religious order for men both in the world and in the U.S. Founded by St. Ignatius of Loyola and approved by Pope Paul III in 1540, the Jesuits soon spread to most of the Catholic countries of Europe. By the end of the sixteenth century, Jesuit missionaries were working in India, China, Japan and most of Latin America.

Jesuit roots in the U.S. go back to 1566, when three Jesuits tried to land on the Florida coast and were killed by Native Americans. The explorations of Father Jacques Marquette* down the Mississippi River and of Father Eusebio Kino* in the Southwest are well known.

The most important Jesuit ministry in the U.S. has long been education. Currently there are nineteen Jesuit universities and nine colleges in the U.S. Worldwide the Jesuits publish 1,400 periodicals. Jesuits such as the late Karl Rahner* and Bernard Lonergan* are esteemed theologians.

Society of St. John the Evangelist. Anglican* monastic order. Also known as Cowley Fathers, the society was the first officially recognized Anglican monastic order. Ideologically, its origin can be traced back to the Oxford movement.* The order, which encourages a mystical* spirituality* based on discipline and prayer, became established in Boston in 1870.

Society of St. Vincent de Paul. An international Roman Catholic-sponsored association of laypersons seeking to help the poor. From its founding in Paris in 1833, the group has engaged in nonpartisan charitable acts that are not restricted to Catholics.

The society came to North America in 1845 and quickly made its mark. "Vincentians" founded the first Catholic institutions for children, struggled for just wages for workers and were among the first Catholics to recognize and cooperate with efforts of other Christians to contribute to the public welfare.

Society of the Woman in the Wilderness. *See* KELPIUS, JOHANNES.

Sockman, Ralph Washington (1889-1970). Methodist* preacher. Sockman was the senior minister of the Madison Avenue Methodist Episcopal Church from 1917 until his retirement in 1961. A frequent traveler, Sockman preached and spoke around the country, yet never once in forty-four years did he fail to deliver a scheduled Sunday sermon at Christ Church. In his concern to communicate the relevance for Christian faith to his day, Sockman was greatly influenced by his fellow liberal* pulpiteer Harry Emerson Fosdick.* Sockman served as president of the Methodist Board of World Peace (1928-1960), wrote a weekly newspaper column and for twenty-five years was the voice of the National Radio Pulpit.

Sojourners Community. A community of Christians committed to a life of radical discipleship. The community had its origins with a group of seminarians at Trinity Evangelical Divinity School (Chicago, Illinois) who in the fall of 1971 started publishing a magazine entitled the *Post-American* under the leadership of Jim Wallis. It subsequently moved to Washington, D.C., and changed its name to Sojourners. The community seeks to live out a pattern of discipleship characterized by a sharing of material resources, identification with the poor and commitment to the values of social peace and reconciliation.

Sola Scriptura. A Latin phrase (literally "by Scripture alone") describing the Protestant* theological principle that Scripture is the final norm in all judgments of faith and practice. Initially used by Protestant theologians as a polemical device in their debates with Roman Catholics,* *sola scriptura* soon became a fundamental tenet of laypeople as well.

In America this principle was manifest in the New England Puritan* "Bible Commonwealth," as well as the primitive* or Restorationist* impulse which sought to bypass the centuries of Christian institutional, liturgical and doctrinal development and restore the primitive church in the New World.

Sommer, Peter Nicholas (1709-1795). Colonial Lutheran* pastor. Sommer was a staunch proponent of Lutheran orthodoxy* and opponent of Pietism,* insisting on the acceptance of all the

Lutheran confessional writings and not just the Augsburg Confession.*

Sorin, Edward Frederick (1838-1893). Founder and first president of the University of Notre Dame.* In 1842 Sorin established the University of Notre Dame near South Bend, where he served as president (1842-1865) and first chairman of its board of trustees (1865-1893).

By the 1860s Sorin had come to believe that European Catholicism had become a sterile, ossified, moribund faith. Much like American Catholics Isaac Hecker* and Orestes A. Brownson,* he concluded that the future of Catholic Christianity lay not in the Old World but in the New.

Apart from founding Notre Dame, Sorin founded or administered six other Catholic institutions of higher education in America.

Soul Winning. Revivalistic* and evangelistic* term referring to the activity of making converts to Christianity. Books by R. A. Torrey* and England's C. H. Spurgeon seem to be the first written specifically on "soul winning."

South America Mission. A nondenominational mission agency founded to evangelize unreached tribal peoples. The missionary organization that would become the South America Mission (SAM) originated in 1914 out of the vision of Joseph A. Davis, who established his initial station in Paraguay. By the 1940s the mission consisted of almost one hundred workers operating out of thirty stations and reaching thirty tribes.

Southeastern Baptist Theological Seminary. Southern Baptist Convention* seminary. The seminary was established in 1951 on the campus of Wake Forest College, Wake Forest, North Carolina. When the college moved to Winston-Salem, North Carolina, in 1956, the seminary remained on the campus. By 1986 the student body had grown to over 1,200 students. The seminary's character was altered in a conservative direction as a result of a fundamentalist* takeover of the board of trustees in 1987. In 1992 Paige Patterson became president.

Southern Baptist Convention. Largest Baptist* body in the U.S. The Southern Baptist Convention (SBC), organized in 1845, comprises fifteen million baptized believers in about thirty-eight thousand churches in all fifty states of the U.S., making it the largest Protestant* denomination* in the U.S.

Theologically, most Southern Baptists are evangelicals* and subscribe to the authority of the Bible. They baptize* by immersion believers who publicly profess faith; they hold that neither baptism nor the Lord's Supper* convey sacramental* grace. A heavy evangelistic* and missionary emphasis has helped to shape the denomination into one of the most aggressive missionary bodies in Christendom. In their doctrine of salvation, Southern Baptists can be generally classified as modified Calvinists.*

Although not a member of the World Council of Churches, the Southern Baptist Convention took the lead in bringing disparate Baptist unions and conventions together into the Baptist World Alliance* in 1905. Southern Baptists jealously guard the autonomy of the local church. Yet the principle of cooperation commands the loyalty of most Southern Baptists. Congregations send messengers to area associations and state conventions, each of which is an autonomous body but closely interrelated.

See also THE BAPTIST CHURCHES IN THE U.S.A.

Southern Baptist Theological Seminary. Southern Baptist Convention* seminary. The Southern Baptist Theological Seminary opened its doors in 1859 in Greenville, South Carolina. In 1877 it moved to Louisville, Kentucky. Its history has included some notable Southern Baptist figures, such as James Petigru Boyce,* John Albert Broadus,* Basil Manly Jr.,* William H. Whitsitt,* E. Y. Mullins* and John R. Sampey.* During the Southern Baptist fundamentalist* controversies of the 1980s and 1990s, fundamentalists established control over the seminary's board of trustees. In 1993 Albert Mohler was named president. In 1992 the seminary enrolled more than 2,000 students.

Southern Christian Leadership Conference (SCLC). An organization advocating nonviolent social change, particularly in the area of civil rights.* Formed in 1957 in the aftermath of the Montgomery (Ala.) bus boycott of 1955-1956, the SCLC elected Dr. Martin Luther King Jr.* as its first president. The guiding principle of the SCLC was nonviolence, derived in part from the tactics of Mohandas K. Gandhi in India, but in a broader sense from the religious faith of its members. The SCLC is best known for its leadership of nonviolent campaigns in Albany (1962), Birmingham

(1963), St. Augustine (1964) and Selma (1965).

King's death slowed the momentum both of the nonviolent movement and SCLC. His successor, Ralph David Abernathy (president from 1968 to 1977), continued the basic program of nonviolent direct action.

Southern Christianity. Recognized as a distinctive religious region in North America, the South is dominated by Protestantism*—particularly conservative or evangelical* forms of it. Baptists* are by far the largest and most influential tradition within both white and African-American populations.

The Span of Popular Southern Christianity. What truly distinguishes the South is the span of popular forms of Christianity. It extends as far as the Presbyterians* on the classical end but knows no boundaries on the innovative or radical end. That is to say, fundamentalists,* Restorationists,* independents, and Holiness* and Pentecostal* churches and people are plentiful and, while regarded by the majority as having gone too far with their zeal, are viewed as basically on the right track. In the substantial middle are the major Baptist denominations and the Methodists.*

Roman Catholicism,* despite the early settlement of the Spanish and the French in the lower South, has always been weaker in the region than anywhere else in the nation. In the late twentieth century, active immigration from other regions has expanded centers of Catholic strength to many places.

The Changing Face of Southern Christianity. In the late 1980s the region continued to reflect the strength and cultural dominance of the popular Southern religion forged around 1830 by the Baptists and Methodists—and to a degree by the Presbyterians also. But the span had widened and extended leftward to include several million Pentecostal, Holiness and fundamentalist people who were no longer confined to the margins of the society or its religious life. On the more traditional end, it stretched to embrace Catholics, Lutherans and Episcopalians, as well as the liberal bodies. The center of gravity remained well to the left of the center of the traditional Christian heritage and the pull was, if anything, somewhat more to the left.

A "limited options culture" is about as concise a characterization of historic Southernness as any. Homogeneity with respect to ethnicity, politics and forms of commerce has been joined by religion in Southern society and culture from the Old South down to World War II.* Since then, the racial desegregation of the region has driven a wedge into this homogeneity. In addition, since the 1950s diversity in population and in economic and political life have made a heavy imprint.

Southern Presbyterians. *See* PRESBYTERIAN CHURCH IN THE UNITED STATES.

Southern Sociological Congress. A congress called by Governor Ben Hooper of Tennessee to meet in Nashville in May 1912 for the purpose of addressing the "social, civic and economic problems" of sixteen Southern states. The congress met until 1920, when it moved its headquarters to Washington, D.C., and changed its name to the Southern Cooperative League of Education and Social Service. The congress was an example of government, social agencies and the church working together.for social betterment.

Southwestern Baptist Theological Seminary. Southern Baptist Convention* seminary. The roots of the seminary are traced to the religion department of Baylor University, which in 1905 became Baylor Theological Seminary. The seminary separated from the university in 1908 and in 1910 moved from Waco to Fort Worth, Texas. In 1925 its ownership was transferred from the Baptist General Convention of Texas to the Southern Baptist Convention. In 1991 enrolled over 4,000 students in its main campus and extension programs.

Spalding, John Lancaster (1840-1916). Bishop of Peoria. Spalding became curate of the cathedral* in Louisville (1865), attended the Second Plenary Council at Baltimore* (1866), organized the first African-American parish* in Louisville (1869) and became chancellor of the diocese* (1871). He also led in the Catholic Prohibition movement.*

In 1877 Pope Pius IX* named Spalding to the see at Peoria, Illinois. Active in educational circles, in 1898 he opened a boy's school, the Spalding Institute, and he was instrumental in the promotion of and the founding of the Catholic University of America.*

Spalding, Martin John (1810-1872). Bishop of Louisville, archbishop of Baltimore and Catholic* apologist.* Spalding served his church in Kentucky from 1834 to 1864, when he became archbishop of Baltimore. He earned national fame as a lecturer and writer of Catholic apologetics* and history. As bishop of Louisville, his pastorals on the sacraments,* marriage and education attracted national attention, as did his personal and written opposition to the anti-Catholic and nativist* attacks of the 1850s. As priest and bishop, Spalding reached out to African-Americans, established orphanages and charities, and introduced several religious orders* to Kentucky.

Throughout his life Spalding argued that education was the foundation of faith and civic responsibility. To that end, he built parochial schools,* promoted the American colleges in Louvain and in Rome* and urged the creation of a national Catholic university.

Spangenberg, Augustus Gottlieb (1704-1792).

Moravian* bishop and assistant to Count Nikolaus L. von Zinzendorf.* Spangenberg joined the Moravians in 1733, becoming Zinzendorf's assistant. In 1735 Spangenberg led Moravian colonists to Georgia. He then moved to Pennsylvania in 1736, where he remained until 1739. In 1744 he was consecrated* bishop and put in charge of the settlement at Bethlehem, Pennsylvania (1744-1748). In 1752 he led Moravians in settling the Wachau district of North Carolina.

Spanish-American War and the American Churches.

When Cuban insurgents rebelled against Spanish rule in 1895, most Americans sympathized with the revolutionaries. Christian leaders supported intervention in Cuba through diplomatic means. American churches rather overwhelmingly opposed both U.S. attempts to annex Cuba or filibustering as a means of settling the conflict.

In 1898 after the sinking of the *Maine,* the religious press, unlike the yellow press, counseled patience pending full investigation. After the official U.S. declaration of war in April 1898, the churches strongly supported the war effort. Some Christians viewed it as a holy crusade. Victories against the Spanish at Manila, Philippines, and Santiago, Cuba, it was said, were signs that God was on the American side.

Most churches agreed with the decision that Cuba should be given independence, while Puerto Rico should be annexed. Opinion favored annexing the Philippines, for churches saw an opportunity to extend the gospel to a "barbarous" people.

Speer, Robert Elliott (1867-1947).

Evangelist and Presbyterian* missions* leader. From 1891 until his retirement in 1937, Speer served as a lay* secretary of the Presbyterian Board of Foreign Missions in New York. Advocating the unique authority of Christ amid the religions of the world, his book *The Finality of Christ* (1933) was widely influential. Speer was a leader in the Federal Council of Churches*—elected as its president in 1920—as well as in the Foreign Missionary Conference of North America.*

Spellman, Francis Joseph (1889-1967).

Catholic* archbishop of New York. Spellman excelled in his personal connections and his abilities in diplomacy, administration and finance. One of these connections in the late 1920s was with Eugenio Pacelli, who later became Pope Pius XII* (1939-1958). Within months of his election, Pacelli appointed Spellman archbishop of New York.

During World War II,* Spellmen had an important role as the Vatican's chief contact with the U.S. government. At war's end, he nearly became Vatican Secretary of State, and Pacelli named him a cardinal in 1946.

Spellman took controversial public stands on birth control,* movie censorship and public aid to private schools. His American nationalism was matched by the ardor of his anticommunism.

During a period known for the "Romanization" of the Catholic hierarchy in the U.S., Spellman, for better or worse, succeeded, where his Americanist* predecessors had failed, in bringing Catholics into the American mainstream. He was one of the most politically influential churchmen in U.S. history.

Spirit Baptism. *See* BAPTISM IN THE SPIRIT.

Spiritual Director.

A person whose ministry is to guide a fellow believer into deeper Christian experience. Normally spiritual direction takes place on an individual or small-group basis. This office is most widely recognized in the Roman Catholic* and Anglican* traditions.

Spirituality.

The goal of *Catholic** spirituality is the profound union of the individual with God in prayer,* something which can never be earned or achieved by human effort, but which is a pure gift from God. The predisposing conditions for and obstacles against such a union, as well as the means and methods conducive to it are all subjects of Catholic spiritual writings throughout the centuries. Since Catholics believe that God is accessible to the individual, Catholic spirituality is always incarnational, sacramental,* integrative and unitive. Until recently, American Catholic spirituality reflected Western European traditions that developed after the Council of Trent (1545-1563) rather than any specific American adaptations.

For *Orthodox** Christians spirituality is a way of living and thinking centered on the mystery of the risen Christ as encountered through personal prayer, the reading of Scripture, the sacraments* and devotional practices of the Orthodox Church. Its basis is the experience of new creation in Christ by the power of the Holy Spirit and its goal is *theosis* (deification or divinization), understood as glorification by participation in the eternal resurrection light commonly shared by the Holy Trinity. Orthodox spirituality is closely related to Orthodox piety,* from which it cannot be empirically separated because both are at once deeply rooted in the same worship,* theology and life of the Orthodox Church as a living community guided by the Holy Spirit.

The spirituality of *Protestants** generally emphasizes the priority of God's saving grace—the spiritual life begins with God justifying believers and granting them assurance of the forgiveness of sins. Two issues tend to dominate Protestant spirituality: the proper role of human effort and divine grace in attaining personal holiness,* and the proper goal of spirituality in this life. There is a great breadth of Protestant traditions, including spirituality those we may designate as Anglican,* Lutheran,* Reformed,* Pietist,* Quaker,* Anabaptist,* Puritan,* Wesleyan,* Evangelical,* Pentecostal and Charismatic,* and African-American.

Sprague, William B(uell) (1795-1876). Presbyterian* minister, author and biographer. Sprague ministered at the Second Presbyterian Church in Albany, New York (1829-1869). His greatest literary achievement was his nine-volume *Annals of the American Pulpit* (1857-1869).

Spring, Gardiner (1785-1873). Presbyterian* minister. In 1810 Spring was called as pastor to Brick Church (old First Presbyterian Church) in New York City, where he served for sixty-three years.

Spring was very active in denominational politics. He is perhaps best known for the so-called Spring Resolutions, presented at the General Assembly of 1861, which affirmed that churches should "do all in their power to strengthen, uphold, and encourage the federal government." By adopting these resolutions, the Old School* Assembly broke its traditional silence on political issues, leading to the withdrawal of the Southern group.

Springfield Will and Testament (1804). Document dating the beginning of the Christian Churches in America. Prepared by five Presbyterian ministers in Ohio who in 1803 had formed the Springfield Synod, this document dissolved the synod, expressing a concern for Christian union.

See also RESTORATION MOVEMENT.

Stam, Elizabeth Alden Scott ("Betty") (1906-1934). Missionary martyr. Growing up in China as the daughter of missionary parents, Betty returned in 1931. She married John Stam in 1933. Three months after the birth of a daughter, she and John were murdered by communist bandits. Their deaths inspired others to give their lives and resources to missions.

Standing Conference of Canonical Orthodox Bishops in America. An association of Orthodox* jurisdictions in the U.S. The Standing Conference (SCOBA) was established in 1960 by the primates of eleven jurisdictions, with Archbishop Iakovos* of the Greek Orthodox Archdiocese (Ecumenical Patriarchate) serving as the chairman. From the start, SCOBA was essentially a voluntary association of the major jurisdictions, designed to foster cooperation. SCOBA is presently composed of nine jurisdictions, which contain the majority of five million Orthodox in the U.S.

Stanton, Elizabeth Cady (1815-1902). Women's rights leader. Elizabeth's marriage to abolitionist* Henry Stanton brought her into close contact with antebellum reform movements, including the nascent women's rights movement nurtured by Lucretia Mott.* In 1848 she helped to organize the first women's rights convention in Seneca Falls,* New York. She became the chief architect of the ideology of the women's rights movement.

Her fifty-year friendship with Susan B. Anthony* was the main impetus for Stanton's increasingly public role as orator and leader of the movement. Stanton's religious pilgrimage took her from the revivalism* of Charles G. Finney* to Unitarianism* and skepticism.

Stanton, Robert Livingston (1810-1885). Presbyterian* minister, church statesman, educator and writer. An adviser to Lincoln* on Southern affairs, Stanton emerged during the Civil War* as a leader of the strongly nationalistic midwestern faction of Presbyterian clergymen. Stanton's election as moderator of the 1866 Old School* General Assembly* (St. Louis) signaled the triumph of radical forces in the church, especially in regard to postwar policies for Southern congregations.

Starr, Ellen Gates (1859-1940). Cofounder of Hull House. Starr spent 1877 at Rockford (Ill.) Seminary, where she became a close friend of Jane Addams.* While on a trip to Europe together, schoolteachers Starr and Addams conceived Hull House, which they founded in 1889. Starr also battled child labor and belonged to the National Women's Trade Union League.

Stations of the Cross. A representation of Christ's progressive suffering from condemnation by Pilate to burial in the tomb, erected for devotional purposes. The origin of this practice lies with pilgrims to the Holy Land who traced the steps of Jesus along the *via dolorosa* in Jerusalem. The fourteen stations, which combine biblical information with pious legend, can be set up in churches or other areas.

Stearns, Lewis French (1847-1892). Congregational* theologian. Stearns taught at Albion College, Michigan (1876-1879) and at Bangor (Me.) Theological Seminary (1880-1892). In the experience of the human Jesus, Stearns believed, one had a way to interpret human suffering and a basis for the liberal Protestant* insistence on the immanence of God and progress in human social development.

Stearns, Shubal (1706-1771). Baptist* separate* in North Carolina. In 1755 Connecticut-born Stearns led a company of fifteen, including his sister and brother-in-law Daniel Marshall,* to Sandy Creek in Guilford (now Randolph) County, North Carolina. Within three years the Sandy Creek Church had planted two sister churches

and formed the Sandy Creek Association. In 1772, Stearns's associates counted forty-two churches and 125 ministers who had arisen from the original Sandy Creek Church.

Stebbins, George Coles (1846-1945). Composer, hymn writer and music evangelist. As music director of Chicago's First Baptist Church, Stebbins became acquainted with George F. Root,* Philip P. Bliss* and Dwight L. Moody.* With James McGranahan and Ira D. Sankey,* Stebbins edited several editions of *Gospel Hymns.* He wrote "Jesus Is Tenderly Calling" and "Take Time to Be Holy."

Steinmeyer, Ferdinand "Farmer" (1720-1786). Colonial Catholic* missionary. In 1752 Steinmeyer arrived in Lancaster, Pennsylvania, where he began his ministry.* In 1758 St. Joseph's Church in Philadelphia became a central base for his mission journeys in nearby states, where he gathered German Catholics into congregations.

Stelzle, Charles (1869-1941). Presbyterian* minister and social reformer. In 1903 Stelzle began a special mission to workers under the auspices of the Presbyterian Board of Home Missions. The project became the Department of Church and Labor in 1906. Stelzle served as superintendent of this agency, the first established by any denomination* primarily to implement social Christianity. Throughout his ministry he maintained that Christianity should be concerned with everyday affairs, and particularly with the lives of working-class people.

Stephan, Martin (1777-1846). Original leader of the Saxon Lutheran* immigrants to Missouri in 1839. In Germany, with earnest preaching,* sensitive counseling and personal magnetism, Stephan attracted many followers, including clergy as well as laity. Increasingly in trouble with civil and church authorities, Stephan and some six hundred followers immigrated to Missouri.

His followers later founded the denomination now known as the Lutheran Church—Missouri Synod.*

Stetson, Augusta Emma (Simmons) (1842-1928). Christian Science* leader and schismatic. Stetson founded the New York City's First Church of Christ, Scientist (1887) and the New York City Christian Science Institute (1891). Her charismatic leadership stimulated the growth of Christian Science. Actions taken in 1902 restricted her official activities, and a heresy trial in 1909 led to her excommunication.

Stevenson, Joseph Ross (1866-1939). Presbyterian* minister and Princeton Seminary* president. Stevenson is best known for serving as Princeton Seminary president from 1914 to 1936—tumultuous years in the school's history. While theologically conservative, Stevenson had an irenic approach toward the presence of liberalism* within Presbyterianism, believing the seminary should serve the entire denomination.*

Steward. The chief overseer of the everyday affairs of a local Methodist* church. Stewards were elected by the charge conference, based on nominations made by the preacher in charge.

By the time of the Evangelical United Brethren and Methodist merger, which formed the United Methodist Church* (1968), the steward's responsibilities had been replaced by various boards and committees.

Stewart, Charles James (1775-1837). Canadian Anglican* bishop. Sensing a definite missionary call to Canada, in 1807, under the auspices of the Society for the Propagation of the Gospel,* Stewart became rector in a village southeast of Montreal. From 1818 to 1826 his ministry under the society was entirely itinerant,* covering many of the settled areas of Lower and Upper Canada (Quebec and Ontario). In 1826 Stewart became the second bishop of Quebec, with oversight for all of Quebec and Ontario.

Stewart, Lyman (1840-1923) and Milton (1838-1923). Fundamentalist* businessmen and philanthropists.* The Stewart brothers, both active Presbyterians* who were involved in oil-related business enterprises, used their resources widely for the support of Christian work. Arising out of their concern about modernism* within American Christendom was their most famous project: the publishing and distribution of *The Fundamentals* (1910-1915).

Stiles, Ezra (1727-1795). Congregational* minister and president of Yale College.* In 1755 Stiles accepted a call as pastor of the Second Congregational Church in Newport, Rhode Island, where he remained until war forced him to evacuate in 1776.

During his presidency at Yale (1778-1795), Stiles raised academic standards and helped reconcile warring factions, allowing the institution to begin to grow from a sectarian college to a university. Stiles was a religious moderate for whom tolerance was a matter of both principle and temperament.

Stillman, Samuel (1737-1807). Baptist* minister. In 1765 Stillman became pastor of First Baptist Church of Boston, a post he occupied for the rest of his life. His forty-two-year pastorate was regarded as a remarkable success. The church was in decline when he arrived, but Stillman's emphasis on evangelism,* combined with a number of successful revivals,* ushered in extended periods of growth and progress.

Stoddard, Solomon (1643-1729). Colonial minister. Stoddard was the second pastor of the Congregational* church in Northampton, Massachusetts. The town was small in 1672 when he arrived, but by the 1720s his strong leadership was felt throughout the Connecticut Valley, and the church grew to be the largest outside of Boston.

In 1727 Stoddard presided over the calling of Jonathan Edwards,* his grandson, to an associate pastorate in Northampton. When Stoddard died two years later, his well-trained congregation was prepared for repeated harvests which would be known as the Great Awakening.*

Stoever, John Casper, Jr. (1707-1779). Pioneer Lutheran* pastor. Beginning soon after his arrival in Pennsylvania in 1728, Stoever served a large number of parishes* as pastor, in most places beginning their first record books, which list hundreds of infant baptisms,* confirmations, marriages* and funerals* under his ministry. After 1735 he ministered also in Maryland and Virginia.

Stone, Barton Warren (1772-1844). Leader of the "Stonite" wing of the early Restoration movement.* After preaching a few years for the Presbyterian* congregations at Cane Ridge* and Concord, Kentucky, Stone was ordained* in 1790.

In 1801 Stone planned a gathering at Cane Ridge, which became a camp meeting* attracting thousands. Under criticism from the synod over his revival methods, Stone and several other revivalists in 1804 organized their own body and then soon after dissolved it, agreeing to be known as "Christians only" and to follow only the Bible.

In 1831 the followers of Stone and of Alexander Campbell* united to form a group that became known as the Christian Church (Disciples of Christ).*

Stone, John Timothy (1868-1954). Presbyterian* minister. Stone was pastor of such prominent churches as Brown Memorial in Baltimore and Fourth Presbyterian in Chicago. His evangelistic* commitment expressed itself in his books and in his support for the YMCA* and Moody Bible Institute.*

Stone, Lucy (1818-1893). Pioneer in the women's rights movement. In 1855 Stone married Henry Blackwell, issuing a protest against the legal disabilities of women and choosing to keep her own name. In 1869 she became head of the American Woman's Suffrage Association and editor of the *Woman's Journal.*

Stonehouse, Ned Bernard (1902-1962). Presbyterian* biblical scholar. Stonehouse was a member of the original faculty of Westminster Theological Seminary, Philadelphia, where he remained until his death. Combining a cordial commitment to Reformed* theology* with breadth of learning, Stonehouse was among the more widely respected conservative New Testament scholars of his day.

Stough, Henry Wellington (1870-1939). Evangelist and founder of the America-Israel movement. In 1901 Stough became an independent evangelist, working under the title of his "Stough Evangelistic Campaigns" (1901-1939). He was associate editor of the periodical *America-Israel Message.*

Stowe, Harriet Elizabeth Beecher (1811-1896). Author. After marrying Calvin E. Stowe in 1836 and bearing seven children, Harriet wrote *Uncle Tom's Cabin,* drawing on earlier experiences in Ohio to depict the evils of slavery. The book was published in serial form in 1852 in the *National Era,* an antislavery newspaper in Washington, D.C. It became an immediate, unprecedented popular success, although its factual inaccuracies as a portrayal of slavery were criticized in both the North and South.

Strachan, John (1778-1867). Educator and first Anglican* bishop of Toronto. Strachan came to Upper Canada (Ontario) in 1799. In 1839 he became bishop of the newly created Diocese of Toronto. He helped found McGill University and Trinity College and was the first president of King's College, later known as the University of Toronto.

Strachan, Robert Kenneth (1910-1965). Director of the Latin America Mission.* An intense, energetic and intellectually restless figure, Kenneth Strachan directed the mission from 1945 to 1965. The mission was then moving toward Latin American control, which was finally achieved in 1971. Strachan's major contribution was Evangelism-in-Depth,* which began in Nicaragua in 1960.

Strang, James Jesse (1813-1856). Leader of Mormon* sect. In 1844, on a visit to the Mormon community at Nauvoo, Illinois, Strang converted to Mormonism. Strang claimed that on the day that Mormon leader Joseph Smith* was killed, June 27, 1844, he was visited by angels who ordained him as the successor to Smith. He also produced a letter, allegedly from Joseph Smith, naming Strang as prophetic successor. A struggle over leadership ensued. Strang and his followers left the main body of Mormons, which was led by Brigham Young, and departed to Voree, Wisconsin. In 1847 Strang moved with his followers to Beaver Island in Lake Michigan, where he established a new Zion, and on July 8, 1850, he was enthroned as king. Dissension within the community eventuated in Strang's assassination and the dispersal of the sect.

Straton, John Roach (1875-1929). Fundamentalist* preacher and social-rights activist. Straton had an outspoken ministry at Calvary Baptist Church, New York City (1918-1929), where he championed Christian fundamentals from the pulpit and founded the Fundamentalist League of Greater New York (1922). He made wide use of the media, including radio broadcasting.

Stringfellow, Frank William (1928-1985). Lawyer, Episcopal* lay theologian and social activist. An adamant supporter of equal rights, Stringfellow was uncompromising in his belief that the gospel demands identification with the disenfranchised of society. His works in ethics and theology are marked by a frequent denunciation of both church and nation for promoting the "collective evils" of racism, sexism, national idolatry and military imperialism.

Throughout the 1960s Stringfellow was a frequent adviser to those who faced criminal charges for resisting the Vietnam War.* He was known for his strong and often vehement espousal of women's ordination.

Stritch, Samuel Alphonsus (1887-1958). Cardinal archbishop of Chicago. In 1930 Stritch became archbishop of Milwaukee. During his years in Milwaukee (1930-1939) he coped with the effects of the Great Depression* by inaugurating a highly successful charity drive.

Stritch was transferred to Chicago in 1940 and in 1946 was elevated to cardinal. He directed a major program of parochial and institutional expansion of the Chicago diocese. He also gave serious attention to the problems of the urban church, working to preserve urban Catholic communities and quietly but firmly dealing with Catholic resistance to African-American admittance in Catholic schools, hospitals and neighborhoods. He was not kindly disposed to ecumenical or interfaith gatherings and prohibited Catholic participation in the World Council of Churches* meeting held in Evanston* in 1954.

Strong, Augustus Hopkins (1836-1921). Northern Baptist* theologian. In 1872 Strong began forty years of service as president and professor of systematic theology* at Rochester Theological Seminary. From about 1885 to 1910, Strong reigned as the most influential Northern Baptist and one of the most influential conservative Protestant* theologians in the U.S.

Throughout his long life Strong endeavored to avoid theological controversy, but by 1916 his apprehension over the havoc that modernism* seemed to be wreaking on the mission* field prompted him to publish *A Tour of the Missions*. The uncharacteristically polemical tone of this volume, coupled with its revelations of theological drift among Baptist foreign missionaries, did more than a little to precipitate the fundamentalist-modernist controversy* in the 1920s.

Strong, James (1822-1894). Biblical scholar. Strong was an expert in biblical and ancient languages and served as professor of biblical literature at Troy University (1858-1863) and later as professor of exegetical theology at Drew Theo-

logical Seminary (1867-1893). Through monumental labor he compiled biblical reference works such as *A New Harmony and Exposition of the Gospels* (1852), *The Exhaustive Concordance of the Bible* (1890) and, with John M'Clintock, edited the *Cyclopaedia of Biblical, Theological, and Ecclesiastical Literature* (10 vols., 1867-1881). He was the author of several biblical studies, including *The Tabernacle of Israel in the Desert* (1888).

Strong, Josiah (1847-1916). Social Gospel movement* leader, expansionist, interdenominationalist. As general secretary of the Evangelical Alliance* (1886-1898), Strong displayed exceptional organizational abilities, setting up three major national conferences devoted to Social Gospel* themes. As he worked for a wider unity among Protestant* churches and missionary* agencies, he played an important part in the formation of the Federal Council of the Churches of Christ in America* (1908).

Strong, Nathan (1748-1816). Congregational* clergyman. Strong was known as a commanding pulpit orator whose later sermons* were often revivalistic* in nature. His interest in evangelism* was further evidenced by his leadership of the Connecticut Missionary Society,* which he helped establish in 1798.

Stuart, George Hay (1816-1890). Philadelphia merchant and evangelical* philanthropist.* When the Civil War* began, Stuart was serving as chairman of the central committee of the vigorously evangelistic YMCA.* He also was chairman of the United States Christian Commission,* for which he collected $6 million and enlisted five thousand volunteers.

In 1869 Stuart accepted an appointment to the Board of Indian Commissioners, where he fought corruption.

Stuart, John (c. 1740-1811). Anglican* clergyman and missionary. In Ontario from 1785, Stuart was the first Anglican missionary (to both whites and Native Americans) in the western settlements. He was chaplain of the legislative council.

Stuart, Moses (1780-1852). Biblical scholar and trinitarian opponent of Unitarianism.* Stuart was professor of sacred literature at Andover Theological Seminary* from 1808 to 1848. An indefatigable scholar, Stuart revolutionized American biblical studies by introducing European biblical studies to America.

In the early 1800s Stuart contributed mightily on behalf of orthodoxy* in New England's tumultuous Unitarian controversy,* championing trinitarian theology against William Ellery Channing* and Henry Ware.*

Stub, Hans Gerhard (1849-1931). Lutheran* pastor, professor and synodic leader. Stub was a professor in several Lutheran institutions in the Midwest and, for two decades, a pastor in Decorah, Iowa. He also was founder and first president of the Norwegian Lutheran Church in America.

Student Foreign Missions Fellowship. An association of college and university students interested in foreign missions. The Student Foreign Missions Fellowship (SFMF) was founded in 1936 to spark interest in foreign missionary service on college campuses. In 1945 it merged with Inter-Varsity Christian Fellowship* (IVCF), becoming the student arm of IVCF on Christian campuses. The national head of SFMF serves as missions director for IVCF.

See also URBANA CONVENTIONS.

Student Volunteer Movement for Foreign Missions. Student voluntary association promoting world missions.* Conceived in 1886, the Student Volunteer Movement (SVM) was formally organized by 1888, with John R. Mott* as chairman and Robert E. Speer* as traveling secretary. The movement's watchword—The evangelization of the world in this generation—challenged students to dedicate their lives to the task of world evangelization. Before its decline after 1920, the SVM stimulated an estimated twenty thousand North American college students to become Christian missionaries.

See also STUDENT FOREIGN MISSIONS FELLOWSHIP.

Stuyvesant, Peter (Petrus) (c. 1610-1672). Dutch soldier and last governor of New Netherland. Stuyvesant's personality was characterized by paternalism, fierce determination, a compulsion for orderly action and an active commitment to traditional institutions—the Dutch Reformed Church, the Orange Monarchy and the Dutch West India Company. He joined the company in 1635, and in 1646 was commissioned director-general of New Netherland, Curaçao, Bonnaire and Aruba.

Stuyvesant governed New Netherland from May 1647 to September 1664, when an invading English naval force compelled him to surrender the colony to the English Duke of York. Although not appreciated for his aristocratic leadership, he brought honest, efficient administration to the stumbling colony, reforming city government in New Amsterdam (later New York City).

Subscription Controversy. Eighteenth-century dispute within the Presbyterian Church.* The controversy concerned whether candidates for Presbyterian ordination* ought to be required to subscribe to doctrinal creeds* or articles of church government.*

In the U.S. in the 1720s this controversy exacerbated preexisting tensions between Scotch-Irish newcomers (*see* Scottish Presbyterians), who favored subscription, and Presbyterians hearkening to the traditions of Puritan* New England, who opposed the practice.

Subsidiarity, Principle of. As expressed in *Quadragesimo Anno,** the principle that a higher group (e.g., the state) should never intervene to do for a lower group (e.g., the family) what the latter can do for itself.

Sudermann, Leonhard (1821-1900). A leader of the Mennonite* emigration* from Russia to North America in the 1870s. Sudermann moved from Prussia to Russia in 1841, later becoming elder* of a Mennonite Church. In the 1860s, believing that new laws would threaten the Mennonites' century-old exemption from military service, he began research on emigration. Sudermann and his family emigrated in 1876, eventually settling permanently in Kansas.

Sulpicians/Priests of St. Sulpice. A group of diocesan* priests released by their bishops to serve in the formation of priests and future priests. Forming a community under a general superior (they are not a religious order*), they take no special vows and work in each of their houses as a collegial* body.

From the founding of the first Sulpician seminary in the U.S. in Baltimore in 1791, the Sulpicians have spread to direct seminaries around the country. In addition to forming thousands of American priests and bishops, they were involved in the formation of the Catholic University of America* and of the National Catholic Welfare Conference.*

Sunday. A Christian holy day. As the early Christians distinguished themselves from Judaism, they emphasized Sunday as the Lord's Day, the day of the resurrection.

English Puritanism* insisted on a strictly observed Christian sabbath (Sunday), and this idea was brought to New England. After the American Revolution and the disestablishment of the church, many Protestants* desired to maintain a strict Christian sabbath in American society.

Christian groups such as the Seventh-Day Baptists and the Seventh-day Adventists have maintained the sanctity of the seventh day.

See also BLUE LAWS; SABBATARIANISM.

Sunday, William (Billy) Ashley (1862-1935). Urban evangelist. In 1886 Sunday, who was a major league baseball player, surrendered his life to Christ at Chicago's Pacific Garden Mission.* By 1891 he had walked away from his sports career to devote his full time to Christian ministry.*

Beginning revival* meetings in Iowa in 1896, Sunday by the eve of World War I was preaching in major cities all over the U.S., including Chicago, Boston and New York City. By the time of his death, millions of people had heard his message, and approximately 300,000 men and women were led to faith in Christ in his meetings. His flamboyant antics, theatrical poses and impassioned gestures attracted the attention of the press and helped make him a household name.

Sunday is credited with helping pass the Prohibition* Amendment.

Sunday and Adult School Union. *See* AMERICAN SUNDAY SCHOOL UNION.

Sunday-School Movement. Originating in England, the Sunday school is traced to the efforts of Robert Raikes (1735-1811), who hired teachers to aid children in desperate circumstances. Transported to the U.S., the institution was aided by movements for social reform. Schools were founded in Virginia in 1785, and in the 1790s Sunday schools spread to Boston, New York and other places. They were intended to aid children who had no other opportunities for education, many of whom were employed in factories.

After 1800 the purposes for the Sunday school became both instruction and evangelism.* The first national Sunday-school effort was founded in 1824, the American Sunday-School Union.* Its purpose was both to evangelize and to civilize.

From 1820 through the 1870s, with the rise of public education, the Sunday school existed in two forms: as the mission Sunday school, it evangelized children in rural and inner-city areas, and as the church Sunday school, it taught denominational distinctives to the children of members.

See also CATECHETICS, CATHOLIC; CHRISTIAN EDUCATION; CONFRATERNITY OF CHRISTIAN DOCTRINE; INTERNATIONAL SUNDAY SCHOOL ASSOCIATION; RELIGIOUS EDUCATION ASSOCIATION.

Sunderland, La Roy (1804-1885). Methodist* abolitionist* minister and one of the founders of the Wesleyan Methodist Church. Sunderland became one of the most ardent abolitionists in the Methodist Episcopal Church.* He founded the American Anti-Slavery Society in 1833 and in 1836 established the abolitionist weekly *Zion's Watchman.*

After censure by the General Conference, Sunderland withdrew his membership and joined Orange Scott* in 1843 at the first conference of the Wesleyan Methodist Church.

Superintendent. A Methodist* pastoral administrator responsible for a district. Appointed by the resident bishop, the district superintendent's pastoral responsibilities include assuring compliance by the local congregation with the *Discipline,* counseling with local pastors regarding their pastoral and personal responsibilities, and recruiting candidates for the ministry.

Supreme Court Decisions on Religious Issues. Religious liberty,* which is the cornerstone of the American Bill of Rights, was fundamental in the development of American civilization. The principle of complete religious liberty has long been viewed by Americans as being near the center of their national life. Supreme Court decisions on religion are generally based on the religion clauses of the First Amendment:* "Congress shall make no law respecting an establishment of religion, or prohibiting the free exercise thereof." The only other reference to religion in the Constitution is to be found in Clause 3 of Article VI: "No religious test shall ever be required as a qualification to any office or public trust under the United States."

Free-Exercise-Clause Cases. While state courts from their beginning have been frequently called upon to resolve questions bearing upon the free exercise of religion and the separation of church and state,* very few U.S. Supreme Court decisions on religion and state were handed down during the first century of the nation's history. Not until *Watson v. Jones* (1872) did the Court render an opinion based on the religion clauses of the First Amendment. It did so by ruling that it could not involve itself in deciding which of two factions represented the true faith in a church dispute. The Court declared, "The law knows no heresy,* and is committed to the support of no dogma,* the establishment of no sect.*"

The first major church-state case in America involved the Mormons* in *Reynolds v. United States* (1878), in which the Court rejected the contention of the plaintiff that his practice of polygamy was a religious obligation. Quoting Thomas Jefferson,* the Court affirmed that the purpose of the First Amendment was to build "a wall of separation between Church and State," but that this did not deprive the state of the right to limit actions based on religious beliefs.

In a landmark church-state case, *Cantwell v. Connecticut* (1940), the Court unanimously upheld the right of Jehovah's Witnesses* to propagate their faith in public and to engage in door-to-door solicitation without a permit or "certificate of approval." For the first time, the Court specifically "incorporated" the free-exercise clause into the Fourteenth Amendment, thus making the clause applicable to the states.

In more than a half dozen cases, the Court has applied the free-exercise clause to conscientious objection to war. Conscientious objection did not become a serious legal question until there was a universal or national conscription for military service at the time of World War I.* First restricted to members of peace churches,* Congress extended it in 1948 to those with "religious training and belief."

A landmark case bearing on religious tests for state office came in *Torcaso v. Watkins* (1961), in which the Court unanimously held unconstitutional a Maryland law requiring "a declaration of belief in the existence of God" for state office. The significance of Torcaso is that the Court categorically denied religious tests for office at any level of government and any preferential treatment of theistic over nontheistic faiths, or religion over against nonreligion as a qualification for public office.

Establishment-Clause Cases. During the twentieth century, no church-state issues have provoked as much discussion or prompted as much litigation as the relation of the state to church schools and the role of religion in state schools. In *Pierce v. Society of Sisters* (1925), the Court outlawed an Oregon statute that required all parents to send their children to public schools and affirmed that the right to maintain and attend a church or private school is constitutionally guaranteed.

Government aid to church schools has been the subject of more than a dozen decisions by the Court based upon the establishment clause of the First Amendment. In *Everson v. Board of Education* (1947), the Court upheld a New Jersey law providing for bus transportation of pupils in parochial schools.* This landmark decision marked the first time that the Court attempted to define the establishment clause and to "incorporate" it into the Fourteenth Amendment and thereby make it applicable to the states.

In approximately a dozen cases since 1971 involving the establishment clause, the Court has applied a three-pronged test in judging the constitutionality of legislation or a government act: The statute must have a "secular legislative purpose"; it must have a "primary effect that neither advances nor inhibits religion"; and its administration must avoid "excessive entanglement" with religion. With few exceptions, all of these cases have had to do with tax aid to religious schools.

Sverdrup, Georg (1848-1907). Lutheran* churchman and theologian. Sverdrup became professor of theology (1874) and then president for thirty-one years of Augsburg Seminary in Minneapolis. He helped form the Lutheran Free Church in 1897 and participated in conflicts over theological education for Norwegian-American clergy.

Swain, Clara A. (1834-1910). Medical missionary to India. Swain, the first woman missionary doctor in the world, served under the Woman's Foreign Missionary Society of the Methodist Episcopal Church.* By 1872 she had opened the first women's hospital in Asia. She ministered in India until 1895.

Swedenborg. *See* CHURCH OF THE NEW JERUSALEM.

Swedish Baptist General Conference. *See* BAPTIST GENERAL CONFERENCE.

Sweet, William Warren (1881-1959). Methodist* minister and American church historian. Himself a product of the late frontier, Sweet in his later work as a historian emphasized indigenous factors and the role of religion on the frontier.* In 1927 he went to the Divinity School at the University of Chicago,* where his chair in the history of American Christianity was the first such post in the country.

Sweet's writings, most notably *The Story of Religion in America* (1930), called attention to the importance of religion within the broader field of American history.

Sweet Daddy Grace. *See* GRACE, CHARLES MANUEL.

Swing, David (1830-1894). Presbyterian,* later independent, pastor in Chicago. A popular preacher who attracted several thousand worshipers every Sunday,* Swing came to national attention in 1874 when he was charged with heresy.* The Presbytery of Chicago acquitted Swing of all charges, but Swing later withdrew from the denomination,* in 1875 becoming the pastor of the newly organized and independent Central Church of Chicago. His liberal evangelicalism helped give rise to the New Theology.*

Synod. A meeting of ministers and lay representatives from the congregations within several presbyteries* or associations. In the context of the Presbyterian Church,* a synod is an assembly of all ministers and ruling elders who are members of the constituent presbyteries. The Congregational* churches of New England also had periodic synods, where ministers and lay delegates addressed problems concerning the collective churches. In episcopal forms of church government, a synod may refer to a periodic gathering of the clergy of a diocese called by the bishop.

See also CHURCH GOVERNMENT.

Syrian Orthodox Church of Antioch. The Syrian Orthodox Church of Antioch—begun, according to tradition, by St. Peter the Apostle—participated in and fully accepted the teaching of Nicea (325), Constantinople (381) and Ephesus (431) but rejected the terminology of the Council of Chalcedon (451). By 1236 it numbered some twenty thousand parishes.

The Syrian Orthodox Church of Antioch is in full communion with the Armenian, Coptic and Ethiopian Churches, being one of what are referred to as the Oriental Orthodox Churches. The church is a member of both the World Council of Churches* and the National Council of the Churches of Christ in the United States of America.*

The presence of the Syrian Orthodox Church of Antioch in America dates back to the late nineteenth century, when religious persecution forced immigration from Ottoman Turkey to the U.S. In 1907 the Very Reverend Hanna Koorie was ordained* to serve as the first Syrian Orthodox priest in the U.S. and stationed in New Jersey. In 1992 there were a reported sixteen parishes and approximately thirty-three thousand faithful, served by fourteen priests.

The church has translated a number of church service books from Syriac, the church's official language, into English. The American experience has also encouraged the church to participate actively in ecumenical* activities.

Systematic Theology. The intellectual reflection, within the context of a specific worldview, on the act and context of Christian faith, including its expression in beliefs, practices and institutions.

In America the older term *dogmatics* has generally been replaced by *systematic theology,* or even *constructive* or *doctrinal theology.* Its task focuses on the intellectual reflection on faith, especially the belief system itself (doctrine), but also the nature of believing and the integration of commitment and life are subjects for systematic inquiry. The result is a coherent presentation of the themes of Christian faith. Traditionally these include God, humanity and creation, Jesus Christ, salvation, the Holy Spirit, the church and the consummation. It is not to be equated with religious studies, for theology is pursued within the context of a faith stance.

T

Tache, Alexandre-Antonin (1823-1894). Roman Catholic* missionary bishop in western Canada. From its base among the French-Canadian *metis,* or half-breeds, in the Red River (Winnipeg) area, Roman Catholicism hoped to make western Canada Francophone and Catholic. The key figure in the attempt to realize this ideal was A. A. Tache. Gradually building up an establishment on the Red River and importing teaching orders, he laid the foundations of a strong western Canadian Roman Catholicism with all its ethnic diversity.

Talbot, John (1645-1727). Anglican* missionary in colonial America. Appointed a missionary of the Society for the Propagation of the Gospel in Foreign Parts* in 1702, Talbot traveled from Maine to North Carolina, preaching* to large crowds in New Jersey, New York and Pennsylvania, and establishing the first formal presence of the Anglican Church in several colonies. In 1704 he helped found St. Mary's Church, Burlington, New Jersey, and remained as its rector.

Talbot, Louis Thomson (1889-1976). Evangelical* minister and president of the Bible Institute of Los Angeles. From 1932 to 1948 Talbot was pastor of the Church of the Open Door and president of the Bible Institute of Los Angeles (1932-1952). After 1953 he served as chancellor of Biola College (now Biola University), and the board named the newly founded Talbot Seminary in his honor. He was an active promoter of evangelical foreign mission* endeavors.

Talmage, T(homas) DeWitt (1832-1902). Dutch Reformed* and Presbyterian* preacher. Accepting a call in 1869 from the badly divided Central Presbyterian Church in Brooklyn, New York, Talmage remained there until 1895, developing it into one of the largest churches in the U.S. During his tenure there he attracted considerable atten-

tion and became involved in lecturing and journalism, in addition to his preaching.

Probably the most popular preacher during the last quarter of the nineteenth century, Talmage published in 3,500 newspapers. Considered a master of sensational rhetoric and having an unconventional style of organizing and delivering his sermons, he was both strongly admired and criticized.

Tanner, Benjamin Tucker (1835-1923). African Methodist Episcopal* editor and bishop. Tanner was editor of the denomination's widely influential newspaper, the *Christian Recorder* (1868-1884), and in 1884 became founding editor of the *A.M.E. Church Review,* a quarterly he quickly established as a leading cultural journal among African-Americans. In 1888 he was elected bishop, a position he held until his retirement in 1908.

Tant, J(efferson) D(avis) (1861-1941). Church of Christ* evangelist and debater. A colorful and controversial figure, Tant was a farmer and preacher for most of his life and participated in over 350 debates. There was an urgency about his evangelism, and in his lifetime he baptized eight thousand people.

Tappan, Arthur (1786-1865), and Lewis (1788-1873). Evangelical* businessmen and social reformers. The Tappan brothers, partners in a silk business in New York City, are best known for their careers in evangelical social reform, expressed in a Calvinistic* activism. The brothers gave liberally of their administrative talents and wealth gained in business to movements for revival,* missions* and many other causes. They supported Lane Seminary and helped establish Oberlin* Seminary and Kenyon College.

Tappan, David (1752-1803). Congregational*

minister and Harvard* professor. Tappan, the third Hollis Professor of Divinity at Harvard (1792-1803), was a respected proponent of moderate Calvinism.* Controversy erupted over the selection of his successor.

Taschereau, Elzear Alexandre (1820-1898). Roman Catholic* archbishop of Quebec and first Canadian cardinal. Taschereau served the Quebec Seminary as teacher, director, prefect of studies and supervisor. He helped found Laval University in Quebec City and was rector for a time before his consecration* as archbishop of Quebec in 1870.

Taschereau was almost immediately in conflict with the ultramontanes* led by Bishop Bourget* of Montreal. Taschereau held his ground, defending Laval University against attack before the papacy.

Taylor, Clyde W. (1904-1988). Evangelical* statesman. After earlier ministry as a missionary and pastor, Taylor joined the National Association of Evangelicals (NAE) in 1944. For more than forty years, Taylor served American evangelicals through this premier unifying organization, from 1963 to 1974 as general director. He helped write key immigration legislation and resisted the Federal Council of Churches'* attempts to obtain a monopoly on religious broadcasting time.

Taylor, Edward (c. 1645-1729). Puritan* minister and poet. Taylor was called to the church at Westfield, Massachusetts, in 1671 and remained there until his death, serving the town as both minister and physician.

Taylor's poetry, discovered only in 1937, establishes him as the most accomplished American poet of his era. He explores the soul's journey to salvation against the background of Puritan cosmology and covenant theology.

Taylor, Graham (1851-1938). Dutch Reformed* and later Congregational* minister, sociologist. In 1892 Taylor joined the faculty of the Chicago Theological Seminary as professor of Christian sociology and English Bible in what was the first department of Christian sociology in the U.S. In 1894 Taylor, his family and four students moved into a poor West Side Chicago community and established "Chicago Commons," a settlement house which achieved a wide reputation. There he developed a great variety of social and educational programs.

Taylor, Herbert John (1893-1978). Businessman and philanthropist.* In 1930 Taylor was called in to rescue Club Aluminum Company from bankruptcy, where he eventually became president (1932-1952) and chairman of the board (1952-1968).

He developed the "Four-Way Test" as a business strategy: (1) Is it the truth? (2) Is it fair to all concerned? (3) Will it build goodwill and better friendships? (4) Will it be beneficial for all concerned? In 1942 the Four-Way Test was adopted by Rotary International.

Taylor, John (1752-1835). Pioneer Baptist* preacher, missionary and author. In 1779 Taylor moved west to Kentucky to engage in mission work. Taylor's work was characterized by the starting of new churches on the frontier and then the pastoring of each new church for a number of years. He was the major force in establishing several Baptist churches in Kentucky.

Taylor, Nathaniel William (1786-1858). Congregational* minister and theologian. Taylor served from 1811 to 1822 as the pastor of New Haven's First Church. In 1822 he became the first incumbent of the Dwight Professorship of Didactic Theology at the newly formed Yale Divinity School, where he remained until 1857. From this prestigious position at the heart of Connecticut Congregationalism, Taylor developed a distinct theological outlook known as Taylorism, or New Haven theology.* More than any other New England theologian of the period, Taylor helped shape a synthetic theological system that borrowed from two of New England's most prominent religious traditions: Congregationalism and nineteenth-century revivalism.*

Taylor became an apologist for a version of American Calvinism that preserved many of the emphases of traditional Reformed* theology and yet encouraged aggressive evangelistic efforts. He effectively loosed New England theology* from its traditional ties to the Reformed doctrine of innate or imputed depravity.

Taylor, William (1821-1902). Methodist* missionary bishop. After an itinerant* ministry in North America (1856-1861), Taylor literally made the world his parish by evangelizing and establishing missions on six continents.

Successive assignments took him to England and Australia (1862-1866), South Africa (1866), India (1870-1875, where his method of establishing self-supporting mission congregations was most successful), South America (1877-1884), and Africa (1884-1896). Taylor University in Upland, Indiana, is named after him.

Taylorism. *See* NEW HAVEN THEOLOGY.

Teen Challenge. A drug rehabilitation agency for adolescents. In 1960 Pentecostal* minister David R. Wilkerson met with a number of interested New York City clergymen and officially organized the ministry of Teen Challenge. By the end of that same year, the first Teen Challenge Center opened its doors. Approximately one hundred Teen Challenge centers have been established across the U.S., caring for the needs of teens, particularly those addicted to drugs. Approximately 150 ministries have been established in foreign countries.

Tekakwitha, Katherine (Kateri Tegah-Kouita, also Tegawita) (c. 1656-1680). Native American and Roman Catholic* convert. In 1676 Tekakwitha, from upstate New York, was baptized* by Jacques de Lamberville. She became widely known for her life of deep spirituality* and asceticism.

Temperance Movement (1820s-1860). The initial phase of the century-long effort to curb consumption of alcoholic* beverages in America. As America's population moved west and grain production increased, so also did alcoholic consumption, since grain was more easily marketed as liquor. Intemperance posed a serious threat to a nation extolling individualism,* democracy* and Christianity* as its foundation.

The American Temperance Society (ATS) was founded in Boston in 1826 to promote voluntary total abstinence* from distilled liquor. Temperance enthusiasm often followed on the heels of religious revivals;* the movement was one manifestation of the perfectionist* impulse of the era. In the 1850s the "Maine Law," a prohibition statute enacted through the efforts of Neal Dow, became the model for state prohibition campaigns throughout the country.

The temperance movement proved to be the most widespread reform effort of the antebellum era.

See also ANTI-SALOON LEAGUE; PROHIBITION MOVEMENT; WOMEN'S CHRISTIAN TEMPERANCE UNION.

Templin, Terah (1742?-1818). Pioneer Presbyterian* minister of Kentucky. Templin ministered in central and western Kentucky for over thirty years, preaching and establishing churches.

Neither a powerful intellect nor a charismatic preacher, Templin's gifts lay in the consistent and sacrificial dedication of his service to the church over a long period of time. He was respected for his integrity and unassuming modesty.

Ten Boom, Corrie (1892-1983). World War II* Nazi death camp survivor and popular evangelical* author. As a result of her family's involvement in helping Jews escape the Nazis, ten Boom spent time in a Nazi concentration camp at Ravensbruck. Upon her release, she began sharing her testimony through her writing and worldwide speaking tours that took her to more than sixty countries.

Tennent, Gilbert (1703-1764). Presbyterian* minister and revivalist* during the Great Awakening.* In the late 1720s and early 1730s, Tennent was involved with his father's efforts at the Log College* (*see* William Tennent), and this involvement, coupled with his revival zeal, made him the leader of a vigorous minority within the Presbyterian Church.

Tennent became the chief spokesman for supporters of the Great Awakening* and is frequently remembered for his sermon "The Danger of an Unconverted Ministry" (1740).

Tennent, William (1673-1746). Presbyterian* minister and educator. In the late 1720s, with controversy building in the Presbyterian Church over ministerial subscription to the Westminster Confession* (*see* Adopting Act), Tennent began tutoring young men for the Presbyterian ministry. By 1735 these efforts had become sufficiently formalized that Tennent built a simple log building which became known as the Log College.*

His son Gilbert* was a noted leader of the New Side* Presbyterians.

Tent Meetings. Borrowing from the camp meeting* tradition, itinerant* evangelists often took a tent with them, setting it up wherever they decided to hold meetings. Charles Finney* had an enormous tent erected on the campus of Oberlin

College when he arrived there in 1835. Tents provided an economical and portable means of accommodating the crowds that attended preaching and revival services. Enthusiastic singing, aisles layered with wood chips forming a "sawdust trail"* to the altar* and fiery preaching characterized the tent-meeting atmosphere. Tent meetings were still used extensively after World War II.*

Terry, Milton Spenser (1846-1914). Methodist* minister, theologian and biblical commentator. In 1884 Terry began a long teaching career at Garrett Biblical Institute, Evanston, Illinois. He was an effective teacher and prolific writer whose long career was dedicated to the task of integrating modern trends in biblical interpretation* with Methodist theology. Terry's *Biblical Hermeneutics* (1883) well reflected this theological task.

Testem Benevolentiae. An apostolic letter in 1899 addressed by Pope Leo XIII* to James Gibbons,* cardinal archbishop of Baltimore, and communicated to all the bishops of the U.S. Although it mentions the term only once, this letter is remembered as the Vatican's condemnation of Americanism.* It is a brief treatise, framed in Neo-Scholastic categories, on the relationship between the church and the modern age.

Testimony Meeting. A gathering where individuals are invited to share their personal religious experience before the entire assembly. This practice became firmly established through the early Puritan* requirement that prospective church members* confess their experience of faith.

Thanksgiving Day. A legal holiday, celebrated in the U.S. on the fourth Thursday of November and in Canada on the second Monday of October. It is a day on which people assemble to express gratitude to God. Churches and synagogues hold special services; interfaith observances are common. Food is gathered and distributed to the poor, and families come together for a dinner of uniquely North American foods, including turkey, squash and pumpkin.

Theism. Theism in the sense of God as the personal creator and sustainer of the world has been the dominant view of God throughout American history. The form in which theism first arrived in British North America was what the Puritan divines called covenant* theology.* Puritan theology had a christocentric focus and emphasized the knowledge and experience of God possible through conversion* and the life of faith.

Jonathan Edwards* adapted the empiricism of John Locke, reasoning that rather than matter acting upon our senses, it is God who acts to give us experience. Edwards's influence continued among those thinkers known as the New Divinity.* Scottish Common Sense philosophy* later became widely embraced, which in turn had decisive impact on Charles Hodge,* whose formulation of Reformed theology has deeply influenced much evangelical* theology, even into the latter part of the twentieth century.

Liberal Reactions to Puritan Theology. Locke's emphasis on "reasonable" Christianity led in Britain to deism, a view of God as first cause, including belief in immortality and, above all, an emphasis on virtuous living.

Charles Chauncy* pioneered a movement that was to have a more far-reaching influence than deism, and indeed was partly a reaction against deism's distant and detached God. Chauncy emphasized God as the epitome of love, with the consequence that he downplayed the depravity of human nature and the threat of eternal judgment. His views eventually led to the emergence of Unitarianism.*

Progressive Orthodoxy. Seeking to adapt New England theology* to the nineteenth-century American mind, Nathaniel W. Taylor* replaced the concept of a sovereign, almighty God with one of God as the moral governor of the universe. His emphasis on moral agency had lasting influence, especially in revivalists* Lyman Beecher* and Charles G. Finney.*

Charles Darwin's *Origin of Species* (1859) introduced a new, scientific view of origins, which fit well with the developmental and evolutionary categories of German idealism. Darwin's world of chance adaptation and chaos soon replaced Common Sense philosophy as the dominant philosophical framework.

Horace Bushnell* best adapted his thought to these currents, developing the transcendentalists'* notion of the interconnectedness of reality for more Christian purposes.

Twentieth-Century Theism and Atheism. Bushnell had a major influence on twentieth-century liberalism. His evolutionary and communitarian* emphases prepared the way for the social theology of Walter Rauschenbusch* and even, in a sense, for the political theology* of Reinhold Niebuhr.*

Though the formulations of the progressive orthodoxy and twentieth-century liberalism differed from their Puritan ancestors, there is a clear continuity as well. New England theology had a grand conception of Christian faith as world forming and God's purposes as decisive for all of life. The continuing challenge for orthodox theism has been to maintain its biblical dynamic, while being open to the cultural currents in which that faith must be expressed.

Theocracy. A term literally meaning "rule by God." The term has been used to describe the government of New England in the seventeenth century because of the way in which scriptural principles were employed not only in the polity* of the church but also in the civil realm, particularly in the Massachusetts Bay Colony. If the term is understood as civil rule by the clergy or by the church as an institution, then it is inaccurate to apply it to seventeenth-century New England.

Literary debates between Boston minister John Cotton* and Roger Williams* led to a limitation of the power of the civil government in controlling individual conscience.*

Theologian. A person who systematically studies theology or some aspect of theology.* Throughout Christian history the title *theologian* or its equivalent has frequently been reserved for the professional scholar or minister who, as teacher, thinker and writer, identifies the central tenets of the Christian faith, ranks subtopics in respect to those centers and systematically fleshes out interrelations and further subdivisions in the light of Scripture, Christian tradition and contemporary culture.

Theology. The study of God and of his relationship with created reality. While the term *theology* may refer even to simple and unsophisticated statements about God and his relationships, it most frequently refers to the academic disciplines of professional theologians and ministerial students.

A dominant motif may describe theology, as in the case of covenant* and dispensational* theology and, more recently, process, narrative, liberation* and feminist* theologies.

Theonomy. *See* RECONSTRUCTIONISM, CHRISTIAN.

Thiessen, Henry Clarence (1883-1947). Evangelical* biblical scholar and educator. Thiessen, an exacting scholar with a dispensational* orientation, taught at Dallas Theological Seminary* (1931-1935) and then Wheaton College* (1935-1946). His *Introduction to the New Testament* (1943) and *Introductory Lectures in Systematic Theology* (1949; rev. ed. 1979) were widely used.

Third Awakening. *See* PRAYER MEETING REVIVAL.

Thirty-Nine Articles of Religion. Anglican* statement of faith adopted by the Episcopal Church* in 1801. These articles derive from a set of theological articles prepared in 1551 by Thomas Cranmer, in which he attempted to sketch out a Protestant* middle ground between Roman Catholicism* and Anabaptism.*

By the time of the American Revolution* some New England Anglicans opposed subscription,* objecting particularly to the article on predestination.*

Thoburn, James Mills (1836-1922). Methodist* missionary to India. Thoburn served a long and distinguished career as missionary in India (1859-1908). He was the first of his church to perceive the significance of "people movements."

Thomas, Norman M(attoon) (1884-1968). Presbyterian* minister, social activist and leader of the Socialist Party in America. In 1918 Thomas resigned his pastorate and joined the Socialist Party, assuming leadership from 1926 to 1950. Six times—from 1928 to 1948—he was a presidential candidate for the Socialist Party.

Intellectually, Thomas was eclectic, borrowing from the Social Gospel,* progressivism and moderate socialist thinkers.

Thomas, Samuel (c. 1672-1706). First missionary sent to South Carolina by the Society for the Propagation of the Gospel.* Arriving in the colony in 1702, Thomas became well liked and eventually saw a significant increase in the number of communicants in his area. He showed great sensitivity toward the plight of both Native Americans and African-Americans.

Thomas, W(illiam) H(enry) Griffith (1861-1924). Evangelical* Anglican* clergyman. Thomas united Anglican churchmanship and Augustinian Protestantism* with dispensationalism* and support of the "higher"* or "victorious"* Christian life. He spoke often at Keswick* and prophetic gatherings in England and North America, helping found Dallas Theological Seminary.* Adept at popular scholarship, he wrote many books, articles and reviews on the Bible, theology,* apologetics* and Christian living.

Thomism. A philosophical system derived from the writings of Thomas Aquinas, distinguished by (1) a high reliance on reason (e.g., to prove God's existence and know the natural moral law [vs. fideism*]); (2) the primacy of *esse,* the act of existing, and the real distinction between essence and existence (vs. essentialism); (3) objective realism (vs. Kantian subjective idealism) and empiricism (vs. Platonic intellectualism), in which all knowledge begins in sensation; and (4) the substantial unity of body and soul (vs. Platonic and Cartesian dualism).

Thompson, Charles Lemuel (1839-1924). Presbyterian* minister and home mission* board executive. In 1898 Thompson left his New York pastorate to become secretary of the Board of Home Missions, a position he held until 1914. The challenges of home missions extended his vision and made him the champion of ministries to Native Americans,* the immigrants* filling American cities, rural churches and the Hispanic* population.

At the time of his death he was recognized as the "Home Missionary Statesman" of his generation.

Thoreau, Henry David (1817-1862). New England transcendental* essayist and philosopher. Thoreau is perhaps America's best and best-known prose essayist. In *Walden* (1854) he focuses on the central question of how a person ought to live. In this profoundly moral book, Thoreau mines his New England heritage (including its Puritan* roots) for radical answers to the problems clamoring for social reform and the issues confronting individuals striving to live morally in an increasingly materialistic society. Thoreau's most famous essay, "Resistance to Civil Government," became a key document in later American social conflicts and has received worldwide recognition.

Thornwell, James Henley (1812-1862). Southern Presbyterian* theologian and educator.

Thornwell served many years at South Carolina College, as professor of philosophy (1838-1839), chaplain and professor of sacred literature and Christian evidences (1841-1851), and as president (1852-1855). From 1855 to 1862 he occupied the chair of theology at Columbia Theological Seminary.

A leader in the formation of the Presbyterian Church in the United States* (1861), he wrote the "Address to All the Churches of Jesus Christ Throughout the Earth," justifying its separation from the Northern church.

Thornwell had a passion for orthodoxy* and a sense of duty to truth and sought to defend traditional institutions and standards against liberal and ungodly assaults. He defended the South and its institutions, including slavery.* His theology was essentially that of the Westminster* Standards. A brilliant Old School* preacher, theologian and churchman, he was the youngest General Assembly* moderator ever (1847) and perhaps the most influential Southern minister before the Civil War.*

Tichenor, I(saac) T(aylor) (1825-1902). Southern Baptist* preacher, educator, agriculturist and denominational* leader. Tichenor was president of the Alabama Agricultural and Mechanical College, later Auburn University (1871-1882). He was leader of the Home Mission Board of the Southern Baptist Convention (1882-1899).

Tillet, Wilbur Fisk (1854-1936). Methodist* theologian and hymn writer. Becoming professor of theology* at Vanderbilt University in 1886, Tillet quickly emerged as one of the leading theologians of the Methodist Episcopal Church, South.* From 1886 he also served as dean of the Vanderbilt Divinity School, guiding it through a time of being accused of spreading heresy.

Tillich, Paul Johannes Oskar (1886-1965). Lutheran* theologian. After teaching at various German universities between 1919 and 1932, Tillich held professorships at Union Theological Seminary* in New York City (1933-1955), Harvard University* (1955-1962) and the University of Chicago* (1962-1965).

Tillich's most significant work was his three-volume *Systematic Theology* (1951, 1957, 1963), in which he employed his method of correlation by which philosophy and other modes of "autonomous" human reflection uncover certain problems in human existence. Revelation provides answers to these problems.

Tillich was the last major theologian to argue that theology had something to say to all of culture. He believed that a deep-level commitment to the creation of culture and to the living of our personal lives puts us into contact with the realm of theology. Theology, without violating the autonomy of culture's disciplines in their status as preliminary, surface concerns, can provide insights into the religious character of all serious cultural creation. Tillich's theology of culture has elicited stiff resistance from those who wish to deny that scientific or artistic or other "secular" activity needs any religious foundation. Precisely these insights into the religious identity of all serious culture, however, may be one of his more lasting accomplishments.

Tilly, Dorothy Eugenia Rogers (1883-1970). Methodist* civil rights* activist. Tilly's major concern was race relations, lecturing in churches and frequently speaking on race relations. She was one of the first Georgians to join the Association of Southern Women for the Prevention of Lynching. Defying opposition from the Georgia legislature, Tilly was responsible for the establishment of a school for delinquent African-American girls. In response to the rise of the Ku Klux Klan, she formed, in 1949, the Fellowship of the Concerned, an activist group which addressed lynchings and promoted integration.

Tittle, Ernest Fremont (1885-1949). Methodist* minister. An intense, intelligent and ambitious young man, Tittle was ordained* in 1910 and soon gained a favorable reputation as a theological liberal* and Social Gospel* prophet.

After service in World War I* as a YMCA* secretary in France, Tittle became an absolute pacifist.* After the war he became pastor of the First Methodist Church of Evanston, Illinois (1918-1949), where he preached prophetically—and to increasingly large and appreciative audiences—on economic and racial injustice and the sinfulness of prideful nationalism and international war. He became the recognized leader of Methodism's liberal and pacifist ministers.

Tocqueville, Alexis de (1805-1859). French political thinker and observer of nineteenth-century America. In 1832 Tocqueville and a companion traveled throughout the U.S. interviewing persons at all levels of society. He concluded that three countervailing forces—the law, voluntary associations and religion—kept American society from degenerating into selfishness and materialism.

Tocqueville's classic *Democracy in America* remains one of the best studies of American democracy and of the relationship between liberty and religion.

Toews, David (1870-1947). General Conference Mennonite* Church leader in Canada. A church statesman of considerable repute, Toews was moderator of the Conference of Mennonites in Central Canada, founder and chairman of the Canadian Mennonite Board of Colonization, which settled more than 20,000 Russian Mennonite immigrants in 1923-1930, and a vigorous advocate of Mennonite nonresistance during both world wars.

Toleration, Act of (Maryland, 1649). Legislation providing for religious toleration of trinitarian Christians. The act gave legal protection to the religious freedoms* of the colony's Catholics* and Protestants.* Although liberal for its time, the bill did not go beyond what had been common practice in Maryland from its founding in 1634.

The act was repealed (1654) and reenacted (1657), only to be repealed once again after England's Glorious Revolution and the establishment of Anglicanism* in Maryland.

Tolton, Augustine (1854-1897). Roman Catholic* priest. In 1877 in Quincy, Illinois, Tolton became catechist* for African-American children. In 1889, after studies in Rome and ordination,* he became pastor of Chicago's St. Monica's Church for the Colored. His chapel, built in 1893, remained the center of African-American Catholic life in the city for the next three decades.

Tomlinson, Ambrose Jessup (1865-1943). Pentecostal* minister and founder of the Church of God of Prophecy. In 1909 Tomlinson was elected the full-time leader of the denomination* now known as the Church of God.* The church eventually moved completely from the Holiness movement* into the Holiness segment of the Pentecostal movement.

A controversy in 1922-1923 resulted in Tomlinson's leaving the Church of God and starting over with approximately two thousand adherents, a group later designated the Church of God of Prophecy.

Tongues, Speaking in. Speaking in tongues, as practiced by Christians, particularly those within the Pentecostal* and charismatic* movements, has two principal manifestations: *glossolalia* refers to a speech pattern with which humans are not familiar, and *xenolalia* refers to the miraculous use of a known language not learned by traditional methods. While practitioners argue that these are genuine manifestations of the gifts of the Holy Spirit, they also discern human imitations and diabolically inspired representations. Tongues speech may occur in Pentecostal or charismatic public worship,* small-group gatherings and private devotion.

In some non-Pentecostal and noncharismatic Christian circles, the phenomenon of tongues speech has been controversial. Critics of the phenomenon have taken various approaches, some arguing theologically, as did Benjamin B. Warfield,* that the gift of tongues was a sign intended only to authenticate the apostolic message. Other Christians are open to the authenticity of tongues speech, though they may not practice it themselves.

The dawning of the twentieth century saw the most extensive practice of tongues speech, which became a distinctive feature of the Pentecostal movement. Charismatics, however, generally regard tongues as only one of several possible gifts given to Spirit-baptized believers.

Torrey, C(harles) C(utler) (1863-1956). Biblical scholar and Semitist. At Andover Theological Seminary* Torrey taught Semitic languages, biblical theology and history (1892-1900); at Yale* he was professor of Semitic languages and literature (1900-1932). In 1900-1901 he established the American School of Archaeology (later the American School of Oriental Research).

Torrey, R(euben) A(rcher) (1856-1928). Evangelist and Congregational* minister. In 1889 Torrey became superintendent of Moody's Chicago Training Institute (later called Moody Bible Institute*), where he remained until 1908. Between 1902 and 1905, accompanied by singer Charles M. Alexander,* he conducted a worldwide evangelistic tour, during which he preached to more than 15 million persons in England, Scotland, Ireland, Germany, France, Australia, New Zealand, Tasmania, India, China and Japan. From 1906 to 1911 he conducted numerous campaigns in the U.S. and Canada.

Torrey was one of the most prolific writers among the evangelicals* of his generation. He wrote or edited forty books and scores of booklets and articles on a wide range of subjects, devoting special attention to the defense of the authenticity of Scripture and the cardinal doctrines of the Christian faith.

Toth, Alexis Georgievich (1853-1909). Archpriest of the Russian Orthodox* Diocese of Alaska and the Aleutian Islands. Ordained* to the priesthood of the Greek Catholic Church in 1878, Toth was sent to the U.S. in 1889 to serve as a missionary to Greek Catholic immigrants.*

When Toth's Catholicity was not recognized by the Americanist* Archbishop John Ireland,* he sought relations with Orthodoxy. In 1891 he and his entire parish in Minneapolis became the first Greek Catholics in America to come over to the Orthodox Church.* Toth eventually organized seventeen parishes in Pennsylvania and brought thousands to the Orthodox faith.

Townsend, William Cameron (1896-1982). Founder of Wycliffe Bible Translators* and the Summer Institute of Linguistics. In 1917 Townsend went to Guatemala, where he became burdened for the large number of Indians who could not read Spanish. Without linguistic training, he embarked on a program of language learning, reducing the language to writing and translating the New Testament.

In 1934 Townsend and L. L. Letgers founded Camp Wycliffe in Arkansas. Out of this small beginning emerged the Summer Institute of Linguistics (SIL) and Wycliffe Bible Translators (WBT), destined to become the largest independent Protestant* mission in the world. The WBT and SIL now are involved in over sixty countries around the world and, in the mid-1990s, have a force of over six thousand members.

Toy, Crawford Howell (1836-1919). Baptist* professor of Old Testament and Hebrew. In 1869 Toy became professor of Old Testament interpretation at Southern Baptist Theological Seminary,* from which he was forced to resign in 1879 because of his acceptance of Darwin's theory of evolution* and the Kuenen-Wellhausen theory of Pentateuchal criticism. He later went to Harvard,* where he gave three decades (1880-1919) to his teaching and scholarship both in the University and the Divinity School.

Tozer, A(iden) W(ilson) (1897-1963). Christian and Missionary Alliance* minister and popular evangelical* author and mystic. Self-educated, Tozer read widely, with a special love for poetry, the church fathers and the mystics* of the church. He pastored the Southside Alliance Church of Chicago (1928-1959) and the Avenue Road Alliance Church of Toronto (1959-1963).

Tract. A short pamphlet written with a religious or evangelistic* message. The American Tract Society* (1825) was the earliest national tract distribution society in America.

Tractarianism. Common name for the movement also known as the Oxford movement or Puseyism, which was concerned with asserting the spiritual nature of the Church of England (*see* Anglicanism). The name *Tractarianism* is derived from the *Tracts for the Times,* authored by its most noted leaders, including John Henry Newman (1801-1890). The movement's openness to Catholic theology* and piety* led by the end of the 1830s to increasing criticism from Anglican evangelicals.* The movement effectively ended in 1845, with the secession of Newman and a number of others to Roman Catholicism.

American Episcopalians* only gradually became interested in the movement. In the long run Tractarianism did contribute to the erosion of the older Hobartian (*see* Hobart, John Henry) high church tradition among some American Episcopalians in favor of the emerging Anglo-Catholicism.* Yet another effect of Tractarianism among American Episcopalians was in increasing the high church/low church* polarization of the communion.

Transcendentalism. A broad-ranging intellectual reform movement centered in New England. Although the movement away from the philosophy of the Enlightenment* had begun in the U.S. as early as 1820, it was not until 1836 that it took definite shape. For the next decade transcendentalism exerted a major effect on American literature, art, religion and social reform.* The movement was an American manifestation of the romantic* mood that had transformed European intellectual life during the first third of the nineteenth century.

Transubstantiation. Catholic* doctrine concerning the Eucharist.* The Roman Catholic Church from early times has taught that Jesus intended his statements "this is my body" and "this is my blood" to be understood literally. The first use of a term equivalent to *transubstantiation* seems to have been around A.D. 1130. The standard Catholic doctrine was formulated by Thomas Aquinas in the thirteenth century—in the Eucharist the substance of bread and wine are miraculously transformed into the body and blood of Christ, while the accidents remain unchanged. *Transubstantiation* is also commonly used in a looser sense, designed to emphasize merely that a real and complete physical change has taken place in the Eucharistic elements.

The Protestant* Reformers all rejected this Catholic doctrine to one degree or another. The Council of Trent (1545-1563), as part of its general refutation of Protestant doctrine, strongly reaffirmed transubstantiation.

See also MASS, THE.

Trappists. Popular name for the Order of Cistercians of the Strict Observance, a Roman Catholic* religious order* known for its austerity and dedication to prayer. The Cistercians began as a reform movement in 1098, with strict observance being reinforced in the seventeenth century.

Lasting Trappist monasteries were established in Gethsemani, Kentucky (1848), and New Melleray, Iowa (1849). Interest in the Trappists was spurred by Gethsemani monk Thomas Merton,* whose writings presented the contemplative ideal to modern Americans.

Triennial Convention. First national organization of Baptists in the U.S. Founded in Philadelphia in May 1814 by delegates from eleven states, the convention was organized to sponsor missionaries Adoniram and Ann Judson.* The leading spirit in its formation was Luther Rice.* In 1817 its work was broadened to include home missions and education. In 1845 the convention was renamed the American Baptist Missionary Union.

Trifa, Valerian (1914-1987). Romanian Orthodox* archbishop. In the U.S. since 1950, Trifa rose quickly from editor of *Solia,* the journal of the

Romanian Orthodox episcopate, to its bishopric. Through *Solia*'s pages and other writings, he brought vitality to a failing church. In 1970 he became a founding father of the Orthodox Church in America.

Trinitarianism. *See* THEISM.

Trotman, Dawson Earle (1906-1956). Founder of the Navigators.* In 1933 Trotman began a Bible study* in his home and developed a discipleship* process emphasizing Bible memorization, prayer* and personal evangelism. The group was first called Navigators in 1934. Trotman also developed the follow-up program used by the Billy Graham Evangelistic Association.*

Trotter, Melvin Ernest (1870-1940). Evangelist and founder of urban rescue missions.* Converted in 1897 in Chicago's Pacific Garden Mission,* Trotter immediately began volunteering his spare time at the mission. He eventually planted urban missions in several states and worked as an itinerant* evangelist.

Trueblood, D(avid) Elton (1900-1994). Quaker* philosopher and theologian. Trueblood taught at Guilford College (1927-1930), Haverford College (1933-1936), Stanford University (1936-1945) and Earlham College (1945-1970). Active as a Quaker throughout his life and converted as an adult to evangelical* faith, Trueblood became known for his provocative slogan "abolish the laity," by which he meant that all believers are called to be ministers. Trueblood authored over thirty books, preached and lectured widely, and founded the Yokefellows, a small-group movement devoted to helping laypeople live out their Christian callings to ministry. Among Trueblood's many books are *The Company of the Committed* (1961) and *The Incendiary Fellowship* (1967).

Truett, George Washington (1867-1944). Baptist* pastor and denominational* leader. Truett was pastor of the First Baptist Church, Dallas (1897-1944), where his ministry was distinguished by pulpit eloquence and pastoral effectiveness. He served as president of the Southern Baptist Convention* (1927-1929) and of the Baptist World Alliance* (1934-1939).

Held in greatest esteem by all Baptists, Truett was widely viewed as an example of what a preacher and Southern Christian gentleman ought to be.

Trumbull, Charles Gallaudet (1872-1941). Leader of American Keswick movement.* Trumbull, who began editing the *Sunday School Times* in 1903, converted to Keswick sanctification in 1910. His most significant contribution was to help gain widespread acceptance for Keswick Holiness* teachings among American and Canadian evangelicals.

See also TRUMBULL, HENRY CLAY.

Trumbull, David (1819-1889). First Protestant* American missionary to Chile. In Chile, Trumbull found that he could work freely among the Roman Catholic* population. Trumbull's cooperation with all denominations* has been credited with the absence of sectarian divisions in Chile that have afflicted missionary work in the neighboring republics.

Trumbull, Henry Clay (1830-1903). Leader in the American Sunday-school movement.* As chair of the Fifth National Sunday School Convention (1872), Trumbull promoted the International Uniform Sunday School Lessons. A prolific author, he became editor of the *Sunday School Times* in 1875 and wrote numerous books on topics dealing with Christian education as well as theology.

Trusteeism. A lay movement seeking to adapt European Catholicism* to American republican values. Trusteeism emphasized the centrality of lay participation at the congregational level and exclusive lay control of ecclesiastical temporalities. Lay and clerical claims and counterclaims gave rise to a series of contracted debates and hostilities within a number of Catholic congregations during the antebellum period.

Lay trusteeism arose from a variety of sources, but it was legally grounded in the trustee system. According to American law, every congregation that wanted legal protection for its property had to elect a board of trustees who would be responsible for ecclesiastical temporalities. Such legal sanctions, the general republican atmosphere, the congregational practices of other Christian denominations and the European Catholic practice of patronage gave many of the elected lay trustees support for their demands for lay leadership and even control of their congregations.

The antitrustee party charged that the trustees'

claims, if fully implemented, would destroy Catholic identity. The trustees had identified Catholicism with a republicanism and Protestantism* which asserted that all authority, ecclesiastical as well as political, arose from the people. This was absolutely contrary to the Catholic view, which held that all ecclesiastical authority arose from divine commission.

From 1829 to 1855, the bishops—through individual efforts, conciliar* legislation, papal support and new American laws—were able to crush the republican lay assertiveness behind trusteeism and to gain for themselves legal control over ecclesiastical properties and temporalities.

See also HOGAN SCHISM.

Truth, Sojourner (Isabella Baumfree) (c. 1797-1883). Abolitionist* and women's rights lecturer. In 1843 Baumfree left New York in response to a vision of God. Asking God for a new name to complement her mission, she became "Sojourner Truth." Tall and stout, head wrapped in a Madras handkerchief turban, unable to read or write, Sojourner Truth spread the abolitionist message of freedom, using biblical references and stories in her heavy Dutch accent. She became famous throughout the North as an itinerant* preacher, abolitionist and advocate for the poor and women's rights.

Tucker, Henry St. George (1874-1959). Episcopal* missionary bishop and ecclesiastical statesman. In 1899 Tucker went as a missionary to northern Honshu, Japan, moving to Tokyo in 1902. In 1912 he became missionary bishop of Kyoto. Beginning in 1923, Tucker taught pastoral theology at Virginia Theological Seminary.

Tucker, William Jewett (1839-1926). Congregational* theologian and educator. In 1880 Tucker became professor of sacred rhetoric at Andover Theological Seminary.* He became one of the foremost leaders in a liberal theological movement sweeping Congregationalism, known as the New Theology.*

In 1893 Tucker became president of Dartmouth College, where his educational vision and business acumen made that struggling college into a nationally respected institution.

Turkevich, Leonty (1876-1965). Russian Orthodox* Metropolitan* of All America and Canada. For nearly six decades Turkevich provided

leadership in the Russian Mission and later in the Metropolia. He authored its statutes, led its councils, edited its publications and advanced the somewhat unpopular cause of theological education. As the first dean of the North American Seminary in Minneapolis, he modified the prescribed Russian curriculum to fit the American situation.

Turner, Henry McNeal (1834-1915). Born a free African-American at Newberry Courthouse, South Carolina, Turner became a popular revivalist* for the Methodist Episcopal Church,* South, in Georgia and other Southern states. Joining the African Methodist Episcopal Church (AME)* in 1858, he filled pastorates in Baltimore and Washington, D.C.

A vigorous human rights advocate, he denounced Supreme Court decisions in 1883 and 1896 denying federal civil rights* protection to African-Americans.

Turner, Nat (1800-1831). Leader of a slave revolt and lay preacher. Turner, a slave in Virginia, was an exhorter, or lay preacher. Inspired by certain biblical texts, Turner began to receive visions of liberating his people. In August 1831 he led a revolt, with about sixty men joining him in killing fifty-seven white Virginians. By November he had been captured and executed.

Tuttle, Daniel Sylvester (1837-1923). Episcopal* bishop. In 1867 Tuttle set out for the Rocky Mountain Jurisdiction, which included Montana, Idaho and Utah. The new territory stretched out across 340,000 square miles without even a single ordained priest.

For the next nineteen years "Bishop Dan" labored in his pioneering ministry, often preaching* in places where clergy had never traveled. Churches in the territory soon developed under his care, as did a hospital and a number of schools.

Tyler, Bennet (1783-1858). Congregational* minister, educator and theologian. In 1829 Tyler engaged in a dispute with Yale theologian Nathaniel W. Taylor.* Joining with other conservatives in what soon was called the Tyler-Taylor controversy, Tyler attempted to revive the theological outlooks of the Puritan* tradition and Jonathan Edwards.*

In 1833 the Theological Institute of Connecticut (later renamed the Hartford Theological Seminary) was founded to offset the growing influence of Taylor and Lyman Beecher.* Tyler served the institute as president until his death.

Tyler-Taylor Controversy. See TYLER, BENNET.

Tyng, Stephen Higginson, Jr. (1839-1898). Evangelical* Episcopal* rector and premillennialist* leader. Following the Civil War* Tyng organized the Church of the Holy Trinity in New York City. He developed an outstanding church, combining a strong evangelical witness and an effective outreach to the urban poor. Tyng organized the first International Prophetic Conference in 1878, which was held in his church.

Tyng, Stephen Higginson, Sr. (1800-1885). Episcopal* minister. A convinced evangelical low churchman,* Tyng was a vehement opponent of both the Tractarian movement* and broad-church* liberalism.* He was a commanding orator and pulpiteer. Thousands flocked to hear Tyng at St. Paul's in Philadelphia (known as Tyng's Theatre). He was also a vigorous promoter of Sunday schools,* attracting more than two thousand children to his own Sunday school in Philadelphia.

UFM International. Nondenominational foreign missionary agency. Unevangelized Fields Mission (UFM) began as a faith mission in London in 1931, comprising missionaries formerly with Worldwide Evangelization Crusade.

Over the years UFM has grown through several mergers. In 1977 the Australian, British and North American branches of UFM recognized each other as separate, independent organizations with their respective mission fields. The North American agency officially changed its name to UFM International in 1980.

Ukrainian Catholics in America. Christians whose church is under the jurisdiction of the pope of Rome but whose church law is that of Eastern Orthodoxy.* They are also called Ruthenian Catholics, Byzantine Rite Catholics or Uniates.

In North America, Ukrainian Catholics experienced considerable religious conflict at the hands of Latin rite* Catholics. Eventually a papal decree in 1929 confirmed their right to maintain their distinct religious practices.

Ultradispensationalism. A movement within dispensationalism* which argues that the church began sometime after the Day of Pentecost. All dispensationalists make a sharp distinction between Israel and the church and are thus concerned to show when the administration of God's redemptive plan shifted from one to the other. Most believe that the shift occurred in the events described in Acts 2, on the Day of Pentecost. But some others, labeled "ultra" by the majority, point to later times—specifically, Acts 13 or Acts 28.

Ultramontanism. The movement in Roman Catholicism* to centralize authority in the papacy.* Meaning literally "over the mountains," it initially referred to those in the French church who resisted Gallicanism* and looked over the Alps to the pope for direction.

See also VATICAN-U.S. CATHOLIC CHURCH RELATIONS.

Unction. The sacrament* of healing in the Roman Catholic* and Eastern Orthodox* churches, based on the New Testament and on early Christian tradition.

Medieval practice in Western Christianity limited the sacrament to those who were dying, hence the phrase *extreme unction.* Vatican II* restored it to its earlier healing purpose.

Unevangelized Fields Mission. *See* UFM INTERNATIONAL.

Unger, Merrill F. (1909-1980). Old Testament scholar, writer and popular conference speaker. From 1948 to 1967 Unger served as professor of Semitics and Old Testament at Dallas Theological Seminary.* He also pastored several churches and published widely. Beginning in 1956 he was assistant editor of *Bibliotheca Sacra.*

Uniates. *See* EASTERN RITE CATHOLICS.

Unification Church, The. A religious movement founded in 1954. The founder of the church, Sun Myung Moon, was born of Presbyterian* parents in Korea in 1920. Moon first toured the U.S. in the 1970s, when his group achieved visibility in the media as increasing numbers of young adults joined. Followers of Moon, popularly known as Moonies, became known for their zealous recruitment tactics and fundraising efforts. Moonies believe that Moon is the designated Messenger of God sent to unite all religions.

Union Theological Seminary (New York). Protestant* mainline* seminary. Founded in 1836 by a group of New School* Presbyterian* leaders, the school quickly became one of the nation's larger seminaries, in great measure because of the prominence of biblical scholar Edward Robinson* and theologian Henry Boynton Smith.* Originally an independent institution, Union became affiliated with the (Northern) Presbyterian Church in 1870. By 1904 it had become fully nondenominational. It is renowned for its theological library of more than half a million volumes.

Unitarian Controversy. The series of theological debates (1805-1825) between orthodox* Calvinists* and liberals* that split Massachusetts Congregationalism* and led to the formation of the American Unitarian Association.* Theological dispute had been building within Puritan* Congregationalism throughout the late eighteenth century, but the controversy was sharpened dramatically with the 1805 election of Henry Ware* as Hollis Professor of Divinity at Harvard.* The dispute centered on two key issues: the nature of biblical interpretation and authority,* and the extent of human capacity for spiritual development. The Unitarians moved increasingly toward historically and rationally conditioned biblical interpretation. And in rejecting the Calvinist doctrine of innate sinful* depravity, the Unitarians stressed the cultivation of the spiritual resources inherent in the self.

Unitarian Universalist Association. The Unitarian Universalist Association (UUA) was established in 1961 with the merger of the American Unitarian Association* and the Universalist Church of America. Both were small denominations,* primarily of New England origin, that exemplified two separate courses of the development of religious liberalism* in America.

The term *Unitarianism* refers most generally to a belief that God is one Person rather than a trinity. In the U.S. its most immediate origins were among a group of mid-eighteenth-century Boston-area clergy who became skeptical both of the revivalism* of the Great Awakening* and of traditional Puritan* Calvinism.* These men, led by Charles Chauncy,* Ebenezer Gay* and Jonathan Mayhew,* were New England Arminians* who were especially hostile to the doctrine of original sin.* In 1825 the American Unitarian Association was founded in Boston as a loose institutional alliance of liberals and included eighty-eight of the hundred oldest congregations in eastern Massachusetts.

Meanwhile, another liberal movement was taking shape, not in cosmopolitan Boston, but primarily in smaller towns along the Atlantic coast. Universalism,* the doctrine that all of humanity would ultimately be saved, was first preached in New England by John Murray* and was given systematic theological articulation and leadership through the work of Hosea Ballou.* Although the movement resisted tight organization, legal pressures led to the forming of the Universalist Church of America in 1833.

In 1961 the two denominations, which were facing many common pressures, merged to form the Unitarian Universalist Association. Membership in 1991 stood at about 191,000, with 978 churches and fellowships in the U.S. and about 6,000 members and 42 churches in Canada.

Unitarianism. *See* UNITARIAN CONTROVERSY; UNITARIAN UNIVERSALIST ASSOCIATION.

United Church of Canada, The. Canada's largest Protestant* denomination.* The United Church of Canada was formed officially in June 1925, out of the union of the following groups: the Methodist* Church, Canada (representing the large majority of Canadian Methodists); the Congregational Union of Canada (representing virtually all Canadian Congregationalists*); the Council of Local Union Churches (numbering about three thousand congregations at the time); and about two-thirds of the Presbyterian* Church in Canada. Some joined the church in the interests of sparking a renewal of evangelical* piety* and outreach; others saw it as the beginning of a national church that would manifest the concerns of the modern mainline* ecumenical movement;* still others, especially on the prairies, saw it as a way of avoiding the costly duplication of resources, whether pastors or church buildings, in small communities.

Declining in numbers since the early 1960s, the church in 1992 claimed 771,548 full communicant members in 4,019 congregations.

United Church of Christ, The. Formed in 1957, the United Church of Christ (UCC) was a merger of the Congregational Christian Churches and the Evangelical and Reformed Church. Through its denominational* traditions the Congregational wing of the UCC goes back to the original Congregationalism* of Puritan* New England.

Congregationalists first united in 1871, establishing the National Council of Congregational

Churches (NCCC). In 1892 the NCCC was joined by a body of Congregational Methodist* churches in Georgia and Alabama, and in 1925 the Evangelical Protestant Churches, a group of Ohio Valley congregations, also joined the NCCC.

In 1931 the General Convention of the Christian Church, or Christian Connection,* united with the NCCC to form the General Council of Congregational and Christian Churches.

The other church tradition represented in the UCC union of 1957, the Evangelical and Reformed Church, was itself the product of a union of two church traditions, both of them tracing their histories back to German immigrants* to America.

The contemporary UCC denomination is noted for its social consciousness, having been influenced by the Social Gospel movement.* In 1992 the UCC reported an inclusive membership of over 1.5 million in 6,264 congregations throughout the U.S.

See also REFORMED TRADITION IN AMERICA.

United Council for Christian Democracy. A nondenominational, social activist organization. Organized in 1936, the council sought to bring together the more radical Christians from various denominations who were concerned with the inequities in the social and economic order. Reinhold Niebuhr,* a socialist and outspoken critic of the capitalistic system, served as its chairman.

United Domestic Missionary Society. *See* NEW YORK MISSIONARY SOCIETY.

United Holy Church of America. A predominantly African-American Holiness* denomination.* The church was founded in May 1886 in North Carolina. A trinitarian body, it accepts the faith confessed in the Apostle's Creed and delimited by the Protestant Reformation. Tremendous emphasis is placed on sanctification* as essential for Christian life. Equal emphasis is placed on Spirit baptism,* which, like sanctification, is regarded as subsequent to conversion.* The United Holy Church practices charismatic manifestations of the Spirit, including speaking in tongues.*

The church experienced unsurpassed growth in the first half of the century through a program of evangelism* and missions* centered in district convocations.

United Methodist Church. The United Methodist Church came into existence in 1968 through a union between the Methodist Church* (10 million members) and the Evangelical United Brethren (800,000 members)—two denominations* that traced their roots to revivals* in eighteenth-century Britain and America.

In 1769 the British Methodist conference, under John Wesley's* leadership, officially sent missionaries to America. In 1784 Wesley set apart Francis Asbury* and Thomas Coke* as "superintendents"* of the Methodists in America. That year, at the Christmas Conference* in Baltimore, the Methodist Episcopal Church was formed.

After 1784 the Methodist Episcopal Church grew especially through the agency of circuit riders,* who traveled on horseback to organize classes and congregations on the frontier,* and of camp meetings,* which maintained the revivalist zeal. By 1840 the church, with 580,000 members, was the largest Protestant denomination in America.

Growth continued even after debate over slavery divided the denomination in 1844 into two regional denominations. In 1939 the two bodies reunited as the Methodist Church. Seven years later the Evangelical United Brethren Church was formed, which joined the Methodist Church in the 1968 merger.

See also METHODIST CHURCHES; REVIVALISM, GERMAN-AMERICAN; WESLEYAN TRADITION.

United Pentecostal Church, International. Oneness* Pentecostal* denomination.* Formed in 1945 by the merger of the Pentecostal Assemblies of Jesus Christ and the Pentecostal Church, Inc., the United Pentecostal Church is the largest white oneness Pentecostal denomination. The group administers baptism* "in the name of Jesus" and believes that there is only one Person in the Godhead, Jesus Christ.

United Presbyterian Church in the United States of America. *See* PRESBYTERIAN CHURCH (U.S.A.).

United Society of Believers in Christ's Second Appearing. *See* SHAKERS.

United States Catholic Conference, The. The public policy* agency of the Catholic* bishops of America. As an organization of Catholic laypeople, clergy and religious,* the United States Catholic Conference (USCC) serves as a consultative body for the American Catholic Church in such areas as education, social action and immigration.* The USCC was formed in 1966 as a result of the post-Vatican II* restructuring of the National Catholic Welfare Conference.*

United States Catholic Mission Council. *See* MISSIONS, ROMAN CATHOLIC FOREIGN.

United States Center for World Mission. An evangelical* foreign missions* center in Pasadena, California. Begun in 1976 by Ralph (a professor at Fuller Seminary's* School of World Mission) and Roberta Winter, the center houses dozens of specialized mission agencies which collectively encourage the whole church in the task of establishing reproducing congregations in every people group by the year 2000.

United States Christian Commission. Northern Protestant* charitable organization during the Civil War.* The commission was formed in 1861 under the guidance of the New York YMCA* to provide charitable assistance to Union forces. It ultimately donated and dispersed over $6 million in money, goods and services.

Unity School of Christianity. A New Thought religious movement. The Unity School of Christianity traces its origin to Kansas City, Missouri, where, in 1889, its cofounders, Myrtle and Charles Fillmore, decided to dedicate their lives to the study and teaching of practical Christianity. From modest beginnings, Unity has grown in size and impact so that today it daily affects the lives of over two million persons through its devotional magazine, the *Daily Word.*

Unity, which has discernible theological and historical links with Christian Science,* teaches the unreality of evil and the innate divinity of humanity.

Universalism. The belief that ultimately all individuals will be saved. Universalism has traditionally sought to defend its viewpoint on the grounds that eternal punishment for sin* is inconsistent, from the standpoint of both Scripture and reason, with belief in the existence of a loving and merciful God who desires the salvation* of all.

A form of Universalism was held by the New England Congregationalists* Jonathan Mayhew* and Charles Chauncy.* The founder of American Universalism, however, is considered to be John Murray.*

Following the publication of the *Humanist Manifesto* in 1933, Universalism struggled with the challenge of humanism.* By the 1950s most Universalists had come to hold that all religions are to be valued as a means of realizing the potential inherent in all of mankind. This religious inclusivism made possible a greater cooperation with Unitarianism, a relationship which resulted finally in the merging in 1961 of the Universalist Church of America with the American Unitarian Association to form the Unitarian Universalist Association.*

Unruh, Tobias A. (1819-1875). A leader in the emigration of Mennonites* from Russia to North America. Unruh was a conservative member of the delegation of twelve Mennonites and Hutterites* from Russia and Poland who traveled to North America in 1873 to determine the prospects for Mennonite emigration. He and his family emigrated in 1875, settling in South Dakota, where he died a few months later.

Urban Churches and Ministries. While the Spanish and French established trading posts and forts like St. Augustine (1560), the Puritans* brought with them an urban vision. John Winthrop* spoke of their being "a city on a hill"; Boston was to be the capital of a new holy commonwealth, the foundation for the imminent establishment of the kingdom of God* in America.

While the "city on a hill" ideal lives on, lingering in the rhetoric of America's political leaders, the reality of the holy city quickly fell prey to secularism.* Boston quickly lost its Christian vision, as speculation, dissent and factionalism came with the emigration from the Old World. For men such as Winthrop, urban ministry was essentially paternalistic, consisting of the "high and eminent" caring for those who were "mean and in subjection." It was assumed that the godly and the moral would become materially prosperous, while the poor usually deserved their own plight.

The Second Great Awakening* of the early nineteenth century brought some focus on the cities, with evangelists such as Lyman Beecher,* Albert Barnes* and Charles G. Finney* conducting urban revivals.* The revivalism of this period united evangelism with social reform in the conviction that the converted person would, out of disinterested benevolence, act for the good of society. This bore fruit in a number of benevolent societies which focused on urban needs.

The greatest growth in urban ministry followed the Civil War.* Cities such as Boston, Philadelphia and New York experienced phenomenal growth between 1860 and 1890, which in turn placed tremendous pressure on urban social and economic order. Western cities also flourished.

New efforts to redeem the city were attempted. Among them, urban evangelists such as Dwight L. Moody and Billy Sunday* argued for conversion, not social reform. Advocates of a Social Gospel,* in contrast, established so-called institutional churches* and settlement houses* to educate, train, socialize and Americanize the immigrant poor.

In the twentieth century, a few white churches have chosen to remain in the city, while many have fled to the suburbs. In the wake of the exodus of the white church, blacks,* Asians* and Hispanics* have established their churches in the city. Catholic* churches, with their geographically determined parish system, have also remained in the urban centers as transmitters and guardians of religion and immigrant culture.

See also RESCUE MISSION MOVEMENT; SOCIAL GOSPEL MOVEMENT.

Urbana Conventions. Popular name for triennial student missions conventions sponsored by InterVarsity Christian Fellowship* of Canada and the U.S. Beginning in 1946, these conventions have challenged college and university students to become a part of the evangelical foreign missions movement. Since 1948 the conventions, attracting upward of eighteen thousand people, have been held on the campus of the University of Illinois at Urbana.

Urshan, Andrew (Bar-) David (1884-1967). Oneness Pentecostal* minister. Born in Persia, Urshan was ordained* by W. H. Durham* in 1910 and four years later returned to Persia as a missionary. He traveled throughout Eastern Europe, baptizing and rebaptizing converts with a "Jesus only" formula. Urshan proved to be an influential thinker among oneness Pentecostals.

Ursulines. A name used to refer to a variety of women's religious* communities, most often engaged in teaching, and identified with St. Angela Merici, who formed the Company of St. Ursula in 1535 for the protection and Christian education of young girls who, without entering a cloister or leaving their homes, chose a life of consecrated virginity.

The first convent of women in the present-day U.S. was Ursuline, established in New Orleans. Expansion from the New Orleans convent introduced Ursulines to America, where over 1,900 now minister.

Valentine, Milton (1825-1906). Lutheran* theologian and educator. Following several pastorates, Valentine became a teacher at the Lutheran Theological Seminary in 1866, president of Gettysburg College (1868-1884) and president and professor of systematic theology at the Seminary (1884-1903). He moved away from the earlier evangelical position of Samuel S. Schmucker* by accepting a milder form of the confessionalism* predominant in his day.

Van Alstyne, Fanny Jane Crosby. *See* CROSBY (VAN ALSTYNE), FANNY JANE.

Van Cott, Margaret Ann Newton (1830-1914). Methodist* evangelist. Van Cott was granted a local preacher's license* in 1869—the first American woman licensed to preach from a Methodist pulpit. She conducted revivals* for more than thirty years, during which an estimated seventy-five thousand people were converted.*

Van Dusen, Henry Pitney (1897-1975). Protestant* theological educator and ecumenical* leader. Van Dusen served from 1926 to 1963 at Union Theological Seminary,* New York (as president from 1945), which he led to a position of great prominence and prestige among liberal Protestant seminaries.

Van Dusen was a leading American Protestant* advocate of the ecumenical movement,* actively promoting the formation of the World Council of Churches.* In 1941 he was a cofounder of the journal *Christianity and Crisis.*

Van Dyke, Henry (1852-1933). Presbyterian* minister, educator, author and diplomat. Van Dyke's literary career began with the publication of *The Reality of Religion* (1884), followed by a great variety of works. His literary renown led to his appointment as professor of English literature at Princeton* University (1899-1913; 1919-1923).

President Woodrow Wilson* appointed him ambassador to the Netherlands and Luxembourg (1913-1916).

Van Dyke's theology can best be described as mediating, with a liberal tendency. A leader in the movement for creedal revision, he particularly opposed the traditional Reformed* doctrine of reprobation and was a convinced evolutionist.*

Van Til, Cornelius (1895-1987). Reformed apologist.* Van Til taught at Westminster Theological Seminary in Philadelphia from 1929 to 1975. He built his apologetics* around an original application of traditional Reformed* theology.* Borrowing from, as well as correcting, the Princeton* traditions of B. B. Warfield* and the Dutch contributions of Abraham Kuyper* and Herman Bavinck, he constructed a presuppositional apologetic based on two fundamental assertions: (1) the Creator-creature distinction demands that human beings presuppose the self-attesting triune God in all their thinking; (2) unbelievers will resist this obligation in every aspect of life and thought.

Vancouver Assembly. The sixth assembly of the World Council of Churches,* meeting in 1983 in Vancouver, Canada. The theme of the assembly, "Jesus Christ—The Life of the World," provided occasion to emphasize the life-affirming nature of Christianity and the church's mission to deny the ultimate power of the world's oppression, death and destruction. The assembly did not concern itself with substantial reports but with wide participation and worship.

By far the largest WCC assembly ever held to that date, Vancouver had 4,500 participants, including 847 voting delegates from 301 member churches.

Varick, James (c. 1750-1827). Cofounder and first bishop of the African Methodist Episcopal

Zion Church.* Varick's Zion Society became one of several African-American churches in the Methodist Episcopal denomination between 1799 and 1816. With the Zion congregation, Varick refused to join the new African Methodist Episcopal* (AME) denomination out of Philadelphia and later created an independent organization, another AME Church—the title of *Zion* being officially added in 1848.

Vasey, Thomas (c. 1746-1826). Methodist* missionary to America. Ordained* by John Wesley* for the purpose of establishing a church in America, Vasey joined Thomas Coke,* Richard Whatcoat* and Francis Asbury* in organizing the Methodist Episcopal Church at the 1784 Christmas Conference* in Baltimore. He assisted in the ordination of Asbury and others.

Vassar, Matthew (1792-1868). Baptist* philanthropist* and founder of Vassar College. In 1861 Vassar provided an endowment of almost unprecedented size ($400,000) for the first true liberal arts college for women in America. Vassar College's early board of trustees included Henry Ward Beecher* and Samuel F. B. Morse.* Vassar was committed to an educational experience that was Christian but never sectarian, one that would foster "gifted, cultivated Christian women."

Vatican Council I (1869-1870). The First Vatican Council is counted by the Roman Catholic* Church as the twentieth ecumenical (or general) council. Membership was restricted to Roman Catholic cardinals and bishops, along with the superiors general of male religious orders.* A total of 793 participated at one time or other in four solemn public sessions and eighty-nine working sessions.

The council considered six draft proposals but accepted only two final documents. One was the constitution *Dei Filius,* which reaffirmed the inspiration and divine authorship of Scripture, as well as the church's authoritative role in determining the meaning of the revealed books. The other was the constitution *Pastor Aeternus,* which declared the meaning of the "primacy" and "infallibility"* attributed to the pope.

The council was called by Pope Pius IX,* whose papacy is the longest on record (1846-1878). The council's main focus was to be on contemporary rationalism, which was seen to be challenging religious faith, and on liberal political and intellectual orientations, which weakened the papacy's position in the church. The council would also have to deal with a division that had grown within Catholicism, between the centralizing forces of "ultramontanism,"* with its romantic* emphasis on the papacy, and liberal Catholics.

Vatican I was a European council of a European church. Asia, Africa, Australia and Oceania were represented by missionary bishops from Europe; not a single native of East Asia, India or Africa was present. Contrast with the situation a century later is sharp. By the late twentieth century well over half the world's Roman Catholics lived in Third World countries, and their churches are largely led by native bishops.

Although papal infallibility was not on the council's formal agenda, it had been discussed in the committee which prepared the agenda and was the major topic of Roman conversation during the winter of 1869-1870. Petitions which circulated indicated that approximately four-fifths of the council fathers supported the doctrine. Others ("inopportunists"), including most U.S. bishops, accepted it but felt the time was not right for a pronouncement. A small group opposed the definition because they judged it inadequately grounded in the church's tradition. The final vote was virtually unanimous in defining papal primacy and infallibility as Roman Catholic dogmas.*

The papal prerogative of infallibility has been used only once, when on November 1, 1950, Pope Pius XII* proclaimed the dogma of Mary's assumption* into heaven.

See also PAPACY AND U.S. CATHOLICS; PAPAL INFALLIBILITY; VATICAN COUNCIL II.

Vatican Council II (1962-1965). The Second Vatican Council had a revolutionary impact on American Catholic practices and self-awareness. It reformed liturgical* patterns, governing styles and ecclesiastical discipline. These changes had an even more significant influence upon the consciousness of many Catholics who had believed that their divinely established church was the one bastion of transcendence, stability and divine purpose in a world that was ceaselessly changing, apparently directionless and increasingly secular.

Vatican II was a pastoral council. It was called to revitalize Christian living among Catholics, to reform changeable ecclesiastical practices and structures, to nurture Christian unity, to engage

Catholicism in a compassionate dialogue with the modern world, to help promote world peace and social justice and to contribute to whatever advanced the dignity and unity of humanity. Internal and external renewal for the sake of Christian integrity and a more effective Christian mission in the world were the hallmarks of the council's intentions.

The American Contribution. The council enabled the American bishops to share their pastoral experiences with other bishops. With the help of their own theological experts, the American bishops contributed to the conciliar discussions on a number of issues that had received some preconciliar theological reflection.

Perhaps the most distinctive and creative American contribution to the conciliar debates was in the area of religious liberty.* John Courtney Murray's* previous twenty-year discussions on religious liberty prepared him to take a leading role in formulating the council's *Declaration on Religious Liberty.*

Conciliar Reforms. The council produced sixteen documents that described the church's understanding of its role and mission in the modern world. The documents on the liturgy, church, revelation, ecumenism, religious liberty, and the church and the modern world were the most significant of the sixteen.

The council fostered a reform mentality. Pope John XXIII used the Italian term *aggiornamento,** bringing the church up-to-date, to describe one of the council's chief purposes. For the pope, this meant that the council should enable Catholics to renew their faithfulness to the gospel in the modern world. The conciliar talk of renewal, change and reform, however, represented a dynamic shift of consciousness for many Catholics who were reared in a church that was accustomed to speaking about the church's irreformable nature and its unchanging practices. In its call for dialogue, the council ended the post-Tridentine confrontational and polemical posture toward Protestants and modernity.

Conciliar Reforms and American Realities. The council and the postconciliar reforms tended to complicate, intensify and justify for many American Catholics the cultural and social dynamics of change, diversity, openness to secularity and freedom during the 1960s and early 1970s. Visible changes in the liturgy, ecclesiastical discipline and piety,* more democratic and lay-involved patterns of governing parish* and diocesan*

churches, friendly relations and dialogues with other churches and religions, increased participation of religious and clergy in political and social-justice movements, new content and methods in catechetics* and theology, and departures of clerics and religious from their active ministries had profound effects upon the American Catholic sense of religious identity. Change itself was becoming a part of Catholic identity, replacing the former sense of permanence and stability.

Although the postconciliar reforms were generally accepted, they produced conflicts within the church that reinforced the dynamics of diversity and change. Reactions to the reforms and interpretations of the council's intentions varied considerably and created new ideological divisions within American Catholicism. Catholic traditionalists rejected the validity, not just the abuses, of postconciliar liturgical reforms. Other conservatives questioned the extent and uncontrolled pace of the reforms or thought that the elite liberal episcopal* and clerical leadership was imposing reforms that were unwarranted by the council. Liberals thought many of the reforms were minimal and did not really meet the needs of modernity. Many of them sought to extend the implications of Vatican II and also began to revise Catholic theological concepts and methods.

See also NEO-CONSERVATIVE CATHOLICISM; VATICAN COUNCIL I; VATICAN-U.S. CATHOLIC CHURCH RELATIONS.

Vatican-U.S. Catholic Church Relations. In the Catholic understanding of the church, the pope, as the bishop of Rome, is also the chief pastor and teacher of the whole church. His ministry, however, is not meant to replace or impede that of local bishops, who are believed to have their office not by papal delegation but from Christ through episcopal* ordination.* The need to discern the respective pastoral responsibilities of pope, local bishops and the priests who assist them, as well as the administrative difficulties generated by any large organization, have sometimes created tensions between the Vatican and the Catholic Church in the U.S.

America as Mission Territory. From the Vatican point of view, the new nation was a mission territory and remained under the supervision of the curial office for evangelization until 1908. Religious toleration, combined with disestablishment, presented the Vatican with a novel political situation. Occasionally, from colonial times until the present, the Vatican has intervened in an extraordinary way in matters having to do with church doctrine or discipline.

The area of church life in which it has exercised the greatest influence in the U.S. has been the selection of bishops. By 1917 the arrangement of local recommendation and papal appointment of bishops, operative in the U.S. since 1822, had become universalized.

Rome and the Emerging American Catholic Identity. As the nineteenth century progressed, the Vatican exerted greater influence on American church affairs. The papacy had gained in stature on a wave of ultramontane* resistance to state control of the church in modern Europe. The ensuing trend to Roman centralization of administration grew stronger under Pope Pius IX.*

A series of events, culminating in the First Vatican Council* (1870), brought significant numbers of American bishops to Rome for firsthand contact with the reinvigorated papacy. Leo's censure of "Americanism"* in 1899 joined with Pius X's* condemnation of modernism* in 1907 to cast a smothering cloud over American Catholicism and its incipient theological gropings.

The years after Vatican II* brought lively attempts to realize its calls for liturgical reform and collegial structures. Ensuing tensions became apparent with widespread dissent by American Catholics over *Humanae Vitae,* Pope Paul VI's* 1968 encyclical* on birth control.*

Recent Relations and Tensions. Reemphasizing the need for Catholic unity in faith and discipline for the sake of the church's mission to the world, Pope John Paul II* has made a number of interventions into the life of the Catholic Church in the U.S., including personal visits in 1979 and 1987.

Under Pope John Paul II, the selection of bishops has remained the Vatican's single most effective means of influencing the church in the U.S. Despite historical precedent for popular elections, present church law provides no role for the people in the selection of their bishops and parochial pastors.

With the Vatican's doctrinal commitment to religious freedom, formal diplomatic relations between the U.S. and the Vatican City State, established by President Reagan* in 1984, and the 1985 agreement between the Vatican and the Italian government separating church and state in Italy, few Americans any longer regard the Vatican's relations with the U.S. Catholic Church as the intrusion of a foreign government inimical to Ameri-

can political institutions.

See also CONCILIAR TRADITION, AMERICAN; PAPACY AND UNITED STATES CATHOLICS; TRUSTEEISM.

Veniaminov, Innocent (Ivan Veniaminov) (1797-1879). Russian Orthodox* missionary bishop. Veniaminov accepted his bishop's 1822 call to mission in the Aleutian Islands with reluctance, but by the time he left Unalaska ten years later, most of the inhabitants of the region were practicing Orthodox Christians. This was the result of his dedication to establishing schools and studying the local language and culture.

See also MISSIONS TO ALASKA, RUSSIAN ORTHODOX.

Verbeck, Guido Herman Fridolin (1830-1898). Reformed missionary to Japan. Verbeck was one of the first six Protestant* missionaries to arrive in Japan in 1859, the year that four ports were opened to foreigners. From 1868 to 1878 he helped the government set up a new school in Tokyo, which developed into what is now Tokyo University. The last twenty years of his life he gave to evangelism and Bible translation.

Verot, Jean-Pierre Augustin Marcellin (1805-1876). Bishop of Savannah and of St. Augustine. In 1858, consecrated* a bishop, Verot was appointed vicar apostolic of Florida. In 1861, while retaining authority in Florida, Verot also was appointed to the See of Savannah.

In time Verot became a social critic, endorsing Southern nationalism, supporting the Confederate war effort and becoming known as the rebel bishop. During Reconstruction, Verot launched the church's most ambitious missionary program among the freedmen, which included building special schools for them.

Vesey, Denmark (c. 1767-1822). African Methodist* and slave-rebellion leader. After purchasing his freedom in 1799, Vesey became a lay leader in the African Methodist Episcopal Church* in Charleston, South Carolina.

Citing various liberationist and apocalyptic biblical texts, Vesey planned an elaborate conspiracy for July 1822. Fearful slaves revealed the plot to authorities, who arrested, tried and executed Vesey and several others. Vesey has been honored in the memory of African-Americans as a revolutionary advocate for liberation.

Vesey, William (1674-1746). Colonial Anglican* rector in New York City. The first rector of Trinity Church in New York City, Vesey served in that post for half a century (1697-1746), overseeing the development of the colony's wealthiest parish and aggressively promoting the interests of the Church of England.

Vespers. The evening hour of prayer. Liturgically, vespers is a service of praise and thanksgiving. Besides Catholics, the Lutherans* and Episcopalians* include an evening prayer service in their liturgies.

See also EVENING SERVICE.

Vestry. Originally a room for keeping vestments, the term became attached to the parishioners who administer parish* business in the Episcopal Church.* Vestries historically were a source of opposition to an episcopate.*

Victorious Christian Life. An evangelical* spiritual movement proclaiming the possibility and means for attaining immediate freedom from the whole power of every known sin.* The outreach of the American Wesleyan*/Holiness* tradition to Great Britain through meetings led by Hannah Whitall Smith,* Robert Pearsall Smith* and William E. Boardman* led to the spirituality of the Keswick movement,* which began in 1875 with annual conferences in Keswick, England, and soon spread to the U.S.

Victorious Life spirituality became identified with fundamentalism* as expressed in *The Fundamentals.* The perspective has played a profound and often unrecognized role in shaping twentieth-century evangelical spirituality.

Vietnam War and the American Churches. In 1955 the U.S. began to send financial aid to the government of South Vietnam. The aid accelerated after 1964, when Congress authorized the president to provide military assistance to South Vietnam, although this act was not an official declaration of war. Americans began to engage in combat early in 1965. By March 1973, when the last American troops left Vietnam, over 46,000 Americans had been killed and over 300,000 wounded. The war stimulated violent emotions, pro and con, among Americans and was the most unpopular war of the twentieth century. Religious people and institutions participated in the controversy.

The most visible reaction among religious people was opposition. Many who opposed the war for Christian reasons tried to influence the general population and the government through extensive writing. They asserted that the war was immoral for a variety of reasons. It was an intrusion into a civil war between North and South Vietnam. It was a racist war in two senses: It was aggression by a white nation against Asian people, and the white nation used its own racial underclass to do the bulk of the fighting—the majority of Americans drafted being poor and African-American.

Opposition took the form of action as well as writing. Religious people conducted marches in the streets and prayer vigils at theological seminaries, churches and synagogues. Others took more direct and controversial action, such as destroying draft board records.

It should not be thought that all religious people or institutions opposed the war. Many believed America's cause in Southeast Asia was proper as a defense against "godless communism." America was a defender of liberty and democracy,* and thus the war was not inconsistent with Judeo-Christian moral principles. A highly visible exponent of such a view was Francis Cardinal Spellman,* archbishop of New York.

But by 1969 the nation had grown weary of the war and perhaps had been sensitized by the religious arguments against it. In a survey, 75 percent of those having no religious preference thought it had been a mistake to send troops, while 64 percent of the Jews, 59 percent of the Protestants* and 53 percent of the Roman Catholics* agreed that it had been wrong.

Many believed that the Vietnam War affected American religion in ways that would be felt for the remainder of the twentieth century, primarily in terms of redefinitions of the role of local clergy in the social arena and the development of theological conservatism as a reaction to the overt radicalism of the 1960s and early 1970s.

Vincent, John Heyl (1832-1920). Methodist* bishop and educator. In 1861 Vincent held the first Sunday School Teacher's Institute in America. His Sunday-school interests led to the founding, with Lewis Miller, of the Chautauqua institutes in 1874. The Chautauqua meetings developed into the era's most extensive American lay educational movement.

Virtues, Cardinal. In traditional Catholic philosophy all other virtues depend upon the four cardinal virtues—prudence, courage, moderation and justice—because they describe the fundamental structures of health of the soul. The cardinal moral virtues are distinguished from the intellectual virtues (wisdom, science and understanding), and both are distinguished, as natural virtues, from the three supernatural virtues (faith, hope and charity), which have God as their object.

Vocation. The term *vocation* describes both God's general election* of his people to salvation* and fellowship in the covenant* community and his particular assignment to serve one's neighbor through daily work. Biblical teaching focuses directly on the former and provides a sound basis for the latter, which was positively articulated by the Protestant* reformers.

The Puritans* adopted this concept of vocation, which had important consequences for New England's colonial period. Characterized by a this-worldly asceticism and a strong sense of personal calling and responsibility in their employment, Puritans showed themselves serious and purposeful in their civic and economic affairs.

See also PROTESTANT WORK ETHIC.

Voluntarism. *See* VOLUNTARYISM, VOLUNTARISM.

Voluntary Societies. *See* PARACHURCH GROUPS.

Voluntaryism, Voluntarism. Scholars of American religion have used both *voluntarism* and *voluntaryism* to refer to the principle that individuals are free to choose their religious beliefs and associations without political, ecclesiastical or communal coercion. One of the distinctive traits of American religion, voluntaryism places value on individual choice while assuming the separation of church and state* and a plurality* of voluntary religious denominations* and societies.

While voluntaryism has roots in the Protestant* tradition as a whole, which emphasizes the individual's direct access to God, it received a clear religious impetus from the First* and Second* Great Awakenings. Religious voluntaryism has shaped and been sustained by related American cultural values such as democracy,* individualism and the entrepreneurial spirit.

Volunteers of America. A nondenominational social service organization. The Volunteers of America was founded in 1896 by the husband-and-wife team of Ballington* and Maud* Booth. Similar to the Salvation Army in its mission but more democratic in its structure, it has blended social welfare with evangelism,* and temporal efforts with an emphasis on spiritual priorities, while utilizing military organization and garb.

Voodoo. Rites and beliefs derived from West African religions and syncretized with Catholicism. As an underground African-American church developed in the slave states, a distinctive variety of this "invisible institution" emerged as the voodoo cult associated with South Louisiana. Voodoo appeared in New Orleans between 1780 and 1810, especially with the arrival of refugees from Haiti.

Vos, Geerhardus (1862-1949). Presbyterian* theologian and author. Vos was the first professor of biblical theology* at Princeton Theological Seminary* (1893-1932). He did pioneering work in the discipline of biblical theology, based on a firm commitment to Scripture as God's inerrant Word. Among American orthodox* Protestant* theologians, Vos was among the first to grasp the fundamental significance of the progressive character of God's special, redemptive revelation.

Waddel, Moses (1770-1840). Presbyterian* educator in South Carolina and Georgia. In 1804 Waddel established at Willington, South Carolina, what was to be one of the most distinguished college preparatory schools in America.

In 1819 he became president of Franklin College at Athens, Georgia, a moribund institution of seven students. He built it up, laying the foundations for what would become the University of Georgia.

Walker, Williston (1860-1922). Congregational* churchman and church historian. Walker taught at Hartford Theological Seminary (1889-1901) and Yale University* (1901-1922). He was active in church unity and missionary efforts but is best known for his work in Congregational history.

In contrast to the overtly spiritual interpretations of Philip Schaff* and other contemporaries, Walker emphasized scientific, "secular" explanations of historical causation, with natural factors predominating over (but not eliminating) the supernatural.

Wallace, Foy E(sco), Jr. (1896-1979). Church of Christ* evangelist, debater and editor. A preacher for over sixty years, Wallace was best known as a controversialist, a man who refused to compromise with any view he considered wrong. In his debating, editing and writing, he is credited with stopping the spread of premillennialism* among the Churches of Christ.

Wallace, Lewis ("Lew") (1827-1905). Religious author. *Ben Hur* (1880) was the most popular of Wallace's seven books, selling 300,000 copies in ten years. He was perhaps the best-selling religious author in the America of his day, though he was never a member of any church.

Walsh, James Anthony (1867-1936). Co-founder and first superior general of the Catholic Foreign Mission Society of America* (Maryknoll). Beginning in 1910, Walsh and Father Thomas Frederick Price (1860-1919) actively promoted the establishment of a Catholic Foreign Mission Society of America. It received tentative approval from the U.S. bishops and Rome in 1911, and the seminary was established at Ossining, New York, in 1912.

Walther, Carl Ferdinand Wilhelm (1811-1887). Lutheran Church—Missouri Synod* theologian. In 1838 Walther joined a band of emigrants led by Pastor Martin Stephan* and settled with them in Perry County, Missouri. After Stephan had betrayed the group's trust, Walther remarshaled its strength in 1841 by developing a rationale for its existence as a free church.*

Walther began pastoring a congregation in St. Louis in 1842, and soon a group of like-minded pastors and congregations was drawn to him. In 1847 they formed the Evangelical Lutheran Synod of Missouri, Ohio, and Other States, with Walther serving as president (1847-1850, 1864-1878). From 1854 to 1887 he served as president of Concordia Seminary, which moved from Perry County to St. Louis in 1849. Walther's influence spread far beyond his own synod* through his books and his editorial work in *Lehre und Wehre,* a theological periodical founded in 1853.

Walworth, Clarence Augustus (1820-1900). Catholic* preacher and pastor. Deeply affected by the Tractarian movement* in England, Walworth became a Catholic in 1845 and with Isaac Hecker* and James McMaster joined the Redemptorists* and was ordained* for that community in 1848. In 1851 in the U.S., he acquired a reputation for compelling and eloquent pulpit oratory.

Wanamaker, John (1838-1922). Business entrepreneur, Sunday-school* leader and supporter of evangelical* ministries.* In 1858 Wanamaker founded Bethany Sunday School in a rough neighborhood of Philadelphia. In 1861 he began his mercantile business, which grew into an immense enterprise. He never relinquished his Christian undertakings, which in fact grew as phenomenally as his secular ones. He led Bethany in becoming the largest Sunday school in America, providing numerous social and recreational activities for people of all ages and economic levels.

Ward, Nathaniel (c. 1578-1652). Puritan* minister, legal scholar and author. After briefly pastoring the church in Agawam (Ipswich), Massachusetts, Ward turned to work in law in 1638. He authored the code of laws adopted in 1641 by the Massachusetts General Court, which helped establish government by law in America.

Warde, Frances (1810-1884). American founder of the Sisters of Mercy.* Warde led the first foundation of Sisters of Mercy to the U.S., arriving in Pittsburgh in December 1843. Warde and successive groups of Sisters of Mercy moved from Maine to California, not the least deterred by the hardships of travel by Conestoga wagon, stagecoach and steamer. Altogether Warde was responsible for establishing thirty-nine convents in the U.S. within the space of thirty-seven years.

Ware, Henry (1764-1845). Unitarian* theologian. By the time the Hollis Chair of Divinity was vacated by the death of David Tappan,* Ware had distinguished himself and was nominated by the Unitarian party to fill the post. Despite strong opposition from trinitarians, Ware became the first Unitarian professor at Harvard* in 1805. The ensuing Unitarian Controversy* was a significant struggle between orthodox Calvinists* and the emerging New England Unitarianism. Under Ware's leadership, Harvard established its own divinity school in 1816.

Warfield, Benjamin Breckinridge (1851-1921). Princeton* theologian. Warfield began his teaching career in New Testament at Western Seminary in Allegheny, Pennsylvania (1878-1887), and then, in 1887, succeeded A. A. Hodge* as professor of didactic and polemic theology at Princeton. From 1890 to 1903 he was editor of the *Princeton Review.*

Warfield's most lasting contribution was his exposure and refutation of liberalism's* naturalistic worldview and reinterpretation of traditional Christian teaching. To their acceptance of human autonomy and skepticism of the uniqueness of Christian revelation, Warfield responded by buttressing Princeton's main themes: (1) an authoritative Scripture and its supernaturalistic worldview, and (2) a strict Calvinistic* theology. Warfield honed a rigorous apologetic* method as a prolegomena to theology. In lengthy articles he defended traditional doctrines of the person and work of Christ and the distinctive teachings of Augustine, Calvin and the Westminster* standards.

Warner, Anna Bartlett (1827-1915). Hymn writer and novelist. Warner expressed her faith and her art in two collections of verse: *Hymns of the Church Militant* (1858) and *Wayfaring Hymns, Original and Translated* (1869). She is best known for her poem "Jesus Loves Me" (1859).

Warner, Daniel Sidney (1842-1925). Founder of the Church of God* (Anderson, Ind.). After experiencing entire sanctification* in 1877, Warner affiliated with the Northern Indiana Eldership of the Churches of God and began editing the group's *Herald of Gospel Freedom,* which eventually became the *Gospel Trumpet* (1881).

In seeking to restore the primitive* church, Warner alienated himself from his denomination.* He then began to organize like-minded individuals into a new movement which eventually became the Church of God (Anderson, Ind.).

Washington, Booker T(aliaferro) (1856-1915). Educator and founder of the Tuskegee Institute. Washington founded the Tuskegee (Ala.) Institute in 1881. In 1895 he delivered his famous "Atlanta Address," in which he encouraged African-American self-reliance in agriculture, mechanics and commerce. This speech and his subsequent autobiography, *Up from Slavery* (1901), gained Washington a national reputation, and he soon found himself the adviser to presidents and prominent American businessmen.

See also BLACK COLLEGES.

Washington, George (1732-1799). Statesman, soldier, first U.S. president and key founder of American civil religion.* Washington combined in his career many outstanding achievements in business, warfare and politics, taking the leading part in three great historical events: the American Revolution,* the drafting and ratification of the U.S. Constitution, and the establishment of the American republic and its institutions, especially the office of president. It was largely because of his leadership that the thirteen colonies became the U.S., a sovereign and independent nation. Because of his courage and integrity, Washington conferred on the presidency a prestige so great that political leaders afterward considered it the highest distinction in the land to occupy the chair he had honored.

Washington was not an orthodox* Christian,* as some have claimed, nor an orthodox deist,* as others have proposed. His personal theology,* based on his own understanding of the Bible and his reading of many Enlightenment* thinkers of his time, was most likely broadly Unitarian,* as was that of most deists of his time.

Quickly elevated to civil sainthood following his death, Washington also became the Moses figure who reminded his people that they enjoyed a common heritage and that God had chosen them as his New Israel for a new era. Washington provided not only critical leadership as the key founder of a new nation dedicated to republican ideals and human rights but also formative leadership as the key founder of the public faith of that new nation.

Watchtower Bible and Tract Society. *See* JEHOVAH'S WITNESSES.

Water Street and Bowery Missions. Urban rescue missions. In 1872 former convict Jeremiah McAuley* opened a facility in the Lower East Side of Manhattan where drifters could find food, clothing and shelter, and also hear the gospel of Jesus Christ. In 1876 it was renamed the McAuley Water Street Mission. Eventually the mission became—and still is—a model for urban missions* all over the U.S.

See also RESCUE MISSION MOVEMENT.

Way International, Inc., The. Religious group founded on the teachings of Victor Paul Wierwille. Considered a cult* by many observers, The Way International began in the 1940s under Wierwille's radio ministry and assumed its current name in 1974. The movement experienced dramatic growth through the 1960s and 1970s. Since Wierwille's death in 1985, the organization has declined. Its beliefs derive from the writing and

teaching of Wierwille, who believed that God gave him the only correct interpretation of Scripture since the first century.

Wayland, Francis (1796-1865). Baptist* minister and educator. Wayland was the president of Brown University* (1827-1855). He brought to the office a forceful personality, a wide range of knowledge and a concern for educational excellence, as well as strong convictions about teaching methods, curricula and textbooks. His determination to initiate change led to a reorganization of the university in 1850 with an expansion of the curriculum to include courses in science, modern languages, economics and a system of elective courses.

Respected as an administrator, a teacher and an author, Wayland touched thousands of students with his innovative ideas, intellectual breadth and passion for analysis, combined with a personal interest in them.

Wealth, Gospel of. A clear expression of social Darwinism and American confidence in progress, "the gospel of wealth" maintained that strong and moral people grow wealthy, while the poor deserve their fate. This view, which helped lead to capitalism, was opposed by Christian socialists* and the Social Gospel movement.*

See also POSITIVE THINKING.

Weaver, Rufus Washington (1870-1947). Baptist* minister and educator. Ordained* in 1893, Weaver held pastorates in several states prior to his election as president of Mercer University, where he served from 1918 to 1927. Under his leadership the school flourished.

Wedel, Cornelius H. (1860-1910). Mennonite* educator and historian. In 1874 Wedel immigrated with the entire Alexanderwohl village in southern Russia to central Kansas, where they established a congregation of the same name near Goessel. When Bethel College was established in 1893, Wedel became professor of Bible and the college's first president, a position he held until his premature death. His numerous textbooks present a comprehensive Mennonite worldview shaped by German culture.

Wedel, Cynthia Clark (1908-1986). Ecumenical* leader. Wedel was the first woman to serve as an associate general secretary of the National

Council of Churches* (1962-1969), as vice president (1957-1960) and as its president (1969-1972). She also was president of the World Council of Churches* (1975-1983).

A leader for racial justice, economic welfare and world peace, Wedel was a staunch advocate of women's full participation in the church and world issues.

Weems, Mason Locke ("Parson") (1759-1825). Anglican* minister, bookseller and author. Weems served Episcopal* parishes* in Maryland from 1784 until 1792. He began printing books in 1791, and from 1792 he devoted the rest of his life to the selling and writing of books and moralistic tracts, considering his profession a broadened scope of ministry.

Weigel, Gustave (1906-1964). Catholic* ecumenical* theologian. Weigel, who taught ecclesiology at Woodstock College, Maryland (1949-1964), tried to awaken American Catholics to the significance of the movement toward Christian unity, which he saw as "the most striking ecclesiological event since the sixteenth century." He encouraged American Catholics to study Protestant* traditions from their own sources. His openness to the mutual learning that took place in interconfessional conversations made him one of the earliest American Catholic ecumenists.

Weld, Theodore Dwight (1803-1895). Revivalist,* abolitionist* and temperance* reformer. Ward was converted* in 1825 under the ministry of Charles G. Finney* and immediately became a disciple of Finney.

Weld left Finney in 1827, becoming an abolitionist and temperance lecturer. He later attended Lane Seminary in Cincinnati (1832-1834), where he staged the famous Lane debates over the issue of slavery, converting a majority of the students to his cause. Expelled from the seminary, Weld became an agent of the newly founded American Anti-Slavery Society and began an itinerant campaign to spread the abolitionist message. He personally trained seventy other itinerants, including his future wife, Angelina Grimké.*

While his role in the abolition movement was for many years overlooked by historians, today many scholars regard Weld as having been the most important of the antislavery crusaders.

Weninger, Francis (1805-1888). Jesuit* missionary-preacher. Between 1848 and the mid-1880s, Weninger traveled extensively in the U.S. (usually alone), conducting over eight hundred parish missions* and delivering more than thirty thousand sermons.* He became widely known for his work with German-speaking Catholic immigrants.*

Wesley, John (1703-1791). Founder of Methodism.* At Oxford (1729-1735), Wesley directed the Holy Club, a group of serious-minded students who were also called Methodists. He had a disastrous missionary experience in Georgia (1735-1737), but on his return experienced an evangelical* conversion* in 1738 at a society meeting on Aldersgate Street, London. Less than a year later, a revival* broke out which continued until his death. In his fifty-two-year itinerant* ministry, Wesley preached over forty thousand sermons and averaged four thousand miles of travel annually.

Wesley's peculiar genius was the formation of societies which gathered and sustained those being awakened and converted. It was these societies that spread to America during the 1760s. Although basically a lay movement, the Methodist Societies on both sides of the Atlantic had a discipline and style directed by Wesley himself.

In spite of the American Revolution,* which in spirit despised all things British, the Methodists continued to grow, primarily under the leadership of Francis Asbury,* one of several missionaries appointed in England by Wesley to serve in America.

Wesleyan Church. A Holiness* denomination. The Wesleyan Church was formed in 1968 through the union of the Wesleyan Methodist Church (organized in 1843 by abolitionists* who were protesting the tolerance of slavery by the Methodist Episcopal Church*) and the Pilgrim Holiness Church (formed in 1922 as the result of several mergers). Both bodies had a theological kinship in their acceptance of the Wesleyan tradition* as it had been transformed through the Holiness movement of the late nineteenth century.

The denomination has maintained a strong emphasis on foreign missions and now has churches established in thirty-four countries outside of the U.S. and Canada.

Wesleyan Methodist Church. *See* WESLEYAN CHURCH.

Wesleyan Tradition. Generally speaking, the phrase *Wesleyan tradition in America* identifies the theological impetus for those movements and denominations* in America who trace their roots to a theological tradition finding its initial focus in John Wesley.* These include the various Methodist denominations (e.g., Wesleyan Church;* Free Methodist;* African Methodist Episcopal;* African Methodist Episcopal, Zion;* Christian Methodist Episcopal;* and United Methodist*), as well as those arising from the Holiness movement* and the Pentecostal movements.*

After his evangelical* conversion in 1738, Wesley sent his preachers to America (e.g., Francis Asbury* and Thomas Coke*), through whom he established a tradition that sought to emphasize justification* by faith as the gateway to sanctification* or "scriptural holiness." While Wesley's doctrine of justification is similar to that of the Continental Reformers, his insistence that *imputed* righteousness must become *imparted* righteousness marks the greatest distinction between the Wesleyan and the Reformed* or Lutheran* traditions, both of which maintain that Christian perfection cannot be obtained in this life. Wesley clearly speaks of a process that culminates in a second, definite work of grace, identified as entire sanctification. Its characteristics are: loving God and loving one's neighbor as oneself; living in Christlike meekness and lowliness of heart; abstaining from all appearance of evil and walking in all the commandments of God; being content with any state in life and doing all to the glory of God.

The Wesleyan tradition in America is far more than a theological expression, however. Wesley developed societies, bands and classes specifically for the purpose of discipling those who were earnest about maintaining a lively faith in Jesus Christ. These covenant fellowships became the heart of the Wesleyan revival, both in England and America.

Between 1784 and 1840 Methodist membership in the U.S. grew from approximately 18,000 to 580,000, making it the fastest-growing American church in the early nineteenth century. The legendary circuit rider* extended the influence of the Methodist not only across the frontier* but quite literally throughout the land.

More recently, much of the clarity which marked the earlier movement has been lost. Class meetings, if they exist at all, are no longer required. Furthermore, Wesleyans in America have tended to fragment over a variety of issues. The smaller denominations have traditionally emphasized doctrine. Larger groups tend to be more issue-oriented, focusing on social justice, human rights, racial equality, peace and justice. Unfortunately, many have forgotten that Wesley emphasized both personal and social aspects of the gospel.

See also HOLINESS CHURCHES AND ASSOCIATIONS; METHODIST CHURCHES; PERFECTIONISM; SANCTIFICATION.

West, Nathaniel (1826-1906). Presbyterian* premillennialist* and Bible conference* leader. One of the founders of the Niagara Bible Conference,* West was widely admired for his piety* and knowledge of the Scriptures. His numerous writings won many to premillennial eschatological* views.

West, Stephen (1735-1819). New Divinity* Congregational* minister. West was the pastoral and theological successor to Jonathan Edwards* at Stockbridge, Massachusetts. He spent his entire career (1759-1818) ministering to the whites and Native Americans of this western New England village. He developed the moral government theory of the atonement.*

Westminster Confession of Faith. A Reformed* confessional* document. Most of the colonists until 1776, and most American churches through much of the nineteenth century, were significantly influenced by the Westminster Confession of Faith (WCOF). Presbyterians,* Congregationalists* and Baptists* all subscribed to the WCOF with slight variations.

Historically, Presbyterians firmly subscribed to the WCOF until the 1880s. Efforts to broaden the confession led eventually to revisions in 1903. Today, the Presbyterian Church (U.S.A.)* gives allegiance to both the WCOF and other documents.

Whatcoat, Richard (1736-1806). Methodist* bishop. In 1784 John Wesley* ordained* Whatcoat for the soon-to-be-established church in America. With Thomas Coke* and Thomas Vasey,* Whatcoat took part in organizing the 1784 Christmas Conference* in Baltimore. In 1800 he was elected bishop, the second in American Methodism.

Wheatley, Phillis (c. 1753-1784). African-American poet. Encouraged by her master to read the Bible and classical literature, Wheatley learned to write poetry using the styles of the psalms and neoclassical poetry. In 1770 she published her first work, "An Elegiac Poem, on the Death of . . . George Whitefield." In London in 1773 she astonished the British aristocracy with her poetry.

Wheaton College. An independent evangelical* liberal arts college. Originally founded as Illinois Institute in 1848 by Wesleyan Methodists,* the school was rechartered as Wheaton College in 1860 by Congregationalists,* with Jonathan Blanchard* as its president. In the beginning the program of studies was uniformly classical, preparing students for the ministry and the professions. By the turn of the century, the curriculum had become broadly diversified.

Since the 1930s it has been a premier educational institution and intellectual haven, first for a broad, interdenominational fundamentalism* and then for the new evangelicalism* of the latter half of the twentieth century.

See also BILLY GRAHAM CENTER.

Wheaton Declaration. A broad-based international statement on evangelical* foreign missions* issued in 1966 in Wheaton, Illinois. The declaration specifically upheld the priority of evangelism,* repudiated both syncretism and universalism,* cautioned against uncritical optimism about changes in the Roman Catholic Church,* and urged greater unity among evangelicals in the missionary enterprise.

Wheelock, Eleazar (1711-1779). Colonial missionary to Native Americans and founder of Dartmouth College.* In the 1740s Wheelock emerged with Jonathan Edwards* as the strongest Connecticut supporter of the Great Awakening.*

In 1754 Wheelock opened Moor's Charity School in Lebanon, Connecticut, to instruct both white and Native American missionaries. He later raised funds enough to move his school to Hanover, New Hampshire, where in 1769 he founded Dartmouth College, naming it after a benefactor, the Earl of Dartmouth.

Wheelwright, John (1594-1679). Puritan* minister and major figure in the antinomian controversy* of 1636-1638. Upon his arrival in Boston in 1636, Wheelwright was plunged into the religious controversy surrounding his sister-in-law

Anne Hutchinson.* Wheelwright, who differed from his ministerial colleagues in placing greater emphasis on God's gift of grace to the unregenerate, was subsequently brought to trial and banished.

Whidden, Howard Primrose (1871-1952). Baptist* minister, politician and educator. In 1923 Whidden was appointed chancellor of McMaster University, a Baptist institution then located in Toronto. The move to Hamilton, Ontario, was accomplished in 1930 under Whidden's direction. Earlier he was deeply embroiled in the fundamentalist-modernist controversy.*

Whitaker, Alexander (1585-c. 1616). Colonial Anglican* minister. In 1611 Whitaker went with Sir Thomas Dale to Virginia, where he served Dale as chaplain and the settlements as minister until 1616 or 1617. Whitaker is generally credited with helping to steer the infant colony's religion toward low church* Anglicanism.

More so than his English peers, Whitaker was favorably impressed by the Native Americans he encountered.

White, Andrew (1579-1656). Catholic* missionary in Maryland. White was part of the first colonization voyage to Maryland in 1633. As Jesuit superior of the mission from 1634 to 1638, he established the system of self-supporting plantations worked by Jesuit priests as gentleman adventurers. In 1639 he began ministering to the Native American tribes indigenous to Maryland, a ministry greatly aided by his writing a grammar and dictionary of Algonquin.

White, Ellen Gould Harmon (1827-1915). Cofounder of the Seventh-day Adventist Church.* Ellen's family joined the Millerites in 1843. When Christ failed to return in 1844, Ellen, then seventeen years of age, experienced the first of over two thousand visions she would have over the course of her lifetime.

After a second vision, Ellen began traveling among the Millerite (adventist) companies, reporting what she had seen. She soon met James White, an adventist preacher, whom she eventually married in 1846. That same year the Whites began observing Saturday as the Sabbath.

Ellen's personal experience of illness led to an interest in health. After a vision in 1863 she began promoting health reform within the newly organized Seventh-day Adventist Church. After her husband's death, White traveled to Europe (1885-1887) and Australia (1891-1900).

White, John Campbell (1870-1962). Presbyterian* minister, educator and leader of the Laymen's Missionary Movement.* In 1906 White was a cofounder of the Laymen's Missionary Movement, which he served as general secretary (1907-1915).

In 1915 White turned his attention to education, serving as president of the College of Wooster (1915-1919) and then as vice president (1920-1927) and acting president (1938-1939) of Biblical Seminary in New York.

White, [Mollie] Alma Bridwell (1862-1946). Founder of the Pillar of Fire Church. Claiming to have experienced sanctification* by faith in 1893, White, with her husband, began conducting revivals* and preaching* at camp meetings.* In 1901 she founded the Pentecostal Union in Denver. The group became known as the Pillar of Fire, the name of her periodical.

White later conducted evangelistic services throughout the U.S. and in London and established approximately fifty branches to further her church's goals of evangelism* and education.

White, William (1748-1836). Episcopal* bishop. White became one of the assistant ministers of the United Parishes of Christ Church and St. Peter's Church in Philadelphia. As a supporter of the American cause in the American Revolution,* White succeeded a Tory as rector of the United Parishes in 1779. From 1777 until 1789, he also served as chaplain to the Continental Congress, continuing in the same capacity with the Federal Congress until the capital moved from Philadelphia.

In the years following the Revolution, White played the dominant role in guiding and inspiring the scattered Anglican parishes of the thirteen colonies to unite into a national church; he is truly the Father of the Episcopal Church. Theologically a low churchman* of the eighteenth-century type, White's abhorrence of enthusiasm caused him to distance himself from the Episcopal evangelicals* who emerged in the nineteenth century.

White's influence on his contemporaries was substantial. Many of the early leaders of the U.S. attended Christ Church; his relations with George Washington* were especially close.

Whitefield, George (1715-1770). British itinerant* revivalist* of the Great Awakening.* Whitefield was deeply affected by his contact at Oxford with John* and Charles Wesley. While parting company with these eventual founders of Methodism* on the issue of free will and predestination* (he remained a Calvinist*), Whitefield imbibed much of the Wesleys' teaching on piety* and the necessity of spiritual regeneration,* or new birth.*

Immediately on his ordination* in 1737 Whitefield began preaching* to English audiences with enormous success. Not content to preach within Anglican churches, he took his message of spiritual regeneration* and free grace to the open fields of England, preaching to all who gathered. He attracted notice both for his powerful delivery and for his curious habit of preaching without any notes. Extemporaneous preaching, like itinerancy, became identified with Whitefield's ministry and was soon widely imitated by evangelical* speakers from all denominations.

From the fields of England Whitefield took his novel brand of preaching to the cultural periphery of the British Empire in Scotland and North America. His greatest North American success came in 1740, when he toured urban areas in New England. In a whirlwind forty-five-day tour of central places in Massachusetts and Connecticut, Whitefield delivered over 175 sermons to thousands of hearers that included virtually every New England inhabitant.

Whitefield was, by all accounts, the greatest English-speaking preacher in the eighteenth century and perhaps the greatest revivalist Anglo-America has ever seen.

Whitehead, Alfred North. *See* PROCESS THEOLOGY.

Whitfield, James (1770-1834). Fourth archbishop of Baltimore. Whitfield became archbishop of Baltimore in May 1828. During his brief tenure, he presided over the first provincial council of Baltimore* in 1829 and a second provincial council in 1833, both of which promoted a sense of ecclesial unity.

Whitman, Marcus (1802-1847), and Narcissa Prentiss Whitman (1808-1847). Pioneer missionaries in the Oregon Territory. Marcus Whitman and Narcissa Prentiss married in 1836, both Presbyterians* and both equally dedicated to missionary work. Commissioned as pioneer missionaries to the Oregon Territory under the American Board of Commissioners for Foreign Missions,* they began their missionary venture in the spring of 1835 among the Cayuse Indians.

In 1847, less than twelve years after their work in Oregon was initiated, their mission compound was attacked by a small group of Cayuse Indians, and fourteen residents were killed, including Marcus and Narcissa.

Whitsitt, William Heth (1841-1911). President of Southern Baptist Theological Seminary* and professor of church history. In 1872 Whitsitt became the professor of ecclesiastical history at Southern Baptist Theological Seminary in Greenville, South Carolina. In 1895 he succeeded John A. Broadus* as president of the seminary.

Only four years after assuming the presidency, Whitsitt was forced to resign under pressure from Landmarkers,* who believed that Whitsitt had opposed their views. Shortly thereafter he became professor of philosophy in Richmond (Va.) College, where he taught until his death.

Whittemore, Emma Mott (1850-1931). Rescue mission* leader and founder of Doors of Hope. In 1890 Whittemore, an officer in the Christian and Missionary Alliance, established the first Door of Hope, "home for fallen and unfortunate women," in New York. By the time of her death, ninety-seven homes were in operation.

Wieman, Henry Nelson (1884-1975). Philosopher of religion.* Wieman taught philosophy at Occidental College (1917-1927), in California, and then at the University of Chicago Divinity School (1927-1947), where he was a prominent figure in the so-called Chicago school.* He was responsible for introducing the empirical metaphysics of Alfred North Whitehead* to the Chicago Divinity School, thus fostering the birth of process theology* as a public and self-conscious theological movement.

Wigglesworth, Michael (1631-1705). Puritan* minister and poet. Wigglesworth served as pastor in Malden, Massachusetts.

His most remarkable work was poetic. Wigglesworth put Puritan theology* into verse that was memorized for generations. *The Day of Doom* (1662), describing the final judgment, sold all 1,800 copies and went through numerous editions to become the colonial bestseller.

Wightman, Valentine (1681-1747). Pioneer Baptist* minister. Wightman was a Six-Principle* Baptist who rejected many Calvinistic* emphases of the Regular* Baptists. He established the earliest lasting Baptist churches in Connecticut (1705) and New York City (1714).

Wilbur, John (1774-1856). Quietist Quaker* minister. In a period of the social transformation of much of American Quakerism into mainstream evangelical* Protestantism,* Wilbur was a conservative and a spokesman for the quietist Friends' tradition of radical dependence on direct leadings of the Spirit. The dispute between quietists and evangelicals resulted in a parting at the New England Yearly Meeting of 1845, with 500 Wilburites being outnumbered by the 6,500 Gurneyites.*

Wilder, Robert Parmelee (1863-1938). Missions* leader and Student Volunteer Movement* organizer and promoter. In 1886 Wilder was instrumental in forming the Mount Hermon Hundred,* soon to become the Student Volunteer Movement for Foreign Missions (SVM). In 1891 he sailed for England en route to a Presbyterian* missionary appointment in India. There he assisted in the formation of the Student Volunteer Missionary Union of Great Britain and Ireland.

Wiley, Henry Orton (1877-1961). Church of the Nazarene* minister and theologian. After pastoring a Nazarene church in Berkeley, California (1905-1909), Wiley served as president of two Nazarene colleges, Pasadena (Calif.) College (1910-1916), and Northwest Nazarene College, Nampa, Idaho (1916-1926).

Wiley's most significant publication was his three-volume *Christian Theology* (1941), which has remained the standard systematic theology* for the Church of the Nazarene and others of the Wesleyan*-Arminian* Holiness* tradition.

Willard, Frances Elizabeth Caroline (1839-1898). Methodist* educator, temperance* leader, reformer and feminist.* Willard was president of the Chicago and Illinois Woman's Christian Temperance Union* (WCTU) groups (1874-1877) and also served as first corresponding secretary of the National WCTU (1879-1898). During 1877 she curtailed her temperance work and led meetings for women in Boston under Dwight L. Moody.*

Willard was a prominent figure in national reform politics. Her genius lay in her ability to combine conservative ideals with a commitment to radical social reform.

Willard, Joseph (1738-1804). Congregational* minister and president of Harvard College.* Willard, a founding member of the American Academy of Arts and Sciences (1780), became famous for his work in astronomy, mathematics and the classics. Willard was inaugurated as the president of Harvard in December 1781 and then devoted himself to repairing the damages caused by the war.

Willard, Samuel (1640-1707). New England theologian and president of Harvard College.* Willard served as teacher to the Old South Church, Boston (1676-1707) and as president of Harvard (1701-1707). In his prolific writings, Willard combined traditional Puritan* interest in predestination* and scriptural authority* with a new concern for human happiness and moral integrity, thus anticipating the thought of Jonathan Edwards* by a generation.

Willett, Herbert Lockwood (1864-1944). Disciples of Christ* minister and biblical scholar. Willett spent most of his teaching career at the University of Chicago (1896-1929). His respected scholarship and excellent organizing and speaking skills in the classroom and on the Chautauqua and Lyceum circuits promoted a constructive encounter with biblical criticism.

William and Mary, College of. The second-oldest college in the U.S., originally founded as a colonial Anglican* institution. Founded at Williamsburg, Virginia, in 1693, the college owes its existence to James Blair,* who successfully obtained the royal charter in London and named the school after the joint sovereigns of England. Blair became the college's first president (1693-1743).

In 1888 William and Mary was given an annual appropriation from the Virginia legislature, which paved the way for it to become a true state institution in 1906.

Williams, Channing Moore (1829-1910).

Protestant Episcopal* missionary bishop to Japan. After brief missionary work in China, Williams began his work in Japan in 1859. In Nagasaki he conducted services in the first Japanese Protestant* church building. He was consecrated* bishop of Japan and China in 1866; by 1874 he had moved permanently to Japan.

Williams, Daniel Day (1910-1973). Process* theologian.* Williams taught theology,* first at Chicago Theological Seminary and the Federated Theological Faculty at the University of Chicago* (1939-1954) and then at Union Theological Seminary,* New York (1954-1973). He was known as the senior statesman of process theology.

Williams, Roger (1603-1683). Christian* minister, statesman, founder of Rhode Island and first champion of religious liberty* in America. Williams arrived in Massachusetts in 1631 with the conviction, that the Puritans* in New England should explicitly separate from the Church of England. After a series of clashes, the colonial General Court (legislature) in 1635 banished him to England. Before he could be deported, Williams fled to the uninhabited regions to the south, outside the limits of Massachusetts, and in the summer of 1636 founded there a settlement which he named Providence.

As leader of the new colony, Williams purchased land from the Narragansett Indians and distributed it for use, befriended the Native Americans and learned their language. In 1642 Williams sailed for England to procure a charter for the cluster of settlements in the Narragansett region. His trip resulted in the acquisition from Parliament in March 1644 of a charter uniting the several towns into the colony of Rhode Island, fixing its boundaries and guaranteeing its independence, and for the first time in American history granting complete religious liberty to all of its inhabitants.

In 1639, shortly after settling Providence, Williams became a Baptist,* and during that year joined with a dozen others in forming the first Baptist church on American soil. However, a few months later Williams withdrew from the Baptists and pronounced himself a Seeker after "the true church." For the remainder of his life Williams was a religious loner searching for a church which he could recognize as created in the image of the first apostles.

Williams, Samuel Wells (1812-1884). Missionary to China, diplomat and Sinologist. Williams went to China in 1833 to work as a printer at a mission press. He developed an extraordinary knowledge of the Chinese language and produced several monographs on the Chinese language and Chinese affairs. From 1856 to 1876 he was connected with the U.S. legation to China.

Williams, Smallwood Edmund (1907-1991). Presiding bishop of Bible Way Church of Our Lord Jesus Christ World Wide, Inc. In 1923 Williams was licensed to preach in the Church of Our Lord Jesus Christ of the Apostolic Faith, and in 1925, at age eighteen, he was ordained* by the denomination and organized the Bible Way Church of Our Lord Jesus Christ in Washington, D.C. Immensely popular as a preacher, his Sunday radio program drew an audience of 500,000. He served as general secretary of his denomination from 1948 to 1952, directed its training program for ministers and Christian workers, and was an active leader in the National Association for the Advancement of Colored People and in the Southern Christian Leadership Conference.* In 1957 Williams, discontent with denominational leadership, led seventy congregations out of the denomination to form the Bible Way Church of Our Lord Jesus Christ World Wide, Inc., with Williams consecrated as presiding bishop.

Williamson, Atkin (fl. 1681-1696). Anglican* missionary in colonial South Carolina. Williamson was the first rector of St. Philip's Church, the first Anglican Church in Charleston, South Carolina, serving from 1681 to 1696.

Wilmer, William H. (1782-1827). Episcopal* clergyman. In 1808 Wilmer was ordained to ministry* in the Protestant Episcopal Church* and spent most of his ministerial career in the diocese of Virginia. In 1812, on the death of James Madison,* bishop of Virginia, Wilmer with other young ministers became instrumental in a successful movement to renew the moribund Episcopal Church in Virginia. In addition to his successful pastoral work and service in the leadership of the church, Wilmer actively fostered theological education. His efforts led to the founding in 1823 of the Theological Seminary in Virginia (now Protestant Episcopal Theological Seminary in Virginia). From 1826 until his death in the following year, he was president of William and Mary College.*

Wilson, J. Christy, Sr. (1881-1973). Presbyterian* missionary to Iran. In 1919 Wilson went as an evangelistic* missionary to Iran under the Presbyterian Board of Foreign Missions. He served there for twenty years and was chairman of the Near East Relief Committee* for Iran. His missionary work also took him to Russia and countries of the Middle East.

In 1939 Wilson returned to the U.S. to teach ecumenics at Princeton* Theological Seminary (1940-1962).

Wilson, Robert Dick (1856-1930). Presbyterian* Old Testament scholar and educator. In 1900 Wilson began teaching Semitic philology and Old Testament criticism at Princeton Seminary.* He devoted his scholarship to defending the historical character of the Old Testament in general and of the book of Daniel specifically. In 1929 he joined J. Gresham Machen* in the establishment of Westminster Theological Seminary.

Wilson, Thomas Woodrow (1856-1924). Historian, educator, reformer, Presbyterian* churchman and twenty-eighth U.S. president. Wilson taught at Princeton* (1890-1902) and then became the first layperson ever chosen as president of the university (1902-1910).

Elected governor of Pennsylvania in 1910, Wilson launched a successful program of progressive reforms which brought him national attention and made him a leading contender for the Democratic presidential nomination in 1912. Wilson was nominated and won election by enunciating his proposed "New Freedom"—a program to liberate American economic energies by drastically reducing tariffs, strengthening antitrust laws and reorganizing the banking and credit system.

Wilson won reelection in 1916, largely because of his successful progressive reforms and the fact that he had kept America out of the European conflict (see World War I). With great reluctance Wilson finally asked for a declaration of war against Germany and its allies in 1917.

Wilson made his greatest contribution to the war effort by formulating war aims that for the first time gave some meaning to the conflict, especially in the enunciation of his Fourteen Points in January 1918. A Republican-controlled Congress, however, rejected the Versailles Treaty, with its provision for Wilson's League of Nations.

Wilson's political philosophy rested firmly on his understanding of Christianity; throughout his life he drew his greatest strength from the resources of his Calvinist* faith, with its emphasis on order, reason and righteousness. The mainspring of Wilson's public life was his crusading idealism, which grew out of his evangelical faith. He represented the last gasp of both the evangelical urge to reform the nation along Christian lines and the progressive movement in American politics.

Wimmer, Boniface (1809-1887). Benedictine* archabbot. In 1846 Wimmer arrived in New York with several German Benedictine candidates, intending to found a monastery. He founded Benedictine parishes* and monasteries across the U.S. One—St. John's Abbey and University in Collegeville, Minnesota—became a powerful force in the renewal of the liturgy* in the American Roman Catholic Church after 1950.

Winchell, Alexander (1824-1891). Methodist* layman and natural historian. Winchell taught in several universities before becoming professor of geology and zoology at Vanderbilt University in 1875. In most of his 250 articles and books, Winchell intended to reconcile the apparent conflict between science and religion.

Winchester, A(lexander) B(rown) (1858-1943). Canadian evangelical* Presbyterian* minister. Winchester organized missions to the Chinese in Victoria and Vancouver, where he remained until he became pastor of Knox Church, Toronto, in 1901. His ministry was characterized by biblical exposition within the framework of orthodox* doctrine, a strong missionary program, premillennial* prophetic teaching and a loyalty to presbyterianism which would cause the congregation to be a bulwark of opposition to the church union* scheme which would produce the United Church of Canada* in 1925.

Winchester, Elhanan (1751-1797). Universalist* minister and evangelist. A gifted orator, Winchester became one of the best-known itinerant* evangelists of his day. Having begun as an Arminian* Baptist,* he subsequently embraced a hyper-Calvinism.* Finally, in 1780, after adopting a Universalist theory of the atonement,* he became perhaps the eighteenth century's most celebrated exponent of Universalism.

Winebrenner, John (1797-1860). Church of God* leader and social reformer. Winebrenner's

adoption of revivalistic* measures led to his eventual separation from the German Reformed Church. With a number of like-minded ministers in south-central Pennsylvania, he organized the Church of God (known today as Churches of God, General Conference) in 1830 and remained a leader in the church until his death.

Winrod, Gerald Burton (1898-1957). Fundamentalist* preacher, publisher and anti-Semitist. In 1925 Winrod organized the Defenders of the Christian Faith to oppose evolution* and modernism.* In 1926 he began publishing the *Defender Magazine* as the voice of the organization and enlisted many prominent fundamentalists to write for it.

A premillennialist,* Winrod wrote many articles on prophetic themes and was especially interested in the place of the Jews in God's plan. His own views led him to see a Jewish conspiracy behind world events, which he blamed for the major evils in the world.

Winslow, Edward (1595-1655). Puritan* separatist* and Plymouth Colony leader. One of the signers of the Mayflower Compact,* Winslow was the colony's principal envoy to Massasoit; next to William Bradford its most important chronicler; a lay leader of the church; one of the colony's governors (in 1633, 1636 and 1644); and its most active explorer and trader, establishing posts in Maine, on Cape Ann, on Buzzard's Bay and on the Connecticut River. In 1629 he became the agent for Plymouth and in 1633 the agent for Massachusetts Bay.

Winthrop, John (1588-1649). First governor of Massachusetts Bay. After being elected governor of the Massachusetts Bay Company, Winthrop departed aboard the ship *Arbella* in 1630. During passage Winthrop delivered his lay sermon "A Modell of Christian Charity," in which he offered the famous description of New England as "a citty upon a hill" for the world to witness and to emulate.

Winthrop served as governor of Massachusetts Bay several times between 1630 and 1649. Winthrop's journal, published as *The History of New England from 1630 to 1649,* remains one of the most authoritative accounts of early Massachusetts.

Wisconsin Evangelical Lutheran Synod. Conservative Lutheran* denomination.* The Wisconsin Synod was founded in 1850 and established a theological seminary in 1863. In 1892 it joined forces with the synods of Minnesota and Michigan for the purpose of cooperation in education and mission work. Historically, the Wisconsin Synod has moved from a weak confessionalism* to a more staunchly conservative Lutheran stance. In 1990 it numbered 316,813 full communicant members in 1,211 congregations.

Wise, John (1652-1725). Congregational* minister. Wise, pastor of a Congregational church in Ipswich, Massachusetts (1683-1725), authored treatises in 1710 and 1717 attacking the Saybrook Platform,* which Wise saw as restricting rightful freedoms. Reprinted in the 1770s, these treatises were used as effective arguments in the colonial struggle with England.

Wishard, Luther Deloraine (1854-1925). Promoter of student Christian work and foreign missions.* Wishard became the catalyst behind a vast expansion of the YMCA's* collegiate program and the world's first full-time Christian worker among students. His work led to the Mount Herman One Hundred,* which inspired the Student Volunteer Movement.*

In 1893 Wishard helped organize the Foreign Missions Conference of North America.* His global vision culminated in 1895 in the World's Student Christian Federation.*

Witch Trial. *See* Salem Witch Trial.

Witherspoon, John (1723-1794). Presbyterian* minister and educator. In 1768 Witherspoon accepted the invitation of New Side* Presbyterians to serve as president of the College of New Jersey.* From Scotland, he brought Scottish Common Sense Realism* and from that perspective sought to train his students. After the Revolution* Witherspoon was instrumental in the establishment of the Presbyterian General Assembly (1789), of which he was the first moderator.

Witherspoon, the only clergyman to sign the Declaration of Independence, was a delegate to the Continental Congress (1776-1782).

Woman's Bible, The. A bestselling treatise essentially summarizing the religious ideology of Elizabeth Cady Stanton.* Selections from the King James Version of the Bible are followed by commentaries on the text (the majority by Stanton),

focusing on those sections of the Bible that mention women or that Stanton thought should have included them. Her main intent was to correct the prevalent antifemale interpretation of the Holy Scriptures.

Woman's Christian Temperance Union. Protestant* temperance* organization. Begun in 1874, the Woman's Christian Temperance Union (WCTU) was the largest women's organization of any kind in the U.S. before 1900. Francis Willard,* president of the WCTU from 1879 until her death in 1898, introduced a "do everything" policy which incorporated many reforms, including equal rights for women and women's suffrage.* For Willard, only with the vote could women have power to eliminate alcohol and protect the home.

Women's Suffrage Movement. The rise of American feminism had its roots in the Christian reform movements* of the 1830s and 1840s, which in turn were generated by the Second Great Awakening.* Following the Civil War,* as the women's movement increasingly focused on the suffrage issue, the traditional link with Christian thought remained strong. Because of the prevailing national attitude that women should represent the spiritual conscience of the family, many suffrage activists argued that granting women the ballot would elevate American politics to a higher moral plane. Ultimately, this religious argument represented an important part of the women's suffrage position that eventually won the ideological victory and paved the way for the Nineteenth Amendment (ratified in 1920).

Wood 'n Ware Controversy. A controversy over human nature and the question of freedom between Unitarian* theologian Henry Ware* and trinitarian theologian Leonard Woods.* In his *Letters to Unitarians* (1820) Woods defended a moderate Calvinist* view of human depravity. Ware responded to Woods's challenge in a literary debate that lasted for four years and produced five major volumes. Ware defended the essential goodness of humanity and charged that the Andover theology was "immoral."

See also Sin; Unitarian Controversy.

Woodrow, James (1828-1907). Presbyterian* theologian and scientist. In 1861 Wilson was made professor of "Natural Science in Connexion with Revelation" at the Presbyterian seminary in Columbia, South Carolina. During many of his years at the seminary, he served simultaneously at South Carolina College as professor of science (1869-1872, 1880-1897) and president (1891-1897).

Woodrow held that God's Word and the world both reveal divine truth and that there is no contradiction between them when they are each rightly interpreted. After some years of opposition to the evolutionary* hypothesis, he came to hold that theistic evolution—what he called "mediate creation"—was probably true.

Woods, C(harles) Stacey (1909-1983). Student ministry* leader. Woods served as leader of the InterVarsity Christian Fellowship* both in Canada (1934-1952) and in the U.S. (1940-1960). He helped organize the first InterVarsity student missionary convention (1946-1947), later held triennially in Urbana,* Illinois.

Woods, Leonard (1774-1854). Congregationalist* minister and theologian. Woods was professor of theology at Andover Theological Seminary,* from its opening in 1808 until 1846. In his *Letters to Unitarians* (1820) he justified Calvinist doctrine on the Trinity, depravity and predestination.* Unitarian Henry Ware* replied, initiating the famous Wood 'n Ware controversy,* which lasted until 1824. His finest work, *An Essay on Native Depravity* (1835), was specifically pointed against Nathaniel W. Taylor* and the New Haven theology.*

Woodsworth, J(ames) S(haver) (1874-1942). Canadian Methodist* clergyman and political figure. Woodsworth is best known as the first leader of the Co-operative Commonwealth Federation, the predecessor to the New Democratic Party. Woodsworth was charged with seditious libel for editorials written during the Winnipeg General Strike of 1919. Following the strike, Woodsworth was elected as a member of parliament and was influential in establishing the Canadian Parliament as a multiparty system. He was known as "the conscience of Canada."

Woodward, Samuel Bayard (1787-1850). Asylum superintendent and cofounder of the Association of Medical Superintendents of American Institutions for the Insane (now the American Psychiatric Association). Through his annual reports Woodward became a nationally respected authority on the nature and treatment of mental disorders. A devout Congregationalist,* he considered proper religious views to be important for mental well-being.

Woodworth-Etter, Maria Beulah (1844-1924). Holiness*-Pentecostal* evangelist. Woodworth-Etter first began holding revivals* around 1880. After 1912, her ministry was primarily with Pentecostal* groups. She is best remembered for her charismatic ministries, which included teachings on postconversion spiritual experience and faith healing.

Woodworth-Etter became one of the best-known Pentecostal evangelists at the turn of the century and certainly the best-known woman preacher. Her public ministry opened doors for other women, such as Aimee Semple McPherson* and Kathryn Kuhlman.*

Woolman, John (1720-1772). Quaker* minister. A paragon of Quaker quietism, Woolman sought to "divest himself of all self-interest" and obey only the "pure leadings" of God. In 1748 he was recorded as a minister of the Society of Friends.* Woolman's life was characterized by an inward and outward motion: searching his heart in silent worship* in order to lay aside his own will and discover God's, and laboring on behalf of the poor and oppressed. From this arose his concerns to live a simple life exemplifying "the right use of things" and to end war, slavery and injustice toward the poor and toward Native Americans. He spoke to oppressor as well as oppressed, gently urging a conversion of heart.

Worcester, Elwood (1862-1940). Episcopal* clergyman. In 1904 Worcester was called to Emmanuel Church in Boston, where he subsequently combined forces with several prominent physicians to evaluate and treat emotionally troubled individuals, using a combination of medical assessment and a liberal Protestant* interpretation of contemporary psychological thought.

Worcester, Noah (1758-1837). Liberal Congregational* pastor and pacifist.* Worcester was pastor in Thornton, New Hampshire, for twenty-two years (1787-1810) and the first missionary employed by the New Hampshire Missionary Society when it formed. In 1813 he became the first editor of the liberal monthly *Christian Disciple* (later the *Christian Examiner*).

Worcester, Samuel Austin (1798-1859). Missionary among the Cherokee Indians. In 1827 Worcester moved to the Cherokee capital at New Echota, Georgia, where he worked with Elias Boudinot* in publishing a variety of religious literature in the Cherokee language. In 1835 Worcester went west with some of the Cherokee who were being forced out of Georgia.

Word Movement. *See* FAITH MOVEMENT.

Work Ethic. *See* PROTESTANT WORK ETHIC.

World Alliance for Promoting International Friendship (1914-1948). An organization that developed from a peace conference held in Germany in 1914. In addition to encouraging peacemaking, the alliance was one of the precursors of the World Council of Churches.*

World Alliance of Reformed Churches. International organization of Presbyterian,* Reformed* and Congregationalist* denominations.* The alliance was formed in 1970 from a union of two organizations: the World Alliance of Reformed Churches Throughout the World Holding the Presbyterian System (formed in 1875) and the International Congregational Council. Today about 160 denominations with congregations in more than eighty countries and approximately 70 million members belong to the alliance.

World Congress on Evangelism. International evangelical* congress held in Berlin in 1966. Convened to focus attention on the resurgence of evangelical Christianity on the occasion of the tenth anniversary of *Christianity Today,* the congress was chaired by Carl F. H. Henry* and Billy Graham.* The congress brought together twelve thousand delegates from one hundred nations, the vast majority of them from outside North America. Anglicans* and Pentecostals* at the ecclesiastical extremes joined with a broad spectrum of denominational representatives and Roman Catholic,* Jewish and ecumenical* observers.

World Council of Churches. An ecumenical* organization of over three hundred Protestant,* Anglican* and Orthodox* churches from some one hundred countries on all six continents. While not a full member, the Roman Catholic Church* does officially participate in various programs.

The vision of a world Christian body linking the churches was expressed many times in the nineteenth and twentieth centuries. Organized finally in 1948, the World Council of Churches (WCC) has several functions and purposes: (1) to call the churches to visible unity in faith and worship;* (2) to facilitate the common witness of the churches; (3) to support the churches in their worldwide missionary and evangelistic task; (4) to express the common concern of the churches for human need, the breaking down of barriers between people and the promotion of justice and peace; (5) to foster the renewal of the churches in unity, worship, mission and service.

The nature of the WCC can best be understood in the language of its doctrinal basis, expanded in 1961 as follows: "The World Council of Churches is a fellowship of churches which confess the Lord Jesus Christ as God and Saviour according to the Scriptures and therefore seek to fulfill together their common calling to the glory of the one God, Father, Son and Holy Spirit."

Important to the WCC's witness are its assemblies, which have met at Amsterdam (1948), Evanston* (1954), New Delhi (1961), Uppsala (1968), Nairobi (1975), Vancouver* (1983) and Canberra (1991).

See also INTERNATIONAL COUNCIL OF CHRISTIAN CHURCHES; WORLD EVANGELICAL FELLOWSHIP.

World Evangelical Fellowship. An international alliance of evangelical* bodies serving as a resource and catalyst to help local churches fulfill their scriptural mandate. The historical roots of the World Evangelical Fellowship (WEF) ultimately go back to the founding of the World Evangelical Alliance in Britain (1846).

Formed in 1951, the WEF provides both the structure and forum for evangelicals worldwide to join together, defend the faith and cooperate in advancing the gospel.

World Gospel Mission. Holiness* missionary* society. Founded in 1910 by the National Association for the Promotion of Holiness (*see* Christian Holiness Association), the World Gospel Mission (WGM, so named since 1950) was created to establish, maintain and conduct interdenominational missions and missionary work in home and foreign fields and to spread scriptural holiness, largely through a properly qualified national ministry.

World Home Bible League. International and interdenominational Bible-distribution agency. The American Home Bible League was founded in 1938 by William and Betty Chapman. In 1950, as the scope of its evangelistic efforts advanced beyond the borders of the U.S. and into Mexico, Japan and India, the agency changed its name to the World Home Bible League.

World Literature Crusade. Evangelical* interdenominational agency dedicated to placing gospel literature in every home in the world. Founded in Canada in 1946, the World Literature Crusade (WLC) opened a U.S. office in 1952. Literature, including tracts* written by national Christians in their own languages, is made available to individual Christians, denominations* and missionaries who organize and implement their systematic distribution.

World Vision. An international and nondenominational Christian humanitarian aid organization. World Vision was founded in 1950 by American evangelist Bob Pierce,* who raised relief funds among American churches during the Korean War. After the war, World Vision began raising support for war orphans through a program of child sponsorship. It later expanded its work to other countries in Asia and in Africa and Latin America, and to other ministries, including evangelism, pastors' conferences and emergency relief.

World War I (1914-1918). The name commonly given to history's most tragic and fateful conflagration, originally called the Great War, and a major watershed in the development of modern civilization. In the generation before 1914, Europeans and Americans, including many theologians, believed themselves heading for a new era of peace and progress. Most important, the Western intelligentsia were convinced that humans had matured to the point that they could settle international disputes without resorting to violence. This worldview came into serious question when in 1914 the nations of Europe, through arrogance and miscalculation, blundered into a disaster the magnitude of which had hitherto been unknown in human history.

The conflict began in Europe on July 28, 1914, with a declaration of war by the Austro-Hungarian Empire (Austria) against Serbia. This followed the assassination on June 28 in Sarajevo, Bosnia, of the heir apparent to the Austro-Hungarian throne by a Bosnian terrorist acting at the behest of the intelligence section of the Serbian General Staff. The term *world war* is properly applied to the conflict of 1914-1918 because the various parts of the British Empire on all continents as well as many countries in Asia and North and South America participated in it. For the first time, all the great powers of the world were engaged in the hostilities; it is estimated that by the end of the war about 93 percent of the population of the world was involved.

When the war began in Europe, most Americans assumed that it was just another in a long series of the Old World's conflicts and therefore none of their business. However, as the war dragged on and the casualties mounted, so did American interest in the hostilities. Finally, on April 6, 1917, Congress declared war against Germany, and the president proclaimed that the U.S. had gone to war "to make the world safe for democracy."

Wilson was determined to offer the defeated Germans a just and humane peace, a position which he outlined in his celebrated Fourteen Points on January 8, 1918. However, the British and French had no intention of abiding by Wilson's idealistic Fourteen Points when the victorious powers—with representatives of none of the defeated countries present—convened the peace conference at Versailles in 1919. Forced to compromise on all of his other points, Wilson preserved the fourteenth, his proposal for a League of Nations, only to have that part of the treaty become the main reason for the U.S. Senate to reject ratification.

Wilson was supported in his decision to go to war with the Central Powers by the vast majority of America's religious leaders, but not all shared the president's high ideals and humane goals. Like the American public, the majority of church leaders could be classified as militants or moderates in their attitude toward the prosecution of the war, with about an equal number taking each position. Moreover, there appears to have been no theological dividing line between these two groups, with conservatives and liberals present in large numbers in each group. Only a small number of American Christians opposed the war.

Based on the most reliable statistics, the total cost of the war was nearly $338 billion. The number of casualties in World War I far exceeded those of any other war before in history. Civilian deaths from military action, massacre, starvation and exposure between 1914 and 1918 are estimated at 12.6 million. Of the more than 65 million people mobilized by all countries during the war, 57.6 percent, or more than 37.5 million, became casualties.

Above and beyond these stark figures, the war deeply affected nearly all of those who served and badly scarred most of those who saw combat. Moreover, the harshness of the peace terms, coupled with continued violence in eastern Europe, the Balkans, the Middle East and Asia, mutual distrust among the victors, and a sharp recession following the immediate postwar boom produced a widespread sense of disillusionment in both Europe and America.

American Christians, too, were swept along in many of these currents. The war had taught Americans to hate not only the enemy but each other as well. The violence and brutality of the war years and the raw emotions aroused by wartime rhetoric blunted the moral consciences of many Christians and readied them for the internecine religious warfare that was to follow in the fundamentalist-modernist controversy* of the 1920s.

World War II. Beginning with the German assault on Poland on September 1, 1939, and ending with the Japanese surrender six years later, World War II was the greatest conflict in history. Measured in terms of lives lost, damage caused, money expended and countries participating, this struggle was without parallel.

After entering the war in December 1941, the U.S. took the lead in forming a global alliance (the United Nations) against the Axis and devoted its vast industrial potential and seemingly inexhaustible human and physical resources to achieving total victory and a better world. With a few exceptions, American Christians supported their country's involvement in the war. They saw the cause as a just one because the Axis powers had committed numerous acts of aggression during the previous decade.

Isolationism. The American failure in the 1920s and 1930s to exercise responsible world leadership was a significant factor in the coming of a second global conflict. Although liberal clerics were involved in various peace movements and

internationalist causes during the interwar years, they did not really speak for the mass of the American people and could not direct their parishioners away from the path of storm-cellar neutrality which simply abetted the aggressive actions of the rising dictatorships. Fundamentalist* leaders distanced themselves from peace activism because of their political conservatism and hatred of modernism.*

Threats to Civil Liberties. One of the first victims of the war effort was civil liberties. By the end of the 1930s partisans of both the political left and right were labeling each other's positions as un-American, subversive and totalitarian, and charges of communism and fascism were flung with abandon.

Race and Ethnic Prejudice. World War II saw some important gains for minority groups, but there were setbacks as well. The intense hatred for German-Americans that so marked World War I did not recur, but the five million Italian-Americans were viewed with suspicion.

The African-American population suffered as usual from white oppression during the war years. African-Americans were disadvantaged in employment, and unrest broke out in various cities, the most serious being the Detroit riots in June 1943. Segregation was such a way of life in the armed forces that no African-American officer was allowed to outrank or command a white person in any unit. The navy did better and began integrating ships after May 1944.

An egregious violation of civil liberties occurred with the internment of 120,000 people of Japanese birth or ancestry, two-thirds of whom were American citizens. Attempts by church groups and liberals to moderate the policy and allow people to leave the camps were stoutly resisted by hard-line segregationists in Congress.

Religious Life in the Armed Services. Although servicemen and servicewomen were uprooted from their homes and churches, a great deal of religious activity went on in their new environments. The military chaplaincy* underwent a dramatic increase from less than two hundred chaplains in the interwar years to around eleven thousand on active duty. Chapels were built on posts and provided on ships; many chaplains served in combat and were killed or wounded.

The National Conference of Christians and Jews* sent interfaith teams to over three hundred camps to promote mutual understanding among religious groups.

The War and Missions. When the Nazi government curtailed financial support to German works abroad and the spreading war in Europe left the continental missions cut off from their home bases, the International Missionary Council* and Lutheran World Federation* assisted these "orphaned missions" to continue their work.

The most vital dimension in the postwar surge of American Protestant missionary activity was the experiences of the GIs themselves. They had witnessed conditions overseas and some even came into contact with existing mission enterprises. They returned home enthused about missionary work, entered Bible colleges and seminaries in droves, and returned to their former places of service ready to win the world for Christ.

*The War and Ecumenism.** The Commission on a Just and Durable Peace (1941) (*see* Dulles, John Foster) focused its attention on the postwar international structure and generated public support for a United Nations Organization. Three of its people, well-known Protestant* ecumenists, served as consultants to the American delegation at the San Francisco Conference in 1945 which created the UN.

The White House itself expanded the scope of ecumenical relations by establishing unofficial ties with the Holy See. In late 1939 Roosevelt named Myron C. Taylor as his personal envoy to the Vatican* to secure Catholic participation in dealing with refugee problems. In 1943 Roosevelt encouraged the National Catholic Welfare Conference* to create the Catholic War Relief Services (now Catholic Relief Services).

*Roosevelt and Civil Religion.** A liberal ecumenical Episcopalian,* Roosevelt had done much during his presidency to advance interfaith relations. He backed candidates and chose advisers without regard to their religious beliefs, and he addressed Protestant, Catholic and Jewish organizations alike. He saw idealism, patriotism and faith as inseparable, and under his aegis the principle of the "three great faiths" was firmly established in the American civil religion.

In 1939 Roosevelt declared that the storms abroad challenged the three institutions indispensable to Americans—religion, democracy and international good faith—and wherever democracy was overthrown, free worship disappeared. The defense of religion and democracy was the same fight.

See also WORLD WAR I.

World's Christian Fundamentals Association. Interdenominational association of fundamentalist* churches. Growing out of a series of prophecy conferences held during World War I, the World's Christian Fundamentals Association (WCFA) originated from a group that gathered at a meeting in Philadelphia in 1919. Faced with the threat of liberal theology and the teaching of evolution, the WCFA continually encouraged its supporters to purge their denominations* of heretics and produce theologically sound graduates from their schools.

World's Parliament of Religions (1893). International Congress on Religion held at Chicago Columbian Exposition. The World's Parliament of Religions was the longest, most ambitious, most visited and most admired of the many international meetings that took place during the summer of 1893 as adjunct activities of the World's Fair held in Chicago. John Henry Barrows, a liberal* pastor at Chicago's First Presbyterian* Church, chaired the committee, which also contained fifteen other members representing various Christian churches (Episcopal,* Roman Catholic* and Protestant*) and Judaism.

World's Student Christian Federation. Ecumenical* association of autonomous Christian student groups. The World's Student Christian Federation (WSCF) grew out of an 1895 meeting which culminated in the union the Student Christian movements of North America, Britain, Germany, Scandinavia and the "mission lands." The WSCF's purpose was to help organize local SCMs, provide ecumenical training with a view toward preparing future leaders and demonstrate the ecumenicity required by the gospel.

Worldwide Church of God. An adventist* sect.* In 1934 the founder of the Worldwide Church of God, Herbert W. Armstrong, then associated with the Church of God (Seventh-Day), began a radio ministry called *The Radio Church of God* and began publishing the magazine *Plain Truth.* He left his denomination in 1937 and in 1947 moved his headquarters to Pasadena, California, where he founded Ambassador College. There the movement continued to prosper, with the radio broadcast (renamed *The World Tomorrow* during the 1960s and hosted by his son, Garner Ted Armstrong), followed by a television ministry, reaching an ever-widening audience.

Worldwide Marriage Encounter Movement.
A Catholic*-based movement to enrich marriage
and family life. Marriage Encounter began in
Spain in the 1950s. A priest, Father Gabriel Calvo,
developed a series of conferences geared toward
questions that encouraged husbands and wives to
improve their communication on a deeper level.
The movement grew within the structure of the
Christian Family movement,* spreading through
South and Central America and, in 1967, beginning also in the U.S. Well over a million people
have taken part in the U.S.

Worship. Public worship in the Roman Catholic*
tradition is liturgical* in nature and regulated according to norms established by the Roman See.
It revolves around the sacraments*—primarily
the Eucharist*—the community and the proclaimed Word. When the first Catholic Mass* was
celebrated in the New World (1494), it was a
worship that had not yet seen the reforms of the
Council of Trent (1545-1563). The earliest Spanish missionaries brought with them a worship
shaped by the Middle Ages, rich in symbolism
and action but subject to the fanciful and even
magical notions of folk religion. The liturgical reforms of Trent did much to reform and standard-
ize Catholic worship, particularly the doctrine of
the sacraments. For the most part, the worship
that was introduced into North America during
the later European migrations and missions* of
the sixteenth through the nineteenth centuries
was post-Tridentine. But even this unity of form
and language (Latin) came through an inevitable
variety of ethnic expressions—from the Hispanic
Catholics of the Southwest to the Polish Catholics
of Chicago. Indeed, even a diversity in rites
would come to be embraced by the inclusion of
Eastern-Rite Catholics* with their own liturgies
authorized by Rome.

In the Orthodox Church,* the Eucharist, generally known as the Divine Liturgy, is the principal
service of common worship. It may be celebrated
normally only once a day. It is always celebrated
on Sunday* and on major feast days. While the
daily celebration is not the norm in parishes,* it
may be celebrated on any day with the exception
of Good Friday* and most of the weekdays of
Lent.* Consistent with the pattern found in the
early church, the Orthodox Eucharist has two major parts. The first is centered on the reading of
Scripture and its explication. The second includes
the offering of the bread and wine, the intonation

of the Great Eucharistic Prayer (the Anaphora*)
and the reception of Holy Communion.* While
various themes are found in the prayers* and
hymns,* the spirit of joyful thanksgiving for the
presence of God and for his mighty acts pervades
the rite. Many of the hymns and prayers of these
rites date back to the early centuries and reflect
the liturgical practices of particular centers of the
early church.

Protestant* worship in America is rooted in Reformation worship, which in turn traces its lineage
back through the worship of the Western church
to that of the ancient and apostolic church. Consequently, there is an obvious historical link between Protestant and Catholic worship. In general
the history of Protestant worship can be viewed
as a variety of attempts, some of them in successive order, to restore biblical forms of worship.
For many Protestants this has been negatively defined as purging their worship of ritual and traditions that are unbiblical. These attempts began
with the Protestant worship of the Lutheran,* Reformed,* Anglican* and Anabaptist* varieties and
continued with the Puritans,* the rise of Free
Church* and finally charismatic* worship in the
twentieth century.

Numerous differences which exist in Protestant
worship today can also be traced to the Reformation. A fundamental disagreement remains over
how much continuity Protestant worship should
have with its Catholic past. Lutherans and Anglicans
have retained much from their Catholic heritage,
while Anabaptists have rejected the past in favor of
restoring what they believe to be a simple biblical
pattern of worship. The Reformed community,
standing in the tradition of John Calvin,* has attempted to forge a mediating position. In matters
of ceremony Lutherans and Anglicans have been
willing to practice what the Bible does not forbid,
while the Reformed and Anabaptist traditions have
shaped their worship according to what they perceive is the explicit teaching of Scripture.

Wrangel, Karl Magnus von (c. 1730-1786).
Lutheran* missionary in Delaware and Pennsyl-
vania. In 1759 Wrangel was sent to America as
provost of Swedish Lutheran congregations in
Delaware and Pennsylvania. He became a close
friend and confidant of Henry Melchior Muhlen-
berg* and took an active role in Muhlenberg's
German Lutheran Pennsylvania Ministerium.*
Wrangel became an outspoken champion of
Pennsylvania German rights.

Wrieden, Jane Elizabeth (1906-1970). Salvation Army* social worker. Initially involved in evangelistic work, Wrieden earned a master's degree in social work and served as administrator for family services and consultant for the Salvation Army.

Wright, G(eorge) Ernest (1909-1974). Presbyterian* Old Testament scholar and archaeologist. Wright taught at McCormick Theological Seminary in Chicago (1939-1958) and at Harvard Divinity School (1958-1974). He was president of the American Schools of Oriental Research (1966-1974) and curator of the Harvard Semitic Museum. Wright figured prominently in the biblical theology movement.*

Wright, George Frederick (1838-1921). Congregational* theologian and scientist. In 1881 Wright accepted a professorship at Oberlin.* Two years later he became editor of *Bibliotheca Sacra,* maintaining the highly regarded theological journal for forty years.

Asa Gray* and Wright formed an imposing partnership in a quest to advance the cause of Darwinism* in the U.S. in the late nineteenth century. Their scientific and theological labors emphasized the theistic (not atheistic or agnostic) interpretation of Darwinism.

Wright, Isaac. *See* COKER, DANIEL.

Wycliffe Bible Translators, Inc. A nondenominational agency devoted to the scientific study of linguistics and the translation of the Bible. Wycliffe Bible Translators (WBT) began in 1934 as a summer training program in linguistics, particularly focused on the needs of Bible translators. Fieldwork began with Mexican tribes in 1935, spreading eventually to work around the world.

In 1942 a unique dual corporate structure was established, encompassing Wycliffe Bible Translators and the Summer Institute of Linguistics (SIL), the latter a scientific and educational organization.

See also TOWNSEND, WILLIAM CAMERON.

X-Z

Yale Band. *See* ILLINOIS BAND.

Yale University and Divinity School. Educational institution with origins in colonial Congregationalism.* Yale came into existence in 1701 in part as a conservative Congregationalist reaction to the growing departure of Harvard* from its traditional Calvinist* orientation. By 1716 it had a permanent campus at New Haven.

Yale's Divinity School, beginning as a department of theology in 1822, was to become the most potent theological force in nineteenth-century America. Nathaniel W. Taylor,* its first professor of theology, was prominent in shaping the New Haven Theology,* which provided a theological rationale for the emergent evangelical revivalism* of Jacksonian America.

See also NEW ENGLAND THEOLOGY.

Yeatman, James Erwin (1818-1901). Businessman and philanthropist. During the Civil War,* Yeatman became the head of the Western Sanitary Commission, which supplied vast quantities of medical and sanitation equipment and material aid to Union troops in Missouri, Arkansas, Kentucky and Tennessee.

Yeo, John (c. 1639-1686). Early Anglican* minister in Delaware and Maryland. From 1677 to 1682 Yeo served as the first Anglican clergyman in Delaware, with the English fort at New Castle the focus of his efforts. In 1682 Yeo moved to Calvert County, Maryland, to establish a parish.

Young, Brigham (1801-1877). Second president of the Church of Jesus Christ of Latter-day Saints.* After Joseph Smith* was murdered in 1844, Young's position as Mormon* apostle, allegiance to the church and personal charisma resulted in his choice as Smith's successor. Young led the Mormon exodus from Illinois to the Great Salt Lake Basin (1846-1848). He used the immense power he possessed as governor of the Utah Territory and church president to establish some 350 communities and numerous economic ventures and instructed his people in everything from doctrine and architecture to fashion and family relations.

Young, Edward Joseph (1907-1968). Presbyterian* Old Testament scholar. Young taught Old Testament at Westminster Theological Seminary from 1936 until his death. He was widely regarded as the leading evangelical* Old Testament scholar of his day, giving direction especially to the reasoned defense of the authority* and integrity of Scripture against destructive criticism.

Young Life. An evangelical* youth movement working primarily with high schoolers. The ministry centers on weekly club meetings consisting of music, skits and a talk based on the Bible. These weekly clubs are supported by Bible studies,* camping* experiences and personal conversations with Young Life leaders.

The movement grew out of the ministry* in 1938 of a young Dallas Theological Seminary* student, Jim Rayburn.

Young Men's Christian Association. Nondenominational community service organization. Founded in London in 1844 by George Williams, the Young Men's Christian Association (YMCA) provided young men with a wholesome alternative to the evils of urban life. Growing rapidly, it was transplanted to Montreal and Boston in 1851. It quickly became a leading nonsectarian organization in the movement to preach the gospel to the unchurched masses in the burgeoning cities. Along with evangelism,* its members cared for the sick, fed the poor, organized Sunday schools,* worked for temperance,* distributed Bibles and engaged in a host of other good causes.

By the 1980s the YMCA had become the largest

health and social service agency in the U.S. The movement has become a flexible community service organization responsive to local needs.

Young Women's Christian Association. A movement originally devoted to meeting the social, physical, intellectual and spiritual needs of young Protestant* women. The first Young Women's Christian Association (YWCA) was organized in America in 1866. In time the YWCA took on an increasingly ecumenical* character, and today membership transcends religious faith, being open to all who wish to identify with the movement.

Youth for Christ, International. An international evangelical* youth organization for evangelism* and Bible study.* Youth for Christ (YFC) originated from evangelistic youth rallies in the 1930s. Some coordination of the ministries came in 1945 when leaders met at Winona Lake, Indiana, and established Youth for Christ, International. Torrey Johnson was elected president, and Billy Graham* became a traveling evangelist for the organization.

In the 1950s YFC began emphasizing high-school Bible clubs.

Youth Ministry/Minister. Today's emphasis on youth ministry in the American church grew out of changing family and cultural patterns in the late 1800s. As public education increasingly grouped children and youth according to ages, a distinct youth culture emerged. Churches began to plan specific programs and activities for youth.

Following World War II,* the fledgling Young Life* (1941) and Youth for Christ* (c. 1945) organizations reached out successfully to youth who were then outside the church through rallies, clubs and camps.* At the same time, most major denominations* established democratically organized and student-led youth fellowships.

By the late 1970s, a new style of youth ministry had become an established institution in many American churches. Medium and large-sized congregations commonly had full-time youth ministers or directors to coordinate biblically oriented and openly Christ-centered ministries with youth. A forthright focus on Christian discipleship* and evangelism with youth often provided a spark which led to renewal of entire churches.

Youth With A Mission. A nondenominational and international evangelistic* organization. Established in 1960 by Loren Cunningham, an Assemblies of God* minister, Youth With A Mission (YWAM) is dedicated to presenting Jesus Christ in a loving way to all members of this generation. With 350 permanent centers throughout the world, YWAM operates in over one hundred countries with some six thousand full-time workers.

Zahm, John Augustine (1851-1921). Catholic* scientist and educator. In 1871 Zahm joined the Congregation of Holy Cross.* He served at the University of Notre Dame as professor of physics and chemistry (1875-1892) and, from 1876, as vice president. His numerous campus projects included an annual public lecture series on modern science and the construction of the university's first science classroom and laboratory.

Zahm was the most important nineteenth-century intellectual in the Congregation of Holy Cross and American Catholicism's most erudite and respected writer on the relationship of Darwinian* evolution and Christian belief in Victorian America.

Zeisberger, David (1721-1808). Moravian* missionary to Native Americans. After studying the Iroquois language, Zeisberger went on a mission in 1745 to the Mohawk Valley. This began sixty-four years of living, working and preaching among the Delaware Indians in Pennsylvania, New York and Ohio.

Throughout the Revolutionary* period he attempted to maintain a pacifistic stance among the Native Americans. Zeisberger later followed the refugee Native Americans as they were forced to migrate to Canada and Michigan.

Zinzendorf, Nikolaus Ludwig von (1700-1760). Pietist* and Moravian* leader. Zinzendorf offered his estate in Saxony as a haven for Moravian exiles from Bohemia and Moravia. In 1727 he devoted his time to renewing the *Unitas Fratrum*, otherwise known as the Church of the Brethren, or Moravian Church. The community became known as Herrnhut (The Lord's Protection) and was viewed by Zinzendorf as an ecumenical* renewal movement within the church at large.

From 1732 Zinzendorf devoted both his time and his fortune to Moravian mission ventures, visiting the West Indies (1738-1739) and America (1741-1743).

Zionism and American Christianity. Zionism as a concept is rooted in the traditions of ancient Israel. It relates to the persistent belief that God's covenant with his people, the Jews, is linked to Palestine and Jerusalem in particular and that the land is rightfully theirs. Since biblical times, this land tradition has been an integral component of Jewish hopes and dreams, an unshakable expectation during nineteen centuries of exile of returning to Zion. Christian Zionists reject the view that the biblical promises made to ancient Israel were abrogated by the coming of Christ or were superseded by the establishment of the church.

In the late nineteenth and twentieth centuries Zionism became enfleshed in a movement that has attracted a broad spectrum of American Christians, although they are a minority numerically speaking. Among many conservative evangelical* Christians, Zionism has been accorded a prominent role as a fulfillment of prophecy and as one of the preconditions for the return of Christ. Christian Zionism has also been prominent among mainline* Protestants,* as well as Catholics,* throughout the twentieth century.

Zouberbuhler, Bartholomew (d. 1766). Anglican* minister in colonial Georgia. Zouberbuhler served as rector at Christ Church Parish in Savannah from 1745 until his death. He was fluent in English, French and German and was particularly suited to the position in Savannah, where he ministered to nearby German communities and also to nearby French Protestants.

Zwemer, Samuel Marinus (1867-1952). Reformed* missionary to the Arab world. Ordained* in 1890, Zwemer went to Arabia under the auspices of the Syrian Mission of the Presbyterian Church in the U.S.A.* Based in Bahrain, Zwemer evangelized the Gulf from Basra to Muscat and in 1912 was assigned to literature work in Egypt. After seventeen years in Cairo, Zwemer was called to be professor of missions and the history of religion at Princeton Theological Seminary.* Zwemer was energetic and stately, a prodigious author and editor.